Advance Praise

[This book] by Dr Hira Sadhak is a valuable book on Indian pension systems in the context of the so-called LPG (liberalization-privatization-globalization) and economic reforms in India. The book examines critically the evolutions of social security and pension systems in India and the associated risks against the backdrop of the ever changing socio-economic-demographic-technological environment and new financial architecture. The book is the product of research for a number of years by an internationally acknowledged financial expert. I am confident that the Book would provide valuable guidance to the managers of pension funds in both public and private sectors.

—**Dr Tarun Das**
World Bank Technical Expert, Ministry of Finance, Dhaka, Bangladesh

The subject of Retirement Savings and Pension are engaging best of the brains in politics, economics and financial services industry throughout the world. Very many conflicting interests of many stakeholders make any agreement on almost any aspect of the problem quite difficult. Yet every one interested in the topic—governments, regulators, industry, media, academics, politicians—must debate, think afresh, design solutions and most importantly implement those solutions that may not be popular with the governments or the public.

[The book] has covered very many aspects of the subject and the debates within 15 chapters of this book—quite an achievement in my view. The author provided wealth of data and information very objectively with his interpretation and views, leaving the readers to explore alternative hypothesis too. Dr Sadhak is bold enough to raise many contentious issues, again with the detachment of an unbiased academician. India badly needs urgent reform and liberalisation of pension and other financial services industry, and private provision is the only way forward. The book does carry this central message, but with a humane face. Dr Sadhak, an ex-colleague, who has the unique combination of theoretical and practical knowledge of Pension and Savings in India. I heartily recommend the book to the students, practitioners and stakeholders of the industry in India.

—**Dilip C. Chakraborty**
Senior Advisor, India, Towers Watson

Indian retirement system is facing enormous challenges to modernize and rationalize the nation's resources and policy to facilitate retirement savings and social protection for the emerging old-age populations. With its unprecedented rise of middle class population and the large portion of rural and non-organized population, the challenge is unique and enormous. The author Dr Sadhak has a long and distinguished career in various senior executive positions in financial industries across asset management, insurance, banking and consultant. His rich experience provides a comprehensive view of the history and environment of this important issue that India is facing, as well as a guidance on the future directions and opportunities. I will recommend this book as one of the must-read books for anyone who wishes to understand India and its financial industry opportunities and the pension policy makers who are looking to review the experience and inspiration on recent pension reform.

—Vanessa Wang, FSA
Managing Director and Asia Pacific Head, Pension Fund Services, Citigroup

India is emerging as the most populous country of the world with fast growing elderly population. Hence it is required for India to have a well structured Social Security System to provide adequate old age income through pension system.

National Pension System (NPS) is an attempt in this direction, but as the author says, there are a number of structural issues which need to be addressed to achieve the desired goal. Dr Sadhak has made a very good effort to analyse the state of existing social security and pension system in India and the wide gap that exist in the form coverage and structure and the role of NPS in that context. While providing a structural framework of NPS, he has pointed out a number of issues and suggested measures to create awareness and confidence among the investors, amend regulatory deficits, strengthen the system of risk governance, valuation and payout system, capacity building etc. The book has provided a synoptic view of global perspective of pension reforms and particularly the experience of many emerging market economies and the challenges confronted by them, which can be immensely useful for policy makers and regulator in India. The book is very informative and rich in terms of facts and statistical information and can be very handy for policy makers, professionals, researchers, students and general public.

—R. Vaidyanathan
UTI Chair Professor in Capital Market Studies, Indian Institute of Management Bangalore

How to design a pension system that works in India? This is the main focus of Hira Sadhak's analysis through out the pages of this must-read book. With a very intelligent approach, the author discusses the problematic of pensions in India, taking into account the domestic institutional framework, recent developments in the country, as well as lessons from the global agenda, in order to point out the main challenges and recommendations to spur a real pension reform in India.

—David Tuesta
Chief Economist, Pensions–BBVA Research

Pension Reform in India

Pension Reform in India

The Unfinished Agenda

H. Sadhak

SAGE | Response Business Books
www.sagepublications.com
Los Angeles • London • New Delhi • Singapore • Washington DC

First published in 2013 by

SAGE Response
B1/I-1 Mohan Cooperative Industrial Area
Mathura Road, New Delhi 110 044, India

SAGE Publications Inc
2455 Teller Road
Thousand Oaks, California 91320, USA

SAGE Publications Ltd
1 Oliver's Yard, 55 City Road
London EC1Y 1SP, United Kingdom

SAGE Publications Asia-Pacific Pte Ltd
33 Pekin Street
#02-01 Far East Square
Singapore 048763

Published by Vivek Mehra for SAGE Publications India Pvt Ltd, typeset in 11/13 Berthold Baskerville by RECTO Graphics, Delhi, and printed at De-Unique, New Delhi.

Library of Congress Cataloging-in-Publication Data

Sadhak, H.
Pension reform in India : the unfinished agenda / H. Sadhak.
pages cm
Includes index.
1. Pensions–India. 2. Social security–India. I. Title.
HD7105.35.I5S23 331.25'220954–dc23 2013 2012050563

ISBN: 978-81-321-0979-2 (HB)

The SAGE Team: Sachin Sharma, Shreya Lall, Nand Kumar Jha and Rajinder Kaur

To
My late Father
Raj B. Sadhak

Thank you for choosing a SAGE product! If you have any comment, observation or feedback, I would like to personally hear from you. Please write to me at contactceo@sagepub.in

—Vivek Mehra, Managing Director and CEO,
SAGE Publications India Pvt Ltd, New Delhi

Bulk Sales

SAGE India offers special discounts for purchase of books in bulk. We also make available special imprints and excerpts from our books on demand.

For orders and enquiries, write to us at

Marketing Department
SAGE Publications India Pvt Ltd
B1/I-1, Mohan Cooperative Industrial Area
Mathura Road, Post Bag 7
New Delhi 110044, India
E-mail us at marketing@sagepub.in

Get to know more about SAGE, be invited to SAGE events, get on our mailing list. Write today to marketing@sagepub.in

This book is also available as an e-book.

Contents

Contents

List of Tables, Figures and Annexures

TABLES

FIGURES

ANNEXURES

Foreword

With changing demographic structure, increased longevity and population ageing, social security and pension have emerge as the important policy issues and institutional concern. Growing cost of pension increased burden on exchequer and tending to be unbearable in the days to come. Added to this is the shrinking of jobs in the organised sector and emergence of a huge informal unorganised economy which normally do not have any provision for retirement pension or social security. Though Life Insurance Corporation of India and other agencies quite active along with civil services and public sector pension system, yet a huge number of workers in the unorganised sector remain beyond the purview of formal social security net. These have necessitated a fresh look into pension system and to initiate reform to introduce a viable and sustainable pension system in India. National Pension System (NPS) in India is a bold step to reform pension system and expand the pension coverage in the country. However the vast majority of Indians still need to know and understand the NPS.

There is also a huge gap between savings and retirement savings—though India has maintained a high level of domestic and household savings, pension and retirement occupy a smaller space in the household basket of savings, perhaps due to lack of financial literacy and absence of multiple financial products for different classes of investors.

This book has attempted to reduce the understanding and knowledge gap and address several critical issues which are important for a well designed and sustainable pension system. The author has provided a critical overview of NPS, and discussed in detail some of crucial issues like Pension Payouts, Pension Annuity, Pension Products, Investment Management, Role of Capital Market, Risk Governance and Risk Management, Regulation and Supervision, Financial Literacy etc. Finally there is set of valuable suggestions, which if implemented will put in place a robust pension system in India. The NPS is in the evolution phase, but globally, many countries have initiated pension reforms long back and the author has successfully provided a global picture of reforms, and discussed about the outcome of such reforms, which would not only provide better a understanding about pension reforms but would also help to realise the weak areas of NPS to strengthen it further.

There cannot be a better author than Dr Sadhak, who has got in-depth knowledge and first-hand experience in Indian financial market spanning over three decades particularly in Life insurance, Mutual Funds and Pension Fund. As the MD/CEO of LIC Pension Fund he has seen the NPS roll out in India and experienced the strength and weakness. He also worked closely with the regulator PFRDA and his vast experience reflected throughout. This book is store of information, knowledge and strategic thoughts of Dr H. Sadhak. This book is a valuable contribution to the Literature of Pension Reform and will help to reduce knowledge and Policy Planning gap. Congratulations to Dr Sadhak for such an immensely useful contribution backed by tremendous amount of painstaking hard work over several years.

D.K. Mehrotra
Chairman
LIC of India

Preface

Pension Reform is perhaps the most critical issue of political economy of the current century as we are moving towards an ageing world. A new global demographic structure characterized by the decline in mortality, increase in longevity, rise in old age dependency ratio emerging are fast making old age living more vulnerable as we need to necessitating arrangement for old age income securities for a larger number of population for a longer duration. However, in the new economic era of market led macro economy management, the states are gradually withdrawing from social security regime and managing the old age income security/retirement pension virtually left to the individual.

Most of the developed countries have experienced early growth and faster ageing, have in the past initiated measures to reform their pension system and many are still experimenting with reforms mostly by introducing parametric changes within the pay as you go pension framework. On the other hand developing countries have still recently experienced higher mortality with relatively lower percentage of their elderly population (60+ age) but with better economic growth and increased longevity started feeling the burden of ageing and many have already put in place pension reforms and others have initiated such reforms. India, the second most populous country of the world emerging as the most populous country beyond 2030, and will be inhabited by a large percent of elderly population but at present about 90% work force do not have any formal social security. Growing burden of public pension, low coverage and increased number of elderly population forced India to initiate reforming its pension system and the National Pension System (NPS) was introduced in 2004 In many ways this is a bold step but still a long way to go as there are several structural constraints, implementation flaws, capacity deficiency. Successful implementation of Indian reforms would be a lesion for those developing countries who are contemplating to reforming their pension system. But at the same time, India needs to look beyond and learn from the pension reform experience of those countries who are early starter like countries in Latin America. There are certain unique features of newly established pension system in these countries and India can learn a lot from their experience of reforms.

Pension reform is a social-political-economic issue and calls for fine balancing act directed to enhancing economic value and welfare of the members. While financial health of the system needs to be carefully promoted but by protecting stakeholders' interest. Market based system has many plus points but cannot achieved the ultimate objectives of reforms; hence state has a role to play carefully craft its involvement. While a new system led by the reforms must have a well-designed integrated institutional framework, the implementation needs to be driven by commitment and capacity of higher order. Institutionalization of reform, building required capacity and competent leadership are important to design develop and carry forward a viable and robust pension system. These issues are the core of this study. The basic objective of this book is to disseminate information on emerging challenges of population ageing and recently initiated pension reform through NPS in India. To understand Indian reforms and probable gaps it was thought, that experience of some emerging economies would shed some lights on the gaps and shortcomings of Indian reforms and provide further inputs for improvement and strengthen the Indian reform.

This book is divided into three sections and 15 chapters for clarity of discussions. Three chapters in section one provides a global perspective, genesis and challenges in social security and pension reforms. A brief review of pension reforms in selected countries—structural change, challenges and impact of pension and social security reforms. In section two, discussions focus on the social security and pension system and the ongoing reforms in India in six chapters, which include changing trend in economy, demography and ageing in India, social security and retirement savings system in India, the structure, architecture and administration of NPS and the performance and structural constraints experienced.

A robust pension system cannot be established unless the system structure based on investors-centric policy clearly defined payout mechanisms, prudent guidelines on investment management and distinctly defined regulatory and supervisory responsibility. These issues have been discussed in section three in the context of NPS keeping in view the global practices. There are six chapters in this section which focused on issues like pension payouts, annuitization and state of annuity market in India; pension products; investment, risk management, governance and the role capital market; issues and challenges of pension fund regulation and supervision and financial literacy—promoting awareness and protecting and investors. In the final chapters some suggestions have been provided to remove structural weaknesses of NPS and make it a robust system with more accountability of stakeholders to enhance and protect the interest of the members of the NPS.

Finally, I would like to mention that pension reform is an evolving process. There may be some changes in the process, regulation operating results and statistical information which might not have been captured due to the time gap between the completion of manuscript and publication of this book. These and any other unintentional omission may be ignored by the esteemed readers.

Acknowledgements

Writing an acknowledgement is probably the most difficult task for an author as a book is an outcome of direct and indirect support of many, but only some of them end up receiving a mention due to space constraint. Yet, I would be failing in my duty if I do not mention the names of at least a few of the many institutions and individuals without whose support this work would have remained incomplete.

Of the many institutions which offered me invaluable help by allowing me to study and use their publications, I would specially mention and thank the International Bank for Reconstruction and Development/The World Bank, The Organisation for Economic Co-operation and Development (OECD) Paris; International Federation of Pension Fund Administrators (FIAP), Santiago, Chile; Organisation International Social Security Association (ISSA), Geneva, Social Security Administration (SSA)Washington.

I have also freely quoted from publications of Pension Fund Development and Regulatory and Development Authority (PFRDA); Insurance Regulatory and Development Authority (IRDA); Securities and Exchange Board of India (SEBI); Reserve Bank of India, Government of India etc. and many other institutions and would like to thank them all.

In addition to the ones mentioned there are many other institutions and authors whose work has enlightened me and they have been cited in this book to make it richer in content. I am grateful to them and would like to thank them all. There are many eminent experts who have provided immense technical support and encouraged me during this work and I am thankful to them all. But I would like to express my sincere thanks to Dr Tarun Das (World Bank Technical Expert Ministry of Finance, Government of Bangladesh), Vanessa Wang (Managing Director, Region Head of Pension Services Citi Asia Pacific); Dr Ryan Tewari (Managing Director, Mahler Fund Management BV, The Netherlands), Prof. B. Vaidyanathan (IIM, Bangalore), Ananta Barua (Executive Director, Securities and Exchange Board of India). Arunava Dutt (Addl. Controller General, Defence Accounts, Govt. of India), Dilip C. Chakraborty (Sr. Advisor, Towers Watson); David Tuesta (Chief Economist, Pensions–BBVA Research); Dr Steward Doss (Asst. Professor, National Insurance Academy, Pune). I would specially mention here that a large number of authors and researchers have allowed me to quote their works/publications and enriched work. Though I have mentioned them while quoting their works, I remain thankful to them.

There are many friends who have provided immense mental and moral support to bring out this edition. To name just a few of them, I would like to mention my friends and colleagues namely Mr D.K. Mehrotra (Chairman, LIC of India), S. Roychowdhury (Member IRDA), S. Sarker (MD, LIC), Jagdish Capoor (Former Dy. Governor, Reserve

Bank of India), Ajit Kamath (CMD, Arch Pharmalabs, Mumbai), Deepak Chatterjee (MD/SBI Mutual Fund). There are also many friends and collegues who have extended their support during the long years of study and I thank them all.

I would also like to thank the anonymous referee who had painstakingly gone through the first draft and offered many valuable suggestions which have improved the quality of this book. Some special mention need to be made here about my publisher SAGE Response Books, for bringing out this book, which is third in a row. The management, editors, and other staff members of SAGE Response, as in case of earlier publications have taken personal care to ensure editorial excellence and production quality and I remain thankful to all of them.

Last but not the least I owe a great deal to my wife Manjushri, son Partha and daughter Cosmica, who stood by me when I used to struggle after office hours. Finally, I would like to mention that while I share my success with all those mentioned above, I alone remain responsible for any shortcomings.

SECTION ONE

Social Security and Pension Reform

A Global Perspective

1 Social Security and Pension Reforms

Genesis and Challenges

INTRODUCTION

The debate on social security reforms has taken the centre stage in developed and developing countries as one of the most critical policy issues during recent times. The policymakers and researchers are intensely searching for an appropriate mechanism to confront the complex challenges arising out of changing population dynamics, ageing, growing inability of the government to finance unfunded pensions, increasing costs of retirement and so on. Pension reforms have, therefore, become a serious policy concern for planners, policymakers, market analysts and elderly population.

Old-age income security is one of the oldest socio-economic concerns of the society, which in course of time with the progress of civilisation and economic progress became the cornerstone of policymaking and socio-economic governance system. The thoughts of *ensuring old-age income support for those who contributed to our growth* gradually emerged as an important factor influencing state policy. Though the concept and importance of old-age economic support to the elderly remained the same, the format has changed over time with the changing dynamics of social policy and philosophy of economic policy. Faster economic growth has induced higher employment and income generation leading to better medical service and good health care which has improved the per capita consumption and improved the average longevity of people. Increased longevity forced the states and statesmen to pay serious attention to old-age pension and social security through innovative strategy and policy within the given limitation of resources and political framework.

A new dimension has been further added to the problem of old-age social security due to the gradual dismantling of the concept of welfare states in many developed and emerging market economies, reducing the responsibility for social assistance and passing the responsibility to the individual. In the new world, economic security of its members is no more the sole concern of the parental state with the economic restructuring advocates passing the same to the private enterprise. Like many other areas of economic functions, pension has also become an area of dual control—public as well as private sectors, through the process of reforms. An intense debate has been going on since the 1980s about the right type of pension reform model. A variety of measures and models have been suggested by many economists and policymakers. A large number of such models are centred on the arguments of privatising pensions and passing the funds management to private asset managers through introduction of funded defined contribution (DC) system. The concern for social security, which began with Bismarck's social security legislation in 1881, got serious global attention with the World Bank's publication, *Averting the Old Age Crisis: Policies to Protect the Old and Promote Growth* (1994).

Many authors have mentioned that the roots of modern social security to the social insurance was introduced by German chancellor Otto von Bismarck during 1881–92. Three laws considered to be the foundation of Bismarck's social security are: laws concerning health insurance for workers (15 June 1883), followed by Accident Insurance Act (6 July 1884) and the law on invalidity and old-age insurance for workers (22 June 1889). All these acts were finally promulgated afresh in the form of the Health Insurance Act on 10 April 1892 (Eurofound 2009). Bismarck's health insurance regulation brought to the fore the importance of social security for the old and disabled and the role of state in protecting them through legislative measures.

Subsequent to this development many countries introduced laws regarding social insurance and social security, particularly for the workers and elderly population, the important among them being the Social Security Act (1935) of the United States, which was signed by President Roosevelt on 14 August 1935. This act, in addition to several provisions for general welfare, created a social insurance programme to pay retired workers aged 65 years and above a continuing income after retirement (Social Security USA Administration). Another landmark development which aimed at strengthening the social security programme was the International Labour Organization (ILO) Declaration of Philadelphia in 1944 and its income security recommendation 1944 (No. 67). Social security was declared as a fundamental human right. Subsequently, ILO came out with various recommendations for strengthening social protection and diffusion of social protection programme. The ILO's social protection policy basically centred around social insurance. The ILO also relied more on existing models of social protection. A new dimension to social security movement was added when the World Bank published its policy research report, *Averting the Old Age Crisis* in 1994, which provided not only a blueprint of impending crisis owing to increased longevity and ageing population but also a strategic model for pension reforms which were based on public private partnership (PPP). *Averting the Old Age Crisis* was considered to be the most powerful guide map for future pension strategies and reforms, which many countries adopted worldwide. *Averting the Old Age Crisis* provided a strategic perspective and a broad framework of the pension reform model which can be adjusted in any economy. Three components of the model are: a publicly managed mandatory system with limited goal of poverty reduction, a privately managed mandatory private savings system for old-age pension and a complementary voluntary savings system to augment old-age retirement income.

The crisis in social security, though basically arising out of increased longevity, improved health care and improved medical facility, gets accentuated by increased unsustainable pressure on the exchequer due to Pay-as-You-Go (PAYG) defined Benefit (DB) pension system and low coverage of formal social security. We would, therefore, make an attempt in this section to examine the nature of pressure exerted by the demographic transition, weakness of DB pension system and various initiatives taken by the countries to protect and promote social security and pension system. Pension reforms have, thus, taken the centre stage in developed and developing countries as one of the most critical policy issues during recent times.

THE OLD-AGE CRISIS

The major concern for old-age social security and pension arises out of increased longevity and people living much beyond their normal working life. This creates several socio-economic and political problems. Increased longevity creates burdens on the national exchequer due to higher spending on pension and social security, increased expenses on health care, imbalance in intergenerational transfer of resources, growing burden on youth and adverse impact on national savings. Changes in population, age structure and ageing will adversely impact economic growth; it will reduce working age population, and hence labour supply. It will also reduce total productivity due to reduction of working age population and impact earnings. Ageing will also adversely impact domestic savings as the elderly population have higher propensity to consume and lower propensity to save than the working age population. It is an important political issue since ageing will emerge as a very strong political agenda which may overshadow the issues of youths as well as development. Peter G. Peterson in his paper, 'Gray Dawn: The Global Aging Crisis' (1999) said:

> *Global aging will become not just the transcendent economic issue of the 21st century, but the transcendent political issue as well. It will dominate and daunt the public policy agendas of developed countries and force the renegotiation of their social contracts. It will also reshape foreign policy strategies and the geographical order.*

We may look into the changing dynamics of world population and changing scenario of population ageing with the help of data from World Population Prospects (United Nations 2009).

Social Security and Social Protection

There is often confusion about definition of the term social security. Sometimes it is used to denote social protection, while it includes only old-age pension at other times. While social security basically concerns providing old-age income security, social protection aims at protecting population against various economic risks through unemployment benefits and health insurance in addition to old-age income security through pension. While pension is linked to workers and labour market, social protection covers all citizens including non-labour. Therefore, social security has broader (used mostly in Europe) and narrow sense (used mostly in developing countries). The term social security is generally used in a broader sense to cover various types of risks associated with old age, health, unemployment and so on. In the European Union, social security includes social insurance and social assistance programme as mentioned by Dethier in the 2020 Focus Brief on the World's Poor and Hungry People:

> *Social insurance denotes publicly provided or mandated contributory programs that cover workers and their dependents against major life risks—essentially unemployment, health risks, and old age. Beneficiaries receive income or services in exchange for contributions to an insurance scheme. Social assistance refers to noncontributory transfer programs that are means tested and targeted in some way to the poor or those vulnerable to poverty and shocks. (Dethier 2007)*

Social Insurance may be provided through mandatory contribution or through exchequer-supported programmes to cover major risks like unemployment, health, old-age income and so on, while social assistance is usually a means-tested programme to protect the poor.

The core objective of social security reforms is to introduce affordable old-age economic support and social protection for people, particularly those who cannot afford old-age savings. Therefore, while talking about social security we need to take a holistic view of old-age economic security as any such reforms of social security must contain old age–related cash and health benefits. It is possible if social security is considered as a package of at least two important ingredients—namely old-age pension and old-age health insurance. However, a major amount of focus of social security globally and in developing countries is particularly centred around pension system. Health insurance as an important component of the social security is mostly prevalent in developed countries and 'with the exception of United States, all the developed countries now have universal health insurance' (Dethier 2007). Along with universal health insurance, most of the developed and many developing countries have introduced universal old-age pension.

Population Growth and Global Ageing[1]

World demographic changes are distinctly characterised by three important factors, namely reduction in mortality and fertility, increase in longevity, decrease in the growth rates in population in the younger cohort (age 0–14); slow growth in working age population (aged 15–59); and rapid growth in elderly population (aged 60+). The United Nations' publication, *World Populations Prospects—The 2008 Revision* has estimated that there will be a sharp decline in average annual growth rate during 2009–50. The average annual rate of change in the world population during 1975–2009 was 1.53 per cent, while the same for the developed countries was 0.48 per cent as against 1.82 per cent in less-developed countries. The average annual growth rate between 2009 and 2050 for the world as a whole is expected to be 0.71 per cent, while the same for the developed countries would be 0.08 per cent as against 0.83 per cent for the less-developed countries. In spite of the sharp decline in growth rates of world population, world population will grow by 2.3 million during 2009–50; that is, the population will increase from 6,829 million in 2009 to 9,150 million in 2050 at a medium variant, but it will be 11,030 million at a constant fertility rate. While population of less-developed countries will increase from 5,596 million in 2009 to 7,875 million in 2050, the same for more developed countries will increase at a much lower rate from 1,233 million in 2009 to 1,275 million in 2050 at a medium variant. At a medium variant, the share of developed countries in world population will decline from 18 per cent in 2009 to 13.9 per cent in 2050 and that of less-developed countries will increase from 67.9 per cent to 86.1 per cent during the same period.

The UN estimates also indicate that by 2028 India will surpass China in terms of population and by 2050 the projected population of India will be 1,775.2 million as against Chinese population of 1,437 million. Slower growth rate in working age population is a result of decline in fertility. Decline in growth rates in younger cohort hence; slower growth rate in working age population is a result of decline in fertility. Fertility projection by the United Nations shows total fertility decline from 2.56 in 2005–10 to 2.02 in 2045–50 at the medium variant. Though the fertility of less-developed countries will decline from 2.73 to 2.05, the same would increase, however, from 1.64 to 1.80 in more developed countries (Table 1.1) during the same period.

Earlier we had problems of high fertility and growing population, today one of the major economic concern is declining fertility and slow growth of working age population. Various measures to reduce over population through birth control, improvement in standard of living due to increased earnings and improved health care and general awareness about personal well-being through micro family, and so on, resulted into decline in fertility, which is an emerging global concern.

---

[1] Population-related data in this section has been drawn from the *World Population Prospects—The 2008 Revision*, and *World Population Ageing 2009*, published by the United Nations (2009).

Table 1.1 World Population Trend

Column 1	*Column 2*	*Column 3*	*Column 4*	*Column 5*	*Column 6*	*Column 7*	*Column 8*	*Column 9*	*Column 10*	*Column 11*
			World			*More developed countries*			*Less-developed countries*	
		1950	*2009*	*2050**	*1950*	*2009*	*2050**	*1950*	*2009*	*2050*
A	Population	2,529	6,829	9,150	812	1,233	1,275	1,717	5,596	7,875
	Per cent of world population				32.1	18.1	13.9	67.9	81.9	86.1
	Item		*World*			*More developed*			*Less developed*	
		1950–75	*1975–2009*	*2009–50**	*1950–75*	*1975–2009*	*2009–50**	*1950–75*	*1975–2009*	*2009–50**
B	Population: Average annual rates of change (%)	1.89	1.53	0.71	1.02	0.48	0.08	2.25	1.82	0.83
	Year		*2005–10*	*2045–50**		*2005–10*	*2045–50**		*2005–10*	*2045–50**
C	Life expectancy at birth		67.6	75.5		77.1	82.8		65.6	74.3
		1970–75	*2005–10*	*2045–50**	*1970–75*	*2005–10*	*2045–50**	*1970–75*	*2005–10*	*2045–50**
D	Estimated and projected total fertility	4.32	2.56	2.02	2.17	1.64	1.8	5.18	2.73	2.05
E	Average annual rates of change of population in broad age groups 2009–50			2009–50*			2009–50*			2009–50*
		0 – 14		–0.08			–0.09			–0.08
		15 – 59		0.57			–0.35			0.73
		60+		2.44			1.11			2.96
		80+		3.3			2.07			4.14
		Total		0.71			0.08			0.83

Source: Population Division of the Department of Economic and Social Affairs of the United Nations Secretariat (2009). *World Population Prospects: The 2008 Revision.* Volume I. Comprehensive Tables (United Nations publication).

Note: * at medium variant.

Economic prosperity in the 20th century enhanced income, and per capita income, new discovery in medicine and ability to afford better health care by people in general significantly reduced the mortality rates. *World Population Prospects—The 2008 Revision* mentioned that the average life expectancy in 2005–10 was 67.6 years as against 47 years in 1950–55, which is further expected to go up to 75.5 years in 2045–50. The life expectancy in the more developed countries will go up to 77.1 per cent during 2005–10 and to 82.8 years in 2045–50, while the same in less-developed countries will go up from 65.6 years to 74.3 years. The general improvement in life expectancy, particularly in less-developed countries, will push up the number of elderly population and increase old-age dependency and the social and state concern for old-age social security.

The UN publication, *World Population Ageing 2009,* indicated (Table 1.2) that,

> *Globally the population of older persons is growing at a rate of 2.6 per cent per year considerably faster than the population as a whole, which is increasing at 1.2 per cent annually. At least until 2050, the older population is expected to continue growing more rapidly than the population in other age group.*

It has been further estimated that the population aged 60 years and above, numbered 600 million in 2000, surpassed 700 million in 2009 and is expected to be 2 billion in 2050. The oldest of the old (aged 80 years and above) will grow at a faster rate than the older persons. As a result the ratio of the oldest of the old to the old will decline from currently one oldest for every seven old persons to one oldest of the old to five old

Table 1.2 Demographic Trend and Ageing—Continent-wise

	Total Population Millions		*Percentage of Population over 60*		*Percentage of Population over 80*		*Old-age Dependency Ratio*		*Life Expectancy at Birth*	
Country	*2009*	*2050**	*2010*	*2050**	*2010*	*2050**	*2010*	*2050**	*2005–10*	*2045–50*
Asia	4,121	5,231	9.9	23.6	1.1	4.4	9.9	26.7	68.9	76.8
Africa	1,010	1,998	5.4	10.6	0.4	1.1	6.1	10.8	54.1	67.4
Latin America and Carribbean	582	729	10.0	25.5	1.5	5.5	10.6	30.7	73.4	79.8
Europe	732	691	22.0	34.2	4.2	9.6	23.8	47.5	75.1	81.5
North America	348	448	18.4	27.8	3.8	8.0	19.5	35.9	79.3	83.5
Oceania	35	51	15.4	23.9	2.9	6.5	16.6	30.0	76.4	82.1
World	6,829	9,150	11.0	21.0	1.5	4.3	11.6	25.3		

Source: Population Division of the Department of Economic and Social Affairs of the United Nations Secretariat (2009). *World Population Prospects: The 2008 Revision.* Volume I. Comprehensive Tables (United Nations publication).
Note: *at medium variant.

persons. Slow growth in working age population and faster growth in older population will see a sharp decline in Potential Support Ratio (PSR) and increase in the dependency ratio (DR). The PSR is the number of working age population per older person aged 65 years or more, which will decline from nine in 2009 to four in 2050. A decline in old-age support ratio will increase old-age dependency ratio as more old people need to be supported by less number of working age population. Though population ageing and old-age dependency are more pronounced in the industrially developed countries, they have emerged as worldwide phenomena, and old-age dependency is going to pose serious problems in these countries in the near future and the developing countries will witness a dramatic shift from 'young' to 'elderly' dependency; the share of elderly in the least developed countries is nevertheless projected to double between 1995 and 2050, from 5.6 per cent to 11. 2 per cent; in the less-developed regions, the rate is forecast to increase from 11.2 per cent to 21.3 per cent (Group of 10 1998). Dependency ratio, however, also includes the youth dependency ratio; that is, the number of children below working age group supported by the working age group. Youth dependency may, however, decline due to the negative growth in population in the age group 0–14 years, but the wide gap in the rate of growth of older population and working age population may not offset the social burden.

The population ageing and the growing number of older and the oldest of the old has thrown unprecedented challenges to the policymakers to provide secure and broad-based source of old-age income to this growing number of older and the oldest of the old. Because living an active life after normal retirement is a right of every citizen who has contributed to the growth and development of the nation while they were young and working. They can't be thrown out, but the ability of the nation is also to be considered along with this right.

As mentioned by the Organisation for Economic Co-operation and Development (OECD) Secretary General Donald J. Johnston at the opening of the Active Ageing Session, G8 Meeting of Employment Ministers, turn on 10 November 2000,

> *The concept of Active Ageing Captures the essence of the policy challenge of ageing populations. It emphasises the importance of providing opportunities for people to contribute longer in the Labour Market and to be more active in the community as they grow older. Active ageing is a good deal for social economic policy and provides opportunities for win-win solutions, at least in the medium and Long run.*

However, the concept of active ageing can be implemented by providing opportunity to older people to remain engaged in productive activities and by ensuring the flow of income when they cease to be employed. In order to keep the older people engaged in productive activities, initiatives have been taken by many countries to move retirement and pension entitlement age upwards. To ensure flow of sustainable old-age income, pension system reforms have been introduced by a large number of countries, which is also a political initiative. Therefore, social security is no more a sociopolitical but a social–fiscal–economic–political problem being confronted by developed as well developing countries. To confront the challenges arising out of ageing and old-age income instability, there is a need to put in place a well-meaning sustainable pension and old-age social security system. It is no doubt a very complex issue and a number of stakeholders with cross purpose diverse interests are present. It is also very difficult to satisfy these cross purpose–interested group with a single set of solutions, but a solution that aims at attaining the long-term socio-economic objectives to protect the interest of older people and create space for economic growth needs to be attempted.

SOCIAL SECURITY MEASURES IN PRACTICE

The term social security refers to a number of programmes which include old-age income security, health-care benefits, financial support for unemployment, and so on, provided through cash payments to the members and dependent persons as per the law of the country, to offset the income loss when a member ceases to work due to retirement or is unable to work due to disability. There are a number of institutionalised social security measures in most of the developed and less-developed countries, though the developed countries have been more generous in providing social security for their citizens. Broadly, three important programmes are followed to provide cash benefits to the members—namely universal pension/social security, means-tested pension and employment-related pension.

State-Supported Universal Social Security or Social Insurance

Under this programme, many states provide old-age pension to their citizens/residents, which is often means-tested. This programme may be simple universal pension or means-tested pension system.

Universal Pension

Universal pensions are flat-rate cash benefits given to all the residents or citizens, irrespective of their income level. Benefits under universal social security may be more than one—they may include old-age pension, disability pension, dependents pension and so on. Universal pension is generally non-contributory and usually financed from general revenues. *Means-tested programmes* are administered to provide pension benefits to a select group of citizens/residents who have insufficient income means and are unable to sustain their needs through self or family income and are thus eligible for benefits under this. Primary test for eligibility is the income of self and sometimes the total family income.

Occupational Pension

Occupational pensions are privately managed and fully or partially funded by the employers, encouraged through tax incentives. Sometimes the government also contributes to an occupational pension fund. Occupational pensions are employment related in nature of social insurance and the members and dependent family members are entitled to receive long-term pension benefits and also short-term benefits for sickness, health care and so on. Occupational pension can be defined as DB PAYG pension or as individual account-based DC pension.

PAYG Pension

It is in the form of DB pension; benefits depend on the pay and length of service. The scheme is generally publicly administered.

Individual Account–Based DC Pension

A recent trend globally is to introduce and encourage DC pensions which are fully funded by the subscribers. In fact, pension reforms to a large extent are based on implementation of DC pension system.

Provident Funds

Provident funds are also being used as an instrument to provide social security, primarily in developing countries. Provident funds are basically mandatory saving programmes under which employees make regular contributions from their wages; sometimes matching contribution is made by the employers. Sometimes provident funds allow partial withdrawal before retirement for certain specific purposes. Sometimes there is a provision to use certain accumulated amount to purchase annuity.

Annuity and Voluntary Savings

There are certain voluntary savings to generate old-age income through self financing. Life annuity and pension-oriented mutual fund products are major instruments in this category. Life insurance companies offer pension annuities which are subscribed on voluntary basis by workers and others for pension annuity. Tax incentives are provided to encourage purchase of such pension plans by the individual.

Prior to the recent pension reforms movement which began with introduction of individual account–based DC system in Chile in 1981, many countries depended on basically publicly managed *DB* type social security financed through payroll taxes and organised around certain predetermined formulae. But due to certain inherent weaknesses, the unfunded DB or PAYG systems were not sufficient enough to face the challenges of increased longevity and the growing fiscal burden on the exchequer. The switchovers that are taking place through reforms are moves towards the fully funded DC system organised around employees' contribution and retirement pension determined solely by the history of individual contribution. The PAYG DB benefit system is a publicly managed pension system financed through payroll taxes and organised around certain predetermined formulae. The DB system is post-retirement pension based on the history of employment and earning record. In a DB system pensions are guaranteed and the amounts tentatively predetermined irrespective of the funding position and investment return received by the pension providers (employers). In the DB System, both the investment risks and longevity risks are solely borne by the employers and the members are not concerned about the risks.

Individual Account–Based DC System

The individual account–based DC system on the other hand is organised around employees' contribution rate and flows of retirement pension determined solely by the history of individual contribution. The DC system is a fully funded system, financed solely by the individual unlike unfunded PAYG system under DB system. In the DC system, no such guarantee exists and the employees are not sure about the extent of accumulated pension savings and post-retirement annuity. Accumulation of assets will solely depend on the performance fund management and return thereon. So the employees will fully depend on fund managers and will remain uncertain about future pensions. In the DC system the employers are in no way accountable for these risks. Both the risks are transferred to the employees, since they own their individual account. In a DC system in general, neither the employers nor the fund managers are accountable for either fund management–related risks or longevity-related risks. However, some states which have introduced the DC system have tried to mitigate the investment risks through minimum return guarantee (MRG).

Many experts have pointed out that state-supported DB system is unable to provide a sustainable solution to the pension challenges arising out of the changing demographic dynamics and population ageing. There are several arguments about the inherent weakness of the state-supported PAYG DB system. Some such arguments are given in the following sections.

❖ ISSUE OF SOLVENCY

A PAYG system is basically unfunded and current pension payments are made out of current contribution received, and there is a hidden liability increase over time with decline in pension support ratio and increase in dependency ratio.

❖ BURDEN ON EXCHEQUER

DB System has been criticised on the ground that the system imposes burden on the exchequer. When anticipated liabilities are larger than the actual assets portfolio, the system tends to be insolvent and is rescued by government subsidy. However, the nature of insolvency will depend on the nature of funding. Hidden pension liability of the government may be lower in a partially funded system than in an unfunded system.

❖ POLITICAL RISKS

A state-mandated PAYG system runs into political risks since the legislature and political parties control the system. Often the political interest prevails over the economic interest of the pensioners and external shocks are resisted through internal changes to protect interest of the pressure groups. Often there are parametric changes in benefits, taxation, indexation, and so on, due to legislative measures. Such changes may or may not be beneficial for the pensioners and the future generation. Therefore, misdirected political intervention in the social security system may cost the exchequer dearly and harm the pensioners' interest adversely.

❖ LACK OF TRANSPARENCY

It is often argued that the PAYG system is not transparent enough since the fund information is not publicly available and workers are unable to track the performance and progress of the fund and the country is unaware of the changing trend in the hidden pension liability which generates public debt.

❖ DOES NOT PROMOTE SAVINGS

Since pension is assured and amount is assumed there is no incentive to save extra amount which may tend to be a disincentive to savings growth.

❖ PASSIVE INVESTMENT

Pension amount in DB system is mostly predetermined and there may not be any serious attempt to earn risk-based higher return. Fund managers mostly follow a passive investment and safe strategy by investing in low-risk government securities. This in turn is reflected in poor resource allocation in the economy.

There is a wider agreement that the politically vulnerable social security system needs to be replaced by market-based social security system through individual accounts with rule-based approach to risk allocation (Valdés-Prieto 2005). Individual account–based social security is basically a DC pension system fully funded by the members and the funds are managed by the professional fund managers. The DC system has several potential strengths and can avoid some inherent weaknesses of the PAYG DB system.

❖ BETTER RETURN

Since this is a market-based system, the investment portfolio contains a higher portion of equity which has the potential to generate a relatively higher rate of return. Total return of the portfolio is expected to be higher in DC than in PAYG DB system, which depends on the wage growth and debt-centric investment strategy.

❖ REDUCED POLITICAL INTERVENTION

Since the DC system is fully funded by the individual, and there is minimal state role in running the system, the scope of political intervention is also minimal and can serve the interest of the members better.

❖ NO BURDEN ON EXCHEQUER

DC is a fully funded individual account–based system and therefore there is no burden on the exchequer except in case of any subsidy (as in case of new pension system) or minimum return guarantee (as in many Latin American and East European pension funds).

❖ SOLVENCY

Since pension funds under the DC system are pre-funded and there is no agreed pension liability, long-term insolvency problem does not arise as in case of unfunded DB system, which assures certain guaranteed pension to the members.

❖ WIDER OPTION AND ACTIVE CHOICE

In a DB system the members generally participate in portfolio selection, but in DC system members can exercise active choice and select a fund/portfolio depending on individual risk tolerance level.

❖ MORE TRANSPARENCY

Pension funds in an individual account system operate in a more transparent way and there is continuous information disclosure by the fund managers, trusts and regulators. Members through their fund ID or permanent account number can also see the performance of investment, accumulation of amount and so on. This transparency is not there in the PAYG DB system.

In addition to the above, there are several other potential advantages of individual account–based DC system; for instance, it supports capital market development and boosts the growth of domestic savings. This reduces the burden on the exchequer as there is less public expenditure on pension spending and finally generates momentum of growth in the economy.

As indicated above, there are several positive features in an individual account–based DC system which attract policymakers, economists, social scientists and researchers to the system. DC has emerged as the main plank of pension reforms globally. However, experts have also pointed out several weaknesses in the individual account based–DC system.

❖ HIGH COSTS OF DC SYSTEM

Experts have pointed out several costs associated with individual account–based DC system. These costs arise out of product marketing, accounting and fund administration, investment management fees, system regulation and oversight fees, costs of purchasing annuity and so on.

❖ ADMINISTRATION COSTS

A major criticism of the individual account–based funded system is the cost of system administration. This cost arises out of product marketing, administration and fund management costs which are fully borne by the individual. Such costs are required in PAYG DC system, and even if some implicit costs are incurred, the same is borne by the employers and retirees are not affected. Quoting the World Bank, Baker and Kar (2002) mentioned that the cost of running a privatised individual account is

10 to 50 times higher than running the public social security system in the United States. Further, the cost of converting accumulated assets into annuity is between 11 to 22 times the cost of operating the social security in the United States. The cost of running a public agency which supervises such a system is much higher than the whole social security in the United States. Many authors have pointed out that administrative costs are higher in Latin American countries, while some have pointed out that it is quite low when compared with other fund management industries. According to Vial and Melguizo (2007), the issue is clouded because contribution to pension is expressed as fraction of wages, while financial market fees are calculated as a fraction of the assets under management. Administrative costs are calculated as a difference of the internal rate of return of pension investment, with or without fee. These were estimated as 0.39 per cent for men and 0.42 per cent for women.

❖ COSTS OF ANNUITY

Another argument relating to the costs is the costs of annuity. There are two stages in DC pensions, namely accumulation and payouts. The payouts stage provides regular flow of annuity income which a member purchases at the end of accumulation period. Though investment return in the accumulation may be higher, it may not be sufficient to purchase an annuity which would provide real income higher than that would have been possible through a life annuity policy at the beginning. 'The issue is the cost that would be required for private market to offer the same level of longevity and inflation protection to all participants' (Heller 1998).

❖ UNCERTAIN MARKET DEVELOPMENT RISK

Uncertain market developments may wipe equity investment gain. Pension funds have experienced such uncertain market development on several occasions. A severe decline in pension assets and return was noted in the financial crisis in 2007–08. According to the OECD Pension Market Focus (December 2008), the total pension assets of OECD countries declined by 3.3 trillion or nearly 20 per cent from December 2007. Including other pension assets like assets in personal pension plans, this loss was about US$5 trillion. The crisis in the financial market also impacted the return on pension fund investment, which marked a decline of more than 30 per cent. This decline was significant in countries having higher investment in equities; for example, a country like Ireland which has 66 per cent exposure in equities witnessed more than 30 per cent decline in return. Alicia H. Munnel, Director, Center for Retirement Research, Boston College, Carrol School of Management, in her testimony before the Committee on Education and Labour, US House of Representative on 24 February 2009 stated:

> *Participants in 401(k) plans approaching retirement held about two-thirds of their balances in equities. As a result, the market value of assets in 401(k)s/IRA tumbled by about 30%. That decline means that the median 401(k) holdings for a person 55–64 went from around $60,000 in 2007 to roughly $42,000 at the end of 2008.*

❖ INVESTMENT-RELATED RISKS

Individual account–based pension system relies on market, particularly the equity market, to provide higher return on investment to enhance the value of accumulated amounts. However, it also has an implicit cost associated with inefficiency of fund managers, inappropriate portfolio composition, unethical practices, hidden motives of self advancements, and so on, which may arise out of weak oversight and regulation.

❖ INFLATION RISKS

Inflation in absence of any indexation reduces the consumption level; hence the worst enemy of pensioners mostly depends on the pension income. In a DB system, inflation risk is automatically covered by indexation but in an individual account–based private pension no such indexation is usually available. A member needs to purchase annuity after the accumulated period is over and the ordinary annuity is not inflation adjusted. There will be additional cost for inflation protection.

❖ RISK OF IRREGULAR CONTRIBUTION

The individual account–based mandatory pension system also suffers from irregular contribution by the members. Valente (2008) pointed out that according to the International Association of Latin American Pension Fund Supervisors (AIOS), they had 76 million pension fund affiliates in late 2007, but only 32 million, that is, 37 per cent of economically active population made regular payments.

❖ OTHER PROGRAMMES

There are several arguments in favour and against both the systems. Though major debates and initiatives on pension reforms the world over centred around the privatised and funded DC (PFDC) model, Latin America experimented in few other non-privatised publicly managed models that provided low-cost retirement benefits. Such models are: notional DC system in Sweden, central provident fund (CPF) system in Singapore and employees' provident fund (EPF) system in Malaysia. There are, therefore, two schools of thoughts—one suggests minimising or eliminating the role of state and transferring the pension system to the private sector, while other prefers to reform the system remaining within the public system. Advocates of total privatisation, however, argue that privately managed systems have the superior capability to promote savings, to reduce pressure on the exchequer, to produce better return on retirement savings, to develop the capital market and to generate better growth rates. However, 'ultimately the decision to adopt a public private system of pensions [for the second non distributive pillar] depends not on economics, but rather on one's view of what role the state ought to have in society' (Willmore and Bertucci 1998).

PENSION REFORM MODELS

Though both the developed and emerging countries are facing pension reform dilemma, there is no uniformity among them with respect to an appropriate model of reforms. Each country has adopted its own pension system depending on sociopolitical and economic needs and circumstances. However, in course of time distinct trends have emerged among the groups of countries that can be clustered around few models, which can be grouped into two broad categories, namely parametric (non-structural) reforms and systemic (structural) reforms.

In a parametric or non-structural reform the system is strengthened by improving financial viability of the system—lowering the pension benefits by increasing the pensionable age and so on. While in reform through structural change, the PAYG DB system is primarily replaced by the contributory DC system. Structural or systemic reforms, however, are two distinct types, namely the World Bank proposed and supported multi-pillar individual account–based funded pension system and a low-risk notional DC (NDC). However, there is no uniform pension reform model and each country has adopted its own pension system depending on social–political and economic needs and circumstances. Most of the OECD countries retained their PAYG DB system, while most of the Latin American and many East European countries have adopted the individual account–based DC system. Some countries like Sweden, Italy, Latvia, and so on, adopted the NDC system, while social security in countries like Singapore and Malaysia centred around provident funds system. India has adopted a distinct model which is a combination of PAYG DB system and individual account–based DC system, which can be termed as semi-systemic system (SSS). The implicit objectives of pension reforms are to enhance pension entitlement and ensure uninterrupted flow of regular income. However, there is a difference between the parametric and systemic reforms regarding longevity risk. In the parametric reforms longevity risk is borne by the pension providers since there is no change in the basic structure of the

DB pension system, but in case of systemic reforms the longevity risk is transferred to the pensioners. Now let us see the major policy parameter of various reform models.

Parametric Reforms

In a parametric reform model the basic structure of pension does not change and it remains a DB system but substantial changes are made in the underlying rules regarding pension. Parametric reforms may be implemented by introducing changes in the contribution side or benefits side. Parametric changes on the contribution side may be affected by changing the percentage of income that need to be paid or the income threshold, while benefits side may be affected by changing indexation or updating pension benefits (Zaidi 2006). Parametric reforms have been undertaken by countries which want to retain the existing unfunded PAYG system through substantial changes in rate of contribution to enhance the benefits, to take care of increased longevity (most of the OECD countries have adopted parametric reforms). The important instruments needed to implement parametric reforms are increasing of pension age, changes in the rate of contribution, calculation of earnings base for pension, revaluation of past earnings for pension, indexation of pension and so on.

❖ RETIREMENT AGE

This is the most common instrument of parametric pension reforms and is carried out by increasing the retirement age, particularly in the OECD countries, which are burdened with ageing and longevity risks. Even many countries which have implemented other types of pension reforms are resorting to increasing the retirement age to tackle the increased pension burden due to increased longevity. With increased longevity more elderly people depend on lesser number of working people. This increases the burden on the latter. However, the pressure can be reduced by allowing the elderly to work for a longer period. This would generate more tax revenue, and more funds to pay pension; working longer also helps people to stay out of poverty (Leibfritz 2003). Increase in retirement age will also improve pension entitlement and reduce the incidence of old-age poverty. Lower pension entitlement can be reversed by increasing the working age since older persons would work longer.

In most of the OECD countries, the retirement age is 65 years and many countries are proposing to increase it further in a phased manner. According to a Mercer Release (2007), Denmark will increase retirement age from 65 to 67 years during 2024–27 and Germany will increase it from 65 to 67 years during 2012–29. According to an OECD release, *Pension at Glance* (OECD 2009) the option to retire early has been restricted in Belgium, Denmark, Greece and the Netherlands.

❖ CONTRIBUTION RATE

Another important instrument of parametric reform relates to the rate of contribution and minimum period of contribution for full pension. The modification of contribution rate, particularly scaling up, has been adopted to enhance pension entitlement in many countries like Czech Republic, Denmark, Germany, Italy, the Netherlands, the United Kingdom and so on. Many countries like Austria, France, Italy, and so on, have introduced minimum contribution period full pension. The contribution rate has also gone up in case of retirement before the legal retirement age. These measures aim at ensuring that the pensioners receive substantial pension annuity after retirement.

❖ CALCULATION OF PENSION ENTITLEMENT

Many countries attempted to increase the pension entitlement by extending the period of calculation and also by revaluing the past earnings of the pensioners. Many OECD countries like Austria, Finland, Germany, Hungary, Poland, and so on, have adopted the base calculation and some have also adopted revaluation method.

❖ PENSION BENEFIT INDEXATION

Another important parametric change that many countries (Austria, Germany, Hungary, Spain, etc.) have followed is the change in the benefit indexation by linking the benefits indexation with prices. Many countries like Austria, Finland, France, Hungary, Spain, UK, and so on, have changed the pension formula for calculation of benefits. Pension formula can be altered by effecting changes in accrual of pension or by changes in pensionable salary.

Systemic Reforms

Systemic reforms are also called structural reforms since the basic structure of PAYG undergoes a structural change in this kind of reform. While parametric reforms aim at improving the pension entitlement through measures like increasing the retirement age, changing the rate of contribution, changing the formula for calculation of pension, benefit indexation, and so on, by keeping the basic pension structure as PAYG DB structure, systemic reforms on the other hand adopt a new system of funded DC pension by replacing unfunded DB structure.

There are two types of DC models, namely multi-pillar World Bank model and NDC. Under the DC, many countries have transformed their pension structure from DB to

DC through mandatory privately managed individual pension accounts. The switchover to a new pension model has also encouraged replacement of single-pillar system by a multi-pillar model.

The World Bank published its policy research paper *Averting the Old Age Crisis* in 1994 which provided a new dimension to the thoughts of pension reforms globally and set the pension reform strategy in many countries, particularly in the less-developed regions. According to John Rust (2002) the book is the first comprehensive and global examination of old-age security, it identifies three functions of old-age financial security programmes—redistribution, saving and insurance. It evaluates the policy options for meeting these functions using two criteria: their impact on the aged and their impact on the economy as a whole (Rust 2002). In *Averting the Old Age Crisis*, the World Bank advocated the introduction of a multi-pillar system.

❖ A MANDATORY PUBLICLY MANAGED TAX-FINANCED FIRST PILLAR

The first pillar is considered to be the anti-poverty pillar, non-contributory and financed through payroll taxes to provide a minimum pension in old age. The first pillar is also an attempt to ensure distributional justice.

❖ A MANDATORY PRIVATELY MANAGED FULLY FUNDED SECOND PILLAR

The second pillar is the core to the World Bank prescription which is individual account–based fully funded pension saving scheme. Under this pillar, an individual account is built up through contribution of members. Funds are managed by the specialised fund managers and accumulated wealth is fully or partly used to purchase annuity policy. More the contribution, more the accumulated assets and monthly pension.

❖ A VOLUNTARY THIRD PILLAR

This is a voluntary saving provision to augment retirement pension received from the first and second pillars. The first pillar is just like a public pension plan, which provides a social safety net for the old and focuses on redistribution. The second pillar is the most talked about and controversial component of World Bank's three-pillar model, which is fully funded and privately managed. Benefits under this model are linked to the contribution and investment return is derived out of it. The third pillar, voluntary savings, is aimed at providing supplementary benefits to those who want a luxurious old age.

However, the World Bank subsequently advocated the five basic elements of the multi-pillar system consisting of (*a*) non-contributory zero pillar, (*b*) a contributory first pillar, (*c*) a mandatory second pillar, (*d*) a voluntary third pillar and (*e*) informal intra-family or intergenerational financial and non-financial support to the elderly including health care and housing (Holzmann and Hinz 2005). One of the most important elements of systemic pension reform is the incorporation of individual accounts which provides ownership claims to the workers in the system. The important reasons cited for individual accounts are: improving the overall performance of economy, increasing the overall rate of return, allowing individuals to assume greater responsibility for their well-being reducing current implicit government liabilities, and more closely linking benefits to contribution (Thompson 1999).

The professional fund managers who manage these pension accounts are considered to be more efficient and are able to provide better returns. These specialised fund managers invest the money and purchase retirement benefits (in some countries) according to the regulatory provisions laid down by the government or regulators. The individual account–based funded multi-pillar system has been widely seen as an answer to the growing pension problems and many authors and experts have suggested replacement of PAYG DB system by the multi-pillar system. According to Holzmann (1998),

> *the multi pillar reform is a welfare enhancing approach starting with reforms of first pillar PAYG, the second pillar enable rapid and nearly complete shift to a mandatory funded system, and the third is a gradual shift to a multi pillar scheme in which there is some mix between PAYG and funded pensions.*

Professor Rust (2002) cited several reasons in favour of multi-pillar system including such as increase in long-term savings, capital market deepening, growth, risk diversification, insulation from political risks and so on. According to Lawrence H. Thompson(1999), the individual accounts system supports and improves the overall performance of economy, increases the overall rate of return, allows individuals to assume greater responsibility for their well-being reducing current implicit government liabilities, and more closely linking benefits to contribution. Several other advantages of the multi-pillar system have also been outlined, such as a distinction between poverty reduction and income replacement goals, risk diversification through wider portfolio choice and minimisation of fiscal burden.

The World Bank has made serious attempts to support the pension reform and implementation of multi-pillar system including fund-based and non-fund-based activities like providing credit, advisory services, capacity building through training, information dissemination and so on. Beginning with 1984, the World Bank has issued more than 350 papers and publications. The World Bank has helped 68 countries to reform their pension system and total lending amounted to US$34 billion. All these efforts to a great extent helped to increase our understanding about emerging pension problems and pushed the countries to initiate necessary measures with seriousness.

However, there are *other views* also and many experts are very critical about the concept of the multi-pillar system, individual account and excessive focus on contributory second tier and less focus on first-tier universal pension. Further, experts have pointed out the high cost of administration and potential reduction of coverage under the multi-pillar system. Orszag and Stiglitz (1999), in their paper *Rethinking Pension Reform: Ten Myths about Social Security System,* tried to dismantle many of the benefits proposed to be achieved through implementation of multi-pillar system and concluded the following:

> *Unfunded public pension systems represent a potential threat to the fiscal soundness—and, more broadly, economic stability—of many countries. The World Bank's study Averting the Old Age Crisis, provided an invaluable service in drawing attention to this problem and in discussing specific policy changes to address the issue. Unfortunately, as often happens, the suggestions have come to be viewed narrowly focusing on a second pillar limited to a private, non-redistributive, DC pension plan.*

Though in the multi-pillar system the first pillar has an important role in poverty mitigation, scant attention was paid to it by most of the countries while concentrating on mandatory contribution-based second pillar.

Multi-pillar DC system has also been criticised for high cost of administration. For example, according to International Confederation of Free Trade Unions (ICFTU) (2003) system-decentralised private accounts are far more costly to manage than a single government fund. The resources used to run these accounts are a waste from an economic standpoint as the capital and labour could have been used in some alternative productive use.

Another criticism often voiced by critics is the inability of the multi-pillar system to expand pension coverage. For example, Willmore (2000) commenting on the World Bank proposed multi-pillar system said,

> *[T]he privatisation promoted by the World Bank, which favours DC schemes and individual accounts, does nothing to expand coverage. On the contrary, it typically results in decreased coverage because benefits are linked more tightly to contributions, so there is less re distributional less reason for the poor to participate.*

He, further suggested a universal first pillar which covers every citizen and a voluntary second pillar, where everyone would have this second pillar option (a system successfully functioning in New Zealand).

The independent Evaluation Group (2006) of the World Bank in its report *Pension Reform and Development of Pension System,* stated, 'while addressing the funding gaps, too often the bank has not addressed sufficiently the primary goal of a pension system to reduce poverty and provide adequate retirement income *within a fiscal constraint.* It has also focused insufficient attention on the income of the aged.' The Independent Evaluation Group (IEG) has further commented:

> *[T]he bank's activities in Latin America and the Caribbean tended to be limited to funded reforms, even when pensions covered a small percentage of the population.... it (World Bank) also often failed to prioritize the need for developing options for old-age safety nets outside the formal pension systems in low income and low coverage countries.*

The basic concept of the World Bank has provided a very useful framework of pension reforms. Even then there cannot be disagreement that there are several advantages in a fully operational three-pillar system which the World Bank has outlined in *Averting the Old Age Crisis.* The problem, however, arises out of myopic implementation by focusing on the second pillar and ignoring the most important first pillar, which was visualised as an important instrument of wealth redistribution and mechanism of poverty eradication. However, while implementing the multi-pillar system many governments (including India) virtually ignored the existence of the first pillar. Further no economic solution to poverty can be a unique solution hence country specific model of pension reform is needed.

Notional Defined Contribution

Notional Defined Contribution (NDC) system attempts to integrate some characteristics of DB and DC system. NDC is a shift from DB plans to a notional account under which pension depends on the contribution of the members but the rate of return or interest rate (notional) is decided by the government. Further, NDC system does not pass the entire system's risks to the investors while building the pension assets through individual pension accounts as in the DC system. According to Börsch-Supan (2003), NDC systems are accounting devices that treat a PAYG system like a DC system. NDC system consists of an accounting method which credits all life time earnings, a mechanism that links final balance with macroeconomic and demographic environment and an actuarial rule which converts all the final balance into an annuity. In an NDC system individual accounts are opened like a DC system and individual contributions are credited to this account kept by the pension system. However, money is not kept in individual account, no capital is accumulated and the balance is only notional pension wealth. The rate of return is not determined through any market mechanism but through a centrally determined mechanism; for example, in Sweden, this rate is determined by the rate of growth of wage. Thus, the system of determining the rate of return is closer to the PAYG system. Therefore, the rate of return and risk of investment depends on the centrally determined interest rate by the government and, thus, individual investment risk is relatively lower compared to the risk in the DC system under which individual chooses funds and fund managers which may generate different level of return and risk.

At the payout stage the notional pension wealth is converted into an annuity by using an 'annuitization divisor' often called 'G-values' (Sweden), which is a number that reflects the average life expectancy at retirement discounted by a notional interest rate. The annuity divisor mechanism plays an important role in NDC system since it adjusts longevity and converts notional account into a pension account. Another advantage of the NDC system in comparison with the multi-pillar system is the lower administrative cost since the accounts under NDC is notional and administration is simple, whereas in a multi-pillar system there are several entities, namely trustees, fund managers and custodians, which increases costs. According to Börsch-Supan (2003),

> *it (NDC System) creates a homogeneous paradigm for the first, second and third pillar of a multiple pillar system; hence it may increase the acceptance of second and third pillar, which are regarded as 'alien' system components in those countries that used to have a monolith first-pillar dominated pension system.*

NDC system as a reform strategy is gradually getting attention since it provides certain advantages of DB system and at the same time discounts the certain major disadvantages implicit in the multi-pillar systemic reforms. Under NDC, people of all income groups bear the same risk and return. Implication of the centrally determined rate of return is that the investment risk is not transferred to the investors as is the case in a DC system. Since in NDC pension depends on the contribution of the member it does not create financial burden on the state as in the case of DB system. There is an automatic balance mechanism for asset liability mismatch, which is corrected through notional interest. NDC system has been introduced by Sweden, Italy, Poland, and so on, and some countries like France and Germany have adopted some features of NDC and have not replicated the NDC fully.

Public Pension Expenditure

Depth and development of social security and pension can be considered in terms of public pension expenditure. Public pension expenditure is also used as an instrument of parametric reform and to enhance the pension benefits of beneficiaries. Public pension expenditure is also an indication of concern of the government about the social security and the average well-being of the elderly population and the extent of development of social security system of a country. Increased awareness about impending economic crisis due to population ageing, particularly in the developed world, prompted the governments to increase public pension spending. According to data in the *World Development Report* (2007), highest public pension expenditure as percentage of GDP has been noted in countries like Poland (15.8 per cent), Uruguay (15 per cent), Sweden (14 per cent), France (13,3 per cent) and Germany (13.2 per cent) in 2007. Average pension as percentage of per capita income was quite high in some countries; for example, 125.4 per cent in Uruguay, 124.2 per cent in Iran and 119.8 per cent in Egypt, though public pension expenditure as percentage of GDP was 1.1 per cent in Iran and 4.1 per cent in Egypt (Table 1.3). In India this expenditure is estimated to be around 2 per cent of GDP (not in Table 1.3). International Labour Organization (ILO), in its *World Social Security Report 2010/11* indicated that 'on an average, 17.2 per cent of global GDP is allocated to social security. However, these expenditures tend to be concentrated in higher-income countries, so this average does not reflect the situation for the majority of the world's population.'

The social structure of low-income, developing countries like India was based on joint family system, where economic needs of the elderly people were taken care of by the other earning members of the family, so government was not under much pressure. Second, since the average longevity of the population was much lower in developing countries as compared to the developed countries ageing and ageing-related economic problems were not an issue of importance in such countries and the social security expenditure constituted an insignificant portion of total budget expenditure.

Importance of Pension Funds in National Economy

Pension reforms have provided a boost to pension savings and pension funds have emerged as an important constituent in national economy supporting the development of capital market, national savings and overall growth of economy (will discuss in detail in subsequent section). Pension funds are important players in the financial market by virtue of the size of the investment in various types of securities. The importance of pension funds in national economy can be gauged by the growth of assets as a percentage of national GDP. In some cases of OECD countries, pension assets exceeded the GDP; for example, it was 134 per cent in Iceland, 132 per cent in the Netherlands, 119.4 per cent in Switzerland and 105.4 per cent in Australia in 2007 (Table 1.4).

As can be seen from the data in Table 1.4, growth has been significant in these countries since 2001. However, more significant is the growth of pension assets in the non-OECD emerging countries since they introduced pension reforms. For example, pension assets as percentage of GDP went up from 55.8 per cent in 2002 to 64.4 per

Table 1.3 Pension Contributors and Public Expenditure on Pension

	Pension contributors	*Column 1*	*Column 2*	*Public expenditure on pensions*	*Column 3*	*Column 4*	*Column 5*
Country	*Year*	*Percentage of labour force*	*Percentage of working-age population*	*Year*	*Percentage of GDP*	*Year*	*Average pension per cent of per capita income*
Algeria	2002	36.7	22.0	2002	3.2	2002	89.1
Austria	2004	80.8	58.8	2003	11.6	2002	93.2
Belgium	1995	86.2	65.9	2003	8.5	2002	62.8
Bulgaria	1994	64.0	63.0	2005	8.9	2002	75.2
Canada	2003	57.0	63.0	2003	5.4	2002	57.1
Chile	2003	58.0	35.2	2001	2.9	2002	53.5
Colombia	2000	19.0	14.0	1994	1.1	2002	54.4
Czech Republic	2003	86.0	61.0	2003	10.5	2002	58.2
Denmark	2003	92.0	74.0	2003	9.6	2002	54.1
Egypt, Arab Rep.	2004	55.4	27.7	2004	4.1	2002	119.8
Estonia	2000	91.0	66.0	2003	6.3	2002	60.9
Finland	2003	90.3	67.0	2003	9.0	2002	78.8
France	2003	90.0	62.0	2003	13.3	2002	65.0
Germany	2003	88.0	64.0	2003	13.2	2002	71.8
Hungary	1996	77.0	65.0	2003	11.0	2002	90.5
India	2004	9.1	5.7	–	–	–	–
Iran, Islamic Rep.	2001	35.0	20.0	2000	1.1	2002	124.2
Ireland	2002	93.0	64.7	2003	4.7	2002	36.6
Italy	2003	90.0	56.0	2003	15.5	2002	88.8
Japan	2003	94.0	73.0	2003	8.9	2002	59.1
Korea, Rep.	1996	58.0	43.0	2003	1.3	2002	43.3
Mexico	2002	34.6	22.6	2003	1.3	2002	45.1
Netherlands	2002	94.0	72.0	2003	9.0	2002	84.1
New Zealand	–	–	–	2003	7.4	2002	39.5
Peru	2003	16.3	12.3	2000	2.6	2002	43.9
Philippines	2000	27.0	18.6	1993	1.0	–	–
Poland	2005	84.8	54.5	2003	15.8	2002	69.7
Portugal	2003	92.0	71.0	2003	11.9	2002	79.8
Sweden	2003	90.0	72.0	2003	14.0	2002	68.2
Switzerland	2003	99.0	84.0	2003	12.1	2002	67.3
United Kingdom	2003	94.0	73.0	2003	8.3	2002	47.6
United States	2003	91.0	71.0	2003	7.5	2002	51.0
Uruguay	2001	57.7	44.3	1996	15.0	2002	125.4

Source: World Development Indicators (Washington: World Bank, 2007).

cent in 2007. During the same time the same went up from 15.5 per cent to 22.2 per cent in Bolivia, 0.1 per cent to 14.3 per cent in Columbia, 0.9 per cent to 19.1 per cent in Costa Rica, 9.3 per cent to 17.1 per cent in Brazil, and so on (Table 1.5). The increase in pension assets relative to GDP has several implications. Pension assets significantly

Table 1.4 Importance of Pension Funds Relative to the Size of the Economy in Selected OECD Countries (as a percentage of GDP)

Countries	*2001*	*2002*	*2003*	*2004*	*2005*	*2006*	*2007*
Australia	57.7	58.1	56.1	51.4	58.0	94.3	105.4
Austria	4.0	3.9	4.3	4.5	4.7	4.8	4.7
Belgium	5.6	5.1	3.5	4.1	4.2	4.3	4.0
Canada	53.3	47.8	52	48.9	50.4	53.4	55.3
Czech Republic	2.6	3.3	2.5	3.6	4.1	4.6	4.7
Denmark	27.4	25.7	27.7	29.8	32.9	32.4	32.4
Finland	8.2	8.1	8.3	45.3	66.1	71.3	71.0
France	3.9	6.6	5.4	6.0	5.8	1.1	1.1
Germany	3.4	3.8	3.6	3.8	3.9	4.2	4.1
Greece	–	–	–	–	0	0	0
Hungary	4.0	4.5	5.3	6.9	8.5	9.7	10.9
Iceland	87.3	88.0	102.0	108.0	123.2	132.7	134.0
Ireland	–	–	–	42.0	52.8	49.9	46.6
Italy	1.8	1.8	2.5	2.6	2.8	3.0	3.3
Japan	13.6	14.1	13.1	15.2	18.8	23.4	20.0
Korea	–	1.5	1.6	1.7	1.9	2.9	3.1
Luxembourg	–	–	–	0.3	0.4	1.1	1.0
Mexico	4.4	4.9	5.7	6.3	7.2	11.5	12.1
Netherlands	107.2	89.6	94.1	108.7	124.9	130.0	132.0
New-Zealand	8.4	7.6	5.7	11.3	11.3	12.4	11.1
Norway	4.0	4.0	4.6	6.6	6.8	6.8	7.0
Poland	2.6	4.2	5.5	7.0	8.7	11.1	12.2
Portugal	12.1	12.0	12.4	10.6	12.9	13.6	13.7
Slovak Republic	10.7	16.7	9.4	0	0.6	2.8	4.2
Spain	6.0	6.0	6.5	9.0	9.1	7.6	7.5
Sweden	8.3	7.7	7.8	12.4	14.5	9.5	8.7
Switzerland	109.4	125.5	–	108.5	117.4	122.1	119.4
Turkey	–	–	–	0.1	0.3	1.0	1.2
United Kingdom	72.7	66.5	65.7	68.8	66.2	77.1	86.1
United States	66.9	57.8	66.0	99.6	98.9	73.7	74.3

Source: Pension Market in Focus, OECD, December 2008 (issue 5), November 2007 (issue 4), October 2006 (issue 3), December 2005 (issue 2) and June 2005 (issue 10).

boosted domestic savings which in turn were channelised to investment, and strongly supported the diversified growth of capital market, induced innovation of new financial instruments and supported improvement in corporate governance.

Coverage

It seems not much could be achieved in terms of expanding coverage. Social security and pension reforms could touch only a small section of society, particularly in the developing countries. Several studies have brought to the fore these dismal facts, which need the urgent attention of policymakers and government economic managers.

Table 1.5 Importance of Pension Funds Relative to the Size of the Economy in Selected Non-OECD Countries (as a percentage of GDP)

Countries	*2001*	*2002*	*2003*	*2005*	*2006*	*2007*
Argentina	–	11.3	13.5	4.7	29.0	11.5
Bolivia	–	15.5	20.9	9.2	2.0	22.2
Brazil	–	9.3	13.1		166.0	17.1
Bulgaria	0.5	1.0	2.3	2.8	1.0	4.1
Chile	–	55.8	64.5	64.9	88.0	64.4
China	–	–	–	0.5	11.0	0.6
Colombia	0.1	0.1	0.1	15.3	21.0	14.3
Costa Rica	–	0.9	1.8	1.9	4.0	19.1
El Salvador	–	7.4	11.0	9.0	3.0	19.4
Estonia	2.0	14.7	–	3.2	1.0	4.6
Fiji	–	–	69.3			
Hong Kong	15.0	17.0	17.6	19.1	53.0	31.2
India	–	–	0.2	5.3	51.0	5.4
Indonesia	2.3	2.6	2.1	0.1	8.0	2.2
Israel	–	–	–		48.0	33.6
Kazakhstan	5.6	7.1	8.8	4.1	5.0	
Malaysia	–	–	56.7	56.7		
Pakistan	–	–	1.7	1.4		0
Panama	–	–	3.6			
Peru	–	8.1	10.6	12.0	14.0	18.0
Philippines	–	–	3.8			
Russia	–	–	0.6	0.7	15.0	1.5
Singapore	–	64.0	61.9	62.6	71.0	56.2
Slovenia	0.1	0.4	0.2	2.4	1.0	3.1
South Africa	–	–	30.4	33.9	72.0	
Sri Lanka	14.6	–	–			
Thailand	7.5	8.0	7.1	4.9	10.0	5.2
Ukraine	–	–	0	0		
Uruguay	–	9.3	11.4	12.8	3.0	14.7

Source: Pension Market in Focus, OECD, December 2008 (issue 5), November 2007 (issue 4), October 2006 (issue 3), December 2005 (issue 2) and June 2005 (issue 10).

Holzmann et al. (2000) in their study, 'Extending Coverage in Multi-Pillar Pension System', indicated, 'of the world's 6 billion people in 1999, only 15 per cent or less have access to a formal system of retirement income support'. According to the *World Social Security Report 2010/11*,

> *Only one-third of countries globally (inhabited by 28 per cent of the global population) have comprehensive social protection systems covering all branches of social security as defined by ILO Convention No 102. Taking into account those who are not economically active, it is estimated that only about 20 per cent of the world's working-age population (and their families) have access to comprehensive social protection. (ILO 2010)*

The report further mentioned that worldwide nearly 40 per cent of the population of working age is *legally* covered by contributory old-age pension schemes. While in North America and Europe this number is nearly twice as high, it is about 20 per cent in Asia, the Middle East, and North Africa and only 5 per cent in Sub-Saharan Africa. However, it is seen from the coverage data that in spite of so much efforts, social security has remained beyond the reach of most of the people, which forces us to rethink the ongoing reform models. Probably there is a need for out of the box thinking to introduce an affordable social protection for all.

Emerging Trends in Pension Reform

In the foregoing paragraphs an attempt has been made to indicate the urgency and the emerging reform models. It has been demonstrated that there are three major reform variants, namely parametric reform, systemic reform and NDC type of reform. However, it has also been observed that many countries in their reform system incorporated multiple features borrowed from parametric, systemic and NDC systems. Most of the OECD countries have introduced parametric reforms while some have also gone for wholesale change in pension system and introduced the systemic reform. Countries like Austria, New Zealand Turkey, UK, and so on, brought reforms through parametric changes; many OECD countries introduced parametric as well as systemic changes, namely Finland, France, Germany, Hungary, Italy Poland, Sweden and so on. Among these countries some have gone for DC, while others have introduced NDC. For example, Hungary, Poland, Slovakia, and so on, introduced the DC system along with parametric changes, while Italy, Poland, Sweden, and so on, introduced NDC along with parametric changes in pension system. Further, there is also variation in NDC system among the countries which have introduced it. For example, the entire pension system in Italy is based on NDC system, while it (NDC) has been incorporated as a first tier of mandatory system in Sweden, Poland, Latvia and so on.

Though population ageing is not as serious as in developed countries at present, it is going to be a serious problem and, therefore, needs urgent attention. Given the increase in the number of pensionable population, exchequer-financed DB pension system is gradually becoming unsustainable. Also, the system of DB pension, which primarily covers organised sector employees, left out a large number of employees in the unorganised sector, which is a growing trend in most of the developing countries. All these considerations prompted the developing countries to reform their pension system and most of them introduced a mandatory DC system as well as brought parametric changes in their DB pension system.

❖ LATIN AMERICAN COUNTRIES

Pension reforms also gained momentum outside the OECD and in most of the developing countries, beginning with Chile, which took the first initiative to reform its pension system in 1981. Increased problem of ageing, deteriorating dependency ratio, growing burden of DB pension system, low coverage, and so on, forced many Latin American countries to revamp their pension system. According to *World Population Prospects (2008 Revision)*, Latin American countries (and the Caribbean) together had 8.5 per cent (582 million) of the world's population in 2009, which is likely to be 8 per cent (729 million) medium variant in 2050, but the percentage of the 60+ population will go up from 10 per cent in 2010 to 26 per cent in 2050. Most of these countries, however, introduced the multi-pillar system mostly on the lines of the World Bank–suggested three-pillar system. Chile (1980/81) was followed by other Latin American countries like Peru (1992), Argentina (1999/94), Colombia (1995), Uruguay (1996), Mexico (1995/96), Bolivia (1993–2000), Costa Rica (2000) and so on. The multi-pillar system was also introduced in Poland (1998), Hungary (1998), Kazakhastan (1998), Bulgaria (200), Russia (2002), Ukraine (2004), and so on. Europe also switched over from their DB pension into DC pension.

Latin America is the pioneer in pension reform and in the introduction of the mandatory DC pension system. 'Mandatory pension schemes have had a long tradition in LAC (Latin American Countries). Chile and Uruguay led the way with the establishment of such system in early 1920s. Over the following half century, all other LAC countries set up mandatory schemes of their own' (Dayoub and Lasagabaster 2008). Among the Latin American countries, Chile took the lead in reforming PAYG DB pension system and to introduce a new system based on individual savings and capitalisation-based mandatory pension system. However, all the Latin American countries did not follow the same kind of reform model. According to Mesa-Lago, three general models of structural reform exist in Latin American countries: substitutive model, parallel model and mixed model. In case of the substitutive model the old PAYG pension was replaced by privately managed individual account–based DC system in countries like Chile, Bolivia, Mexico and so on. The parallel system was introduced in Peru and Columbia where public system was not abolished but reformed and simultaneously a privately managed individual account–based DC system was introduced with the option to the workers to select either of these two systems. However, in a mixed model as adopted in Argentina, Brazil, Uruguay and other countries, a privately managed individual–based DC system was introduced by retaining the public system. Therefore, reform in these countries combined both the public and private pension systems. In Latin America, there are three general models of structural pension reforms which can be identified as substitutive, parallel and mixed (Mesa-Lago 2005). In a substitutive model the old system is replaced with a new system, while in the parallel model the old system is allowed to run along with a new system and in a mixed model, a combination of old and new systems form the reform. The substitutive model has been implemented by Chile, El Salvador, Mexico and so on. The parallel model has been introduced by Peru and Columbia, while the mixed model has been introduced by Argentina, Uruguay and Costa Rica. The most important feature of the newly reformed pension system are the integrated supervision of private fund managers, centralised contribution collection and specialised private fund managers called pension fund administrators. In the new pension system, individual pension funds are managed by specialised financial institutions.

❖ CENTRAL AND EAST EUROPEAN COUNTRIES

Ageing in Central and East European (CEE) countries, particularly in Eastern Europe, was not as serious as in Western, Southern and Northern Europe. However, it is slowly catching up. CEE countries had a population of 295 million in 2008 and this is likely to fall to 231 million in 2050 (2008 World Population Data Sheet) and the percentage of total population of 60+ is likely to increase from 20 per cent in 2002 to 37 per cent in 2050 (United Nations 2002). The Increase in percentage of elderly population is the consequence of decline in fertility and mortality and will exert tremendous pressure on the social security system.

Transitional economies in CEE countries, which have switched over from command economy to market economy were compelled to introduce pension reforms due to changing economic environment and increased pension burden. During the socialist regime these countries had PAYG DB pension system which was virtually managed by state and providing pension was the responsibility of the government through transfer of funds from the state-owned firms to social security budget. However, transition brought about sharp decline in employment and output, decline in contribution and increase in dependency ratio and benefit costs. In the mid-1990s, some CEE countries particularly the East European countries undertook major pension reforms and in late 1990s other countries followed them but the pace of decision-making and implementation has differed markedly from country to country. The early starters were countries which were earlier in the Soviet Block, such as Hungary, Poland and Latvia.

Among the CEE countries, Hungary was the first country to initiate pension reform in 1993 by introducing a supplementary system of voluntary and funded pension funds followed by Czech Republic (1994) and Poland (1997). The CEE countries before switching over to market economy were under the socialist regime and followed a system which was mostly the PAYG-defined type. Pension was primarily determined under the state regulation based on the years of service. However, the old system could not be retained when these countries switched over to market economy due to excessive pension cost on the exchequer. To overcome pension burden on the exchequer, most of these countries introduced non-structural parametric reforms by increasing the retirement age, eliminating sectoral privileges, increasing pensionable contribution period and so on. However, a large number of countries have also adopted the multi-pillar system and introduced structural reforms by introducing the fully funded privately managed second pillar. Individual account–based mandatory pension system has been introduced in Hungary (1998), Poland (1999), Lativia (2001), Estonia (2002), Bulgaria (2002) and so on. Many such countries have also retained PAYG DB as a first pillar as in the case of Hungary, Estonia, Bulgaria and so on. Some countries like Poland and Lativia have reformed their first pillar and by following Sweden, Italy, and so on, have introduced the first-pillar NDC system. As a result of reforms, social security has been separated from the state budget and provided separate financing or accounting for various types of benefits. One distinctive feature of reform in these countries is to separate social security budget. According to Fultz (2001), 'All countries now have a pension budget, account, or fund which is distinct from the state budget or segregated within it.'

❖ ASIAN COUNTRIES

Asia is the home of more than half of the world population. Of the world population of 6,829 million, 4,121 million inhabited Asia in 2009. In terms of percentage it was 60.3 per cent of the world population. At a medium variant growth rate of 0.58 per cent, population of Asia will grow to 5,231 million, having 57.2 per cent share of world population of 9,150 million in 2050. India and China are the two most populous countries of the world and were home to 37 per cent of world population in 2009. By 2028, Indian population is expected to surpass population of China and together these two countries will account for 36 per cent of world population (World Population Prospects 2008). The general trend of decline in population growth rate, decline in fertility and increase in longevity will add up to the number of older population, particularly the oldest of the old. The percentage of people aged 60+ will go up from 414 million (10 per cent of total population) in 2010 to 1,236 million in 2050 (24 per cent of total population) and people aged 80+ will go up from 47 million (1 per cent) to 228 million (4 per cent) during the same period.

Asia has a distinct family culture system and family bond which created an informal family-based old-age system and old-age economic support was virtually coming from family. However, faster economic growth, urbanisation and shifting jobs from agricultural enterprises to manufacturing and service sector forced the workers to move outside. This impacted the joint family system, which was replaced by the nuclear family system. As a result, old-age family support is also gradually diminishing. Moreover, countries in Asia adopted market economy which resulted in reducing the share of public sector in economy, particularly in employment, the major segment of organised sector employment. Further inefficiency in operation of many public sector organisations also imposed severe fiscal burden on the state exchequer. These developments forced the countries to rethink about social security and pension reforms. However, there is no uniformity in reform models in Asia though many countries are moving towards the DC system while others are strengthening the existing DB/DC system. Some countries have already initiated pension reforms and others are taking steps to reform pension and social security. While in some countries, the provident fund system (as in Singapore and Malaysia) is doing very well, China after adopting market economy has gone for reforming its public sector–based pension system. India, which quite successfully managed its dual system of PF and DB pension is also facing fiscal constraints and has initiated several steps to reform the system.

The pension systems in Malaysia, Indonesia, Singapore and Sri Lanka are basically DC system, while the same in South Korea, Philippines, Vietnam are DB system. China has introduced the NDC system. India has undertaken pension reform with introduction of mandatory DC system for new entrants (excluding armed forces) to central government services. In Asia some publicly managed provident fund systems have been providing quite successfully low-cost retirement benefits. Such models exist as the CPF System in Singapore, the EPF system in Malaysia and EPF in India. Over the years, the CPF in Singapore and EPF in Malaysia have functioned very successfully. While DC and NDC suggest minimising or eliminating the role of the state and transferring the pension system to the private sector, there are few who suggest that CPF- and EPF-type reforms should take place within the public system. EPF in India is also undergoing some reforms along with the introduction of DC NPS.

❖ AFRICAN COUNTRIES

In 2009, Africa was the home of 14.8 per cent (1,010 million) of the world population but it will witness the highest rate of growth and its population will be more than double (2,999 million) with 21.7 per cent share of global population in 2050. Ageing is not a serious problem at present as only 5 per cent of population was aged 60+ in 2010, but the same is going to be more than double 11 per cent in 2050 since the average rate of change of population during 2009–50, of the population aged 60+, is estimated to be 3.35 per cent as against the global rate of 2.44 per cent. Though fertility rate will decline from the current rate of 4.615 (2005–10) to 2.40 per cent (at medium variant), it will be much higher than any other region's and the global average of 2.02. Therefore, changing the demographic situation and ageing is a growing concern for Africa. However, the immediate concern is the poverty, unemployment and growing number of HIV/AIDS cases which render many families income-less. Some countries, such as Mauritius, Botswana and Namibia established meaningful universal pension system, while South Africa has its means-tested public pension. Occupational and private pensions are also available in few countries like Kenya, Nigeria and so on.

However, pension and social security has drawn the attention of policymakers and many African countries have initiated major pension reforms. Most such reforms are parametric in nature but many countries have also initiated systemic reforms to establish funded private pension systems. The immediate reason for reforming the pension system is the increasing fiscal burden, changing demographic situation and consideration of coverage expansion and so on. Reform is also being driven by an increasing awareness of old-age provision as an integral part of social policy, fixing unsustainable existing schemes and making them more efficient in terms of administrative costs and return as well as the desire to increase savings and develop the financial market in the regions (Stewart and Yermo 2009).

India is not an exception to the ageing and pension problems; though the average age of its population is about 26 years, growth rate of elderly population is much higher (3 per cent) than the growth rate of average population (1.8 per cent). DB pension is a strain on the exchequer and fiscally unsustainable in the long run. Moreover, coverage of the existing DB pension is quite low, and about 11 per cent of the labour force is covered under the formal pension system. Pension reforms, therefore, became inevitable and the Ministry of Welfare (later renamed Ministry of Social Justice and Empowerment), Government of India commissioned the Project Old Age Social and Income Security (OASIS) in July 1998. A number of committees and expert groups were formed which suggested various recommendations to reform the Indian pension system. Most of these committees were in favour of introducing the DC pension system. Subsequently, the Government of India introduced NPS with effect from 1 January 2004 for the employees of the central government (excluding armed forces) who joined services on or after that date. Following the central government, state governments also joined the NPS. Subsequently, NPS also opened to all citizens. NPS is a two-tier mandatory contributory pension system opened also to state government employees and all citizens in the organised sector on voluntary basis in 2009. However, NPS has several structural weaknesses which need to be rectified to make it a viable instrument for providing affordable social security to all. India has introduced a reform model which has incorporated several features of reforms from other countries, yet there are certain unique features which can be followed by other countries having similar problems. However, there remain a few unresolved issues which need closure scrutiny and remedial actions. Therefore, the study of NPS will provide some generic guidelines for other developing countries which are planning to reform pension and social security system.

REFERENCES

Baker, Dean and Kar Debayani (2002), *Defined Contribution for Workers, Guaranteed Benefits for Workers: The World Bank's Approach to Social Security Reform*, Centre for Economic Policy Research, Washington DC, 16 July 2002. Available at: http://www.cepr.net/world_bank_social_secyrity.htm.

Börsch-Supan, Axel H. (2003), 'What Are NDC Systems? What Do They Bring to Reform Strategies?' In *Pension Reforms: Issues and Prospects for Non-Financial Defined Contribution (NDC) Schemes*, ed. Robert Holzmann and Edward Palmer, 35–36, Washington, DC: World Bank. Available at: http://ideas.repec.org/p/mea/meawpa/03042.html (accessed 16 December 2003).

Dayoub, Mariam and Experanza Lasagabaster (2008), 'General Trends in Competition Policy and Investment Regulation in Mandatory Defined Contribution Markets in Latin America'. Policy Research Working Paper 4720, World Bank, September.

Dethier, Jean-Jacques (2007), 'Social Security: What Can Developing Countries Learn from Developed Countries'. 2020 FOCUS BRIEF on the World's Poor and Hungry People-October, IDEAS (a service hosted by the Research Division of the Federal Reserve Bank of St. Louis). Available at: http://conferences.ifpri.org/2020Chinaconference/pdf/beijingbrief_dethier.pdf.

Eurofound (2009), 'Bismarck's Social Security Legislation'. Available at: http://www.eurofound.europa.eu/emire/GERMANY/BISMARCKSSOCIALSECURITYLEGISLATION-DE.htm.

Group of Ten (1998), 'The Macroeconomic and Financial Implications of Ageing Populations'. Bank for International Settlements, 1998. Available at: http:www.bis.org.

Heller, Peter S. (April 1998), *Rethinking Public Pension Reform Initiatives.* IMF Working Paper no. WP/98/61, International Monetary Fund.

Holzmann, Robert, Truman Packard and Jose Cuesta (2000), 'Extending Coverage in Multi-Pillar pension Systems: Constraints and Hypothesis, Preliminary Evidence and Future Research Agenda'. *Social Protection Discussion Paper Series.* Washington, DC: World Bank, January 2000.

Holzmann, R. (1998), *A World Bank Perspective on Pension Reform.* Washington, DC: World Bank.

Holzmann, R. and Richard Hinz (2005), *Old-Age Income Support in the Twenty-first Century: An International Perspective on Pension Systems and Reform.* Washington, DC: World Bank.

IEG-World Bank (Independent Evaluation Group-World Bank) (2006), 'Pension Reform and Development of Pension Systems-An Evaluation of World Bank Assistance'. *IEG Study Series.* Washington, DC: World Bank.

Orszag, Peter R. and Joseph E. Stiglitz (1999), 'Rethinking Pension Reform: Ten Myths about Social Security Systems'. Presented at the conference on 'New Ideas about Old Age Security'. Washington, DC: The World Bank, 14–15 September.

ICFTU (International Confederation of Free Trade Unions) (2003), 'World Bank Involvement in the Privatisation of Public Pension System in Developing and Transition Countries'. Report prepared by D. Baker and D. Kar. Available at: www.policyarchive.org/handle/10207/bitstreams/20807.pdf.

ILO (International Labour Organization) (2010), 'Providing Coverage in Times of Crisis and Beyond'. *World Social Security Report 2010/11.* Geneva: International Labour Office.

Leibfritz, Willi (2003), 'Retiring Later Make Sense'. *OECD Observer,* January 2003. Available at: http://www.oecdobserver.org/news/fullstory.php/aid/824/Retiring_later_makes_sense.html.

Mercer (2007), *Global Report: Increase in Normal Retirement Ages Underline Impact of Longevity.* Press Release, 5 December 2007.

Mesa-Lago, Carmelo (2005), 'Evaluation of a Quarter Century of Structural Pension Reforms in Latin America'. In *A Quarter Century of Pension Reform in Latin America and the Caribbean.* Ed. Carolin A. Crabbe. New York: Inter-American Development Bank, 45.

Munnell, Alicia H. (2009), *The Financial Crisis and Restoring Retirement Security.* Testimony before the Committee on Education and Labour, US House of Representatives, 24 February 2009.

OECD (Organisation for Economic Co-operation and Development) (2009), *Pension at a Glance: Current Trends and Policy Topics in Retirement Income Provision in OECD Countries.* Available at: http://www.oecd.org/dataoecd/12/60/43098050.pdf.

Peterson, Peter G. (1999), 'Gray Dawn: The Global Aging Crisis'. *Foreign Affairs.* New York, January/February 1999.

Pugh, Colin (2009), 'Brazil: Regulation and Supervision of Close Ended Pension Funds'. Presented at International Organisation for Pension Supervisors (IOPS)/OECD Global Forum, 14–15 October.

Rust, John (2002), 'Main Points from World Bank Report on: Averting the Old Age Crisis'. *Econ 698s,* Fall 2002. Available at: http://gemini.econ.umd.edu/jrust/econ698s/avert_lec.pdf.

Salvador, Valdés-Prieto (2005), 'Market-based Social Security as a Better Means of Risk-Sharing'. Pension Research Council Working Paper, PRC WP 2005–16. Available at: http://prc.wharton.upenn.edu/prc.html.

Stewart, F. and J. Yermo (2009), 'Pensions in Africa'. OECD Working Papers on Insurance and Private Pensions, No. 30, OECD publishing, © OECD. doi:10.1787/227444006716.

Thompson, Lawrence H. (1999), 'Administering Individual Accounts in Social Security: The Role of Values and Objectives in Shaping Options'. *The Retirement Project Occasional Papers Series.*

Social Security USA Administration, 'Traditional Sources of Economic Security'. Social Security Online. Available at: www.ssa.gov/history/briefhistory3.html.

United Nations (2009), 'World Population Prospects: The 2008 Revision, Highlights', Working Paper No. ESA/P/WP.210. Department of Economic and Social Affairs, Population Division.

Valente, Marcela (2008), *Latin America: Future of Private Pension Funds in Doubt.* Available at: ipsnews.net/news.asp?idnews=44872.

Vial, Joaquín and Angel Melguizo (2007), 'Moving from Pay as You Go to Privately Managed Individual Pension Accounts: What Have We Learned after 25 Years of the Chilean Pension Reform?' BBVA Working Paper, Economic Research Department.

Willmore, Larry (2000), 'Three Pillars of Pensions? A Proposal to End Mandatory Contribution'. United Nations DESA Discussion Paper No. 13, 1 June.

Willmore, Larry N. and Guido Bertucci (1998), 'Public versus Private Provision of Pensions'. DESA Discussion Paper No. 1, Department of Economic and Social Affairs, United Nations.

World Bank (2007), 'World Development Report: Development and the Next Generation'. Available at: http://go.worldbank.org/TF89PWOF70.

Zaidi. A. (2006), 'Pension Policy in EU25 and Its Possible Impact on Elderly Poverty', *Policy Brief September*, European Centre for Social Welfare Policy and Research, Vienna.

2 A Brief Review of Pension Reforms in Selected Emerging Market Countries

INTRODUCTION

The goal of pension reform should be 'to provide adequate, affordable, sustainable and robust retirement income, while seeking to implement welfare improving schemes in a manner appropriate to the individual country' (Holzman and Hinz 2005). To achieve this goal quite a few strategies have been adopted by many countries, the most significant being the World Bank–suggested multi-pillar pension system having a defined contribution (DC) pillar, largely introduced by the emerging market countries while developed countries, have undertaken reforms, mostly retaining the Pay-as-You-Go (PAYG) system but attempted to strengthen it through parametric reforms to strengthen the funding and enhance the pension entitlement to face the challenges of ageing.

Since Latin America is the pioneer in pension reform; seven countries of Latin America have been included in this study to get an understanding of the process of reforms, challenges and outcome. Most of these countries have certain unique feature to learn from; for example, Chile is the pioneer in pension reform and Bolivia's Bonosol and Columbia's health-care programmes are unique. We have included two East European Transitional countries, namely Hungary and Poland which have adopted market economy and switched over from public pension system to privately managed pension system. Sweden has successfully experimented with Notional Defined Contribution (NDC) System which attracted attention of reformers throughout the world. Reforms in African countries are in the early stage. We however included the case of Mauritius, which has promoted a developed pension system and undertaken reforms. Asian countries have initiated reforms quite recently and changes are taking place. We have restricted study only to reforms in China which have lots of demographic and economic similarity with India. All these countries are experiencing the problems of population ageing as the population of over 60 years and 80 years is growing alarmingly (Table 2.1) and moving fast to reform the social security and pension system. It needs to be mentioned here that perhaps some latest changes remain to be included, but the information here would provide an emerging and valuable indication of reforms and post-reform impact. Further, intention here is not to make any critical evaluation of reforms and post-reform impacts but to acquaint the readers with some

Table 2.1 Demographic Trend and Other Statistics in Selected Emerging Market Countries

Country	*Total Population in Million*		*Percentage of Population over 60*		*Percentage of Population over 80*		*Old age Dependency Ratio*		*Life Expectancy at Birth*		*Pensionable Age*		*GDP Per Capita (US $)*
	2009	*mid-2050*	*2010*	*2050*	*2010*	*2050*	*2010*	*2050*	*Men 2009*	*Women 2009*	*Men 2009*	*Women 2009*	*2009*
Argentina(a)	40.7	52.2	14.7	24.9	2.6	5.3	16.6	30.2	72.5	80.0	65	60	13,238
Bolivia(a)	10.0	16.7	7.2	17.5	0.7	2.8	8.0	18.6	65.0	69.4	65	65	4,206
Brazil(a)	195.4	259.8	10.2	29.3	1.5	6.5	10.2	35.9	69.9	77.2	65e	60e	9,567
Chile(a)	17.1	20.2	13.2	28.7	2.1	7.6	13.5	36.0	76.2	82.3	65	60	13,880
Colombia(a)	46.3	59.2	8.6	23.1	1.1	5.0	8.6	27.3	70.4	77.7	60	55	8,587
Mexico(a)	110.6	131.6	9.4	28.2	1.4	6.2	10.0	35.9	74.9	79.7	65	65	14,104
Peru (a)	29.5	39.3	8.7	22.5	1.1	4.3	9.3	25.7	71.6	76.9	60	60	7,836
Uruguay (a)	3.4	3.7	18.4	27.4	3.7	6.8	21.8	34.8	73.7	80.7	60	60	11,216
Hungary (b)	10.1	8.9	22.4	33.0	3.8	6.9	23.8	44.3	69.2	77.4	62	61	17,887
Poland	38.2	31.4	19.4	38.0	3.4	8.5	18.8	52.2	71.3	79.8	65	60	13,847
Sweden	9.0	10.4	23.3	30.2	5.3	9.2	28.1	40.5	78.7	83.0	65	65	32,525
Mauritius (d)	1.3	1.5	11.6	26.1	1.3	5.9	10.7	32.7	–		60	60	12,715
China(c)	1,351.5	1,437.0	12.3	31.1	1.4	7.2	11.4	38.0	71.3	74.8	60	60	6,757
India(c)	1,220.2	1,755.2	7.5	19.6	0.7	2.6	7.7	20.2	63.2	66.4	60	60	3,452

Source: (1) Population Division of the Department of Economic and Social Affairs of the United Nations Secretariat (2009). (2) Social Security Programmes Throughout the World: The Americas, 2009, Africa 2009, Europe 2008, Asia 2008, Office of Research, Evaluation and Statistics, Social Security Administration Washington DC.

Note: (a) Data relates to the year 2009, (b) data relates to the year 2008, (c) data relates to the year 2008, (d) data relates to the year 2009 and (e) urban workers.

salient features of various reform models/systems, particularly the individual account–based private system. Some findings on reform impact are presented in the Chapter 3.

PENSION REFORM IN CHILE

Chile was the first country in Latin America which introduced structural reforms in its social security and pension system and set the trend of pension reforms in Latin America, which has in course of time emerged as the Latin American model. Many emerging economies and developing countries—having population pressure, demographic transition and fiscal constraints—that are trying to reform their social security and pension system have been encouraged by the Chilean reforms and have adopted many of the Chilean practices. Chile has thus set a trend and provided an outline for pension reform globally.

Demography

Chile is a country in Latin America with an average population. Its population is higher than Uruguay's and Bolivia's and much lower than in Brazil, Mexico, Colombia and Peru (the countries referred to in our study). In 2009, Chile had a population of 17.1 million and expected to go up to 20.2 million in 2050. However, population ageing is one of the highest in Chile among Latin American countries. The percentage of population aged over 60 years will go up from 13.2 per cent in 2010 to 28.7 per cent in 2050, while the percentage of population aged over 80 years will go up from 2.1 per cent to 7.6 per cent during the same period. Old-age dependency will be a serious problem in Chile, which will increase from 13.5 per cent in 2010 to 36.9 per cent in 2050.

Reform and New Pension System

Before the introduction of pension reform, Chile had almost 30 different PAYG defined benefit (DB) pension plans with wide differences in contribution and benefits and poorly administered scheme proving low investment return. According to Vial and Melguizo (2007), each operator (*caja*) had different rules concerning benefits and contributions to the scheme and many of them had major fiscal liabilities built into their financial structure. 'Heterogeneity of pension regimes, contributions and benefits, inter and intra-generational redistribution, and efficiency among SSIs was large, reflecting differences among participating groups in their political weight in securing special benefits provided by ad hoc laws or administrative/budgetary decisions granted by the executive' (Schmidt-Hebbel 1999). Implicit pension debt of the Chilean government estimated as 130 per cent of GDP (Gill et al. 2005). The system also generated a large deficit, making it unviable for the future. Therefore, Chile took drastic steps to replace the old PAYG by individual savings and capitalisation system through a decree of law on 4 November 1980.

Structure of New Pension System

Pension reform in Chile was radical in the sense that it introduced a new three-pillar system by replacing the old PAYG system in May 1981. The new system is a DC fully funded privately managed pension system under which benefits depend on the accrued amounts in the individual accounts, which was made mandatory for the dependent employees but was optional for all the self-employed workers. The workers, who were the members in the old PAYG system, were given an option either to continue with old PAYG system or to join the new system. The state ensured minimum pension for those who were unable to finance the individual capitalisation account. Chilean reform has undergone several changes since 1981, and in January 1981 Chilean Congress passed a reform based on the three-pillar system. The government kept an active role in the first pillar ('solidarity pillar') through the minimum pension guarantee (MPG).

Three-Pillar Pension System

The reform introduced in 2008 added a new pillar called the solidarity pillar and now the three pillar areas are discusses in the following paragraphs.

❖ FIRST PILLAR (SOLIDARITY PILLAR)

It is an integrated pillar with old age, disability and survivorship benefits financed through solidarity fund. The aim is to gradually replace current MPG by universal pension for those who do not receive pension from the contributory system.

❖ SECOND PILLAR (MANDATORY CONTRIBUTION PILLAR)

The second pillar is the old-age saving and insurance programme; participation is mandatory for all new dependent workers. This is an individual account–based DC pension scheme based on participant contributions. Funds in the second pillar are managed by private pension fund managers known as Administradoras de Fondos de Pensiones (AFPs) under government regulation and supervision.

❖ THIRD PILLAR (VOLUNTARY SAVING PILLAR)

The third pillar is voluntary old-age saving, to augment old-age pension. The dependent and independent workers are authorised to save over and above their mandatory contribution to AFPs. Voluntary savings are also eligible for tax benefits.

Transition to the New System

When the mandatory DC system was implemented in 1981, the members of earlier PAYG system were given the option to either switch over to the new system or to remain with the old system. The state issued recognition bonds to those who opted to switch over to the new capitalised system from the earlier PAYG system, which was equivalent to contribution and real rate of return at 4 per cent. Transition from PAYG to fully funded private pension in Chile was considered to be highly costly and according to David Langer (1998), employees and workers needed to pay an additional combined contribution of 1.52 per cent of taxable pay roll.

Pension Coverage

New pension introduced in 1981 made the participation mandatory for all the private and public sector employees entering the workforce. But it was voluntary for the self-employed. After privatisation the number of members/affiliated workers with the new system went up significantly. Immediately after introduction in December 1981, there were 1,400,000 members. This went up to 3,739,542 in December 1991; 6,427,656 by December 2001 and further 7,526,696 by June 2006 (International Federation of Pension Funds Administrators [FIAP] 2006). This shows that during the recent times growth of members has slowed down.

Contribution and Collection

In Chile, each dependent worker, that is, each member of an AFP deposits a percentage of the taxable salary, which in June 2006 was 10 per cent of taxable salary (with upper limit of 60 UF) for financing old-age pension, invalidity and survival benefits. There is also a provision of an additional contribution by the members to the fund managers. In June 2006 this was 2.37 per cent of the taxable salary. Out of this 2.37 per cent, 1.06 per cent goes towards insurance premium (risk of invalidity and death) and 1.31 per cent for the cost of fund management by the AFPs. (AFPs in Chile may either charge a fixed monthly commission or a variable commission.) Chile has adopted a decentralised system of collection, with contribution being collected by the individual AFPs. In Chile mandatory contributions are to be paid to the AFPs while voluntary contribution can be paid to banks, mutual funds, insurance companies and others.

Pension Benefits

The workers in Chile are entitled to receive three types of benefits, old-age pension, disability pension and survivors' pension. Disability or death benefit is given with an insurance policy. The responsibility to pay pension to those workers who remained with the old system rested with the state.

Old-Age Pension

The retirement age in Chile is 65 years for men and 60 years for women. Under the mandatory individual account the members are entitled to receive old-age pension on retirement. At retirement, the accumulated amount can be used to buy an immediate life annuity, temporary income with a deferred life annuity and programmed withdrawals. Alternatively, the accumulated amount can also be used to buy an immediate life annuity with programmed withdrawals.

Guaranteed Minimum Pension

Persons who have not opted for the new disability solidarity benefit but who received the guaranteed minimum pension prior to 1 July 2008 are entitled to it (the guaranteed minimum pension has been replaced by the disability solidarity benefit).

Basic Old-Age Solidarity Pension

Men and Women aged 65 years, who have resided in Chile for at least 20 years, including at least 4 of the last 5 years, and with no entitlement to a pension, are eligible for basic solidarity pension of 75,000 pesos a month. There is also basic disability solidarity pension for those aged between 18 and 64 years, who have resided in Chile for at least 5 years in the past 6 years, assessed with a disability but are not entitled to a pension. The family of the pensioners must be among the poorest 50 per cent of the population.

Social Insurance

Social insurance is available to wage earners and self-employed persons with earnings lower than three times the legal monthly minimum wage (MW).

Solidarity Pension

Chile has introduced significant changes in its pension system through introduction of solidarity pension in January 2008, which aimed at removing certain shortcomings in the pension system. Chile maintains its three-pillar system but abolished old MPG and instead introduced minimum pension benefits to anyone who is unable to make regular contributions to save for the old age. The minimum pension benefits under solidarity pension are administered under a new PAYG system. The new solidarity system has two important components, namely basic solidarity pension and solidarity contribution. Basic solidarity pension is provided to people living in poverty and having no other means to save to fund their pension, while solidarity contribution is provided to those with insufficient savings to fund their pension. The new system replaced the minimum guarantee pension and welfare pensions (Marcel and Tapia 2009). The new system also aimed at improving coverage, to reduce in equity among men and women in respect of pension entitlement and so on.

Minimum Return Guarantee

There are minimum return guarantee in Chilean pension system. All the AFPs must guarantee that the average real return in the last 36 months is not less than that of the lower of the following two measures:

1. Average real return of the funds minus two percentage points for the funds C, D, and E and minus four percentage points for the funds A and B.
2. Fifty per cent of average real return of all funds. However, if the average yield exceeds by 2 per cent, 4 per cent or by 50 per cent the excess of return is transferred to a yield fluctuation reserve, which is used to make up the guaranteed return if funds under an AFP are under the guaranteed minimum.

Tax Benefits

Chile has introduced exempt exempt tax (EET); that is, while the full mandatory contributions and investment income is exempted from tax, pension payments are taxable. However, voluntary contributions up to a certain ceiling are tax exempted.

Investment Management in Multi-Fund System

Since the introduction of mandatory contributory pension fund in 1981, the pension fund managers in Chile could offer only one fund, but in February 2002, through a new

Act 19795, three new types of funds were introduced but since August 2002, there have been five different funds, namely the riskiest fund A; the risky fund B; intermediate fund C (the original, which has been maintained since the launch of the system); conservative fund D; and the most conservative fund E. The basic difference between the five funds is the maximum and minimum limits of investment in equity instruments. It is obligatory for the AFPs to offer four least aggressive funds, while the riskiest fund A is voluntary. Fund managers also had an option to offer a fifth fund to the investors. Multi-fund system thus introduced to offer a wide variety of options to the investors, who could select one according to their risk appetite and risk tolerance level. However, there is a limiting factor which prohibits investors who retired or are likely to retire, to invest in high risk funds.

> *The reason for limiting the participants' option to choose any type of fund is based on the State's role as guarantor. Excessive variation in the funds of contributors who are close to retirement age and pensioners increases the probability and the amount of public spending on pensions due to the welfare pension programs. (Hormazábal 2010)*

Chile has also introduced a default option for those participants who do not select any type of fund. The default option funds are assigned to the members according to their age, so that younger members (men and women under 35 years of age) will have their savings in the risky fund B. Subsequently their funds will be transferred at a rate of 20 per cent per year to the intermediate fund C and then to the conservative fund D, when women reach 50 years of age and men 55 years of age.

Funds Management

The new system is managed by the private pension funds managers known as AFPs, who are specially created for pension fund management. They are regulated by state regulation. The AFPs must fulfil the diversification requirement set out by the law. In Chile, workers can choose only one AFP at a time and annuity provider, but they have no say in investment within AFPs. AFPs are supervised by the superintendence of AFP. By June 2006, there were 6 fund managers (AFPs) in Chile, though in the beginning (1981) there were 12 AFPs. Though Chile has liberalised pension fund investment, state regulation is quite strong. Pension funds are allowed to invest up to 37 per cent funds in equity and up to 45 per cent funds in state securities. Regulations have been prescribed for maximum limits for each class of investment instruments, rating requirement, liquidity and so on.

Expenses and Commission

Chilean AFPs charge for expenses incurred for administration, marketing, advertisement and investment management. There are no limits to the level of commission charged by AFPs. Two types of commissions, fixed and variable aggregate commission, are around 3.1 per cent of salary (Shah 1997). Some authors have further pointed out the high administrative costs of Chilean pension funds; for example, according to Steve Idemoto (2000), 'steep advisory fees of per cent to per cent are paid by many.... Total expenses appear to be in the range of 15 percent to 20 percent of annual contribution'.

Role of the Government and Regulator

Though Chile has introduced privately managed contributory individual account system, the government plays a significant role in ensuring orderly regulation and protection of members/workers interest in terms of minimum pension and guaranteed return. The superintendent of pension funds (SAFP), who represents the government, is the supervisory authority for pension fund administrators (AFPs) in Chile. The AFPs are the single purpose private institutions. The AFPs are required to maintain a legal reserve, a cash reserve and a profitability/liquidity fluctuation reserve. There is free entry and exit into the industry.

PENSION REFORMS IN PERU

Peru was the next Latin American country to introduce privatised funded pension system after Chile, but in many respects adopted a reform structure that was different from the Chilean. While Chile abolished the PAYG old system, Peru established a private pension fund system through the Law 25897 on 6 December 1992.

Demographic Trend

According to the UN population projection, the total population of Peru will go up from 29.5 million in 2009 to 39.3 million in 2050, but population over 60 will go up by about 3 times (8.7 per cent to 22.5 per cent) and that of over 80 will increase by 4 times (from 1.1 per cent to 4.3 per cent) during the same period. Similarly, the old-age dependency will increase sharply imposing serious burden on the declining working population. Per capita income of people in 2009 was US$7,836, and pension assets as percentage of GDP was 18.0 per cent in 2007 in Peru.

Reform and New Pension System

Before introduction of the private pension system (PPS) through Law 25897 on 6 December 1992, Peru had national pension system (NPS) which is PAYG DB system, while PPS is a capitalised DC system. Peru introduced the private pension system PPS as an alternative to PAYG public system NPS. Peru, thus established a two-pillar system consisting of a PAYG public component and a fully funded private component and there is also a voluntary system.

NPS

The public pension provision consists of two different programmes; that is, social assistance for low-income individual and a contributory social insurance programme. Through the social assistance programme, Peru provides minimum benefits for low-income individuals. The minimum benefit also provided to all the members of the private pension system who, at retirement, could not accumulate enough funds in their personal accounts to finance a pension of an amount equal to or greater than the minimum pension, on the fulfilment of certain requirements as specified by law.

PPS

The PPS, created through Law 25897 in December 1992, is based on an individual capitalisation model and operates parallel to the public system. Pension fund management firms (AFPs) manage affiliates' accounts and are supervised by the Superintendencia de Banca, Seguros y AFP (superintendence of bank, insurance and private pension funds [SBS]). This second pillar was voluntary for all the dependents and self-employed workers and managed by private fund managers called AFPs. Workers who did not opt for the new system remained the members of publicly defined benefit system.

Voluntary Pension Saving

Peru has also introduced voluntary savings by workers to augment old-age pension and non-pension income. The voluntary saving for pension purpose can be withdrawn only on retirement while non-voluntary saving can be withdrawn three times in a year. 'Voluntary saving in Peru is poorly developed as it does not offer any tax benefit and there is no limit on the base contribution salary to the mandatory system' (FIAP 2006).

Transition

While introducing the funded private system, Peru did not discard the old DC system and allowed both the systems to compete with each other. The new entrants to the labour force were given an option to decide within a period of 10 days whether to join the PPS or the NPS. In case a worker did not make any choice, she/he was automatically affiliated to the private system. While the workers in NPS had an option to switch over to PPS or to remain with NPS, the workers who had once affiliated with PPS were not allowed to switch back to the public system.

Contribution and Collection

In Peru, the entire contribution to the PPS system was charged to the workers. The total contribution to the funded PPS system is 12.75 per cent (2006) of their taxable salary for old age, survivor and disability coverage. Out of the total contribution of 12.75 per cent, 10 per cent is transferred to individually funded account, 1.83 per cent for funds management fees and 0.91 per cent going to insurance company for invalidity, survival and burial expenses.

Collection of contribution in Peru is decentralised and performed by the fund managers through main banks. In Peru, members are allowed to switch over from one AFP to another AFP as per the rule.

Coverage

In Peru, the pension system is mandatory for all the Peruvian workers and all the workers must join either the public pension system or the private pension system while self employed may voluntarily join one of the pension systems. FIAP data indicate that though there is a steady increase in the number of members since the introduction of private system, the members do not contribute regularly. By the end of June 2006, there were only 1,396,296 contributors as against the total number of 3,775,230 members. That means about one-third members did not pay their contribution. The reason behind nonpayment, according to some authors, is the predominant presence of informal sector workers in Peru.

Pension Benefits

Under the funded PPS system, pension benefits include retirement pension, grants for ageing, disability and survival benefits. Retirement age in Peru is 65 years for both men and women, and on retirement accumulated balance (and converted recognition bond if any) is converted into monthly pension payment. Early retirement is permissible on certain conditions in addition to other benefits.

Minimum Pension

Peru has introduced an MPG under the first pillar through the state supplementary acknowledgement bonds to those who are unable to get an individual pension.

Minimum Return Guarantee

Before the introduction of multi-fund law in November 2005, Peru had minimum return guarantee on investment by private fund managers. However, with the introduction of multi-fund law, the minimum guarantee was replaced by reference index or 'benchmark'. Accordingly, each AFP will select a bench mark index which reflects the composition, diversification, risk and return for each class of securities.

Taxation

Peru has introduced EET. Under EET, mandatory contributions are taxed, but the investment incomes and benefits are tax exempted. However, there is no tax exemption for voluntary contribution.

Investment Management

In Peru, pension funds under the private scheme PPS are managed by specialised private fund management called AFPs. AFPs are not allowed to do any business other than pension fund management, and are set up as joint-stock companies. AFPs are allowed to do business if licenses are issued by the SBS, which also regulate and supervise the AFPs. Initially (1993), AFPs could only offer one pension fund to their affiliates. However, following the practices in Chile and Peru, in July 2005, through Law 279883, introduced a multi-fund scheme and AFPs were allowed to offer three types of funds with different levels of risk, which arise due to different proportion of equity investment in schemes. While the more aggressive fund with highest level of expected risks can invest up to 80 per cent funds in equity, the balance fund can invest up to 45 per cent of funds in equity and more conservative fund can invest up to 10 per cent funds in equity. In 2010, there were five AFPs operating in the pension market in Peru, each one was managing three.

Composition of asset classes in three different funds aimed at diversification and risk return optimisation. Equity exposure varies from 80 per cent in growth fund type-1, to only 10 per cent in fund type-2; similarly, fixed-income securities vary from 100 per cent in fund type-1 to 70 per cent in fund type-3. Though AFPs can invest up to 80 per cent in equity, it was observed that in September 2009, equity investment in type-1, type-2 and in type-3 funds were 5.57 per cent, 25.9 per cent and 49.7 per cent respectively, while investment in fixed-income securities in type-1, type-2 and type-3 funds were 78.2 per cent, 45.5 per cent and 14.2 per cent respectively. Further overwhelming percentage of funds invested in domestic securities which varied from 84.8 per cent in type-1 to 67.2 per cent in type-3 funds (BBVA Research 2010).

In Peru no explicit default option/product is available, but in case a member does not exercise any option to select a fund, the regulator assigns a fund according to the age of the member. According to the current rule, a member aged below 60 years will be assigned to a mixed fund, while a member older than 60 will be assigned capital maintenance, conservative fund with higher investment in fixed-income instrument.

PENSION REFORMS IN COLOMBIA

Pension Reform in Colombia has a distinctive feature as it emphasised upon reforming the pension and health-care system through the law 100 passed in December 1993 by the Colombian Congress. This law made the participation of dependent and independent workers in pension and health-care system mandatory in Colombia, which is quite significant, since in many countries reform focus remained to the pension system only.

Demographic Trend

Colombia is the third-largest country, next to Brazil and Mexico, in terms of population among Latin American countries studied by us. However, population ageing is one of the highest in Colombia among Latin American countries and the percentage of population aged over 60 years will go up by nearly 3 times from 8.6 per cent in 2010 to 28.2 per cent in 2050, while the percentage of population over 80 years will go up from 1.1 per cent to 5.0 per cent during the same period. Old-age dependency ratio will be a serious problem in Colombia, which will increase from 8.6 per cent in 2010 to 27.3 per cent in 2050.

Reform and New Pension System

Prior to the introduction of the pension reform in 1993, Columbia had a 'fragmented pension system comprising of six broad categories of pension plans and institutions'

(Schmidt-Hebbel 1997). These included pension funds for government and public sector employees, mandatory pension fund for private sector employees and most of these systems were PAYG DB schemes, which were administered by Instituto de los Seguros Sociales (ISS). Several considerations like low coverage, changing demographic scenario, growing cost of unfunded PAYG system, and so on, prompted pension reform in Colombia. The Law 100 provided a general framework to reform both the pension and health-care systems. Participation of dependent and independent workers in both the systems was mandatory. The Law 100 introduced the general pension system, with two mandatory subsystems—state managed PAYG public system, which is DB scheme, and privately managed fully individual account system, which is a DC system. Both the systems coexist and compete with each other. There is also a voluntary saving system. Therefore, currently Colombia has multi-pillar pension and social security systems comprising the following: state-managed DB PAYG scheme run by ISS, privately managed individually funded DC system run by AFPs and a voluntary saving scheme.

The DC system is managed through individual accounts; it is an alternative to the old system. The private system is managed by the private fund managers called AFPs. Workers can also make voluntary contribution to voluntary pension fund (FPV) on regular or occasional basis. FPVs can be managed by AFPs, trust companies or life insurance companies. In addition to the above there are a number of insurance companies which manage voluntary pension funds.

Solidarity Pension Fund

An important feature of reform is the introduction of solidarity pension fund financed through solidarity tax. Workers earning more than four times of MWs are to pay 1 per cent of income to solidarity pension fund with matching grant of government contribution. Another important feature of Colombia's pension reform was the introduction of non-contributory pension, financed out of general revenue and paid to retirees who do not fulfil the conditions for receiving social insurance benefit.

Health Care

The health-care system was one of the twin focuses of the Law 100. Prior to this Law 100, insurance and services in the social sector were provided by ISS and public and private hospital structures.

Law 100 dismantled the previous system and put in place a single insurance system based on 'cross subsidies' between the contributive system (CS) and the subsidised system (SS). The contribution to CS is 12.5 percent of payrolls, 67 percent paid by employer and the 33 percent paid by employee. The subsidised SS meant for individuals who lack financial means to pay for health care contributions. The insurance component of the health care system is based on the Empresas Promotoras de Salud (EPS), offering the mandatory basic health care plan known as Plan Obligatorio de Salud (POS). The service component is provided through the Instituciones Prestadoras de Salud (IPS). In Colombia, health care coverage has increased significantly, from 28 percent of the population in the early 1990s up to 86 percent by end-2006. (Clavijo 2009)

Transition

Participation in the general pension system was compulsory for self-employed and dependent workers. There is also an option to switch over from one system to another in each 5th year, but will not be allowed before 10 years of retirement. The new system also allowed the right of employees to switch back and forth between the old and new systems. Also, at the time of transition, full pension benefits were recognised for the existing contributors. However, those who did not exercise any option automatically became members of the public system.

Pension Coverage

New general pension system covers all the workers in Columbia. Pension social security coverage including health care in Colombia is extended to all employees and self-employed workers though social insurance (medium premium pension) and individual account system (individual saving regime) and non-contributory pension system. There are old-age retirement, disability benefits (full and partial), medical and other benefits to Colombian workers. There has been a significant increase in membership in individual account system since implementation in 1994. Total membership to individual account increased from 991,620 in December 1994 to 6,701,261 in June 2006. However, number of contributors still remained low at 2,677,620 in June 2006; that is, contributors are only 39.95 per cent of membership of the individual system.

Contribution

Pension system in Colombia is financed through the contribution of employers and employees. According to the amendment of Law 100/93, the contribution will increase progressively from 13.5 per cent in 2003 to 14.5 per cent in 2004, 15.0 per cent in 2005, 15.5 per cent in 2006, 16.5 per cent in 2008 (FIAP 2002). At this rate workers contribute 25 per cent and 75 per cent is contributed by the employers. Total contribution is distributed between medium premium regime (public pension) and individual saving regime (individual account). Total contribution in June 2006 was 15.5 per cent (employers at 11.62 per cent + employees at 3.88 per cent) and allocated to funded individual account system (14 per cent) and MPG fund (1.5 per cent). Out of the 14 per cent allocated to the funded system, an amount of 11 per cent was allocated to individual accounts, 1.59 per cent was fund managers' commission and 1.41 per cent to invalidity and survival insurance premium.

Benefits

New general pension system in Colombia provides liberal pension, health care and other social security benefits to the members. Major benefits fall under social insurance and individual funded account and under medical benefit schemes. In Colombia, under the social insurance scheme retirement age is 60 for men and 55 for women, while under the private system the retirement age for men is 62 years and for women it is 60 years. Old-age pension is available under social insurance and individual account system.

Under the social insurance old-age pension, men and women are eligible for old-age pension at 60 and 55 respectively, if certain stipulated contributions are made. Minimum social insurance pension is available if the pension is less than the minimum pension set by law; the government makes up the difference. There is also a social insurance old-age settlement available to those insured who do not meet the qualifying conditions of contribution at the normal retirement age. Pension benefits are adjusted according changes in consumer price index.

Individual Account

Pension under individual account depends the value of contribution (and accrued interest) of the member. At retirement, a member can buy an annuity policy or can opt for periodical withdrawal from own account survival benefits, death benefit and disability benefits; various types of medical benefits are also available under social insurance and individual account systems.

Guaranteed Minimum Pension

Under the new system there is a guarantee for minimum pension to the Colombian workers, under the social insurance and individual account systems. However, the workers must contribute 23 years to be eligible for minimum pension.

Taxation

Colombia has introduced EET taxation for pension funds. Contribution to pension funds is deductible from income tax. Pension benefits are tax-exempt up to 25 MWs. In Colombia there is no restriction on commission and AFPs can charge commission as percentage of salary of the affiliates.

Investment Regulations

Investment regulation for pension funds in Colombia has been designed to avoid risks through diversification. Accordingly, up to 40 per cent can invested in equities with high, medium and trading liquidity but only up to 5 per cent of the fund value can be invested in equity low trading liquidity. Investment in public debt up to 50 per cent, in Retail Investment Funds and private investment fund up to 5 per cent in each, up to 10 per cent deposit with central bank is allowed but no loan and Real estate investment is allowed (OECD 2010). Investment by private pension funds and, accordingly, investment in government sector, corporate sector, financial sector and foreign sector was 47.33 per cent, 19.43 per cent, 18.89 per cent and 14.35 per cent respectively in June 2006.

Minimum Return Guarantee

Private pension fund managers in Colombia need to provide a guaranteed return which is the average real rate of return in the last 36 months and is equal to at least 70 per cent of the system's average (Dayoub and Lasagabaster 2008).

Fees

In Colombia, there is an upper limit on commission that can be charged by a fund manager. A fund manager can charge a fee including premium for disability and survivors insurance, which should not exceed 3 per cent of salary of the member. The actual commission charged by the fund manager in June 2006 was 3 per cent (1.59 per cent as fund management fees + 1.41 per cent as insurance premium). By June 2006, there were six private pension fund managers in Colombia and they managed US$1,402.8 million. AFPs are allowed to manage more than one fund in Colombia. Investment regulations are much more relaxed in Colombia than in Peru and Chile.

Administration and Supervision

The PAYG system is managed by ISS, which is regulated and controlled by Banking Superintendency of Colombia. Private funds are managed by prevision entities administrators of private funds (AFPs) which are controlled and supervised by Superintendencia Bancaria de Colombia.

PENSION REFORMS IN ARGENTINA

Argentina is an important case study since it was the first country in Latin America which after experiment with pension reform nationalised the private pension system. Argentina reformed its PAYG pension system and introduced a mixed system in 1994 but through the senate approval in November 2008 nationalised US$24 billion in assets under management currently handled by the country's 10 private pension fund managers (AFPs) (Business News Americas, 21 November 2008).

Demography

Argentina is the fourth-largest country (among the Latin American countries studied here) in terms of population, 40.7 million in 2009. Argentina's population is expected to go up to 52.2 million in 2050. Life expectancy in 2009 was 72.5 years for the male and 80 years for the female. But Argentina is next to Uruguay (the country with highest percentage of elderly population) in terms of ageing population. Population over 60 years of age in 2010 was 14.7 per cent, estimated to go up to 24.9 per cent in 2050. Further, elderly population over 80 years of age will increase from 2.6 per cent to 5.3 per cent during the same period. Old-age dependency ratio will be almost double from 16.6 in 2010 to 30.2 in 2050. GDP per capita in 2009 was US$13,238 and pension assets in terms of GDP were 11.5 per cent in 2007.

Pension Reform

Argentina has a very long history of social security and pension fund.

> *The first pension fund was created as early as 1904, before some developed and most developing countries. However, this scheme targeted only some civil servants. Coverage progressively extended to the rest of the population, especially during the 1940s with the creation of pension funds for industrial and commerce workers. Although initially, most pension. (Arza 2005)*

Before pension reform in 1993, the country had a well-developed PAYG DB pension with the contribution of employers and employees and it was administered by the state. But the system suffered from a 'very extensive evasion, low retirement ages, very high targeted replacement rates, multiple pension for some workers' unmarried and widowed daughters and sisters, resulting into high dependency, large deficits and transfer from budget' (Vittas 1997), which prompted the Government of Argentina to reform its pension system.

Argentina introduced the new integrated system of retirement and pension (Sistema Integrado de Jubilaciones y Pensiones [SIJP]) through the Law 24241 was passed on 23 September 1993, which made affiliation to SIJP mandatory for most employed and self-employed persons. The system is a multi-pillar mixed system having public and private pension funds competing with each other. The first pillar is a universal basic pension (Prestación básica universal [PBU]) which is as a PAYG scheme, managed by the national social security administration (ANSES). The second pillar consists of two alternative regimes, namely a PAYG regime, managed by ANSES, and an individual account–based funded regime, managed by private fund management companies called Administradoras de Fondo de Jubilaciones y Pensiones (AFJPs). The fully funded system based on individual capitalisation was operating since 1994. It stopped in November 2008.

Transition

Joining the SIJP system was mandatory for the dependent and the independent workers. It was also compulsory for self employed over 18 years. Existing workers were allowed to remain with the old public system or to join the new system but those who did not exercise options automatically became members of the private system. Members were allowed to switch over from public system to the private pillar but not allowed to switch over from private system to the public system in the second pillar.

Coverage

Pension and social security coverage in Argentina is provided basically through social insurance and social assistance programme. The new pension system was able to attract a sizeable number of workers and the membership to the funded pension, which increased substantially during 1994 to 2000 from 3,121,681 in September 1994 to 8,103,974 in June 2000; that is, an annual average growth rate of 26 per cent. However, there was a significant decline in the growth rate in membership during 2000–06. Membership by June 2006 stood at 10,958,574 which means annual average growth rate during 2000–06 was little less than 9 per cent. Further, the quantity of contributors as a percentage of membership was also very low as the total amount of contributors by June 2006 was 4,340,729 as against the total membership of 10,958,574; that is, 39.6 per cent of members were active contributors. It seems that the declining rate of membership, low ratio of contributors to membership, and so on, were among the few reasons for nationalisation of private pension system in Argentina.

Contribution

Under PAYG public system managed by ANSES, employees are to contribute 11 per cent of their taxable salary and a 16 per cent is to be provided by the employers. But self-employed workers pay 27 per cent contribution out of which 16 per cent goes to the public system. The contribution to the AFJP system is 27 per cent of workers' income—11 per cent contributed by workers and 16 per cent contributed by employers. The AFJP component of the second pillar is financed by 11 per cent contribution of employees. Out of the 11 per cent, 7.5 per cent is used as retirement capital in individual account and the remaining 3.5 per cent used for financing survivors insurance and disability benefits.

Pension Benefits

In Argentina, retirement for men and women are 65 years and 60 years, respectively, and the retired employees receive several benefits under various provisions. There are several types of pensions and social security benefits available to workers in Argentina. Pension benefits under the public system include universal old-age pension or PBU available to men aged 65 and women aged 60 who have served up to 45 years and contributed for at least 30 years. Compensatory pension is (Prestacion Compensatoria [PC]) provided by the state to those who are eligible for PBU. Advanced-age old-age pensions are available to men and women aged 70 or more with certain stipulated years of service. There is also non-contributory old-age pension for the needy residing in Argentina. In addition to pensions, workers are also entitled to disability benefits, survivors' benefits, death benefits and medical benefits under the social insurance scheme. The private system pension depends on the accumulated funds (contribution and investment income). Pension benefits can be availed on retirement by opting to use accumulated amount for purchasing annuity. A member can also opt for programme withdrawal according to a life expectancy schedule. Under the private system of the second pillar, workers are entitled for disability and survivors insurance and can purchase life annuity or opt for gradual withdrawal of accumulated amount.

MPG

Argentina has introduced guaranteed minimum return by the fund managers. Each administrator must guarantee a real rate of return in the last 12 months, which is equal to 70 per cent of the system average or this same profitability minus two percentage points (Dayoub and Lasagabaster 2008).

Investment Management and Regulations

The private pension funds were managed by private fund management companies called AFJPs. Each AFJP operates only one account. AFJPs invest within the parameters of investment guidelines issued by the Regulator. In June 2006, there were 11 fund managers (AFJPs) in Argentina which managed the funded pension scheme.

Investment activities of AFJPs are heavily regulated in Argentina. This regulation includes quantitative and qualitative rules that govern the upper limit in any instrument as well as specific restrictions on investment. Accordingly, in 2007, a pension fund could invest up to 50 per cent in national public bonds, treasury notes and credits to the national state, up to 40 per cent in corporate bonds with maturity of two years or more, up to 40 per cent in convertible corporate bonds, up to 50 per cent in equity, up to 40 per cent in mortgage-backed bonds, up to 20 per cent in mutual fund shares, up to 10 per cent each in foreign sovereign bonds and foreign corporate bonds and so on (OECD, October 2007). The fund managers of AFJP were allowed to charge variable and fixed commission on the basis of salary of affiliates. Administration cost is one of the highest in Argentina.

Guarantee of Minimum Return

Argentina introduced minimum return guarantee by the fund managers. Each AFJP had to deliver a minimum yearly return (calculated every month) which should be 70 per cent of the weighted average return for the overall system or the weighted average return minus two percentage points. In case an AFJP fails to achieve this minimum return over a month, it must compensate by funding the difference.

Administration and Supervision

The PAYG system is managed by the public social security agency—ANSES. The private pension system in Argentina is managed by AFJPs. They manage the pension funds and the retirement benefits. The Superintendencia de Administradoras de Fondos de Jubilaciones y Pensiones (SAFJP) regulates and supervises pension funds.

Private Pension System Was Nationalised

There are several points and counterpoints about nationalisation of private pension system in Argentina. However, our concern here is not that debate, but to mention some expert findings which might have prompted the Argentine government to nationalise the private pension system. According to World Bank Evaluation (Independent Evaluation Group [IEG] 2006), real return (11.7 per cent) of funded pension system in Argentina since inception (1994) outperformed real wage growth rate (–0.8), which was considered to be a proxy for the implicit rate of return to the PAYG system. This return was even better than in many Latin American countries including Chile. However, coverage remained low (declining) during the post-reform period in Argentina. The World Bank had assigned 'Moderately Satisfactory' rating to the multi-pillar reform and indicated that 'fiscal problems continued to plague the system'. A presentation made by Camila Arza (Arza 2009) in The United Nations Research Institute for Social Development (UNRISD) Conference in Geneva (12–13 November 2009) provided some important insight into the private pension system which prompted nationalisation of pension system in Argentina in October 2008. Accordingly, up until 2004, contribution revenue fell, expenditure remained stable and non-contributory financing rose from 31 per cent to 62 per cent. Coverage as a percentage of economically active population (EAP) fell among the poor by 78 per cent and rose among the rich by 28 per cent during 1993–2006. The system witnessed new risk and high cost. Though historical return was 9.9 per cent, it was quite volatile, about one-third of contribution was used to pay operation cost and during 2006–08, private pension fund lost 1.2 million affiliates. These developments, therefore, seem to be implicit in the World Bank evaluation quoted earlier. Nationalisation of private pension system, though political (as commented by many experts), point out the necessity of critical evaluation of performance of the private pension system.

SOCIAL SECURITY AND PENSION REFORMS IN URUGUAY

Uruguay is considered to be the pioneer in introducing social security pension programmes in Latin America beginning with the introduction of a fund for teachers in 1896, which was subsequently extended to other sectors. In the year 1943 a system of family allowances was introduced, and consolidated further in 1950. However, the most significant reform in pension system was introduced on 3 September 1995 through the Law 16713 but unlike many other Latin American countries, Uruguay did not follow the Chilean model, rather it introduced a mixed model by reforming it PAYG DB pension system. The reform of the pension system aimed at increasing the value of benefits and increase public social expenditure, which aggravated the problem of how to adequately finance the system and to address the financing problem that confronted the public system (Antia and Lanzara 2011).

Demography

Uruguay is a small country, and the smallest among the countries included in our study but having highest percentage population over 60 years of age. In 2009, Uruguay had a population of 3.4 million, which is likely to go up to 3.7 million in 2050. However, the population over 60 years of age will shoot up from 18.4 per cent in 2010 to 27.4 per cent in 2050 and the population over 80 years will go up from 3.7 per cent to 6.8 per cent during the same period. Uruguay has one of the highest old-age dependency ratios, 21.8 per cent in 2010 which would go up to 34.80 per cent in 2050. Therefore, ageing is a very serious concern for Uruguay though Uruguay has a very liberal pension and social security systems and the pensionable age for men and women is 60 years. The average per capita income in Uruguay was US$11,216 in 2009 and the pension assets as percentage of GDP were 14.7 per cent in 2007.

Pension Reform

Uruguay followed Argentina in introducing a mixed pension system instead of following total privatisation like Chile, Bolivia and so on. Uruguay adopted a partial privatisation model by retaining the earlier PAYG system through social security reforms in 1995. The mixed social insurance and individual account system are mandatory for employed and self-employed persons born after 1 April 1956, with monthly earnings greater than 19,805 pesos and voluntary for those with monthly income of 19,805 pesos or less. All others are covered only by the social insurance system (ISSA 2009). Pension system after 1995 was based on a multi-pillar model consisting of three pillars discussed in the following paragraphs.

❖ FIRST PILLAR

It is a publicly managed social insurance (Régimen de Jubilación por Solidaridad Intergeneracional). Participation and contribution is mandatory for all workers. In addition to workers contribution, employers and the state also contribute to finance. This pillar, 'social insurance', is managed by the Banco de Previsión Social (BPS). Funds under this first pillar are used to pay retirement benefits, survivor's benefits, extreme old-age benefits and disability benefits.

❖ SECOND PILLAR

It is a privately managed fully funded System (Régimen de Jubilación por AhorroIndividual Obligatorio). The second pillar is a privately managed fully funded scheme to which contribution is mandatory for all workers in income brackets above a certain minimum level, and voluntary for those who are below the stipulated income level. The second pillar is managed by a private fund management company called Adiministradoras de Fondos de Ahorro Previsional (AFAPs). AFAPs are public limited companies set up to manage private pension funds. As on June 2006, there were four AFAPs in Uruguay.

❖ THIRD PILLAR (VOLUNTARY SAVINGS)

This individually funded system allows the voluntary deposits by workers to increase the savings accumulated in the individual account. The contributions can be directly paid by the workers or company to the personal saving account.

Transition

In transition from the PAYG system to the mixed system in Uruguay, a flexible option was given to the existing members of the old system and both the system were compulsory for workers. The social security system was made mandatory for all people who were under 40 years of age as on 1 April 1996; it was also made mandatory for the workers who entered labour market after that date. However, the new system was made voluntary for the workers above the age of 40 years.

> *As a general rule, affiliates with wages below a threshold continue being served exclusively by the public–PAYG pillar, unless they explicitly opt for sending half of their personal contributions to a savings account. Until now, most workers in this situation made this option and are currently contributing to both pillars by halves. Affiliates with higher wages are obliged to make personal contributions to both pillars. Employers' contributions go exclusively to the public–PAYG pillar. Accordingly, low-wage workers who did not opt for the savings accounts receive their full pension from the BPS, while other workers' pensions are financed by both the BPS and the funds accumulated in their savings accounts. (Alvaro 2004)*

Contribution and Collection

The new system is a joint regime, receiving the contributions to the workers and grants benefits in a combined way. A portion of the contribution is allocated to the intergenerational joint regime and the other to the mandatory individual saving regime

(FIAP 2002). In Uruguay (as in June 2006), total contribution to the public system was 27.5 per cent, out of which 15 per cent was contribution by workers and 12.5 per cent was contribution from employers. In privately managed funded system, contribution is 15 per cent of the income of workers, and no contribution is made by employers. Out of the 15 per cent contribution in funded system, 12.14 per cent is transferred to individual account of the members, 0.976 per cent is paid to insurance company and 1.887 per cent goes to the fund managers' account as AFAP's commission (FIAP 2007). Uruguay has adopted a centralised collection system through social security bank (BPS) which is a government agency.

Coverage

Social security and pension coverage in Uruguay extended through three important instruments, namely social insurance, individual account and social assistance programme. Social insurance covers employed and self-employed workers, while individual accounts provide mandatory covers to employed and self-employed persons with earnings above certain stipulated amount and voluntary cover for employees and self-employed with earnings below certain amount. Social assistance tested by non-contributory means is provided to elderly or disabled persons. Membership and number of contributors to the privatised individual system was 702,923 and 431,399 (FIAP 2006) respectively; that is, little more than 61 per cent members were active contributors, which compares well with other Latin American countries. The number of affiliates in the private system, however, increased marginally during 1998 to 2002; the number of affiliates increased from 0.5 million to 0.6 million. In fact, there was a marginal decline in 2002.

Pension Benefits

Uruguay is considered to be one of the countries in Latin America providing liberal pension and social security to its employees. These benefits are available through the first pillar social insurance scheme, the second pillar individually funded scheme and social assistance programmes. Benefits include basic pension (first pillar) equivalent to 50 per cent of pensionable salary that one is entitled to after 35 years of service on retirement (at the age of 60 years), which increases with the increase in the number of years' contribution beyond 35 years. There is also a provision of advanced age pension for those who are not eligible for basic pension. Second pillar benefit is provided through mandatory purchased annuity. Disability and survivor's benefits are provided partly by public system and partly by private system, insurance companies provide supplementary benefits to total disabled and to the very old.

Old-Age Pension (Social Insurance and Individual Account)

Men and women, 60 years of age with at least 30 years of contribution, are eligible for old-age pension and those who are 70 years old with 15 years' contribution are eligible for advanced-age pension under social insurance and individual account. There is also a provision for survivor pension under social insurance and individual account system.

Uruguay workers are also entitled to receive permanent disability pension and partial disability pension under social insurance and individual account under certain situations. Non-contributor means tested pension (social assistance) is available to a resident of Uruguay for at least 15 years. This benefit is available to those who are with a total and permanent disability and are assessed as needy.

MPG

There is minimum pension. There is also a provision for social insurance for those who retire without sufficient pension due to low income.

Taxation

Uruguay has introduced EET tax system; that is, contribution and investment income get tax incentive, while benefits are taxable as per the law of the country.

Funds Management and Regulation

In Uruguay, the specialised pension fund management companies (AFAPs) manage the assets under the mandatory private pension system. AFAPs are established as public limited companies and manage one pension fund. AFPs can be formed by banks and financial institutions. Uruguay has introduced strict quantitative investment norms for private fund managers and there are certain legal restrictions on investing in certain asset classes, foreign investment, investment in single issuer and so on. Investments of AFPs are overwhelming in government securities. Uruguay has laid down a strict investment requirement for pension fund investment. Initially 100 per cent in government bonds—minimum 60 per cent and maximum 20 per cent in Uruguayan corporate or public stocks. All AFPs are required to have 100 per cent funds in government securities initially and 60 per cent in the long run. Asset allocation in 2001 indicates that 61.2 per cent of funds are invested in government securities, 19.2 per cent in bank deposits and 8.5 per cent in corporate bonds. According to FIAP (2006) data, investment in government sector, corporate sector, financial sector and others was 84.55 per cent,

4.05 per cent, 8.89 per cent and 2.51 per cent, respectively. There was no investment in the foreign sector in June 2006.

Guaranteed Rate of Return

Uruguay has introduced return guarantee by the AFAPs. Each AFAP must guarantee an annual average real rate of return, calculated every month, that is, the lowest of 2 per cent or the system's average minus two percentage points (Dayoub and Lasagabaster 2008).

The Central Bank of Uruguay controls and supervises the AFAPs including investment regulation. The funds under the publicly managed social insurance system are managed by the social insurance bank (BPS). It also manages non-contributory benefits, unemployment insurance, sickness insurance and family allowances.

Administration and Supervision

Uruguay system is a public–private combination; while payroll taxes are collected by the government, capital accumulation and benefit payments are handled by private pension, funds and insurance companies. Payroll taxes collected by Dirección General Impositiva (DGI) are sent to BPSs, who in turn forward it to AFPs for investing. The pension saving fund administrator (AFAP) is allowed to administer the individual capitalised saving account. Commissions charged by the AFAPs can be fixed or calculated on the basis of collection. Pension systems in Uruguay are supervised by the central bank of the country.

PENSION REFORM IN BOLIVIA

Pension reforms in Bolivia were to a great extent influenced by Chilean reforms but at the same it was unique in certain respects. In 1997, Bolivia totally eliminated the old system of publicly managed PAYG system and introduced a substitutive model—fully funded system based on individual contribution and managed by private fund managers. The unique feature of Bolivian reform was the linking of pension reform with disinvestment of large public sector and selling of 50 per cent shares of six public-owned companies to foreign companies. The capitalisation process was thus the decisive factor which permitted the universal old-age benefits (Escobar and Nina 2004).

Bolivia is a small country in terms of population, 10 million in 2009, which is going to be 16.7 million in 2050, but population of above the age of 60 will be more than double from 7.2 per cent to 17.5 per cent during this period and elderly population over 80 years will go up from 0.7 per cent of total population to 2.8 per cent and old-age dependency ratio from 8.0 per cent to 18.6 per cent during 2009 to 2.8 per cent in 2050. Life expectancy at 65 for men and 69.4 for women (2009) was one of the lowest in Latin America's average per capita income (US$4,206), and was also lower than many Latin American countries.

Process of Pension Reform

Though the Bolivian social security pension at the beginning of 1990s was serving different sectors, a comprehensive social security law was passed in December 1956 and the new pension system that was introduced was basically a PAYG DB system. Rationalisation Law was introduced in 1972 and Bolivian Institute of Social Security (IBSS) was created in 1973 to bring uniformity in pension and old-age benefits. In the 1970s many workers' unions also launched complementary pension funds. In 1996 the Bolivian pension system consisted of a basic pension administered by a public agency (Fondo de Pensiones Básicas [FOPEBA]) and 38 complementary funds, including 8 social security funds of public universities and one for the armed forces, with compulsory participation in the basic pension and voluntary participation in the complementary funds (Gersdorff 1997). The old PAYG system was very liberal but running with high deficit and administrative costs, which necessitated the reform of the DB PAYG system.

Bolivia introduced pension reform by enacting the Law 1732 on 29 November 1996. According to the new law, the old PAYG DB system was totally closed and established an individual capitalisation accounts–based mandatory long-term social security (SSO) for all workers. In addition to this, an old-age social security programme was also established through Bonosol. The old-age relief is financed by the share of capitalised enterprises. Under the new system the capitalisation shares was transferred into a fund called Fondo de Capitalización Colectivo or FCC which is managed by private fund managers called AFPs. All eligible Bolivians are owners of FCC and are benefited through the Bonosol programme. The pension fund administrators (AFPs) thus operate two funds as discussed in the following paragraphs.

❖ INDIVIDUAL CAPITALISATION FUND (FCI)

Mandatorily financed by individual member through regular contribution.

❖ COLLECTIVE CAPITALISATION FUND (FCC)

Financed with resources coming from the privatisation of public sector companies.

❖ VOLUNTARY SAVING

Over and above the contribution for the individually funded system, Bolivia allows the members additional contribution into the individually funded account to augment retirement benefits.

With the introduction of the new DC system in 1997, the earlier DB system was closed down and all the existing contributors to the old system were transferred to individual capitalised accounts. While it was mandatory for all the dependants to join the new system, it was voluntary for the self-employed. After the introduction of a new system, the old contributors were issued recognition bonds. Additional contribution as voluntary saving is allowed in the funded account, but there is no tax incentive for such contribution.

Contribution and Collection System

Under the new system, each member contributes 12.21 per cent of taxable salary. The employer makes an additional contribution of 1.71 per cent for the insurance premium for illness or accidents causing invalidity or death (FIAP 2006). Individual capitalisation accounts are managed by fund administrators called AFPs. Out of 12.21 per cent contribution, 10 per cent is saved in individual capitalisation accounts, 1.71 per cent towards premium for accidents causing invalidity and death and 0.5 per cent for AFP's service.

Collection system is decentralised and the fund managers collect the contribution through banks in Bolivia. Contribution for voluntary saving is paid directly to the members account.

Pension Coverage

Bolivia has attempted to cover its citizens through three types of social security programmes, namely mandatory individual account, voluntary coverage for self employed persons and universal pension called Renta Dignidad for all citizens aged over 60 years or older.

With the introduction of mandatory individual accounts, there has been a significant growth of membership. Total affiliates of pension funds in Bolivia have increased from 383,123 in June 1998 to 966,466 as on 30 June 2006. One of the reasons for this growth was the introduction of regulations during 1999–2000 to force self-employed workers to contribute to AFPs and the share of self-employed workers in total affiliates increased from 1.3 per cent in 1999 to 5.0 per cent in 2000. However, the share of self-employed workers in total affiliates declined subsequently to 4.3 per cent in 2002 (Escobar and Nina 2004). Further, all the members are not contributing regularly and there is a huge gap between affiliates and contributors.

Pension Benefits

Bolivian citizens are entitled to various types of old-age benefits which include old-age pension, survival and disability benefits and so on. Old-age pension is paid out of accumulated capital (contributions plus accrued interest). The amount is used to purchase a fixed or variable life annuity, depending on the total amount of the accumulated capital. The first monthly amount paid under a variable life annuity is not to be less than 70 per cent of the members' earnings in the last five years. But for armed forces personnel, the pension is 100 per cent of the earnings in the last five years. In addition to this, there is compensatory pension for those who have contributed to the old PAYG system. Disability and death pension are contracted by the AFPs to insurance companies. Guaranteed minimum pension is paid if the pension is less than the minimum pension set by law, which is 70 per cent of the average earnings in the last five years. The government makes up the deficit if members fulfil certain conditions. Universal pension (Renta Dignidad) is paid to resident citizens aged 60 or older.

Bonosol Programme

Bolivian pension reform is unique in the sense that it linked the old-age social assistance programme to capitalisation. This programme aimed at providing social safety net to the large number of poor people in their old age. Through Bonosol programme, Bolivia has set up a universal old-age assistance support to all Bolivians above 65 years.

> *Bonosol is an annuity, intended to distribute the benefits of the capitalisation programme to all resident Bolivian citizens who were 21 year or older as of end-1995, once they reach age 65. The benefit is financed by the principal and investment income on the portfolio consisting of the capitalisation enterprises. (Gersdorff 1997)*

The Bonosol Law, revised in November 2002, provided pension rights to all Bolivian citizens domiciled in the nation land who were 21 years old as on 31 December 1995. As a right they received pension from 65 years till death and annual and permanent benefit called solidarity bond Bonosol. Besides, they will also receive an additional Bonosol and funeral service expenses.

No Minimum Guarantee

In Bolivia, the government does not guarantee any minimum pension, or any minimum yield on investment. The government neither guarantees any pension in case of bankruptcy of any AP or payment of Bonosol benefit if FCC becomes insolvent.

Administration and Market Allocation

Another distinctive feature of Bolivian reform is limiting the number of fund managers in order to keep the administrative cost low, to make fund management a good business proposition and attract the efficient fund managers into the system. Through a competitive bidding process, Bolivia selected only two AFPs for the initial five years, but no more fund managers were added further. Another unique feature is the division of geographical areas of the country into three zones. Two fund managers were assigned one exclusive zone and the third was a common zone where both AFPs could operate.

Investment of Pension Fund Assets

Pension fund assets in Bolivia are highly concentrated in the government sector. According to the FIAP data for June 2006, 75.8 per cent funds were invested in the government sector, while 11.5 per cent funds were invested in the corporate sector, 8.7 per cent in the financial sector, 2.5 per cent in the foreign sector and 1.5 per cent in others.

Supervision and Regulation

Pension funds in Bolivia are regulated and overseen by the superintendents of El Sistema de Regulación Financiera (SIREFI), of pension and of the capital markets, which was established in 1997.

Bolivian reform has been praised by many pension experts due to its uniqueness, such as linking capitalisation with pension reforms, introduction of Bonosol programme for social assistance, completely abolishing old system by a new one but incorporating all the old members and so on.

PENSION REFORMS IN MEXICO

Mexico has a long history of social security and providing welfare measures to its workers. In 1925, it had introduced civil pension for government employees; in 1942 it passed social security law and in 1943 established the Mexican Social Security Institute (Instituto Mexicano de Seguridad Social [IMSS]) to insure and protect private sector workers. Federal Government Institute of Social Security Services (Instituto de Seguridad y Servicios Sociales de los Trabajadores del Estado [ISSSTE]) was created in 1959 to strengthen pension and medical services for state employees. In 1972 National Workers' Housing Fund Institute (Instituto del Fondo Nacional de la Vivienda para los Trabajadores [INFONAVIT]) for private sector workers and the ISSSTE for the government employees were created. Thus, Mexican social security initiatives attempted to extend support to various needs of the workers.

Demographic

Mexico is one of the most populous countries in Latin America with a population of 110.6 million in 2009, which is likely to go up to 131.6 million in 2050. Life expectancy at birth for men and women was 74.9 per cent and 79.7 per cent, respectively, in 2009. Though ageing at present is not an acute problem it is going to be in the future, as population over 60 years will go up from 9.4 per cent in 2010 to 28.2 per cent in 2050 and population over 80 years will go up from 1.4 per cent to 6.2 per cent during the same period. Mexico had the highest GDP per capita, US$14,104, among the Latin American countries included in our study.

However, before the introduction of the present system, Mexico had a PAYG social security system which was being managed by the IMSS. The IMSS managed the old age, severance, disability and life insurance. The social security system of Mexico for formal private sector workers and the self-employed evolved for almost 50 years through 1992, consisted of retirement, pensioners' health benefits and disability (Invalidez, Vejez, Cesantia en Edad Avanzada, y Muerte [IVCM]) and specialised housing fund administered by INFONAVIT (Grandolini and Cerda 1998).

Mexico made an attempt to reform its pension system by introducing the retirement savings system (Sistema de Ahorro para el Retiro [SAR]) in May 1992, as a mandatory individual retirement savings account and by raising the contribution as the second pillar. The SAR was introduced as a response to the deficiencies in the PAYG DB pension system and to complement the first pillar. The SAR consisted of two sub-accounts: individual retirement sub-account and a housing sub-account managed by INFONAVIT. Subsequent to reform in 1992, the National Commission for the Retirement Saving System (Comisión Nacional del Sistemas de Ahorro para el Retiro [CONSAR]) was set up in 1994 to regulate SAR.

However, the reform could not achieve the desired result and there continued imbalance between contribution paid in and benefits received, depletion of reserves and relatively high contribution rates of 31.5 per cent of nominal salary (Carstens 1997). Finally, Mexico took a drastic step to replace its PAYG system by a fully funded individualised capitalised system in 1997. The new social security system established by enacting a law in 1997 replaced the previous public social security based on PAYG managed by IMSS, by an Individual capitalisation and savings system. This new system was made mandatory for all workers affiliated with IMSS. The reform in 1997 followed the World Bank approach of multi-pillar system and Chilean reform.

Transition

The 1997 reform abolished the PAYG DB pension system and the workers who were members of the previous system were given an option either to join the new system and transfer their accumulated balance under the new system or to retire with the old system and receive benefits under the old system as in 1997, but all the new workers entering to the work force were to join the new system compulsorily.

Pension Coverage

Pension coverage in Mexico extended though the second-pillar individual account which is mandatory for all the private sector employees and members of cooperative entering labour force after 1997 but voluntary for public sector employees who were members of IMSS, self-employed persons and the workers covered under social insurance scheme before 1997. After privatisation of pension system through 1997 reform the number of affiliates increased rapidly, from 4,917,570 in June 1997 to 36,284,649 in June 2006. In fact, Mexico had the largest number of members among Latin American countries, which have introduced pension reforms. However, the number of contributors in June 2006 was only 13,702,588, that is, only about 38 per cent of membership. This low percentage of contributor is a serious concern in Mexico like other Latin American countries.

Contribution and Collection System

In Mexico, contribution to the new system is made by the employers, the employees and the government. For the second pillar meant for retirement, advance age unemployment and old-age sub-account (Retiro, Cesantía y Vejez [RCV]), contribution is 6.5 per cent of taxable salary which is split among the government, the employers and the employees. Out of this 6.5 per cent, an amount of 5.12 per cent is transferred to individually funded accounts while 1.38 per cent goes to the retirement fund administrators (Administradoras de Fondos para el Retiro [AFOREs]) towards commission in different ways. In addition to the above, the government adds a social quota (welfare allocation) to each individual account of 5.5 per cent of the general MW.

IMSS manages the invalidity and life insurance (IV) which is financed by 2.5 per cent of the taxable salary contributed by employers (1.75 per cent), workers (0.62 per cent) and the government (0.13 per cent). The housing sub-account contribution of 5 per cent taxable salary comes from the employer only and is deposited to the national housing fund managed by INFONAVIT. The individually funded system allows voluntary deposit in the voluntary sub-account by the members or employers to augment pension at the time of retirement. Voluntary savings can be short term, which can be withdrawn after two months, or long term, which can be kept in individual accounts to augment retirement pension. The collection system is centralised in Mexico and carried out by IMSS, an autonomous government agency which takes the help of banking institutions.

Pension Benefits

The workers in Mexico are entitled to receive several old-age benefits and retirement benefits under the mandatory individual account and social insurance scheme.

Mandatory Individual Account

The first pillar provides a MPG which is equivalent to the minimum salary in Mexico and under the second pillar with individual account, the option is given to the affiliates for a schedule withdrawal or purchase of an annuity from a private life insurance company. (The first) 'pillar is used if the, second pillar, individualised resources cannot provide the pension with an annuity equal to a MW' (Villasenor-Zertuche 2000).

Mandatory Scheme Old-Age Pension

Men and women aged 65 with at least 1,250 weeks of contributions are eligible for this benefit. The pension benefits depend on the value of the accumulated capital plus accrued interest. At the time of retirement, the insured can either purchase an annuity or opt for programmed withdrawals. There is a provision of early pension at the age of 60 years or older.

Guaranteed Minimum Pension

Guaranteed minimum pension and disability pension is available to an insured person when the value of the accumulated capital plus accrued interest is less than the minimum pension.

Unemployed Worker's Pension

Available to men of 60 years and women of 64 years who have made certain weekly contributions, and who are unable to find suitable paid employment.

Disability Pension

Disability pension is available to the insured who have certain weekly contributions.

Social Insurance

Under social insurance scheme similar benefits like old-age pension, early pension, unemployed worker's pension, disability pension, survivor pension, and so on, are available.

Tax Benefits

EET is applicable to pension fund savings, that is, contribution and investment returns are tax exempted, while benefits are taxable as per taxation law in Mexico. In Mexico tax-free benefits depend on the balance accumulated over an individual's working life—contribution and return on that contribution (Carstens 1997).

Investment Management

Initially, when the new system was launched in 1997, there was a single pension fund called Sociedades de Inversión Especializadas en Fondos para el Retiro (SIEFOREs) mostly investing in debt instruments. However, this model was replaced in 2004 by a model containing two SIEFOREs, namely SB1 and SB2. SB1 invested only in fixed-income instruments, while SB2's investment was a combination of fixed income and equity securities. This model was not sufficient to take into consideration the wide range of risk-return profiles of investors and was further replaced by a multi-fund model in 2008. The new multi-fund model for the AFOREs was introduced in April 2008. Three new SIEFOREs were added to the fund system with wider investment alternatives to the investors. With the reform being introduced in 2008, AFOREs had a family of five pension funds—SB1, SB2, SB3, SB4 and SB5—within the DC scheme of the SAR. A new investment regime for SIEFOREs was approved by the board of directors of the CONSAR.

As on 31 March 2008, accordingly, all 18 AFOREs restructured their SB2s into three new funds—SB3, SB4 and SB5. The new system created a multi-fund family of five SIEFOREs, and all of them except SB1 were allowed to have equities exposure through stock indexes and structured notes, but direct investment in stocks remained prohibited. New norms also allowed the SIEFOREs to invest in infrastructure, real estate and private capital. However, foreign investments still remain limited to 20 per cent. A key characteristic of the new multi-fund model is the life cycle focus of its design. It offers an all-in-one approach to monitor, diversify and reallocate assets in three new investment societies specialised in retirement funds. SIEFOREs were added to the range of investment alternatives available for retirement funds. 'The new multi-fund model represents a major step forward for the SAR in Mexico. In the medium term, it is still possible to strengthen the SIEFOREs' investment regime to the benefit of the affiliates' (Gómez 2008).

Investment management activities are carried out by AFOREs, which are the specialised firms promoted by private sector entities and trade unions. AFOREs are also the single purpose corporation authorised by the regulator and are required to maintain minimum paid up capital as per law.

Administration and Supervision

In Mexico, there is more than one agency to regulate the pension fund administrators and other service providers. The CONSAR is the Mexican pension fund regulation agency which supervises over AFOREs and SIEFOREs. CONSAR issues licenses and monitors the operation of AFOREs.

The housing and disability benefits to the private sector employees are provided by the IMSS and the housing for workers by INFONAVIT. Pension and health services for the government employees are provided by the ISSSTE and the housing and related facilities are provided by the fund for housing of the ISSSTE called Fondo de la Vivienda del Instituto de Seguridad y Servicios Sociales de los Trabajadores del Estado (FOVISSSTE).

PENSION REFORMS IN BRAZIL

Brazil has a long history of social security and the 'first Bismarck-style Social Security system started in 1923 and somewhat equivalent programme traced back to 1793 and 1821' (Pugh 2009). The basic social security, Regime Geral de Previdência Social (RGPS), in Brazil is a DB PAYG. Brazil has also initiated pension reforms but it did not follow the conventional Latin American model that began with Chile and was subsequently followed by other countries in the region. Brazil has not replaced the PAYG public pension by mandatory private pension. Though Brazil introduced private pension funds, but they are only complementary and voluntary. One of the focus areas of Brazil is to strengthen rural and informal sector pensions, since it has a large number of informal sector workforce, and introduce the rural pension system. Brazil is the largest in terms of population and also in terms of pension fund assets among the Latin American countries. The social security and pension systems in Brazil are quite complex like that of India and suffer from structural weaknesses such as non-coverage of a large number of informal sector workers and costly DB schemes for civil servants which pose challenges to reform.

Demographic Trend

Brazil is the largest country in terms of population, which was 195.4 million in 2009 and will go up to 259.8 million in 2050. Though population over 60 years in 2010 at 10.2 per cent was lower than in some countries, such as Uruguay, Argentina and Chile, Brazil is going to have the largest percentage of population (29.3 per cent) in 2050. Population over the age of 80 will increase from 1.5 per cent in 2010 to 6.5 per cent in 2050 and old-age dependency ratio will increase from 10.2 per cent to 35.9 per cent in 2050 and life expectancy in 2009 was 69.9 per cent for male and 77.2 per cent for female—lowest in Latin America.

Pension System Reform

The Brazilian pension system witnessed several changes, particularly after the approval of the Organic Law of Social Security (Lei Orgânica da Previdência Social [LOPS]) in 1960, which attempted to establish uniformity in the contribution system. Further reforms followed and in July 1977, Brazil legalised the private social security, which was further revised in May 2001 to legalise the private pension social security. The new law introduced a pension system having three components, namely general regime of social security (RGPS), special pension regime for government workers (Regimes Próprio de Previdência Social [RPPS]) and complementary pension regime (Regime de Previdência Complementar [RPC]). The current structure of social security in Brazil structured into three components (Reis and Paixão 2004).

❖ THE GENERAL REGIME (RGPS)

It is a mandatory PAYG public system managed by IMSS, which covers all private sector employees up to a certain amount of pensionable ceiling. The recent reforms were oriented to strengthen the redistributive role of the basic scheme, increase coverage and correct actuarial distortions.

❖ SPECIAL PENSION REGIME FOR GOVERNMENT WORKERS (RPPS)

The special regime for civil servants cover all the public sector and states' employees. Special system for civil servants is a mandatory PAYG system operated by the federal and state governments.

❖ COMPLEMENTARY PENSION REGIME (RPC)

The RPC system is voluntary and complementary to the first pillar and was established in 1977. This complementary system has two components, namely closed pension funds (Entidades Fechadas de Previdência Complementar [EFPC]) and open private pension entities (Entidades Abertas de Previdência Complementar [EAPC]).

Close-ended EFPCs are privately managed by non-profit organisations established by single or multiple employers or labour union or professional group financed by employees and/or employers. Close pension funds can be DB, DC or mixed pension plans. On the other hand, open pension fund (OPF) EAPC managed by insurance companies, banks' subsidiaries and non-profit organisations which offer pension plans to employees, employers and the self-employed and so on. They are non-profit organisations set up for providing retirement pension death, disability benefits and health coverage. In 2003, there were 360 close pension funds sponsored by 2,108 companies, with accumulated assets of US$82.9 billion, and 43 open private pension fund providers with 2,085 plans and accumulated assets of US$15.2 billion (Reis and Paixão 2004).

Rural Pension

One of the important features of the Brazilian pension system is the rural pension. Rural workers receive social security benefits equivalent to MWs from the ages of 60 (men) and 55 (women) subject to the proof of 10 years' rural activities. According to Maciel (2010),

> *Rural Workers retirement systems are an important progressive program that does not only create incentives for workers staying in the rural sector (avoiding migration to the urban centers) but it is also important for small municipal's public accounts and economies. Given its non-contributive bias this program works as a social assistance program.*

Rural retirement benefit in Brazil is provided just for subsistence agriculture (*agricultura familiar*) workers. Their contributions are based on a fraction of commercialised products from worker's excess production, but most workers rarely have excess production. However, the Brazilian Constitution granted the right of retirement to rural workers independent of their contribution.

Informal Sector

Brazil has a large growing informal sector which often is a constraint for expansion of social security in the country. In the last decade the Brazilian economy observed a sharp increase in the rate of informal workers in the economy. There has been a sharp increase in the informal sector workers during the 1980s and the 1990s. Barbosa Filho (2005) estimated that by using the number of workers that do not have a signed work card (called *carteira assinada*), the rate of informal workers corresponded to 28 per cent of total workers in 1980. This number increased to 38 per cent at the end of the 1990s. However, if the size of the informal sector is measured by using the rate of workers that do not contribute to the social security system, the rate was 52.8 per cent in 1985 and increased to 62 per cent in 1999. This large size of the informal sector has restricted the coverage of social insurance (social security) as only 1 in 2 dependent workers and 1 in 10 independent workers contribute to the system (Barrientos 2002).

Pension Coverage

Social security coverage in Brazil extended through RGPS, RPPS and RPC. Further, rural pension has been an important initiative to expand coverage in the rural and informal sectors. Maciel (2010) mentioned that 48.4 per cent Brazilian workers belong to the RGPS (general social security regime), 7.3 per cent contributors belong to RPPS (for civil public servants and the military regime), 8.8 per cent are special beneficiaries (specific categories) and 34.1 per cent of the workers are unprotected by the system (informal economy) where 15.7 per cent (most women) receives less than a MW and 17.8 per cent more than MW. Pension and private pension funds in Brazil have been able to increase coverage gradually and in 2003; close private pension funds covered 1.7 million workers. By October, the private pension funds covered 2.5 million active members and 0.8 million retirees totalling 3.3 million (Predtechensky 2010).

Contribution

Contribution to public system made by individual employees and employers. Individual contributions depend on their earning. The employers contribute 20 per cent of covered earnings. As of 2007, insured individuals contributed 8 per cent of earnings if their monthly earnings were up to 868.29 reais, 9 per cent if the earnings were between 868.3 reais and 1,447.14 reais or 11 per cent if earnings were between 1,447.15 reais and 2,894.28 reais. The government covers administrative costs and any deficit. Under complementary pension system there are no general legal rules regarding the contribution levels. For the DC plans, the contribution rate is around 4–6 per cent of the payroll, while for the DB plans it varies between plans (http://pension3.com/br/).

Pension Benefits

Pension benefits of general regime are based on age, length of contribution nature of work and so on. Members are also entitled for old-age assistance, sick pay, accident insurance and maternity pay and so on.

❖ RETIREMENT PENSION DUE TO AGE

Those who are at a minimum age of 60 years (women) and 65 years (men) are eligible for age pension. However, rural workers can retire five years earlier. Minimum length of contribution is 15 years.

❖ RETIREMENT PENSION DUE TO LENGTH OF CONTRIBUTION

Those insured, who have a minimum length of contribution of 35 years for men and 30 years for women (rural workers and teachers can retire five years earlier). Minimum age is 53 years (men) and 48 years (women).

❖ SPECIAL RETIREMENT

Those insured, who exercise activities subject to special conditions that are harmful to their health or physical integrity are eligible for special retirement. According to the risk, length of contribution varies from 15 years to 25 years. Insured workers also receive survival pension and disability retirement benefits.

❖ SOCIAL ASSISTANCE PROGRAMME

Under this scheme one MW is given to over 65-year-old elders whose income is less than 1/2 MW (formal or informal sector) or to families with a physically disabled member whose income is less than 1/2 MW. Most of the closed pension funds are DB and

> *rights usually accrue at a steady rate of between 1.5 per cent and 2 per cent per year of service, with a total benefit target (including social security benefits) of 45 per cent to 70 per cent of final salary after a maximum period of between 30 and 35 years. (International Organisation of Pension Supervisors [IOPS] 2011)*

Pension benefits under DC plans depend on the funds accumulated and investment return. Benefits can be paid as lump sum or through annuity.

Investment Rules and Regulations

The investment regulations for pension funds are issued by the National Monetary Council (Conselho Monetário Nacional [CMN]). The investment regulations laid down a quantitative limit across and within asset classes taking into consideration credit risk of financial instruments and governance. According to CMN Resolution 3792, maximum invest limit to various financial instruments in 2010 was as follows: up to 100 per cent in fixed-income securities, up to 70 per cent in variable income, up to 20 per cent in structured investment, up to 10 per cent in offshore investment, up to 8 per cent in real estate and up to 15 per cent for operations with members (loan). However, actual investment in fixed income, variable income, real estate, loans and others in 2009 was 59 per cent, 33 per cent, 3 per cent, 2 per cent and 2 per cent respectively (Predtechensky 2010). This trend in equity investment is to a great extent similar to many countries in Latin America which have adopted fully privatised systems.

Supervision and Administration

National Institute of Social Security (Instituto Nacional do Seguro Social [INSS]) is responsible for the activities of administration relating to collection and processing of tax revenue and benefits payments including public assistance (pension and retirement benefits) for RGPS and state-run employees. The INSS reports to the ministry of social security. Closed pension funds in Brazil are supervised by the state secretariat of pension funds (Secretaria de Previdência Complementar [SPC]), a public body which issues licenses and supervises compliances.

However, the regulatory decisions are made by the National Board of Complementary Pension (Conselho de Gestão da Previdência Complementar [CGPC]) attached to the ministry of social security. The OPFs are supervised by Superintendence of Private Insurance (Superintendência de Seguros Privados [SUSEP]) linked to the ministry of finance. The National Board of Private insurance (Conselho Nacional de Seguros Privados [CNSP]) is attached to the Ministry of Finance.

PENSION REFORMS IN HUNGARY

Hungary is the first country in Central and Eastern Europe (CEE) which reformed its pension system to introduce funded contributory pension managed by private fund manager. Hungary is also the first country in this region to nationalise the private pension system. In 1993, Hungary introduced voluntary and funded pension and a mandatory privately managed second pillar was introduced in 1998. However, Hungary reversed the reform of 1998, and the Hungarian Parliament approved a legislation in December 2010 to roll back the pension reform. The new legislation effectively eliminates a pillar for Hungary's three-pillar pension system. The legislation gives members of mandatory private pension funds until 31 January 2011 to opt out of a transfer of their pension savings to the state pillar. Members who decide to stay in the funds will lose all future contributions to the state pension system by their employers (http://www.realdeal.hu/20101214/parliament-approves-nationalisation-of-mandatory-private-pension-funds).

Demographic Trend

Population projection in East European countries indicate an overall decline during 2009 through 2050 and Hungary will witness a sharp decline in population. Total population of Hungary will decline from 10.1 million in 2009 to 8.9 million in 2050 due to low fertility rate (1.3) and low rate of natural increase (–0.4 per cent). However there will be a sharp increase in elderly population in Hungary during this period. Population over 60 years will go up from 22.4 per cent in 2010 to 33.0 per cent in 2050, while population over 80 years will go up from 3.8 per cent to 6.9 per cent during the same period. In 2009, life expectancy at birth was 69.2 years for men and 77.4 years for women. GDP per capita in Hungary was US$17,887 in 2009, which compared well with other emerging economies.

Pension Reform

Hungary was the first country among the former communist block and Eastern Europe which reformed the pension system and introduced mandatory pension fund in 1997 which was implemented since 1 July 1998. However, the funded pension fund is not new in Hungary. 'The Hungarian statutory pension system was established in 1929. This scheme was fully funded, benefit defined, as opposed to the subsequent PAYG system' (Zoltán and Kopint-Datorg 2005). During the Second World War the Hungarian funded pension system collapsed and the then socialist government introduced a unified unfunded (PAYG) system in 1949, for the salary and wage earners. Subsequently, several systemic and parametric changes were brought into the state-controlled pension system in Hungary. In 1992, an independent Pension Insurance Fund (PIF) was established with separate budget and responsible to Parliament. A similar Health Insurance Fund (HIF) was also created to finance health-care institutions, distribute benefits and so on.

Pre-reformed (1998) pension system in Hungary had several shortcomings and strength, which have been summed up by Simonovits (2002):

> *The pre-reform Hungarian pension system has relatively favored the poorest pensioners but sacrificed the social insurance principle at the altar of the solidarity. Like in other (but not all) public pension systems, Hungarian citizens saw less and less incentives to properly contribute to its financing, meanwhile they have expanding possibilities to avoid paying contributions.*

The old system gradually became fiscally unsustainable due to wage indexation. There is also huge evasion of pay roll tax, calling for radical reform of the old system.

New System Introduced in 1998

The move towards establishing private pension funds in Hungary was initiated in 1993 when the supplementary funded pension funds were introduced on a voluntary basis. Subsequently, the whole public pension system was reformed in July 1998 and the mandatory second pillar was introduced to move towards the three-pillar system. The three-pillar pension was a mixed public and private pension system and membership to the mandatory private pension system was made compulsory for new entrants to the labour force. According to Borbély (2001), 'the core of the system is insurance based, which means that coverage for pension, unemployment and health insurance is provided for persons engaged in an economically gainful activity, and who pays contribution'. The new pension system is an employer–employee financed pension insurance. Hungary also introduced the means-tested social assistance programme. The new system consisted of the three pillars given in the following paragraphs.

❖ FIRST PILLAR

The first pillar is a uniform publicly managed PAYG contributory DB mandatory social security pension system, created by reforming the pre-reform PAYG system. Social security pension under this pillar is available at the retirement age of 62 years (for both men and women) after 20 years of contribution.

❖ SECOND PILLAR

The second pillar is a mandatory fully funded DC private pension fund. Participation is compulsory for all the new entrants to the labour force (employed and self-employed) hired after 1 January 1998. Members contribute to their individual accounts and the retirement pension depends on the individual savings and investment income earned by the fund managers. On retirement, savings are converted into life annuity. After paying for 15 years, the member is eligible for annuity. The fund guarantees a minimum pension of 25 per cent of first-pillar pension. The second pillar of Hungarian pension system is managed by private pension trusts, financed by contribution of 8 per cent wages of employees.

❖ THIRD PILLAR

The third pillar is a voluntary tax-favoured private pension fund, which became effective after the adoption of Mutual Pension Insurance Act of 1993. These are privately established non-profit legal entities. Memberships are voluntary. There is no maximum limit of contribution but tax deduction is allowed up to 30 per cent of the contribution. Voluntary pension funds are controlled and supervised by a state agency.

Means-tested Old-age Benefits

The Hungarian government provides means-tested social benefits as old-age assistance. This pillar is financed by local and central budget.

Transition and Switching Arrangements

When the mandatory system was introduced in January 1998, members of the previous system who were older than 43 years on that day were given an option to switch over to the new mandatory system or to remain with the old PAYG system. Workers were allowed the freedom to remain with the first pillar or switch over to the second pillar within two years from August 1999. Those who did not join the new two-pillar system remained with the earlier PAYG scheme, which, however, is similar to the first pillar of the new system with certain exception in respect of contributions and benefits. But the new entrants had to mandatorily opt for the second pillar.

Coverage

A resounding 94 per cent of members voluntarily chose the mixed pension system, while for the remaining 6 per cent of new entrants to the labour force entry was mandatory. About 40 per cent of the EAP chose the reformed (mixed) system. The majority (75 per cent) of fund members consists of people from the 20–40 age group (Golinowska and Kurowski 2010). Since the introduction of the new system in 1998, membership of private pension funds has gone up significantly and in 2007 about 62 per cent of the labour force were members of the two-pillar scheme.

Contribution

The contribution rate to the mixed pension system (May 2008) was 33.5 per cent of taxable salary of employees. Out of this, 24 per cent was paid by the employers and 9.5 per cent was to be paid by the employees. The entire 24 per cent contribution of employers goes to the state pension scheme. Out of 9.5 per cent contribution of employees, 8 per cent goes to their individual account and 1.5 per cent goes to state scheme (Guardiancich 2010a).

Pension Benefits

The first pillar provides earnings-related old-age disability and survivors' benefits, which are financed mainly from separate pension contributions. There are several other benefits in addition to old-age pension which includes social allowances like pension allowance, family and child care allowance, unemployed allowance, sick pay and so on. Under the revised system the retirement age for men and women was increased to 60 years. The number of years of contribution for pension entitlement was 40 years. Under the private individual account benefits are paid as annuities. A member is entitled for full pension at the retirement age of 62 years.

MPGs

In Hungary, there is MPG for the first- and second-pillar arrangements. Under the first pillar the minimum pension amount is determined by the number of years of service and the MW. The second-pillar minimum guarantee is at least 25 per cent of the first-pillar pension for those who pay contribution for 15 years. This guarantee is provided out of the central guarantee fund (CGF). 'The Guaranteed Fund is pre funded, pension funds pay 0.3–0.5 per cent of the fund members contribution. The commitments of the Guarantee Fund are backed up by the Government' (INPRS 2001).

Minimum Return Guarantee

In Hungary, there is a minimum return guarantee under the second pillar. Private pension funds are required to build a reserve fund against yield fluctuation to protect individual savings. When investment return is higher than benchmark return, a part of the excess return is transferred to this reserve fund and when it is lower than bench mark return, funds are transferred from reserve fund. The benchmark is the market index of government bonds with maturity of more than one year.

Minimum GF

GF is a central financial institution and legal entity. It is a pre-funded entity through contribution of pension funds, which pays 0.3–0.5 per cent of contribution of members of pension funds. Two main objectives of this fund are to provide claim amount of a member in case of switching from one fund to other. If the former fails to pay the claim amount the GF transfers the missing amount and claims from the new fund. Second, the GF also provides minimum pension to those who have spent 15 years in the system.

Funds Management

In Hungary the private pension funds are non-profit organisations, primarily set up by the financial institutions, such as banks and insurance companies. Before conducting any business they must undergo a two-stage licensing process. By mid-1990s there were 19 mandatory pension funds which insured three million members (70 per cent of economically active and collected HUF 1,766 billion. In the voluntary pension market 250 funds were issued licenses but only about one-third was active and collected HUF of 749 billion assets (Guardiancich 2010a). Investment regulations provide the limits of investment in various instruments. In Hungary, there is no limit to investment equities of listed companies by the pension funds, but is restricted to 10 per cent in non-listed companies. Investment in real estate by mandatory pension fund is restricted to 5 per cent while the same for voluntary pension fund is restricted to 10 per cent. There is no limit to investment in government bonds but it is restricted to 10 per cent in corporate and municipal bonds. There is also no limit to investment in retail investment funds, while up to 5 per cent investment in derivative fund is allowed. There is also no limit to invest in bank deposit if it is listed. Investment of up to 20 per cent in foreign assets is allowed (OECD 2010).

Regulation and Supervision of Pension Funds

The regulatory responsibilities of Hungarian pension funds are entrusted to the Ministry of Finance. The Central Administration of National Pension Insurance (CANPI) manages the Hungarian public pension. The Ministry of Social Affairs and Labour is responsible for legislation. The Hungarian Financial Services Authority (HFSA) is the regulatory and supervisory authority for funded pension system.

Impact of Reforms

While analysing the reforms and fund governance in Hungary, Róbert I. Gál (2001) commented:

> *The characteristics form of pension fund is a given society is linked to the mandate if it is loaded on employees or employees. If the mandate of pre-funding for old age is imposed on employers, closed funds will be more frequent. If it is employee who is mandated the typical pension, fund will not restrict on membership.*

It was also observed by Gál that in Hungary occupational funds cover a large share of the voluntary funds whereas open funds are almost exclusive in the mandatory sector (Gál 2001).

Why Was Funded Pillar Abolished?

A note of the Ministry for National Economy, Hungary, 'The Reform of the Hungarian Pension System (A Reformed Reform)', dated 30 November 2010, gives an indication of the scope and objectives of the new reform. The note has referred to some problems of Hungarian pension system which includes: (*a*) The first key problem is that due to the modifications of the Hungarian pension system the financing of the state pension pillar has become questionable. In the 2011 budget revenues (contributions) of the first pillar of only HUF 2,100 billion stand against the benefit payment obligations of over HUF 3,000 billion. (*b*) The second, a structural problem of the Hungarian pension system, is that there are both solidarity and social care–type obligations in the state pension pillar. Solidarity items are related to old-age pension liabilities and social items to disability allowance and early retirement benefits. (*c*) The third problem of the Hungarian pension system is that it gives insufficient incentives for voluntary pension savings, resulting in suboptimal accumulation of long-term savings in the voluntary private pension funds. (*d*) The last but most pressing problem of the Hungarian pension system is that there is a shortage of one million legally employed workers paying contributions in the short and medium term, and one million children who could make the system sustainable in the long run.

Apart from the inherent structural problems mentioned above there were other problems linked to the three-pillar system such as the transition from a PAYG system to a multi-pillar system had serious financial implications. The pension system reforms' macro-financial impact will deteriorate the Hungarian budget situation until the 2040s.

Another negative feature of the multi-pillar system is that it provides solution only to the segment of the population that is entitled to old-age pension benefits, moreover, exclusively to those who have been able to accumulate sufficient savings during their active years. It is again the state budget that has to cover the old-age pensions of those with insufficient or no savings at all.

Yet another disadvantage of the multi-pillar system is that the guarantee and prudent management of the portfolio by private funds represent significant risks—as the ever-spreading financial crisis since 2008 well demonstrates. Even by appropriate regulation, the reduction of such risks requires additional resources and their elimination is impossible. The operation of private pension funds is also costly, especially in Hungary as experience shows.

There is also an indication of the reformed two-pillar pension system in Hungary that was brought in after the abolition of the previous multi-pillar system. The first pillar will be managed and monitored by the state and financed from the central budget. The second main pillar will be a system, supported by the state and managed by the private sector alongside the guidelines set by the state to promote the interest of members, which will enable the accumulation of voluntary pension savings. This new pillar will keep the advantages eliminate the disadvantages of the current compulsory private pillar (http://www.liaa.gov.lv/uploaded_files/EKSPORTETAJIEM per cent20sadala/Ungarija/The per cent20reform per cent20of per cent20the per cent20Hungarian per cent20pension per cent20system.pdf).

PENSION REFORMS IN POLAND

Poland was the next to introduce pension reforms and the first to introduce the NDC model in Eastern Europe. Pre-reform state-managed PAYG DB system was reformed and replaced by NDC system which constituted a part of the first pillar of multi-pillar pension system advocated by the World Bank. To some extent Poland followed the Chilean reform to introduce funded pension but did not totally scrap the PAYG system; instead of that the benefits of first pillar was linked to NDC system as in case of Sweden.

Demographic Trend

Population projection in East European countries indicates an overall decline during 2009–50 and Poland is not an exception to this trend, though this decline is not as sharp as in the case of Poland as is with the other countries discussed by us in this study. Total population of Poland will decline from 38.2 million in 2009 to 31.4 million in 2050 due to low fertility rate and low rate of natural increase. However, there will be a sharp increase in elderly population in Poland during this period. Population over 60 years will be nearly double as this percentage will go up from 19.4 per cent in 2010 to 38.0 per cent in 2050 while population over 80 years will go up from 3.4 per cent to 8.5 per cent during the same period. In 2009, life expectancy at birth was 71.3 years for men and 97.8 years for women. GDP per capita in Poland was US$13,847 in 2009, which was much below Hungary's.

New System

Pre-reform pension system in Poland was PAYG DB pension. Sharp rise in elderly population, deterioration in dependency ratio, declining contribution, growing pressure on exchequer, and so on, forced the government to undertake pension reforms in Poland. Gomulka and Styczen (1999) have mentioned about some pre-reform key problems including 'low effective retirement ages, excessive liberal disability criteria, high replacement ratio large redistributive components in pension formula and excessive privileges for some categories of workers'.

The reform called security through diversity implemented in January 1999, followed by two important laws relating to pension reforms. The social security system law was signed by the Polish president in November 1998 and the social security pension funds system law was signed by the Polish president in December 1998 (FIAP 2002). The new system is a multi-pillar pension system called 'security through diversity', which replaced the old PAYG DB system by NDC system, introduced an individual account–based funded second pillar and also a third-pillar private or occupational pension.

Multi-Pillar Polish Pension System

The multi-pillar Polish pension system consists of mandatory first pillar, universal second pillar and voluntary third pillar. The first and second pillars have been designed as basic social security, while the voluntary third pillar as a supplementary pension benefits. The new system has entirely replaced the previous system and is focused on annuitisation, minimum pension, and so on, through pillar system.

❖ FIRST PILLAR

It is the reformed social insurance institute. Currently, the first pillar is based on the concept of NDC to the Social Insurance Fund (Fundusz Ubezpieczeń Społecznych [FUS]). This is a public PAYG mandatory pillar for all employees and the only one available to people over 50 years of age. Under this pillar members receive DB pensions. The contributions are allocated to individual accounts, managed by a central agency called Social Insurance Institute (Zakład Ubezpieczeń Społecznych [ZUS]). The capital value of deposits is adjusted by the factors-based consumer price index (CPI). The first pillar is a safety net and redistributive mechanism. Another important feature of the new first pillar, which is an NDC system, is the demographic reserve fund or buffer fund to stabilise contribution rate in the system in the face of demographic fluctuation. The 'buffer fund' will consist of any surplus in the first pillar, privatisation revenues and, temporarily, one percentage point of total contributions. Interest, and any extra revenues of ZUS, will be added to the fund (Gora and Rutkowski 1998).

❖ SECOND PILLAR

It is one of the two components of public pension but managed by private fund managers. The second pillar is a fully funded mandatory DC pension system, which is parallel to individual account–based Chilean type mandatory pension system, introduced in Poland in 1999. Any person covered by the national social security system and born after 31 December 1968 is required to join a mandatory personal pension plan, that is, an open pension. People born between 1 January 1949 and 31 December 1968 were given an option to choose whether or not to join the new mandatory system introduced in 1999. Both employees and self-employed persons are covered by the second-pillar pension or OPFs which are managed by dedicated pension fund management companies called General Pension Societies (Powszechne Towarzystwa Emerytalne [PTE]) formed as joint stock companies. OPFs are fully funded pension funds run through contribution of employees. Members have the option to select an OPF, which acts as a mutual fund. Functioning of OPF is monitored by the Superintendency of Pension Funds (UNFE). OPF is expected to provide additional pension benefits to people after retirement. Accumulated capital at the time of retirement is used to purchase life annuity policy.

❖ THIRD PILLAR

The third pillar is voluntary personal pension investment opportunity in order to augment personal pension on a voluntary basis. The third pillar is also called employees' pension programme, which constitutes employee pension funds (Pracowniczy Fundusz Emerytalny [PFE]), employee pension programmes (Pracowniczy Program Emerytalny [PPE]) and personal pension accounts (Indywidualne Konto Emerytalne [IKE]).

Though the third pillar is a DC system and operates like the second pillar, investment regulations are more flexible here and it does not offer any guarantee for return. In the third pillar, contributions will be paid into life policies, pension and investment funds.

Social Assistance Programme

There is a provision for non-contributory social assistance to those whose income falls below certain threshold limit. This programme has been designed for poverty alleviation in Poland.

Transition

Reform in 1999 closed the old PAYG DB system for the workers who were born after 1948 and those who were born after 1968 were covered by both the first and second pillars. For the new entrants, membership to both the pillars was mandatory. Those who contributed to the old system retained the accumulated funds under the new system.

Contribution

Under the new system, the contribution for the first and second pillars is registered in individual account. In the new social security system, out of total contribution of 19.52 per cent, of taxable salary of workers, the amount being paid by the employer and the employee is 50 per cent each. Of the total contribution of 19.5 per cent, an amount of 12.22 per cent goes into the public NDC plan, of which 9.76 per cent is paid by employers and 2.46 per cent by workers. The remaining 7.3 per cent is credited to a private individual account, which is paid entirely by the employee (Guardiancich 2010b). Poland has introduced a centralised collection system, and the collections are taken by ZUS.

Pension Benefits

Under the new system there are several retirement benefits including pension, disability benefits, illness support and accident benefits and so on. In the new system there is old-age pension under the first pillar as well as under the mandatory individual account.

The ZUS covers old-age pensions, disability and survivors' pensions, sickness and work accidents. These are financed through the four sub-funds of the social insurance fund (FUS). The first-pillar pension depends on the value of contribution paid divided by the average life expectancy at the time of retirement. Pension under the second-pillar mandatory individual account depends on the funds accumulated in an individual account. This amount is used to purchase an annuity policy. There is also provision of means-tested guaranteed minimum pension, which is paid when the total pension amount of the first- and second-pillar pensions (old-age pension and the individual annuity) is less than the legal minimum old-age pension.

Coverage

Reformed pension system attempted to cover Polish citizens under the pension and social security net through first-pillar NDC system, second-pillar individual account and the third-pillar voluntary pension. Mandatory coverage was necessary for all economically active persons and voluntary coverage for others.

Funds Management and Investment Regulations

❖ FUNDS MANAGEMENT

In Poland mandatory private pension funds are OPFs which are managed by pension societies and conduct the activities in the form of a joint stock company. In May 2010 there were 14 OPFs (Otwarty Fundusz Emerytalny [OFE]). Accumulated asset size of OPFs from 1999 to May 2010 was worth PLN 152.7 billion (Guardiancich 2010b). Since 2004, each pension entity is allowed to set up a second OPF with a different type of investment strategy and risk level. One fund must be invested with higher proportion of equities, whereas the other fund must be invested mainly in fixed-income instruments (Tapia 2008).

Under the third pillar, voluntary private pension system is made up of occupational pension plans (PPE) and individual pension plans (IKE). Occupational pension plans are established and managed by life insurance companies, investment funds and foreign management companies. There may be more than one PPE. Individual pension plans are offered and administered by investment funds, insurance companies and broking companies. Switching from a PPE to an OPF is not allowed, but it is possible to move to an IKE. The PPE investment regime is similar to that of the OPF's and default products are provided by PPEs.

❖ INVESTMENT REGULATION

An upper limit has been fixed for investment in different financial instruments and a cap on foreign investment. OPF funds can invest a maximum of 40 per cent in listed equity in the primary market and 7.5 per cent in the secondary market or non-listed equity, no limit of investment in treasury bonds but up to 40 per cent in mortgage, 40 per cent in municipal bonds and up to 40 per cent in corporate bonds. OPF funds can also invest in retail investment funds. A loan equal to investment in the shares of the borrower is permitted, but no investment is permitted in private investment funds. Investment in foreign assets is permitted up to 5 per cent by OPF.

Minimum Rate of Return Guarantee

Poland has introduced minimum rate of return for the pension funds. The law of OPFs provides that in case the funds return rate for a period of 24 months is lower than the minimum, the OPF is obliged to cover the deficit within three days (Borowczyk 2002). The minimum rate of return is considered against the benchmark return, which is arrived at by calculating the average rate of return of all funds over 24 months of consecutive operation of funds. Minimum rate of return is thus the rate lower than the 50 per cent value of the weighted average rate of return and the weighted average rate of return minus four percentage points, whichever is lower. All the entities involved in management of pension system are involved executing the minimum return guarantee.

The mechanism of guarantee consists of reserve fund, share capital, GF and state treasury. If a fund fails to generate return less than minimum rate of return then the management company is to make good of the deficit in the account. When the pension funds and pension society fail to cover the deficit through their reserve account and share capital, pension GF comes into picture and covers the deficit. Pension GF is created by compulsory payments of all universal pension societies. However, if all the above security measures fail the state treasury guarantees the coverage of the OPFs deficits, which supplements it to a level of minimum rate of return (Borowczyk 2002).

Administration and Supervision

While the Polish pension system for employees is under the responsibility of the Ministry of Labour and Social Policy for employees, and the ministries of defence and of internal affairs for soldiers and policemen. Farmers in Poland are covered by the Agricultural Social Insurance Fund (Kasa Rolniczego Ubezpieczenia Społecznego [KRUS]) and the Ministry of Agriculture and Rural Development is entrusted with the responsibility of pension for farmers. The ZUS administers pensions for workers, collects contributions for the first pillar and distributes the same among first-tier NDC system and OPF, supervises the management of the demographic reserve funds, manages the payouts of the first-pillar pension, maintains the central database for the second pillar and so on. The OPFs are managed by PTE and asset management and investment in OPFs is supervised by the Polish Financial Supervision Authority (Komisja Nadzoru Finansowego [KNF]).

SOCIAL SECURITY AND PENSION REFORMS IN SWEDEN

Most of the OECD and developed countries have introduced parametric reforms, and in most Latin American and CEE countries the pension reform is based on the World Bank concept of third pillar. Beyond these two basic reform models a significant development is the concept called NDC, introduced for the first time in Sweden and in many countries including Poland, Italy, Latvia and so on. The NDC system is sometimes called the DB in DC, as it contains several features of DB and DC systems and attempts to solve several problems that arise out of demographic changes and weakness of capital market. NDC is thus a new dimension in the social security reform arena and is gradually becoming more popular among countries going for pension reform.

Demographic Trend

Population projection in European countries indicates an overall decline during 2009–50. However, the Swedish population will increase from 9 million in 2009 to 10.4 million in 2050. However, there will be a sharp increase in elderly population in Sweden during this period. Population over 60 years will go up from 23.3 per cent in 2010 to 30.2 per cent of total population in 2050. Similarly, population over 80 years of age will increase from 5.3 per cent to 9.2 per cent during this period, which will exert serious pressure on the social security system in Sweden. Life expectancy of men and women in 2009 was 78.7 years and 83 years respectively. This growing pressure of ageing and demographic challenges forced Sweden to introduce radical reform in its DB pension system in 1998.

Pension System before the 1998 Reform

Prior to the introduction of the NDC system, Sweden had the allmän tilläggspension (ATP) which was introduced in 1960. The ATP system was a combination of flat rate basic pension and an earnings-related contribution-based defined-benefit, PAYG, price-indexed adjusted system, where the benefit was determined as a percentage of the average of a person's 15 highest paid years. Thirty years of contributions were enough for a full pension. There was a floor and a ceiling on benefits, but not on contributions (Kruse 2010). Due to demographic changes and liberal benefits the ATP system created severe fiscal pressure forcing Sweden to opt for radical pension reform.

New Pension System

The new pension system introduced in 1998 is a multi-pillar system which replaced the previous income related DB PAYG System. The new reform consists of two types of DC systems, which was complemented by a guaranteed pension. The important guiding principles of pension reform were:

> *One to one relationship between contributions paid to the system by or for an individual, and the pension credit of that individual, the financing of the pension payments should be guaranteed by a fixed contribution rate, the average pension in relation to the average income in the new system should be the same as in the old system and there should be a guaranteed minimum pension. (Settergren 2003)*

The new pension system is a three-pillar system. The first pillar contains three tiers, namely the zero tier—the universal guarantee pension (*garantipension*); first tier—the earnings-related pension (ATP); the notional DC pension (*inkomstpension*) and the second tier is the fully funded premium pension (*premiereservsystem*). The second pillar is a supplementary and quasi-mandatory funded pension and the third pillar, a voluntary private pillar, is the accumulation for old age to pension funds or insurance companies (Natali 2004).

❖ FIRST PILLAR

State-administered mandatory pension scheme—a combination of three tiers. The zero tier is a universal, tax financed, flat rate price index–linked guaranteed pension meant for the people with little or no income. Residents of Sweden are eligible for guaranteed pension at age 65. To receive a full guaranteed pension, an individual must in principle have resided in Sweden for 40 years after age 25. A resident in another EU/EES country is also credited towards a guaranteed pension (Settergren 2005). Means-testing applies for income earned through the income pension, premium pension, supplementary pension (*tilläggspension*), widow's pension (*änkepension*), but not through income form capital, occupational pensions (*tjänstepension*) or private pension insurance. In 2009, the full guarantee pension amounted to SEK 6,777 per month for a married person and SEK 7,597 for a single one (Guardiancich 2010c).

The first tier of the first pillar is the inkomstpension, the NDC system which is a PAYG system. This tier is financed through the contribution paid by the employers and employees. Out of total contribution of 18.5 per cent to the mandatory public system, 16 per cent goes to this inkomstpension account. The NDC system was introduced in 1998 for the cohorts born after 1954. (However, a mixed system applies for those born between 1938 and 1953.)

The NDC system works through a notional account and annuity divisor, buffer fund. A notional account is created for each contributor and 16 per cent of annual pensionable income is credited yearly to the notional account. The corresponding amount is transferred in monthly instalments to the system buffer fund, which finances pension payments. The interest earned on the notional account is either the increase in nominal average (pensionable) income as measured by an income index or an approximation of the internal rate of return in the system, as measured by the balance index. At the time of retirement, pension is calculated by dividing the notional account balance by a so-called annuity divisor, which reflects the life expectancy at the time of retirement. Further, final annuity divisors are determined for every age group over age 64 for all individuals in the same birth cohort, the year the cohort reaches the age of 65 (Settergren 2003). Pension savings thus built up cannot be withdrawn before the minimum pensionable age of 61 (inkomstpension and premium pension).

The second tier of the first pillar is the premium pension. Premium pension is a fully funded scheme and is a part of Swedish public pension, introduced in 1998. Out of a total contribution of 18.5 per cent, an amount of 2.5 per cent goes in premium pension account. An individual member can select maximum 5 funds out of more than 800 funds to invest their money in and may also switch unrestricted number of times. In case an investor does not select any fund, money is invested in a default fund called Seventh AP Fund managed by a government agency. As of 2008, 785 investment funds were registered with Premiepensionsmyndigheten (PPM). At the end of 2008, 57 per cent of contributors had selected a fund (PPM 2009). On retirement an investors in premium pension fund can opt either for fixed interest annuity or for variable annuity. Premium pension contributions are collected by the national tax board and managed by the premium pension authority (PPM). However, the Swedish government has introduced changes in premium pension and its regulatory structure. 'On May 1, Sweden's AP7, which manages assets of the mandatory individual premium pension accounts, replaced its premium choice and default funds with low-cost equity and fixed-income funds' (SSA online, 2010–11).

The NDC system aims at attaining financial stability in providing pension through a stabilising mechanism supported by buffer fund, annuity divisor, imputed interest rate mechanism and so on. As indicated in the *Swedish Pension System Annual Report* 2005, the primary purpose of the buffer fund is to stabilise pension label and pension contributions in relation to economic and demographic variation. The buffer fund of the national public pension system consists of five different funds: the first to fourth, and sixth national pension fund (NPF). The annuity divisor is a number that reflects remaining life expectancy at retirement, taking into account an imputed interest rate on the pension to be paid. There are three kinds of divisors, for inkomstpension, for premium pension and for economic annuity. Divisor for inkomstpension is used for calculation of individual balance pension and divisor for premium pension is used for calculation of balance capital, while the divisor for economic annuity is used for calculation of pension liability. Under the NDC model, interest rate on the inkomstpension account is determined by the growth in average income which is measured by the income index, while the interest on premium pension account is determined by the changes in the value of the premium pension funds chosen by the insured. NDC system aim at balancing the average pension and average income through indexation of both notional capital and pension based on the average growth of income.

> *The growth in average income will normally deviate from the internal rate of return of the NDC system. Hence, assets may increase faster than liabilities, or vice versa. If and when liabilities should exceed assets, the basis for indexation is automatically switched to an approximation of the system's internal rate of return, thus automatically adjusting pension levels as well. (Settergren 2005)*

The second pillar is a non-public quasi-mandatory occupational pension based on collective agreements. About 90 per cent of employees in Sweden are part of a voluntary occupational pension scheme. There are two main schemes: Svenska Arbetsgivareföreningen–Landsorganisationen (SAF–LO) for blue-collar workers and the Industrins och handelns tilläggspension (ITP) plan for white-collar workers. The SAF-LO plan is a DC plan, while ITP occupational pension consists of two parts—Part I and Part II. The ITP occupational pension plan Part I, introduced in 2007, is DC in nature and covers all employees born in or after 1979. Part II has been in effect for years and covers all employees born before 1979. It is mainly DB in nature and based on final earnings.

There are a large number of individual pension plans under which contribution can be made annually or in a lump sum. Employer contributions are 4.5 per cent for earnings under 7.5 income base amount (IBA), and 30 per cent for earnings over 7.5 IBA. Members are eligible to contribute from the age of 25. On reaching 65, a member with 30 years of service receives benefits as a life annuity, although the option of withdrawing a pension entitlement over a period as short as five years was introduced in 2007. A life annuity benefit may be broken down as is shown in the following paragraphs. The usual retirement age in ITP is 65, although early retirement is possible from the age of 55 (http://pension3.com/se/).

The third pillar is the voluntary, supplementary pension schemes for old age to pension funds or insurance companies. Its growth is favoured by tax incentives.

Contribution

The overall contribution of employer and employee under Swedish public pension is 18.5 per cent. The individual insured pays 7 per cent of her/his earnings, while employers pay 10.21 per cent of that individual's earnings.

> *The total pension contribution is thus 17.21 per cent where as the pension credit and pension contribution is 18.5 per cent of the pension base. The difference is due to the fact that the pension base is reduced by the individual pension contribution of 7 percent when pension credit is calculated. (Settergren 2005)*

Out of 18.5 per cent, 16 per cent are deposited in the four buffer funds of inkomst-pension system and the remaining 2.5 per cent goes to the second individual account to finance the fully funded scheme called PPM.

Benefits

New pension system in Sweden provides old-age retirement and disability pension. Under the first-pillar minimum guaranteed pension, a person is eligible for the pension with minimum three years' residency; full guaranteed pension is available after 40 years' residency. Benefits under NDC are calculated on life expectancy. The actual benefits depend on the amount accrued in the notional account and in the individual, premium funds rate of growth of per capita wages are used to calculate a yield.

On retirement, the notional account is converted into an annuity by using a discounted rate of 1.6 per cent, which is assumed to be the long-term growth rate of the economy, and an expected age of death for the cohort to which the person retiring belongs. Under the guaranteed component of public pension, the state supplements the difference between the guaranteed minimum pension and entitlement of contribution-related pension to all citizens who have lived for 40 years in Sweden. Guaranteed pension in Sweden is linked to the price index.

❖ TAXATION

Employee contribution to the social security is not taxable income, while employer contribution to public social insurance is tax deductible. Contribution to occupational pension by employee is not considered taxable income while contribution by employer is eligible for tax deduction within limit as per law. However, the benefits received from public and private social insurance are taxable.

❖ INVESTMENT REGULATIONS

Sweden has introduced a flexible investment regulation. Investment regulation has set up the maximum limit of investment—up to 60 per cent in equity shares, up to 10 per cent in single company and 5–10 per cent in foreign securities. Further, funds are not allowed to hold more than 5 per cent voting rights in a single company.

Supervision and Regulation

The Ministry of Social Security and Labour is responsible for Swedish public pension and the National Insurance Board (Försäkringskassan) administers the guarantee pension and the income pension. The PPM manages the individual accounts and annuities in the premium pension. Private managers administer the funds. The National Tax Board collects contributions for income-related schemes. The Swedish Financial Accounting Standard Council oversees the standards for the privately managed occupational pension. On 1 January 2010, the Swedish Pension Agency replaced the Swedish Insurance Agency as the state pension administrator, and the premium pension authority, which had been established in 2000 to manage the individual premium pension plan accounts, was abolished. The government expects the new organisational structure to help cut waste and improve customer service (SSA online, 2010–11).

NDC Is Unique in Many Respects

NDC system in Sweden is a combination of non-contributory income-tested guaranteed pension and a fixed contribution–based mandatory PAYG DB and DC pension system. An interesting feature is that it is a DC in a DB framework, as risk is partially borne by the pension provider, which is also outside the capital market fluctuation as in the case of pure DC system, though benefits are fully certain. Benefits are linked to the contribution in such a manner that it does not create payout burden on the fiscal system and provides fiscal stability to the system. Another important feature of the NDC system is automatic balancing 'that uses a complex formula to correct for increases in life expectancy and slow wage growth by lowering initial benefits (for those who have not yet retired) and benefit indexation (for retirees) until the system comes back into balance' (Weaver 2011).

Since the pension amount will depend on real and notional account, it will provide an incentive to work. The system has introduced a flexible retirement age for workers. Finally, the system is partly funded and will provide a boost to national savings. The reforms, in spite of partially privatising the pension system, have taken care of the safety aspect through the centralised publicly managed second individual account, which is invested in real assets. 'The changes are noteworthy and beneficial which provides greater incentives to work, increased national savings, flexible retirement age, lower taxes, less Government spending, fairness and more retirement income (Normann and Mitchell 2000). The guarantee provided to the 'early transition' generation of retirees also lowered the prospects for political opposition. Moreover, increasing the linkage between social insurance pension benefits and contributions allowed politicians to claim that the new system was more 'fair'. This helped to defuse opposition from those who would stand to lose in the new system. All of this meant that politicians were unlikely to incur voter retribution for supporting cuts in pension obligations (Weaver 2011). In fact, the Swedish NDC model has emerged as a trendsetter in pension reforms in many transitional European and Asian countries.

SOCIAL SECURITY AND PENSION REFORMS IN CHINA

Chinese pension reform initiative has attracted global attention due to several reasons—the most populous country of the world, ageing is catching up fast in China and the country is going to emerge as the home of the highest number of elderly population in the world in the near future. China has emerged as one of the fast growing economies in the world, after it dismantled centralised planning and adopted market economy. China is also another country which is experimenting with NDC model as a part of social security and pension reform. It has also introduced special social security for rural areas, which is a unique pension reform model. Chinese experiment could provide certain guidance to Indian policymakers since India is facing similar challenges.

Demographic Trend

Chinese policy to check population growth and introduction of one child policy played a critical role in demographic changes. China's demography has changed from one of 'high birth rate, low death rate, and high growth rate' to that of 'low birth rate, low death rate, and low growth rate', a transformation that took many developed countries nearly a century to complete (Sze 2006). China, in 2009 with a population of 1,351.5 million was the most populous country of the world. Total population of China will increase to 1,437 million in 2050 and will be placed next to India with population of 1,755.2 million. However, the growth of elderly population is expected to be fastest in the world. Consequently, the population over 65 years will go up from 12.3 per cent in 2010 to 31.1 per cent in 2050, while the population of individuals over 80 years will rise from 1.4 per cent to 7.2 per cent during the same period. However, China has been making serious efforts to introduce a unified pension system after the State Council announced in 1997 the decisions to establish a unified basic pension insurance system for enterprise employees, and to establish a unified pension programme for cities/township enterprise employees.

Pre-reformed Pension System

Social security in China was established in the 1950s which was mostly administered by local-level trade unions. When the Communist Party came to power in 1949, it introduced a comprehensive social security system for its citizens, which was administered first by trade unions then by state-owned enterprises (SOEs) which provided social insurance through their own funds. But in 1969 SOEs were made responsible for pension. Chinese pension system started facing the problems of declining worker to retirees' ratio, erosion of pension benefits, reduction in coverage and so on. Also the relaxation eligibility from 20 years to 10 years increased the number of pensioners.

> *The liberalisation of eligibility criteria contributed to a rapid increase in pensioners and led to a sharp decline in the workers to retirees ratio from 30 state and urban collective workers for every pensioner in 1978 to only 13 in 1980. The ratio of workers to pensioners has continued to decline, reaching 7.1 in 1986 and only 5.1 in 1994. (Loraine 1997)*

Further economic reforms in China saw the decline in jobs in SOEs and rapid growth in non-state sectors, having no or little old-age benefits. In 1978, 72 per cent of new job entrants were assigned to the state sector, but by 1990 the proportion had fallen to 60 per cent (Guan 1994). All these factors prompted Chinese leadership to reform its old pension system.

> *In 1993, in its decisions for the establishment of a socialist market economic system in China, the Third Plenary Session of the 14th Central Committee of the Chinese Communist Party pointed out the need to revamp the state enterprise employees pension system, to facilitate the combination of social pooling and individual account. The basic objective of this programme was to change the pension fund system from a pay-as-you-go system, to a mixture of pay-as-you-go and fully-funded system. (Y. Wang 2005)*

Though the basis objective of the reforms is to slowly move away from PAYG to fully funded pension, the Chinese leadership focused on basic social pillar first, to provide a decent living for the retirees. In 1995, the State Council Circular that first introduced the new system set the goal of establishing a unified and socialised pension system by the end of 1999 (Hussain 2001). The government also introduced individual pension account system in 1995. A further initiative was taken to reform pension system and to introduce a unified pension in China in 1997 when the State Council announced the decisions to establish a unified basic pension insurance system for enterprise employees, and decided to establish unified cities/township enterprise employees' pension programme. This document broadly specified the first pillar, which is PAYG DB, and aimed at delivering a pension of 20 per cent of city average pay based on contributions paid over 15 years, and a second pillar which is individual accounts–based. Other important steps were the establishment of rural pension system and National Social Security Fund (NSSF).

A Multi-Pillar Pension System

In order to establish a unified pension system, the State Council Decree, 26 July 1997, introduced a three-pillar retirement system consisting of mandatory public pension and voluntary private pension. Public pension in China comprises the urban pension system and the rural pension system. Urban public pension has two components, namely PAYG DB common pool endowment insurance and fully funded DC individual account. In 2004, China has also introduced voluntary funded DC enterprise annuity (EA). The mandatory public pillar is termed as pillar one, EA as pillar two, and other voluntary savings as pillar three. One important feature of Chinese reform is that the pension reform first started at the provincial level, following the pilot project experiment in Shanghai and Guangzhou. Public pension in China is mandatory and participation is compulsory for employees and self-employed persons in urban areas. It is a mixed system like Swedish public pension, which consists of DB universal basic pension and a mandatory DC fully funded individual account system. The third pillar is a contributory voluntary occupational pension.

❖ PILLAR ONE

Basic pension consists of two mandatory components, namely pillar 1A and pillar 1B. Pillar 1A is a common pool mandatory DB PAYG public pension. This is a PAYG system which provides basic pension to workers on their retirement and is intended to provide replacement rate of 35 per cent of the employees' final salary. The pension amount is determined by prevailing local wages rather than the salary of the workers. Pension is available with minimum contribution for 15 years. This pillar is financed by the employers' contribution—20 per cent of wages and the deficits, if any, will be made up by the government. Pillar 1B is the second component of the first pillar and is an individual account–based mandatory DC public pension which is fully funded. This component of first pillar is financed by the 8 per cent contribution of employee and the payout is determined by accumulated reserve in the individual account. This individual account–based second pillar is similar to NDC system in Sweden. However, unlike Sweden, investors do not have any choice of investment portfolio. Entire assets are invested in government bonds and deposits of banks and managed at the provincial level. Pension is calculated on the basis of balance in the individual account and is payable to a worker on retirement. The individual account is financed by employee within the public pension.

❖ PILLAR TWO

The second pillar of Chinese urban pension system is the voluntary EA, formed as a trust and sponsor by the employer with the approval and registration with the Ministry of Labor and Social Security (MOLSS). Funds are managed by each individual firm or private insurance company. The EAs are funded DC individual accounts. The EA plans are administered by a managing council jointly represented by employer and employee union representatives. The trust can take the form of either an internal or external trustee model. The internal trustee in China is known as pension council, while financial institutions can be selected as an external trustee referred to as a professional trustee (Allianze Global Investors 2007) (http://www.allianzglobalinvestors.com).

Employers fulfilling pillar one contribution requirements may establish an EA subject to the approval of the employee union or representatives. Total of employers' and employees' annual contributions must not exceed one-sixth of the previous year's total payroll. Allocation of employee contributions must be equal to the individual's own contributions. There is a great deal of flexibility in the allocation of employer contributions (Sze 2006). EA funds are managed by licensed financial institutions, and by the end of 2005 licenses were granted to 37 financial institutions including 15 asset management companies to manage EA funds.

❖ PILLAR THREE

The third pillar consists of a voluntary DC programme and is a complementary private savings account meant for people who want to augment higher pension income during the post-retirement period. However, the third-pillar savings are not supported by tax incentives.

Rural Pension

Rural pension, particularly in developing economies, virtually remained out of the purview of pension reform. It is the organised urban employees which became major beneficiaries of any reforms due to their massive organised strength. Even highly populous countries like India and China which have a strong rural base and where the rural economy plays a critical role in overall development, the rural workers receive minimal pension benefits. China has been making serious efforts to promote a pension insurance scheme for rural people. According to Shen and Williamson (2010), 56 per cent of China's total population and 70 per cent of its elderly population live in rural areas. In the year 1986, China began the work of establishing a grass-roots social security system, and in 1991 China introduced pension for rural employees to be financed by 3 per cent of their wages. But it failed to expand coverage in the rural areas and in 2008 only 56 million or 12 per cent of 473 million rural area employees were covered by public pension and the average pension was very low (Oksanen 2010). Necessity for a comprehensive rural pension policy became apparent and the government introduced the new rural social pension plan. In January 1991, the State Council decided to develop old-age social insurance in rural areas under the 'basic plan for old age social insurance in the countryside'. Ministry of Civil Affairs was made responsible for the rural pension scheme.

Shen and Williamson (2010), quoting from various issues of *China News*, provided some insight into the new rural pension scheme of China. Accordingly,

- The new rural pension has two components, namely a basic pension component financed by local and central government and a personal account component based on contributions from enrolled individuals.
- In relatively poor regions the central government will pay approximately 80 per cent of the cost of the basic pension component and the local government will bear the rest. The contribution from local government will be higher for more affluent regions and as high at 90 per cent in some of the most affluent areas.
- It is a voluntary programme and all rural residents aged 16 and above are being given strong incentives to participate. To qualify a resident must be at least 60 (for males) or 55 (for females) and have contributed for at least 15 years.
- The minimum annual contribution for participating workers are required to make generally ranges between 4 per cent and 8 per cent of the county's average personal income during the previous year.
- Residents who contribute for more than 15 years will receive higher pension benefits. For those who are currently 60 years old, the required years of payment will be shortened.
- Those who are already 65 years old can receive the benefit from the basic pension (US$8 a month being the minimum) without having contributed anything to the programme subject to the condition that all of their family members aged 16 and above participate in the pension plan.

This plan also encourages local governments of relatively developed areas to make additional contributions. A major feature of this scheme is that, for the first time in China's long history, the government will make direct contributions to a rural pension scheme. This government involvement will have major implications not only for millions of old people living in rural areas, but also for economic and social development in rural China more generally (Shen and Williamson 2010).

New Health-Care Policy

Along with the introduction of various measures to reform old-age pension system and to expand coverage China has also taken a bold step to improve the health-care system and to bring the entire population under the health-care network. In 2009, China announced a three-year health-care programme to ensure affordable health-care provision for the entire population by 2020. The principal goals are to make health care more equitable by building up health-care service facilities in rural areas and increasing access to health-insurance schemes and by reducing costs through a range of programmes, and to improve quality by increasing training and research, improving the supervision, regulation. By the end of 2011, the government intends to cover 90 per cent of the population by some form of health insurance scheme (Barnett and Chalk 2010).

The Urban Minimum Livelihood Guarantee Scheme

To alleviate poverty, in 1999, the government implemented the urban minimum livelihood guarantee scheme to ensure urban residents, whose total average family income was below the standard for the local area, could obtain assistance with their living costs. The urban minimum livelihood guarantee scheme is a new social relief system, replacing the 'five guarantees' 10 scheme in urban areas. Approximately 20 million people receive payments, which are calculated on the basis of the average family income for a given area and average living costs, and are indexed to inflation. To provide further assistance, supplements for education, housing and health are available to recipients of payments under the urban minimum livelihood guarantee scheme. All funds required for the urban minimum livelihood guarantee scheme come from the budgets of the central, provincial and municipal governments, while policy responsibility for it lies with the Ministry of Civil Affairs. Administrative responsibility for the scheme rests with communities at the street office and community residents' committee levels (Murton 2010).

NSSF

One significant aspect of Chinese pension reform is the establishment of the NSSF in 2000 as a fund of last resort. On 1 August 2000, the Central Committee of Communist Party of China (CPC) and the State Council decided to establish NSSF, and set up the National Council for Social Security Fund (SSF). NSSF aims to serve as a strategic reserve funds accumulated by the central government to support future social security expenditures and other social security needs. The NSSF is managed by the SSF, which reports directly to the state. The SSF was set up to promote a long-term national strategic reserve fund in order to finance future social security expenses in view of the growing social security expenditure due to fast-changing population dynamics and the increased number of elderly population. The SSF consists of five government representatives from the Ministry of Finance and the Ministry of Labour and Social Security to the trade unions. The council also has five regional representatives and five representatives from the central government. The National Council for Social Security fund (NCSSF) is responsible to administer the assets of the NSSF, formulate and implement the investment strategies, selecting the fund managers and custodians for the NSSF assets, monitor their performance and so on.

According to the NCSSF (http://www.ssf.gov.cn/Eng_Introduction/), a government agency on the ministerial level directly under the State Council of the People's Republic of China is responsible for the management and operation of NSSF and has the responsibilities as follows:

1. To operate the fund allocated by the central government, capital and equity assets derived from reduction of state-owned shares and capital raised in other manners.
2. To formulate the operation schemes for investments of SSF and to organise the operation.
3. To select investment managers and custodians of the NSSF, to mandate them with and to monitor the investment operation and custody of the NSSF assets, invest directly in prescriptive markets in accordance with the related laws and regulations.
4. To be responsible for the financial management and accounting of the NSSF, and to prepare periodical financial accounting statements and financial accounting reports.
5. To regularly publish the financial conditions, such as NSSF's assets, proceeds and cash flow to the public.
6. To earmark fund for social security purposes in a way instructed and designated jointly by the Ministry of Finance and Ministry of Labour and Social Security.
7. To perform other duties as assigned by the State Council.

Sources of NSSF Funds

The NSSF has multi-source funding including fiscal allocation of the central government, allocation from the lottery, public welfare fund, capital derived from reduction or transfer of state-owned shares, capital raised in other manners with approval of the state. In 2005, 65 per cent came from the fiscal transfer, 16.2 per cent was the proceeds from the privatisation of SOEs, 10.5 per cent as investment income and 8.3 per cent from lottery proceeds. In 2006, total assets of NSSF were to the tune of RMB 283 billion (Allianze Global Investors 2007). NSSF is one of the largest of such funds in the world. The bulk of the NSSF's assets comes from fiscal transfers (65 per cent in 2005), followed by the proceeds of privatisation (16.2 per cent), investment income (10.5 per cent) and lottery income (8.3 per cent). In 2006, the NSSF's total assets amounted to EUR 27.5 billion (RMB 283 billion). Asset allocation was very conservative in the initial period of operation, but investment in deposits has decreased gradually since then. Meanwhile, the share of outsourced assets has increased steadily, from 24.1 per cent in 2003 to 37.3 per cent in 2006.

The NSSF's investment policy is based on the priorities of asset security and liquidity. As a result, regulations determine that deposits and government bonds combined must amount to at least 50 per cent of assets. At least 10 per cent must be invested in deposits alone. The maximum limit for corporate bonds is 10 per cent, and the combined limit for shares and mutual funds is 40 per cent. In 2003, the NSSF began outsourcing some of its assets. As of 2005, five national and/or joint ventures were selected to manage NSSF assets. In 2006, the NSSF allotted five investment mandates to foreign asset managers to manage international investments of EUR 758 million. In the future, the central government's contribution to 'refill' pillar 1B will be managed by the NSSF. The initial amount is EUR 972.1 million, that is, RMB 10 billion (Fuhrman 2010).

Expansion of Coverage

Reform has enabled China to expand the pension coverage. According to some news in Xinhua News Agency (14 January 2006),

> *China plans to make its pension system coverage expand from the present 174 million to more than 220 million people in 2010, with an annual increase of 10 million, Minister of Labor and Social Security (MLSS) Tian Chengping said in Beijing on Friday. The ministry said that 174 million people have participated in the corporate old-age pension system at present, as compared with 112 million in 1998. (Xinhua News Agency 2006)*

Though significant progress has been made by China to expand coverage, it still remains lower than expected, but though many experts say the progress is very slow, by 2005, 136 millions urban employees had individual accounts—implying a 42.4 per cent coverage rate for urban workers under mandatory occupational pension. Under occupational voluntary pension, 9.6 millions urban employees were covered, implying a 3.0 per cent coverage by 2006 (http://www.oecd.org/dataoecd/53/46/38766497.pdf [January 2011]). A recent study by Heikki Oksanen (2010) on the assessment of Chinese pension reform has provided some insight about the impact of reform on the coverage. Accordingly, 'under the basic pension scheme for urban employees, pension expenditure was 2.5 per cent of GDP and revenue from contributions was 2.7 per cent, as a result reserves have accumulated, amounting to 3.3 per cent of GDP in 2008'.

Oksanen further mentioned in his paper, 'the current system is supposed to cover all 302 million (in 2008) urban employees, but in fact contributions are paid by or on behalf of 55 per cent of them'. Regarding coverage of rural pension, it is stated that of the 473 million rural area employees, in 2008, only 56 million, that is, 12 per cent, were covered by the public pension system. The number of retirees was 5.1 million, who received quite low pensions—in 2005 their monthly average pension was RMB 58 (Birmingham and Cui 2006).

Extending coverage to the rural population is a challenge that is clearly recognised by the Chinese authorities, as demonstrated by the government plan issued in August 2009. According to Jianguo there are 'more than 80 million rural people in more than 2000 counties in 30 provinces. Accumulated funds under the rural social pension insurance have reached nearly 120 billion yuan'. The number of participants under these three plans is about 345 million—about 26 per cent of the total population or just 44 per cent of those employed.

The central government has put forward a proposal that would create universal coverage by 2020. However, workers in both rural areas and urban informal sectors are reluctant to join the system because of the high contribution rate (28 per cent of salary for the urban employee pension plan) and unclear benefits (Lianquan 2011). Salditt et al. (2007) mentioned a few reasons of low coverage including the incentive problem (unattractive return on the individual accounts), low degree of willingness to contribute (limited public trust in the system), administrative procedures (for contributing to and benefiting from the public old-age insurance might turn out to be too difficult to understand) and so on. Heikki Oksanen (2010) also mentioned some reasons for low coverage which include relatively high contribution rate, 'problems in implementation (including fraud) probably because people do not trust the system due to unclear rules and suspicion that the system is not sustainable and that contributions might be used for other expenditures than their declared purpose'.

Contribution

Pension system in China is financed by the members (insured person), enterprises (employees) and the government. As noted earlier, the DB basic pension is financed by the employers and the contribution is 20 per cent of the wages, while the individual account–based mandatory pension is financed by the employee contribution only (8 per cent wages). EA is a voluntary pension and is financed by employers and employees. For basic pension insurance central and local government subsidies are provided to city/county retirement pension pools as needed. In all total contribution of employer and employee comes to 28 per cent plus voluntary contribution.

Benefits

The retirement age in China is generally 60 years for men and 50–55 years for women (*China Daily* 2011). However, a debate is presently on to increase the retirement age as well as to introduce equal retirement for men and women. The basic pension pays 1 per cent of the average of citywide average earnings for each year of coverage subject to minimum of 15 years of service. The pension payment is indexed to a mix of wages and prices. Under the individual account system, the accumulated balance of the fund is converted into stream of pension payments at the time of retirement by dividing it with a government determined annuity factor, which reflects individual retirement age and average local life expectancy (OECD 2009). There is a provision of early pension and minimum pension which is equal to the amount between 40 per cent and 60 per cent of the local average provincial wage during the previous year.

❖ TAX BENEFITS

The EA is subject to exempt tax tax (ETT) tax. Contribution to EA by employer receives 4 per cent of wages but no tax incentives for employees' contribution. But investment income and payout annuity is taxable.

Investment Management and Regulation

Investment regulation and practices are quite different in different types of programmes. We, however, discussed here the investment regulation of EA. Investment regulations for EA funds aim at increased return through portfolio diversification and at the same time providing enough liquidity. As such quantitative restrictions have been imposed on investment. Accordingly, the regulations stipulate (Allianze Global Investors 2007) that at least 20 per cent of assets must be invested in high-quality money market instruments such as deposits, central bank notes and short-term bond repos, a maximum of 50 per cent of assets can be invested in term deposits, contractual deposits, government bonds and corporate bonds but at least 20 per cent should be invested in government bonds, a maximum of 30 per cent assets can be invested in stocks, investment-linked insurance products and equity funds but investment in equities should not exceed 20 per cent. The official guidelines for investment of funds under DC schemes 'specify that 80 percent of accumulated funds are said to be invested in government bonds and 29 per cent in Bank deposits. In practice some funds are said to be diverted into investment in local projects in pursuit of higher yields' (Feldstein 2001).

Administration and Supervision

Pension funds management and surveillance have been combined and the responsibility has been entrusted to the social security agencies at various levels in the hands of administrative regime of China. This is a contrast to the international practice of centralised supervision. However, the supplementary pension system will be based on market process.

China, however, took a pragmatic step in 2000, by establishing the NCSSF, which was assigned the task of

> *managing National Social Security Funds (NSSF), the Pool Assets coming from State Owned Assets sales, Fiscal Appropriation and the Insurance of Lottery Tickets etc. In principle, the NCSSF will not be involved in the direct investment management of Funds of NSSF but will delegate the management to qualified asset managers. (X. Wang 2001)*

China Promoting a New Model of Pension Reform

It seems from the above that China has made commendable attempt in transforming its pension system without sacrificing its basic social goal to protect the workers in their post-retirement period. It has also set its goal to protect rural workers through rural pension insurance. But the most significant is that it has successfully linked pension reforms to the reforms of SOEs. According to Martin Feldstein (2001), 'China is noteworthy for its decision to develop a mixed system of DB and DC social security pensions. In doing so it can provide protection for future retirees while strengthening national savings and expenditure and expanding the market for enterprise securities.'

The new Chinese rural pension scheme, as indicated by the basic feature mentioned above, is a programme of combined participation of central government, local government and local workers. While the government participation through subsidy/contribution will induce individual confidence, it will also encourage voluntary participation. It seems this rural pension programme also indirectly aims at attacking rural poverty and intra- and inter-regional disparity in development. Countries like India which are witnessing rapid urbanisation, industrialisation, large-scale rural migration and rapid changes (decline) in traditional family–based social support to elderly population need to introduce special rural pension programme and China can be a role model. Further, in all such developing countries one can notice significant intra- and inter-regional disparity in development. Affirmative action for less-developed regions are a necessary precondition to remove economic backwardness and rural pension, though the primarily aim of providing old-age social security would not only be an instrument to enhance social welfare but would also contribute to increase rural productivity as such; in the long run the net national cost of subsidy may be marginal.

NDC Model as we have discussed earlier, seems to be more appropriate in emerging countries which do not directly transfer risks to the investors as in case of pure DC schemes adopted in Chile and other countries. Moreover, it reduces pressure on exchequer as the pension benefits finally depend on the contribution. Though slow in implementation it will strengthen the system in the long run. Health care is mostly neglected in developing countries and it is emerging as an equally serious problem along with old-age security in developing countries. By having a separate health insurance programme, China has taken a bold step in the right direction. Finally establishment of NSSF is a unique attempt to protect and strengthen the old-age social security system. There is also evidence that social security has emerged as an integral part of overall economic policy in China, which finally developed a unique model for pension reform appropriate and suitable for developing countries. More or less the same view has been echoed by Salditt et al. (2007):

> *Social security in China is currently in the process of building the largest pension system in the world, and it is doing this at a time of unparalleled economic and demographic transition. The 11th five-year plan (2006–2011) of the government has put the creation of a 'harmonious society' as the ultimate Goal of all its actions and a functioning old age insurance scheme seems essential to reach this goal.*

PENSION SYSTEM IN MAURITIUS

In our country study Mauritius is an exception in many ways—a small country, but well advanced in providing social security to its people through much developed and more comprehensive social security, particularly through non-contributory universal social security measures, highly appreciated throughout the world. Mauritius is also well ahead in introducing the five-pillar pension system. Many of the countries embarking upon pension reforms and concerned about providing social security to its people can learn from Mauritius' experience. However, like other countries, Mauritius will also experience the age quake in terms of faster increase in the number of elderly population, worsening dependency ratio, increased burden on exchequer for providing basic pension to its citizens and initiated pension reforms well in advance to confront any potential crisis.

The Country and Economy

Mauritius is a small country located in the Indian Ocean and is home to 1.3 million people. Since its independence in 1968, Mauritius has made rapid progress in economic development, and is considered to be an upper-middle-income country with an estimated GDP of US$8,590 million in 2009 and GNI per capita at US$7,250. The poverty rate, whether measured as relative poverty, absolute poverty, or with respect to food poverty, is low. The country is ranked high in terms of competitiveness, investment climate and governance. The remarkable performance of the economy is attributed to sound economic governance, accelerated reforms to sustain long-term growth and effective state business relations. These factors together with timely and targeted responses helped Mauritius to weather the negative effects of the global crisis (World Bank 2011). Mauritius has been able to promote a well-developed financial system along with a growing vibrant offshore sector, which contributes significantly to the growth of economy. Mauritius has a well-capitalised banking system and banking assets are about 100 per cent GDP, while contractual savings are more than 40 per cent of GDP, and the assets of NPF only account for 17 per cent of GDP (International Monetary Fund [IMF] 2003).

Mauritius has made significant progress in social security sector which is often not much known, as Willmore (2003) puts it, 'What is less known is that every elderly resident of Mauritius receives income support from a system of non contributory pensions that dates from 1950, subject to a minimum residency test.' Mauritius is more advanced than many advanced countries in respect of pension and social security measures for its people. Mauritius has a relatively well-developed pension system—much better than other countries at this economic development stage (World Bank 2004). Advance pension system in Mauritius has also given a boost to the growth of contractual savings—insurance and pension. According to Vittas (2003), Mauritius belongs to a select group of developing countries where contractual savings—savings with insurance companies and pension funds—exceed 40 per cent of GDP and represent a major potential force in the local financial system. Pension funds account for 75 per cent of contractual savings.

Demographic Trend

According to the World Population Projection (2008), Mauritius is a small country with a population of 1.3 million in 2009 which is estimated to go up to 1.5 million in the mid-2050s. However, Mauritius will experience faster rise in elderly population comparing to average rise in Asia, Africa and the world as a whole. There will be sharp increase in people over age 60 in Mauritius from 11.6 per cent in 2009 to 26.1 per cent in 2050, as against overall rise from 5.4 per cent to 10.6 per cent in Africa, 9.9 per cent to 23.6 per cent in Asia, and 11 per cent to 21 per cent in the world as a whole. Similarly, percentage of population of Mauritius aged 80 years and above will go up from 1.3 per cent in 2010 to 5.9 per cent in 2050 as against overall rise from 0.4 per cent to 1.1 per cent in Africa, 1.1 per cent to 4.4 per cent in Asia, and 1.5. per cent to 4.3 per cent in the world as a whole. Life expectancy at birth is quite high in Mauritius. Combined life expectancy in Mauritius increased from 71.3 in 2000 to 72.1 in 2009. However, it was much higher among female (75.8) than among male (68.5) in 2009. Further, life expectancy at 60 years of age (for both sexes) increased from 18.1 years during 1995–2000 to 18.9 years during 2000–2010. Changes in population dynamics, increased life expectancy of people will increase the old-age dependency ratio from 10.7 in 2010 to 32.7 in 2050 in Mauritius (International Labour Organisation [ILO] 2010). However, the World Bank (2004) projected a little different view and accordingly during 2010–2050, total population of Mauritius expected to increase from 1.3 million to 1.5 million, working age population (15–59 years) expected to decline from 66 per cent to 56.3 per cent of total population, old-age dependency ratio to rise from 17.3 per cent to 45.1 per cent and life expectancy to rise from 16.5 to 19.5 for male and 22.3 to 24.3 for female. To sustain the present pension benefits to its people, which are one of the best in the world, Mauritius needs to initiate proactive pension reforms (which has already been initiated).

Pension System in Mauritius

It seems Mauritius is much ahead of time as it implemented a five-pillar pension system well before the same was advocated by the World Bank. The pension system in Mauritius very much resembles the five-pillar model which the World Bank recommended in the World Bank published report (*Old-Age Income Support in the Twenty-first Century: An International Perspective on Pension Systems and Reform* in 2005). These five pillars are: a non-contributory zero pillar for poverty alleviation, an earnings-related contributory; first pillar an individual accounts–based mandatory; second pillar, a voluntary third pillar and informal intra-family support of various kinds, including health care, as fourth pillar.

The present pension system in Mauritius looks like a five-pillar pension system consisting of a well developed universal basic pension financed by budgetary support, a mandatory earnings–related scheme for private sector employees, a DB plan for civil services and public sector, occupational pension for un organised sector and a voluntary plan and social assistance programme.

Basic Retirement Pension

BRP is a flat rate non-contributory universal pension introduced in 1951, financed by consolidated revenue. BRP is paid to all citizens and non citizens aged 60 years subject to a residency test of having resided in Mauritius for an aggregate period of 12 years since attaining the age of 18. However, the residence qualification does not apply to a Mauritian citizen aged 70 years or above. Non-citizens are also entitled for basic pension if they have resided in Mauritius for at least 15 years in aggregate since attaining the age of 40; 3 of those 15 years should be immediately before the claim is made. There is also a provision for basic widow's pension, basic invalid's pension, basic orphan's pension and inmate's allowance (pocket money). This programme is administered by the Ministry of Social Security and National Solidarity.

NPF

The NPF was created in 1978 through the National Pensions Act 1976. The NPF is a mandatory earnings–related DB pension scheme for the all employees of private sector firms, except those on very low wages and some sugar industry employees. The NPF is a partially funded scheme requiring 9 per cent contribution (6 per cent employer contribution, 3 per cent employees). Workers in large sugar estates contribute 50 per cent more (13.5 per cent with employers paying the additional). Contributions are converted into points which are accumulated on the basis of the declared cost of a point at the time of contribution. It covers over 60 per cent of the labour force. Pension benefits depend on the accumulated points and the value of a point at the time of retirement. Declared aim of NPF is to provide 33.3 per cent replacement after average life time earnings for 40 years. This programme is administered by the Ministry of Social Security and National Solidarity. Members are entitled to retirement pension, contributory widow's pension (CWP), contributory invalid's pension (CIP), contributory orphan's pension (COP) and industrial injury benefits.

National Savings Fund

The National Savings Fund (NSF) was established in 1995 under the National Savings Fund Act. The NSF is a fully funded DC scheme. Participation in NSF is mandatory for all the employees including civil services and statutory bodies. There are minimum and maximum monthly earnings for contribution purposes. The NSF is not open to non-citizens of Mauritius and self-employed workers. The contribution rate amounts to 2.5 per cent of basic wages/salary and the same is paid by employers. Employees of the NPF also contribute an additional 1 per cent of their basic wage or salary to the NSF, subject to the same ceiling. Under the NSF, a lump sum is paid to insured employees (or their legal representatives) on retirement, death or redundancy. The lump sum is made up of contributions paid and accrued interest, after deduction of administrative charges. Benefits are also available for loss of employment on or after attaining 45 on certain grounds or if retired on medical ground.

The Civil Service and Parastatal Pension Scheme

This is an unfunded non-contributory scheme which covers all civil servants (as well as local government employees) and benefits are paid from the budget. Under the scheme, civil servants are entitled to two-thirds of salary after 33.3 years of services. The civil service plan has some 50,000 contributors and the local government schemes have a further 5,000. Currently 20,000 civil service pensioners, and a further 10,000 survivors' pensions are payable (World Bank 2004). The pension scheme for various statutory bodies is known as parastatal pension. The scheme is also non-contributory and offers benefits similar to civil service pension scheme. However, the pension schemes of statutory bodies are required, by virtue of the Statutory Bodies Pension Funds Act of 1978, to create a fund covering their actuarial liabilities. These funds are administered by the State Insurance Corporation of Mauritius (SICOM).

Voluntary Occupational Pension

Mauritius has a long history of occupational private pension system. Private sector companies in Mauritius establish their pension schemes under the Employees Superannuation Fund Act 1982. Most of the private company pension schemes are non-contributory and operate as DB plans offering pensions equal to two-thirds of final salary on the last month of employment after 40 years of service. They are thus somewhat less generous than the civil service pension scheme or the statutory bodies' pension funds. Moreover, annual pension increases are limited by tax regulations to no more than 3 per cent per year. Private company pension schemes tend to be paternalistic, operating on a non-contributory basis and offering several additional services, including in particular housing loans (Vittas 2003). Usually 12–19 per cent earnings are contributed only by employers to superannuation funds. 'However some private pension schemes in Mauritius are converting their DB schemes to DC schemes' (Becceea 2010). A large number of funds are insured and/or administered by insurance companies. These funds are formed as associations and registered with registry of association.

❖ SOCIAL SAFETY NET

In addition to the universal flat rate basic pension, Mauritius has also introduced means-tested pension benefits which is paid under the Social Aid Act (as social assistance) and the Unemployment Hardship Relief Act. There are provisions under the Labour Act, for payment of sick leave, maternity leave and maternity allowance by employers and there is a free medical service available to every person in Mauritius.

From the discussion about the structure of pension funds above, Mauritius pension system can very well be compared with five-pillar system of World Bank. In fact 'at the conceptual level, the Mauritian pension system seems to be fully in line with the new five-pillar model proposed by the World Bank'. (Gopee 2006). The non-contributory BRP is the zero pillar. While the mandatory DB NPF is the first pillar, DC NSF can be treated as the second pillar. Private and occupational pension are similar to the third pillar. Finally the means-tested social assistance programme, health care, can be treated as the fourth pillar.

Coverage

Mauritius has been successful in providing 100 per cent pension coverage to its citizens (also resident non-citizens) through universal basic pension, mandatory DB and DC, social assistance and private voluntary occupational pension. While universal pension scheme applies to the entire population, including non-citizens, it is subject to a residency test. The contributory NPS scheme applies to employees and employers of the private sector, which also includes employees in domestic service. Employers are also required to pay contributions in respect of casual workers, part-time workers, even if they employ only one worker (provided earnings exceed the prescribed minimum level). Various studies have noted the full coverage in Mauritius. ILO (2010) has observed that in Africa while 10 per cent of elderly or fewer have any pension entitlement, Mauritius, which spends more than 5 per cent of GDP on pension and other social security benefits, has the highest coverage (around 100 per cent). According to Willmore (2003),

> *Pension coverage in Mauritius has been truly universal since 1977. In fact, since 1994 coverage has been more than universal, reaching an estimated 103 per cent to 108 per cent of the population older than 60 years of age. Some of this apparent over coverage may reflect under estimation of the elderly population by Central Statistical Office.*

❖ CONTRIBUTION/FINANCING

The non-contributory universal pension is financed from the government budget on a year-to-year basis. For the contributory NPF employers pay contributions at the rate of 6 per cent and employees contribute at the rate of 3 per cent. However, large employers of the sugar industry pay contributions at a higher rate of 10.5 per cent but their employees contribute at the standard rate of 3 per cent. The employees of large employers of the sugar industry are entitled to a higher level of contributory pensions. For NPS, public sector employers (including the government) and the private sector contribute 2.5 per cent of the basic salary of their employees. For superannuation funds usually, 12–19 per cent earnings are contributed only by employers. Therefore, in Mauritius, except NPF and private schemes, contributions are made by the government and employers.

❖ INVESTMENT MANAGEMENT OF THE NPF AND NSF

The funds under NPF and NSF are invested by an investment committee, set up under the act. This committee determines the manner in which surplus funds of the NPF and NSF are to be invested. This committee is assisted by an external investment adviser. the investment committee comprises representatives of government, employers and employees under the chairmanship of the financial secretary.

❖ INVESTMENT PRINCIPLES

The objective of NPF investment process is to provide a level of return adequate to meet its long-term pension obligations and asset protection and all investment decisions are based on three basic investment objectives, namely return, security and liquidity as per the investment guidelines of the NPF and the NSF. The committee targets investment return of CPI inflation + 4 per cent for the NPF and CPI inflation + 3 per cent for the NSF. The committee aims to hold a well-diversified portfolio comprising many investment classes, currencies and regional exposures (NPF-NSF Investment Committee 2010).

❖ ASSET ALLOCATION PATTERN

In order to meet its objectives, the NPF investment committee aims to hold a well-diversified portfolio. Diversification helps reduce the impact that a single, poorly performing investment can make on the overall portfolio. The asset allocations of the NPF and NSF (on a market value basis) MUR 7.3 billion (NPF) and MUR 1.8 billion (NSF) respectively. The combined assets of NPF and NSF were approximately MUR 83.6 billion in by 31 December 2010. Both the funds invested heavily in the government; 56.2 per cent by NPE and 72.4 per cent by NSF. Equity investment by NSF was lower at 3.3 per cent as against 12.3 per cent by NPF. However, the long-term return was more or less same. The overall returns are dominated by the substantial holdings in local fixed-income instruments, especially government of Mauritius bonds and treasury notes (NPF-NSF Investment Committee 2010).

❖ TAXATION

The basic pension is taxed as ordinary income, with some tax applied to those who continue to work or have other sources of income. Those over 90 pay some tax.

❖ ADMINISTRATION AND SUPERVISION

The Ministry of Social Security and National Solidarity, Senior Citizens Welfare and Reforms Institutions (MSS) is responsible for the administration of universal non-contributory basic flat rate pensions under the national pensions scheme (NPS), Contributory pensions under the NPS, NSF, means-tested social assistance scheme (social aid) for needy persons/families and the unemployment hardship relief scheme (UHR) financed by the government.

Emerging Challenges and Reform Initiatives

Mauritius has introduced one of the most advanced pension systems of the world and so far managed very successfully in the interest of its citizens with liberal pension benefits. However, there are severe challenges emerging due to fast-changing population profile. Increased per capita income, improved health care, increased longevity and so on are slowly emerging as a threat and growing burden on exchequer. It is estimated that the share of people over 60 in the total population will be more than triple in the next 50 years. The World Bank (2004) has estimated that currently public sector outlays for pension are about 4.2 per cent but going to increase sharply. Expenditure on basic pension alone expected to be 5.9 per cent of FDP in 2020, and the civil service pension as the share of wage bill expected to increase from 20 per cent to 30 per cent over the next 15 years. World Bank (2004) has thus, recommended to reduce fiscal risk by modernising the BRP, render the system more equitable and efficient, improve transparency in management through introduction of regulation and a supervisory agency for pension and Introduce flexibility in the system, especially regarding the retirement age.

Mauritian authority is well aware of the potential challenges and has already taken several steps to reduce fiscal challenges. The Deputy Prime Minister and Finance Minister of Mauritius in his budget speech (2006–07) on 9 June 2006 also expressed concern about the financial sustainability of various pension schemes in Mauritius. The minister said that the number of persons of working age to support one pensioner will decline from seven to around two in some 40 years due to population ageing. A set of guidelines on the future reforms was also spelt out in his speech which includes, gradual increase of retirement age from 60 to 65 years by 2018, the gradual increase in entitlement age to the BRP, to reach 65 years by 2018, CPI-based increases, making the BRP a part of chargeable income for the top income brackets, introduction of modified DB for the public sector pension, aligning the NPF age for pension eligibility to the other schemes, increase in the pension contribution by the members of the national assembly (MNA), increasing the pension entitlement age to 65 for new members, review of the composition of the investment committee of the NPF, strengthening the regulation of occupational pension plans and so on.

REFERENCES

Allianze Global Investors (2007), 'Asia-Pacific Pensions 2007: Systems and Markets'. Allianz Global Investors AG, International Pensions, Nymphenburgerstr, Munich. Available at: http://www.allianzglobalinvestors.com.

Antia, Florencia and Arnaldo Provasi Lanzara (2011), 'Multi-pillared Social Insurance Systems: The Post-Reform Picture in Chile, Uruguay and Brazil'. Available at http://saopaulo2011.ipsa.org/sites/default/files/papers/paper-1296.pdf.

Arza, Camila (2005), 'Aims, Outcomes and Prospects of Pension Reform in Argentina: An Assessment Ten Years After'. Economics Working Group, Policy Paper No. 6, The Argentina Observatory.

——— (2009), 'Back to the State: Pension Fund Nationalisation in Argentina'. FLACSO-Argentina, UNRISD Conference, Geneva, 12–13 November, 2009. Available at http://unrisd.org/80256B3C005BD6AB/(httpAuxPages)/74D443AA6702F00AC125767A003D3006/$file/2-6Arza.pdf.

Barbosa Filho, Fernando de Holanda (2005), 'Labor Legislation and the Size of Informal Sector in Brazil'. 22 December 2005. Available at: http://www.sbe.org.br/dated/ebe28/pdf/15.pdf.

Barnett, Steve and Nigel Chalk (2010), 'Building a Social Safety Net'. *Finance & Development*, September, 47(3).

Barrientos, Armando (2002), 'Comparing Pension Schemes in Chile, Singapore, Brazil and South Africa'. Institute for Development Policy and Management Discussion Paper No. 67, University of Manchester. Available at: http://idpm.man.ac.uk.

BBVA Research (2010), 'Long Term Returns in Perus's Private Pension Fund'. Available at: www.bbvaresearch.com.

Becceea, Namratta B. (2010), 'Services in Public Sector: The Pension system in Mauritius and Superannuation'. Paper presented at the International Research Symposium in Service Management, University of Mauritius.

Birmingham, Bill and Shaomin Cui (2006), 'An Introduction to Pension Schemes in China'. EU China Affairs Publications. Available at: ec.europa.eu/economy_finance/publications.

Bonturi, M. (2002), 'The Brazilian Pension System: Recent Reforms and Challenges ahead', OECD Economics Department Working Paper No. 340, OECD Publishing. Doi: 10.1787/251552114651.

Borbély, Szilvia (2001), 'Social Security System in Hungary'. Available at: http://socialsecurity.fgov.be/bib/frames/engels/btsz_01_borbely.htm.

Borowczyk, E. (2002), 'Guarantees Brought by the Compulsory Open Pension Funds in Poland'. Paper presented at the European Regional Meeting New and Revised Approaches to Social Protection in Europe. Budapest, 13–15 November 2002, International Social Security Association.

Budget Speech (2006–07), 'Securing the Transition: From Trade Preferences to Global Competition'. Hon. Deputy Prime Minister, Minister of Finance and Economic Development of Mauritius, 9 June 2006. Available at: http://www.gov.mu/portal/site/MOFSite/menuitem.5b1d751c6156d7f4e0aad110a7b521ca/?content_id=646739f4fb4bb010VgnVCM1000000a04a8c0RCRD.

Business News Americas. Published on Friday, 21 November 2008. Available at: http://www.bnamericas.com/news/insurance/Senate_approves_nationalization_of_private_pension_fund_managers.

Carstens, Augstin G. (1997), 'The Reform of Social Security in Mexico'. in Steven A. Sass and Robert K. Triest (eds), *Social Security Reform Conference Proceedings*. Boston: Federal Reserve Bank of Boston, USA.

China Daily, 2011. 'China to Review Women's Retirement Age'. *China Daily*, **Sunday, 29** May 2011. Available at: http://www.chinadaily.com.cn/china/2011-02/28/content_12084830.htm.

Dayoub, Mariam and Esperanza Lasagabaster (2008), 'General Trends in Competition Policy and Investment Regulation in Mandatory Defined Contribution Markets in Latin America'. World Bank, Latin America and Caribbean Region Finance and Private Sector Development Unit, September 2008.

Escobar, Federico and Nina Osvaldo (2004), 'Pension Reform in Bolivia: A Review of Approach and Experience'. Development Research Working Paper Series No 04/2004, Institute for Advance Development Studies.

Feldstein, Martin (2001), 'Social Security Pension Reform in China'. Working Paper 6794, National Bureau of Economic Research, Cambridge, November 2001. Available at: http://www.eucss.org.cn/fileadmin/research_papers/policy/Pension/PensionschemesChina.pdf.

FIAP (International Federation of Pension Fund Administrators) (2002), *Annual Report 2002*, FIAP, Santiago. Available at: http://www.fiap.cl/p4_fiap_eng/site/artic/20031013/asocfile/ASOCFILE120031013202239.pdf.

——— (2006), *20th Bi-Annual Report*, FIAP, Santiago.

——— (2007), 'Contribution Rates and Tax Ceilings in Countries with Individually Funded System', FIAP, Santiago, March, 2007.

Försäkringskassan (2005), Swedish Social Insurance Agency, 28 November 2005.

Forteza, Alvaro (2004), 'Uruguay, Options for Pensions Reform'. Available at: http://129.3.20.41/eps/pe/papers/0406/0406002.pdf.

Fuhrman, Peter (2010), 'China's National Social Security Fund: the World's Largest Investor in PE Firms'. Available at: http://en.21cbh.com/HTML/2010-11-10/5NMDAwMDIwNTM5Ng.html (accessed on 10 November 2010).

Gál, Róbert I. 2001. 'Pension Fund Governance in Hungary in an International Context'. TÁRKI Social Research Center, Budapest. Available at: http://www.pfsprogram.org/archive/pfsorg/ovr01/publications_governance.html.

Gersdorff, Hermann von (1997), 'The Bolivian Pension Reform, Innovative Solutions to Common Problems'. Financial Sector Development Department, World Bank.

Gill, Indermit, Truman Packard and Juan Yermo (2005), *Keeping the Promise of Social Security in Latin America.* Stanford: Stanford University.

Golinowska, Stanisawa and Piotr Kurowski (eds) (2010), 'Rational Pension Supervision'. Part 6, *Development of Pension Funds and Pension Supervision in Central and Eastern Europe.* Warsaw: Centre for Social nod Economic Research. Available at: http://www.case.com.pl/upload/publikacja_plik/rc36part2.pdf.

Gómez, Carlos A. Herrera (2008), 'Mexico Strengthens Its Pension System with a Multi-Fund Model'. Pension Systems Analysis Unit, BBVA. Available at: icacionespensiones_05_tcm268-166818.pdf.

Gomulka, S. and M. Styczen (1999), 'Estimating the Impact of the 1999 Pension Reform in Poland 2000–2050'. Case CEU Working Paper No. 27.

Gopee, R. (2006). 'The Adequacy of Current Social Security Benefits. Meeting of Directors of Social Security Organizations in English-Speaking Africa'. Mahe, Seychelles, International Social Security Association, 1–12.

Gora, Marek and Michal Rutkowski (1998), 'The Quest for Pension Reform: Poland's Security through Diversity'. Social Protection Discussion Paper No. 20111, World Bank, October 1998.

Grandolini, Gloria and Luis Cerda (1998), 'The 1997 Pension Reform in Mexico: Genesis and Design Features'. Draft—22 April 1998. Available at: http://www-wds.worldbank.org/external/default/WDSContentServer/WDSP/IB/1998/06/01/000009265_3980709144952/additional/111511322_20041117141527.pdf.

Guan X. (1994), 'Social Security System—An Outline of Its Reform and Problems Since 1979', in R. Krieg and M. Schadler (eds), *Social Security in the People's Republic of China.* Hamburg: Institute for Asian Studies.

Guardiancich, Igor (2010a). 'Hungary—Current Pension System: First Assessment of Reform Outcome and Output'. European Social Security Observatory. Available at http://www.ose.be/files/publication/2010/country_reports_pension/OSE_2010_CRpension_Hungary.pdf (accessed on 11 September 2012).

——— (2010b), 'Country Report Poland—Current Pension System: First Assessment of Reform Outcomes and Output'. *The Quest for Pension Reform: Poland's Security through Diversity.* European Social Security Observatory, May 2010.

Guardiancich, Igor (2010c), 'Sweden Current Pension System: First Assessment of Reform Outcomes and Output'. European Social Observatory.

Holzman, Robert and Richard Hinz (2005), 'Old Age Income Support in the 21st Century'. Washington DC, The International Bank for Reconstruction and Development/World Bank.

Hussain, Athar (2001), 'Pension Reform in China: Its Progress and Challenges'. Asia Research Centre, London School of Economics, 11–13 September 2001. Available at: http://www.hks.harvard.edu/m-rcbg/Conferences/financial_sector/PensionReforminChina.pdf.

Idemoto, Steve (2000), 'Social Security Privatisation in Chile: A Case for caution'. Seattle: Economic opportunity Institute, 29 September 2000.

IEG (Independent Evaluation Group) (2006), *Pension Reform and the Development of Pension Systems: An Evaluation of World Bank Assistance.* IEGKE.

ILO (International Labour Organisation) (2010), 'World Social Security Report 2010/11—Providing Coverage in times of Crisis and Beyond'. Geneva: International Labour Office.

IMF (International Monetary Fund) (2003), 'Financial Sector Assessment Mauritius'. Joint IMF-World Bank Financial Sector Assessment Programme, Africa Region Vice Presidency, Financial Sector Vice Presidency, August 2003.

INPRS (2001), 'Recent Developments in Selected CEEC: Romania, Poland, Hungary and Czech Republic'. International Network of Pension Regulators and Supervision, Private Pension Conference, Sofia, Bulgaria, 23–26 April 2001.

IOPS (International Organisation of Pension Supervisors) (2011), 'Country Profile—Brazil', January 2011. Available at: http://www.iopsweb.org/dataoecd/61/10/41548295.pdf.

ISSA (International Social Security Administration) (2009), 'Social Security Administration throughout the World: Asia and Pacific (2008)', International Social Security Association Social Security Observatory, Geneva.

——— (2009), 'Social Security Administration throughout the World: Asia and Pacific (2008)'. International Social Security Association Social Security Observatory, Geneva.

——— (2010), 'Social Security Programs throughout the World: The Americas, 2009'. Social Security Administration, Office of Retirement and Disability Policy Office of Research, Evaluation, and Statistics, Washington, DC 20254. SSA Publication No. 13-11804, March 2010.

Kruse, Agneta (2010), 'A Stable Pension System: The Eighth Wonder'. in T. Bengtsson (ed.), *Population Ageing—A Threat to the Welfare State? Research Monographs.* Available at: http://www.demogr.mpg.de/books/drm/008/4.pdf.

Langer, David (1998), 'The Lesson of Chilean Social Security'. Contingencies, March-April 1998.

Lianquan, Fang (2011), 'Rethinking Public Pension Reform: Could China Adopt a Notional Defined Contribution Model?' *AARP International,* Winter 2011.

Loraine, A. West (1997), 'Pension Reform in China: Preparing for the Future'. Eurasia Bulletin, Summer 1997, US Census Bureau.

Maciel, Pedro Jucá (2010), 'Social Security in Brazil: Importance'. Available at: http://www.pedrojucamaciel.com/Social per cent20Security per cent20and per cent20Fiscal per cent20Policy.pdf.

Marcel, Mario and Waldo Tapia (2009), 'The Impact of Financial Crisis of Private Pension Funds in Latin American Countries'. Paper presented at Pension Reform and Developments in Latin America-Conference Proceedings of the OECD/IOPS Global Forum on Private Pension. Rio de Janeiro, Brazil 2009.

Murton, Tim (2010), 'Recent Developments in the Social Security System'. Available at: http://epress.anu.edu.au/cb/pdf/ch12.pdf) (OECD 2010—investment).

Natali, David (2004), 'Sweden: The Reformed Pension System'. Open Method of Coordination: Pensions and European Integration. Brussels, Belgium: European Social Observatory (OSE). Available at: http://www.ose.be/files/mocpension/SwedenOMC.pdf (accessed on 3 August 2007).

Normann, Goran and Daniel J. Mitchell (2000), 'Pension Reforms in Sweden: Lesson for American Policy Makers'. Heritage Foundation (No. 1381), 29 June.

NPF-NSF Investment Committee (2010), Press Meeting, Friday, 20 August 2010, Press Meeting Brief.

OECD (2008), *Pension Markets in Focus.* Newsletter, December 2008, Issue 5.

——— (2009), *Health at a Glance 2010: OECD Indicators.* Paris: OECD Publishing.

——— (2010), *Survey of Investment Regulation of Pension Funds.* February 2010. Paris: OECD.

Oksanen, Heikki (2010), 'The Chinese Pension System: First Results on Assessing the Reform Option'. Economic Papers 412/June 2010, European Commission, Director General for Economic and Financial.

PPM (Premiepensionsmyndigheten) (2009), Årsredovisning *2008.* Stockholm: PPM.

Predtechensky, Alexej (2010), 'Brazilian Pension System—An Overview'. Paper presented in sixth Asian Conference on Pension and Retirement Planning, 1–2 February, Singapore.

Pugh, Colin (2009), 'Brazil—Regulation and Supervision of Close ended Pension Funds'. IOPS/OECD Global Forum, Rio de Janeiro, October 2009.

Reis, Adacir and Leonardo André Paixão (2004), 'Private Pension in Brazil'. Available at: http://www.oecd.org/dataoecd/26/40/42601981.pdf.

Salditt, Felix, Peter Whiteford and Willem Adema (2007). 'Pension Reform in China: Progress and Prospects'. OECD Social, Employment, and Migration Working Papers, OECD.

Schmidt-Hebbel, Klaus (1997), 'Fiscal and Macroeconomic Effects of Columbia's Pension Reform'. *Revista de Análisis Económico* 12(2): 37–69.

——— (1999), 'Chile's Pension Revolution Coming of Age'. Available at: http://schmidt-hebbel.com/pdf/SH99PR.pdf.

Sergio, Clavjio (2009), 'Social Security Reforms in Colombia: Striking Demographic and Fiscal Balances'. IMF Working Paper, International Monetary Fund WP/09/58.

Settergren, Ole (2003), 'The Reform of the Swedish Pension System-Initial Results'. Available at: http://www.sante.gouv.fr/IMG/pdf/rfos2000304-art12-uk.pdf.

——— (2005), 'Two Thousand Five hundred Words on the Swedish Pension System Annual Report'. Swedish Social Insurance Agency.Shah, Hemant (1997), 'Towards Better Regulation of Private Pension Fund'. World Bank Working Paper, 19 April. Available at: http://elibrary.worldbank.org/docserver/download/1791.pdf?expires=1348127734&id=id&accname=guest&checksum=BB33045C36E4759630325B4170AA966D.

Shen, Ce and John B. Williamson (2010), 'China's New Rural Pension Scheme: Can It Be Improved?' Available at: www.emeraldinsight.com/0144-333X.htm.

Simonovits, András (2002), 'Hungarian Pension System: The Permanent Reform'. Social Security Reform Co-operation Project, ASIE/2004/3252. Institute of Economics, Hungarian Academy of Sciences, Budapest, 25 February 2002.

Social Security Reform Co-operation Project, ASIE/2004/3252. Available at: http://www.eucss.org.cn/fileadmin/research_papers/policy/Pension/PensionschemesChina.pdf.

Soledad, Hormazábal (2010), 'Multi-funds in the Chilean Pension System'. Working Papers, BBVA, No. 10/28, 14 October. Santiago: Chile.

SSA online (2010–11), 'Sweden—Social Security'. Swedish Pension System: Director of the Department of Pensions. Available at: http://www.ssa.gov/policy/docs/progdesc/intl_update/2010-06/index.html.

Sze, Michael (2006), 'Enterprise Annuity in China', International Section News, Society of Actuaries, Issue No. 39 (July 2006). Available at: http://www.soa.org/library/newsletters/international-section-news/2006/july/isn-2006-iss39-sze.pdf.

Tapia, W. (2008), 'Description of Private Pension Systems', OECD Working Papers on Insurance and Private Pensions, No. 22, OECD Publishing. doi: 10.1787/237831300433.

United Nations (2002), 'Population Ageing.2002'. Population Division, Department of Economic and Social Affairs.

United Nations (2009), 'World Population Prospects, The 2008 Revision (Vol. 1)'. Department of Economic and Social Affairs/Population Division.

Vial, Joaquin and Angel Melguizo (2007), 'Moving from Pay As You Go to Privately Managed Individual Pension Accounts: What Have We Learned After 25 years of the Chilean Pension Reform?' BBVA Economic Research Department's Working Paper No. 0805.

Villasenor-Zertuche, Jaime A. (2000), 'An Overview of the New Pension System in Mexico'. Private Pension System and Policy Issues. Paris: OECD.

Vittas, Dimitri (1997). 'The Argentine Pension Reform and Its Relevance for Eastern Europe'. Washington DC: Financial Sector Development Department, World Bank.

——— (2003), 'The Role of Occupational Pension Funds in Mauritius'. Policy Research Working Paper No. 3033. The World Bank Financial Sector Operations and Policy Department, April.

Wang, Xin (2001), 'China's Pension System Reform and Capital Market Development'. Research Department, China International Capital Corporation, paper presented to the Kennedy School, Harvard University, International conference on China and the WTO, The Financial Challenge, 12 September 2001. Available at: http://finntrack.co.uk/finance/pensionsystemrefr.pdf.

Wang, Yanzhong (2005), 'Reform of Yanzhong Wang China's Pension System'. China & World Economy 44–55, 13(3). Available at: http://en.iwep.org.cn/download/upload_files/lypk4ja1m2bixn45lmiyhrub20090324125944.pdf.

Weaver, Kent (2011), 'The Politics of Automatic Stabilization Mechanisms in Public Pension Programs'. Available at: http://bibliothek.wz-berlin.de/pdf/2011/i11-201.pdf.

Willmore, Larry (2003), 'Universal Pension in Mauritius: Lessons for the Rest of Us'. DESA Discussion Paper No. 32, United Nations, Department of Economic and Social Affairs, April.

World Bank (2004), 'Mauritius—Modernizing an Advanced Pension System'. Report No. 29588-MU, Southern Africa Region, World Bank Document, 30 June.

World Bank (2011), 'Mauritius: Country Brief'. Available at: http://web.worldbank.org/WBSITE/EXTERNAL/COUNTRIES/AFRICAEXT/MAURITIUSEXTN/0,,contentMDK:20211139~pagePK:1497618~piPK:217854~theSitePK:381974,00.html (accessed in April 2011).

Xinhua News Agency (2006), 'Pension System to Cover 220 Million People in 2010'. 14 January. Available at: http://www.china.org.cn/english/2006/Jan/155140.htm.

Zoltán, Ádám and Kopint-Datorg Rt. (2005), 'The Hungarian Pension Reform'. Paper presented at the Lancut Economic Forum for Reverse Learning, Lancut, Poland, 15–16 April. Available at: www.kopdat.hu.

3 Pension Reforms

Structural Change, Challenges and Impact

INTRODUCTION

In the previous chapter an attempt has been made to identify the process and structure of pension reforms in few selected countries across the world. It was observed that each country took its own course of action, which was sometimes quite diverse in terms of structure of new pension system, implementation and regulation but some common threads were also found among the group of countries. The experience of these countries in pension reforms enlightened us about the constraints and challenges, which will prove useful while reforming pension system in a country like India. In this chapter, an attempt has been made to summarise broadly some important issues relating to reforms. Second, an attempt has also been made to examine broadly the major impact of reforms and their success in achieving macro-financial objectives.

SOME IMPORTANT FEATURES OF PENSION REFORMS

Pension reforms are related to multidimensional issues involving the system, components, benefits, regulations and so on. Some of these issues have been summarised here from the reform experience of the individual countries.

Multi-Pillar System

Most of the countries, studied in the previous chapter, developed multi-pillar system by reforming the existing social security system. They have either transferred their Pay-as-You-Go (PAYG) defined benefit (DB) system to defined contribution (DC) system or added a new DC pillar to the existing DB system. The new system, in many countries, is a mixture of public and private pension funds and social security. While the first pillar basically remained as universal social security or social insurance or basic minimum pension programme financed by states, the second pillar is usually a fully funded DC pillar managed by private pension fund managers. The third pillar is primarily voluntary savings plan for additional retirement benefits. The first and second pillars are mandatory in most of the countries studied in the previous chapter.

A radical departure from the old pension system has been noted in many Latin American countries. Out of the seven countries studied—three countries, namely Chile, Bolivia and Mexico have adopted a totally contributory system by replacing the old PAYG system, while Peru and Colombia established a parallel system of public or private pension system and Uruguay has established a combined public and private system. Brazil, though introduced second-pillar private pension, it mostly remained a DB system. Pension reforms can be non-structural (parametric) or structural. Non-structural reforms are carried out by raising contribution, increasing the retirement age, modifying the pension payout formula and so on. On the other hand, structural reform redesigns the entire pension system, particularly by changing the public system. There are several models of structural reform. Mesa-Lago (2002) has pointed that in Latin America there are three basic structural models: substitutive model, where public system is replaced by private system, for example, Chile, Bolivia and Mexico; parallel model, where public system is reformed but it remains in place, and private system is developed as a competitor to the public system, for example, Peru and Colombia and mixed model, where the private pillar functions as complementary to public pillar; another type of model, which has been gradually adopted by many countries, is notional defined contribution (NDC). The NDC was developed and implemented by Sweden, subsequently adopted by many countries including Poland, Italy, China and other countries. NDC attempted to incorporate the important characteristics of DB and DC systems.

❖ TRANSITION CHOICE

There is no uniformity in respect of workers' choices in transition. Many countries have accepted the workers right in deciding their future pension system. Joining the new system was made mandatory for all workers in Argentina, Bolivia and Mexico, while it was mandatory for new entrants in Chile, Hungary and voluntary for others. In Poland the new system was mandatory for workers below 30 years and voluntary for workers aged 30–50 years. In Colombia and Peru membership for one of the pillars is mandatory.

❖ COLLECTION SYSTEM

Pension reforms through introduction of privately managed funds have compounded the problems of collection for contribution, record keeping compliance and so on. In a publicly managed system collection is normally through centralised government agency, which can be managed and controlled efficiently at a relatively low cost. The complexities in collection are associated with the structure of system. Among the Latin

American countries two major types of collection system have been noticed. For example, Chile, Bolivia, Colombia and Peru have introduced decentralised collection though Administradoras de Fondos de Pensiones (AFPs) but countries like Argentina, Mexico and Uruguay have introduced centralised collection system. Hungary has introduced a unified collection system. However, contribution of collection to the second pillar is collected by the individual pension funds. Poland has established a single clearing house for collection of contribution which will be transferred to the funds selected by the contributors. Collection of social security contribution in Poland is administered by National Social Security Institutions, known as Zakład Ubezpieczeń Społecznych (ZUS).

Similarly, collection costs vary across the country from 0.66 per cent of contribution in Argentina to 0.12 per cent of contribution in Bolivia in 2006 (FIAP 2006). There are certain advantages and disadvantages in both the centralised or decentralised systems of collection. While centralised system can save time to transfer contribution to the individual system in a cost-effective way, it can also enjoy benefits of economies of scale and is therefore cost-effective and also has the advantage of quick and cost-effective compliance.

Safety Net

Public sector DB plans have been criticised for implicit policy risks, but market risks are borne by the pension providers. In case of privately managed DC plans risks are fully transferred to the members. In order to reduce the intensity of such risks and to provide some comforts to the investors/members, most of the reformed countries have introduced some safety measures either through minimum pension guarantee (MPG) or through minimum/benchmark return for the second-pillar DC plans which are managed by independent fund managers. The major safety net instruments are universal pension, MPG, earnings-related first pillar, flat rate pension and so on. A non-contributory universal pension for citizens regardless of earnings or occupation has been advocated as a simple and superior means for poverty relief as it avoids targeting the beneficiary group. World Bank's three-pillar model with the first pillar as the basic pension and universal pension can be ideal, though only few countries have introduced it. According to Willmore (2006), a total of nine countries (including Bolivia and Mauritius) and one large city (Mexico City) provides universal pension. However, many other countries have introduced means-tested residence base social assistance or minimum pension as the basic pillar.

MPG

One of the most important features of pension reforms in many countries is the introduction of MPG. Public pension system was the backbone of social security, which has been dismantled/disturbed due to the reform of PAYG DB system and often the workers were put into hardship. By introducing the social assistance/MPG the state has tried to mitigate these problems and implicitly carried out its social obligation. These steps have reduced the hardship of retirees and fulfilled the social obligation of state. In Latin America most of the reform countries have introduced MPGs, which are often in the form of social assistance. In Chile there is a provision for minimum pension. Argentina has prestación básica universal (PBU) in addition to the second pillar, Colombia has minimum pension, Mexico has a minimum pension benefit equal to minimum wages (in 1997), and Uruguay has guaranteed pension benefit under the first-pillar national pension system, while Peru has MPG social assistance based on legal minimum wages. However, Bolivia does not have guaranteed minimum pension. The transitional countries like Hungary and Poland have also made provision for minimum pension. Hungary has introduced a minimum pension under the first and second pillars. In China there is a basic social pension under the first pillar of newly introduced multi-pillar system. This basic pension is DB PAYG pension financed by employers and shortfall if any is made up by the government. There is targeted means-tested social assistance programme in India.

Minimum Rate of Return Guarantee

One of the most crucial issues associated with fully funded second pillar managed by private fund managers in a multi-pillar pension system is the uncertainty in investment return. While, in DB system pension amount is predefined, in a DC system pension depends on capital invested and rate of investment return. Investment restrictions and diversifications imposed through investment regulations are attempts to protect the account holder's interest. Moreover, most of the countries which have introduced DC system managed by private fund managers have introduced some benchmark return or some guaranteed return to be provided by the private fund managers. Countries like Chile, Argentina, Colombia, Peru and Uruguay in Latin America, Hungary and Poland in Eastern Europe have introduced minimum return. In Chile each AFP must ensure minimum return equal to lower of average return of all AFPs minus 2 per cent for last 12 months or 50 per cent of the average industry return; in Argentina it is related to the market average, 30 per cent higher or lower than the average return; in Peru, each AFP must ensure return within a range of 50–150 per cent of industry average return; in Uruguay, the real return on investment in Adiministradoras de Fondos de Ahorro Previsional (AFAPs) must not fall below 20 per cent per year and an individual AFAP may not earn less than 2 per cent below the average of all AFPs. Colombia also has a bench mark relative to synthetic portfolio. In Hungary an anticipated average rate and minimum and maximum rate is determined. Individual savings are protected by a minimum return guarantee, funds are required to make shortfalls in rates of return that are more than 15 per cent but less than the return of a portfolio of long-term government bonds. Also, in Poland, there is a rate of return guarantee, for all the private funds. If the value of a given fund falls below the 50 per cent average, nominal return of 4 per cent below the average industry return, the fund administrator should make up for the shortfall.

There are various practices regarding guarantee providers and arranging the resources for guarantee. Guarantee providers can be the fund managers, sponsors, central pension guarantee fund or the government. In many Latin American countries fund managers are required to set up the yield fluctuation reserve fund and the sponsors are required to set up the cash reserve (CR) fund. For example, in Chile the yield fluctuation fund (YFF) is made up of a pension fund's actual yield surplus over the last year, which has exceeded the average actual yield of all the funds for that year by more than two percentage points or by more than 50 per cent, whichever is higher. CR is equivalent to at least 1 per cent of the value of pension fund and is paid by using the AFP's own resources; that is, out of shareholders fund. When a pension fund is unable to provide guaranteed minimum return even by using YFF and CR, the government steps in and makes up the deficits and proceeds to wind up the fund. In countries like Poland and Hungary, central pension guarantee funds are established through contribution of fund managers. For example, in Hungary the central guarantee fund (GF) is a pre-funded institution. Pension funds pay 0.3 per cent to 0.5 per cent of members' contribution into the guarantee fund. The government steps in when resources of GF are exhausted to fulfil the guarantee. Minimum return guarantee makes the DC partially DB pension and transfers a part of investment risks to the fund managers. Second, guarantee is a sort of insurance which may make the fund managers take unmanageable higher risks. However, advantages seem to underscore disadvantages while a minimum return guarantee offered by a fund managers.

First, pension savings is a critical old-age income generated by investors through savings and pension funds with expectation of higher return than the risk free return on bank deposits and bonds, in anticipation that the pension fund managers are experts. Therefore, pension funds need to perform to provide the expected return so that investors in their old-age receive regular income.

Second, when the responsibility of providing minimum return is put on the fund managers, a more cautious and scientific investment approach is followed by them by minimising the risk of decline in return. This will strengthen the risk governance and regulatory oversight which is a precondition for efficient supervision of pension funds. Third, when some responsibility for good performance is fixed for the sponsors, only the best and competent organisations will enter into pension business, which will promote a healthy fund management industry in the pension sector. Fourth, minimum return guarantee on pension fund returns induces confidence among the investors in investing in pension funds which will provide a boost to domestic savings through pension funds.

Health Care through Pension Reforms

Old-age health care is a costly affair and a vast number of older people are unable to afford it. Government-sponsored health-care support is grossly inadequate in most of the developed and emerging market countries. We have noted in the previous chapter that health insurance and health-care benefits are part of the new system in some countries, particularly in countries like Colombia and China. In Colombia, health-care system is a part of social security and pension reforms. The Law 100 put in place a single insurance system based on 'cross subsidies' between the contributive system (CS) and the subsidised system (SS). The contribution to CS is 12.5 per cent of payrolls, 67 per cent paid by employer and 33 per cent paid by employee. The SS is meant for individuals who lack financial means to pay for health-care contributions. The insurance component of the health-care system is based on the Empresas Promotoras de Salud (EPS), offering the mandatory basic health-care plan known as Plan Obligatorio de Salud (POS). The service component is provided through the Instituciones Prestadoras de Salud (IPS).

> *In Colombia, health care coverage has increased significantly, from 28 percent of the population in the early 1990s up to 86 percent by end 2006.... Special health care programs (including the military) account for an additional coverage of 2 percent, so total health care coverage is currently close to 88 percent of the Colombian population. (Clavijo 2009)*

China has also taken a bold step to provide affordable health-care facilities to its citizens along with the introduction of various measures to reform old-age pension system and to expand coverage. It has also taken a bold step to improve health-care system and to bring the entire population under health-care network. In 2009, China announced a three-year health-care programme to ensure affordable health-care provision for the entire population by 2020. The principal goals are to make health care more equitable by building up health-care service facilities in rural areas, and increasing access to health insurance schemes and by reducing costs through a range of programmes, and to improve quality by increasing training and research, improving the supervision, regulation. By the end of 2011, the government intends to cover 90 per cent of the population by some form of health insurance scheme.

Rural Pension

Historically, the organised and urban workers, due to their massive organisational strength, influence the policymakers and corner the lion's share of social security and pension benefits, though the informal and rural sector play a critical role in economy and contribute substantially to growth. Countries with large informal and agriculture economy like China, India, Brazil, and so on, fall in this category, and it is a concern and core issue of pension reform. Most of the workers in the informal and agriculture sectors do not have any formal social security and pension to take care of old-age income needs. Countries undertaking pension reforms, therefore, face the critical challenges to design appropriate pension system for them. It is a difficult task, because they lack regular income and are often unable to contribute regularly. Also, those who are engaged in informal sector change their jobs very frequently. Therefore, pension plans designed for urban and organised sector workers are often not suitable for rural and unorganised sector workers, and special pension plans are required to be designed for this sector. Some countries have, therefore, introduced rural pension scheme; for example, Brazil and China, which have large informal sector employment and vast rural, population have specially designed pension system for population.

Under the rural pension system Brazilian workers, having proof of at least 10 years' rural activities receive non-contributory social security benefits equivalent to minimum wages from age of 60 (men) and 55 (women). Rural pension not only provides old-age subsistence to agricultural workers but also helps reduce incidence of migration from rural to urban areas. However, it may be mentioned here that Brazilian constitution granted the right of retirement for rural workers independently of their contribution (Pedro 2010). China has been making serious efforts to promote pension insurance scheme for the rural people. In the year 1986, China began the work of establishing a grass-roots social security system. According to Shen and Williamson (2010), 56 per cent of China's total population, but 70 per cent of its elderly population, live in rural areas. After 1991, China introduced pension for rural employees to be financed by 3 per cent of wages and in 2008 only 56 million or 12 per cent of 473 million rural area employees were covered, which was quite low comparing to elderly rural population. However, Chinese policy to provide pension to the rural sector is an important policy direction of pension reform.

Administrative Cost

Under the individual account system pension providers charge various fees to cover various operating costs like marketing, funds collection, funds management, record keeping and so on. The fees charged for managing pension funds in Latin America can be classified into categories discussed in the following paragraphs.

❖ FEES ON CONTRIBUTION

Variable fee is charged on an affiliate's (member's) salary at a given rate. However, a percentage of fees/commission out of the fees on contribution is transferred to life insurance companies as a premium for survival and disability insurance. Fees on assets are variable fees that are charged as a percentage of assets managed keeping in view the fund management's objectives and asset maximisation. Fees on return are variable fees, which the fund managers charge on the return on the fund.

❖ FEES ON TRANSFER/EXIT

Transfer/exit fee is charged when a member exits from the scheme or transfers his/her assets to another fund manager. Though various types of fees are charged by pension funds, two most common fees are fees on contribution and fees on assets. While all countries charge fees on contribution, few charge fees on assets and return. As Tapia and Yermo (2008) have mentioned that there is no limit on the fees on contribution in countries like Chile, Mexico, Peru and Uruguay but there is a cap on such fees based in Argentina (1 per cent), Bolivia (0.5 per cent of salary), Colombia (3 per cent of salary), Hungary (6 per cent of contribution) and in Poland (7 per cent of contribution). Fees on assets can be charged in Bolivia (0 per cent–0.223 per cent), Mexico (no limit), Hungary (0.9 per cent) and in Poland (0.45 per cent). Commission can be charged on return in Poland (0.45 per cent). There are certain criticism about the fees/commission charged by pension funds which erode the investors assets and are finally reflected in the value of assets. However, some arguments in favour of fees are that initial establishment and operational costs are higher and in course of time with the maturity of system, fees will come down.

Taxation of Pension Savings

There are several critical issues to be addressed by the policymakers of pension reforms and one such issue is the tax treatment of retirement savings of funded pension. The tax policy of a funded pension has to achieve several objectives; often they are conflicting in nature. For example, tax policy must encourage retirement savings by keeping revenue loss and cost of tax concession at minimum, it also needs to encourage pension savings, by attaining distributional justice and to ensure incentives for deferred consumption and so on. While unrealistic higher tax rate on pension contribution or pension payment will discourage pension savings, excessive tax benefits for retirement savings on the other hand are not socially tenable and also generate adverse revenue consequences. The very purpose of retirement savings is to ensure the post-retirement consumption remain possibly at the pre-retirement level by deferring the current consumption. The longer the period of savings, the higher the amount of accumulated financial assets, which can be transferred for post retirement consumption. Imposing taxes on the financial savings would reduce the available financial assets for consumption. The investor may also consider future increase in income and increase in tax exempt contribution limit. There are four major types of taxation that can be imposed on pension savings. These are exempt exempt tax (EET) which exempts pension contributions and investment incomes from tax but pension payments or benefits are taxed; tax exempt exempt (TEE) which imposes tax on contribution but exempt investment income as well as pension payments; tax tax exempt (TTE) which imposes tax on the contribution and investment income but pension payments are tax exempted, and exempt tax tax (ETT) which exempts the contribution but imposes taxes on investment income and the pension payments. Most of the emerging countries, which have undertaken pension reforms, have adopted EET tax system. These countries include Argentina, Chile, Columbia, Uruguay, Hungary, Poland and India.

Tax incentives are important instrument to encourage savings but may not be the only instrument to influence the individual decision to save and may not be necessarily a sufficient condition for substantial increase in savings for individual retirement in a funded pension system. According to Whitehouse (1999), 'A generous tax treatment seems neither a necessary nor a sufficient condition for large private pension funds. The regulatory and industrial o regimes, historical factors as well as the public pension system will also affect the size of private funds.' However, higher tax incentives often provide a boost to retirement savings. Cifuentes (2003) in his study on tax incentives for retirement savings in Chile has observed that 'despite the fact that the tax incentives mechanism is relevant for the workers with higher incomes only, the impact on the total amount of funds is considerable'. According to his study, this change comes from a shift on the payment of income taxes, from active life to retirement.

Retirement Age

Though this measure comes under the parametric/non-structural reform model, most of the countries have included the retirement factor in their package of reforms and retirement has been increased in the new system; for example, Argentina has increased retirement age from 60 years to 65 years for men and 55 years to 60 years for women, Colombia has increased from 55 years to 60 years for men and 50 years to 57 years for women under public pillar and to 62 years and 60 years for men and women under private pillar. Similarly, Hungary has increased retirement age from 60 years to 62 years for men and 50 years to 62 years for women. Poland has also increased retirement age from 59 years to 65 years for men and 55 years to 60 years for women. By increasing the retirement age, a country can defer pension payment for a certain period, which temporarily reduces pension liability.

IMPACT OF PENSION REFORMS ON EXPANDING COVERAGE

Extending social security and pension coverage is one of the most important objectives globally, particularly in the emerging market and less-developed countries. According to the ILO estimates, only the one-third of the countries inhabited by 28 per cent of global population is covered by comprehensive social security and only 40 per cent of working age population is legally covered by contributory pension schemes (ILO 2010). However, this coverage is concentrated mostly around developed countries and on formal sector employees. Extending coverage, therefore, remains a major concern of any public policy and one of the primary objectives of pension reforms is to expand the coverage. Since the PAYG DB system primarily covers the organised sector employees, self-employed and informal sector employees remained beyond the system. Fragile pension system based on DB mostly provided benefits to a limited number of organised sector employees and a vast majority of workers in the unorganised sector remained beyond the formal social security network. It has been argued by the reform experts that privately managed DC system would remove this shortcoming of PAYG system and extend the coverage system to include self-employed and informal sector employees. However, this objective is yet to be achieved in many countries which have introduced pension reforms.

The increase in members and the number of contributors can be seen from Table 3.1. There has been a significant increase in coverage in countries like Argentina and Bolivia which have totally changed the PAYG DB system to fully funded DC system managed by private fund managers. However, based on active contribution, coverage was highest in Uruguay (61.37 per cent) followed by Chile (50.73 per cent), while Chile was transformed into fully private system or Uruguay was a mixed public–private system. So it cannot be said certainly that privatised system provides better coverage. Further, with the reform there has been a significant switchover to the private system. In Bolivia and Mexico, workers were to compulsorily opt for new system. But in a parallel system like Peru about 95 per cent workers opted for private system and in Peru 49 per cent

Table 3.1 Membership and Contributors in Mandatory Individual Account System

Column 1	*Column 2*	*Column 3*	*Column 4*	*Column 5*	*Column 6*	*Column 7*	*Column 8*
Country	*Year of Reforms*	*June 2000 Membership*	*June 2000 Contributors*	*June 2000 Contributors as per cent of Membership*	*June 2006 Membership*	*June 2006 Contributors*	*June 2006 Contributors as percentage of Membership*
Argentina	1994	8,395,368	327,994	39.06	10,958,574	4,340,729	39.61
Bolivia	1997	633,152	587,873	92.84	966,466	448,877	46.44
Colombia	1994	3,954,007	1,916,199	48.46	6,701,261	2,677,620	39.95
Chile	1981	832,976	3,196,991	47.66	7,526,696	3,818,842	50.73
Mexico	1997	17,844,956	10,379,823	58.16	36,284,649	13,702,588	37.76
Peru	1993	2,471,593	1,031,366	41.72	3,775,230	1,396,296	36.98
Uruguay	1996	577,729	293,282	50.76	702,923	431,399	61.37

Source: FIAP Annual Reports 2000 and 2006.

accepted the private system. So, it can be assumed that privatisation, through various ventures, encouraged existing workers to switch over to the private system.

It seems that pension reforms failed to provide enough coverage due to low replacement ratios for women employees, only dependent workers being mandatorily covered, exclusion of self-employed from mandatory participation, high informality, rotation between formal and informal sectors, large informal sector, frequent changes in jobs, and so on, and many workers did not contribute regularly. It seems that the option to join pension system voluntarily has not been very successful and restrained the coverage expansion in the reformed system. In some countries there was even a decline in the number of self-employed workers in the system. For example, In Chile self-employed workers account for 15 per cent of the employed labour force and their coverage declined from 12 per cent to 5.4 per cent in 1986–2004, and in 2004–05, the self-employed were only 4 per cent of total insured in Bolivia and Columbia and so on (Mesa-Lago 2007). A similar observation was also made by Valente (2008) quoting International Association of Latin American Pension Fund Supervisors (AIOS) that the 10 Latin American Countries that make up the association had 76 million pension fund affiliates as of late 2007, but only 32 million (37 per cent) of the economically active population made regular payments. Some experts, therefore, suggested the minimum contribution for pension to be reduced, MPG to be made attractive, minimum rate of return, barriers to entry and liberal scheme for covering informal sector workers. Independent Evaluation Group (IEG 2006) evaluation has shown that post-reform participation increased somewhat in Chile and Colombia but plummeted in Argentina. Small gain in Bolivia was associated with the pension reform. One explanation for the stagnation of the coverage rates could be the presence of minimum guarantees which may encourage low-income workers to limit their years of contributions in the formal system. Others are high contribution rates and lack of economic growth. Some experts, therefore, suggested that minimum contribution for pension to be reduced, MPG to be made attractive, minimum rate of return, barriers to entry and liberal scheme for covering informal sector workers.

IMPACT OF REFORMS ON THE SIZE OF PENSION ASSETS

One of the most significant aspect of pension reforms and introduction of mandatory DC system is the rapid increase in the size of pension assets in the countries which have introduced pension reforms. Countries in Latin America and Central and Eastern Europe (CEE) which have introduced pension reform witnessed significant growth in pension assets. When pension reform was introduced in Chile, pension assets were less than 1 per cent. Though pension reform in CEE countries is comparatively recent, they are making significant progress, particularly Poland, Hungary and so on.

In CEE countries Polish pension market is the largest with 60 per cent market share, and the assets of Polish pension funds increased from zero in 1995 to almost USD$5

Table 3.2 Importance of Pension Funds Relative to the Size of the Economy of Countries

(as percentage of GDP)

Column 1	*Column 2*	*Column 3*	*Column 4*	*Column 5*	*Column 6*	*Column 7*	*Column 8*
Countries	*2002*	*2003*	*2004*	*2005*	*2006*	*2007*	*2009*
Argentina	11.3	13.5	12	4.7	–	11.5	11.6
Bolivia	15.5	20.9	19.5	9.2	21.6	22.2	
Brazil	9.3	13.1	12		15.5	17.1	18.8
Chile	55.8	64.5	64.4	64.9	61.01	64.4	72.2
Colombia	0.1	0.1	10.4	15.3	14.8	14.3	20.2
Mexico	4.9	5.7	6.3	7.2	–	12.1	10.0
Peru	8.1	10.6	11.4	12	–	18	18.7
Uruguay	9.3	11.4	12.7	12.8	–	14.7	
Hungary	4.5	5.3	6.8	8.5	9.71	10.9	13.1
Poland	4.2	5.5	7	8.7	11.03	12.2	13.5
Sweden	7.7	7.8		14.9	–	8.7	
Mauritius							
China			0.5	0.5	–	0.6	
India		0.2	5.3	5.3	–	5.4	

Source: International Federation of Pension Fund Administrators (FIAP) '20TH Bi-Annual Report', Santiago, Chile, June 2006.

billion in 2001 and almost USD$38 billion in 2006. Pension assets of Hungary increased from little over USD$2 billion in 2001 to almost USD$11 billion in 2006 (Hryckiewicz 2009). According to an estimate of Musalem and Baer (2010), pension assets in terms of GDP in Chile went up to 72.2 per cent while that of Colombia was 20.2 per cent, Brazil was 18.8 per cent and Peru was 18.7 per cent (Table 3.2). The growth of pension funds assets as a percentage of GDP in Latin American and in some CEE countries as shown in Table 3.2 looks impressive, particularly in Chile, Colombia, Poland, and so on., which are expected to increase further in the years to come as estimated by many authors. According to Palacios (2003), pension assets in 2015 are expected to reach 90 per cent of GDP in Chile, 44 per cent in Bolivia, 31 per cent in Argentina, 28 per cent in Peru, 26 per cent in Mexico, 25 per cent in Colombia and 13 per cent in Uruguay. Growth in pension assets is expected to provide strong support to growth in national savings, capital formation and growth in GDP.

IMPACT OF PENSION REFORMS ON SAVINGS, INVESTMENT AND GROWTH

Increased pension assets are expected to induce higher domestic savings, boost up capital formation and investment and thus economic growth rate in the country.

However, we are not sure about the impact of reforms on the voluntary savings through other channels. We have noticed in the previous section that the size of the pension assets significantly increased in the countries which have embarked upon pension reforms. Keeping these in view an attempt has been made here to examine the impact on some important macroeconomic indicators like growth rate in GDP, domestic savings, investment, capital formation and so on.

Impact on Savings Growth

One of the well-known arguments for pension reform through introduction of DB system is that it encourages individual savings for retirement income and thus gives a boost to domestic savings. This is possible since mandatory DC forces the workers to save for retirement income subject to the fact that it does not reduce the voluntary savings of the workers. Rise in national savings in the post-reform period will also depend on the rate of contribution to mandatory pension savings. If the rate of contribution is higher in the new system than that was in the pre-reform system, reform will boost up rate growth of national savings. Further, savings growth among others will also depend on the risk free rate of return generated by the pension funds. If the risk free return is higher than the return under PAYG and from other investment, investors will be induced to invest more in the voluntary component of the system giving a boost to national savings. Nature of coverage and system of taxation of the country will also have an impact on savings growth—higher coverage and tax incentives will have positive impact on savings growth. It has been argued that population ageing changes the savings behaviour of household as internal rate of return generated by PAYG pension system decreases which makes own savings as a vehicle for retirement income both necessary and attractive (Börsch-Supan et al. 2004). Savings growth will further depend on the growth in investment and GDP. Growth of savings determined by number of factors such as growth rate, domestic savings, incentives for savings, organisational efficiency to mobilise savings, aid flow and so on. A study of Dani Rodrik (1998) shows that savings transitions are associated with noticeable increase in both the investment and growth rates. The author concludes that growth transition tends to be followed by significant and sustained improvement in savings performance.

In our sample of countries in Latin America, Eastern Europe and Asia, higher growth of savings in terms of GDP has been noted in China and India during 1990 and 2008, which had initiated reforming their pension system in the 2000s. Countries which reformed their pension system earlier in the 1980s and 1990s have generated varied results; for example, significant rise was noted in Argentina, Bolivia and Peru while marginal increase was noted in Chile, Mexico, Uruguay and Poland. Savings in terms of GDP, however, declined in Brazil, Colombia and Poland. However, it is not clear how far this growth or decline was impacted by the pension reforms as the savings growth depends on a variety of factors like general economic environment, GDP growth rate, Investment and taxation regime and so on. There are several studies on the impact of pension reforms on national savings but there is no unanimity among the experts, though a general view is that reforms in general positively contribute to the growth of savings While some of these studies indicate positive impact of reforms on savings growth, others have differed. Jeanine Bailliu and Helmut Reisen (1997) also concluded in their study based on comparable cross-country data over 1982–93 and observed, 'the development of funded pension does indeed contribute to higher aggregate savings'. Bailliu and Reisen (1997) in their two-period life cycle model found evidence of such positive impact and observed

> *mandatory pension schemes will stimulate savings also with tax exempt return if the coverage of low is higher enough or if there are limits on eligibility so as to compensate or avoid the savings income effect of high savers enjoining tax breaks. Voluntary funded pension plans are unlikely to stimulate savings if returns are exempt from taxation.*

However, opposite views have been expressed by Holzmann (1997) who concluded that direct effect of financial market developments on the private savings rate was negative until 1989 and small afterwards. IEG of World Bank commented that the impact of multi-pillar reform on savings is inconclusive, '...the impact of a Chilean-type pension reform on private (national) saving may not hold'. Savings rate in Peru, Kazakhstan and Latvia increased. By contrast savings rate in Bolivia and Uruguay remain virtually unchanged, while rates in Colombia Hungary and Mexico declined. The relationship between pension reform and savings is complex. It depends on the way in which the fiscal deficit has been financed, the reaction of financial market and the reaction of workers (IEG 2006).

The recent trend in savings as percentage of GDP in the countries of our sample study of pension reform, shown in (Table 3.3), and the data do not clearly indicate any significant impact on pension reform on savings growth because the countries which have fully followed systemic reform, like India and China, have maintained high growth rate in savings. A similar view is expressed by Valdez (2011) who observed:

> *Empirical studies at the level of the majority of the countries that have adopted this (individually funded pension system) have not found a clear, positive relationship between the pension funds and national savings. A potentially positive effect depends on the macro economic situation, the special characteristics adopted by the reforms in the various countries and implementation of complementary structural reforms.*

Capital Formation

Increase in gross domestic savings is expected to influence the rate of growth of gross domestic investment and capital formation. But, various studies at different points of

Table 3.3 Gross Savings as Percentage of GDP

Country	*1990*	*2006*	*2007*	*2008*	*2009*	*2010*
Argentina	13	27	27	25	23	23
Bolivia	10	27	29	29	23	–
Brazil	19	18	18	19	15	15
Chile	23	25	25	23	21	–
Colombia	22	19	18	18	18	18
Mexico	20	26	25	25	21	20
Peru	16	23	24	24	26	23
Uruguay	14	16	17	16	17	18
Hungary	26	18	16	17	–	–
Poland	16	17	19	18	17	16
Sweden	22	27	29	30	24	–
Mauritius	–	17	21	16	13	13
China	39	52	52	53	54	51
India	22	35	37	33	35	28

Source: International Bank for Reconstruction and Development/The World Bank. World Development Indicators 2006 and 2010.

time suggest that there is no strong evidence to indicate that reforms have significantly influenced the rate of growth of savings and therefore it is difficult to say that pension reforms through mandatory DC will have very strong impact on capital formation. Data provided in the World Development Indicators (2006 and 2010) shows that there is mixed indication in the gross capital formation as percentage of GDP during 1990 and 2010. It has been noted in general that countries adopting parallel and mixed systems have a better record of capital formation than those who replaced PAYG by DC system. For example, gross capital formation as percentage of GDP increased in Argentina (14 per cent to 22 per cent), Colombia (19 per cent to 22 per cent), Uruguay (12 per cent to 19 per cent). On the other hand, countries following substitutive model fared badly as it declined in Chile (25 per cent to 24 per cent) and Mexico (23 per cent to 21 per cent), but increased marginally in Bolivia (14 per cent to 16 per cent). Further, some countries following mixed system of reform also witnessed decline in capital formation; for example, Sweden (24 per cent to 17 per cent) and Poland (26 per cent to 90 per cent) during 1990 to 2010 and Hungary (25 per cent to 22 per cent during 1990–2008). However, a significant rise in gross capital formation as percentage of GDP was noted in China (35 per cent to 45 per cent) and in India (24 per cent to 32 per cent) (World Development Indicators 2001 and 2010). These are the countries which had initiated pension reforms in early 2000s and basically follow a parallel reform model. The experience of China and India show that higher growth in savings and capital formation can be achieved without radical pension reform as followed in Chile and some other countries.

GDP Growth Rate

Pension reforms on the basis of multiple pillars have been advocated among others on the basis of expected growth effect due to removal of labour market distortions and sustainability of financial stability. According to economist Nicholas Barr (1994), the effects of a funded pension system on national savings, and hence economic growth, is 'arguably the most controversial area', and he further opined that the 'experience of countries in the West is inconclusive both theoretically and empirically'. However, some studies have indicated that pension reforms have lead to the decline of consumption and positive impact on growth rates. Corsetti and Schmidt-Hebbel observed that Chile's consumption (PC/GDP) declined by 21 percentage points from 1971 to 1992; they attributed half of it to pension reforms cum financial market deepening. It has been also noted that final consumption expenditure and per capita consumption increased in the countries, particularly in Chile during the later part of reforms, that is, 1990–99. However, there is no evidence that post reforms, GDP growth rate was better in LAC countries. In fact, rate of growth in Chile after reaching to 10.6 per cent in 1995 gradually declined to 4.5 per cent in 2000. Similarly, in Peru, the rate of growth rate of GDP (Table 3.4) declined from 12.8 per cent in 1994 to 3.1 per cent in 2000. Vial and Melguizo (2007) estimated that the per capita economic growth in Chile increased from just 1.8 per cent per year in 1966–85 to 4.8 per cent for 1986–2004 and the accumulated

Table 3.4 GDP Growth Rates

Column 1	*Column 2*	*Column 3*	*Column 4*	*Column 5*	*Column 6*	*Column 7*
	Average Annual Growth (per cent)	*Annual Growth Rate in GDP (per cent)*				
	1990–2000	*2006*	*2007*	*2008*	*2009*	*2010*
Argentina	4.3	8.5	8.7	6.8	0.9	9.2
Bolivia	4	4.8	4.6	6.1	3.4	4.2
Brazil	–	4.0	6.1	5.2	–0.6	7.5
Chile	6.6	4.6	4.6	3.7	–1.7	5.2
Colombia	2.8	6.7	6.9	3.5	1.5	4.3
Mexico	3.1	5.2	3.3	1.5	–6.1	5.5
Peru	–	7.7	8.9	9.8	0.9	8.8
Uruguay	3.4	4.3	7.3	8.6	2.6	8.5
Hungary	1.6	0.8	0.8	0.8	–6.7	1.2
Poland	4.6	6.2	6.8	5.1	1.7	3.8
Sweden	2.2	4.3	3.3	–0.6	–5.3	5.5
Mauritius		3.9	5.9	5.5	3.0	4.0
China	10.6	12.7	14.2	9.6	9.1	10.3
India	6	9.3	9.8	4.9	9.1	9.7

Source: International Bank for Reconstruction and Development/The World Bank. World Development Indicators 2006 and 2010.

increase in GDP in the first 20 years after the reforms ranges between 4 and 9 percentage points. According to Alonso et al. (2009), these countries could increase their per capita GDP between 1 per cent and 3.6 per cent by 2050 if they invested a higher percentage of portfolios in infrastructure.

IMPACT OF PENSION REFORMS ON CAPITAL MARKET DEVELOPMENT

Development of financial market in any economy is closely linked to the overall development of economy. While on the one hand economic development strongly supports the development of financial market, on the other hand a well-developed financial market also supports the economic growth, since a well-developed financial system of an economy acts as a clearing mechanism to facilitate pooling of resources, transfer of assets and settlement of payments, generating price signals for the market participants. A sound financial system must have speed, transparency and cost efficiency which should provide confidence to participating institutions and stability to the system.

Pension funds as institutional investors, therefore, can play an active and most needed necessary role in promoting financial and capital market, provide depth to it, channelise financial capital for most productive use in the system. Pension reform and privatisation of pension system has been advocated on the ground that they perform this role in a better manner in an environment free from political intervention. Private fund managers invest in diversified portfolio, thus creating demand for financial instruments of various kinds—equity- and debt-related new instruments, securitisation, indexed instruments and so on, and also support innovation of new financial instruments. It is also argued that increased demand for financial instruments like debt equity, and so on, for long-term investments provide immense financial support to corporate sector and provide impetus to the growth of industrial sector. Further, pension funds as institutional investors can play a very significant role in promoting transparency, improving quality of regulations and corporate governance. It has been noted in our earlier discussions that pension reform has accelerated the growth of pension assets in the countries which have reformed their pension system. Pension funds have thus emerged as the important institutional investors impacting the growth of capital market and supporting the improvement in quality of market governance.

Financial market development is closely related to stock market development and economic growth. A mature economy can hasten the process of resource allocation through stock market. In order to examine the changes in stock markets we have selected three important indicators viz. market capitalisation as percentage of GDP which indicates the market value, value traded as percentage of GDP which shows the condition of liquidity in the market and the turnover ratio of share traded as percentage of market capitalisation which is a measure of liquidity as well as transaction cost. Changes in all these parameters have been shown in the Table 3.5, which indicate a significant improvement during 1990–2010 in market capitalisation and liquidities in all

Table 3.5 Changes in Stock Markets

Column 1	*Column 2*	*Column 3*	*Column 4*	*Column 5*	*Column 6*	*Column 7*	*Column 8*	*Column 9*	*Column 10*	*Column 11*	*Column 12*
	Market Capitalization as percentage of GDP			*Market Liquidity (Value Traded as percentage of GDP)*			*Turnover Ratio (Value of share traded as percentage of Market Cap)*			*Listed Domestic Companies*	
Country	*1990*	*2006*	*2010*	*1990*	*2006*	*2010*	*1990*	*2006*	*2010*	*2006*	*2010*
Argentina	2.3	37.2	17.1	33.6	2.1	0.7	0.6	6.4	4.6	101	101
Bolivia	–	19.4.7	17.1	–	0	0.1	–	0	0.4	35	38
Brazil	–	65.3	74.0		23.4	43.2		42.9	66.4	392	373
Chile	45	118.9	176.9	6.3	19.6	26.7	2.6	18.5	19.7	224	227
Colombia	3.5	34.5	72.3	5.6	7	8	0.2	22.2	13.4	114	84
Mexico	12.5	21.5	25.4	44.0	8.4	10.4	4.6	27.3	27.3	131	130
Peru	3.1	19.9	29.3	19.3	4.6	2.6	0.4	8.9	4.7	193	199
Uruguay	–	0.8	2.5	–	0	0	–	1.6	–	10	6
Hungary	1.5	37.2	21.2	6.3	27.6	20.3	0.3	83.7	94.5	41	48
Poland	0.2	43.6	40.6	8	16.1	16.5	0	45.3	47.6	267	569
Sweden	–	143.6	126.9	–	169.7	96	–	138.6	86.8	321	331
Mauritius	–	55.3	66.9	–	2.1	3.7	–	4.4	6.4	41	86
China	0.5	89.4	81	14	60.3	136.6	0.2	102	164.4	1,440	2,063
India	12.2	86.1	93.5	65.9	67.1	61.1	6.9	93.1	75..6	4,796	4,987

Source: International Bank for Reconstruction and Development/The World Bank. World Development Indicators 2006 and 2010.

the countries. Stock market activities of pension funds were primarily influenced by the growth and accumulation of pension fund assets during the post-reform period which boost the demand for financial assets, particularly equity and debt. It can be noted from data in the Table 3.6 that there was a significant rise in market capitalisation in all the countries during 1990–2010. However, in many market the liquidity constraints (value traded) declined in recent times. Contribution of pension funds in capital market development has been noted by Roldos (2007) who states that 'the experience in the region suggests that regulatory limits on pension funds foreign investments have undoubtedly contributed to the development of local financial markets'.

However, this impact has largely been felt in the government bond market, and the rapid growth of pension funds has at times distorted the prices of domestic securities Vial and Melguizo (2007). He has also noted that the change in asset prices have risen significantly in Chile. According to his observation, the total value of traded stock has risen from 2.5 per cent of GDP in 1988 to 12.3 per cent in 2004 and the stock market capitalisation has gone up from 28.4 per cent of GDP to 124.4 per cent of GDP during the same period. Study of pension reforms and capital market development in CEE countries also provides a positive indication. Hryckiewicz (2009) noted, 'economically and statistically significant evidences on the positive effect of the pension reform in

Table 3.6 Pension Funds—Portfolio Composition as of December 2009

Type Assets	*Argentina*	*Brazil*	*Chile*	*Colombia*	*Mexico*	*Peru*	*Total****
Public Debt (National and Local government)	62.5	17.8	9.8	42	66.1	20.1	27.8
Financial Institutions	6.8	41.7	18.9	5.1	2.8	8.7	25.6
Non Financial Institutions	1.9	1.7	11.2	6.4	13.8	11.8	6
Stocks	9.8	16.8	13.9	31.7	9.1	31.2	16.4
Mutual Funds and Investment Funds	4.5	19.4	2.7	1.4	0	2.8	10.4
Foreign Assets	4.8	0	43.7	116	8.2	21	11.6
Others	9.7	2.6	0.3	1.8	0	4.5	2.2
Total Assets under Management (US$ million)	35,840	295,378	116,733	46,124	87,389	23,768	

Source: Musalem and Baer (2010).

CEE countries and stock market development in those countries'. The findings also suggest that much of the development on stock market growth has been achieved due to the pension reform. Effect of pension fund reforms on stock market capitalisation, stock market activity and bond market depth are statistically significant; for example, 'the increase of pension funds' assets by 1 per cent increases the stock market liquidity by almost 5 per cent and bond market capitalisation by 4 per cent. There is also positive effect of the pension reform on the stock market capitalisation. Holzmann (1997) also noted that pension reforms have positively impacted the growth of capital market as he says empirical findings are seemingly consistent with the claim that financial market developments enhanced economic growth and that pension reform has contributed to this development. However, contribution of pension funds to the development of capital market in general cannot be denied. Several studies have noted the influence of pension funds in developing qualitatively better market regulations, institutional development (custodian services, electronic exchange, and so on), promoting new financial instruments like mortgage bonds, corporate bonds, and so on, exerting influence to promote corporate governance standard, and so on.

However, many experts expressed opposite view about the impact of pension reforms on capital market development. Despite reforms in capital market and pension industry in Latin American countries, capital markets in many countries still remained underdeveloped as compared to developed and other emerging economies. The contribution of pension funds in market liquidity in Chile has been overestimated by many analysts and pension funds are not very active traders, either in stocks or bonds. Moreover, the increasing concentration of the Chilean industry in the 1990s probably further aggravated the liquidity problem (Dayoub and Lasgabaster 2008). Similar observation was made in the IEG (2006) study,

> *so far, most capital markets have not developed significantly as a result of multi-pillar pension reform, even when financial sector and capital market has improved. Capital market development relied on equity market development. Still equity markets development has not proceeded in Colombia, or Hungary although there has been growth in Peru. Mexican equity market declined in the post reform period from being one of the strongest in Latin America.*

Data in Table 3.7 shows the recent changes in market capitalisation, market liquidity, turnover ratio and the number of listed companies in the countries studied by us.

FISCAL IMPACT

One of the strongest arguments in favour of pension reforms and introduction of DC system is that it would correct long-term fiscal imbalance and would reduce the pressure on the exchequer. Reforms reduced the role of state in providing the old-age income and encouraged/forced the individual to save for own income. However, it has not been very clear how far this objective has been achieved. Since most of the countries except Chile do not have long track record, it may take little longer time to realise the real impact on fiscal sustainability. What we have at present are contradictory views. While some authors have opined that overall, the long-run fiscal sustainability of pension systems has significantly increased as a result of structural reforms. According to Zviniene and Packard (2002), Bolivia, Chile, El Salvador and Mexico showed the largest falls in the implicit pension debt since the reform closed the PAYG

Table 3.7 Post-Reform Challenges

Post Reform Issue	*Countries*
Low Coverage	Argentina (declining), Peru, Kazakhstan, Kyrgyz Republic, Russia (declining)
Lack of Poverty Alleviation	Mexico, Uruguay, China, Russia, Bulgaria (Women)
Continuing Fiscal Deficit	Argentina, Bolivia, Brazil, Uruguay, Korea (Long term)
Limited Actuarial Capacity	Mexico, Uruguay, Kyrgyz Republic
Under developed Financial Sector	China, Uruguay, Bulgaria, FYR Macedonia, Russia
High Commission	Hungary, Peru
Additional Pension Systems	Mexico, Peru
High Benefits	Brazil, Peru
Administrative Capacity Assistance Untimely and Ineffective	Hungary and Latvia

Source: International Bank for Reconstruction and Development/The World Bank: 'Pension Reform and Development of Pension Systems, An Evaluation of World Bank,' The World Bank, Washington DC 2006.

pillar, but the implicit pension debt also declined in the countries where PAYG pillar was retained with the rationalisation of public pillar. However, IEG (2006) has noted that in a number of countries including Argentina, Bolivia, Mexico, Peru and Uruguay insufficient parametric reforms in civil service pension and other PAYG plans created unsustainable pension deficits. Vial and Melguizo (2007) echoed the same view as IEG in case of Chile in respect to civil service pension burden. They observed that there was a major rise in the civilian pension deficit after reform but

> *what was remarkable in the case of Chile, besides the extra ordinary increase in fiscal outlays in pension,...the overall tax burden was falling by about 10 per cent point of GDP.... In spite of this trends fiscal accounts have remained in surplus for most of the time since the end of the 80s. Vial and Melguizo (2007)*

FINANCIAL DEEPENING

There is a close correlation between financial market development and financial deepening. Financial deepening promotes financial and capital markets, increases the depth and free flow of service delivery on the one hand and on the other hand expands the network of services geographically to cover all sector of the economy and segments of the society. Financial institutions play the critical role in the process of financial deepening by creating financial instruments, financial processes and financial service transmission mechanisms. Pension funds are distinctive institutional investors which induce long-term retirement savings in the country, mobilise the same from the saving market and create assets by investing in the capital market. Pension reforms can significantly influence financial deepening by creating continuous demand for financial instruments for long-term investment by the pension funds. Data in Table 3.6 shows that there was significant improvement in the important financial market indicators like turnover in equity assets, value of stock market asset like equity and so on. We have also noted significant increase in the size of pension funds which influenced financial market deepening. The most important indicator of financial intermediation is the M7-M1, that is, total financial instruments minus liquid money. Cifuentes et al. (2002) have shown that pension reform strongly supported financial deepening in Chile. During the period 1981 to 2000, annual trading value in terms of GDP in stocks, fixed income securities and financial intermediation went up from 1.39 per cent to 8.92 per cent, 0.35 per cent to 64.47 per cent, and 5.54 per cent to 191.83 per cent respectively. Stock market valuation (market capitalisation) went up from 41.87 per cent to 91.74 per cent. Assets of institutional investors such as insurance companies, pension funds and mutual funds in terms of GDP went up from 1.19 per cent to 16.74 per cent, 1.16 per cent to 53.85 per cent and 2.62 per cent to 6.77 per cent, respectively, while M7-M1 went up from 27.72 per cent in 1981 to 87.53 per cent in 2000 in Chile. Privately managed pension funds with huge assets at their command created significant demand for equity, debt securities, money market instruments, mutual funds and annuity products supplied by life insurance companies. During the post-reform period, the Chilean capital market had grown remarkably in size, depth and liquidity and the private pension system was at the root of this important transformation (Cifuentes et al. 2002).

PROMOTING MARKET COMPETITION

One of the desired objectives of pension reforms and privatisation of pension system is to generate higher rate of return, through competitive fund management system. It is expected that a competitive environment in fund management industry by allowing more fund managers will promote competition which in turn will reduce fund management and other costs as well to generate higher rate of return. However, in reality such an objective was not realised and in course of time fund management industry came under the control of a few fund managers. An analysis of market share of fund managers indicates the nature of concentration. Over the period of time there has been a decline in the number of pension fund managers and gradually the market has been concentrated in the hands of few fund managers. As in June 2006, more than 50 per cent of pension funds are concentrated in the top two fund managers, for example, Brazil (56.87 per cent), Columbia (51.87 per cent), Chile (55.28 per cent), Peru (68.50 per cent), Uruguay (74.24 per cent) and Bolivia (100 per cent). Further, the top three fund managers cornered more than 70 per cent funds in Chile (72.53 per cent), Peru (94.04 per cent) and Uruguay (91.60) (FIAP 2006).

The share of the three largest AFPs was 70.3 per cent in 1998. Rates of return on AFPs' own capital—not to be confused with the rates of return on pension funds managed by AFPs or on pension assets held in individual accounts, analysed below—became positive and very high after being negative during the first three years of start-up of the system, when the scale of operation was low and marketing costs were high. Very high returns of 39–48 per cent in real terms on AFPs' own capital reaped during 1989–91 prompted a massive entry into the industry, a substantial reduction in subsequent returns to more normal levels and, again, to industry concentration. (Schmidt-Hebbel 1999). It has also been observed by Dayoub and Lasgabaster (2008) that this concentration has increased over time through mergers and acquisitions. Further, the concentration is significant in countries with small size funds, namely in Bolivia, Peru and Uruguay. Market concentration often comes in the way to promote fair competition which is not in the interest of investors and the reform may fail to generate desired result of fair play by the fund managers, risk management and risk adjusted higher return.

IMPACT OF PENSION REFORMS ON PORTFOLIO DIVERSIFICATION, ASSETS ALLOCATION, INVESTMENT RETURN AND MARKET EFFICIENCY

One of the major arguments for pension reforms is that it liberalises investment regime with greater scope for investment in equity and equity-related instruments which enable the funds to earn better rate of return. The DB public pension mostly invests its funds in government securities, which earn relatively lower return but have wider investment opportunities under privately managed DC scheme. But they also have the potential for higher return and reduction of market risks through portfolio diversification. It is also argued that induction of private fund managers impart efficiency in fund management, hence reduced costs and increased risk-adjusted return. Private pension funds are also allowed to invest in foreign securities which provide further scope for portfolio diversification and opportunity for better return.

Trend in Asset Allocation

However, in reality wider asset diversification and larger equity investment have not been found in newly reformed Latin American countries. Most of the Latin American countries still invest a larger portion of assets in government sector, followed by financial sector. Investment in corporate and foreign remained quite low. It has been noted that in most of the countries pension funds invested a very large portion of assets in the government sector, highest being 84 per cent in Uruguay followed by Mexico 78 per cent, Bolivia 76 per cent and the lowest of 15 per cent by Chile, investment in foreign assets remained below 10 per cent, though it was the highest at 31.21 per cent in Chile, followed by Colombia (31.2 per cent) in 2006 (FIAP 2006). Though strong arguments are forwarded in favour of portfolio diversification and higher investment equities, it is observed in reality that fund managers are very cautious about investing in high risk equities and prefer to invest larger portion of assets in debt instruments. It can be seen from Table 3.6 that equity investment varied between 9 per cent and 31 per cent, the highest being in Chile (31.7 per cent) and the lowest in Brazil (1.7 per cent). On an average investment equity was 16.4 per cent in Latin America. Average investment foreign securities accounted for 11.6 per cent of portfolio, the highest being in Chile at 43.7 per cent followed by Peru at 21 per cent. Mutual fund is a preferred instrument in Brazil at 19.4 per cent. However, investment in financial institutions was second-most preferred instrument (25.6 per cent) next to national debt (27.8 per cent).

It is obvious that the pension funds portfolio is not well diversified in most of the countries and concentration in debt and financial institutions has been noted in most of the countries except Chile. Further, investment in non-financial corporate sector was also minimal. Diversification in Europe and Central Asia was also limited—Hungarian pension fund invested roughly 70 per cent of their assets in government bonds in mid-2003, Polish pension funds invested roughly 60 per cent of assets in government bonds in 2002 (IEG 2007). However, pension funds investment is strictly guided by investment regulation which allows the funds to invest a higher amount in debt instruments. In addition to the quantitative regulation, opportunities in domestic market are also limited due to underdevelopment of capital market as noted earlier.

Investment Return

The proponent of fully privatised pension system strongly argued that private asset managers were in a better position to provide higher return on retirement income. One of the arguments in favour of higher return through privatisation is based on the investment of pension funds in equity. To support the argument of superior return by equity portfolio, they often quote the return of equity in the US market but the return of the US equity should not be taken as the bench market in case of emerging markets like India. In respect of development, efficiency and maturity, emerging markets are much behind the US market. Further the return that was quoted in respect of the US market is the long-term return, and the same may not hold true for a country with a history of recent development of capital market and market capitalism. Evidence suggests that that mostly did not happen in many new systems primarily due to very high operating costs and absence of a mature capital market. While giving his testimony, as mentioned above, Stephen J. Kay said,

> *(for Chile) the figures usually cited shows that pension funds have produced a real average annual return of 11 per cent since 1981, but these are gross returns. Once commissions are factored in, the real average return is considerably lower. Valente (2008) reported that since the creation of Chile's multi-fund system in 2002, returns have ranged between 2.8 and 4.2 per cent depending on the level of risk exposure. But if measured since 1981, returns have averaged 8.8 per cent.*

IEG (2007) report reveals that gross rates of return for the funded pillars of many countries have been favourable compared to wage growth—a proxy for the implicit rate of return to the PAYG. Real rate of return since inception in Argentina is 11.7 per cent, in Bolivia is 16.2 per cent and in Chile it is 10.5 per cent. In many countries, high returns are a result of high interest on government bonds. Willmore and Bertucci (1999), by following Samuelson–Aaron Rule, demonstrated that return from the PAYG system may be higher than privately managed pension portfolio. Out of the 13 countries studied, returns on unfounded public pension for the period 1967–90 was higher in the 5 countries that held private portfolios.

Fund Management Efficiency

One of the important arguments in favour of managing pension funds by private fund managers is that it would impart competition, reduce cost, improve rate of return through improved efficiency in fund management. However, in reality this expectation was mostly not fulfilled and efficiency in fund management was doubtful as noted by Barrientos and Boussofiane (2001). In their study (for the period 1982–99) of pension fund managers efficiency in Latin America, they observed that over all the pension fund management market is inefficient as pension fund managers could have produced the same level of output with around 35 per cent fewer assets.

There has been a structural weakness in the new system as it failed to generate enough competitive environments and to operate a low-cost system. Moreover, private fund managers in many countries failed to beat the public system in terms of rate of return. Even the much talked about coverage expansion through privatised DC system did not materialise. However, the performance of NDC structure in Sweden and Poland was better than Latin American countries. We can, however, conclude by quoting IMF working paper on pension reform: 'It is clear that adoption of a DC/EF scheme does not simply indicate that the issue of redistributional or addressing the basic needs of elderly that were not participants in the DC/EF scheme can be ignored.'

FINANCIAL MARKET TURMOIL, 2007–2008 AND PRIVATE PENSION FUNDS

An intense debate has emerged during post-crisis period about ongoing pension reforms on two counts: (*a*) long-term viability of fully mandatory DC system totally replacing the DB system, and (*b*) designing pension fund portfolio heavily biased in favour of equity. It has been noted during 2008 turmoil that countries with fully DC system and investing a significantly large amount of assets in equity have suffered most in terms of decline of pension fund assets. It has been reported by OECD (2008) that total assets of all pension funds by October 2008 had declined by US$3.3 trillion (nearly 20 per cent) compared to December 2007, out of which only the United States lost US$2.2 trillion. This decline was severe in countries having higher exposure in equities; for example, Irish pension funds with 66 per cent investment in equities. Similar decline was also noted in emerging countries, particularly those that have reformed the pension system by introducing mandatory private pension system.

Crisis in the financial market has also negatively impacted pension funds industry in emerging country markets including Latin America. For example, assets of private pension funds in Chile shrunk from US$94.3 billion on 31 October 2007 to US$69.1 billion on 31 October 2008 (Valente 2008). As reported by Marcel and Tapia (2009), total pension funds in December 2008 reduced by US$52 billion compared to December 2007, the highest impact being felt in Chile, which lost 33 per cent aggregate value of pension funds. A similar fall was also noted in aggregate value in other countries; for example, 23 per cent in Argentina, 15 per cent in Uruguay, 11 per cent in Mexico and so on. Marcel and Tapia (2009) also pointed out that real investment during December 2007–08 declined by 40.3 per cent to 0.9 per cent for various funds in Chile, 9.3 per cent to 0.1 per cent in Mexico, and 42 per cent to 10.2 per cent in Peru. However, countries with mixed system have suffered the least for example Uruguay and others which reformed the pension system and introduced the DC system also retained the old PAYG DBs.

Financial crisis also had an adverse effect on coverage which was felt in 2009. Marcel and Tapia have mentioned that the number of contributors in the Latin American pension system was reduced by 900,000 during December 2008–June 1009. This decline is correlated to decline in employment due to the financial crisis. Therefore ILO (*World Social Security Report* 2010/11) suggested correction. The report states, 'The degree of vulnerability of future pension levels to the performance of capital markets and other economic fluctuations, introduced in so many pension systems during the last three decades, was clearly a mistake that stands to be corrected.' Strong MPGs, which act as 'automatic stabilisers' seem to be an effective instrument in maintain living standard of retired people. Towards correction ILO suggested rebuilding trust in DB schemes, rebalancing pension systems in their DB/DC and Funded/PAYG mixes, reforming of public pension system and so on.

Recent experience of reforms in many emerging countries showed that many of the desired objectives like increased pension coverage, providing risk-free higher return through equity weighted pension portfolio, and so on, have not been achieved. Further vulnerability of private pension fund portfolio with higher equity component in a totally DC system was exposed during recent turmoil (2007–08). Many experts and organisations including ILO have signalled the need for fresh rethinking about ongoing pension reforms. Further, the World Bank evaluation report also pointed out many shortcomings in implementation of multi-pillar system, which deserve immediate attention of the government, policymakers and authorities responsible for implementation of pension reforms. It is high time a thorough evaluation of the process is undertaken and necessary correction is introduced. It is also an important lesson for the countries which have recently introduced pension reforms or are on the verge of reforming the pension system.

CHALLENGES IN NEWLY REFORMED COUNTRIES

We have in the foregoing sections discussed about some of critical issues associated with pension reforms like pension coverage; impact of reforms on domestic savings, investment and growth; development of capital market, fiscal sustainability, financial deepening and so on. We have referred various studies to examine the impact of reforms. Though many positive developments have taken place in the countries studied by us, in most of the countries the reform process is still evolving and most of the expected results are yet to take place, though reform initiatives have been successful in creating awareness about impending crisis due to changing demographic dynamics but have failed to a large extent to achieve the major objectives. There are critics of the multi-pillar reforms who doubt the outcomes. As Willmore (2002) states,

> *[T]he privatisation promoted by the World Bank, which favors defined contribution schemes and individual accounts, does nothing to expand coverage. On the contrary, it typically results in decreased coverage because benefits are linked more tightly to contributions, so there is less redistribution and less reason for the poor to participate.*

Similarly, International Confederation of Free Trade Unions ([ICFTU] 2003) is also very critical about the new system and their outcomes, and states,

> *Privatised DC funded pension systems substantially alter the nature of the state's commitment to support workers in retirement, often producing more inequity and shifting more risk onto workers. In many cases workers risk receiving considerably lower benefits than they would have received under the public systems that were replaced.*

These critical views, should however not be set aside totally, but should be examined with patience to find out the weakness of the reform model and challenges thrown before us for further refinement. IEG, World Bank (2008) listed out several challenges confronted by various countries during the post reforms. The major challenges are low coverage, lack of poverty alleviation, continuing fiscal deficits, high commission rates, limited actuarial capacity and so on. Low coverage is an issue in countries like Argentina and Peru. In fact Argentina has witnessed decline in coverage. Poverty alleviation is an issue in Mexico, Uruguay and China while fiscal deficit continued even after reform in Argentina, Bolivia, Brazil and Uruguay (Table 3.7).

These problems can, however, be solved through further reform on the basis of current experience. Pension reform has long-term significance and impact on the life of millions; therefore, it needs to be articulated with a very long-term perspective by keeping in view the economic welfare along with implicit financial constraint. Pension reform should not be thought of as balance sheet measures but in terms of national welfare account.

REFERENCES

Alonso, Javier, Jasmina Bjeletic, Carlos Herrera, Soledad Hormazabal, Ivonne Ordóñez, Carolina Romero, David Tuesta and Alfonso Ugarte (2009), Projections of the 'Impact of Pension Funds on Investment in infrastructure and Growth in Latin America1'. BBVA Working Paper, Economic Research Department No. 1002.

Bailliu, Jeanine and Helmut Reisen (1997), 'Do Funded Pension Contribute Higher Aggregate Savings? A Cross Country Analysis'. Technical Paper No. 130, OECD Development Centre, December 1997. Available at: www.oecd.org/dev/Publication/Tp130.pdf.

Barr, Nicholas (1994), 'Income Transfers: Social Insurance', in Nicholas Barr (eds), *Labour Markets and Social Policy in Eastern Europe: The Transition and Beyond.* New York: Oxford University Press.

Barrientos, Armando and Aziz Boussofiane (2001), 'Efficiency of Pension Fund Managers in Latin America'. Working Paper No. 11, Centre on Regulation and Competition, Institute for Development Policy and Management, University of Manchester. Available at: http://idpm.man.ac.uk/crc/.

Börsch-Supan, Axel, Jens Köke and Joachim Winter (2004), 'Pension Reform, Savings Behavior and Capital Market Performance'. MEA Discussion Paper Series 04053, Mannheim Research Institute for the Economics of Aging, University of Mannheim.

Clavijo, Sergio (2009), 'Social Security Reforms in Colombia: Striking Demographic and Fiscal Balances'. Western Hemisphere Department, IMF.

Cifuentes, Rodrigo (2003), 'Tax Incentives for Retirement Savings: Macro and Welfare Effects in an OLG-GE Model with Liquidity Constraints and Heterogeneous Consumers'. Central Bank of Chile Working Paper No. 242. Available at: http://www.bcentral.cl/estudios/documentos-trabajo/pdf/dtbc242.pdf.

Cifuentes, Rodrigo, Jorge Desormeaux and Claudio González (2002), 'Capital Markets in Chile: from Financial Repression to Financial Deepening'. The Development of Bond Markets in Emerging Economies No. 11, 86–102, Bank for International Settlements.

Dayoub, Mariam and Esperanza Lasagabaster (2008), 'General Trends in Competition Policy and Investment Regulation in Mandatory Defined Contribution Markets in Latin America'. Policy Research Working Paper No. 4720 of the World Bank, Latin America and Carribbean Region Finance and Private Sector Development Unit, September 2008.

FIAP (2006), *20th Bi-Annual Report.* International Federation of Pension Fund Administrators, Santiago, Chile, June 2006.

Gill, Indermit, Truman Packard and Juan Yermo (2005), *Keeping the Promise of Social Security in Latin America.* California: Stanford University Press.

Holzmann, Robert (1997), 'Pension Reform, Financial Market Development, and Economic Growth: Preliminary Evidence from Chile'. International Monetary Fund Staff Paper, 44(2), June 1997, Washington, DC.

Hryckiewicz, Aneta (2009), 'Pension Reform, Institutional Investors' Growth and Stock Market Development in the Developing Countries Does it Function?' Available at SSRN: http://ssrn.com/abstract=1370886 (31 March 2009).

Independent Evaluation Group (IEG) (2006), *Pension Reform and the Development of Pension System—An Evaluation of World Bank Assistance.* Washington DC: The World Bank.

——— (2007), *The Development Potential of Regional Programs: An Evaluation of World Bank Support of Multicountry Operations.* Washington DC: The World Bank.

International Bank for Reconstruction and Development/The World Bank (2006), 'Pension Reform and Development of Pension Systems'. *An Evaluation of World Bank.* Washington DC: The World Bank.

International Confederation of Free Trade Unions (ICFTU) (2003), 'World Bank Involvement in the Privatisation of Public Pension Systems in Developing and Transition Countries'. Available at: http://www.eurodad.org/articles/default.aspx?id=474.

International Labour Organisation (ILO) (2010), *World Social Security Report 2010/11—Providing Coverage in Times of Crisis and Beyond.* Geneva: International Labour Office.

Marcel, Mario and Waldo Tapia (2009), 'The Impact of Financial Crisis of Private Pension Funds in Latin American Countries'. In Pension Reform and Developments in Latin America-Conference Proceedings of the OECD/IOPS Global Forum on Private Pension, Rio de Janeiro, Brazil, 2009.

Mesa-Lago, Carmelo (2002). 'Reassessing Pension Reform in Chile and Other Countries in Latin America'. Available at: http://www.adb.org/Documents/Events/2002/SocialProtection/lago_paper.pdf.

——— (2007), *Reassembling Social Security—A Survey of Pension and Health Care Reforms in Latin America.* New York: Oxford University Press.

Musalem, R. Alberto and Fernando Baer (2010), 'Latin American Pension Funds Investing in Private Equity and Venture Capital'. Working Paper No. 36, Centre for Financial Stability, New York, July 2010.

OECD (2008), 'Pension Markets in Focus'. Issue 5, December 2008.

Palacios, R. J. (2003), 'Pension Reforms in Latin America: Design and Experiences'. *Pension Reforms: Results and Challenges,* International Federation of Pension Fund Administrators, Santiago, Chile.

Pedro, Jucá Maciel (2010), 'Social Security in Brazil: Importance, Problems and Reform Agenda'. Available at: www.pedrojucmaciel.com.

Rodrik, Dani (1998), 'Saving Transition'. World Bank Research Project on Saving. Available at: http://siteresources.worldbank.org/INTMACRO/Resources/rodpaper.pdf.

Roldos, Jorge (2007), 'Pension Reform and Macroeconomic Stability in Latin America'. IMF Working Paper No. 07/108.

Schmidt-Hebbel, Klaus (1999), *Latin America's Pension Revolution: A Review of Approaches and Experience.* Central Bank of Chile, prepared for the World Bank's ABCDE Conference, Washington, DC, 28–30 April 1999.

Shen, Ce and John B. Williamson (2010), 'China's New Rural Pension Scheme: Can It Be Improved?' Available at: www.emeraldinsight.com/0144-333X.htm.

Tapia, W. and J. Yermo (2008), 'Fees in Individual Account Pension Systems: A Cross-Country Comparison'. OECD Working Papers on Insurance and Private Pensions, No. 27. Paris: OECD publishing.

Valdez, Hector (2011), 'Impact of the Pension Funds on Economic Growth: The Case of the Dominican Republic'. In *Advancing in the Strengthening and Consolidation of the Individually—Funded Pension System.* Santiago, Chile: FIAP.

Valente, Marcela (2008), 'Latin America: Future of Private Pension Funds in Doubt'. Available at: http://ipsnews.net/news.asp?idnews=44872 (accessed on 9 September 2010).

Vial, Joaquin and Angel Melguizo (2007), 'Moving from Pay As You Go to Privately Managed Individual Pension Accounts: What Have We Learned After 25 years of the Chilean Pension Reform?' BBVA Economic Research Department's Working Paper No. 0805.

Whitehouse, Edward (1999), 'The Tax Treatment of Funded Pensions'. Social Protection Discussion Paper Series. Washington DC: The World Bank.

Willmore, Larry (2006), 'Universal Pensions for Developing Countries'. *World Development,* 35(1). Available at: www.elsevier.com/locate/worlddev.

Willmore, Larry N. and Guido Bertucci (1999), 'Public versus Private Provision of Pensions'. Revised DESA Discussion Paper No. 1, Department of Economic and Social Affairs, United Nations.

Zviniene, A. and T. Packard (2002), 'A Simulation of Social Security Reforms in Latin America: What Has Been Gained?' Background Paper for the Regional Study on Social Security Reforms, LAC Region. Washington DC: The World Bank.

SECTION TWO

Social Security and Pension Reforms in India

NPS in a Changing Socio-Economic Environment

4 Changing Trend in Economy, Demography and Ageing in India

INTRODUCTION

The brief review of pension and social security reforms in Section One indicates that social security management has emerged as one of the most crucial and strategic issues in macroeconomic management. Due to rapid growth of elderly population and unsustainable fiscal burden of Pay-as-You-Go (PAYG)/Defined Benefit (DB) pension system, it is unsustainable in the long run and continuation of the same would lead the economy into dangerous pension crisis. Another problem, particularly in the emerging economy countries, is the poor coverage of the traditional pension system. Pension is primarily a social security issue and the sociopolitical environment of different countries differs to a significant extent, so the solution cannot be uniform and therefore there is variation in the reform design. The concern for promoting a sustainable pension and social security system emerged as a universal phenomenon irrespective of economic structure and system of macroeconomic management due to increased longevity, ageing and lack of enough state resources to support the PAYG system. India is not an exception to this global phenomenon and ageing is catching up fast and the burden of social security would be unsustainable in the years to come. However, to understand the nature of pension problems in India and potential crisis due to demographic transition let us look into the existing socioeconomic environment in the following paragraphs.

CHANGING TREND IN KEY DEVELOPMENT INDICATORS

Population

India is the largest democracy and the second-most populous country in the world. In terms of population, India is next to China. India occupies only 2.4 per cent of the world's land area but is inhabited by 17.5 per cent of world population. In 1950–51, population of India was only 359 million, but it increased significantly during the subsequent years. According to provisional census data, population of India in 2011 was

1.21 billion (1,210.19 million) as against 1.34 billion population of China. Indian Census 2011 has estimated that out of 1,210.19 million population, 623.72 million were male and 586.46 million were female and for 1,000 males there were 940 females (Sex Ratio) (Table 4.1).

India has witnessed the sharpest fall in decadal population growth during 2001–11. The decadal growth of population for India as a whole has declined from 23.87 per cent in 1981–91 to 21.54 per cent in 1991–01 to 17.64 per cent in 2001–11 (Census 2011). While birth rate declined from 33.9 in 1981 to 29.5 in 1991 and further to 22.5 in 2009 per 1,000 population, the death rate declined at a much sharper rate from 27.4 in 1981, to 7.4 in 1991 and further to 7.3 per 1,000 population in 2009 (Figure 4.1).

Life Expectancy

Due to the various socioeconomic measures of the government and increase in per capita income, etc., India has witnessed a sharp increase in life. Overall life expectancy at birth has improved significantly in India—32.5 years in 1950–51 to 55.4 years in 1981–85 to 63.5 during 2002–06. Life expectancy of the male and the female during

Table 4.1 Selected Population Indicators

Indicator	*1991*	*2001*	*2011*
Total Population (in millions)	846	**1,029**	**1,210**
Rural	629	743	833
Urban	217	286	377
Male	439	532	624
Female	407	497	586
Annual Growth Rate (%)	2.14	1.97	1.64
Density of Population (Per Sq. Km.)	274	324	382
Sex Ratio (Males per 1,000 females)	927	933	940
Literacy Rate			
Person	52.21	64.83	74.04
Male	64.13	75.26	82.14
Female	39.29	53.26	65.46
Age Structure			
0–14 years	37.3%	35.3%	29.7%*
15–59 years	55.5%	56.9%	64.9%**
60 years and over	6.7	7.5%	
65 years and over*			**5.5%**

Sources: The Registrar General & Census Commissioner, Ministry of Home Affairs, Government of India, 'Provisional Population Totals Paper 1 of 2011 India Series' (http://www.censusindia.gov.in/2011-prov-results/prov_results_paper1_india.html); *Population Composition—Census of India* (www.censusindia.gov.in/vital_statistics/srs/Chap_2_-_2010.pdf); Central Intelligence Agency (2012), *The World Fact Book*, 13 September 2012 (https://www.cia.gov/library/publications/the-world-factbook/geos/in.html).
Note: *Central Intelligence, *The World Fact Book* (2011); **for the age group 65 years and over.

Figure 4.1 Changing Trend of Birth and Death Rates

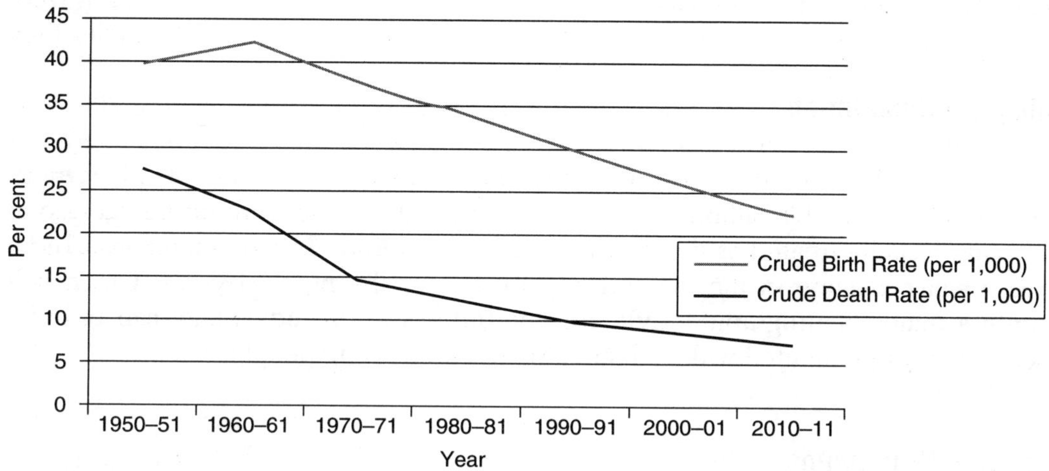

Source: Census of India (2011).

Figure 4.2 Life Expectancy at Birth

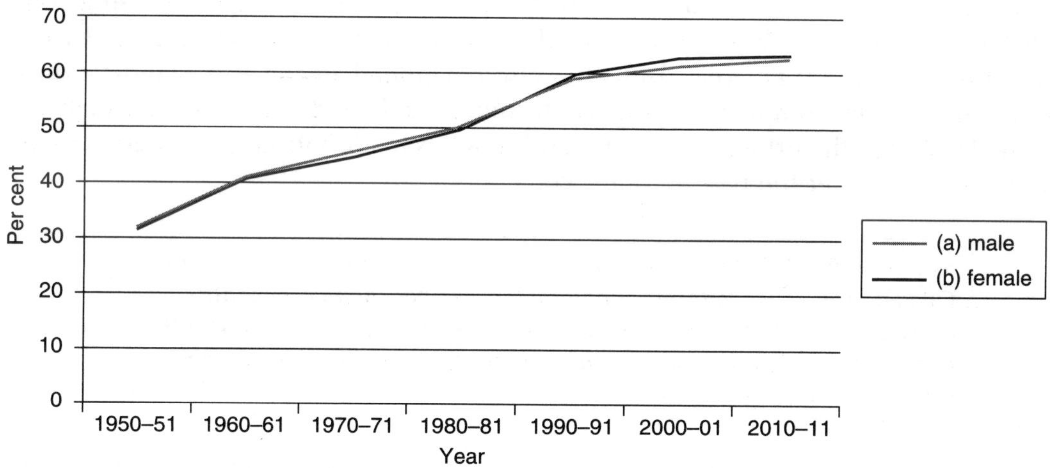

Source: Census of India (2011).

2002–06 was 62.6 years and 64.2 years respectively (Figure 4.2). Estimated population density in 2011 was 382 persons per square kilometre (Census 2011).

Rural and Urban Population

There has been a decline in rural population during 2001–11. Rural population declined from 72.19 per cent to 68.84 per cent while urban population increased from

27.81 per cent to 31.16 per cent. Of the 121 crore Indians, 83.3 crore live in rural areas while 37.7 crore stay in urban areas.

Working-Age Population

According to the Economic Survey 2010–11, India is a nation of young people. Out of a population of above 1.1 billion, 672 million (2009–10) people were in the age group 15–59 years (usually treated as the 'working-age' population). It is predicted that India will see a sharp decline in the dependency ratio over the next 30 years, which will constitute a major 'demographic dividend' for India. But this advantage can only be realised if it is supplemented with skill enhancement of young people.

Health-Care Programme

The health management system in India is a combined initiative of the public and private sectors, with some support by the non-governmental organisations (NGOs). Over the years India has developed a three-tier public health infrastructure, comprising community health centres (CHCs), primary health centres (PHCs) and sub-centres spread across rural and semi-urban areas. India has also developed a wide and well-developed medical care system comprising specialty hospitals and medical colleges, which are primarily located in the urban areas. Though India has made substantial progress in the health-care system over the past decades, yet

> *as per HDR 2010, India fares poorly when compared to countries like China and Sri Lanka in terms of parameters like per capita expenditure on health, number of physicians/hospital beds (per 10,000 persons), and IMR. In addition, within the country, the improvement has been quite uneven across. (Economic Survey 2010–11)*

The private sector plays a dominant role in the delivery of health services in the country, around 70 per cent of all hospitals and 37 per cent of total beds in the country are in the private sector. The major initiatives of government of India to provide affordable health care and to bridge the gap in existing health infrastructure mentioned are discussed in brief as has been discussed in the following paragraphs.

❖ NATIONAL RURAL HEALTH MISSION (NRHM)

One of most important health programmes in India is the NRHM, launched in 2005.

to provide accessible, affordable, and accountable quality health services to rural areas with emphasis on poor persons and remote areas. The NRHM aims to provide an overarching umbrella to the existing programmes of health and family welfare including the reproductive child health project (RCH-II) and malaria, blindness, iodine deficiency, filaria, kala azar, T.B., leprosy and integrated disease surveillance programmes by strengthening the public health delivery system at all levels. (NRHM website: http://www.mohfw.nic.in/NRHM/Documents/Mission_Document.pdf)

❖ JANANI SURAKSHA YOJANA (JSY)

The JSY is a centrally sponsored scheme launched with a view to bring down the maternal mortality rate (MMR) by ensuring that deliveries are conducted by skilled birth attendants. The scheme focuses on improvement in manpower, training and strengthening of infrastructure, and this has resulted in significant improvement of institutional deliveries. The JSY scheme has grown rapidly in the last three years, with the number of beneficiaries reaching 100.78 lakh in 2009–10. The government also launched Integrated Child Development Services (ICDS) in 1975 for holistic development of children below six years of age and for proper nutrition and health education of pregnant and lactating mothers with 33 projects and 4,891 Anganwadi centres (AWCs). There are other programmes like ASHAs/Link Workers Programme, the Revised National TB Control Programme (RNTCP), National Vector Borne Diseases Control Programme (NVBDCP) and National Programme for Control of Blindness (NPCB), etc.

Future Population Growth in India

With the decline in fertility rate from 3.0 in 2001–06 to 2.2 in 2051–56 and further to 2.1 in 2096–2101, India's population is projected to rise to1.82 billion in 2051 and thereafter decline to 2.18 billion, according to Population Foundation of India (2007) study. India is a young country having more than 50 per cent of its population below the age of 25 and more than 65 per cent below the age of 35. However, it is expected that in 2020 the average age of an Indian will be 29 years, compared to 37 for China and 48 for Japan. According to Census 2011, population density was 382 person per square kilometre, and 940 females per 1,000 males.

According to an estimate of UNO, Indian population will rise from 1149.3 million in 2008 to 1,755.2 million in 2050, while population of China would increase from 1324.7 million to 1437.0 million during the same period (Table 4.2).

Table 4.2 Most Populous Countries in the World in 2008 and 2050

Country	*Population 2008 (millions)*	*Population 2 2050 (millions)*
China	1,324.7	1,437
India	1,149.3	1,755.2
United States	304.5	438.2
Indonesia	239.9	343.1
Brazil	195.1	259.8
Pakistan	172.8	295.2
Nigeria	148.1	282.2
Bangladesh	147.3	215.1
Russia	141.9	189.3
Japan	127.7	150.1

Source: The 2008 World Population Data Sheet, Population Reference Bureau. Available at: http://www.prb.org/publications/datasheets/2008/2008wpds.aspx Prb.org.

However, the US Census Bureau International Data Base (IDB) has estimated that in 2010 China had 1.330 billion population as against 1.173 billion population in India and since 1970s the population in India is constantly rising at a higher rate than in China. IDB has projected that India's population is to grow through at least 2050, when it will be 1.656 billion, surpassing China in 2025. China's population is projected to reach a maximum, of 1.395 billion, in 2026 and to decrease thereafter (Davanzo et al. 2011). Population growth rates are affected by crude death rates (CDR), crude birth rates (CBR) and total fertility rates (TFR). IDB had estimated that in 2010 CBR in India was much higher at 21.34 than in China at 12.17 per 1,000 population, while CDR in 2010, per 1,000 population was 7.53 and 6.89 in India and China, respectively. During 2000–35, CBR in India is projected to decline from 26 to 15 per 1,000 population, but CBR will decline from 11.2 to 8.6 during the same period. Currently CDR is higher in India, but according to IDB estimates, CDR in China is expected to surpass CDR in India by 2014. According to IDB estimate TFR in India was 2.65 children per woman as against 1.54 children in China in 2010 which will decline to 2.1 children per woman in India in 2035 and 1.70 children per woman in China in 2025.

Another important aspect of IDB is the working-age population in India and China. Accordingly, India is projected to take over China in 2028 with 971 working-age population as against 956 working-age population in China. An increase in the proportion of working-age population provides an opportunity to reap a Demographic Dividend (Figure 4.3) (Bloom et al. 2003). However, this will depend on socioeconomic policy environment. In India, it will primarily depend on massive growth of job opportunities particularly for the entry level jobs. This will have serious implications on socioeconomic fabrics of the county including long-term consequences on social security, which will be discussed in the following paragraphs.

Figure 4.3 Relative Size of Population of India, China and Other Populous Countries in 2008 and 2050

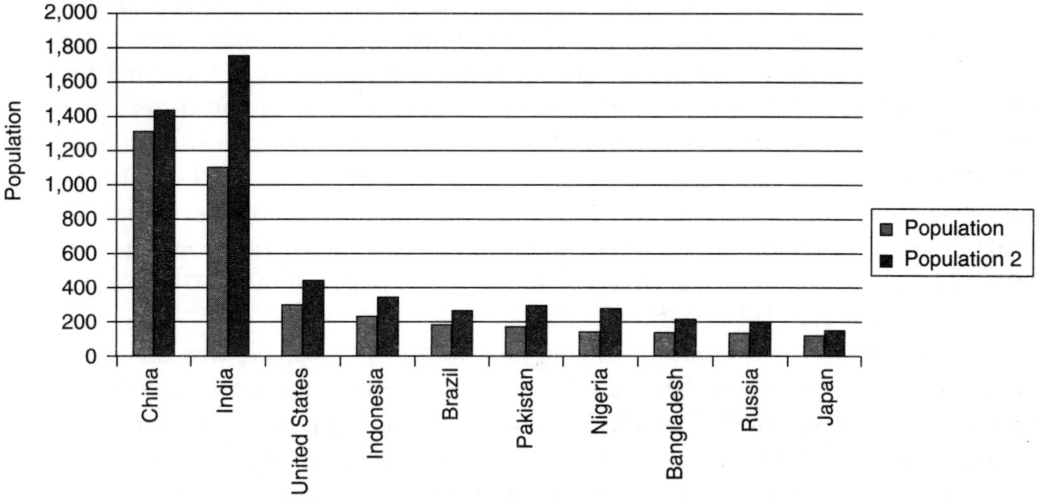

Source: Bloom et al. (2003).

Important Economic Indicators

Indian Economy, since independence in 1947 has come a long way and slowly moved from agriculture-based economy to a modern economy drawing its strength from industry and service sector. Further, management and economic policy has also undergone a radical transformation from state-controlled centralised planning system to a market-based economy keeping pace with changes in the world economy. In the process, the private sector has gradually increased its role in development and moved from bank-financed growth towards capital-market–financed growth model. India has achieved quite reasonable rate of growth in GDP, savings and capital formation, in spite of very high growth rate in population and other internal and external constraints.

❖ ECONOMIC GROWTH

Indian economy since its first five year plan has come a long way to transform itself from a predominant agriculture-based economy to a service-led economy. There has been a significant improvement in economic environment and the total GDP of the country at factor cost at constant prices has gone up from ₹224,786 crore in 1950–51 to ₹4,493,743 crore in 2009–10, while the per capita net national product has gone up from ₹5,708 to ₹33,731 during the same period. India has also registered significant growth in capital formation which has gone up from 8.4 per cent to 36.5 per cent of GDP during 1950–51 to 2009–10, while the rate of growth in domestic savings has steadily moved up from 8.6 per cent to 33.7 per cent in terms of GDP. Growth in domestic savings and capital formation critically supported the steady growth in GDP (Economic Survey 2010–11). With 2.4 per cent growth rate of real GDP in1950–51, India has entered into fast growth trajectory emerging as one of the fastest growing country in the world having achieved an average annual growth rate during 1990–91 to 1999–2000 of 5.7 per cent and 7.3 per cent during 2000–01 to 2009–10, indicating inherent strength of Indian economy. India has shown remarkable resilience during the global financial crisis and global recession, maintained its growth momentum in the year 2010–11 by registering real GDP growth rate of 8.6 per cent in 2010–11 (as against 8.0 per cent in 2009–10) (Table 4.3).

The most significant development during last decades, however, was the structural change in Indian economy which transformed itself from an agriculture-dependent economy to a service sector–led modern economy as can be noted from the contribution of service sector to GDP (Figure 4.4). While the contribution of agriculture declined from 55.2 per cent in 1950–51 to 14.6 per cent in 2009–10, the contribution of service sector had gone up from 34 per cent to 64.9 per cent during the same period. Service sector has also emerged as the major provider of jobs in the country. Employment in the tertiary sector in the country has gone up from 21.2 per cent of total employment in 1993–94 to 25.4 per cent of total employment in 2007–08, while that in the secondary sector increased marginally from 14.3 per cent to 18.7 per cent but employment in the primary sector declined from 64.5 per cent to 55.9 per cent during the same period. Emergence of service sector as the dominant sector has also attracted foreign investors

Table 4.3 Sector-wise Growth Rates in GDP Growth at Factor Cost at 2004–05 Prices

Sector	*2005–06*	*2006–07*	*2007–08*	*2008–09*	*2009–10*	*2010–11*
Agriculture Forestry and Fishing	5.1	4.2	5.8	-0.1	0.4	5.4
Mining and Quarrying	1.3	7.5	3.7	1.3	6.9	6.2
Manufacturing	10.1	14.3	10.3	4.2	8.8	8.8
Electricity, Gas and Water Supply	7.1	9.3	8.3	4.9	6.4	5.1
Construction	12.8	10.3	10.7	5.4	7	8
Trade, Hotels, Transport and communication	12.1	11.7	10.7	7.6	9.7	11
Financing Insurance, Real Estate and Business Services	12.7	14	11.9	12.5	9.2	10.6
Community, Social and Personal Services	7	2.9	6.9	12.7	11.8	5.7
Gross Domestic Product at Factor Cost	9.5	9.6	9.3	6.8	8	8.6

Source: Department of Economic Affairs (2011).

Figure 4.4 Changing Trend in Sectoral Growth Rates

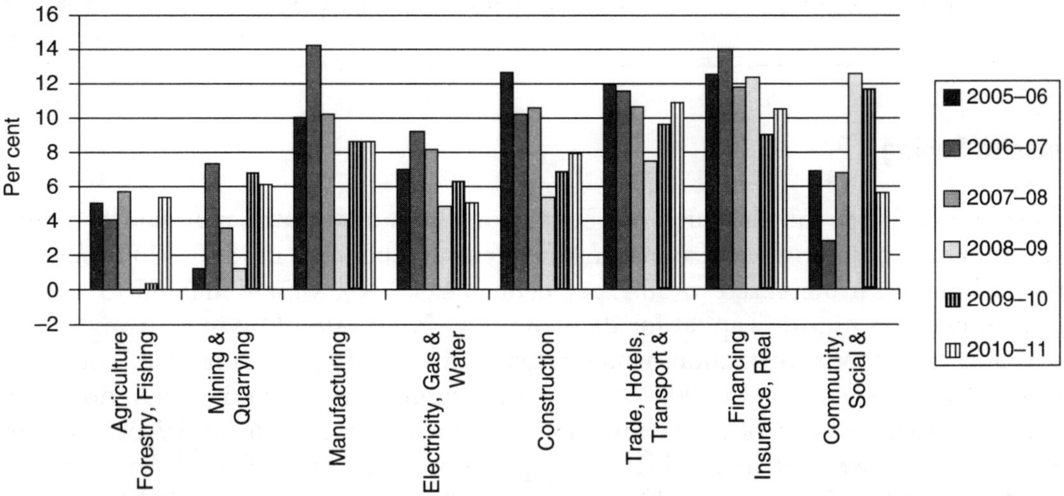

Source: Economic Survey 2010–11.

as indicated by FDI equity inflows which was around 51 per cent of total inflow during April 2000–December 2010 (Economic Survey 2010–11).

❖ INDIAN ECONOMY IN 2050

Economic reforms and structural changes in Indian economy stimulated the growth momentum and India has emerged as the second-fastest growing economy of the world. However, many economists believe that growth rate of Indian economy is going to be faster in future than the current fast-growing economy of China. India, as many believe, will be the second-most powerful economy, next to China in 2050. It is because of the rapidly changing demography and fast-growing ageing population as compared to India. Demographic structure of India is also changing but at a slower rate. In 2050, while China will have 31.1 per cent of total population over 60 years of age, India will have 19.6 per cent population over 60 years. Similarly, 7.2 per cent Chinese will be over 80 years of age as against 2.6 per cent of Indian population. Demographic transition and ageing will thus work against China and will adversely affect labour supply and productivity and old-age dependency. A study by Hawksworth and Tiwari (2011) shows,

> *India has the potential to be the fastest growing large economy in the world over the period to 2050 with GDP at the end of this period 14 per cent larger than the US in PPP terms. PwC study has estimated that by 2050, China will be the no. 1 country in the world with projected GDP at*

PPP (constant 2009) of US$ 59,475 billion as against the no. 2 country India with US$ 43,180 billion, followed by the no. 3 country US with 37,876 billion.

Domestic Saving

India is one of the countries which has continuously improved and maintained a very high rate of growth in domestic savings, from merely 8.6 per cent in 1950–51 (Economic Survey 2010–11), it increased to 33.7 per cent in 2009–10, which enabled to reduce its dependence on outside capital for development. High rate of savings strongly supported domestic capital formation, which registered a steady growth from 8.7 per cent in 1950–51 to 33.7 per cent in 2009–10. The most significant aspect of Indian domestic saving is a steady growth of household savings which increased from 5.7 per cent in 1950–51 to 23.5 per cent in 2009–10. Gross domestic saving increased from merely ₹871 crore in 1950–51 to ₹2,207,423 crore in 2009–10 while fixed capital formation went up from ₹877 crore to ₹2,016,186 crore during the same period (Economic Survey 2010–11). The banking sector still attracts the larger share of financial assets of household sector, which was 54.9 per cent in 2008–09 as against 50.4 per cent in 2007–08. Deposits with banks have increased substantially from 35.7 per cent to 54.9 per cent in 2008–09. No other financial industry registered such an increase except insurance industry which had only 9.8 per cent share in household savings in 1950–51 but went up to 20.1 per cent in 2008–09. However, it was the life insurance sector which attracted the major portion of insurance saving 19.5 per cent in 2008–09.

However, one of the alarming developments during this period was the continuous decline in the share of pension and provident funds—which was 23.2 per cent in 1970–71 but declined to 9.5 per cent in 2008–09 (Table 4.4). This decline was inversely related to the increase in the share of insurance sector in household savings. This is a cause of concern from the point of view of social security and long-term savings. One of the primary reasons for the growth of the share of life insurance was the Unit-Linked Insurance Plan (ULIP) products, often sold as an insurance product but in reality cannot substitute the pension products, since ULIPs are basically investment products.

❖ INADEQUATE AWARENESS ABOUT RETIREMENT SAVINGS

One of the reasons for recent decline in the share of household savings in pension and provident fund may be the inadequate financial literacy and lack of awareness about the importance of retirement savings by the household sector. Some recent studies have thrown some light on savings behaviour of the household sector. The findings of these studies/surveys indicate that there is a low level of financial awareness for retirement savings, a tendency of risk avoidance, etc. (Discussed in detail in Chapter 14.)

Table 4.4 Financial Savings of the Household Sector (gross)

Item/Year	*1970–71*	*1980–81*	*1990–91*	*2000–01*	*2006–07*	*2007–09*	*2008–09*
Financial Saving (Gross)	100	100	100	100	100	100	100
(a) Currency	16.8	13.4	10.6	7.1	10.2	11.4	12.5
(b) Deposits	38.9	48.9	33.3	42	49.1	52.2	58.5
(i) with Banks	35.7	45.8	27.2	32.4	47.8	50.4	54.9
(ii) with Non-Banking Companies	3.2	3.1	2.2	4.9	0.2	0.5	1.8
(iv) Trade Debt (net)	2.4	3	–0.8	–0.7	1	1.3	1.8
(c) Shares and Debentures	3.2	3.4	14.3	2.5	9	12.4	2.6
(i) Private Corporate Business			4.1	1.1	3.7	4.4	4.2
(ii) Banking					0	0.1	0.1
(iii) Units of UTI	0.7	0.3	5.8	–0.4	0		-0.4
(iv) Bonds of PSUs			0.8	0.1	0		0.1
(v) Mutual funds (Other than UTI)			3.3	1.6	5.3	7.9	-1.2
(d) Claims on Government	5	5.9	13.5	15.6	3	–4	-3.1
(i) Investment in Government securities			0.2	1.7	0.3	–2.1	-4.5
(ii) Investment in Small Savings			13.2	13.9	2.7	–1.9	1.4
(e) Insurance Funds	9.8	7.6	9.5	13.5	17.7	18	20.1
(i) Life Insurance Funds			8.5	12.9	17.1	17.4	19.5
(ii) Postal Insurance			0.2	0.3	0.3	0.4	0.3
(iii) State Insurance			0.7	0.4	0.3	0.2	0.3
(f) Provident and Pension Fund	23.2	17.5	18.9	19.3	11.1	9.9	9.5

Source: Central Statistical Organisation, Government of India, cited in Reserve Bank of India: Annual Report, various issues.

INDIAN LABOUR MARKET

The concern for any development initiatives and resultant growth is to see how that impacts the life of people and enhances the standard of living through increased consumption which can be achieved through gainful employment. Therefore, development must be able to create employment for the growing number of people throughout the society to create economic security. Labour market situation is thus a mirror of effectiveness of developmental initiatives. There is no doubt that full employment is practically impossible but direct and indirect employment can be created for the maximum number of people in the working-age group.

Employment and Unemployment

Though India has achieved significant growth in GDP and population growth rate has been declining during the past decades, growth in workforce has been constantly lagging behind the growth rate in labour force resulting into growth in unemployment. Indian labour force increased by 2.28 per cent annually during 1984–88 to 1993–94 and by 2.8 per cent annually during 1999–00 to 2004–05, while workforce increased by 2.61 per cent and 2.62 per cent respectively. It may be mentioned here that structural reforms in India began in 1990–91 and there might be some relationship between reforms and decline in the workforce during 1993–94 to 1999–00. During 1999–00 to 2004–05 both registered an increase but labour force increased at a faster rate (2.84 per cent) compared to workforce (2.62 per cent) resulting into growth of unemployment from 26.68 million in 1999–00 to 34.74 million (Economic Survey 2007–08). Growth of employment in the post-reform period declined primarily due to the decline in jobs in the organised sector, particularly in the public sector. According to Economic Survey 2009–10, during 1983–94, jobs in the organised sector increased by 1.20 per cent per annum (1.53 per cent in public sector and 0.44 per cent in private sector) but there was a sharp decline in employment by 0.03 per cent during 1994–2007 (in public sector it was 0.57 per cent and in private sector it was 1.30 per cent). According to the latest National Sample Survey (NSS) (64th Round), total employment created between 2005 and 2008 was 2.4 million, that is, by 8 million per year (*Economic and Political Weekly* 2010).

Informal Sector

Another important feature of Indian labour market is dominance of informal sector employment. The share of informal sector in total employment was more than 86 per cent in 2004–05. According to the NSS 55th Round (1999–2000), total employment was estimated at 396 million, 342.60 million being employed in informal sector and the rest 54.20 million in formal sector. NSS 61st Round (2004–05) estimated total employment at 457.5 million, 395 million in informal sector and 62.50 million in formal sector (Economic Survey 2008–09). Though, between NSS 55th Round (1999–2000) and 61st Round (2004–05) there was an increase in employment by 60.70 million (15.30 per cent), the increase was basically due to the increase in employment in informal sector by 52.40 million. This has serious implication on the social security since these informal sector employees are mostly unskilled and not covered by any formal social security. India does not have any universal social security, and the workers usually survive on their income till they are able to work. However, they tend to depend on children or relatives for their survival when they are unable to work.

Employment in Organised Sector

According to NSS 61st Round only 13.66 per cent employment was in the formal or organised sector consisting of public and private sector. However, organised public sector was the major employer as it was the source of employment of 180.02 lakh (66 per cent) employees out of total employment of 272.76 lakh (Figure 4.5). In 1991 the organised sector employment was 267.33 lakh which increased marginally to 279.60 lakh in 2000 but declined sharply to 272.76 lakh in 2007, primarily due to the slow growth of employment in private sector and decline in public sector employment.

Figure 4.5 Employment in Public and Private Sector

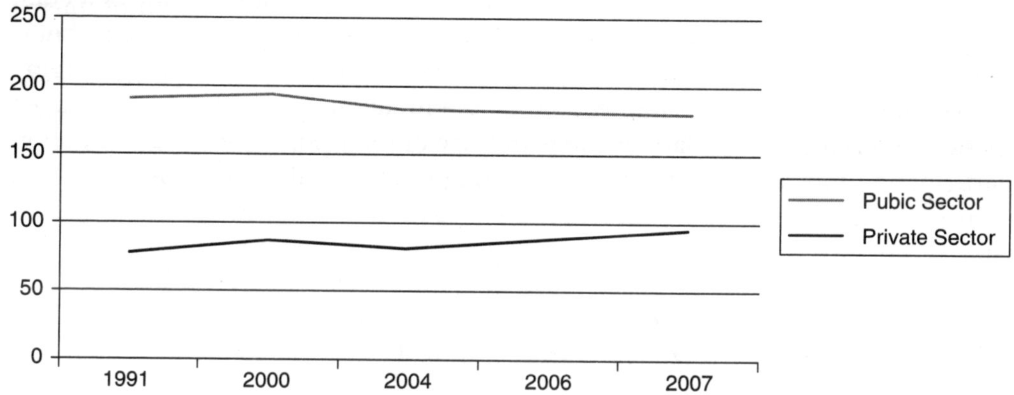

The public sector plays the most crucial role in Indian economy and is the major provider of employment to the growing workforce. However, the share of public sector in organised sector employment declined sharply from 71 per cent to 66 per cent during 1991–2007. Though the employment in organised public sector increased till 2000, it started declining subsequently and it was 180.02 lakh in 2007 as against 193.14 lakh in 2000. In the post-reform period it was expected that the private sector would substantially increase the prospects of overall employment growth but in spite of several market-oriented actions including various incentives allowing private sector to play a more active role in economy could not increase employment in organised private sector in a big way which was only 34 per cent of total organised sector employment in 2007, which declined from 8.69 million in 1997 to 8.65 million in 2001.

Gender Distribution of Organised Sector Employment

Gender distribution of organised sector employment Indicate a wide gap in employment of male and female employees. Figure 4.5 indicates that out of 272 lakh employees in the organised sector in 2007, only 53.12 lakh were female employees, which was only 19.47 per cent of total organised sector employment. Male employees constitute 80.53 per cent of total organised sector employment. This has a serious implication from the social security point of view, since longevity of female in the country has increased significantly, but most of them do not earn a living and have to depend on others for their survival in old age.

Labour Force and Workforce Participation Rates

Labour force and workforce participation rates are important components for measuring changing structure of employment and unemployment. The labour force of a country includes everyone of working-age above certain age (around 14 to 15) and below retirement age (around 60 in India) who are actively employed or seeking employment, while the workforce is the number of people in labour pool who are employed. Participation rate is the ratio of labour force and size of their population cohort. Labour force participation rate is a key component for long term growth of an economy. It can be seen from the data in Table 4.5 that male participation rate was high overall through the year 1983 to 2004–05 than female participation in labour force as well as in workforce. Female participation rate was higher in labour force as well as in workforce.

However, urban female participation rate improved in labour force and workforce significantly during 1999–00 to 2004–05 (Figure 4.6). This is due to the increased literacy rate, changing lifestyle, increased employment opportunity, career consciousness, changing attitude among educated women about non-marital relationship, etc. On the other hand rural India still lacks enough growth to create employment opportunities for the growing number of population, absence of enough educational opportunities, absence of liberal attitude about men–women relationships often prohibit even educated women's entry into job market. Overwhelmingly, a large majority of people live

Figure 4.6 Male and Female Employment

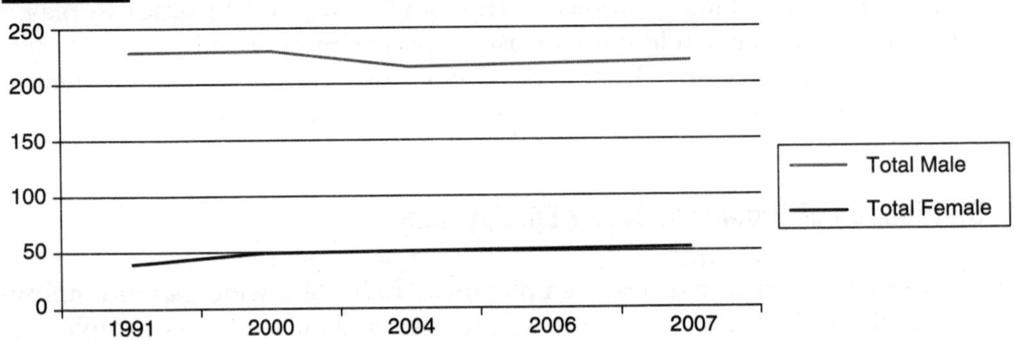

Table 4.5 Labour and Work Participation Rates

Column 1	*Column 2*	*Column 3*	*Column 4*	*Column 5*
	1983	*1993–94*	*1999–00*	*2004–05*
Labour Force Participation Rates (LFPR)				
Rural Male	52.7	53.4	51.5	53.1
Rural Female	21.9	23.2	22	23.7
Urban Male	52.7	53.2	52.8	56.1
Urban Female	12.1	13.2	12.3	15
Work Force Participation Rates (WFPR)				
Rural Male	48.2	50.4	47.8	48.8
Rural Female	19.8	21.9	20.4	21.6
Urban Male	47.3	49.6	49	51.9
Urban Female	10.6	12	11.1	13.3

Source: Various rounds of NSSO survey on employment and unemployment/planning commission cited in Economic Survey 2008–09, Government of India, Ministry of Finance, Economic Division.
Note: LFPR/WFPR represents number of persons/person days in the labour force/workforce per 1000 persons/person days.

in rural areas and most of the workers are unskilled or semiskilled but the percentage of organised sector employment in agriculture, mining, quarrying, etc., to total employment is declining. However, significant growth in employment was noted in the sectors requiring highly specialised skills like finance, insurance, real estate, community and personal services, etc. This development has been reflected in rural unemployment and poverty.

POVERTY, SOCIAL PROTECTION AND HUMAN DEVELOPMENT

Poverty

India has made remarkable progress in economic development and in social sector in terms of growth rate GDP, capital formation, domestic saving, literacy, life expectancy, etc. But the impact of growth has not really been felt throughout the society and the purchasing power has not increased for all sections of the society resulting into existence of chronic poverty. Impact of development should also be reflected in overall human development, which is measured by human development index.

In India, the planning commission is the official agency which estimates the incidence of poverty on the basis of the sample surveys on household consumer expenditure conducted by the National Sample Survey Office (NSSO). Usually two types of data are used to identify the number of poor in the country, namely the uniform recall period

(URP) data which uses a 30-day recall/reference period for all items of consumption and mixed recall period (MRP) which uses a 365-day recall/reference period for five infrequently purchased non-food items clothing, footwear, durable goods, education and institutional medical expenses and a 30 day recall/reference period for remaining items (Economic Survey 2010, p. 272). According to the latest available estimate (URP method) all India poverty ratio declined from 36.0 per cent in 1993–94 to 27.5 per cent in 2004–05. While rural poverty ratio declined from 37.3 per cent to 28.3 per cent, the ratio for urban population declined from 32.4 per cent to 25.7 per cent during the same period. The Government of India and various state governments have taken several initiatives to reduce the incidence of poverty which helped to increase income and consumption of people with low income or no income. Some important central government initiatives are National Rural Employment Guarantee Scheme (NREGS), *Swarnjayanti Gram Swarozgar Yojana* (SGSY), Swarnajayanti Sahari Rozgar Yojana (SJSRY), etc. (Economic Survey 2009–10).

Poverty Reduction and Social Protection

Population explosion, increased unemployment, slow growth in economy, weak redistribution mechanism and absence of universal social protection measures resulted into poverty. However, the government has initiated several measures to reduce the incidence of poverty, but still a large number of people live below the poverty line and future social security measures need to take this poverty issue into account. Poverty reduction through various social protection measures have been initiated by the central and state governments in India. The Asian Development Bank (ADB) has identified over 50 such social protection measures in India. Social protection has been defined by ADB as 'the set of policies and programmes designed to reduce poverty and vulnerability by promoting efficient labour markets, diminishing people's exposure to risks, and enhancing their capacity to protect themselves against hazards and the interruption/ loss of income' (ADB 2007). Social protection in India includes social assistance and social insurance, labour market programmes, localised support programmes, etc. We shall discuss briefly about some of these programmes except social insurance and social assistance programmes which will be discussed in the next chapter.

Poverty alleviation and Employment Generation

Labour market programmes aim at providing additional employment to enhance income earning opportunities and thus consumption in rural areas. These include some central government initiatives discussed in the following paragraphs.

❖ THE MAHATMA GANDHI NATIONAL RURAL EMPLOYMENT GUARANTEE SCHEME

Launched in February 2006 as National Rural Employment Guarantee Scheme but renamed subsequently as the Mahatma Gandhi National Rural Employment Guarantee Scheme (MGNREGS) for

> *enhancing livelihood security of households in rural areas of the country by providing at least one hundred days of guaranteed wage employment in a financial year to every household whose adult members volunteers to do unskilled manual work. It also mandates 33 per cent participation for women. The primary objective of the Scheme is to augment wage employment. This is to be done while also focusing on strengthening natural resource management through works that address causes of chronic poverty like drought, deforestation, and soil erosion and thus encourage sustainable development. (Economic Survey 2010–11)*

❖ SGSY

The SGSY was launched in April 1999 as a major scheme to help poor rural families to cross the poverty line by assisting them to take up income-generating economic activities through a mix of bank credit and government subsidy. The scheme attempts to organise the poor into self-help groups (SHGs), build up their capacities through training and skill development, to creation of infrastructure and technology and provide marketing support. The SGSY specially focuses on vulnerable sections among the rural poor with SCs/STs accounting for at least 50 per cent and women for 40 per cent of the *swarozgaris*. SJSRY was launched by the Government of India in December 1997 and subsequently revamped in April 2009, with the objective to provide gainful employment to the urban unemployed and underemployed by encouraging them to set up self-employment ventures or provision for wage employment. The SJSRY scheme has five components, namely Urban Self Employment Programme (USEP), Urban Women Self-help Programme (UWSP), Skill Training for Employment Promotion amongst Urban Poor (STEPUP), Urban Wage Employment Programme (UWEP) and Urban Community Development Network (UCDN). A total of 680,325 beneficiaries had been benefited till 31 December 2010.

❖ SOCIAL PROTECTION PROGRAMMES

India has a very large informal sector employing a huge magnitude of labour force, which is generally not covered by any formal social security programme. However, the government is making several efforts on expanding the coverage of social security schemes so as to provide a minimum level of social protection to workers in the unorganised sector and to ensure inclusive development. These programmes include: *Aam Admi Bima Yojana* (AABY), Rashtriya Swasthya Bima Yojana (RSBY), the Unorganised Workers' Social Security Act 2008, etc., which will be discussed in the next chapter.

Social Sector Expenditures

Social sector expenditure contributes to human development and social protection and is considered to be a measure taken by the government for eradicating social problems. And recent trend indicates that expenditure on social services as a proportion of total expenditure increased from 21.1 per cent in 2005–06 to 25.2 per cent in 2010–11 (budget estimate), which was 6.63 per cent in 2010–11. Expenditure on education as a proportion of total expenditure has increased marginally from 10 per cent in 2005–06 to 11.3 per cent in 2010–11 while the expenditure on health as a proportion of the GDP has increased from 1.23 per cent in 2005–06 to 1.27 per cent in 2010–11 (BE), its share in total expenditure has increased marginally from 4.7 per cent in 2005–06 to 4.8 per cent in 2010–11 (BE) (Economic Survey 2010–11). Social sector and social services expenditure in India expanded the opportunities of employment and income for the poor, improved the access to health and education for vulnerable section, particularly in rural areas.

> *There is also a significant pro poor bias in the targeting of social protection expenditure—the percentage of social protection expenditure going to the poor as the ratio of poverty rate is 1.24. Nevertheless, despite its high average indicators, the overall contribution of these to the income of the poor remains quite low at only over a quarter of the poverty line income. (ADB 2007)*

Social Protection Index for Committed Poverty Reduction

The ADB in association with Halcrow has developed a Social Protection Index (SPI) to measure poverty reduction. The SPI includes labour market, social security, health insurance and health-care support, micro-credit, targeted education, child protection etc. This study has revealed,

> *India's SPI is 0.46 which gives it a ranking of 10 out of the 31 countries forming a part of the study. This ranking is much higher than its HDI ranking of 22 indicating that it has a higher degree of social protection than one would expect from its level of Human Development. (ADB 2007)*

According to the Human Development Index (HDI) 2010, India's SPI was 0.519 with an overall global ranking of 119 (out of the 169 countries). Although lower in HDI ranking, India has continuously improved its HDI ranking which was 0.427 in 1980 but still in the medium human development category with countries like China, Sri Lanka, Thailand, Philippines, Egypt, Indonesia and South Africa having better overall HDI ranking within the same category. The existing gap in health and education indicators as compared to developed countries and also many of the developing countries indicates a need for much faster and wider spread of basic health and education (Economic Survey 2010–11) (http://indiabudget.nic.in).

Profile of Indian Elderly Population

It was noted earlier that both the birth rates and death rates are declining but this decline is faster in case of death rates than the birth rates and it is expected that there will be a further decline in mortality and increase in life expectancy due to increased per capita income, consumption and improved health-care system. At the same time there has been a drastic fall in infant mortality rate per 1,000 births from 110 in 1981 to 50 in 2009 and the total fertility per woman declined from 4.5 in 1981 to 2.6 in 2008. Decline in birth and death rates as well as declining mortality rate has its impact on the age structure. Decline in birth rate and fertility will reduce the child population and increase in life expectancy will further increase the number of older population. Population below five years is likely to decline from 12.80 per cent in 1991 to 9.7 per cent in 2016, whereas working-age population between 15–59 years will increase from 55.58 per cent to 63.33 per cent during the same period. The age group of 60 plus is projected to increase from the current levels of 7 per cent to nearly 9 per cent by 2016. In India the change in the share of young population (population aged 14 or less) will decline from 4 per cent in 1950–65 to –12.55 in 2010–50, while change in the share of elderly population (population aged 60 or above) will increase from –0.1 per cent in 1950–65 to 12.3 per cent in 2010–50, the change in respect of working-age population will witness marginal increase –3.9 per cent to 0.2 per cent. This implies that there will be higher burden on working population. Since number of young people will come down there will be more older people than younger people that at present. Age structure is an important indicator to assess the potential problems of population ageing for institutional actions. Therefore 'it is important to consider not only the degree of population ageing but also the pace of change in the age structure' (World Population Ageing 2009).

According to United Nations' document *World Population Ageing 2009*, population of older persons is growing at a rate of 2.6 per cent per year while overall population growth is 1.2 per cent per annum. The population over 60 years or more in 2000 was 600 million and the number will triple in 1950. This number increased to 700 million in 2009 and is projected to be 2 billion by 2050. It has been further estimated that 10 per cent of world population are in the age group of 60 plus years while in China and India 8 per cent of the population are in the 60 plus age group. But world average of older population of 60 years or more is going to be 21 per cent in 2050, while India will have 15 per cent of its population in 60 plus age group, China will have 30 per cent of its population in 60 plus age group (Table 4.6).

Table 4.6 Population Aged 60 Years or Older

	India		*China*		*World Total*	
	2002	*2050*	*2002*	*2050*	*2002*	*2050*
Number (in '000)	81,089	324, 316	143,243	436,980	628,874	1,963,767
Percentage of Total Population	8	21	10	30	10	21
Percentage of 80 years	8	15	9	23	12	19
Potential Support Ratio	12	8	10	3	9	4
Life Expectancy at age 60	*2000–05*		*2000–05*			
Men	17		16		17	20
Women	18		20			

Source: United Nations (2000).

The study by Davanzo et al. (2011) indicates that in 2011, 5.3 per cent of Indian population was 65 plus years (against 8.6 per cent in China) which is likely to go up to 7.7 per cent in 2025 (against 21 per cent in China) and will be double (in both the country) in 2035. By 2025, India will have 5.5 per cent of its population aged 85 or more (against 6.6 per cent in China). The Registrar General of India estimated that in 2001 elderly population in India was 71 million and it is estimated to be 114 million by the year 2016. The United Nations projected (medium variation) as 77 million in 2000, 168 million in 2050 and 326 million in 2050. Thus, elderly population which was 20 million in 1951 will increase up to 326 million in 2050. This is frightening situation not only from the point of view of social security for elderly but also from the point of view of management of economy.

United Nations' estimates of Population Ageing 2008 show that by 2050 more people will be beyond 80 years (called oldest old). Oldest old are the fastest growing segment of the older population. In 2002, the oldest (80 years or more) constituted 12 per cent of the population and will grow to 19 per cent of older population (age 60 years or more). The oldest old in India will increase from 8 per cent in 2002 to 15 per cent in 2050 while in China it will grow from 9 per cent to 23 per cent during the same period. The number of people who are 100 years or more is estimated to go up by 15 fold from 210,000 in 2002 to 3.2 million in 2050.

❖ DEPENDENCY RATIO

Age distribution data provides important insight into dependency ratio—youth as well as old dependency ratio. Youth dependency ratio (number of persons 0–14 years per 100 persons of 15–59 years) and old-age dependency ratio (number of person aged 60 years or more per 100 person 15–59 years). The group 15–59 years is considered to be the working-age people and they support the youth and older people (aged 60 years and above). Moreno and Santos (2008) by using UNO data calculated the changes in population shares from 1950–56 to 2010–50 and observed that many emerging market economy (EME) countries entering into the second stage of population growth are characterised by decline of child dependency and increase in elderly dependency. It can be seen that youth dependency ratio has been steadily declining, whereas elderly dependency has been increasing and in the long run the rate of growth of old-age dependency would be higher than the growth of working-age population.

The age structure of Indian population is changing rapidly and a youthful country is tending towards an ageing society with the number of people below 15 slowly declining and the number of people above 65 plus steeply increasing pushing up old-age dependency ratio, though still it is much lower than youth dependency ratio. In 2010, youth dependency ratio was 46.4 (people under the age of 15 for every 100 of working people) as against elderly dependency ratio of 8.3 (people of the age of 60 years and above for 100 working-age people). The old-age dependency ratios (per 1,000) given in Table 4.7 shows that the old-age dependency ratio is higher in rural than in urban areas.

According to the census, the ratio has increased over time. This implies that the 'burden' of the aged on the working population is higher in rural areas as compared to that in urban areas. Increased longevity, low dependency ratio and increase in population over 60 years will exert pressure on economy and necessitate a well-developed pension and social security system. This problem will further aggravate since joint family system is gradually disappearing due to pressure on agriculture, industrialisation, migration and fast-emerging micro-family system.

Table 4.7 Old-Age Dependency Ratio (per 1,000) in India

Source	*Rural*	*Urban*	*Combined*
Census 1981	94	71	89
NSS 43rd Round (1987–88)	111	88	103
Census 1991	123	96	118
NSS 50th Round (1993–94	108	90	104
NSS 52nd Round (1995–96)	92	74	87

Source: National Sample Survey Office (1995–96).

Socioeconomic Profile of Elderly Population

❖ DEMOGRAPHIC BURDEN

Elderly population impose demographic burden on the society, economy and working population since they have to support the aged people. In order to understand seriousness of the problems, we would like to discuss some socioeconomic profile of aged Indian people with the help of data collected by NSSO in its nationwide survey (52nd round July 1995–June 1996). The survey had identified many socioeconomic aspects of aged population in India. According to the survey, there has been strong evidence that demographic burden of the aged population in India is rising rapidly. The number of aged persons, which was 43.5 million in 1981, grew to 61.4 million in 1991 and the number of the aged was 65 per 1,000 persons in 1981 and rose to 74 in 1991. The number of aged persons obtained from the NSS survey (52nd Round) was estimated at 46.4 million during 1995–96 and about 78 per cent were residing in the rural areas and 22 per cent in the urban areas, for every 1,000 persons, in rural India nearly 6 persons were aged as against 5 per 1,000 persons in urban India. The overall share of the aged in the total population in India was 5.5 per cent.

❖ LIVING ARRANGEMENT AND ECONOMIC INDEPENDENCE

The proportion of the aged living alone came down from 6 per cent to 9 per cent in 1986–87 to around 4 per cent in 1995–96. The proportion of the aged who lived with their spouses went up significantly from 37 per cent to 57 per cent in the rural areas and 35 per cent to 55 per cent in the urban areas. The decrease in the proportion of aged persons living with their children between 1986–87 and 1995–96 reflects the gradual breakdown of the extended family system in India in both its rural and urban areas. Two important reasons to live with others are emotional as well as economic support. Dependence on other for day-to-day economic needs arises due to absence of economic independence of elderly population. Data in Table 4.8 shows that as many as 70 per cent of the aged had to depend on others for their day-to-day maintenance.

The situation is worse for elderly females. Among them, about 85 per cent to 87 per cent were economically dependent either partially or fully. In this respect, males were much better off—among them 49 per cent to 52 per cent did not depend on others for their livelihood. Compared to 1986–87, the results of the present survey indicate that the economic condition of the elderly in the urban sector has improved, whereas it has deteriorated in general in the rural. Economic independence of elderly Indians is shown in Table 4.9. It can be seen from data of the economically dependent aged that a majority (about 74 per cent) is supported by their children and a sizable proportion (14 per cent to 16 per cent) by their spouses while 5 per cent to 6 per cent of such aged

Table 4.8 Type of Living Arrangement (per 1,000 distribution of aged persons)

Type of Living Arrangements	*Rural*			*Urban*		
	Male	*Female*	*Person*	*Male*	*Female*	*Person*
(1)	*(2)*	*(3)*	*(4)*	*(5)*	*(6)*	*(7)*
1. Living Alone	25	61	43	30	60	45
	−124	−14	−80	−95	−8	−59
2. With Spouse Only	137	77	107	103	57	80
3. With Spouse and Other Members	613	313	462	648	297	469
4. With Spouse (2 + 3)	750	390	569	751	354	549
	−451	−251	−370	−449	−215	−353
5. With Children	179	481	331	178	512	349
	−368	−660	−486	−396	−673	−510
6. With Other Relations And Non-Relations	38	59	48	35	65	51
	−57	−74	−62	−56	−100	−74
Total (Including Non Relations)	1,000	1,000	1,000	1,000	1,000	1,000

Source: National Sample Survey Office (1995–1996).

Table 4.9 Per 1,000 Distribution of Aged Persons by State of Economic Independence

	State of Economic		*Independence*	
Location	*Not Dependent on Others*	*Partially Dependent on Others*	*Fully Dependent on Others*	*Total*
Rural				
Male	485 (511)	180 (162)	313 (327)	1,000
Female	121 (88)	146 (137)	706 (775)	1,000
Person	301 (340)	163 (152)	511 (508)	1,000
Urban				
Male	515 (457)	169 (169)	297 (374)	1,000
Female	115 (48)	110 (91)	757 (861)	1,000
Person	311 (289)	139 (137)	532 (574)	1,000

Source: 'The Aged in India—A Socio Economic Profile', India NSS 52nd Round (July 1995–June 1996), National Sample Survey Office, Department of Statistics, Ministry of Planning and Programme Implementation, Government of India.

people were supported by their grandchildren and the rest (6 per cent to 7 per cent) had to depend on 'others', including non-relations.

Work participation rate gives an indication poor economic condition of the aged which makes it necessary for them to work even in the old age of 60 or beyond. The WPR among the aged in the rural areas (39 per cent) was higher than that in the urban areas (21 per cent). However, the WPR among the aged females was 17 per cent and among aged males was much higher at 60 per cent—even much higher than that for the overall population in rural India. This percentage was virtually opposite in urban areas—WPR of aged males was 35 per cent as against 8 per cent of aged females.

This also implies that among the aged, more than 60 per cent in the rural areas and about 79 per cent in the urban areas neither did any work nor was available for work during 1995–96.

The survey also provided some information about the possession of assets by the aged population in India. About 54 per cent of the aged had some kind or other of financial assets in 1995–96. The proportion was 8 percentage points lower in 1986–87 in urban areas. Among the aged who were once employed either as wage/salaried employees or as casual labour, about 79 per cent in the rural areas and 35 per cent in the urban areas did not receive any benefit on their retirement.

The brief review of socioeconomic profile of the growing elderly population of India indicate that the country is slowly moving towards *Ageing Trap* which will impose severe burden on the economy and probably retard the growth of economy. Unsustainable population growth and growing number of elderly outside the ambit of working-age group impact the national labour supply, productivity, savings, etc. A high proportion of population in the working-age group will increase labour supply and thus productivity and savings. On the other hand, a large number of people in the older age group will reduce labour supply and thus productivity and savings. Bloom et al. (2008) maintained:

> *The ratio of consumption to production tends to be high for the youth and elderly and low for the working age adults and a country with large cohort of youth and elderly is likely to experience slower growth than one with a high proportion of working age population.*

Population ageing thus has a serious long-term impact on growth in terms of reduced labour supply and productivity unless successful measures are taken to constantly improve the average productivity and incentives are provided to induce saving for capital formation and investment. Some studies have also suggested that savings rate increases with life expectancy in countries with universal pension coverage and retirement savings but not in countries with PAYG systems and high replacement rates (Bloom et al. 2007).

However the long-term impact of population ageing will not only be restricted to macro-economy but it will have an adverse impact on sociopolitical system. Peterson (1999) views this problem as 'global aging will become not just the transcendent economic issue of the 21st century, but the transcendent political issue as well.... Global aging could trigger a crisis that engulfs the world economy'. This crisis may even threaten democracy itself. India is the largest democracy of the world and will be the most populous country by 2050. Though currently the economy is growing with youthful workforce, but it may be difficult to sustain the current rate of growth with huge burden of elderly population over 60 and 100 years. Since a stable democracy needs the support of a vibrant economy, it is absolutely essential to sustain required economic growth to provide old age/retirement income support to the elderly people through a comprehensive social security policy.

REFERENCES

Asian Development Bank (ADB) (2007), 'Social Protection Index for Committed Poverty Reduction'. Volume 9. India *Country Report—Final*. London: Halcrow Group Ltd.

Bloom, David E. (2008), 'Population Aging and Economic Growth'. Working Paper No. 22, International Bank for Reconstruction and Development/World Bank, Washington DC.

Bloom, David E., David Canning and Gunther Fink (2008), 'Population Aging and Economic Growth'. Working Paper No. 32, International Bank for Reconstruction and Development/The World Bank, Washington DC.

Bloom, David E., David Canning and Jaypee Sevilla (2003), 'The Demographic Dividend: A New Perspective on the Economic Consequences of Population Change'. Santa Monica, California: RAND Corporation, MR-127-WFHF/DLPV/RF. Available at: http://www.rand.org/pubs/monograph_reports/MRI1274.

Bloom, David E., D. Canning, R. Mansfeild and M. Moore (2007), 'Demographic Changes, Social Security System and Savings'. *Journal of Monetary Economics*, 54(1): 92–144.

Davanzo, Julie, Harun Dogo and Clifford A. Grammich (2011), 'Demographic Trends, Policy Influences, and Economic Effects in China and India Through 2025'. Working Paper No. WR-849, April 2011, Rand National Security Research Division. Available at: http://www.rand.org/content/dam/rand/pubs/working_papers/2011/RAND_WR849.pdf.

Department of Economic Affairs (2011), *Economic Survey (2010–11)*. New Delhi: Department of Economic Affairs, Government of India.

Economic and Political Weekly (2010), 'Jobless Growth'. 25 September, XLV(39).

Government of India (2011), *Census 2011*. New Delhi: Office of the Registrar General & Census Commissioner, Ministry of Home Affairs. Available at: http://censusindia.gov.in/.

Hawksworth, John and Anmol Tiwari (2011), 'The World in 2050'. PricewaterhouseCoopers. Available at: www.pwc.uk/economics.com.

National Sample Survey Office (NSSO) (1997), *The Aged in India—A Socio Economic Profile*, NSS 52nd Round (July 1995–June 1996), National Sample Survey Office, Department of Statistics, Ministry of Planning and Programme Implementation, Government of India.

Peterson, Peter G. (1999), 'The Global Aging Crisis', *Foreign Affairs*. January/February 1999. New York. Available at: http://homepages.stmartin.edu/Fac_Staff/rlangill/PLS per cent20152/Gray per cent20dawn.doc.

Population Foundation of India (2007), 'The Future Population of India—A Long-range Demographic View'. Population Foundation of India and Population Reference Bureau, August 2007. Available at www.popfound.org.

Moreno, Ramón and Marjorie Santos (2008), 'Pension Systems in EMEs: Implications for Capital Inflows and Financial Markets'. In BIS Paper No. 44. Available at: www.bis.org/pub/bppdf/bispap44.pdf.

Reserve Bank of India (2008–09), *Annual Report 2008–09*. Mumbai: Reserve Bank of India.

United Nations (2000), *World Population Ageing 2000*. New York: Department of Economic and Social Affairs, Population Division, United Nations.

——— (2009), *World Population Ageing 2009*. New York: Department of Economic and Social Affairs, Population Division, United Nations.

5 Social Security and Retirement Savings System in India

INTRODUCTION

It has been noted in the previous chapter that India is undergoing a serious potential threat of population ageing and there is an emerging need for creating a viable and institutionalised social protection for the elderly, the disabled and the sick in the society, particularly for those who are below the poverty line and in informal and rural areas. However, India has so far not been able to put in place any universal social security to protect this section of population. Most of the programmes that have been developed and are being implemented through different agencies in India target the organised formal sector workers while the state governments provide need-based, old-age support in a limited scale. Moreover, the present system of retirement/pension schemes covers only 10 per cent of organised sector employees.

There were no social security schemes in India to take care of old-age income, health disability, etc., except General Provident Fund (GPF) which was introduced under Workmen Compensation Act in 1923. The introduction of Employees' Provident Fund Scheme (EPFS) in 1952 was a significant step towards retirement provision for Indian employees. At present there are health care and pension support system for civil servants, Public Pension Fund (PPF), pension and health-care system for organised private sector employees and old-age pension, destitute pension and occupation-based, old-age income support schemes run by state (provincial) governments. Apart from the employees' provident fund (EPF) (1952), there are also some mandatory provident funds linked to specific occupations or states, namely,

- *Coal Mines Provident Fund Scheme* introduced in 1945 for covering about 25 lakh employees working in coal mines;
- *EPFS* introduced for employees of six major industries in 1951 (it was expanded further);
- *Assam Tea Plantation Employees' Provident Fund Scheme* introduced in 1955;
- *Seamen Provident Fund Scheme* introduced in 1966;
- a separate *Provident Fund* introduced in Jammu and Kashmir in 1961;
- a restructured *GPF* was introduced in 1980 for government employees; and

- an *Employees' Family Pension Scheme* introduced in 1971 which was merged with, *Employees' Pension Fund Scheme* (EPS) introduced in 1955.

However, the social security system in India is inadequate to tackle the problem of ageing and old-age security. The important schemes of pension in the organised sector are: civil services and defined benefit (DB) pension schemes, government provident funds, additional benefits for government employees, unfunded part of employees' pension fund, and tax concession–centric PPF. Another problem being confronted by us is that of low pension fund contributors. There is a reasonable and well-structured pension system, particularly for the civil services and the public sector. The organised sector schemes can be divided into two categories, namely the organised private sector schemes and organised public sector schemes including civil servants' retirement schemes. In India pension is not covered by any statute but by the *Directive Principles of State Policy. However,* the government introduced the National Pension System (NPS), and made it mandatory for the employees who join services w.e.f. 1 January 2004. But those who have joined services before that date are covered under DB pension. Government pension includes employees of central and state governments. The employees of public sector, which include banks, insurance and public sector enterprises, also receive pension, provident funds and benefits of gratuity under the Gratuity Act. In addition to pension and social assistance discussed above, one can avail the benefits of some voluntary schemes like Public Provident Fund (PPF), superannuation schemes, plans sold, life insurance companies and mutual funds. There are also several voluntary pension schemes for organised sector employees and savings schemes for organised and unorganised sector employees. There are different social security and pension programmes for unorganised/informal sectors which include targeted social assistance programme of the government, NPS and voluntary savings for retirement income. The pension schemes for organised/formal sectors include pension and other benefits of organised private and government/public sector. Organised sector pensions in India can be divided into three categories—those schemes which were formed under an act or statute, the pension system for government employees (also followed by the public sector) and voluntary pensions (Table 5.1).

TARGETED SOCIAL ASSISTANCE PROGRAMME

There is no universal social insurance or social security programme in India. But there are a large number of subsidised schemes which have been launched for the most poor people and the vulnerable section of society through directly targeted programmes and through support to the non-governmental organisations (NGOs), which operate both at the state and national levels. Some kind of means-tested pensions are also provided to elderly poor, particularly those who are below poverty line (BPL). In addition, there are subsidised social security schemes sponsored by the central and state governments.

Table 5.1 Pension System in India

Unorganised Sector	Organised Sector	National Pension System
Targetted Social Assistance	EPFO Special PF ESIS	Government Employees Corporate Pension
Social Insurance Public Provident Fund	Civil Servant Pension	All Citizens Scheme NPS Lite

Source: Author's own.

The state governments also run certain scheme through Life Insurance Corporation of India (LIC). Social security in India is used in a broad sense and consists of a variety of schemes such as centrally funded social assistance programmes, social insurance programmes, social assistance through welfare funds of central and state governments and public initiatives.

Centrally Funded Social Assistance Programmes

These include programmes to address the social security need of the people below the poverty line like *National Social Assistance Programme (NSAP), Annapurna Scheme, Antyodaya Anna Yojana, Swarnjayanti Gram Swarojgar Yojana and Jawahar Gram Samridhi Yojana.* We would discuss some of these programmes in the following paragraphs.

❖ NATIONAL SOCIAL ASSISTANCE PROGRAMME

The NSAP is considered to be the first national programme of a cash-transfer nature in the country. The programme intends to protect poor and destitute persons in events of insecurities during old age, death of the breadwinner and maternity. The scheme is a measure of social protection to the poor and old persons throughout the country. NSAP came into force on 15 August 1995 and is a fully funded centrally sponsored programme and was transferred to the state plan from the year 2002–03. The Ministry of Finance releases funds under the scheme to the states/union territories in the form of Additional Central Assistance (ACA). This ACA is over and above the normal allocation of the state for welfare schemes as reflected in the state's budget so as to ensure a minimum level of expenditure on the welfare schemes. This programme has three components, namely the *NSAP*, *Indira Gandhi National Widow Pension Scheme (IGNWPS)*, *Indira Gandhi National Disability Pension Scheme (IGNDPS)* and *Indira Gandhi National Old-Age Pension Scheme (IGNOAPS)*.

The IGNOAPS benefits are available to those who have little or no regular means of subsistence from her/his own income or through the support of family members or other. The age of the applicant (male and female) shall be 60 years and financial assistance ₹200/per month given to the beneficiary. During 2010–11 this scheme covered 170.59 lakh beneficiaries as against 163.33 lakh beneficiaries in 2009–10 (http://nsap.gov.in/).

❖ INDIRA GANDHI NATIONAL WIDOW PENSION SCHEME

Widows belonging to a BPL household and who are in the age group of 40–64 years are entitled to receive benefits under this scheme. The amount for monthly widow pension is ₹200. During 2009–10, IGNDPS covered 34.25 lakh beneficiaries as against 32.13 lakh in 2009–10.

❖ INDIRA GANDHI NATIONAL DISABILITY PENSION SCHEME

Pensions under IGNDPS are available to those who are disabled and are in the age group of 18–64 years and are suffering from severe or multiple disabilities as defined in Persons with Disabilities Act and National Trust Act (1999). An amount of ₹200 is paid per month as pension. During 2009–10, 510,354 persons received pension and an amount of ₹3,279.96 was spent by the state governments through central assistance.

❖ NATIONAL FAMILY BENEFIT SCHEME (NFBS)

NFBS is targeted at BPL households after the death of the primary breadwinner in each of these families. The person entitled to this benefit should be in the age group of 18–65 years. A lump sum financial assistance of ₹10,000 is given to the targeted family. The NFB Scheme covered 3.35 lakhs the year 2010–11, as against 3.43 lakhs beneficiaries covered in 2009–10.

❖ ANNAPURNA SCHEME

This was launched on 1 April 2000 as a 100 per cent centrally sponsored scheme to provide food security to the senior citizens eligible for pension under the National Old-Age

Pension Scheme, but who were not getting the same. Under the scheme certain quantity of food grains were supplied free of cost per month. The scheme had been transferred to states in 2002–03. During 2009–10, an amount of ₹1,399.75 was disbursed by the states for 740,417 beneficiaries (Economic Survey 2010–11).

❖ ALLOCATION OF FUNDS

There has been a progressive improvement in allocation of funds under these schemes. Combined allocation under the Social Assistance Programme increased from ₹680 crore in 2002–03 to ₹5,162 crore in 2010–11. Similarly, total funds released under all the schemes increased from ₹657.09 crore to ₹5,162 crore (National Social Assistance Programme, Ministry of Rural Development, http://rural.nic.in/nsap_1.htm). The trend in combined allocation and funds released is shown in Figure 5.1.

THE SOCIAL INSURANCE SCHEMES

The Government of India also operates certain social insurance schemes for poor and weaker section of the society through LIC. The social insurance schemes include several schemes launched by the central and the state governments for the benefit of weaker

Figure 5.1 Combined Allocation and Release of Total Funds

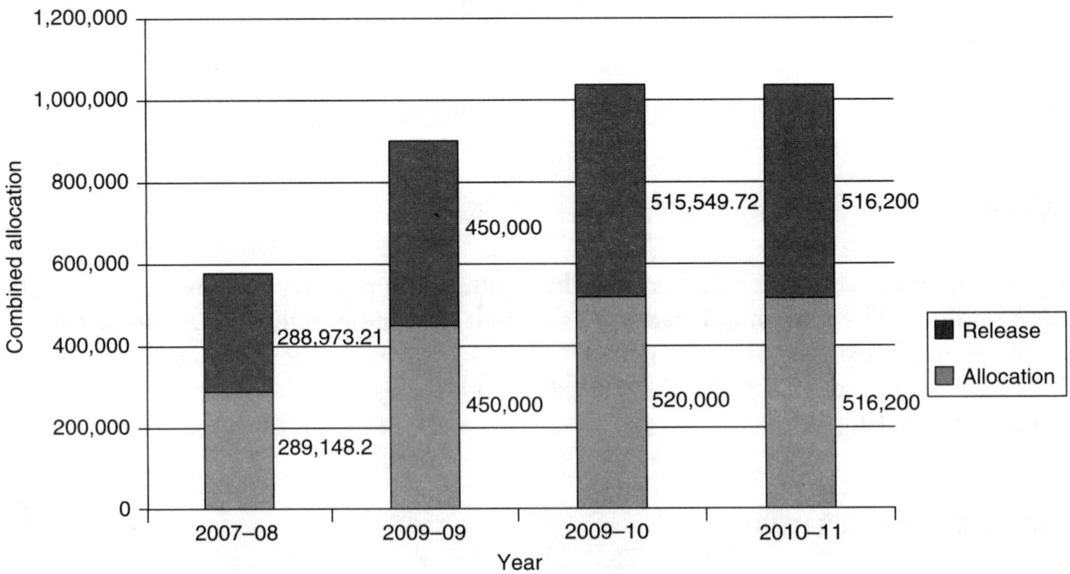

Source: National Social Assistance Programme, Ministry of Rural development. Available at: http://rural.nic.in/nsap_1.htm.

sections through the LIC and General Insurance Corporation of India. There are schemes for the employees of shops and commercial establishments and other weaker sections. The LIC has introduced a number of group insurance schemes devised by the central government for economically weaker sections of India (LIC social security schemes).

Some of the ongoing schemes are *Aam Admi Bima Yojana, Kendriya Bhed Palak Bima Yojana, Janashree Bima Yajana for National Rural Employment Guarantee Act* (NREGA) workers, *Bima Yojana for Powerloom Workers, Khadi Karigar Janashree Bima Yojana, Bima Yojana for Handicraft Artist, Mahatma Gandhi Bunkar Bima Yojana, Bima Yojana for Primitive Tribal Group and Siksha Sahayog Yojana.* Some closed schemes are *Landless Agricultural Labourers Group Insurance Scheme, Rural Group Life Insurance Scheme, Social Security Group Scheme, Krishi Shramik Samajik Suraksha Yojana, Bunkar Bima Yojana,* etc.

Rashtriya Swasthya Bima Yojana (RSBY)

The RSBY was launched on 1 October 2007 and became operational from 1 April 2008 for BPL families (a unit of not more than five) in the unorganised sector. The objective of RSBY is to provide the insurance cover to BPL households afflicted with major health problem that involve hospitalisation. The premium is shared on 75:25 basis by the centre and the state governments. In case of north-eastern states and Jammu and Kashmir, the premium is shared in a 90:10 ratio. Under the scheme, BPL households are entitled to a cost of up to 30,000 rupees per annum for a nominal registration fee of 30 rupees. A smart card is issued by the insurance company through the smart card service providers and the beneficiary is entitled to cashless transactions.

Universal Health Insurance Scheme

The Universal Health Insurance was the first attempt to provide medical benefits to the poor through health insurance launched on 14 July 2003. This policy is available to groups of 100 or more families and is being operated by National Insurance Company, New India Assurance Company, Oriental Insurance Company and United India Insurance Company. Premium for an individual is of ₹1/per day and ₹365 per annum. The benefit of family will operate on floater basis, that is, the total reimbursement of ₹30,000 can be availed of individually or collectively by members of the family. This policy covers people between the ages of 3 months and 65 years. The scheme also provides benefits like medical reimbursement, personal accident cover and disability cover. The policy provides reimbursement of hospitalisation expenses up to ₹30,000 to an individual/family subject to certain conditions. Other benefits include Personal Accident Cover of ₹25,000 for death of the earning head of the family (as named in the schedule) due to accident; Disability Cover, which is a compensation of ₹50 per day which is paid to a family if the earning head of the family is hospitalised due to an accident/illness. A compensation of ₹50 will be paid per day of hospitalisation up to a maximum of 15 days after a waiting period of 3 days.

UNORGANISED SECTOR WELFARE FUNDS

With a view to providing social security to the unorganised sector workers the Government of India has launched some welfare funds for the workers which are outside the framework of specific employer and employee relationship and the finances for the funds are raised by imposing cess on the commercial activity of the target group on a non-contributory basis and delivery of welfare services is effected without linkage to individual worker's contribution. The Ministry of Labour (Labour Welfare Fund Wing of Labour Welfare Division) is responsible for the administration of these funds which have been set up under the Acts of Parliament. These welfare funds include the Mica Mines Labour Welfare Fund Act (1946); the Limestone and Dolomite Mines Labour Welfare Fund Act (1972); the Iron Ore, Manganese Ore and Chrome Ore Mines Labour Welfare Fund Act (1976); the Beedi Workers' Welfare Fund Act (1976); and the Cine Workers' Welfare Fund Act (1981). The welfare funds provide several benefits to the workers which include public health and sanitation, medical facilities and the prevention of disease; water supply and facilities for washing; educational facilities; housing and recreational facilities including standards of living, nutrition and amelioration of social conditions. Presently, this is not for cine workers; family welfare, including family planning education and services; social security; transportation to and fro from place of work (for mine workers only); such other welfare measures and facilities as may be prescribed, etc.

Social Security Fund

The social security fund was set up in 1989 for providing subsidy for insurance cover to the weaker sections of the society. The initial fund was made by the LIC and the Government of India. The Fund is being managed by LIC. During 1989–90, out of a total contribution of ₹91.40 crore, LIC contributed ₹85.40 crore and the Government of India contributed ₹6 crore. During the period 1989–90 to 2004–05 the fund disbursed ₹362.86 crore towards premium subsidy in respect of Janashree Bima Yojana and social security group insurance schemes and Landless Agricultural Labourers' Group Insurance (LALGI) claim payment. The total corpus fund by the end of the financial year 2007–08 was ₹605.13 crore. The finance minister, while presenting the Union Budget 2010–11, in the Lok Sabha had announced the formation of the National Social Security Fund for unorganised sector workers with an initial allocation of ₹1,000 crore. This fund will support schemes for weavers, toddy tappers, rickshaw pullers, *beedi* workers, etc.

The Unorganised Workers' Social Security Act 2008

Another important step towards social security for the unorganised sector is the Unorganised Workers' Social Security Act 2008 passed by the Indian parliament. The Act aimed at providing social security to unorganised workers. The Unorganised Workers' Social Security Rules 2009 have also been framed. The Act has come in to force w.e.f. 16 May 2009. It provides for constitution of a National Social Security Board and State Social Security Boards, which will recommend social security schemes for these workers. The National Social Security Board has since been constituted and has met twice. The Board has made some recommendations regarding extension of social security schemes to certain additional segments of unorganised workers.

SOCIAL SECTOR EXPENDITURE BY CENTRE AND STATE GOVERNMENTS

Social sector expenditure as percentage of total expenditure from 20.3 per cent in 1990–91 to 23.8 per cent in 2009–10, and in terms of social sector expenditure as percentage of GDP during the same period, has increased from 3.3 per cent in 1990–91 to 7.23 per cent in 2009–10 (Figure 5.2). This trend is an indication of the growing concern of the government to mitigate social sector problems like old-age income security,

Figure 5.2 Social Sector Expenditure as Percentage of Total Expenditure and GDP

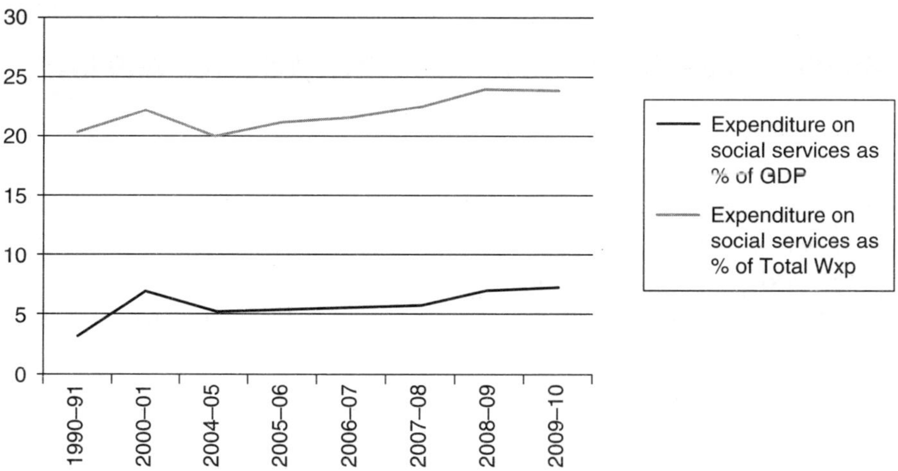

Source: Department of Economic Affairs (2010).

health problems, education and societal problems. However, this growth seems to be inadequate considering the nature of socioeconomic problems in terms of growth of population, ageing, unemployment and inadequate health-care system.

However, according to a study conducted by ASSOCHAM Research Bureau (2008), 'an industry organization in India', social sector ranking of India is the lowest among the BRIC (Brazil, Russia, India and China) nations. While India with its unabated growth momentum stands out as a preferred investment destination, the country lags far behind its peers in social sector achievements. Despite the sustained rise in budgets over the years, India's public spending on health as a percentage of GDP is second-lowest among the BRIC countries and the lowest in terms of education. According to this study, 'Public health and education expenditures among the BRIC countries' revealed that India's public expenditure on the two most significant social sectors, health and education stood, at 5 per cent and 9.2 per cent respectively as a percentage of GDP in FY 2005–06. The study shows that Brazil and Russia spent 7.9 per cent and 5.2 per cent respectively on health as a percentage of GDP in FY 2005–06, and India is marginally above China (share of 4.9 per cent of public expenditure on health) with public expenditure on education at 5 per cent of GDP in 2005–06 expenditure on health. In terms of government education expenditure (per primary student) as a percentage of GDP per capita, India is at the lowest of the pile of BRIC economies with 9.2 per cent of GDP for the year 2004–05. While Russia, Brazil and China spend 12.9 per cent, 12.8 per cent and 10.2 per cent expenditure, respectively, per primary student as a percentage of GDP per capita, India contributes just 9.2 per cent of GDP per capita towards primary education (Table 5.2). The study concludes that 'India needs to keep its pace with other developing countries in its social sector development, to meet the twin objectives of rapid progress and inclusive growth. We need to invest in more quality education and health services.'

PENSION AND PROVIDENT FUNDS FOR ORGANISED PRIVATE SECTOR AND CIVIL SERVICES

Present system of social security in India for the organised sector includes *employees' provident fund (EPF); employees' pension fund, Central Service Pension Scheme, the government provident fund, special provident fund.* Tax preferred voluntary component includes PPF, superannuation plans and personal pensions. For the organised private sector workers, there are a few funded social security schemes namely a DC *Employees' Provident Fund Scheme (EPFS)* and a DB *Employees' Pension Fund Scheme (EPS),* which are operated by the Employees' Provident Fund Organisation (EPFO). These two programmes are mandatory. However, there are also voluntary pension plans for workers in the unorganised sector. These pension plans are either managed privately by the managers appointed by them or through LIC.

Table 5.2 Trends in Social Services Expenditure by Central Government (Central and State Governments Combined) (₹ crore)

Items	*1990–91*	*2000–01*	*2004–05 Actual*	*2005–06 Actual*	*2006–07 Actual*	*2007–08 Actual*	*2008–09 (RE)*	*2009–10 (BE)*
Total Expenditure	163,673	595,595	869,757	959,855	1,109,174	1,295,903	1,659,109	1,870,955
Expenditure on Social Services	33,255	131,805	172,812	202,672	239,340	288,500	398,828	4,5,751
Of which:								
1. Education	17,094	67,036	84,111	96,365	114,744	127,547	167,981	198,842
2. Health	7,309	27,960	37,535	45,428	52,126	60,869	76,489	89,314
3. Others	8,852	36,809	51,166	60,879	72,470	100,084	154,358	157,595
As per cent of GDP								
Total Expenditure	8.36	31.30	26.85	25.90	25.89	26.19	29.76	30.35
Expenditure on Social Services	3.3	6.93	5.33	5.47	5.59	5.83	7.15	7.23
Of which:								
1. Education	3.35	3.52	2.60	2.60	2.68	2.58	3.01	3.23
2. Health	1.43	1.47	1.16	1.23	1.22	1.23	1.37	1.45
3. Others	1.73	1.93	1.58	1.64	1.69	2.02	2.77	2.56
As per cent of total expenditure								
Expenditure on Social Services	20.3	22.1	19.9	21.1	21.6	22.3	24.0	23.8
Of which:								
1. Education	10.4	11.3	9.7	10.0	10.3	9.8	10.1	10.6
2. Health	4.5	4.7	4.3	4.7	4.7	4.7	4.6	4.8
3. Others	5.4	6.2	5.9	6.3	6.5	7.7	9.3	8.4
As per cent of social services expenditure								
1. Education	51.4	50.9	48.7	47.5	47.9	44.2	42.1	44.6
2. Health	22.0	21.2	21.7	22.4	21.8	21.1	19.2	20.0
3. Others	26.6	27.9	29.6	30.0	30.3	34.7	38.7	35.4

Source: Economic Survey 2009–10, Government of India, Ministry of Finance, Department of Economic Affairs, February 2010.
Notes: BE: budget estimates; RE: revised estimates.

EPFO

The EPFO is the largest social security organisation in India, which administers three schemes. The programmers are administered by a tripartite body headed by the Union Labour Minister and the EPFO functions under the overall superintendence of the policies framed by the Central Board of Trustees. The EPFO manages *EPFS 1952, Employees' Deposit Link Insurance Scheme 1996, employees' pension fund 1995, under EPF Schemes.*

The EPF 1952 is the largest and the most important scheme. It is a fully funded contributory scheme mandatory for the establishment employing 20 or more persons. The Employees' Provident Funds and Miscellaneous Provision (EPFMP) Act 1952 which is the legal basis for social security for employees in India provides two choices to employer. An employer can select a scheme run by the central provident commissioner, or can manage its own provident fund trust by seeking an exemption. In addition to EPFS (1952) EPFO manages EPS 1995, Employees' Deposit Linked Insurance Scheme (1971) (EDLI). These three programmes are applicable to 186 classes of industries and establishments within these industries with 20 or more employees. The primary objectives of these schemes are to inculcate savings habit among the employees and to provide them social security. On its 50th golden jubilee celebration on 25 February 2003, it established a nationally *Unique Social Security Number* that remains constant and permanent and is able to establish one permanent number and one account for each member of the workforce regardless of geographical location or employer. The salient features of the EPFO schemes are shown in Annexure 5A.1.

EPFS (1952)

EPFS was the first serious attempt to regularise functioning of existing provident of the country and to expand the coverage. At the time of passing of the EPF Act, it covered only six industries. By 31 March 2008, 186 industries/classes of establishments were covered under the EPFMP Act. An employee who received a monthly salary of up to ₹6,500 was eligible to join the scheme as a member. The qualifying service period to join the scheme is from the date of joining the factory/establishment is *eligibility for Membership of the Scheme.* However, some *establishments are exempted* from joining the EPFO and can establish their own provident fund scheme offering benefits to their employees equal to or better than those provided under the statutory scheme. Though the functioning of exempted establishments is the responsibility of the Board of Trustees in each establishment, the EPFO exercises its control over such establishments through periodic inspections for ensuing proper compliance to conditions of exemption.

Coverage

There are provisions of compulsory coverage and voluntary coverage. Participation is mandatory for employees and employers as per the EPFMP Act, 1952. The Act extends to the whole of India except the state of Jammu and Kashmir. The Act is applicable to every establishment which is engaged in any one or more of the industries specified in Schedule I of the Act or any activity notified by the central government in the official gazette and employing 20 or more persons. However, the Act does not apply to co-operative societies/establishment, employing less than 50 persons and working without the aid of power. The establishments which are not otherwise coverable under the Act can also join the scheme voluntarily with the mutual consent of the employer and the majority of its employees.

Contribution and Membership Coverage under EPF Scheme

The normal rate of contribution payable to the provident fund by the employees and the employers under the Act has been revised from time to time. The rate of contribution presently applicable is 12 per cent except in respect of some category of industry notified by the government (Annexure 5A.1). There has been a significant increase in the amount of contribution over the years. Total contribution (exempted and un-exempted) went up from ₹7,795 crore in 1998–99 to ₹24,667.21 crore in 2007–08. As on 31 March 2008, the EPFO covered 532,702 establishments out of which 2,697 were exempted establishments and the rest 530,005 were un-exempted. Total membership stood at 44,919,278 out of which 3,760,722, were members of exempted establishment while the membership under un-exempted establishment was 41,158,556 (Table 5.3).

Benefits under EPF

While the members received accumulated amount along with interest in lump sum on retirement under EPF, they are entitled to monthly pension under EPS. Full benefits, that is, refund of employees and employers contribution with interest is payable to employees in case of retirement at the age of 55 years. Partial withdrawal is allowed in situations like illness invalidation and to provide funds to enable them to discharge their social responsibilities like marriage of self, sister/brother/daughter/son or higher education of children and construction of a dwelling house.

Table 5.3 EPFO Performance Statistics 2007–08 at a Glance

1. Coverage				
No. of Industries/**Classes of Establishments** to which EPF & MP Act, 1952 applied as on 31.03.2008				186 (182)
	Exempted		*Un-exempted*	*Total*
No. of **Establishments** Covered as on 31.03.2008	EPS 03 (03)	EPF 2,697 (2,586)	530,005 (469,089)	**532,702 (471678)**
Membership *(As on 31.03.2008 (in lakh)*	*Exempted*		*Un-exempted*	*Total*
1. In EPF	37.61 (40.01)		411.58 (404.03)	
2. In Pension Fund			405.86	**405.86 (357.30)**
2. Contributions Received (₹ In Crore)	*Exempted*		*Un-exempted*	*Total*
1. EPF				
a. During the year	5,884.91 (5,048.07)		18,782.30 (14,414.01)	**24,667.21 (19,462.08)**
b. Progressive	73,017.01 (67,132.10)		110,001.01 (91,218.71)	**183,018.02 (158,350.81)**
2. Employees' Pension Fund	*Un-exempted*			
	Employer's Share		*Government's Share*	*Total*
a. During the year	8022.46 (6710.66)		990.00 (1340.00)	**9,012.46 (8,050.66)**
b. Progressive				**87,754.27 (78,741.81)**
3. Employees' Deposit Linked Insurance Fund				*Total*
a. During the year				**308.44 (250.65)**
b. Progressive				**7,089.29 (6,780.85)**
Total Contribution (a+b+c)	*Exempted*		*Un-exempted*	*Total*
a. During the year	5,884.91 (5,048.07)		28,103.20 (22,715.32)	**33,988.11 (27,763.39)**
b. Progressive	73,017.01 (67,132.10)		204,844.57 (176,741.37)	**277,861.58 (243,873.47)**

Source: EPFO Annual Report 2007–08.

❖ INVESTMENT MANAGEMENT

Assets of EP funds are invested according to the guidelines issued by the Government of India. The contributions received by the EPFO in respect of un-exempted establishments as well as Board of Trustees and exempted establishment are to be invested according to the pattern laid down by the Government of India from time to time (Annexure 5A.2). RBI was handling the investment of EPF monies since inception to 1995. However, from 1 April 1995 investment management was handed over to the State Bank of India. Further in the year 2008, the EPFO appointed four private sector fund managers on contractual basis which is to be reviewed further.

As on 31 March 2008, an amount of ₹121,503.70 crore was invested by EPFO. Instrument wise break up indicate that highest percentage of 43.04 per cent was invested in the Special Deposit Scheme of Government of India. Out of the balance funds 43.04 per cent was invested in public sector financial institutions/undertakings (including private sector bonds/securities), 19.76 per cent was invested in central government securities, 13.52 per cent in state government securities and 1.23 per cent in government guaranteed bonds that amounted to ₹6, 278.22 crore.

❖ ADMINISTRATIVE AND INSPECTION CHARGES

The administrative expenditure of Provident Funds Scheme is met out of the administrative charges received from the employers of the un-exempted establishments and inspection charges from the employers of exempted establishments. The prevailing rate of administrative charges and inspection charges are 1.10 per cent and 0.18 per cent on the aggregate wages on which contribution to provident fund is payable.

EPS

The EPS (1995) was conceived as a 'Benefit defined Social Insurance Scheme', which came into force on 16 January 1995. The objective of the scheme is to provide economic sustenance during old age and survivorship coverage to the member and his family without any additional contribution. The Pension Scheme (1971) derives its financial resource by partial diversion from the provident fund contribution. The eligibility for EPS membership is fixed at a minimum 10 years of service in aggregate of Employees' Family Pension Scheme (1971) and EPS (1995). The maximum pay on which employers' and employees' contribution is computed is ₹5,000. The scheme is made mandatory for all the existing members of the provident fund who were contributing to the Employees' Family Pension Scheme and also for all the new entrants to the membership of provident fund from 16 November 1995.

Superannuation/retirement pension under the EPS (1995) is payable on fulfilling the minimum 10 years of eligible service, and attaining the age of 58 years. On ceasing employment earlier than 58 years, pension may be availed of by a member at his option, before attaining the age of 58 years but not below 50 years subject to discounting factor at the rate of 3 per cent for every year of shortfall from 58 years. No pension will be payable to any member before attaining the age of 50 years but in case of pension entitlement on disablement or pension payable to the family members on death of the member no such age restriction or eligibility requirement shall apply, for membership one month contribution will suffice in such cases. The scheme is financed by diversion of 8.33 per cent of wages from the employer's share of the provident fund contribution and central government also contributes 1.16 per cent as government contribution. All accumulations in the ceased family pension fund constitute the corpus of pension fund. The contribution is received year-wise. EPS 1995 provides several benefits to the members and their family. The members of the scheme are entitled for superannuation/retirement and permanent total disablement benefits and capital return (corpus accretion) on option formulae basis. There is also a provision of commutation of pension up to 1/3rd of pension amount. The widow/widower of the family upon death of the member is entitled to pension for life or till remarriage, two children at a time up to 25 years of age are simultaneously entitled to widow/widower pension/ orphan pension. Children/orphans with total and permanent disability are also entitled to children pension or orphan pension.

❖ INVESTMENT MANAGEMENT

The scheme provides for investment of the pension funds as per pattern prescribed by the government from time to time. As on 31 March 2008, total investment under EPS fund was ₹94,101.42 crore. Instrument-wise investment of this fund indicate that 21.56 per cent funds were invested in central government securities, 12.64 per cent funds were invested in state government securities, 1.72 per cent funds were invested in government guaranteed securities, 1.49 per cent funds were invested in Special Deposit Scheme, 23.47 per cent was in public sector financial institutions/undertakings (including private sector bonds/securities) and 39.12 per cent was invested in Public Account (*EPFO Annual Report 2007–08*). By 31 March 2008 pensionary benefit had been extended to 2,952,622 beneficiaries.

Employees' Deposit Linked Insurance Scheme (1976)

Launched in August 1976 in order to provide insurance and additional savings avenue, Employees' Deposit Linked Insurance (EDLI) Scheme came into force from 1 August 1976. No contribution is payable by the employee for availing the insurance cover. The scheme covers the employees of all factories and establishments to which EPFMP Act 1952 applies. The employee members are not required to contribute to the insurance fund, the employers are required to pay contributions to the insurance fund at the rate of 0.5 per cent of pay. The EDLI Scheme provides life insurance and death cover. If a member of the EPF or of the exempted provident fund dies while in service, the person is entitled to receive the provident fund accumulations and an additional amount equal to the average balance in the provident fund account of the deceased during the preceding 12 months wherever the average provident fund balance is less than ₹35,000.

❖ INVESTMENT

The contribution received in the insurance fund was kept in the Public Account in 1996–97. The rate of interest on such accumulations in the Public Account was 8.5 per cent. From 1997–98 onwards net accretions are being invested as per prescribed investment pattern. By 31 March 2008 total investment corpus of EDLI Scheme was ₹627.88 crore. Investment pattern indicate that 67.59 per cent of these funds was invested in Public Account, 13.83 per cent was invested in public sector financial institutions/undertakings (including private sector bonds/securities), 9.51 per cent in central government securities, 8.56 per cent in state government securities and rest in government guaranteed bonds and Special Deposit Scheme.

❖ ADMINISTRATIVE AND INSPECTION CHARGES

EPFO charges fees for administration to insurance funds from all establishments covered. The rate of administrative charges is 0.01 per cent of basic wage, dearness allowance, etc., subject to a minimum of ₹2 per month. The employees of establishments covered are granted exemption under the EDLI Scheme and are required to pay the inspection charges of 0.005 per cent of basic wage, dearness allowance, etc., subject to a minimum of ₹1 per month (EPFO Annual Report 2007–08).

Some Critical Observations about EPF/EPS

EPFO has played a very important role in providing pension to the organised corporate sector in India. The size of the EPF and EPS funds, number of employees covered, etc., is a testimony of its successful operation. However, the operation of the organisation recently came under critical comments by many experts, particularly the investment regulation, withdrawal of funds, supervision, etc. Investment regulation has been described as the constraint for higher return as most of the funds are invested in government securities and public deposit schemes. As noted by Gillingham and Kanda (2001), investment rules have constrained investment in corporate bonds and proscribed investment in equities, thus drastically reducing the return on investment to provident and pension funds. The lower returns on EPF have imposed an implicit 'tax' on EPF contribution.

Another weak area of EPFO is liberal provision of withdrawal which defeats the very purpose of retirement savings. EPFO allows withdrawal for children education, housing, funerals, wedding, etc. The provision for premature partial withdrawal cannot be totally withdrawn in view of lower income of employees who may not be able to have the alternative savings for these important functions. But strict provision can be introduced to avoid misuse of the provisions. Regulation of EPFO is also an area of critical observation. EPFO is a fund manager as well as supervisor of its operation. EPFO unlike other fund managers in mutual funds, insurance or pension funds is not under any regulatory body. Neither the trustee-managed pension funds nor funded gratuity schemes supervised by any statutory body. This is considered as an important weakness of the operation of EPFO.

SPECIAL PROVIDENT FUNDS

Though these funds are managed by separate trusts and fund managers basically to follow the rules and investment guidelines applicable to EPFO. These funds have been set up under a special Act.

Coal Mines Provident Fund

Coal Mines Provident Fund Scheme, was introduced in 1948, even before the introduction of EPF in 1952. Initially the scheme was introduced on 12 May 1947. The scheme extends to all coal mines in India. This is a contributory scheme—10 per cent of total emoluments being the rate of contribution. The contribution of employer should match employee contribution. An employee can also make excess voluntary contribution but not exceeding 12 per cent of total emoluments. An employee receives full benefits at any time on attaining the age of 50 years.

Coal Mines Pension Scheme (1998)

Coal Mines Pension Scheme was introduced on 5 March 1998. The scheme covers employees of coal mines joining service on or after 5 March 1998, who were members of Coal Mines Pension Scheme (1971) but had not attained the age of superannuation, an employee who did not join the Coal Mines Family Pension Scheme (1971). The Pension Fund is financed through transfer of 2/3 per cent of the salary of the employee diverted from the provident fund, and 12/3 per cent of the salary of the employee (maximum ₹600 per month) being contributed by the government. Monthly pension is payable to a member on retirement/superannuation/termination/resignation/death or on attaining the age of superannuation after the completion of 30 years of pensionable service. There is also the provision for disablement pension and Orphan Pension Ex-gratia Payment.

Railway Pension Fund

Indian Railways is the single-largest employer in India employing over 1.6 million employees. In the year 1957, the Railways introduced a DB non-contributory pension fund for its employees. Initially, pension payments to retired employees were made from the general revenue but a pension fund was set up in 1964, and the Railways started to contribute on this fund and pay pension to the employees. There has been a significant increase in pension expenditures over the period. With deceleration in recruitment of fresh employees, the dependency ratio, that is, the ratio of pensioners to workers for the railways has increased sharply from 0.17 in 1980–81 to 0.66 in 1999–2000. As a result, the share of pensions in the working expenses of the Railways has risen from 4.65 per cent in 1981 to 13.3 per cent in 1998 (Mathur 1998). The working group on government of India's pension liability has further estimated that total pension expenditure of Railways increased from ₹886 crore in 1990–91 to ₹4,018 crore in 1999–2000 and to ₹5,800 crore in 2001–02 (Sehgal 2001). If the current system continues the pension will increase further and the system will be under tremendous stress.

The Assam Tea Plantations Provident Fund Scheme

This is the only institutionalised social security cover for the tea garden workers of Assam. The Scheme came into force w. e. f. 12 September 1955. After introduction of provident fund schemes on 12 September 1955, a series of legislations were introduced to strengthen the system. The following schemes are operational (Barua 2010) *Assam Tea Plantations Provident Fund Scheme (1955), Pension Scheme (1967), Family Pension Scheme (1972), Deposit Linked Insurance Scheme, (1984).* Presently, an employee working 60 day in a period of three months and drawing less than ₹5,000 per month is entitled to be a member of the scheme. The rate of contribution increased from 6.25 per cent in 1955–56 to 12 per cent in 2003–04. Rate of interest on pension fund accumulation amount increased from 1.5 per cent in 1955–56 to 11 per cent in 1995–96 but declined to 9 per cent in 2003–04. A growth was witnessed in the pension funds from ₹74,108 lakh in 1994–94 to ₹256,241 lakh in 2003–04.

Pension–cum–Family Pension Scheme

There is also provision of pension and family pension. But neither the employee nor the employer is required to pay any extra contribution to the pension fund. The board and the Government of India contribute 21/3 per cent and 1/6 per cent of the total wages of the members of the provident fund. On retirement a member is paid a pension for a period that varies according to the years of service rendered and the amount of provident fund accumulated. There is also a Deposit Linked Insurance Scheme that came into force from 1 February 1984 and is applicable to all pension fund members under ATPPF and PF Scheme. The employees contribute 0.5 per cent of the ιotal wagers and the Government of India contributes 25 per cent of the total wages of members. In the event of death of a member, the nominee is paid the insurance benefit under the scheme.

The Seamen's Provident Fund Scheme

Introduced w.e.f. 1 July 1964, it was the first social security scheme for Indian Merchant Navy Seamen, which was brought under statute by enactment of the Seamen's Provident Fund Act (1966) (April 1966). The objective of the scheme was to provide provident fund for seamen as old-age retirement benefit and their family members in the event of death of member seamen. This is a contributory provident fund and the employers are required to deposit the provident fund contributions in respect of the seamen employed by them with their matching contribution with the Seamen's Provident Fund Organisation after the termination of each voyage. The rate of contribution since its establishment has gone up from 8 per cent to 12 per cent. However, employers can contribute more if they desire. Fund is invested as per guidelines of the Finance Ministry. As on 31 March 1999, the organization covered 33708 accounts and the total amount of provident fund accumulations is ₹.3,047,745,305.59 (http://www.dgshipping.com/dgship/final/spfc.htm). The needy seamen members are also allowed non-refundable withdrawals for the longer period of unemployment, sickness, purchase of dwelling house, marriage (for self and/or member of the family) or higher education of the children.

THE EMPLOYEES' STATE INSURANCE SCHEME (ESIS)

The ESIS is an integrated need-based social insurance scheme that protects the interest of workers in contingencies such as sickness, maternity, temporary or permanent physical disablement, death due to employment injury resulting in loss of wages or earning capacity also guarantees reasonably good medical care to workers and their immediate dependants. Following the promulgation of the ESI Act the central government set up the Employees' State Insurance Corporation to administer the scheme. The scheme was first implemented in Kanpur and Delhi on 24 February 1952. The design of the scheme is such that the benefits provided to the employees are in conformity with ILO conventions.

Coverage

The ESI Act is applicable to all the factories employing 10 or more persons irrespective of whether power is used in the process of manufacturing or not. The scheme has also been extended to shops, hotels, restaurants, cinemas including preview theatre, road motor transport undertakings and newspaper establishments, private medical and educational institutions employing 20 or more persons. With effect from 1 May 2010, the workers earning ₹15,000 per month are covered under this scheme. As on 31 March 2010, the ESI Scheme has 14,300,000 insured person family units; 13,896,150 employees; 55,484,000 beneficiaries; 2,600,250 insured women and 406,499 employers.

Contribution

The ESI Scheme is a contributory programme and is financed by employees and their employers as a percentage of fixed wages. The rates are revised from time to time. Currently, the employee's contribution rate (w.e.f. 1 January 1997) is 1.75 per cent of the wages and that of employer's is 4.75 per cent of the wages paid/payable in respect of the employees in every wage period. Employees in receipt of a daily average wage up to ₹70 are exempted from payment of contribution but employers will contribute their own share in respect of these employees.

Benefits

The persons who are insured under ESIS are entitled to several benefits including the medical benefit, sickness benefits, extended sickness benefits, enhanced sickness benefits, maternity benefits, disablement benefits, dependents' benefits (family pension) and some other benefits. The ESIS allows full medical care in the form of medical attendance, treatment, drugs and injections, specialist consultation and hospitalisation to insured persons and also to members of their families. Insured persons are entitled to sickness benefits in cash in the event of sickness resulting into absence of work. Maternity benefits are payable to an insured woman in the case of confinement, miscarriage or medical termination of pregnancy (MTP), sickness arising out of pregnancy, premature birth. Disablement are payable to an insured person if she/he suffers from employment injury or occupational disease as an employee. There is also Dependents' Benefits Family Pension.

Administration

The ESIS is administered by Employees' State Insurance Corporation, which comprises employees, employers, the central and state governments, representatives of parliament and medical profession. A standing committee, constituted from among the members of the corporation, acts as an executive body. The Medical Benefit Council, constituted by the central government, is yet another statutory body that advises the corporation on matters related to effective delivery of medical services to the beneficiary population.

GRATUITY UNDER THE PAYMENT OF GRATUITY ACT (1972)

A gratuity is payable to an employee or beneficiary upon termination of employment after such employee has rendered continuous service for not less than five years. The condition of completion of five years' continuous service is not applicable where termination of the employment of an employee is due to death or disablement. The payment of the gratuity benefit is a statutory requirement for employers with a workforce of 10 or more employees, and it is applicable to all permanent employees, regardless of category or salary. The benefit is paid in lump-sum form. As per the existing provisions in payment of Gratuity Act 1972, the maximum gratuity payable is ₹10 lakh even though the individual is eligible for higher amount based on his length of service and last pay drawn.

CIVIL SERVANTS' PENSION SCHEME

Civil servants' pension though primarily covers the central government employees; similar pension benefits are extended to state government employees. In addition to these categories almost same benefits are available to central and public sector employees. However, we would restrict ourselves to the pension and related benefits that are available to the central and state government employees. Latest data (2007) indicates that 272.76 lakh persons were employed in the organised sector, 180.02 lakh (66 per cent) in the organised public sector and 34 per cent in the organised private sector. Employment in organised public sector, which includes central government, state government, quasi government and local bodies, has declined from 181.88 lakh persons in 2006 to 180.02 lakh persons in 2007. Out of 180.02 lakh persons 28 lakhs were employed in central government, 72.09 lakh persons were employed in state government, 58.61 lakh in quasi governments and 21.32 lakh in local bodies. These organised public sector employees enjoy the pension benefits and other social benefits. We shall discuss in brief some such benefits in the following paragraphs.

Pension Scheme for Central Government Employees

Central government employees who joined services before 1 January 2004 are entitled for DB pension commutation of pension, gratuity and other benefits. In addition to these, they are also entitled to certain non-pensionary benefits. Civil servants in India used to receive pension even before the introduction of EPF in 1995. A bulk of salaried employees was employed in the central government departments. As per the Census of Central Government Employees undertaken by Ministry of Labour, 'the total regular employment under the Central Government as on 31st March, 2001 was 38.76 lakhs, as against 39.82 lakhs as on 31st March, 1995. The employment has thus recorded a decrease of 2.66% in 2001 over 1995.' The employment in Ministry of Railways was highest (39.02 per cent) followed by Communications & IT (15.94 per cent), Defence (civilian) 15.21 per cent, Home Affairs (14.80 per cent), and Finance (4.37 per cent). Other Ministries/Departments collectively shared the rest of 10.66 per cent of the total central government regular employment (Census of Central Government Employees 2001). Among the central government employees, the largest single component of the pension bill goes to retired Defence personnel and their dependents next to Defence and the second-largest component goes to Railways' Pension Scheme. 'It has also been estimated that pension spending for Indian civil servants has risen dramatically during the last few years for the central government, in terms of GDP it has been doubled between 1995 and 2000' (Sehgal 2001). In addition to pension the central government employees receive other benefits like gratuity and GPF. Civil Services Pension in India is unfunded DB pensions which is paid out of current revenue. The maximum replacement rate is 50 per cent of the average salary during last 10 months of service (Sehgal 2001). Pensions are indexed according to inflation and structure of salary of serving employees. There are various types of pension, namely

- *Superannuation Pension*: A government servant is entitled to superannuation pension when he retires from services on attaining the age of compulsory retirement.
- *Retiring Pension*: When a government servant retires prior to the age of compulsory retirement Article 459 of Civil Service Rules (CSR) or opts for voluntary retirement on being declared surplus, he/she is entitled to this kind of pension.
- *Invalid Pension*: When a government servant retires from service on account of any bodily or mental infirmity, due to which she/he permanently incapacitates for the service, the employee is eligible for invalid pension. But this pension is granted only on the recommendation of a Medical Board constituted for the purpose.
- *Compensation Pension*: A government servant who is discharged from service owing to the abolition of his/her permanent post is granted this pension.
- *Compulsory Retirement Pension*: If a government employee is compulsorily retired from service as a measure of penalty, she/he is granted this pension.
- *Compassionate Allowance*: A government servant who is dismissed or removed from service by the competent authority, and if the case deserves special consideration, he is granted this allowance.
- *Family Pension*: If a government servant dies while in service or after retirement, family pension is payable to the widow/widower or to an eligible family member.

An employee may receive full pension or partial pension. An employee is eligible for full pension after 20 years of service and maximum number of years taken into account is 33 years and partial pension is received after 10 years of service. There is a provision for commuted value, that is, an employee is entitled to take a lump sum amount of money as commuted value at the time of retirement and before monthly pension payments starts. On retirement DB formula is calculated on accrual rate so slightly more than 10 per cent per year of service is multiplied by the average of the civil servant during his final 10 months before his retirement. The process of determining the initial pension level is further complicated by the fact that part of the pension can be 'commuted', in other words taken as lump sum. Most pensioners appear to take full advantage of the Commutation Option (World Bank 2001). This unfunded DB pension is paid from current revenue. The maximum replacement rate (the ratio of income from retirement benefits to pre-retirement income after mandatory deduction is 50 per cent of the average salary during last 10 months of service. There is also a maximum limit on the absolute amount of pension, which is 50 per cent of the highest pay in the government. The pension benefits are paid out of current revenues, in the case of non-commercial departments. As per present government policy, pensions are indexed not only to inflation but also to change in the salary structure of serving employees (Sehgal 2001).

❖ GPF

In addition to the pension, the central government employees are also covered under the GPF scheme. The GPF is a DC programme where only employees themselves contribute a minimum percentage of their monthly earnings (as decided from time to time). The accumulation value comprising of contribution and investment return under the GPF are returned to the employee at the time of retirement.

❖ OTHER NON-PENSION BENEFITS FOR CENTRAL CIVIL-SERVICE EMPLOYEES

The central government employees are also entitled for certain other non-pension benefits like Gratuity, GPF, and Central Government Employees' Group Insurance Scheme (CGEGIS).

❖ GRATUITY

The central government employees are also entitled to gratuity under the Gratuity Act of 1972. There are three types of gratuity depending on the period of service, namely retirement gratuity, death gratuity and service gratuity. All three types of gratuity are based on basic pay and dearness allowance.

Retirement Gratuity

It is a one-time lump sum benefit and it requires a minimum of five years of qualifying service and eligibility to receive service gratuity/pension. There is no minimum limit for the amount of gratuity but the maximum retirement gratuity payable is 16.5 times the emoluments plus dearness allowance limited to ₹10 lakh.

Death Gratuity

It is a one-time lump sum benefit payable to the widow/widower or the nominee of a permanent or a quasi-permanent or a temporary government servant including CPF beneficiaries dying in harness. There is no stipulation regarding minimum length of service rendered by the deceased employee.

Service Gratuity

It s paid to a retiring government servant if the total qualifying service is less than 10–12 years. There is no minimum or maximum monetary limit on the quantum. This one-time lump sum payment is distinct from and is paid over and above the retirement gratuity. Government of India while giving wage revision to central government employees through Sixth Pay Commission enhanced the ceiling of retirement/death gratuity to ₹10 Lakhs w.e.f 1 January 2006.

❖ CENTRAL GOVERNMENT EMPLOYEES' GROUP INSURANCE

In addition to the above benefits, the central government employees are also entitled to *Central Government Employees' Group Insurance Scheme (CGEGIS)*. Under CGEGIS, the employees pay monthly premium depending on their civil service rank. CGEGIS provides a survivor benefit equal to a multiple of the monthly premium in the event a worker dies prior to retirement. Otherwise, it provides a lump sum payment equal to the accumulated premiums.

Pension Scheme for State Government Employees

The civil servants of the state governments, like their counterpart in the central government receive pensions from the state government, which is usually paid from the general revenue of the governments, and in recent times there is a steep rise in pension liabilities adversely affecting the fiscal soundness of the government. According to the report of the group to study the pension liabilities of the state governments (known as *Bhattacharya Committee Report*, October 2003), pension payments of the state governments during the period 1980–2002 have increased at an annual compound rate of 23.6 per cent from ₹268 crore in 1979–80 to ₹28,197 crore in 2001–02. According to the committee, the rapid increase in the outgo of states for pension was on account of increase in state government employees during the previous decade, increase in various facilities to employees and non-government institutions (grant-in-aid institutions [GIAs]), impact of pay revisions, introduction of wage indexation and increase in life expectancy, etc. State government employees in India receive various retirement benefits in addition to pension as mentioned below.

❖ PENSION

State government employees in India are entitled to a variety of pension schemes which includes retirement pension, superannuation pension, compensation pension, invalid pension. There is also a provision for family pension which is payable to the widow/widower or to an eligible family member from the date following the date of death of an employee, while in service or after retirement. Pension schemes cover all state government employees including the GIAs which are mostly educational institutions. In case of GIA employees though grants were initially given by many state governments to meet the gap between their receipts and expenditure but over the years, many state governments have accepted the entire burden relating to both the salary and pension expenditure of such institutions. The minimum eligibility period for receipt of pension on retirement, other than voluntary retirement, is 10 years of service for state government employees while in the case of voluntary retirement, minimum service period is 20 years which is calculated on the basis of completed six monthly periods. The maximum period of service that is taken into account for calculation of pension is 33 years. In general, the minimum pension/family pension payable is ₹1,275 per month. The maximum limit on pension is ₹12,250 per month and on family pension it is restricted to ₹7,350 per month. Most of the states follow the DA formula as per the central government pattern. Dearness relief on pension/family pension is revised twice a year, that is, on 1 January and most of the states follow full wage indexation for the pensioners.

Gratuity

State government employees are also entitled to gratuity depending on the period of service. There are three types of gratuity for the state government employees, namely (*a*) retirement gratuity, (*b*) death gratuity and (*c*) service gratuity. Gratuity amounts are calculated on the basis of basic pay and service period.

❖ RETIREMENT GRATUITY

It is available after a minimum five years of qualifying service, which is calculated at the rate of one-fourth of the last basic pay for each completed six-month period of qualifying service. It is one-time lump sum benefit payable to the nominee of the deceased employee. An employee is entitled to receive gratuity (and not pension) if total qualifying service is less than 10 years. Admissible amount of state government employees are also entitled for gratuity on death and on fulfilment of certain conditions.

❖ NON-PENSIONARY BENEFITS

In addition to pension and gratuity, the state government employees are also entitled to certain other additional non-pensionary benefits like leave encashment, government employees' insurance schemes, etc. Some state governments also provide survivor benefits to employees dying in harness. For example, under the Tamil Nadu Government Servant Family Security Scheme which is compulsory for all employees who have a family, the employee contributes ₹20 per month and in the event of the death of the employee, a sum of ₹1 lakh after deduction of any advance towards funeral expenses is paid to the nominee.

VOLUNTARY PENSIONS PLANS

In addition to the pension plans offered by EPFO, there are few options before individuals to make provisions for their post retirement income through voluntary pension arrangements. These pension plans are offered by publicly managed LIC and other privately managed life insurance companies. The Unit Trust of India (UTI) and other mutual funds like Kothari Pioneer also offer pension plans.

Apart from EPF schemes the organised sector employees can also take the benefits of group superannuation plans offered by life insurance companies. Under the Employee Superannuation Scheme an employer can establish an irrevocable trust fund (under Income Tax Act [1961]). The superannuation scheme though intended primarily for post-retirement pension, also provides other contingencies like death in service, etc. The superannuation fund set up by an employer can be privately managed by it or alternatively handed over to LIC for management under group superannuation schemes. In 2003, the Central Board of Direct Taxes (CBDT) amended the Income Tax Rules (1962) and allowed private insurance companies to run group gratuity schemes where companies had approved gratuity funds. We shall discuss about LIC group annuities along with individual annuities.

PPF

The PPF in the country was introduced in 1968 in order to provide a long-term savings avenue for those who are not covered by any formal pension scheme. The PPF is an extremely good instrument for risk-averse investors for long term wealth creation, particularly for building corpus for old-age income. PPF is a safe instrument since it is backed by the government of India. This guarantee is in the form of safety of capital and regular payment of interest.

❖ MAIN FEATURES OF THE PPF

The PPF is a long-term investment and an account is opened for an initial period of 15 years. But it can be continued further. After the initial term of 15 years a PPF account can be extended for five years at a time, but there is a bar on further extension. Investment in PPF provides multiple tax benefits. First, the investment made in PPF is deductible from income under Section 80C of the Income Tax Act. This means that the entire investment in PPF is tax free, subject to the provisions of Section 80C. Second, the interest earned in a PPF account is tax free. Therefore, on maturity of PPF and withdrawal of PPF money attract no tax deduction. The minimum investment in PPF is ₹500 per year. This low amount ensures that even persons falling in low income groups can save for their retirement using a government backed, safe investment avenue. The maximum investment allowed in PPF is ₹100,000 per year. Though the PPF is meant for long-term investments, at times, in order to mitigate the emergency needs there is a provision for withdrawal of PPF, once a year, from seventh year onwards. But an investor can withdraw an amount not exceeding the lower of (*a*) 50 per cent of the balance at the end of the fourth immediately preceding year, (*b*) 50 per cent of the balance at the end of the immediately preceding year. The PPF account can be closed only after 15 years. Loan is allowed after three years and withdrawal is permitted after four years. The PPF funds are invested by providing loans to the state government (3/4 of total funds) and the rest (1/4th) is invested in public accounts of the central government.

❖ FUNDS COLLECTED UNDER PPF SCHEME

Year-wise receipt and outstanding has been shown in Table 5.4. Yearly receipt of the PPF has gone up from ₹1,405 crore in 1990–00 to ₹2,940 crore in 2008–09, that is, by little over two times. Similarly outstanding under PPF increased from ₹4,624 crore in 1990 to ₹25,758 crore, that is, by five times (Figure 5.3). Though the scheme of PPF was launched to create retirement fund for low-income people the scheme failed to achieve this objective as it got presented as tax saving instrument, provision to withdraw funds before maturity, low key publicity and marketing initiatives, etc.

Table 5.4 Pension and Annuity Business of LIC of India (under in-force policies)

Column 1	*Column 2* *2004–05*	*Column 3* *2005–06*	*Column 4* *2007–08*	*Column 5* *2008–09*	*Column 6* *2009–10*
1. Individual Insurance					
A. Sum Assured and Bonus (₹ in Crore)					
i. Assurance	1,288,468.8	1,535,439.6	1,783,426.24	2,113,689.6	2,422,714.4
ii. Annuities	1,189.8	1,296.16	1,592.28	5,181.1	1,569.84
iii. Pension	3,136.27	3,208.08	2,297.59	2,364.93	2,381.2
B. No of Policies (in Lakh)	1,649.35	1,835.77	1,925.27	2,102.53	2,261.59
i. Assurances	9.31	9.79	9.44	9.43	9.62
ii. Annuities	1,938	1,944	18.85	18.18	18.46
iii. Pension	1,649.35				
2. Group Schemes					
i. Sum Assured (₹ Crore)	136,286.92	199,427.16	306,950.5	417,552.26	457,918.61
ii. Annuities per annum (₹ in Crore)	1,916.64	2,189.28	3,211.3	4,176.08	5,197.96
No of Schemes					
i. No. of Group Schemes	106,912	109,995	128,904	121,107	125,019
ii. No. of Superannuation Schemes	7321	6,135	6,463	7,009	5,974
No. of Llives (in Lakh)					
i. Group Insurance	306.5	302.71	495.25	624.48	764.22
ii. No. of Lives	12.73	12.5	15.54	22.6	70

Source: Life Insurance Corporation of India, Annual Report 2005–06, 2007–08, 2009–2010.

Figure 5.3 Public Provident Fund (receipts and outstanding)

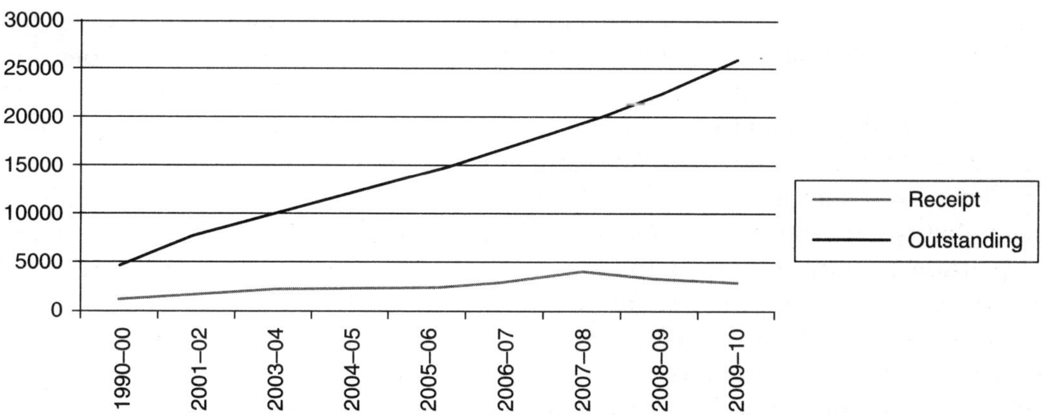

Source: Handbook of Statistics on Indian Economy (2010), Reserve Bank of India, Mumbai.

Pension Schemes of Life Insurance Companies

Individual and group annuities play a very important role in pension system particularly for the unorganised sector, which cannot avail retirement benefits offered to the organised sector employees. In India, employees who are outside of EPF/state or central pension system can very well avail the benefits of annuities as retirement savings. Till the opening of Indian insurance industry, LIC was the only annuity provider of the country. However, a number of new life insurance companies have introduced annuity products, after the opening up of the insurance industry. Yet, the presence of the private sector in life insurance is at best marginal. The LIC remains the dominant player in the annuity market. The annuity market can be sub-divided into *Individual Annuity* and *Group Annuity*. While Individual Annuity purchase is voluntary, Group Annuity became mandatory for employer run superannuation funds. For self-managed superannuation funds accumulation can be managed through trust or by insurance company (LIC of India) while at the time of retirement, fund has to be handed over to LIC for group annuities.

❖ INDIVIDUAL ANNUITIES

LIC and other private insurance companies have introduced pension plans. Though annuities are major pension plans, of late the Unit-Linked Pension Plans (ULPPs) are also becoming very popular in India. The LIC is the primary annuity provider having about 90 per cent of market share. As on 31 March 2010, total in-force general annuity and pension policies reported by IRDA was little more than 31.83 lakh out of which 27.80 lakh, that is, 87 per cent of total policies were in LIC's book. Sum assured under these policies is reported to be ₹52,952.36 crore and the share of LIC was 88.6 per cent, that is, ₹46,962.56 crore.

A clear picture of changing trend in annuity and pension business of life insurance companies in India can be seen in terms of business of LIC during recent time (Table 5.4). It can be seen that during 2004–05 to 2009–10, enforced annuity and pension policies together decreased marginally from ₹28.69 lakh to ₹28.08 lakh, while the combined sum assured declined from ₹4,326.07 crore to ₹3,951.04 crore during this period. In the year 2009–10, LIC sold 0.23 lakh individual annuity policies and 0.19 lakh pension policies for a sum assured of ₹21.35 crore and ₹645.18 crore respectively. This indicates that life insurance companies could not or did not fully exploit the potential of pension annuity market in India. However, though individual annuity growth remained stagnant, group superannuation and annuity did better than individual annuity in extending coverage across the section.

The annuity market in India is still very under-developed, like most of the annuity market outside. In fact, under-development of the annuity market is a global phenomenon. Estelle James (2001) has noted,

> *Annuities markets are still poorly developed in virtually all the countries. The under development of the industry manifests itself in its small size relative to other kind of insurance, the absence of mortality tables which are pre-requisite to sound pricing and funding policies and the relative paucity of long term financial instruments with which to match assets and liabilities, thereby creating substantial reinvestment risk.*

These observations about the worldwide annuity market is also very relevant for India and it need to be corrected to promote a market for long-term retirement security system which is interlinked to the development of active annuities market. James and Sane (2002) has noted the institutional gaps that the industry and government have addressed to make annuities an important instrument for retirement savings.

❖ GROUP SUPERANNUATION SCHEMES

Group superannuation schemes are voluntary in nature and depend on the employers to introduce this scheme or not. A company can introduce a group superannuation scheme either through constitution of a trust or can buy a superannuation scheme from a life insurance company. On retirement the employee can commute one-third of accumulated value and buy an annuity with the remaining amount. The employer and employee receive tax benefits if the scheme is approved by the income tax authority. Investment of superannuation fund is governed by the IRDA investment guidelines. The coverage of group superannuation schemes has shown a continuous increase in terms of the number of lives, with the exception of certain years the number of new schemes offered each year has also shown a rising trend.

Group Superannuation Scheme of LIC

The LIC offers life insurance protection under group insurance policies to various groups such as employers-employees, professionals, co-operatives, weaker sections of society, etc. The LIC provides insurance coverage to people at subsidised rates under social security group schemes. Besides providing insurance coverage, LIC also offers group schemes to employees, which provide funding of gratuity, pension liabilities and leave encashment liabilities of the employers.

Group Gratuity Schemes

Gratuity is a statutory liability of the employers. This is an incremental liability which accrues for an employee for every year of service put in by him. In the group gratuity scheme granted by LIC, in the event of premature death of the member, the dependent can get an amount which will be equal to the gratuity payable on the normal retirement of the member, had he survived up to the date of superannuation. In June 2006, LIC introduced a unit-liked gratuity plan called *Gratuity Plus* for management of gratuity fund. Gratuity Plus is a market linked plan, which offers great flexibility and transparency.

Group Superannuation Scheme

The group superannuation scheme is designed to provide pension to the employees/ beneficiaries on the exit of the member from the service. A decreasing group insurance cover in conjunction with the superannuation benefit can also be provided to supplement the lower accumulation in the event of premature death of the member. The scheme is of two types: (*a*) Money Purchase Scheme and (*b*) Benefits Purchase Scheme. Pension which is linked to the dearness allowance will also be granted. In May 2009, LIC introduced *Group Superannuation Plus* plan. This is a unit-linked DC plan for management of superannuation funds.

Group Annuity Scheme

Employers who have a privately administered superannuation fund where money is invested by the trusties as per income tax rules can purchase pension for employees as and when it is due under group annuity policies from LIC. The LIC offers wide range of benefits options combined with good rate of return on the investment. *Money Purchase Schemes*: Under this scheme the rate of contribution payable by the employer with respect to his employees is decided in advance. These contributions are utilised by LIC to secure appropriate annuities.

Benefit Purchase Plans: Under this scheme the amount of annuity is fixed by the employer in advance in relation to the salary to be drawn by the employee at the time of retirement or the average salary drawn during the last three years prior to retirement.

LIC superannuation scheme can be purchased by an employer for at least 10 employees. This number can be reduced under certain circumstances. The annual contribution of the employer to the superannuation fund together with employers' contribution to any provident fund for an employee should not exceed 27 per cent of the employee's salary. The employee can also contribute partly towards his own pension under the scheme. Pension fund administered by LIC under its Group Superannuation Scheme provides several benefits. In addition to pension, lump sum is payable on death if the employer has taken Group Insurance Scheme in conjunction with Group Superannuation Scheme. There are various types of pension to suit the need of the employees—life pension at death, life pension with return of capital on death, guaranteed life pension for 5,10,15, or 20 years and thereafter, joint life pension, etc. Under the existing rules of Income Tax Act (1962), an employer can set up a privately managed superannuation fund; however, pensions that are to be purchased from such annuity policies are known as Group Annuities.

Pension Funds Launched by Mutual Funds in India

Mutual funds have emerged as a strong player in retirement saving market in many countries, particularly in the United States. According to Investment Company Institute, Mutual funds had 21 per cent share in US$10.9 trillion US retirement market with US$2.3 trillion in assets held in retirement account. In 2001, mutual funds assets in DC plans accounted for US$1.1 trillion, while the assets in 401 (k) plans totalled US$765 billion and in IRAs amounted to US$1.2 trillion. In many other countries like Sweden, Australia, etc., mutual funds are also the dominant player in the retirement market.

Indian mutual fund industry has also emerged as one of the strong players in the financial market. According to the SEBI NCAER—SEBI Survey (2011), there were 3.03 million mutual fund–owning households and 10.50 million investors in India. Out of 10.50 million mutual fund investors, 6.21 million were from urban areas while 4.29 million were from rural areas. There has been a significant increase in net assets of mutual funds in India, from ₹107,946 crore in 1999–2000 to ₹592,250 crore in 2010–11 (SEBI 2011). In India only two pension funds have been launched, namely *UTI Retirement Benefit Plan (RBP)* and *Templeton India Pension Plan.*

❖ UTI'S RETIREMENT BENEFIT PLAN

UTI—Retirement Benefit Pension Fund (RBP) is the first such plan launched by any mutual fund in India. This open-ended pension plan was launched on 26 December 1994. It is a notified pension plan under section 88(2)(xiiic) for salaried class, self-employed persons and professionals, which seeks to provide post retirement income with tax benefit on investment. The minimum contribution is ₹10,000 in units, either in lump sum or instalments till the 52 issue monthly incomes from 58 years onwards. Repurchase is allowed after 70. The net assets of RBP by 30 June 2011 was ₹762.57 crore. The fund has given 10.82 per cent return since inception (http://valueresearchonline.com/funds/newsnapshot.asp?schemecode=281).

❖ TEMPLETON INDIA PENSION PLAN

It is a central government–notified pension scheme which was originally launched as *Kothari Pioneer Pension Plan* by Kothari Pioneer Mutual Fund on 3 March 1997.

It is an open-ended tax saving scheme with a lock-in period of three financial years. Investments in the fund are eligible for tax benefits under Section 80C. Tax deduction of up to ₹1 lakh per year is allowed on investment amount. There are no entry loads/up-front charges and hence units are allotted for 100 per cent of invested amount. Investments have to be a minimum of ₹10,000 in lump sum or in instalments of at least ₹500 and options are either income or growth. After 58, three choices are available under the income plan: regular income leaving the corpus intact, partial withdrawal and still receive income on holdings or full withdrawal. The growth plan offers complete withdrawal at 58. The net asset of the fund as on 30 June 2011 was ₹211.74 crore and return since as on 30 August 2011 was 13.03 per cent.

Mutual funds retirement plans played an insignificant role in the growing retirement/pension market in India. The importance of mutual funds in the pension/retirement market can be seen from the role of mutual fund industry in the US retirement market. The US mutual fund industry is the largest in the world with US$11.8 trillion assets under management, accounting for 48 per cent of global mutual funds assets of US$24.7 trillion by the end of 2010 in mutual fund assets worldwide. At year-end 2010, mutual funds accounted for US$4.7 trillion, or 27 per cent, of the $17.5 trillion US retirement market. The $4.7 trillion in mutual fund retirement assets represented 40 per cent of all mutual fund assets at year-end 2010. Retirement savings accounts were a significant portion of long-term mutual fund assets (48 per cent). Similarly, as a share of households' mutual fund holdings, mutual fund assets held in DC plans and IRAs represented 51 per cent of household long-term mutual funds. Investment of retirement assets in mutual funds primarily come from IRAs and employer-sponsored DC plans, such as 401(k) plans. By the end of 2010, IRAs held US$2.2 trillion, and employer-sponsored DC plans had US$2.5 trillion in mutual fund assets.

As noted above, India has a long history of social insurance and pension but the system that primarily benefitted is the organised sector, mainly the civil servants. Some efforts have been made in the recent past to extend limited social security benefits to the unorganised sectors but they are insufficient. Fragmented efforts by various administrative ministries and organisations made the system further complex. The system is totally inadequate and efforts are insufficient given the size of population, huge number of poor people living below the poverty line. It can be assessed from the facts above that Indian mutual funds failed to penetrate into retirement market as in the United States, primarily due to their short-term obsession for market share and the launching of short-term liquid funds so frequently. Similarly, life insurance industry also failed to focus on annuity market and focused on investment products like ULIP, for capturing market quickly but that also failed recently. Therefore, the pension and social security system need to be restructured and various measures need to be integrated under a robust pension policy.

ANNEXURES

Annexure 5A.1 The Salient Features of the Three Schemes Administered by the EPFO

	Employees' Provident Fund Scheme, 1952	*Employees' Pension Scheme, 1995*	*Employees' Deposit-Linked Insurance Scheme, 1976*
Benefits	• Accumulation plus interest upon retirement, resignation, death • Partial withdrawals allowed for specific expenses such as house construction, higher education, marriage, illness	• Monthly benefits for superannuation/ retirement, disability, survivor widow(er), children • Amount of pension based on average salary during the preceding 12 months from the date of exit and total years of employment • Minimum pension on disablement • Past service benefit to participants of Family Pension Scheme, 1971	• Provides lump-sum benefit upon death while in service, equal to average balance in the EPF account during the preceding 12 months of death, if average P.F. balance is less than ₹35,000 • In case average balance exceeds ₹35,000, amount paid will be ₹35,000 plus 25 per cent of average balance in excess of ₹35,000 limited to a maximum benefit of ₹60,000
Contributions (per cent on wages)			
Employer	3.67 per cent (for 181 industries) 1.67 per cent (for 5 industries)	8.33 per cent	0.5 per cent
Employee	12 per cent (for 181 industries) 10 per cent (for 5 industries)	Nil	Nil
Government	Nil	1.16 per cent	Nil
Administrative Charges by employer: Un-exempted (per cent of wages)	1.10 per cent	Till 05.01.2007 @ 16 per cent paid out of the EPS Fund and rest from PF Administration Fund w.e.f. 06.01.2007 to be met fully from PF Administration Fund	0.01 per cent
Inspection Charges by employer: Exempted (per cent on wages)	0.18 per cent		0.005 per cent

Source: Annual Report (2007–08), Employees' Provident Fund Organisation, New Delhi.
Notes: (*a*) Legal coverage for EPS/EPF extends to 177 types of establishments and (*b*) effective EPS coverage refers to subset of EPF members.

Annexure 5A.2 Investment Pattern of EPFO Funds

	Pattern of Investment	Per Cent of Amount to be Invested
(i)	Central government securities as defined in Sec. 2 of the Public Debt Act, 1944 (18 of 1944); and/or units of such mutual funds which have been set up as dedicated funds for investment in government securities and which have been approved by the Securities and Exchange Board of India;	25
(ii)	1. Government securities as defined in Sec. 2 of the Public Debt Act, 1944 (18 of 1944); created and issued by any state government; and/or units of such mutual funds which have been set up as dedicated funds for investment in government securities and which have been approved by the Securities and Exchange Board of India; and/or 2. Any other negotiable securities the principal whereof and interest whereon is fully and unconditionally guaranteed by the central government or any state government except those covered under (iii) (a) below.	15
(iii)	(a) Bonds/securities of 'Public Financial Institutions' as specified under Section 4(1) of the Companies Act; 'public sector companies' as defined in Section 2(36-A) of the Income Tax Act, 1961 including public sector banks; and/or (b) Short duration (less than a year) term deposit receipts (TDR) issued by public sector banks.	30
(iv)	To be invested in any of the above three categories as decided by their Trustees.	30
(v)	The trusts, subject to their assessment of the risk-return prospects, may invest up to 1/3rd of (iv) above, in private sector bonds/securities, which have an investment grade rating from at least two credit rating agencies.	

Source: EPFO Annual Report 2007–08.

REFERENCES

ASSOCHAM Research Bureau (2008), 'Social Sector Ranking of India Lowest among the BRIC nations'. *ASSOCHAM Eco Pulse* (June), New Delhi.

Barua, Paban (2010). Secretary-cum-PF commissioner, http://assamchahmazdoorsangha.org/atppf_scheme.html (2010).

Department of Economic Affairs (2010), *Economic Survey 2009–10.* Government of India, New Delhi.

Directorate General of Employment and Training, Survey and Study Division (2003), *Census of Central Government Employees.* Ministry of Labour, Government of India, New Delhi.

EPFO (2003), 'Golden Jubilee Year of EPFO'. New Delhi: Employees Provident Fund Organisation (EPFO), February, 2003.

Gillingham, Robert and Daniel Kanda (2001), 'Pension Reform in India'. IMF Working Paper WP/01/125, International Monetary Fund, Washington DC.

James, Estella and Renuka Sane (2003), 'The Annuity Market in India: Do consumers Get Their Money's Worth?' in Anand Bordia and Gautam Bhardwaj (eds), *Rethinking Pension Provision for India.* New Delhi: Tata McGraw Hill Publishing Company Ltd.

LIC. *Booklet on Social Security Group Insurance Scheme.* LIC of India, Central Office, Mumbai, Marketing booklet for agents/distributors.

——— (2010), *Annual Report 2009–10.* Mumbai: Life insurance Corporation of India.

Mathur, S. N. (1998), *Greying of Indian Railways.* New Delhi: Asian Institute of Transport Development.
NCAER–SEBI (2011), 'How Households Save and Invest: Evidence from NCAER Household Survey'. New Delhi: National Council of Applied Economic Research, July 2011.
Reserve Bank of India (2003), *Report of the Group to Study the Pension Liabilities of the State Governments.* Mumbai: Reserve Bank of India.
SEBI (2011), *Annual Report 2010–11.* Mumbai: Securities and Exchange Board of India, June 2011.
Sehgal, A. M. (2001), *An Assessment of Government of India's Pension Liability.* Ministry of Finance, Government of India.

6 Critical Challenges and Pension Reform Initiatives in India

The short review of socio-economic environment, demographic transition, profile of growing elderly population of India and existing pension system in India in Chapters 4 and 5 indicate the inadequacy of the current system to confront the challenges arising out of changing age structure, increased longevity and life expectancy, limited social security coverage, growing fiscal pressure of civil services pension liability, etc. It is a serious challenge that needs immediate institutional solution, to avoid the long-term problem being thrown in by the problem of population ageing, a phenomenon called 'agequake' by well-known author Paul Wallace (1999). The old-age problem is handled with care and through a comprehensive directed programme. The Government of India became fully attentive to the situation and made several attempts o reform Indian social security and pension system, which culminated into introduction of New Pension System (NPS). In this section we focus on some major challenges and recommendations of various expert/study groups to reform pension and retirement system.

DEMOGRAPHIC CHALLENGES

Challenges to pension system arises from many areas including changing population profile, composition of labour market, low coverage, high cost of providing DB pension to organised and civil servants, etc.

Population Growth

India has witnessed the sharpest fall in decadal population growth during 2001–11. The decadal growth of population for India as a whole has declined from 23.87 per cent in 1981–91 to 21.54 per cent in 1991–01 to 17.64 per cent in 2001–11 (Census 2011). While birth rate declined from 33.9 in 1981 to 29.5 in 1991 and further to 22.5 in 2009 per 1,000 population, the death rate declined at a much sharper rate from 27.4 in 1981 to 7.4 in 1991 and further to 7.3 per 1,000 population in 2009. India has also witnessed a sharp increase in the number of old and oldest of the old.

The working group also predicted that the majority of the people in their sixties will be physically and psychologically fit. Senior citizens in their seventies and beyond and those with health problem would require assistance.

Population Ageing

Population ageing is fast catching up in India and the country is moving towards an ageing trap; during coming decades the country will be facing a progressive increase in both the proportion and number of persons beyond 60 years of age. During the post-independence period India has introduced several measures for health care which have reduced infant mortality and increased life expectancy. The population of elderly (>60 years) increased from 19.8 million in 1951 to 62.3 million in 1996. Over the next 20 years the population of more than 60 years is likely to grow from 62.3 million in 1996 to 112.9 million in 2016 (Ramachandran et al. 2000). Planning Commission has estimated that population in the age group of 60+ will increase from 6.3 per cent in 2001 to 8.9 per cent in 2016 (Table 6.1).

Dependency Ratio

One positive feature of demographic and labour market change is the growth of labour force at a higher rate than the growth of working age population in future. The labour force is expected to grow at 2.42 per cent per annum as against the growth of working age population at a rate of 2.41 per cent during 2002–07 and gap between these two rates is likely to widen further in 2012–17, working age population growing at 1.70 per cent per annum against labour force growth of 1.78 per cent (Table 6.2).

Thus, India's age dependency ratio is expected to decline. However, this is a very short-term projection and cannot be fully relied for very long-term scenario. Therefore, creating enough employment for the growing labour force is a huge a challenge. As we have noted earlier that employment growth is very slow and informal sector has to

Table 6.1 Age Structure of Population

Age Group	*2001*	*2006*	*2011*	*2016*
0–4	35.6	32.5	29.7	27.1
15–59	58.2	60.4	62.5	64
60+	6.3	7	7.9	8.9
All age groups	100	100	100	100
Population	1,027	1,113.7	1,194.4	1,267.5

Source: Five Year Plan 2002–2007, Volume 1, Planning Commission, New Delhi 2002.

Table 6.2 Growth in Population and Labour Force

Item	*2002–07*	*2007–12*	*2012–17*
Population (All Age Group)	1.63	1.41	1.2
Population (15–59 years)	2.41	2.08	1.7
Labour Force (15–59 years)	2.42	2.15	1.78
Population (15+)	2.57	2.26	1.93
Labour Force (15+)	2.51	2.25	1.92

Source: Five Year Plan 2002–2007, Volume 1, Planning Commission, New Delhi, 2002.

absorb more than 60 per cent of labourers. With the emergence of service sector economy and replacement of labour-intensive production/service by technology intensive system will make a large number of labour redundant requiring support of the states for some sort of social security.

COVERAGE GAP

One of the most serious inadequacies of the present pension system is the low coverage. It has been estimated that current social security in India only covers a small percentage, 10 per cent of total work force that too in the organised sector only. A large majority of Indian labour force is engaged in unorganised, informal and particularly in the rural areas, which are still outside EPFO net. Any system which fails to cover so large a number of labourers as happened in India can be called anything but social security. According to Gillingham and Kanda (2001), the most serious problem with the current pension system is that it fails to reach majority of population, and does not provide a safety net for those who are not covered.

Coverage Gap in Organised Sector

> *In India, currently only about 35 million out of a workforce of 400 million have access to social security in the form of old age income protection. This includes private sector workers, civil servants, military personnel and employees of state public sector undertakings. Out of these 35 million, 26 million workers are members of the Employee Provident Fund Organisation. (Sing 2003)*

In rural areas, the coverage gap arises because the existing system could not be extended to the workers in the rural areas. Social security in India continues to remain confined to the organised sector in the urban areas, and most of the more than 250 million workers who live and work in the rural areas remain out of present system and thus widen the coverage gap (Anand 2003).

Coverage Gap in Informal Sector

Coverage gap has been further widened due to the non-inclusion of informal sector in the EPFO system and non-existence of any other system to cover the workers in the informal sector. 'Currently, the Indian Labour force is estimated to be 397 million, out of which 93 per cent or about 369 million work in informal economy' (Anand 2003). These informal sector workers are mainly involved in the organised sector through the contract labour system, employed by informal sector micro-units, home-based, piece-related workers and self-employed informal sector workers. This wide coverage gap and exclusion of a large number of workers in rural and informal sector was noted by the Second Labour Commission and it observed:

> *In considering the question of evolving an integrated and comprehensive system of social security in India, one needs to have a broad vision and develop a structure which will encompass the whole population of diverse needs. It cannot be a single scheme but a combination of schemes catering to the needs of different target groups with different needs and different paying capabilities.*

The coverage and benefits of social assistance programme is very insignificant compared to the number of needy people in the country.

Inequity in the Present System

Many authors have pointed out the emerging inequity in social protection pension for public sector vis-à-vis private sector, even among the organised sector employees. It is often mentioned that many central and public sector employees enjoy non-contributory pension benefits linked to inflation index, while private sector employees enjoy the mandatory contributory pension benefits. Many such private pensions are not used to purchase annuity and therefore there is no post-retirement protection.

FISCAL SUSTAINABILITY

The present system of DB unfunded pension system which covers civil services, public sector employees and also EPF is considered to be unsustainable over the long period and needs to be replaced by a more dynamic funded programme. The stressed fiscal burden of present system can be seen in terms of growing pension liability of the central and the state governments as discussed in the following paragraphs.

Pension Liability of the Central Government

In the previous section, we have examined the important features of central government pension funds, which are basically non-contributory schemes with implication of unsustainable future liability. Two important works can be quoted here—the estimate of the working group appointed by the Government of India and the projection by the Planning Commission. The extent of liability has been examined by a working group appointed by the Government of India (Chairman A. M. Sehgal, Controller General of India).

The committee was to assess the likely expenditure on pension payments to the government servants in the short/medium term, and to recommend appropriate formats/information system to facilitate accurate assessment of the pensioner's liability in future. The working group submitted its report on 25 June 2001 indicating the central government's liability arising out of pension payments (Sehgal 2001). The committee has also observed that over 50 per cent of pension payments of central government goes to defence employees, at the end of March 1998, there were 5.2 million central government employees, while the number of pensioners was estimated at 3.5 million, which gives an overall dependency ratio of 67 per cent, the pension expenditure of the Government of India (including post, civil, defence, railways and telecom) has gone up by six times from ₹3,272 crore in 1990–91 to ₹19,446 crore in 1999–2000 and likely to be ₹21,117 crore in 2000–01, as a result of the acceptance of Fifth Pay Commission's recommendation, pension liability has gone up by 86 per cent from ₹11,375 crore in 1997–98 to ₹21,117 crore in 2000–01 and estimated pension liability of the Government of India would rise to ₹29,891 crore in 2009–10 at an inflation rate of 6 per cent per annum and to ₹33,558 crore at an inflation rate of 10 per cent per annum.

The working group also recommended

> *a transition to a funded system of pension payments for new Government employees and a system of incentives to encourage migration of existing employees to funded system. The fiscal impact can only be mitigated for the incremental liability of new employees with the introduction of a defined contribution system.*

Planning Commission Projection of Central Government Pension Liability

The pension bill is another matter of concern, as a percentage of GDP, the pension bill of the central government is increasingly growing over the years. A study conducted by Dr Sen and Swain (2002) indicated that as a percentage GDP, the pension bill of the central government (civil and defence) has increased from 0.24 per cent of GDP in the year 1980–81 to 0.73 per cent of GDP in the year 1991–2000, growing at a rate of about 22 per cent annually in nominal terms during the past two decades. Pension bill constitutes 5.7 per cent of the total revenue expenditure in the union budget reflecting a quantum jump from the 1980–81 level of 2.4 per cent in 2002. Sudden step-ups in the annual growth rate of pension payments (Figure 6.1) at discrete points of time reflect the impact of two Pay Commission awards. The sharp increase that resulted in non-productive committed liability of the government assumed significance because of the non-contributory but DB nature of the present pension scheme a substantial portion of which is indexed. Dr Sen, however, has taken into account civil component of central government pension bill and estimated that there will be an annual average increase of 7.5 per cent of pension bill for central government employees (civil) as against the working group projection of 4.5 per cent annual increase of combined pension bill of the central government by assuming annual inflation rate of 6 per cent (Sen 2004).

Figure 6.1 Pension Liabilities of Central and State Governments

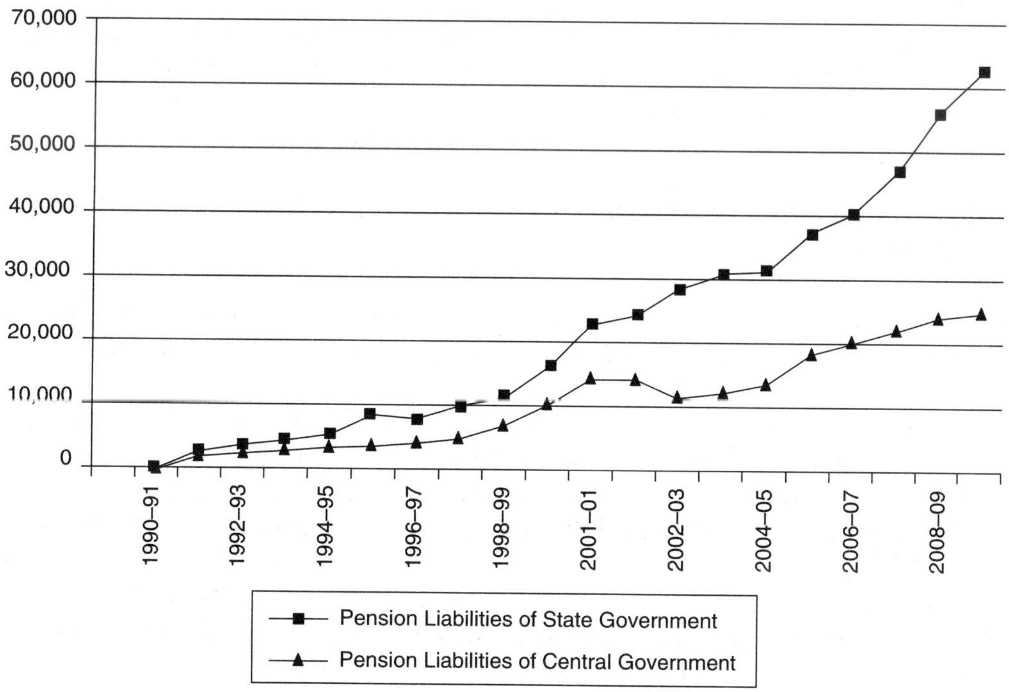

Source: Indian Public Finance Statistics 2009–10, Ministry of Finance, Department of Economic Affairs, Government of India.

Pension Liability of the State Government

The Bhattacharya Group appointed by the Reserve Bank of India (RBI) has made an attempt to assess the future pension liabilities of the state governments. The Group has assessed the likely fiscal implications of increasing pension payments. Accordingly, the Group observed:

> *While pension payments would pre-empt about 20.1 per cent of the total revenue receipts of the states in 2010-11, the pre-emption would be as high as about 30.3 per cent of the States' own revenue receipts. On the basis of the historical growth rates for a longer period (1980–81 to 2001–02), it is observed that total revenue receipts would record a growth of 14.3 per cent, while States' own revenue receipts would rise by 14.6 per cent. Accordingly, pension payments would pre-empt about 22.3 per cent of the total revenue receipts of the States in 2010–11; the pre-emption would be much higher at 33.8 per cent of the States' own revenue receipts.*

Actual Pension Expenditure of the Central and State Government (1990–91 to 2009–10)

Over the years pension liability of the central and state governments has increased rapidly exerting tremendous burden on exchequer. The increase has eroded state revenue impacting development expenditure.

❖ COMBINED PENSION EXPENDITURE OF CENTRAL AND STATE GOVERNMENTS

As per the Indian Public Finance Statistics 2009–10, Government of India, combined pension expenditure of the central and state government has increased sharply by 23 times from ₹5,183.75 crore in 1990–91 to ₹119,385.75 crore in 2009–10, while total tax revenue during this had gone up by 11 times from ₹87,723.28 to ₹996,883.95. GDP at market prices increased by 10.9 times from ₹569,624 crore in 1990–91 to ₹6,231,171 in 2009–10. These rise in relation to tax revenue and GDP shows that pension expenditure as a percent of tax revenue and GDP became more than double from 1990–91 to 2009–10.

Pension expenditure as percent of tax revenue increased from 5.91 per cent in 1990–91 to 11.98 per cent, pension expenditure as percentage of GDP increased from 0.91 per cent to 1.92 per cent during the same period (Table 6.3).

Table 6.3 Combined Pension Liabilities of Central and State Governments

Year	*Pension Liabilities (₹ in Crore)*	*Tax Revenue (₹ in Crore)*	*GDP at Market Prices (₹ in Crore)*	*Pension Liability as per cent to Tax Revenue*	*Pension Liability as per cent to GDP*
1990–91	5,183.75	87,723.28	569,624	5.91	0.91
2000–01	38,818.67	305,320.24	2,102,314	12.71	1.85
2001–02	40,321.2	314,535.19	2,278,952	12.82	1.77
2002–03	43,037.56	356,638.23	2,454,561	12.07	1.75
2003–04	45,226.76	414,084.77	2,754,620	10.92	1.64
2004–05	55,436.72	494,370.1	3,239,224	11.21	1.71
2005–06	60,871.14	587,687.81	3,706,473	10.36	1.64
2006–07	69,068.5	736,707.71	4,283,979	9.38	1.61
2007–08	77,634.2	870,329.09	4,947,857	8.92	1.57
2008–09	97,002.25	947,659.91	5,574,449	10.24	1.74
2009–10	119,385.75	996,883.95	6,231,171	11.98	1.92

Source: Indian Public Finance Statistics 2009–10, Ministry of Finance, Department of Economic Affairs, Government of India, and *Hand Book on the Statistics on the Indian Economy (2009–10)*, Reserve Bank of India, Mumbai.

❖ ACTUAL PENSION EXPENDITURE OF THE CENTRAL AND STATE GOVERNMENT (1990–91 TO 2009–10)

Over the years pension liability of the central and state government has increased rapidly exerting tremendous burden on exchequer. The increase has eroded state revenue, impacting their development expenditure.

❖ COMBINED PENSION EXPENDITURE OF CENTRAL AND STATE GOVERNMENTS

As per the Indian Public Finance Statistics 2009–10, Government of India, combined pension expenditure of the central and state government has increased sharply by 23 times from ₹5,183.75 crore in 1990–91 to ₹119,385.75 crore in 2009–10, while total tax revenue during this had gone up by 11 times from ₹87,723.28 to ₹996,883.95. GDP at market prices increased by 10.9 times from ₹569,624 crore in 1990–91 to ₹6,231,171 in 2009–10. These rise in pension expenditure in relation to tax revenue and GDP shows that pension expenditure as a percent of tax revenue and GDP became more than double from 1990–91 to 2009–10. Pension expenditure as per cent of tax revenue increased from 5.91 per cent in 1990–91 to 11.98 per cent, pension expenditure as percentage of GDP increased from 0.91 per cent to 1.92 per cent during the same period (Table 6.3).

Impact of Sixth Pay Commission on Pension and Other Benefits

However, in the years to come the pension liability of both the central and state governments are going to increase manifold as a result of the implementation of Sixth Pay Commission for the central government employees. Further, the state governments, more or less, accept the central pay commission reports to revise the salary and other benefits for their employees. The retirement age of central government and central government undertakings is 60 years. Salary, pension and other benefits of the employees are revised from time to time on the basis of the government appointed by the Pay Commission. The latest pay commission, that is, Sixth Pay Commission Report has been accepted by the Government of India and pension and other benefits have been revised upwards.

❖ PENSION BENEFITS

On the basis of the Sixth Pay Commission the government has decided to grant full pension benefits to all government employees after 20 years in service, against the earlier provision of 33 years of service. Octogenarians will now be paid an additional 20 per cent of their basic pension, while those aged 85 will get 30 per cent or more, rising to 100 per cent additional pension for centurions. The government has also revised the gratuity provision for the central government and raised the gratuity limit to ₹10 lakh.

❖ PENSION LIABILITY

As a result of implementation of the Sixth Pay Commission recommendation, the central government pensioners would receive an overall increase of 40 per cent in pension. As a result the total estimated pension liability of nearly ₹29,900 crore of the central government will go up by nearly ₹1,400 crore. The central government had estimated 3,321,210 employees (excluding defence personnel) on its rolls in 2007, with the number projected to go up marginally to 3,329,682 in 2008 (http://irse.forumco.com/topic.asp?TOPIC_ID=351&whichpage=4).

OTHER SHORTCOMINGS OF THE PRESENT SYSTEM

Provident Fund System

The Indian provident fund system has many shortcomings—some of which are inherent to the schemes while others have emerged due to poor plan administration.

According to Vittas and Skully (1991), in a provident fund system, the income replacement, investment and inflation risks are borne by the plan participants. According to the principles of social insurance, provident fund is not an ideal substitute for pension. The ILO (1997) argues that provident funds have serious limitations in alleviating old-age poverty because it does not provide protection against the contingency. The experience of provident fund schemes in India also suggests some practical limitations of a pure provident fund arrangement. First, the inability to ensure that lump sum payments are used to provide old-age protection is a serious drawback of the current system. Majority of the workers being low-wage earners, they have little additional savings and much of the lump sum amount is spent in meeting essential needs after retirement. Second, the provision of liberal non-refundable withdrawal facility from provident funds to meet various contingencies during the employment period significantly reduces the quantum of benefit at retirement (OASIS 2000). Low investment yields from provident funds, due to conservative investment norms, further complicate the problem. According to World Bank (1994) estimates, the average real rate of return from the EPF scheme was below 1 per cent in the 1980s. The average annual real rate of return between 1985 and 1997 is only about 2.63 per cent. These returns are too low to generate a sizeable terminal accumulation of pension assets, and they further encourage premature withdrawal of funds allowed under certain defined circumstances as mentioned earlier.

REFORM INITIATIVES

Though India has been experiencing the changes in population structure leading to increasing number of elderly population and poor plight of a large number of elderly population due to absence of any universal social security or any meaningful old-age income provision, no serious attempt was made till the appointment of the Expert Committee on Old Age Social and Income Security (OASIS) by the Ministry of Social Justice and Empowerment, Government of India under the Chairmanship of Dr S. A. Dave in 1998. The committee submitted its report on 11 January 2000 and that was the beginning of a serious attempt for social security and pension reforms in India. Subsequently, many organisations and expert committees have conducted studies on India's pension problems and forwarded many suggestions. Some of the important reports on Indian pension reforms are Project OASIS by Dave Committee (January 2000), India, The Challenge of Old Age Income Security by the World Bank (April 2001), *Pension Reforms in the Unorganised Sector*—a report by the Insurance Regulatory and Development Authority (October 2001), Report of the Group assessing the Pension Liabilities of the State Governments (Chairman: B. K. Bhattacharya), RBI, October 2003.

OASIS Recommendations on Pension Reforms

The Ministry of Social Justice and Empowerment, Government of India, had set up a committee on OASIS in 1998 under the chairmanship of Dr S. A. Dave, which submitted its Repot in January 2000 recommending some drastic changes in the structure of social security in India through introduction of privately managed pension system.

OASIS has focused on transforming Indian Pension System from DB to fully founded defined contribution (DC) system, liberalisation of investment and annuitisation of pension payments. The thrust of the committee was to develop an institutional infrastructure through which individual can take care of their own pension requirements, particularly in the unorganised sector. The committee felt that 'it would be difficult to enforce a mandatory system which may lead to harassment and corruption' and recommended a voluntary contribution system. The committee, which submitted its report on 11 January 2000, made far-reaching recommendations and laid the foundation of Indian pension sector reform. While the committee has primarily focused on introducing a pension system for the unorganised sector, it made several recommendations to improve existing civil services pension, EPF/EPS through parametric changes. We discuss the major recommendations below in the following paragraphs.

The committee suggested the pension reform based on Individual Retirement Accounts (IRA) exclusively financed by the employee and fully portable. The account will remain with employee across job changes and the employee would have an easy access to the IRA account, which can be operated at any points of presence (POP). *Centralised record keeping and depository, professional pension funds manager (PFMs)* needed to be selected for the purpose. The committee also suggested the introduction of predefined funds styled as safe income, balance income and growth funds and investment in international equity up to 10 per cent in the growth fund.

The committee also suggested *Default Allocation* for investors who are not able to take decisions to select an appropriate fund. In order to protect the interest of investors the committee suggested *Minimum Guarantee* for safe income portfolio—fund managers must give guarantee that they would not under perform less than 2 per cent of weighted average return of all managers. The recommendations also included a government guaranteed additional safety net called *Contribution Protection Insurance*—in case the final accumulated amount falls short of the total contribution.

The Committee suggested that the accumulated amount in the account would purchase annuity from a life insurance company and monthly pension would be paid to the member till death. The member would be entitled to receive pension on his/her retirement at the age of 60. The mandatory annuity of ₹200,000 which will be given as a monthly pension of ₹1,500/and beyond that the member will decide what to do with surplus money. Other suggestions include the tax free limit for accretion into IRA up to ₹6,000 per annum, premature withdrawal to be taxable, but the amount used for buying annuity should be tax free. The committee suggested the creation of a new regulator, the Indian Pension Authority (PIA). The PIA would oversee all the aspects of Indian Pension system, enforce the mandatory contribution in the organised sector; register the depository, POP, PFM, annuity provider and retirement advisor. The PIA would also prescribe investment guidelines, accounting policies, implement relative return guarantee, under take research and other regulatory activities.

The OASIS Committee also recommended reform of existing EPF and EPS. In its recommendation of reform of public provident fund, the committee suggested introduction of a new Public Provident Fund (PPF), withdrawal of new PPF at the age of 60 years, professional management of funds, liberalised investment management guidelines, professional management of funds, introduction of single set of benefits, abolition of 1.1 per cent government contribution, etc. Other recommendations include reforming the government pension scheme and introduction of National Senior Citizen's Fund.

❖ REFORMING PUBLIC PROVIDENT FUND

The OASIS committee has also made some recommendations to improve efficiency of PPF and suggested the closure of existing PPF for contribution and Introduction of a new scheme to be called PPF-2. Other suggestions include withdrawal at the age of 60, managing PPF-2 by a professional board of trustees and investing under liberalised guidelines and investment of 40 per cent of assets in state government securities, etc.

❖ NATIONAL SENIOR CITIZENS FUND

The OASIS report suggested setting up a National Senior Citizens Fund for educating people, undertaking research concerning social security for senior citizens, etc. The fund can be set up by channelising 1.16 per cent of government contribution at present given to EPS and by introducing 25 per cent premature and lump sum withdrawal tax to be imposed on provident fund under IRA. The fund should be administered by a professional board of trustees appointed by the Ministry of Social Justice and Empowerment.

The OASIS committee report indicates a move towards a new pension system that would be professionally managed and privately funded under an independent Regulator. The committee has not suggested abolishing the existing defined benefit system like Chile and other countries which have replaced the old DB system by new DC system. In fact new system proposed by OASIS Committee is a parallel system successfully implemented by many countries. Moreover, the suggestion to introduce minimum guarantee and contribution protection insurance is an important direction well tested by many countries but unfortunately ignored by NPS.

The IRDA Recommendations of Pension Reforms

Insurance Regulatory and Development Authority of India (IRDA) had also submitted a report on pension reforms in October 2001. The IRDA report suggested pension system operating 'through a mechanism of trustees'. The pension system should be voluntary and focused on the unorganised sector. The report suggested that 'it would thus be focused on the pillar three and should set up standards that are capable of accommodating other pillars of pension provision as and when needed'. The new system should cover all irrespective of employment and there should not be mandated minimum annual contribution but each contribution should exceed ₹100. Collections of contribution should be done through banks, NGOs, asset management companies, etc. The report indicated that specially selected pension provider (PP), would be allowed to manage pension funds. These PPs can be selected from mutual funds, asset management companies, financial institutions, banks. Pension would be provided in the form of annuity, through life insurance companies. The Report envisaged a variety of schemes with a product mix between debt and equity, investing at least a part of the funds in index funds, no change in the overall limit of existing tax rebate but suggested a favourable tax treatment on terminal benefits. The report also suggested that the Regulation of Pension Funds should be entrusted with Insurance Regulatory Authority of India.

World Bank Suggestion on Pension Reforms

The World Bank has also studied various aspects of Indian pension system and suggested some policy response most of which are in line with OASIS report though some differences are there. The report has made a detail analysis of EPF, EPS, civil services pension, etc., and pointed out various shortcomings in the social assistance schemes, Employees' Provident Fund, Employees' Pension Fund, Civil Service Pension Scheme, voluntary tax preferred schemes, etc. The study identified the major problems of existing system in India including, high contribution, low returns, high incidence of withdrawals, poor benefit designs of EPF/EPS, unfunded civil service pension and growing pension liabilities, inconsistent tax system discouraging contractual saving institutions, etc. (World Bank 2001). The report talked about two types of reforms of unfunded DB system, that is, partial reforms based on changes such as eligibility criteria, benefit calculation formula, financing and tax treatment and systematic reform which implies 'a major paradigm shift in the mandatory retirement savings scheme'. This shift is carried by establishment of a fully funded defined contribution scheme in place of un funded DB scheme and suggested two cases of systematic reform for India. According to the report, pension reform should aim to reduce overall contribution rates, to eliminate unintended intra generational redistribution, to establish a reasonable replacement rate for an average wage worker payable until death and protected against inflation risk, to minimise labour market distortions subject to the other objectives having been reached, etc. The report also suggested minimum pension level, determination of a target replacement rate, basic pension, etc.

Regarding the reforming of EPF System, the report suggested that withdrawal is to be discouraged, investment restrictions have to be gradually relaxed, competition to be introduced by allowing private fund managers to operate, management, supervisory and regulatory framework to be redesigned.

The report suggested several methods to extend the coverage of social security. The Important methods among them are incentives to attract employers and employees, reducing overall contribution by 4–6 per cent, increasing yields, etc. 'A reasonable approach would be to impose a ceiling on the contributions to be made to the earnings related, DC scheme at some level that reflected public policy concerns about reasonable consumption during old age'. Two ways have been suggested to extend statutory coverage of the public pension system, that is, to enlarge the list of the type of establishments that are subject to the EPF Act and to reduce the minimum size of the establishments covered. The report also suggested some tax incentives to attract long term contractual savings/pension and annuities. For instance, it recommended that double taxation was to be avoided and the contributions were be taxed only once—either at the beginning or at the end.

The report also highlighted the problems of maintaining a non-contributory scheme for civil servants, in the form of *civil servants pension*, were highlighted. In order to prevent the accumulation of further unfounded fiscal liabilities, facilitate labour mobility and apply consistent policy criteria to public and private sector workers, younger civil servants or at least new entrants should be shifted into the reformed basic pension and DC schemes. A useful first step might be to shift the government provident fund contribution to the reformed EPF scheme. The World Bank report has made a very significant comment,

> *[I]n addition to giving due consideration to the breadth of the reform program, policy makers must also consider a planning horizon that goes well beyond what is required in most areas of public policy. Decisions made today can have very long term implications and reforms will play out very long periods of time. (World Bank 2001)*

Recommendations of the High Level Expert Group on New Pension Scheme of the Central Government

The Government of India constituted a high level expert group on new pension system in June 2001 (Chairman: Shri B. K. Bhattacharya) to provide a road map for introducing the New Pension Scheme. The group examined the various aspects of the existing pension system and came out with a number of recommendations which include: a two-tier scheme—the first tier would act as a social security scheme with mandatory contribution of 10 per cent each on the basic pay and DA by the employees and government while the second tier would promote personal savings. A cap of 5 per cent of pay plus DA was recommended in the case of matching contribution by the government. The mandatory first tier is a DB at 50 per cent of the average emoluments over the last 36 months. The minimum qualifying service will be 20 years and full pension will be payable on superannuation for qualifying service of 33 years. A second exit point can be provided at any age after 50 years, and the full pension or proportionate pension will be payable only from the date of superannuation. The contribution under the second tier would be portable and tax exempt within the overall ceilings prescribed by the government on approved saving schemes. In case of second tier, the amount on retirement could be either taken as a lump sum or converted into annuities at the choice of the individual. The contribution to the second tier would be invested in separate funds with the fund managers investing the contributions as per more liberalised investment guidelines. The group recommended indexation of inflation up to 5 per cent but did not suggest any wage indexation. Furthermore, the group recommended the new scheme to be applicable only to the new entrants to the civil services.

The group recommended three separate pension funds, each one for Railways, Defence and other Civil ministries, and recommended periodic actuarial valuation of the Fund. The investment pattern should satisfy the twin principles of safety and return. The first tier was expected to be a fully funded scheme, the funds being managed by Professional Fund Managers subject to supervision of Investment Committee of Board of Trustees, Board itself and a Pension Development and Regulatory Authority (PDRA).

The contribution from the second tier would have a separate institutional structure and will be based on investment guidelines that might be more liberal than what was laid down for the first tier. Subsequently, based on the experience gained, individuals might be permitted to exercise their choice of the type of fund in which funds can be invested. The group recommended constitution of an independent Pension Regulatory Authority which can be called PRDA for the pension sector in the country.

Recommendations of the Group to Study the Pension Liabilities of the State Governments

On the basis of the decision taken in the Eleventh Conference of State Finance Secretaries held in the RBI during January 2003, a group was constituted by the RBI in February 2003.

The group has particularly suggested structural and parametric change and introduction of a two-tier scheme for the new employees with the DB in the first-tier of DC-DB scheme supplemented by a mandatory DC scheme, wherein both the employees and the state governments make contributions. The pure DC component could, at the option of the state government, be merged with Tier-II of the proposed Central Government Pension Scheme, which is open to state governments as well. The group proposed that the new pension scheme should be made mandatory for all new employees and optional for existing employees of the state governments. It was suggested that in the states where pay, pension and interest burden have exceeded 90 per cent of state's total revenue receipts, the new contributory scheme is obligatory for even existing employees with less than 10 years of the contributions under the proposed scheme/s and also the earnings from the pension funds may be granted Income tax exemption.

The group has recommended few parametric changes in order to mitigate the immediate and medium-term effect on state finances, like, continuation of the present practice of price indexation, while doing away with wage indexation facility, bringing down the maximum permissible commutation amount from 40 per cent of basic pension to 33 1/3 per cent, enhancing the present discount rate used for calculating commutation factor, bring down the enhanced family pension, etc. The group has recommended the setting up of a dedicated pension fund to meet, at least partially the pension burden of the existing employees and pensioners.

Brief discussions about more critical challenges as above call for pension reform and introduction of a structured social security system in India. Towards this end the various committees have given several suggestions, particularly the OASIS Report recommended far reaching changes in Indian pension system. The need for replacing the existing DB system by a multi-pillar DC system was the core to all recommendations, which influenced the introduction of NPS, which was centred on the lines of individual account–based contributory, defined contributory and management of funds by professional fund managers. Other points that came out of these reports were the extension of coverage to all categories of workers, making the scheme affordable to the subscribers and financially viable. It was also essential keeping in view the prevailing necessity and affordability that the scheme was economically viable and self-financing. The scheme was also required to have certain amount of flexibility, in its scope and administration.

India took the first step to reform the pension system by implementing New Pension Scheme, which was mandatory for central government employees who joined services w.e.f. 1 January 2004. Though India has introduced defined contribution pension for new employees, existing defined benefit pension system was not disturbed. Further, Indian system is not uniform for all sections of employees. While new system for government employees is mandatory, a separate scheme called All Citizens Scheme has been introduced for unorganised sector. New Pension Scheme also included another low component called NPS Lite for economically disadvantaged segment of the society. The salient features of NPS will be discussed in the following chapters.

REFERENCES

Anand, Harjit S. (2003), 'Social security in the Indian Informal Sector'. *50 Golden Years of Unbroken Trust* by Employees Provident Fund Organisation, Ministry of Labour, Government of India.

Beattie, Roger (1997), *Reform and Development of Pension Systems in Asia and the Pacific.* Geneva: ILO.

Government of India (2011), *Census 2011.* New Delhi: Office of the Registrar General & Census Commissioner, Ministry of Home Affairs.

Sen, Pronab and Sibani Swain (2002), 'Technical Study on Retirement and Pension Projection of the Central Government'. Working Paper Series

Paper No. 1/2002-PC, January 2002.

Gillingham, Robert and Daniel Kanda (2001), 'Pension Reform in India'. IMF Working Paper WP/01/125, International Monetary Fund, Washington, DC.

Government of India (2009–10), 'Employment in the Organised Sector'. *Economic Survey* (2009-10), Government of India.

OASIS (2000), *The Project OASIS Report* (Chairman: S. A. Dave), Mumbai: OASIS Foundation.

Ramachandran, Prema, Mohan Singh, A. N. Kapoor, K. K. Lamba (2000), 'Population Growth Trends, Projections Challenges and Opportunities'. Working Paper No. 2/2000, Planning Commission, Government of India.

Reserve Bank of India (RBI) (2003), *Report of the Group to Study the Pension Liabilities of the State Governments* (Chairman: Mr Bhattacharya). Mumbai: RBI.

Sehgal, A. M. (2001), 'An Assessment of Government of India's Pension Liability'. Ministry of Finance, Government of India.

Sen, Pranab and Sibani Swain (2004), 'Pension Liabilities of the Central Government: Projection and Implications'. Planning Commission, Government of India.

Sing, Ajai (2003), 'Comprehensive Social Security to all Workers—Role of the EPFO'. *50 Golden Years of Unbroken Trust* by Employees Provident Fund Organisation, Ministry of Labour, Government of India.

Vittas, Dimitri and Michael Skully (1991), 'Overview of Contractual Saving Institutions'. Working paper, Country Economics Department, WPS 605, World Bank, Washington DC.

Wallace, Paul (1999), *Age quake: Riding the Demographic Rollercoaster Shaking Business, Finance and Our World.* London: Nicholas Brealey.

World Bank (2001), *India: the Challenge of Old Age Income Security.* Report no 22034 in Finance and Private Sector Development, South Asia Region, World Bank, Washington, DC, 5 April.

7 The Structure, Architecture and Administration of National Pension System

INTRODUCTION

We have discussed in detail about the changing population profile and emerging problems due to ageing, growing dependence of elderly population on others in the back drop of virtually non-existence of universal pension and very insignificant social assistance programme. Defined Benefit pension and other related post-retirement income support system only cover the civil servants and a small segment of formal sector employees. Government supported pension for the organised civil services is fiscally untenable and unmanageable. In this background there had been serious concern at the level of policy makers and managers of economy which resulted into appointment of several working/study groups to examine the current system and to suggest a suitable pension system to cover a larger segment of society and to evolve a sustainable pension system. The concern of the central government is reflected in the consecutive budget speech in Indian Parliament of the honourable Finance Minister. For the first time, the then finance minister, in his budget speech 2001–02 (Annexure 7A.1) mentioned,

> *Whereas the organised sector is at present covered by various pension, provident fund and gratuity schemes, the unorganised sector does not have adequate social security coverage. I am asking the Insurance Regulatory Development Authority to look into all these issues and provide a road map for pension reforms by October 1, 2001.*

He further mentioned,

> *The Central Government pension liability has reached unsustainable proportions: as a percentage of GDP, it has risen from about 0.5 per cent in*

1993–94 to 1 per cent in 2000–2001. As such it is envisaged that those who enter central government services after October 1, 2001 would receive pension through a new pension programme based on defined contributions. In order to review the existing pension system and to provide a roadmap for the next steps to be taken by the Government, I propose to constitute a High Level Expert Group, which would give its recommendations within 3 months.

In the next year the finance minister in his Budget speech 2002–03 (Annexure 7A.1) laid down a road map for pension reform.

The present pension scheme for Government employees casts an open-ended financial burden on the Government. I had announced the appointment of a High Level Expert Group to develop a new pension scheme, based on defined contributions, for new recruits entering government service. The Expert Group has submitted its report to the Government. It has proposed a hybrid scheme that combines contributions from employees and the Union Government on matching basis, on the one hand, while committing to the employees a defined benefit as pension. The report is being considered by the Government and the new pension scheme for new recruits will be announced and implemented by June 1, 2002. The expert groups have suggested reform of the current pension system by introducing a funded pension system.On the basis of these suggestions the Government of India introduced the New Pension System (NPS) which is a fully funded Defined Contribution (DC) w.e.f. from 1ST January 2004. The NPS is very low cost retirement saving system with many attractive features comparable to any such system in the world.

In the Budget Speech 2003–04 (Annexure 7A.1), the then Finance Minister further elaborated the structure of the new pension system while he announced,

It will apply only to new entrants to Government service, except to the armed forces, and upon finalisation, offer a basket of pension choices. It will also be available, on a voluntary basis, to all employers for their employees, as well as to the self-employed. This new pension system, when introduced, will be based on defined contribution, shared equally in the case of Government employees between the Government and the employees. There will, of course, be no contribution from the Government in respect of individuals who are not Government employees. The new pension scheme will be portable, allowing transfer of the benefits in case of change of employment, and will go into "individual pension accounts" with Pension Funds. The Ministry of Finance will oversee and supervise the Pension Funds through a new and independent Pension Fund Regulatory and Development Authority.

The budget speeches of finance ministers of India spelt out the need and intention of pension reforms and laid down a road map of reforms, which was followed by the appointments of various working/study groups. These study/working groups came out with a number of suggestions on the need and architecture of reforms and India moved towards reforming its pension system by introducing a defined contribution pension mandatory for selected group of central government and voluntary for others. The Ministry of Finance, Department of Economic Affairs issued a press release dated 27 August 2003 on operationalisation of the budget announcement 2003–04 on new pension system. The press release said,

> *The Government approved on 23rd August 2003 the proposal to implement the budget announcement of 2003–04 relating to introducing a new restructured defined contribution pension system for new entrants to Central Government service, except to Armed Forces, in the first stage, replacing the existing system of defined benefit pension system. The new system will also be available, on a voluntary basis, to all persons including self employed professionals and others in the unorganised sector. However, mandatory programmes under the Employee Provident Fund Organisation (EPFO) and other special provident funds would continue to operate as per the existing system under the Employee Provident Fund and Miscellaneous Provisions Act, 1952 and other special Acts governing these funds.*

The press release further provided an outline on the proposed new scheme including the Architecture of the New Pension System, Regulatory Authority, Investment strategy, Tax treatment and the Scope of the New Pension System (Annexure 7A.2).

Reforms in India followed a parallel path, introduced mandatory DC system for the new employees of the central government (adopted by the state government and many public sector undertakings/enterprises) which is voluntary for others. However, the DB system for the existing employees remained undisturbed. The new system introduced in India has three clearly defined components, namely NPS for government employees (employees include employees of the central government, state governments, union territories and autonomous undertakings). NPS for all citizens (unorganised/informal sector), NPS Lite (for low-income workers) and Swavalamban Scheme.

PFRDA has taken a step-by-step approach to introduce various pension schemes. In the first phase, new pension scheme for central government and central autonomous organisations' employees was introduced with effect from 1 January 2004. Pension contributions of all such employees were kept in a separate account under the Public Accounts of India and funds management began w.e.f. 1 April 2008. Simultaneously, NPS was also extended to all the employees of state governments/union territories and state/union territories' autonomous organisations. In the meantime PFRDA developed the necessary funds management infrastructure including appointment of Central Record Keeping Agency (CRA), three Pension Fund Managers (PFMs), namely LIC

Pension Fund Ltd, SBI Pension Fund Ltd and UTI Retirement Solutions Ltd, NPS Trustee, NPS Trustee Bank and Custodian. Three PFMs started investing NPS funds of the central government employees w.e.f. 1 April 2008. In the second phase, PFRDA extended the NPS to all citizens in India through All Citizens Scheme launched w.e.f. 1 May 2009. PFRDA appointed 6 PFMs and 22 POPs to manage funds for the All Citizens Scheme.

In the third phase, the PFRDA introduced the *Tier-II NPS* for all account holders under *Tier-I*, that is, members of central government/state governments/union territories and central/state/union territories' autonomous organisations' employees. Tier-II was opened for subscription w.e.f. 1 December 2009. In the fourth phase PFRDA introduced NPS Lite Scheme on 22 July 2010. This was a welcome strategy for a new system and past experience helped to modify earlier weaknesses of implementation, (though something more needs to be done). A separate scheme has also been introduced for the corporate sector employees. Following the implementation of NPS by the central government for its employees, the state governments in India also decided to implement NPS for its employees but effective dates were not the same. Implementation dates in some states were even before January 2004; for example, the state of Chhattisgarh implemented NPS w.e.f. November 2003.

THE SALIENT FEATURES OF THE NATIONAL PENSION SYSTEM (NPS)

A Flexible System

NPS is quite flexible as it is not mandatory for all workers but for the new employees of the central government who joined after a specified date, that is, 1 January 2004 and also it is voluntary for other workers. Also it is mandatory for the new employees of the state government, who have joined NPS. For the state government employees effective date is not 1 January 2004 but the date at which the states have joined the NPS or the effective dates decided by the state governments. As on 2 March, 2013, out of 28 Indian states, 23 have joined the NPS and two states namely Maharashtra, Tamil Nadu have notified NPS but yet to adopt and other three states yet to notify. This is significant in view of the fact that India is a federal democratic country and there are different political parties which rule different states.

NPS Is a Combination of Four Schemes

The NPS at present comprises four schemes aimed at covering different segments of workers/citizens. These are:

- NPS for central and state government employees: Participation in NPS is mandatory for central government employees (excluding armed forces) who have joined services on or after 1 January 2004. Participation is also mandatory for state government employees in the states which have joined NPS.
- NPS for All Citizens (Unorganised Sector): This scheme is open to all citizens of India and participation is voluntary.
- NPS for Corporate Sector: This is voluntary scheme specially designed for employees of corporate sector. But POPs play an important role in driving the corporate model and also the corporate unlike All Citizens Scheme; contribute along with the workers to build up pension corpus for old age income. Further, the POPs play an important role in Corporate NPS as the corporate can join through them.
- NPS Lite: NPS Lite is a unique scheme designed for Vulnerable Section of Society and participation is voluntary.

However, in this section, only first three schemes, namely NPS for government employees, All Citizens Scheme and NPS for Corporate will be discussed. (The NPS Lite will be discussed separately in the next chapter due to its own significance as a Micro Pension Product.)

Individual Pension Account

NPS is an individual account–based pension system. Every subscriber is issued a unique Permanent Retirement Account Number (PRAN) by the Central Record keeping Agency (CRA). Through this PRAN, a subscriber can periodically accrete savings into her/his individual account. This account is portable and remains with the member even whenever the member changes employer or location.

Portable Pension Account

The new pension system is a portable system and the members have the option to transfer individual pension accounts in case of change of employment or change of location anywhere in India. This is definitely an important feature of the NPS, as there are frequent changes of jobs from government/public sector to private sector and vice versa or from one employer to another.

Switching Facilities

The NPS allows the subscribers to switch over from one fund manager to another and from one scheme to another.

Two-Tier System

The NPS is a fully funded DC pension system based on individual account, individual contribution and active investment choice. It is a two-tier system. Tier-I is a non-withdrawable and tax deferred pension account, which resembles the second pillar in the three-pillar system. It is mandatory for central government employees but voluntary for All Citizens Scheme and Corporate Scheme while the Tier-II is a voluntary savings plans and a member is free to withdraw part or all of the Tier-II wealth anytime. The Tier-II of NPS thus resembles the third pillar in a three-pillar system. The assets of Tier-II are managed through exactly the same way as the assets of Tier-I. This withdrawable account does not constitute pension investment, and there are no special tax incentives. While the Tier-I account was made available from May 1 2009, the facility of Tier-II account was available w.e.f. 1 December 2009 to all citizens of India and government employees mandatorily covered by NPS. The Tier-I is a pension account while Tier-II savings account serving the members to mitigate two different financial need—long-term retirement income and short-term financial requirement, though a member can maintain the Tier-II account till she/he exit from the scheme. While the members of Tier-I are eligible for tax incentives, there is no such incentives for investing in Tier-II. Another difference is that the Tier-I is a non-withdrawable account while Tier-II is a withdrawable account which allows the investors to withdraw from this account on account of emergency financial contingencies. Through Tier-II savings an account holder would be able to enhance his/her retirement savings to take care of old-age income.

The Tier-II account is available to those investors who are members of NPS through Tier-I. Therefore an active Tier-I is a pre-requisite for opening a Tier-II account. Some important features of Tier-II account are that there are no limits on number of withdrawals. There are no additional CRA charges for opening a Tier-II account and annual maintenance, but separate transaction charges are levied by CRA for each transaction. The subscriber would have the same choice of PFMs and schemes as in the case of Tier-I account in the unorganised sector. An investor can contribute to Tier-II through any POP/POP-SP. No separate KYC for Tier-II account opening will be required. There will be facility of one-way transfer of savings form Tier-II to Tier-I. Significant characteristics of Tier-I and Tier-II are shown in Table 7.1.

Eligibility

❖ SCHEME FOR GOVERNMENT EMPLOYEES

The NPS has been opened to the new employees of the central government who joined services on or after 1 January 2004, and for the state government employees as per the notification issued by the respective governments.

Table 7.1 Comparative Features of Tier-I and Tier-II Accounts

Serial No	*Functionality*	*Tier-I*	*Tier-II*
1.	Registration	Registration through PAOs for government subscribers and through POP-SP for all other subscribers. KYC to be done by POP-SP	Registration only through POP-SP for government as well as all other subscribers. PRAN card to act as KYC, no separate documentation required.
2	Contribution	Government subscriber • Mandatory contribution through PAO/CDDO for government subscribers (10 per cent + 10 per cent of Basic + DA per month) Other Subscribers (all Citizen except those mandatorily covered by NPS) • Minimum four contribution in a year • Minimum contribution ₹6000/- p.a. • Minimum contribution ₹500/- per contribution.	• Voluntary contribution through POP/POP-SP for Government as well as other subscribers • Minimum contribution of ₹1000/- at the time of account opening. • Minimum contribution of ₹250/- per contribution. • Minimum balance of ₹2000/- at the end of each financial year.
3	Scheme Preference	Unorganised sector subscribers • 3 Asset classes and 6 PFMs • Availability of Auto Choice Government Subscribers • Default Scheme under Tier-I • 3 PFMs	All subscriber shall have: • Choice of six PFMs and three assets classes (E,C,G) • Availability of Auto Choice
4	Bank Account	Non-Mandatory	Mandatory
5	Withdrawals	No withdrawals allowed during vesting period except as per the norms prescribed by PFRDA.	No limit on withdrawals.

Source: National Pension System (NPS) Offer Document for both Tier-I vis-à-vis Tier-II, www.pfrda.org.in

❖ ALL CITIZENS SCHEME

All the Citizens Scheme opened for subscription with effect from 1 May 2009. A citizen of India, whether resident or non-resident can join the NPS subject to the fulfilment of two basic conditions. She/he should be between 18–55 years of age as on the date of submission of her/his application to the POP/POP-SP. She/he should comply with KYC norms as detailed in the subscriber registration form.

❖ CORPORATE NPS SCHEME

The Corporate NPS Scheme has been extended to the central public sector enterprises, state public sector enterprises, entities registered under companies act, entities registered under various co-operative acts, registered partnership firm, registered Limited Liability Partnership (LLPs) and anybody incorporated under any act of Parliament or state legislature or by order of central/state government, if they want to extend NPS to their employees, tied up with an approved POP through MOUs. Corporate NPS is open to all resident or non-resident citizens of India subject to the conditions that subscribers should be between 18–60 years of age and comply with the KYC norms.

Funding to NPS

❖ GOVERNMENT EMPLOYEES

In the new system, NPS contributions and investment returns would be deposited in a non-withdraw able Tier-I account. As per the present practice, the employees would contribute 10 per cent of salary and an identical matching contribution will be made by the central government, which is transferred to the pension account of an employee. For state government employees the quantum of contribution is left to the respective state government, but they follow the central government pattern.

❖ ALL CITIZENS SCHEME

Under this scheme entire contribution is made by the members. There is a provision for the minimum contributions. For Tier-I, the minimum amount per contribution is ₹500 and per year ₹6,000. However, the minimum number of contributions can even be only ₹1 per year. The minimum amount of contributions per account under Tier-II account is ₹250 and the minimum balance of ₹2,000 at the end of each financial year and there can be a single contribution per year subject to the following conditions:

- Minimum amount per contribution—₹500
- Minimum contribution per year—₹6,000

❖ CORPORATE NPS

Minimum amount of contribution and minimum payment is the same as in case of All Citizens Scheme. However, there can be equal contributions by employer and employee and also unequal contribution by the employer and the employee or contribution from either the employer or the employee. From 1 April 2012 onwards an employer can contribute up to 10 per cent of the salary (basic and dearness allowance) of employees.

Collection of Contribution

❖ GOVERNMENT NPS

Under the government NPS system contributions of employees are deducted from the salary of employees by the controlling office. Along with the employer contribution money is transferred to the designated Branches of Trustee Bank (Bank of India).

❖ ALL CITIZENS SCHEME

In case of All Citizens Scheme contribution to NPS is collected by the POP and this collection is transmitted to the collecting banker, that is, Bank of India. POPs deduct the pre-determined collection charges from the amount deposited by a member. By the end of September 2011, there were 35 POPs having 12,226 authorised branches which collected 55,611.

❖ CORPORATE NPS

The PoPs play an important role in Corporate NPS. They are authorised to receive consolidated contribution from corporate as per their MOU. PoPs can also provide consolidated acknowledgement to the corporate along with nominal roll of subscribers, and remit funds to trustee banks.

Mandatory Annuitisation

Annuitisation of pension wealth is a debate associated with pension reforms and most of the countries have introduced the provision of annuity in the DC system. In fact the strength of the pension system to a great extent depends on the nature of annuitisation. Under the NPS a member can normally exit at the age of 60 or at superannuation from Tier-I of the pension system. At the time of exit the member would require to invest at least 40 per cent of pension wealth to purchase an annuity (from an IRDA-regulated life insurance in case of government employees the annuity should provide for pension for the lifetime of the employee and his dependent parents and his spouse at the time of retirement. The member would receive a lump sum of the remaining pension wealth, which she/he would be free to utilise in any manner. An individual member of the NPS would have the flexibility to leave the pension system prior to age of 60. However, in that case, the mandatory Annuitisation would be 80 per cent of the pension wealth (Table 7.2).

Table 7.2 Mandatory Annuitisation and Withdrawal under NPS

Vesting Criteria	*Benefits Withdrawal*
Withdrawal at any point of time before 60 years of age	A Member of NPS would be required to invest at least 80 per cent of the accumulated pension wealth to purchase a Life Annuity Policy from any IRDA regulated life insurance company approved as an Annuity Provider by PFRDA and Rest 20 per cent of the pension wealth may be withdrawn as lump sum.
On attaining the age of 60 years and up to 70 years of age	On attaining age 60 years a member can exit from NPS but be required to invest minimum 40 percent of accumulated pension wealth to purchase a life annuity Life Annuity Policy from any IRDA regulated life insurance company approved as an Annuity Provider by PFRDA. The remaining pension wealth can either be withdrawn in a lump sum on attaining the age of 60 or can be deferred upto age 70 years and stay invested in the NPS without any fresh contributions. The deferred lump sum amount can be withdrawn at any time before attaining the age of 70 years by giving a withdrawal notice. Without such notice the accumulated pension wealth would be automatically monetized and credited to the bank account of the subscriber upon attaining the age.
Death due to any cause	In case of death of a member option is available to the nominee to receive 100 per cent of the NPS pension wealth in lump sum. But there is an option the nominee to continue with the NPS, as an individual subscribe after following the KYC norms.

Source: Pension Fund Regulatory and Development Authority (PFRDA)'s NPS Main Scheme-Welcome Kit.

Multiple Fund Managers

In order to provide wider choice and to introduce competition, there are multiple fund managers in NPS. In India, there was a reservation among the government employees to open the NPS to private fund managers at the initial stage therefore a conscious decision was taken to appoint only public sector fund managers to manage pension funds of government employees.

❖ GOVERNMENT EMPLOYEES FUNDS

There are three licensed fund managers, sponsored by three public sector managing government sector funds—The LIC Pension Fund Ltd, SBI Pension Funds Ltd and UTI Retirement Solutions Ltd. However, currently the government employees do not select any fund manager but the contributions are pooled together and distributed among three licensed fund managers proportionately on the basis of the investment performance in the previous year.

❖ ALL CITIZENS SCHEME FUNDS

For managing the funds under the All Citizens Scheme the PFRDA has issued licenses to six fund managers including two public sector fund managers and four private sector fund managers were appointed to manage. They are ICICI Prudential Pension Fund Management Company Ltd, IDFC Pension Fund Management Company Ltd, Kotak Mahindra Pension Fund Ltd, Reliance Capital Pension Fund Ltd, SBI Pension Funds Ltd and UTI Retirement Solutions Ltd. The subscribers to All Citizens Scheme have the option to select fund managers from the multiple pension fund managers.

❖ CORPORATE NPS

Corporate NPS is quite flexible as far as investment option is concerned. They can opt for the investment pattern designed for central government employees or for the All Citizens Scheme and accordingly the fund managers.

❖ NPS LITE

Investment option under the NPS Lite is decided by the Aggregators—which can be the Central Government employee's funds or the All Citizens Scheme. Accordingly the fund managers will also differ.

Fund managers for different schemes are shown in Table 7.3.

Investment Option

Purchasing power, disposable income and risk tolerance are different for different income levels. Keeping this in view NPS offers different types of funds for three groups of investors, namely government employees, unorganized sector and for the low cost NPS Lite. Under the NPS, the pension fund managers will offer multiple schemes to the subscribers. At present, however, schemes offered to the central government employees and other citizens are a bit different. There is also an option for the subscribers to opt for active option or an auto choice (default option).

❖ FUNDS OFFERED TO CENTRAL GOVERNMENT AND STATE EMPLOYEES

There is a provision for Low and moderate low risk funds (schemes) for central government and state government employees who join the NPS.

Scheme-1

According to investment arrangement under this scheme, up to 15 per cent of assets can be invested in equity and mutual funds, up to 55 per cent assets can be invested in

Table 7.3 Fund Managers for Different Schemes

Schemes	*Fund Managers*
A. Government Employees Funds	LIC Pension Fund Limited
	SBI Pension Funds Private Limited
	UTI Retirement Solutions Limited
B. All Citizens Schemes	ICICI Prudential Pension Fund Management Company Limited
	IDFC Pension Fund Management Company Limited
	Kotak Mahindra Pension Fund Limited
	Reliance Capital Pension Fund Limited
	SBI Pension Funds Private Limited
	UTI Retirement Solutions Limited
C. Corporate NPS	
1. Opting for investment pattern followed for Central Govt. Employees	LIC Pension Fund Limited
	SBI Pension Funds Private Limited
	UTI Retirement Solutions Limited
2. Opting for investment pattern followed for All Citizens Scheme	ICICI Prudential Pension Fund Management Company Limited
	IDFC Pension Fund Management Company Limited
	Kotak Mahindra Pension Fund Limited
	Reliance Capital Pension Fund Limited
	SBI Pension Funds Private Limited
	UTI Retirement Solutions Limited
D. NPS Lite	
1. Opting for investment pattern followed for Central Govt. Employees	LIC Pension Fund Limited
	SBI Pension Funds Private Limited
	TI Retirement Solutions Limited
2. Opting for investment pattern followed for All Citizens Scheme	ICICI Prudential Pension Fund Management Co. Ltd
	IDFC Pension Fund Management Company Limited
	Kotak Mahindra Pension Fund Limited
	Reliance Capital Pension Fund Limited
	SBI Pension Funds Limited
	UTI Retirement Solutions Limited
	LIC Pension Fund Ltd

Source: Pension Fund Regulatory and Development Authority (PFRDA).

central and state government securities, up to 40 per cent assets can be invested in corporate debt including PSU bonds and up to 5 per cent assets can be invested in short term money market instruments.

Scheme 2

Under this scheme 100 per cent pension assets will be invested in government securities. However, at present only Scheme I is operational. (Investment pattern for the central and state government employees funds is shown in Table 7.4.)

Table 7.4 Investment Pattern for Funds under Government Employees

	Investment Pattern	*Percentage Amount to be Invested*
(i)	(a) Government securities[1] (b) Other securities[2] the principal whereof and interest whereon is fully and unconditionally guaranteed by the Central Government or any State Government except those covered under (ii) (a) below: (c) units of mutual funds set up as dedicated funds for investment in Government securities and regulated by the Securities and Exchange Board of India; Provided that the exposure to a mutual fund shall not be more than 5 per cent of the total portfolio at any point of time.	**Up to 55**
(ii)	(a) Debt securities with maturity of not less than three years tenure issued by Bodies Corporate including banks and public financial institutions[3]; Provided that at least 75 per cent of the investment in this category is made in instruments having an investment grade rating from at least one credit rating agency. (b) Term Deposit Receipts of not less than one year duration issued by scheduled commercial banks. Provided that the scheduled commercial banks must meet conditions of (i) continuous profitability for immediately preceding three years; (ii) maintaining a minimum Capital to Risk Weighted Assets Ratio of 9 per cent; (iii) having net non-performing assets of not more than 2 per cent of the net advances; (v) having a minimum net worth of not less than Rs.200 crores. (c) Rupee Bonds having an outstanding maturity of at least 3 years issued by institutions of the International Bank for Reconstruction and Development, International Finance Corporation and the Asian Development Bank.	**Up to 40**
(iii)	Money market instruments including units of money market mutual funds	**Up to 5**
(iv)	Shares of companies on which derivatives are available in Bombay Stock Exchange or National Stock Exchange or equity linked schemes of mutual funds regulated by the Securities and Exchange Board of India.	**Up to 15**

Source: Ministry of Finance, Government of India, Circular: F. No.5(88)/2006-PR dated August, 2008.

Note: 1. 'Government Securities' as defined in Section 2(b) of the Securities Contracts (Regulation) Act, 1956.
2. 'Securities' as defined in Section 2(h) of the Securities Contracts (Regulation) Act, 1956.
3. 'Public Financial Institutions' as specified under Section 4A of the Companies Act, 1956.

❖ INVESTMENT OPTIONS OFFERED IN ALL CITIZEN'S SCHEME

One of the most significant features of the NPS is flexible investment option. One can select a scheme depending on her/his risk tolerance capacity from a basket of three schemes under active choice. However, those who are unable to decide on any scheme by themselves can simply opt for a pre determined investment portfolio called auto choice.

Investment by an NPS participant in equity would be subject to a cap of 50 per cent. The subscriber will have the option to actively decide as to how the NPS pension wealth is to be invested in three asset class. Under active choice there are three options to select an investment portfolio with different asset classes with varying degree of risks. Three asset classes are:

Asset Class E: Investment in predominantly equity market instruments
Asset Class C: Investment in Fixed income instruments other than the government securities.
Asset Class G: Investment in government securities.

However, one can select a portfolio with Asset class E (equity) investment maximum up to 50 per cent.

PFRDA has issued detail investment guidelines on PFRDA for Private Sector NPS (Annexure 7A.3) incorporating investment in different asset classes in separate schemes—Investment Universe, Investment Restrictions, Investment objectives, etc. Some significant points from the investment guidelines can be outlined as follows: Asset classes and Schemes. Accordingly the PFs will manage various schemes with different asset classes:

Asset class E (equity market instruments): An NPS participant is allowed to invest up to 50% in asset class E- in shares of the companies listed in National Stock Exchange, Bombay Stock Exchange or/and in derivatives or in part of Nifty Fifty Index or BSE Sensex. Cap of 50% as mentioned above is expected to be maintained at all points in time, but can be exceed by maximum 5% for purposes of portfolio balancing.

Asset class G (Government Securities): The asset class G will be invested in central government and state government bonds subject to certain restrictions.

Asset class C (credit risk bearing fixed income instruments): The asset class C will be invested in bonds issued by any entity other than Central and State Government and money can also be invested in Fixed deposits and credit rated debt securities like rated bonds/securities of Public Financial Institutions and Public sector companies, rated municipal bodies/infrastructure bonds and bonds of all firms (including PSU/PSE), subject to certain restrictions.

Corporate CG: Applicable (currently) to SBI Pension Funds Private Ltd, UTI Retirement Solutions Ltd & LIC Pension Fund Ltd which replicates the scheme as applicable to Central Government employees (subject to instructions from PFRDA/NPS Trust from time to time).

NPS Lite: Investment pattern is similar to that prescribed by the Central Government for its own employees as amended from time to time. (Please refer to Annexure 7A.3 for detail guidelines.)

❖ AUTO CHOICE (DEFAULT OPTION)

In case the subscriber is unable/unwilling to exercise any choice as regards asset allocation, his/her contribution will be invested in accordance with the auto choice option. In this option the investment will be determined by a predefined portfolio.

At the lowest age of entry (18 years) the auto choice will entail investment of 50 per cent of pension wealth in 'E' Class, 30 per cent in 'C' Class and 20 per cent in 'G' Class. These ratios of investment will remain fixed for all contributions until the participant reaches the age of 36. From age 36 onwards, the weight in 'E' and 'C' asset class will decrease annually and the weight in 'G' class will increase annually till it reaches 10 per cent in 'E', 10 per cent in 'C' and 80 per cent in 'G' class at age 55 (Appendix 7.3).

In auto choice life cycle fund pattern of investment changes from higher risk higher return portfolio to lower risk lower return portfolio (Table 7.5). To begin with, higher investment is made in Equity (max 50 per cent) at a lower age, which gradually declined with age of the investors. An auto choice portfolio begins with 50 per cent investment in equity (Asset Class E), 30 per cent investment in asset class C and 20 per cent investment in asset class G (up to Age 35 years) and at the age of 55 years and beyond, portfolio consist of 10 per cent investment in asset class E, 10 per cent investment in asset class C and 80 per cent investment in Asset Class G. (Investment Guidelines for All Citizens Funds provided in Annexure 7A.4.)

Table 7.5 Distribution of Asset under Auto Choice

Age	*Asset Class E*	*Asset Class C*	*Asset Class G*
up to 35 years	50 per cent	30 per cent	20 per cent
36 years	48 per cent	29 per cent	23 per cent
37 years	46 per cent	28 per cent	26 per cent
38 years	44 per cent	27 per cent	29 per cent
39 years	42 per cent	26 per cent	32 per cent
40 years	40 per cent	25 per cent	35 per cent
41 years	38 per cent	24 per cent	38 per cent
42 years	36 per cent	23 per cent	41 per cent
43 years	34 per cent	22 per cent	44 per cent
44 years	32 per cent	21 per cent	47 per cent
45 years	30 per cent	20 per cent	50 per cent
46 years	28 per cent	19 per cent	53 per cent
47 years	26 per cent	18 per cent	56 per cent
48 years	24 per cent	17 per cent	59 per cent
49 years	22 per cent	16 per cent	62 per cent
50 years	20 per cent	15 per cent	65 per cent
51 years	18 per cent	14 per cent	68 per cent
52 years	16 per cent	13 per cent	71 per cent
53 yeas	14 per cent	12 per cent	74 per cent
54 years	12 per cent	11 per cent	77 per cent
55 years	10 per cent	10 per cent	80 per cent

Source: Pension Regulatory and Development Authority (PFRDA)'s Detailed Investment Guidelines for All Citizens Under the New Pension System.

Note: The reallocation among the asset classes in this choice will be done every year on the date of birth of the subscriber.

❖ INVESTMENT OPTION FOR CORPORATE NPS

There is more flexibility in investment choice for corporate NPS. Investment option can be decided either at subscriber level (subscribers option) or at the corporate level centrally (corporate option) for all its underlying subscribers. Each of these options has two choices.

Option 1

Corporate option, where corporate centrally decides on behalf of all underlying subscribers.

Choice I: Choice 1 under the option 1 is similarly to the scheme offered to the Central government employees and the funds are allocated among the three fund managers namely LIC Pension Fund Ltd, SBI Pension Funds Ltd and UTI Retirement Solutions Ltd at a proportion decided by PFRDA.

Choice II: Choice II under option I is similar to the All Citizens Model and funds can be allocated to any of the fund managers authorised to manage assets under the All Citizens Scheme.

Or

Option 2

Subscriber can choose any one of the six fund managers authorised to manage assets under the All Citizens Scheme/Private Sector NPS. The subscribers can also opt for either an Active Choice or Auto Choice.

No Guaranteed Return

NPS in India differs from most of the pension system in Latin America and East European countries which have introduced pension reforms in respect of guarantee. An element of new system in those countries is some guarantee of return by the fund managers/sponsors of funds. But in India no such return guarantee, implicit or explicit assurance of benefits is provided by the fund managers/sponsors/government. Investment return is purely market driven and fund managers are no way responsible for poor performance.

Fee Structure in NPS

Pension reforms are often confronted by fee structure which is often considered to be high, particularly when compared with employee funded DB pension system. It is criticism that no reform system can avoid. PFRDA has been too concerned to keep the cost low under various heads operation to run the system and tried to evolve a low cost system comprising CRA charges, POP charges, fund management fees, trustee bank charges and custodian fees (Table 7.6).

❖ CRA FEES

PFRDA has appointed the National Securities Depository Ltd (NSDL) as the single CRA to carry out record keeping and other related services for an annual fee of ₹10 lakh. This is an exception while there are multiple service providers like PFM, POP there is only one CRA. The logic behind single CRA was that at the initial stage of implementation of a new system it was easy to handle multiple CRA services through a single agency.

There are various charges of CRA which includes account opening charge, account maintenance charge, and transaction charge. NSDL is charging a fee of ₹50 per account as account opening charges. The annual maintenance charges and transaction charges payable by a subscriber is ₹280 and ₹6 respectively (till such time as the number of accounts with the CRA reaches 10 lakh); but this charges would come down to ₹250 and ₹4 respectively, once the threshold limit of 10 lakh accounts is reached and once the number of accounts with the CRA reaches 30 lakh. While in case of All Citizens Scheme all these charges are to be borne by the subscribers, the central government have decided to bear these charges in respect of their employees covered under the NPS.

❖ POPS FEES

POPs charges two types of fees from the subscribers namely, account opening fee and transaction fee. For every new account POP charges ₹40 per account and there after ₹20 for transaction charge for every account. In addition to these charges POP receives from PFRDA ₹150 as supplementary fees to enrol subscribers in NPS.

❖ FUNDS MANAGEMENT FEES

In the first year of operation PFRDA selected three PFMs for managing pension funds of central government employees and fund management fees were decided through a bidding process. There was no uniformity in Fee structure and it was 0.05 per cent for LIC Pension Fund and SBI Pension Fund, while 0.05 per cent for UTI Pension Fund.

Table 7.6 Charges under NPS

Intermediary	*Charge Head*	*Service Charges*	*Method of Deduction*
CRA	PRAN Opening charges	₹50	Through cancellation of units
	Annual PRA Maintenance cost per account	₹280[1]	
	Charge per transaction	₹ 6[1]	
POP (Maximum Permissible charge for each subscriber)	Initial subscriber registration and contribution upload	₹40	To be collected upfront
	Any subsequent transactions[2]	₹20	
Trustee Bank	Per transaction emanating from a RBI location	Zero	Through NAV deduction
	Per transaction emanating from a non-RBI location[4]	₹15	
Custodian[5] (On asset value in custody)	Asset Servicing Charges	0.0075% p.a. for Electronic segment & 0.05% p.a. for Physical segment	Through NAV deduction
PFM charges	Investment Management Fee[3]	Govt. NPS: 0. 0102% NPS Lite: 0.0102% Private & Corporate NPS: 0.25%(max)	Through NAV deduction

Source: National Pension System (NPS) Offer Document for both Tier-I vis-à-Vis Tier-II, www.pfrda.org.in.
Note: When the number of accounts in CRA reaches 10 lakh the service charges, exclusive of Service Tax and other taxes as applicable will be reduced to ₹280 (Rupees two hundred and eighty only) for annual PRA maintenance per account ₹6 (Rupees six only) for charges per transaction. Further, when the number of accounts in CRA reaches 30 lakh the service charges, exclusive of Service Tax and other taxes as applicable, will be reduced further to ₹250 (Rupees two hundred and fifty only) for annual PRA maintenance per account and ₹4 (Rupees four only) for charges per transaction. CRA's charge for maintenance of your permanent retirement would include charges for maintenance of electronic information of the balances in your PRA, for incorporating changes to PRA details received by the CRA in electronic form, for sending annual account information once a year in printed form etc.

The bidding process also followed for deciding the selection of fund managers for All Citizens Scheme in 2009. However, it was mentioned in the RFP for unorganized sector that the selected fund managers have to accept L1 management fees. Further three fund managers for central government and state government employees also had to accept L1 fees quoted for unorganised sector. Accordingly, LIC Pension fund, SBI Pension Fund and UTI Retirement Solution Ltd, the fund managers for central and state government employees, also had to accept L1 fees. The lowest fee (L1) quoted by one of the fund managers for All Citizens Scheme was 0.0009 per cent, which was binding for all the fund managers managing central and state government funds as well All Citizens Scheme with effect from 1 April 2009. It is very difficult to understand why PFRDA changed the bidding process in selecting fund managers for unorganised sector (All Citizens Scheme), which tended to generate a fee structure so low that no one could recover even a part of fund management expenses.

❖ FUND MANAGEMENT FEES IN 2012

There was a significant development in 2012 as the structure and method of determination of fund management fees changed for government and private sector NPS. The system of uniformity in fee structure for managing government employees fund and fund for all citizens was abolished. The following fee structure was introduced with effect from 1 November 2012.

Private Sector NPS

The upper ceiling of the Investment Management fees has been fixed at 0.25 per cent p.a. of the asset under management (AUM) with effect from 1 November 2012 for the schemes spanning all private and corporate sector subscribers. The fund managers can fix their own Investment Management fee for different schemes subject to the upper ceiling of 0.25 per cent p.a., which is inclusive of brokerage except custodian charges and applicable taxes. The PFMs are permitted to revise the Investment Management fee, once in a year.

Government NPS

The investment management fee applicable to the NPS schemes for government employees revised with effect from 18 April 2012 would continue at 0.0102 per cent p.a.

❖ NPS LITE AND SWAVALAMBAN

The Investment Management fee for the NPS Lite/Swavalamban will be at par with the Investment Management fee applicable to NPS Schemes for government employees, which is currently at 0.0102 per cent p.a.

In the revised scheme, the fund managers are not permitted to charge any differential investment management fee for different subscriber class and investment management fee is to be calculated on the AUM on a daily accrual basis and charged to the scheme at the end of every quarter.

❖ CUSTODIAN CHARGES

PFRDA has appointed a single custodian Stock Holding Corporation of India Ltd (SHCIL) as the single custodian for the NPS. SHCIL charges 0.0075 per cent p.a. for electronic segment and 0.05 per cent p.a. for physical segment towards servicing assets. These charges are deducted from the Net Asset Value (NAV) of assets serviced by it.

❖ BANKING CHARGES

PFRDA has appointed Bank of India as the trustee bank which charges ₹15 per transaction emanating from a non RBI location, while no fee is charge on any transaction emanating from RBI location. Almost all the centres in India, however, are connected with RBI and therefore, charges are levied on very few locations.

Costs in NPS

Professionalism, corporate governance, risk consciousness and investment ethics are the pre requisites of good performance and prudent management to protect the long-term interest of investors. High standard of professionalism, however, has its own cost and needs to be inbuilt into the system. Fee structure and regulation in DC private pension system differs widely among the countries. While some countries put the limit on various fees, there are countries which do not put any cap and leave them to market forces. There is also variation in the composition of fee structure globally. Yet the major components are fixed commission, fees on contribution, fees on asset management, fees on exit and switching. In some countries there are also fees on investment return and fees for providing disability and death benefits to the pensioners. In Latin America most of the countries charge fees on contribution and few countries like Peru and Columbia do not charge fund management fees which are included in contribution fees. Countries like Australia, Chile charge both.

Costs of managing private pension also depend on the nature of collection of contribution and record maintenance. In a centralised collection system in countries like Colombia, Uruguay, etc., in Latin America, Poland, Hungary, etc., in Eastern Europe, there is a centralised agency which collects contributions and distributes funds among the pension fund managers, while in a decentralised collection system in countries like Chile, Peru, Hungary, etc., contributions are directly collected by the PFMs. It is said that centralised collection is less costly due to scale economy. However research has not proved this contention. In most of the countries in Latin America or Eastern Europe the, record keeping is done by the pension funds even where separate collection agency is involved in contribution collection.

It may also be mentioned here that in some countries like Chile, Mexico, Peru, etc there is no limit on management fees. However, there is not much variation in actual fee structure even without any cap/limit. Average administrative including fund management fees vary from 1 per cent to 1.8 per cent. Asset management fee is the most debated and important cost factor in private pension system. Generally the asset management fee varies from 0.5 per cent to 1.5 per cent in many eastern European countries.

In India, under the NPS, there are separate cost centres like CRA, POPS, PFMS, trustee bank and custodian. Some costs like CRA charges, often criticised as high at the initial stage. (However, the same declined with the increase in number of accounts.) The most important component of any private pension system is the fees charged by the fund managers, because, entire performance depends on their performance. Currently, the fund management charges 0.0009 per cent (based on assets under management), which is probably the lowest in the world. Even the mutual funds charges in India vary from 1.5 per cent to 2 per cent (often even more). Low cost means more amount for investment leading to higher accumulated wealth at the time of termination from the scheme. It is a fact that such a low cost is not sustainable. However, in over emphasis on low cost, fund management may harm the interest of investors in the long run, low cost may adversely impact the fund management and investment return.

Taxation in NPS

NPS in India has adopted Exempt-Exempt-Tax (EET) regime. The EET is close to the expenditure tax and implemented for funded pensions by a large number of countries in the world. Under the EET, the contribution and investment returns of NPS will not be taxed but withdrawal will attract the tax benefits subject to maximum limit of exemption. Subsequently, the Finance Ministry announced two concessions to NPS in the Union Budget 2009–10, which will immensely benefits the NPS in terms of increasing returns out of NPS investment. Finance Minister proposes to exempt the income of new pension system trust from the income tax and any dividend paid to this trust from dividend distribution tax. Similarly, all purchases, sales of equity shares and derivatives by the NPS Trust will also be exempt from this Securities Transaction Tax. These concessions will significantly improve the investment returns of NPS investment by the fund managers. These will immensely help the pension funds to enhance their investment return.

❖ BENEFITS TO NPS UNDER PROPOSED DIRECT TAX CODES

The new tax code proposed to be implemented will boost pension savings directly and indirectly. It is expected that present EET on pension savings will be replaced by EEE. The new Tax code boosts savings greatly and highly simplifies tax calculation procedures. The tax code proposed to increase the exemption limit for savings. Currently, savings including pension savings of ₹1 lakh is exempted from the tax. Under the new tax code this limit has been extended up to ₹3 lakh. The Tax code also proposes to reduce tax rates. An individual having annual taxable income between ₹160,000 and ₹1,000,000 will be charged tax @ 10 per cent while taxable income above ₹1,000,000 but up to ₹2,500,000 would be charged @20 per cent. For income above ₹2,500,000 tax would be payable @30 per cent.

THE ARCHITECTURE AND ROLE OF VARIOUS ENTITIES IN NPS

Reforming a pension system and its success depends on many factors including a well-conceived system structure which induces confidence among the potential members, a well-designed product basket which fulfils the needs and expectations of a cross section of investors, and a robust architecture with well-defined roles of various entities serving the system. Pension architecture plays an immensely important role in system design as it integrates the various entities and brings clarity in their operational role which helps smooth transaction, keeps the system low cost and manageable and finally enhances value of accumulated assets. India has considered these aspects to make NPS a technology driven low cost pension system and devised an architecture which consists of a CRA, multiple PFMs, several POPs, one centralised custodian, one trustee bank, a centralised trustee for the NPS, under the overall regulatory supervision of the PFRDA.

Pension Fund Regulatory Development Authority

The PFRDA was established by the Government of India on 23 August 2003 to promote old-age income security by establishing, developing and regulating pension funds, to protect the interests of subscribers to schemes of pension funds and for matters connected therewith or incidental thereto. The PFRDA will regulate and develop the pension market in India. The PFRDA will adopt multiple strategies to promote the NPS and maximise retirement wealth of the subscribers, and to regulate the NPS for healthy and orderly growth. The authority shall consist of a chairperson and not more than five members, of whom at least three shall be whole-time members, to be appointed by the central government.

New Pension System (NPS) Trust

On the basis of authorisation of the Government of India, PFRDA appointed the New Pension System Trust (NPS Trust) on 27 February 2008. The deed of NPS Trust was executed by the PFRDA as per the provisions of the Indian Trust Act, 1882. The NPS Trust was registered under the Indian Registration Act 1908 on 5 March 2008.

❖ OBJECTS OF THE NPS TRUST

NPS Trust has been set up for taking care of assets and funds under the NPS. The securities NP will be purchased by the pension funds on behalf of and in the name of trustees and will be held in the custodial account of NPS Trust. However, individual subscribers will remain beneficial owner of these securities assets under the funds.

❖ MANAGEMENT OF THE TRUST

Trust is managed by a board of trustees. The minimum and maximum number of members of the trust can be three and seven members. Out of trustees appointed, one will be designated as chairperson of the board. The PFRDA may also appoint a suitable person as chief executive officer for day to day administration and management of the Trust. Currently the NPS Trust is headed by a chairman and day to day administration and management of the trust is looked after by a CEO.

❖ MANAGEMENT OF THE NPS FUND

According to the objectives of the NPS Trust, trustees shall manage the NPS Funds to realise and fulfil the objectives of NPS Trust. Trustees shall manage the affairs of the NPS Trust with utmost trust and good faith. Trust expenses shall be borne out of the income from fee, payments made by PFRDA/central government/states/union territory governments. Major functions of trustees will include the following: on the basis of investment guidelines and other directions issued by powers and functions of NPS Trust, they should issue instructions to the custodian not to assign transfer, hypothecate, pledge or other-wise dispose off any assets of NPS Trust; the trustee should call for any information, report, etc., from PF(s), trustee bank and custodian and to issue directions to PF(s) for protecting the interest of subscribers; should appoint a panel of independent auditors to undertake compliance audit and obtain compliance certificate from PF(s) at regular intervals; verify that trustee bank is performing its functions as per the provisions of the agreement with the NPS Trust and PF(s) are strictly following the terms and condition of Investment Management Agreement (IMA) and also verify that PF(s) and custodians are functioning as per the tripartite agreement entered into between NPS Trust, custodian and PFs. The trustee should take care to ensure that the funds are managed by the PF(s) in accordance with the NPS Trust deed and the PFRDA guidelines/directions take into its custody or under its control all the property of the pension funds and hold these in trust for the beneficiaries. The trustee should provide information. The trustee should take necessary steps to ensure that the transactions of the PFs are in accordance with the provisions of the NPS trust deed and periodically review the complaints received from beneficiaries.

Pension Fund Managers

Pension funds managers play the most crucial role in NPS by managing investment of retirement savings of the subscribers in various schemes according to the investment management agreement, objects/provision of the trust deeds and guidelines of PFRDA.

All the pension funds shall manage the corpus in accordance with the investment pattern indicated for the various schemes available to the individual subscribers and guidelines issued by PFRDA/GOI from time to time. The PFMs perform many functions including: funds management activities according to the investment agreement signed with NPS trustees; PFMs are responsible for the day-to-day management of the funds, by exercising all due diligence and vigilance in carrying out its duties in order to protect the rights and interest of the subscribers; responsible to furnish periodic reports as specified by the PFRDA and NPS trust as well as any other information and documents as may be required by the PFRDA, NPS trustees and the CRA from time to time and required to submit to the NPS trustees and to the PFRDA quarterly reports of each on its activities and compliance with the agreement, etc. However, the ownership rights and all other rights relating to ownership of all the record/records, data, statistical returns and information in electronic and physical form or in any other form obtained collected and/or required to be maintained by the PF(s) shall vest in the PFRDA. No person other than the PFRDA shall have any ownership rights or any other rights over any data or information in the possession of the PFMs.

Central Recordkeeping Agency

The CRA plays a very critical role in the NPS system by rendering administration and customer service function for all subscribers. The CRA acts as an operational interface between PFRDA and other NPS intermediaries such as pension funds, annuity service providers, trustee and trustee bank. CRA is expected to monitor each subscriber's contributions and instruction and transmit the information to the relevant pension fund and scheme on a daily basis; perform all record keeping, administration and customer service functions for all subscribers of the NPS and maintains liaison with external agencies to carry out its activities as per contract terms and conditions. The CRA issues PRAN to each subscriber, records the transactions related to each subscriber's PRAN, maintains database of all accounts and monitors contributions of subscribers and transmits the information to the relevant pension fund and schemes on a daily basis. The CRA receives instructions from subscribers and transmits required instructions to the PFMs, trustee bank, annuity service provider, etc. The CRA is also responsible to effect subscribers instructions regarding switching between funds and PFMs. It also provides periodic, consolidated PRAN statements to each subscriber and discharges such other duties as determined by the PFRDA and interacts and co-ordinates as necessary for the requirement of the NPS with other stakeholders. In addition to the above the CRA is expected to perform many other functions as required to carry out the administrative and servicing functions. It is in fact the nodal centre of all operation-related activities of NPS.

Point of Presence

The POPs play an equally important role in the whole architecture of NPS. POPs are the first point ground level contract point between NPS architecture and the potential subscribers. In fact they can play a developmental role in educating and popularising the NPS and effectively support the extension of pension coverage. The POPs perform very important functions relating to registration of subscribers, undertaking KYC verification, receiving contributions and instructions from subscribers and transmission of the same to designated NPS intermediaries. They are also required to comply with the provisions of the Prevention of Money Laundering (PML) Act, 2002. The POPs receive the application forms along with the KYC documentation, and register the subscription according to the prescribed rules issued by PFRDA/NPS Trust and accept the contribution from individual subscriber and remit funds to the trustee bank on at least T+1 basis.

They also provide many functions relating to customer services as they carry out changes in subscriber details on the basis of the request of subscribers, send the switching request of the subscribers regarding change in PFM and/or investment option from subscriber to the CRA, to redress the grievances against the PoP-SP normally within seven days from the date of receipt of grievance, etc.

NPS Contributions Accounting Network (NPSCAN)

NPSCAN is a web-based centralised system, set up by the Government of India. It is used by central (civil), ministries, non civil departments, union territories, central autonomous bodies and grant in aid institutions to provide administrative functions to government subscribers.

Trustee Bank

PFRDA has appointed one public sector bank that is Bank of India as the Trustee Bank, which manages the banking of the pension funds. The Trustee Bank is interfaces with pension funds for transfer of funds to the PFM's bank account as per the instructions of CRA, receive funds from the PFM's bank account and transmit to the NPS Trust Bank's account as per instructions of CRA, etc. Trustee Bank also has interfaced with the CRA for uploading of contribution details, transfer funds based on the instructions received from CRA, uploading of statement of closing balance of the NPS Trust account with the Bank to the CRA system, daily reconciliation of balances in various CRA related accounts, downloading of incremental PAO master file and transaction id list file. The trustee bank will also transfer funds on the instructions of CRA to annuity service provided or to the withdrawal account, etc.

NPS Custodian

The custodian provides custodial services to the pension funds, which will ensure that benefits due on the holdings are received, provide detail reports to the PFs, etc. Stockholding Corporation of India Ltd (SHCIL) has been appointed as custodian for all the schemes under NPS.

Annuity Service Providers

There is a provision of mandatory annuitisation in NPS and the annuity service providers (ASPs) will play a critical role, since they will offer annuity to the subscribers when members exit from the system. The ASPs will offer annuity products to the subscribers receive funds from CRA and pay regular monthly annuity to the annuity holders. PFRDA is in the process of appointing annuity service providers.

Subscribers

Subscribers are the most important stake holders in the NPS system as they have complete freedom about selection of fund managers and the scheme depending on their expectations and risk tolerance ability. They will also be free to switch over from one fund to another fund and one fund manager to another fund manager. Subscriber will also have the independent choice to select an annuity product as they like.

SELECTION OF INTERMEDIARIES IN NPS SYSTEM

PFRDA has followed a very transparent and competitive bidding process to select various intermediaries like CRA, PFMs, POPs, trustee bank and custodian. The process involved two ways bidding—technical and commercial. First it invited expression of interest (EOI), and thereafter selected bidders were issued request for proposal (RFP). License was issued after evaluation of commercial bidding. In Phase-1, PFRDA selected CRA, sponsor to form PFMs to manage funds of central government employees, trustee bank, and custodian. In the Phase-2, PFRDA appointed POPs and PFMs to manage funds for all citizens. It may be mentioned here that the initial process of selection would be valid until the PFRDA Bill is passed by the Parliament and will be applicable to management of pension funds relating to pension assets of central government employees including employees of central government, autonomous organisations covered by the NPS notified from 1 January 2004. The pension funds appointed by PFRDA may also be engaged by the state governments who have opted for NPS.

Central Recording Keeping Agency

PFRDA issued an advertisement on 22 January 2007, inviting Expression of Interest (EoI) from public sector entities with experience of developing and managing technology based central administration and recordkeeping systems, for functioning as CRA responsible for opening and maintenance of personal retirement accounts of the subscribers under the NPS and providing a number of related services. Subsequently on the basis of evaluation of the technical and commercial proposals, National Securities Depository Limited (NSDL) was selected as the CRA and the PFRDA and NSDL entered into a formal agreement on 26 November 2007 relating to the setting up of a CRA for the NPS. NSDL's appointment as CRA is for 10 years.

Selection of Sponsors and Pension Fund Managers

The PFMs in India were not appointed directly by the regulator PFRDA, instead, the regulator selected the sponsors through a competitive bidding, who were to incorporate Pension Fund. The PFRDA followed the process of two-way bidding to select efficient and financially sound institutions to select as the sponsors who would in turn form pension fund management companies.

Accordingly, PFRDA issued an advertisement and Preliminary Information Memorandum (PIM) inviting EOI from public sector entities for sponsoring pension funds for government employees under the new pension system. Out of seven institutions who submitted EOIS, only four, namely IDBI Capital Market Services Ltd, Life Insurance Corporation of India, State Bank of India and UTI Asset Management Company Private Ltd were invited for issuance of Request for Proposal (RFP) for sponsoring pension funds under the NPS were issued and finally after technical and commercial evaluation only three, namely Life Insurance Corporation (LIC), State Bank of India (SBI), UTI Asset Management Company (UTI-AMC) were appointed as sponsors on 27 November 2007. The LIC was the first to incorporate LIC Pension Fund Ltd, as a public limited company on 21 November, and thus became the first pension fund management company under NPS, to be incorporated in India. Other pension funds are *SBI Pension Fund Private Ltd and UTI Retirement Solutions Ltd.* Three Pension Funds entered into an investment management agreement with the NPS Trust on 29 March 2008. These three fund managers were initially appointed for a period of three years, and entrusted the investment management functions for pension funds of central government employees, for a fee varying from three to five basis points.

Selection of Pension Fund Managers for All Citizens

Pension Fund Managers for the All Citizens Scheme were also selected through a rigorous two way bidding system as followed for the selection of CRA. The PFRDA put an advertisement in leading financial newspapers as well as on its website on 26th December 2008 inviting EOI to sponsor pension fund for appointment of pension fund(s) for roll out of NPS for All Citizens. Subsequently, PFRDA issued EOI on 26 December 2008 for appointment of Pension Fund(s) for the voluntary sector under the new pension system.

In response to the advertisement, 21 institutions submitted EOI for sponsoring pension fund to manage pension funds of the unorganised sector. However, out of these 21, 15 firms were shortlisted to submit the RFP, and finally six namely ICICI Prudential Life Insurance Company Ltd, IDFC Asset Management Company Ltd, Kotak Mahindra Asset Management Company Ltd, Reliance Capital Asset Management Company Ltd, SBI Pension Funds Ltd, UTI Retirement Solutions were selected as sponsors to set up pension funds to manage pension funds under NPS for all citizens other than government.

Appointment of POPs for NPS

In order to implement the NPS for the voluntary sector the PFRDA appointed 23 POPs. The POPs are acting as collection centres for NPS contribution. Entities other than three existing pension funds were eligible to apply for POPs. POPs were selected on the basis of technical and commercial eligibility. On the basis of technical and commercial criteria the following 22 POPs were selected in the initial stage. It can be seen from the above that PFRDA has followed a transparent method and open parent criteria to select the NPS intermediaries except selection of fund managers in the second phase when fund managers for All Citizens Scheme was decided. The criteria for lowest quotation and having only six fund managers, subsequently generated many operational questions like uneconomical fund management, reflected in poor quality of research, absence of incentive-based motivation, etc.

ANNEXURES

Annexure 7A.1: Budget Announcements Regarding Pension Reforms

❖ BUDGET SPEECH (PART A) 2001–02 BY THE HON'BLE FINANCE MINISTER OF INDIA

Para No. 73. ... Whereas the organised sector is at present covered by various pension, provident fund and gratuity schemes, the unorganised sector does not have adequate social security coverage. I am asking the Insurance Regulatory Development Authority to look into all these issues and provide a road map for pension reforms by October 1, 2001.

Pension Reforms

Para No. 83. The Central Government pension liability has reached unsustainable proportions: as a percentage of GDP, it has risen from about 0.5 per cent in 1993–94 to 1 per cent in 2000–2001. As such it is envisaged that those who enter central government services after October 1, 2001 would receive pension through a new pension programme based on defined contributions. In order to review the existing pension system and to provide a roadmap for the next steps to be taken by the Government, I propose to constitute a High Level Expert Group, which would give its recommendations within 3 months.

❖ BUDGET SPEECH (PART A) 2002–03

Para No. 67. IRDA has recommended a regulatory framework for setting up pension funds to enable individuals to subscribe on a defined contribution basis to obtain the benefit of pensions on their retirement. Action on these recommendations will be taken by June 30, 2002.

Pension Reform

Para No. 91. The present pension scheme for Government employees casts an open-ended financial burden on the Government. I had announced the appointment of a High Level Expert Group to develop a new pension scheme, based on defined contributions, for new recruits entering government service. The Expert Group has submitted its report to the Government. It has proposed a hybrid scheme that combines contributions from employees and the Union Government on matching basis, on the one hand, while committing to the employees a defined benefit as pension. The report is being considered by the Government and the new pension scheme for new recruits will be announced and implemented by June 1, 2002.

❖ BUDGET SPEECH 2003–04

Para No. 44. My predecessor in office had, in 2001, announced a road map for a restructured pension scheme for new Central Government employees, and a scheme for the general public. This scheme is now ready. It will apply only to new entrants to Government service, except to the armed forces, and upon finalisation, offer a basket of pension choices. It will also be available, on a voluntary basis, to all employers for their employees, as well as to the self-employed.

Para No. 45. This new pension system, when introduced, will be based on defined contribution, shared equally in the case of Government employees between the Government and the employees. There will, of course, be no contribution from the Government in respect of individuals who are not Government employees. The new pension scheme will be portable, allowing transfer of the benefits in case of change of employment, and will go into „individual pension accounts with Pension Funds. The Ministry of Finance will oversee and supervise the Pension Funds through a new and independent Pension Fund Regulatory and Development Authority.

❖ BUDGET SPEECH 2004–05

Para No. 70. A 'defined contribution' pension scheme for new entrants into Central Government Service has come into effect from January 01, 2004 for the Central Government employees recruited on or after the date. A suitable legislation to provide a regulatory framework for the scheme will be introduced in Parliament.
Para No. 100. A 'defined contribution' pension scheme for new entrants into Central Government Service has come into effect from January 01, 2004. The tax treatment of contributions made to the scheme has engaged the attention of Government. I propose to adopt the universally accepted formula of EET that is, the contributions will be excluded from income for tax purposes; the accruals will also be exempt from tax; and only the terminal benefits will be taxed at the applicable rate in the year of receipt.

❖ BUDGET SPEECH 2005–06

Para No. 84. With increasing longevity, the problem of old-age income security can no longer be ignored. Government had announced a defined contribution pension scheme for newly recruited Central Government employees which would also be extended to the unorganised sector. I am happy to inform the House that seven State Government—Andhra Pradesh, Chhattisgarh, Himachal Pradesh, Jharkhand, Manipur, Rajasthan and Tamil Nadu—have introduced similar schemes for their employees. Other States have also evinced interest. An Ordinance was promulgated on December 29, 2004 to set up a Pension Fund Regulatory and Development Authority (PFRDA).
Para No. 85. Through the new scheme, it is proposed to offer a menu of investment choices to the subscriber and to provide a strong regulatory mechanism to ensure that the interests of subscribers are protected. I appeal to workers all over the country to join the new pension system.

❖ BUDGET SPEECH 2006–07

Para No. 90. Important Bills to amend the banking laws and for setting up the Pension Fund Regulatory and Development Authority are before Parliament. The Standing Committee on Finance has recommended these Bills. I would urge the Honourable Members to cooperate with the Government and pass these Bills.

❖ BUDGET SPEECH 2010–11

Para No. 90. To encourage the people from the un-organised sector to voluntarily save for their retirement and to lower the cost of operations of the New Pension Scheme (NPS) for such subscribers, Government will contribute ₹1000 per year to each NPS account opened in the year 2010-11. This initiative, 'Swavalamban' will be available for persons who join NPS, with a minimum contribution of ₹1000 and a maximum contribution of ₹12000 per annum during the financial year 2010–11. The scheme will be available for another three years. Accordingly, I am making an allocation of ₹100 crore for the year 2010–11. It will benefit about 10 lakh NPS subscribers of the un-organised sector. The scheme will be managed by the interim Pension Fund Regulatory and Development Authority.
Para No. 91. I also appeal to the State Governments to contribute a similar amount to the scheme and participate in providing social security to the vulnerable sections of the society (http://finmin.nic.in/the_ministry/dept_fin_services/pension/Budgetpercent20Announcements.pdf).

Annexure 7A.2: Operationalisation of the Budget Announcement 2003–04 on New Pension System

The Government approved on 23rd August 2003 the proposal to implement the budget announcement of 2003–04 relating to introducing a new restructured defined contribution pension system for new entrants to Central Government service, except to Armed Forces, in the first stage, replacing the existing system of defined benefit pension system. The new system will also be available, on a voluntary basis, to all persons including self employed professionals and others in the unorganised sector. However, mandatory programmes under the Employee Provident Fund Organisation (EPFO) and other special provident funds would continue to operate as per the existing system under the Employee Provident Fund and Miscellaneous Provisions Act, 1952 and other special Acts governing these funds.

The Government approved the basic features of the new pension system; and setting up of an interim pension fund regulatory and development authority (PFRDA).

The main features of the new pension system are given below:

- The new pension system would be based on defined contributions, which will use the existing network of bank branches and post offices etc. to collect contributions and interact with participants allowing transfer of the benefits in case of change of employment and offer a basket of pension choices.
- The system would be mandatory for new recruits to the central Government service except the armed forces and the monthly contribution would be 10 percent of the salary and DA to be paid by the employee and matched by the Central Government. However, there will be no contribution from the Government in respect of individuals who are not Government employees. The contributions and investment returns would be deposited in a non-withdrawable pension Tier-I account. The existing provisions of defined benefit pension and GPF would not be available to the new recruits in the central Government service.
- In addition to the above pension account, each individual may also have a voluntary Tier-II withdrawable account at his option. This option is given as GPF is proposed to be withdrawn for new recruits in Central Government service. Government will make no contribution into this account. These assets would be managed through exactly the above procedures. However, he would be free to withdraw part or the entire second tier' of his money anytime. This withdrawable account does not constitute pension investment, and would attract no special tax treatment.
- Individuals can normally exit at or after age 60 years for Tier-I of the pension system. At exit the individual would be mandatorily required to invest 40 percent of pension wealth to purchase an annuity (from an IRDA-regulated life insurance company). In case of Government employees the annuity should provide for pension for the lifetime of the employee and his dependent parents and his spouse at the time of retirement. The individual would receive a lump-sum of the remaining pension wealth, which he would be free to utilise in any manner. Individuals would have the flexibility to leave the pension system prior to age 60. However, in this case, the mandatory annuitisation would be 80 per cent of the pension wealth.

❖ ARCHITECTURE OF THE NEW PENSION SYSTEM

- It will have a central record keeping and accounting (CRA) infrastructure, several pension fund managers (PFMs) to offer three categories of schemes viz. option A, B and C.

- The participating entities (PFMs and CRA) would give out easily understood information about past performance, so that the individual would able to make informed choices about which scheme to choose.

❖ REGULATORY AUTHORITY

- An independent pension fund regulatory and development authority (PFRDA) will regulate and develop the pension market. PFRDA will develop its own funding stream based on user charges.
- Till such time when a statutory PFRDA is established, an interim PFRDA, on the pattern of SEBI and IRDA, should be appointed by an executive order.
- The interim PFRDA is to be headed by a Chairman with a status of not less than a Secretary to the Government of India and would be appointed by the Central Government. Other members of the interim body, not exceeding four in number, of whom not more than two shall serve full time, shall be selected by the Central Government from amongst persons having experience and knowledge in economics, finance, legal and administrative matters with one person from each discipline.

❖ INVESTMENT STRATEGY

- There will be different investment choices such as option A, B and C. The option A would imply predominant investment in fixed income instruments and some investment in equity. Option B will imply grater investment in equity. Option C will imply almost equal investment in fixed income and equity.
- Pension fund managers would be free to make investment in international markets subject to regulatory restrictions and oversight in this regard.
- It is proposed to evaluate market mechanisms (without any contingent liability) through which certain investment protection guarantees can be offered for the different schemes.

❖ TAX TREATMENT

Pension contributions and accumulation would be accorded tax preference up to a certain limit, but benefits would be taxed as normal income.

❖ SCOPE OF THE NEW PENSION SYSTEM

- The option of joining the new system would also be available to the State Governments and as and when they decide, the new system would be capable of accommodating the new participants.
- Mandatory programmes under the Employee Provident Fund Organisation (EPFO) and other special provident funds would continue to operate as per the existing system. However, individuals under these programs could voluntarily choose to additionally participate in this scheme. (F. No. 5(26)/2003-ECB & PR New Delhi, dated 27 August 2003.)

Annexure 7A.3: Status of Implementation of NPS by State Governments till December 2010

	State	*Date of Notification*	*Date of Adoption*
1	Andhra Pradesh	22-09-2004	01-09-2004
2	Assam	25-01-2005	01-02-2005
3	Bihar	31-08-2005	01-09-2005
4	Chandigarh	11-07-2009	01-01-2004
5	Chhattisgarh	27-10-2004	01-11-2004
6	Goa	05-08-2005	05-08-2005
7	Gujarat	18-03-2005	01-04-2005
8	Haryana	04-12-2008	01-01-2006
9	Himachal Pradesh	17-08-2006	15-05-2003
10	J& K	24-12-2009	01-01-2010
11	Jharkhand	09-12--2004	01-12-2004
12	Karnatak	19-01-2010	01-04-2006
13	MadhyaPradesh	13-04-2005	01-01-2005
14	Manipur	13-12-2004	01-01-2005
15	Meghalaya	24-03-2010	01-04-2010
16	Mizoram	17-06-2010	01-09-2010
17	Orissa	17-09-2005	01-01-2005
18	Poducherry	07-03-2005	01-01-2004
19	Punjab	02-03-2004	01-10-2004
20	Rajasthan	02-08-2005	01-01-2004
21	Uttar Pradesh	28-03-2005	01-04-2005
22	Uttarakhand	25-10-2005	01-10-2005
23	Nagaland	28-01-2010	01-01-2010
24	Sikkim	18-05-2006	01-04-2010
25	Arunachal Pradesh	01-01-2008	01-01-2008
26	Tamil Nadu	06-08-2003	01-04-2003

Source: PFRDA & Other Sources.

8 NPS Lite

A Low Cost Pension Scheme for the Economically Disadvantaged

INTRODUCTION

Most of the countries, which have reformed the national pension system have generally introduced a uniform structure covering all sections of population with few exceptions. Countries like China and Brazil which have introduced pension reform (as discussed in Section One, Chapter 2) have taken initiatives to introduce exclusive pension for rural population. This is a welcome step, since a large number of population live in rural areas in these highly populous countries and also a large number of workers are engaged in the informal sector. There exists income disparity between rural and urban areas as well as income disparity among workers in formal and informal segments of labour market. Therefore, a uniform pension system may not be essentially suitable for all segments.

India has got a large informal sector and most of the informal sector workers are in rural areas of the country. According to some estimates based on National Sample Survey (NSS) informal sector workers are estimated to be 395 million, that is, 86.34 per cent of total workers of 457 million as per 61st Round of National Sample Survey (2004–05), which was the same as found in 55th Round NSS (1999-2000) (Table 8.1).

However, according to Raveendran, et al. (2006) the total informal employment was 362.08 million out of a total employment of 396.77 million (on the basis of the revised definition of unorganised/informal sector and using the criteria of availability

Table 8.1 Employment Formal and Informal Sector Workers

NSS Round	*Total Employment (million)*	*Formal Sector Workers (million)*	*Per Cent Workers in Formal Sector*	*Per Cent Workers in Formal Sector*	*Per Cent Workers in Informal Sector*
55th round (1999–2000)	396.8	54.2	13.66	13.66	86.34
61st round (2004–05)	457.5	62.5	13.66	13.66	86.34

Source: Economic Survey 2008–09, Ministry of Finance, Government of India.

of provident fund in the case of regular salaried/wage employees). This estimate shows that informal sector employment constituted 91.3 per cent of total work force. The sector wise informal sector employment is shown in Table 8.2. Accordingly, 98.84 per cent of the employment in agriculture is informal. In the non-agricultural sector, the highest numbers of informal employees are in retail trade, construction, land transport, textiles, etc. Indian policy makers and Pension Fund Regulatory and Development Authority (PFRDA) considered this aspect of pension reform and introduced a low cost system deemed suitable for low income workers, seasonal workers and those who do not have enough financial understanding and reach. NPS Lite is thus a welcome step.

In addition to the NPS Lite another scheme launched by the Government of India and administered by the PFRDA is the Swavalamban Yojana (Scheme) for unorganised sector. It is a subsidised scheme applicable to all citizens in the unorganised sector, who join New Pension Scheme (NPS). We shall discuss here some of important features including coverage, benefits and administration of these two schemes.

NPS LITE—2010 SCHEME

NPS Lite is a low cost group model driven by the aggregators. This scheme was specially designed 'to facilitate the economically disadvantaged sections of society with limited investment potential also to take advantage of NPS, PFRDA now makes available a unique platform at ultra low cost with optimised features' (PFRDA—Offer

Table 8.2 Estimates of Informal Employment in India

		Estimated Number (million)		
Sl. No	*Sector*	*Male*	*Female*	*Total*
1	Agriculture			
1.1	Rural	138.67	88.06	226.73
1.2	Urban	4.91	3.28	8.19
	Total	143.58	91.34	234.92
2	Non-Agriculture			
2.1	Rural	47.46	13.91	61.37
2.2	Urban	53.43	12.36	65.79
	Total	110.89	26.27	127.16
3	All India			
3.1	Rural	186.13	101.97	288.10
3.2	Urban	58.34	15.64	73.98
	Total	244.47	117.61	362.08

Source: Raveendran et al. (2006).

Document on NPS Lite). Though NPS Lite is quite similar to All Citizens Scheme for the unorganised sector, there are certain distinct differences between both the schemes. An individual cannot directly become a member of NPS Lite she/he would be able to join NPS as groups through 'aggregators'. In All Citizens Scheme there is a provision for minimum number of contribution and minimum amount of contribution but these restrictions have been removed from NPS Lite making it easier for workers to join the pension scheme. Further, the enrolment cost in the All Citizens Scheme is very high for low income workers, but it is much lower in NPS Lite. However, NPS Lite is regulated like the All Citizens and government NPS. The NPS trust, CRA, pension fund managers, trustee bank, custodian, etc. are same for NPS Lite Scheme. Like other schemes, permanent retirement account number would be available to NPS Lite subscribers. NPS Lite is extended to its target population through specific entities called 'aggregators' who enrol their underlying subscribers in NPS Lite as groups. The aggregators are the main interface between the NPS architecture and NPS Lite subscriber.

Coverage

NPS Lite scheme is open to any citizen of India, between 18–60 years of age as on the date of submission of his/her application by the aggregator and comply with the Know Your Customer (KYC) process carried out by the aggregator. NPS Lite being the scheme for economically disadvantaged section of society there are minimum and maximum limit of investment in the scheme. The maximum investment limit prescribed by RBI vide their master circular number RBI/2008–09/72 dated 1 July 2001 for 'Small Deposit Accounts shall be applicable for each NPS account opened under NPS Lite, till PFRDA prescribes separate limits.' An extract from the RBI circular mentioned above has been provided in the annexure. However, NPS Lite is prohibited for individuals of unsound mind and pre-existing account holders under NPS.

Contribution

Some rigidities that restrict low income/seasonal income people to subscribe to All Citizens Scheme have been removed from NPS Lite to make it more investor friendly. An applicant is required to make the first contribution at the time of applying for registration with NPS Lite through an aggregator, the minimum contribution amount at the time of registration is ₹100 but there is no condition of a minimum yearly contribution. However, minimum contribution of ₹1,000 per year will enable a member to avail benefit of Swavalamaban Scheme. The flexibility in contribution further makes NPS Lite affordable to the low income and financially disadvantaged segment of the society.

Benefits

NPS Lite provides benefits similar to other pension schemes like All Citizens Scheme under PFRDA regulation. It is a pension accumulation scheme and an investor can save for old age pension income. On attaining the age of 60 years a member of NPS Lite can exit from the scheme but would be required to buy a life annuity from any IRDA-regulated life insurance company with at least 40 per cent of the accumulated pension wealth. However, she/he has an option to purchase an annuity for an amount greater than 40 per cent and the remaining pension wealth can either be withdrawn in a lump sum or on attaining the age of 60 or in a phased manner, between age of 60 and 70. Withdrawal before the age of 60 years is allowed subject to the condition that at least 80 per cent of the accumulated pension wealth is used to purchase a life annuity from any IRDA-regulated life insurance company. In case of death there is a provision to pay the entire 100 per cent accumulated savings to the nominee. However, if the nominee wishes to continue in the NPS Lite with the accumulated savings amount she/he has to subscribe to NPS individually after the due process of KYC.

Exit from the NPS Lite system in respect of those who avail Swavalamban Scheme of the Government of India shall also be subjected to conditions prescribed under operating guidelines of Swavalamban Scheme issued by Department of Financial Services, Government of India vide their letter no. 13/10/2006-PR dated 21 June 2010. Accordingly,

> *[T]he exit from the Swavalamban Scheme would be on the same terms and conditions on which exit from Tier-1 account of NPS is permitted, that is, exit at the age of 60 with 40 per cent minimum annuitisation of pension wealth and exit before age of 60 with 80 per cent annuitisation of pension wealth. This exit would be subject to the condition that the minimum pension out of his accumulated pension wealth would be ₹1,000 per month, which may be revised from time to time.*

NPS Lite Architecture

The architecture of NPS Lite is the same as the NPS for the government employees and the All Citizens Scheme except for an additional intermediary called aggregator. NPS Lite is a group concept and the aggregators are the only interface between the subscribers and other intermediaries under NPS Lite. Under the NPS Lite, PFRDA is the regulator and appoints various intermediaries such as Central Record Keeping Agency (CRA); pension funds (PFs), points of presence, trustee bank, NPS trust, custodian, etc., for operationalising the NPS roll out to unorganised sector subscribers. *NPS trust* is responsible for taking care of the NPS Lite Scheme. National Securities Depository Limited (NSDL) has been appointed as the CRA for NPS Lite Scheme which performs the function of record keeping, administration and customer service for all subscribers of the scheme. Bank of India is functioning as trustee bank for the NPS Lite scheme. There are seven fund managers to manage the retirement savings of subscribers under the scheme. However, the choice of fund manager/s rests with the aggregators unlike other schemes that allow the subscribers to choose a fund and fund managers. There are two options regarding the choice of fund manager/s. The aggregators may choose one of the PFMs to whom the entire corpus can be entrusted, or they may also choose to invest the contributions through all the three PFMs as per central government scheme.

❖ OPTION 1

Aggregators may choose one of the Single PFMs from the list of following:

1. ICICI Prudential Pension Funds Management Company Limited,
2. IDFC Pension Fund Management Company Limited,
3. Kotak Mahindra Pension Fund Limited,
4. Reliance Capital Pension Fund Limited, and
5. SBI Pension Funds Limited.6. UTI Retirement Solutions Limited.

❖ OPTION 2

The aggregators may also choose to invest the contributions through all the three PFMs as per central government scheme in the same manner as government employees. The allocation ratio in this case is decided and periodically reviewed by PFRDA. The fund managers under option 2 are:

1. LIC Pension Fund Ltd,
2. SBI Pension Funds Limited, and
3. UTI Retirement Solutions Limited.

Annuity Service Providers

The role of Annuity Service Providers (ASPs) in NPS Lite (Figure 8.1) will be the same as in other schemes to delivering a regular monthly pension to the subscriber for the rest of his/her life.

Figure 8.1 Schematic Representation of NPS Lite Architecture

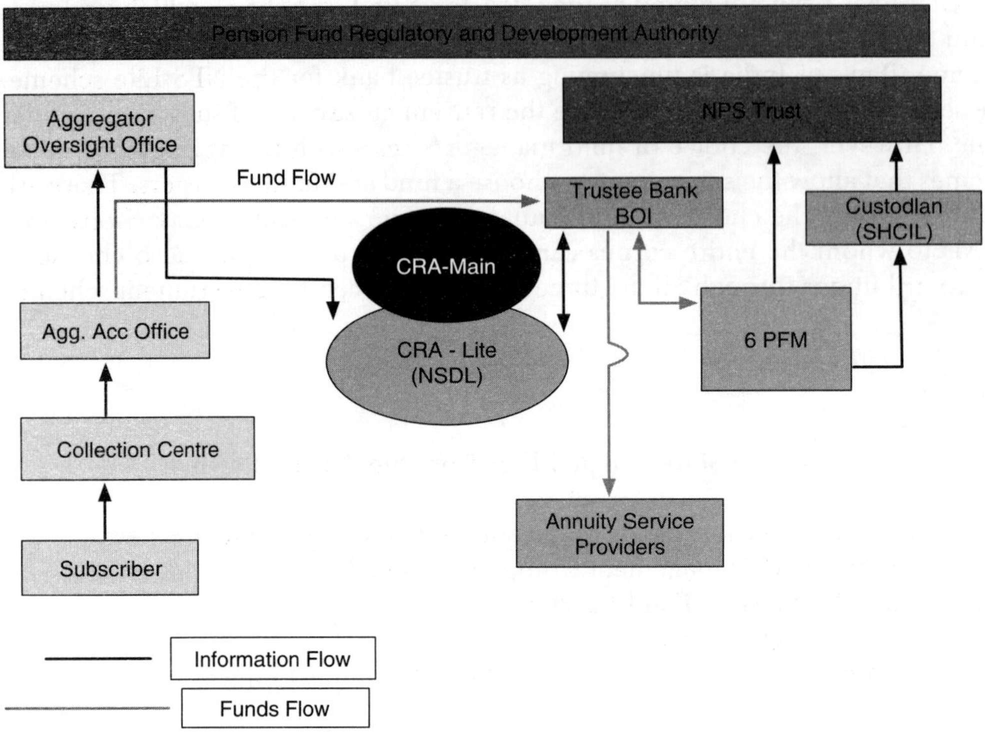

Source: PFRDA.

Aggregators under NPS Lite

NPS Lite is a group concept driven by the appointed aggregators, who play an important role in popularising the scheme, bringing the investors under one umbrella and also performing the role of POPs. The aggregators are intermediaries identified and approved by PFRDA, and perform the subscriber interface functions under NPS Lite for their constituent groups. The aggregators are entities already in existence having continuous functional relationship with a known customer base for delivery of some socio-economic goods/services (NPS Lite Offer Document). According PFRDA, the following entities have been considered as potential aggregators: nodal offices running certain schemes for identified beneficiary groups under central and state governments; micro-finance institutions (MFIs); non-banking finance companies (NBFCs); non-governmental organizations (NGOs); entities running common service centres under the National E-Governance Plan and any other category as identified by PFRDA from time to time.

Eligibility Criteria

Though broad characteristics of potential aggregators have been underlined, PFRDA has also laid down some specific conditions for appointing an entity as an aggregator. Accordingly, before the appointment an aggregator must have been registered under any one of these entities: Societies Registration Act 1860 (or a state amendment of this act); Indian Trusts Act, 1862; Charitable and Religious Trusts Act, 1920; Indian Companies Act, 1956 (Section 25, for nonprofit companies); Indian Companies Act 1956 with necessary certification from RBI (for NBFCs); Indian Companies Act 1956, for any other company or any other act/rule as specified by PFRDA from time to time. However, the PFRDA may, at its discretion, relax some, or all of these eligibility criteria in case of entities which are fully or partly controlled by either central or any state government or have been created under any specific arrangement of the central or state government or any other entity with proven track record, on a case to case basis, in the initial state of the development of the sector.

Aggregators in Consortium

In order to provide opportunities to a large number of entities to act as aggregator and widen the scope of enlisting the aggregators, PFRDA has allowed to form aggregators in consortium. Accordingly, two or more entities may get enlisted as aggregators. However, they need to present to PFRDA the internal arrangement among them regarding the distribution of responsibilities. Further, one of the two entities will be enlisted as primary aggregator, which will be responsible for meeting all eligibility requirements and all responsibilities arising out of their enlistment as aggregator. The total number of aggregators empanelled by PFRDA stood at 20 by 21 March 2011. According to the NPS Lite regulations for aggregators, all the POPs appointed by PFRDA are automatically qualified to become an aggregator under NPS Lite in respect of their own constituent subscriber base. The POPs may also act as 'facilitator' to any other aggregator. However, the terms of engagement, level of service and fees for the same shall be negotiated between the aggregator and POP and settled between them.

Role and Responsibilities of Aggregators

Aggregators are expected to play a very important role in NPS Lite to promote awareness about NPS Lite pension system, to expand coverage and to play the role of POPs as in All Citizens Scheme. The role of promoting NPS is very important since there is no provision for distributors or selling agents in NPS system. Moreover, NPS Lite is meant for low income people who normally do not have much knowledge about old age income saving through pension saving and do not have the reach to subscribe to such a scheme. Aggregators fill the gap and also act as catalysts in market making. The aggregators are expected to perform a number of functions including promoting awareness about NPS, its advantages and general awareness about the necessity for old age income security among its constituent group members; meeting the KYC requirements in respect of potential NPS subscribers as mandated under AML/CFT requirements; collecting applications from subscribers and undertaking KYC verification; distribution of PAN cards; etc.

❖ FEES FOR AGGREGATORS

PFRDA has introduced a performance-based revenue model for the aggregator. Accordingly, the aggregators receive a fixed sum from PFRDA after each completed year of business which is decided on the basis of subscriber acquisition cum retention. The aggregator will be eligible for remuneration if each of the account enrolled and retained by the aggregator during the year have at least a minimum annual contribution of ₹1,000.

❖ CHARGES/FEES UNDER NPS LITE

NPS Lite is a low cost pension system, and charges are much lower than All Citizens Scheme. Account opening charge for NPS Lite is ₹35 (as against ₹50 for All Citizens scheme). Similarly annual maintenance charge for NPS Lite is ₹70 per annum with 12 free subscriber contributions per account (as against ₹280 for All Citizens Scheme) while there is no transaction charge for first 12 transactions and ₹5 per transactions beyond 12 free subscriber contributions each in NPS Lite (as against ₹10 per transaction in All Citizens Scheme). Trustee bank charge and custodian charges, PFM charges for investment management are same as All Citizens Scheme (Table 8.3). The charges and fees as mentioned above and paid to the intermediaries is much lower than in other unorganised sector scheme called All Citizens. This low charge is definitely a positive feature of NPS Lite Scheme. The Regulator should in the light of NPS Lite fees, bring down the fees/charges of All Citizens Scheme.

SWAVALAMBAN SCHEME

The Union Finance Minister in his budget speech in February 2010 expressed his concern about the need for a low cost pension scheme for the unorganised sector and

Tale 8.3 Charges under NPS Lite Scheme

Intermediary	*Activity*	*Charges*	*Method of Deduction*
Central Record Keeping Agency (CRA)	Account opening Charges	₹35 (Digitisation will be carried out by CRA–FC)	Through cancellation of units from each subscriber's pension account
	Annual maintenance charges[1]	₹70 per annum with 12 free subscriber contributions per financial year.	
	Charge per transaction[2]	Nil for first 12 transactions and ₹5 per transactions beyond 12 free subscriber contributions in each year	
Trustee Bank	Per transaction emanating from a RBI location	Zero	Through NAV deduction
	Per transaction emanating from a non-RBI location[3]	₹15 (Trustee Bank, levies collection charges of ₹15 per transaction for collection of funds, only at Non RBI Centres)	
Custodian[4] (On Asset Value in Custody)	Asset servicing charges	0.0075 per cent p.a. for electronic segment & 0.05 per cent p.a. for physical segment	Through NAV deduction
PFM Charges	Investment Management fee[5]	0.0009 per cent P.A. (PFMs get a fee of ₹90,000 for every ₹1,000 crore of corpus they manage)	Through NAV deduction

Source: www.pfrda.org.in

Notes:
1. When the number of accounts in CRA reaches 15 lakh the service charges, exclusive of Service Tax and other taxes as applicable, will be reduced to ₹50 (Rupees fifty only) for annual PRA maintenance per account.
2. Transaction cost will be reduced to ₹4 and ₹3 per transaction when the thresholds of 15 lakh and 30 lakh subscribers respectively are attained.
3. Trustee Bank charges are not charged to subscriber directly. Transaction refers to the entire chain of activities starting from receipt of electronic instructions/receipt of physical instrument to transfer of funds to the designated PFMs. On the outflow side, it would include all activities leading to credit of beneficiary account.
4. Charges for Demat/Remat, Receipt of shares & SEBI charges are extra.
5. The investment management fee is inclusive of all transaction related charges such as brokerage, transaction cost, etc., except custodian charges and applicable taxes. The investment management fee is calculated on the average monthly assets managed by the pension fund.

encouraged them to join NPS. The Finance Minster also announced a subsidy scheme to encourage the potential investors. He announced,

> *to encourage the people from the unorganised sector to voluntarily save for their retirement and to lower the cost of operations of the NPS for such subscribers, Government will contribute Rs 1,000 per year to each NPS account opened in the year 2010–11. This initiative, (called) 'Swavalamban' will be available for persons who join NPS, with a minimum*

> *contribution of Rs 1,000 and a maximum contribution of Rs 12,000 per annum during the financial year 2010–11. The scheme will be available for another three years. Accordingly, I am making an allocation of Rs 100 crore for the year 2010–11. It will benefit about 10 lakh NPS subscribers of the unorganised sector. The scheme will be managed by the interim Pension Fund Regulatory and Development Authority.*

Subsequent to this announcement Department of Financial Services, Ministry of Finance, Government of India issued operational guidelines on 18 June 2010 outlining the various aspects of the scheme including the scope, benefits contribution, etc.

Scope of the Scheme

The Swavalamban Yojana, as it is called, is applicable to all citizens in the unorganised sector who join the NPS administered by the interim Pension Fund Regulatory and Development Authority (PFRDA). The operational guidelines also outlined the definition of unorganised sector for the purpose of Swavalamban Scheme. A person will be considered as a part of the unorganised sector if that person is not in regular employment of the central or state government, or an autonomous body/public sector undertaking of the central or state government having employer assisted retirement benefit scheme, or if she/he is not covered by a social security scheme under EPF and Miscellaneous Provisions Act, 1952 or the Coal Mines Provident Fund and Miscellaneous Provisions Act, 1948 or the Seamen's Provident fund Act, 1966 or the Assam Tea Plantations Provident Fund and Pension Fund Scheme Act, 1955, and the Jammu and Kashmir Employees' Provident Fund Act 1961.

Eligibility

The Swavalamban Scheme will be applicable to all persons in the unorganised sector and the benefit of central government contribution will be available only to those persons whose contribution to NPS is a minimum of ₹1,000 and maximum of ₹12,000 per annum, for both Tier-I and II taken together, provided that the person makes a minimum contribution of ₹1,000 per annum to his Tier-I NPS account.

Benefits under the Scheme

Under this scheme as if they were opened as new accounts in 2010–11 subject to the condition that they fulfil all the eligibility criteria prescribed under these guidelines. The government will contribute ₹1,000 per year to each NPS account opened in the year 2010–11 for the next three years, that is, 2011–12, 2012–13 and 2013–14. The benefit will be available only to persons who join the NPS with a minimum contribution of 1,000 end maximum contribution of ₹12,000 per annum.

Operation

A person can join the Swavalamban Scheme as an individual as per the existing scheme or through the CRA Lite approved by PFRDA. However, at the time of joining the NPS, by giving a self declaration indicating that she/he falls within the definition of unorganised sector, as per the definition above and her/his contribution would range between ₹1,000 to ₹12,000 per annum

Exit from NPS

There is a provision for the exit from the Swavalamban Scheme. The exit conditions are the same as the exit from Tier-I account of NPS. Accordingly if the subscriber, exit at age of 60, a minimum 40 per cent minimum accumulated wealth will be invested in a life annuity, and if she/he exit before the age 60 years, 80 per cent accumulated wealth will be invested in a life annuity policy. This exit condition has been added by another condition that on exit, the minimum pension out of his accumulated pension wealth would be ₹1,000 per month, which may be revised from time to time.

NPS LITE—SWAVALAMBAN PROMOTION FRAMEWORK

PFRDA has taken important step towards promoting NPS Lite and Swavalamban Scheme by introducing an incentive programme to reach to the target group and to extend pension coverage to the unorganised sector.

'To ensure early coverage of NPS in its target population and to achieve the broader agenda of financial inclusion, it has been decided to support the promotional efforts of aggregators by providing additional financial support over and above that prescribed under section 15 of the Regulations' (PFRDA 2010): This incentive programme is called support scheme for aggregators (SSA). The SSA is a combined support of promotional assistance and financial assistance. SSA can be classified at two levels—centralised and decentralised. The SSA centralised non-financial promotional support and decentralised financial support. The centralised support model would focus on PFRDA initiatives in promoting NPS Lite through support to all the aggregators. This programme would contain nationwide media campaign through print media, audio/visual media and targeted media campaign (supporting regional awareness campaign). This would include capacity building programme through national/regional workshops and training programmes for aggregators.

Decentralised support model includes monetary benefits to aggregators through incentivising/subsidising their promotional efforts. The activities approved by PFRDA for promotion by aggregators are: to conduct workshops/training in collaboration with state governments, to produce promotional literature/tools/NPS stationary, adopting new technology in their areas of operation. For these activities the aggregators are providing an additional per capita remuneration of ₹20 per account over and above the regular remuneration per account.

Performance-Based Incentives

In addition to the above, incentives are being given to an aggregator based on performance, which increases with the increase in the number of subscribers, per capita incentives for aggregator may vary from ₹10 for the number of subscribers above 1 lakh under the aggregator to ₹22 for the number of subscribers above 4 lakh under the aggregator. The incentive scheme was introduced to support the promotional objective and the national media campaign and the training programme for capacity building are very positive steps and would fill the awareness gap if carried out with commitment. However, mostly it is seen that such programmes tend to end up as an administrative and academic exercise. PFRDA should also examine whether such incentives could be given to the fund managers/sponsors who have wider network, market confidence and other resources. There active involvement will add further strength to the development/promotional programme.

FUTURE POTENTIAL FOR NPS LITE/MICRO PENSION

NPS Lite, a micro pension product should be promoted separately and vigorously focusing on the target group, as it has tremendous potential and can serve well the poor and low income group and also support the country's financial inclusion programme. A Study conducted by Dhan Foundation in partnership with World Granny, Pension Development Network and Helpage India provided some important insights into the Micro Pension market (Dullemen and Brujin 2010). The studies conducted in 2009 and early 2010 saw participation of 44,000 members of DHAN Foundation (Table 8.4).

The study elicited information about the opinion and willingness about participation in micro pension programme. It has been revealed that over 90 per cent respondents felt opined in favour of the need for micro pensions. The need is higher with people of 60 years or more (93.75 per cent) while need for people between 31 and 50 years was a little lower (90 per cent).

Table 8.4 Need and Willingness for Micro Pension (in per cent)

	> 60 Years	51–60 Years	41–50 Years	31–40 Years	≥ 30 Years
Opinion					
Yes, I need	93.75	91.25	90.00	90.00	91.25
No I don't Need	1.25	3.75	10.00	7.50	8.75
I can't Say	5.00	5.00	–	2.50	–
Willingness					
Yes, I am willing	58.75	45.0	42.5	33.75	36.25
No, I am not Willing	27.5	36.25	45.0	52.5	53.75
I can't say	13.75	18.75	12.5	13.75	10.0

Source: 'Pensions for the Poor; A Case Study of Micro Financing-Demographic Transition and the Need for Innovative Micro Pensions', study conducted by DHAN Foundation. Data quoted in the *paper* presented at Second European Research Conference on Microfinance, by Caroline E. van Dullemen, Jeanne G.M. Bruijin, June 2011.

However, a large percentage of respondents are not willing to use their accumulated savings for micro pension, which was higher in the lower age group as 53.7 per cent in the age group of 30 or less not willing to take micro pension while only 27.5 per cent are not willing in the age group over 60 years (Table 8.4). This study demonstrates that while there is a strong realisation about the necessity of micro pension for old age income security, there is an unwillingness to buy it, may be due to several apprehensions. It is therefore necessary to remove these apprehensions and decision resistance through financial literacy and education.

NPS Lite is a very well-designed concept and can be taken forward as a micro pension product to serve the socially vulnerable section of the society who fails to purchase social security due to low or no savings and purchasing power. Swavalamban subsidy is good initiative but needs to be made an integral part of NPS Lite not as a temporary measure. It is also observed from the list of aggregators that they are basically urban centric. Another weakness is the low visibility of NPS among the low income group, and in the rural and semi urban areas, as the campaign through urban centric media does not reach sufficiently to the rural masses. PFRDA needs to focus more on this area and should aim at increasing the number of aggregators in the rural area. PFRDA should also be alert enough to ensure that aggregators are sufficiently educated, motivated and enterprising to carry the scheme forward with care, due diligence as a social commitment but not merely as an alternative business proposition.

A COMPREHENSIVE MODEL FOR MICRO PENSION

The NPS Lite is a well-conceived micro pension scheme/product to serve the socially vulnerable section of the society who fail to purchase social security due to low or no savings and purchasing power. But it is structurally weak as it failed to take broader view of the needs and expectations of the poor people who are marginalised financially and have very limited reach and understanding of long term savings for survival. Again, except administration costs and aggregator model of mobilisation, it resembles the All Citizens' Scheme open to all. The unorganised poor and financially vulnerable section of society need a simple flexible scheme which can take care of financial needs in respect of longevity risk, health care and old age income. NPS Lite failed to address these issues as the NPS is a way to accumulate savings to buy annuity at a particular age.

Swambalamban subsidy is a good initiative but needs to be made an integral part of NPS not a temporary measure. It was also observed from the list of aggregators that they are basically urban centric. Another weakness is the low visibility of NPS among the low income group, and in the rural and semi urban areas, as the campaign through urban centric media does not reach the rural masses. The PFRDA needs to focus more on this area and should aim at increasing the number of aggregators in the rural area. The PFRDA should also be alert to ensure that aggregators are sufficiently educated, motivated and enterprising to carry the scheme forward with care and due diligence as a social commitment and not merely as an alternative business proposition.

An Outline of a Co-Contributory Composite Micro Pension Model

Micro pension programme and product must be designed keeping in view the fact that there is no universal social security in India, there is an excessive concentration of wealth and income in few families and a huge chunk of population live below poverty line and thus disposable income and capacity to save is minimal. Literacy and particularly the financial literacy of this section is very low but they need to save for personal financial risks, health care and old age income. Therefore, micro pension programme needs to ensure that the economically marginalised section is induced to buy micro pension products through financial incentives, which would take care of multiple needs like pension, life insurance and health insurance. The financial incentive plays an important role in inducing such investors. Therefore, any programme for micro pension needs to have an element of support/subsidy. There are a number of issues which need to be considered for any sustainable target-oriented micro pension programme. Few unavoidable critical issues are discussed as in the following paragraphs.

❖ MULTI-BENEFIT PRODUCT

Though there are various long-term financial needs for poor people, most of them have very little means to buy multiple financial products. It would therefore be necessary to design a pension product which would offer multiple benefits like old age income support, personal financial risk and health care. Hence, a micro pension must offer old age pension, life insurance and health insurance cover. NPS Lite and such products at present offer an avenue to accumulate savings but do not payout annuity. It would be difficult to buy a need-based annuity from a life insurance company at the time of exit. Pension product, therefore, should contain both accumulation and payout/annuity. Moreover, private health care is very costly in India and public health care often fails to fulfil the need. Affordable health insurance is equally necessary for poor. Therefore, multipurpose micro pension must contain health care support.

❖ STANDARISED PRODUCT

Another essential feature of a micro pension product is that it should be simple and easy to understand by a subscriber. Apart from NPS Lite there are many other products launched by NGOs and private entities offering various benefits at varying costs. The cost differentials also arise due to hidden administrative expenses charged to the subscribers. It is, therefore, necessary that one or more standard products are approved to be launched under uniform regulatory mechanism which would prevent the hidden costs and any abnormal administrative expenses charged to the customers.

❖ DEFAULT OPTION

Default options are an essential feature of contributory pension system as a very large number of investors (80–90 per cent even in developed countries) are unable to select a need based scheme. In NPS, there is an option of auto choice with pre designed portfolio relating to age profile and risk content. However, keeping in view the low level understanding and risk tolerance of the subscribers to micro pension, a different default option containing an investment portfolio with lower risk class needs to be designed.

❖ CO-CONTRIBUTORY SCHEME

India does not have any universal social security or pension system. There are, however, scattered measures to provide financial support, which are insignificant compared to the need. Moreover, it is administered by different entities in an uncoordinated manner. Micro pension, therefore, occupies centre stage for providing old age pension to this vulnerable poor section of the society, who should be encouraged and induced to join the system. Financial support is an important inducement and many countries are offering co contribution. Even in India, NPS Lite is such a scheme and the government is contributing a part of subscription through Swavalamban scheme, though for an initial limited period. There has been an encouraging trend in the subscription to NPS Lite. The NPS Lite scheme was launched on 21 June 2010 and the All Citizens' Scheme was launched on 1 May 2009. However, as on 7 July 2012, the number of subscribers far exceeded that of All Citizens' Scheme. As on 7 July 2012, total number of NPS Lite subscribers was 1,150,887 as against 99,082 subscribers of private sector/All Citizens' Scheme. This overwhelming response to NPS Lite is primarily due to the subsidy in the form of Swavalamban contribution. This makes a case for co-contribution to micro pension.

❖ MICRO PENSION FUNDING FUND

NPS Lite is partially funded by the government. A question arises here as to how co contribution could be made to the scheme launched by the non government entities. This issue can be solved by setting up a co contribution fund, which may be called Micro Pension Funding Fund (MPPF). The MPPF is a centralised entity to provide a part of contribution to micro pension subscription. There are several avenues to mobilise required funds for this purpose including the following:

- A small portion of proceeds received from disinvestment of public sector companies may be transferred to MPFF. Such a practice exists in Bolivia, where a part of money received from disinvestment of public sector is transferred to Bonsol programme meant for non contributory old age pension. In China, a part of disinvestment proceeds is transferred to National Social Security Fund.
- Regulators and developers are entrusted the responsibility to promote respective segments of the financial market they supervise. Bodies like IRDA, SEBI, RBI spend large amount as promotional expenses. A small part of such expenses can be transferred to MPPF for co contribution purposes.
- Insurance companies, mutual funds and banks are also active in micro pension, micro insurance and micro credit market and it is an emerging area of business for them. They spend huge amount on publicity and business promotion purpose. These entities must share the burden of micro pension as CSR activities and transfer a small percentage of such expenses to the MPPF.
- State has been withdrawing from business activities of the country making space for private sector and it becomes imperative for the corporate sector to share burden of social security for those citizens who are unable to arrange their old age income security. Therefore, the government should impose micro pension cess on the profit making companies and the amount to be transferred to MPFF.
- There are many other ways including a cess on lottery, IPL, etc., for mobilising funds for MPPF.

❖ SPECIAL ANNUITY PRODUCT

Success of any pension system depends on the annuity products and efficiency in delivery mechanism. Standard annuity may not be cost efficient for small savers in micro pension. The IRDA needs to focus on developing annuity market in India and special annuity for micro pension.

❖ SIMPLICITY, FLEXIBILITY AND ACCESSIBILITY

Target sections of micro pension are people with little or no literacy and those who are unable to understand financial jargon and fail to select a need based product. In a contributory system risk is totally transferred to the buyer and understanding risk return relationship is most crucial. An easily understandable product will not only make it attractive to the buyers but would also provide better tolerable risk return relationship.

Flexibility, is another pre requisite for micro pension product as the market segment is heterogeneous and often a large number of such customers depend on the seasonal income. Flexibility in contribution amount, time and duration would help them to continue with the system. It has been observed in Latin American countries that around 40 per cent members of the pension system contribute regularly. Flexibility is therefore an essential element of micro pension programme.

Accessibility is important as micro pension subscribers are mostly from rural areas having less access to banking and other facilities. Therefore, there is a need to create accessibility for them and a well designed cost effective distribution network would be essential to derive the product. Personalised marketing through well-trained agents who would act as financial literacy trainer would provide strong support to the system.

❖ REGULATION

In view of the special characteristics of the product and product market relationship of micro pension a separate regulatory mechanism needs to be devised, with special emphasis on risk governance, supervision and market development. There is also a possibility of regulatory conflict in the micro pension space as such products are launched by the entities regulated by different regulators.

However, it would be prudent that all micro pension products are regulated by one entity and PFRDA would be best suited under a separate regulatory wing represented by different regulators. The government and financial sector regulators like IRDA, PFRDA, SEBI and RBI need to take precautionary regulatory steps to ensure misadventure of such entities. A well conceived prudentially managed regulatory mechanism needs to be put in place.

Micro pensions should not be treated only as a new business opportunity and an emerging avenue for excess profit. Regulation should have in built provision keep such motivated promoters out of micro pension space for long-run interest of the investors and industry.

❖ CAPACITY BUILDING

Development of a sustainable micro pension industry to achieve desired objectives depends among other things on the capacity to drive the industry by the regulators, fund managers and other stakeholders. While regulators themselves should have a check list about their own capability and skill, such a check list must be for others including sponsors, fund managers, etc.

❖ FINANCIAL INCLUSION

Financial inclusion has emerged as a priority initiative in the country but it mostly remained banking and insurance centric. Also micro finance has attracted a lot of attention but mostly as a new market for business initiative. There are many unscrupulous entities exploiting the naïve poor investors in the name of financial inclusions, which need to stop.

❖ NATIONAL TASKFORCE FOR MICRO PENSION

A number of initiatives have been taken by various stakeholders to carry forward financial inclusion, micro insurance, micro pension and micro credit which need to integrated and all resources need to be channelised under a composite national policy. A National Task Force (NTF) comprising experts from various industries needs to be formed which will not only design a policy framework but also provide inter industry linkages.

In India, access to financial services is still limited to urban agglomerate and limited rural areas. Banks have expanded and integrated well. Insurance and pension still remain urban phenomena though LIC has taken the concept of insurance deep into rural areas. However insurance penetration is very low at 4.1 per cent and pension remains a distant illusion for vast majority of unorganised sector. However, urban market is mostly saturated for life insurance companies though for pension it still offers opportunities. Yet future market opportunities for life insurance and pension industry would be provided by rural areas and a vast majority of unorganised sector. Therefore insurance and pension industry must focus attention on the unorganised micro pension/insurance sector not only as their social responsibility but also as a part of their future business strategy.

REFERENCES

Ministry of Finance (2010), Economic Survey 2009–10. Ministry of Finance, Government of India, February 2010.

PFRDA (2010), 'NPS Lite—Swavalamban Promotion Framework'. NPS Lite—the Low cost Model for the Group'. Offer Document. Available at: http://www.pfrda.org.in/writereaddata/linkimages/Support%20Scheme%20for%20Aggregator2063990585.pdf.

Raveendran, G., S. V. R. Murthy and Ajaya Kumar Naik (2006), *Estimation of Informal Employment in India.* Outline and Progress Report on the Manual on Surveys of Informal Employment and Informal Sector, Expert Group on Informal Sector Statistics (Delhi Group), 11 and 12 May 2006 New Delhi, India. Available at: http://www.docstoc.com/docs/26840146/national-commission-for-enterprises-in-the-unorganized-sector.

9 NPS, Performance So Far and Structural and Regulatory Constraints

NPS—A STATUS REPORT

NPS was introduced with effect from 1 January 2004, in 2007 the interim Pension Fund Regulatory and Development Authority (PFRDA) put in place the Central Record Keeping Agency (CRA), Pension Funds Managers, Trustee Bank, Depository, etc. NPS Tier-I was operationalised and investment of funds received from central government began on 1 April 2008. Subsequently NPS was extended to others and PFRDA introduced the All Citizens Scheme, NPS Lite, and also Tier-II of NPS. Though it is very short period to judge the performance of NPS, yet a closer look can reveal the direction of the ongoing progress. PFRDA has still to evolve a system of periodic data dissemination. Some scattered information is available and on the basis of that an attempt is made here to assess the performance of NPS in terms of the growth of subscribers, accumulation of NPS funds and return on investment, etc.

Growth of Membership NPS

NPS is quite unique in the sense unlike many countries in Latin America which switched over the entire DB system into DC, India has retained existing DB system and made NPS mandatory for the new government employees who joined services after a particular date. Second, NPS is not mandatory for all the citizens but voluntary. NPS is a combination of three major schemes, namely NPS for central and state government employees, NPS for All Citizens Scheme and NPS Lite (including Swavalamban).

Available information indicate that in spite of several constraints and absence of any structured distribution system some positive developments have taken place, though not very significant, in the area of membership and coverage. Total membership of NPS increased by 197 per cent during 30 April 2010 and 8 October 2011 and membership under all the schemes has gone up from 878,713 on 30 April 2010 to 2,615,093 on 8 October 2011 (Table 9.1).

However, most significant is the spread of membership across the segments, particularly the increase in membership in the NPS Lite, state government scheme and unorganised sector (NPS Lite). NPS Lite, which was introduced on 22 July 2010 has

Table 9.1 Status of NPS Subscribers (number)

	As on 30 September 2010		*As on 8 October 2011*	
Sector	*Number*	*Per Cent to Total*	*Number*	*Per Cent to Total*
i. Central Government	609,376	69.35	812,659	31.08
ii. Central Government Autonomous Bodies	7,902	0.9	48,238	1.84
iii. State Governments	255,903	29.12	906,373	34.66
iv. Unorganised Sector*	5,532	0.63	57,378	2.19
v. Corporate Sector	–	–	10,657	0.41
vi. NPS Lite	–	–	779,788	29.82
Total	878,713	100	2,615,093	100

Source: PFRDA.
Note: *Till 8 October 2011, 6,627 Tier-II accounts were activated.

already been subscribed by 779,788 members which was 29.82 per cent of total subscribers. While the per cent share of central government subscribers to the total number of subscribers declined from 69.35 per cent to 31.08 per cent, that of state government increased from 29.12 per cent to 34.66 per cent, which indicates growth in subscription in the central government NPS is getting saturated and will decline further, the subscription by central public sector will increase as more and more such organisations are going to stop DB pension and encourage the new employees to go for NPS. Some progress has also been made in the unorganised sector, though very little, in view of the untapped potential. But it is quite encouraging that corporate sector is expressing interest to opt for NPS for their employees. However, market perception is that this number would be more as the response has relatively increased in the current year compared to the previous year. Further, low response to NPS is witnessed in unorganised sector due to several other factors as the following:

- Low level of financial literacy
- Lack of awareness about the long term benefits of NPS
- Lack of concern for retirement savings
- Some adverse criticism about the initial cost of NPS
- Absence of properly laid down distribution mechanism
- Absence of coordinated efforts by all the stake holders to popularise NPS

We, need to take many more sincere steps to increase coverage significantly.

Contributions to NPS

It has been indicated above that NPS has two segments, namely mandatory segments for central and state government employees and voluntary segments consisting of

Figure 9.1 Percentage Share of Various Schemes in NPS Assets

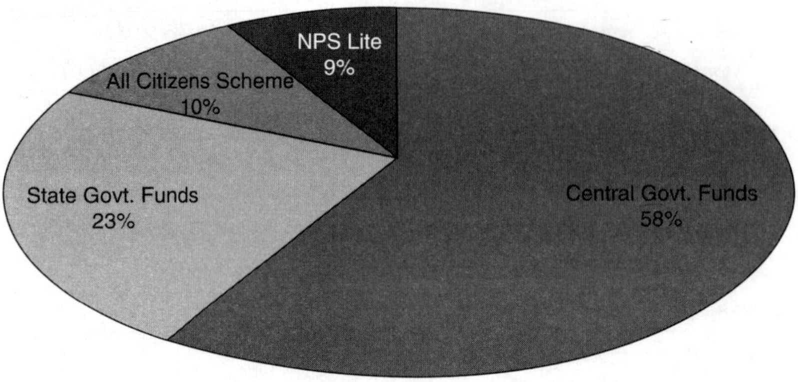

others citizens who can subscribe to All Citizens Scheme, NPS Lite and Swavalamban Scheme (Figure 9.1). Therefore, total fund size under NPS will depend on the voluntary and mandatory contribution.

Mandatory contribution consists of funds contributed by the employees of central government, central government undertakings, state government and state government undertakings. Voluntary contributions consist of contribution raised through the non-government sector under the All Citizens Scheme, NPS Lite and Swavalamban Scheme. Currently, the mandatory contribution of central and state government employees funds distributed by the PFRDA on the basis of previous year's investment performance of each three designated fund managers, namely LIC Pension Fund, SBI Pension Fund and UTI Retirement Solutions, who are authorised to manage NPS funds for government employees. At present the central government employees' funds are pulled and allocated by PFRDA. For the funds contributed by the employees of the state governments, 2010–11, was distributed by the respective government among the three authorised fund managers on the basis of allocation pattern decided for the central government funds. However, for the 2011–12, even the allocation pattern for the state government funds has been decided by PFRDA as shown in Table 9.2. It is significant to note that LIC Pension Fund which received only 5 per cent of central government NPS in 2007–08, due to the fund management fee quoted by them increased their share substantially to 35 per cent in 2010 due to their performance. For the year 2011–12, the share of LIC Pension Fund, SBI Pension Fund, UTI Retirement Solutions in central government NPS is 33.5 per cent, 32.5 per cent and 34 per cent respectively and that of state government NPS is 33.5 per cent, 31.0 per cent and 35.5 per cent respectively for LIC Pension Fund, SBI Pension Fund and UTI Retirement Solutions (Table 9.2).

However, as per the NPS structure, after a period of consolidation allocation of funds of central government and state government by PFRDA will end and employees will be allowed to choose the fund managers and select the schemes as per their choice.

Table 9.2 Allocation of Central Government and State Pension Funds

Sl. No.	Name of Company	Central Government Employees Funds				State Government Employees Funds
		2008–09	2009–10	2010–11	2011–12	2011–12
1.	LIC Pension Fund Ltd.	5 per cent	29 per cent	35 per cent	33.5 per cent	33.5 per cent
2.	SBI Pension Fund Pvt. Ltd.	55 per cent	40 per cent	33 per cent	32.5 per cent	31.0 per cent
3.	UTI-Retirement Solution Ltd.	40 per cent	31 per cent	32 per cent	34 per cent	35.5 per cent

Source: PFRDA.

Size of NPS Funds

Since April 2008, when investment management started by three selected fund managers, some progress has been made in funds mobilisation. It may be mentioned here that NPS was introduced w.e.f. 1 April 2004 and the central government employees who joined services as on that day or after were mandatorily brought under NPS. Their contribution to NPS were deducted from salary and kept in a specified account which was transferred to Pension Fund Managers (PFMs) on 1 April 2008. During the year 2008–09, three fund managers LIC Pension Fund, SBI Pension Fund and UTI Retirement Solutions managed an amount of ₹2,032.20 crore. During the year 2009–10, an additional amount of ₹2,109.69 crore was mobilised by seven fund managers from employees of government NPS and members under All Citizens Scheme. However mobilisation picked up during 2010–11 and after due to NPS Lite which is a low cost scheme and Swavalamban, the Scheme which attracts central government subsidy of ₹1,000 per year per account even under NPS Lite. Mobilisation under all the schemes as on 29 September 2011 stood at ₹11,187.24 crore. The largest amount of ₹8,874 crore (79.32 per cent) came as contribution to central government NPS, next to it was contribution by the state government employees ₹2,113 crore (18.89 per cent). All citizens scheme (which is for the unorganised sector contributed only ₹125 crore (1.13 per cent) while contribution by NPS Lite was only ₹73 crore. (Table 9.3). However, NPS Lite has

Table 9.3 Summary of Funds Mobilisation under NPS

Ministries/Sector	(₹ in '000) As on 29 September 2011	Per Cent Share of Respective Category
Central Government Funds	88,740,092	79.32
State Government Funds	21,136,896	18.89
All citizens Scheme	1,259,572	1.13
NPS Lite	735,877	0.66
Total	111,872,437	100

Source: PFRDA.

attracted investors particularly in the low income segments and collection in NPS Lite is expected go up, once the schemes distribution system strengthen.

Mobilisation under the Central and State Government NPS

We have noted earlier that the NPS for the central and state government NPS elicited better response due to its mandatory nature. Three authorised PFM mobilised ₹8,874 crore by 29 September 2011. Due to historical reason, that is, initial base, the share of SBI Pension Funds Pvt. Ltd stood at 41.36 per cent on 29 September as against 34.02 per cent of UTI Retirement Solutions Ltd and 24.62 per cent of LIC Pension Fund Ltd. (Table 9.4).

It may be mentioned here that there has been a sharp improvement in the share of LIC Pension Fund since beginning while the share of SBI Pension Fund in total subscription of government declined significantly and UTI Retirement Solutions more or less maintained its share. The pattern of asset distribution of PFMs managing the funds of government employees indicates that market concentration is declining due to competition and performance is driving the market growth. It's an important development and in the interest of investors.

Mobilisation under All Citizens Scheme

All Citizens Scheme was primarily introduced for unorganised sector which does not have any major formal pension scheme, though there are life insurance policies, public provident funds, etc., yet they failed to extend pension coverage in the country. Membership for All Citizens Scheme is voluntary. Currently both the Tier-I and Tier-II are operational. Yet this scheme made very little progress and very small amount has been mobilised. It can be noted from Table 9.5 that as on 29 September 2011, an amount of ₹125 crore was mobilised by this under Tier-I and Tier-II of All Citizens Scheme. In terms of per cent share, only 13.09 per cent was mobilsed by Tier-I while

Table 9.4 Mobilisation under Central and State Government Schemes (as on 29 September 2011)

Name of Company	*Central Government Employees Funds (₹ in '000)*	*State Government Employees' Funds ₹ in '000 (2)*	*Total 2+3 ₹ in '000 (3)*	*(3) as Per Cent (iv)*
i. LIC Pension Fund Ltd.	20,841,782	6,210,059	27,051,841	24.62
ii. SBI Pension Fund Pvt. Ltd.	37,579,286	7,862,177	45,441,463	41.36
iii. UTI-Retirement Solution Ltd.	303,1,9024	7,064,660	37,383,684	34.02
Total	88,740,092	21,136,896	109,876,988	100

Source: PFRDA.

86.91 5 were mobilised by Tier-II. However it may be mentioned that Tier-I is basically a saving scheme and does not qualify for any tax incentives. Many countries in Latin America offer tax incentives to encourage voluntary savings under the third pillar which is a saving scheme like our Tier-II.

All Citizens Scheme is wider in terms of investors choice as it offer equity oriented Scheme 'E', corporate bond oriented Scheme 'C' and Low Risk Government Security Fund 'G'. In India a large number of people advocated for higher investment of pension fund assets in equity for better return. However, if investor's choice is any indication, Indian investors do not want to take undue risks by putting their money in a more risky portfolio with higher equity asset concentration. In equity fund E, a maximum investment of 50 per cent in equity is allowed, even then the response indicates risk aversion as only 33.04 per cent of funds were mobilised under scheme E in All Citizens Scheme. Fund C which has a higher concentration of corporate bonds is the least preferred among investors, and only 28.53 per cent funds have been mobilised under this fund. Corporate bond market is poorly developed without much depth, there are very few high quality bond (AAA rated), market is also illiquid, and most of the trades are over the counter (OTC) and also there is, in general, an issue of corporate governance, which deters the investors choice. It is the bond fund which attracted highest funds, 38.43 per cent (of total mobilisation) under the All Citizens Scheme (Table 9.5).

It will be in the interest of investors to offer some balance fund in addition to the existing three active funds. A balance fund with pre-determined assets (percentage) in debt (government and corporate) and equity with an objective of risk minimisation and return maximisation, will also strengthen the fund basket. Though investors under All Citizens Scheme have the option to go for auto choice (default option), no official information is available publicly. However, it is understood that some investors are opting for auto choice.

NPS Lite

NPS Lite has been introduced recently but it is making good progress and is attracting investors mostly in low income segments. There are seven fund managers in this segment, but information available up to 29 September 2011, shows that only four fund managers including three public sector and one private sector fund managers could attract investment from this segments. Among the public sector fund managers LIC Pension Fund had the highest share, 34.90 per cent of total NPS Funds. LIC Pension Fund was followed by SBI Pension Fund (32.59 per cent) and UTI Retirement Solutions (31.68 per cent). Only one private sector fund manager, IDFC Pension Fund Management CO. Ltd. could mobilise 0.83 per cent of total NPS Lite fund (Table 9.6). LIC Pension Fund is expected to increase its share in this segment significantly as it is promoted by the largest financial institution and life insurance companies in the country having track record of more than 60 years. It is also an indication that investors'

Table 9.5 Mobilisation under All Citizens Scheme

(Amount in ₹ '000)

	Tier-I			Tier-II		
Name of Company	*E*	*C*	*G*	*E1*	*C2*	*G3*
SBI Pension Fund Pvt. Ltd.	219,537	185,285	305,612	21,880	25,551	23,875
UTI-Retirement Solution Ltd.	35,262	28,955	39,258	8,448	7,051	6,095
Total (A)	254,799	214,240	344,870	30328	32,602	29,970
ICICI Prudential Pension Funds Ltd.	55,135	41,676	39,640	10,207	19,314	15,856
IDFC Pension Fund Management Ltd.	16,700	13,112	9,828	2,543	2,007	1,411
Kotak Mahindra Pension Fund Ltd	14,330	11,964	13,690	2,355	1,736	1,608
Reliance Capital Pension Fund Ltd	24,173	18,393	22,225	5,571	4,278	5,011
Total (B)	110,338	85,145	85,383	20,676	27,335	23,886
Grand Total (A+B)	365,139	299,385	430,253	51,004	59,937	53,856

Mobilisation under Tier-I (E + C + G) = 1,094,777, Mobilisation under Tier-II: (E + C + G) = 164 797
Mobilisation under All Citizens (Tier-I + Tier-II) = ₹1,259,574
Tier-I as per cent of total mobilisation = 86.91, Tier-I as per cent of total mobilisation = 13.0
Mobilisation under Scheme E (Tier-I + Tier-II) = ₹416,143
Scheme E as per cent of total All Citizens Scheme = 33.04 per cent
Mobilisation under Scheme C (Tier-I + Tier-II) = ₹35,932
Scheme C as per cent of total All Citizens Scheme = 28.53 per cent
Mobilisation under Scheme G (Tier-I + Tier-II) = ₹484,109
Scheme G as per cent of total All Citizens Scheme = 38.43 per cent
Source: PFRDA.

Table 9.6 Funds Mobilised under NPS Lite

Name of Company		*Per Cent Share to Total NPS Funds*
LIC Pension Fund Ltd.	256,844	34.90
SBI Pension Fund Pvt. Ltd.	239,756	32.59
UTI-Retirement Solution Ltd.	233,151	31.68
IDFC Pension Fund Management Co. Ltd.	6,126	0.83
Total	735,877	100.00

Source: PFRDA.

confidence in the institution is an important determinant of investment decision when it comes to taking a long term investment decision.

Though mobilisation marginally improved in 2010–11 under the unorganised sector, it can be considered as insignificant in the context of huge potential in this segment. Several factors as mentioned above are responsible for poor response to the unorganised sector NPS. However, it is expected to pick up in the current year due to more awareness about NPS, Swavalamban Scheme announced in the budget 2010–11 and good performance of the fund managers.

INVESTMENT PERFORMANCE AND RETURN BY PENSION FUNDS UNDER NPS

PFRDA has introduced quantitative regulation and all investment operations need to be carried out by following the norms laid down in investment guidelines. Funds management in NPS is carried out within the investment guidelines (referred earlier). Therefore, investment return is primarily determined by board approved investment strategy, fund managers experience and expertise and market movement. We have no data on the expertise of fund managers and the investment strategy adopted by the boards of PFMs, but a general trend in the market movement, which is one of the determinants of investment performance can be captured. Some information about interest rate/yields of various investment instruments for the year 2010–11 are discussed here.

Market Environment

Pension Funds are allowed to park money for short term in Collateralised Borrowing and Lending Obligation (CBLO). During the year 2010–11, there was a wide variation in CBLO rates; from 2.95 per cent in April 2010 it went up to 6.46 per cent in March 2011.

G Sec and corporate bonds are important instruments of investment in Scheme C and Scheme G funds as well funds under government schemes. The 10 year G Sec in 2010–11 varied from 8.01 per cent in April 2010 to 8.0 per cent in March 2011. In fact, yield began to decline from January 2011 when it was 8.15 per cent. However, there was a steady rise in the yield of AAA rate, five-year corporate bond, from 8.37 per cent in April 2010 to 9.23 per cent in March 2011 (Table 9.7). However, the constraints are lack of sufficient number of AAA or AA+ corporate bonds in the market, as well poor liquidity in the government securities market. Similarly equity market also witnessed severe volatility during the year. CNX Nifty in the month of April 2010 registered an improvement in April 2010 (5,295) over the previous month (5,178); it reached the peak of the year 6,069 in October 2010, and declined to 5,538 in March 2011.

Similarly, BSE Sensex also witnessed volatile movement in index, which was 19,679 in April 2010, reached peak of the year to 20250 in October 2010 and declined to 18,457 in March 2011. Markets lost much of the valuation gains made during the last four months of 2010, when they outperformed most of the international markets. However, during Q4 of 2010–11, the BSE Sensex was the worst performer amongst the major equity indices. Slowdown of net equity investment by the FIIs in India largely contributed to the decline. In terms of the coefficient of variation, the volatility of Sensex between end-December 2010 and end-March 2011 at 3.95 per cent is much higher than the 2.0 per cent of the MSCI emerging market index and 1.9 per cent of the MSCI world index. The equity derivatives segment had gone up substantially over the year and currently constitutes almost 90 per cent of the overall investments. FII investments accounted for 19.8 per cent of the total investments in derivatives

Table 9.7 Rates in Domestic Financial Markets

	Money Market					*Bond Market*		*Forex Market*	*Stock Market Indices*	
	Call Rate (Per cent)*	*Market Repo Rate (Non-LAF) (Per cent)*	*CBLO Rate (Per cent)*	*Commercial Paper WADR (Per cent)*	*Certificates of Deposit WAEIR (Per cent)*	*G-Sec 10-year yield (Per cent)*	*Corporate Bonds Yield - AAA 5-Yr bond (Per cent)*	*Exchange Rate (₹/US$)*	*CNX Nifty ***	*BSE Sensex ***
1	*2*	*3*	*4*	*5*	*6*	*7*	*8*	*9*	*10*	*11*
Mar-10	3.51	3.32	3.15	6.29	6.07	7.94	8.61	45.50	5,178	17,303
Apr-10	3.49	3.04	2.95	5.37	5.56	8.01	8.37	44.50	5,295	19,679
May-10	3.83	3.79	3.67	6.85	5.17	7.56	8.15	45.81	5,053	16,845
Jun-10	5.16	5.29	5.21	6.82	6.37	7.59	8.21	46.57	5,188	17,300
Jul-10	5.54	5.37	5.25	6.93	6.69	7.69	8.27	46.84	5,360	17,848
Aug-10	5.17	5.12	5.01	7.32	7.17	7.93	8.52	46.57	5,457	18,177
Sep-10	5.50	5.35	5.24	7.82	7.34	7.96	8.52	46.06	5,811	19,353
Oct-10	6.39	5.96	5.88	12.15	7.67	7.68	8.58	44.41	6,069	20,250
Nov-10	6.81	6.42	6.14	12.22	8.16	8.03	8.64	45.02	6,055	20,126
Dec-10	6.67	6.27	6.20	10.10	9.15	8.03	8.89	45.16	5,971	19,228
Jan-11	6.54	6.21	6.20	8.81	9.42	8.15	9.05	45.39	5,783	19,289
Feb-11	6.69	6.45	6.43	9.05	10.04	8.12	9.25	45.44	5,401	18,037
Mar-11	7.15	6.56	6.46	10.40	9.96	8.00	9.23	44.99	5,538	18,457

Source: Reserve Bank of India.
Notes: *: Average of daily weighted call money rates. **: Average of daily closing indices. WADR: Weighted Average Discount Rate. WAEIR: Weighted Average Effective Interest Rate.

(RBI 2011). Keeping in view the prevailing market environment in 2010–11, we examine the return generated by the PFMs under various designated schemes.

Mutual Fund Returns

In India returns under pension funds are often compared with return of mutual funds. However, the there are mutual schemes which replicate the portfolios of NPS, but some mutual funds have portfolios little similar to the funds under NPS. In absence of any other comparable funds we have considered returns under four selected mutual funds, namely Multi Cap Equity Funds, Debt-oriented Conservative Funds, Income Funds, Debt Funds–Gilt Medium and Long Term. Multi Cap Funds are identified as funds with 60–80 per cent of assets in large cap companies over the last three years, Debt-oriented Conservative Funds are hybrid funds having equity exposure less than 25 per cent over the last three years and Gilt Funds are funds with medium and long-term investment in gilt securities. Multi-cap funds can be compared with Fund E under All Citizens scheme, though Scheme E allowed investment in equity up to 50 per cent of portfolio assets. Debt-oriented Conservative Funds come closer to government NPS, while Gilt Funds can be compared with Fund G under All Citizens Scheme. It can be seen from Table 9.8 that one year, two year and three year average return under Multi Cap Equity Fund was estimated at 7.85 per cent, 18.17 per cent, and 7.74 per cent respectively while that of Debt-oriented Conservative Fund was 6.05 per cent, 7.39 per cent and 7.44 per cent respectively. The average return of Debt-oriented Gilt Medium and Long-Term Fund by the end of March 2011, was 3.91 per cent, 3.25 per cent and 6.76 per cent respectively for one year, two years and three years (Table 9.8).

Return under Government NPS

NPS for the central government employees became investment effective from 1 April 2008 and that for state government employees became effective from 25 June 2009. These schemes are mostly debt centric and maximum permissible investment in equity including mutual fund is 15 per cent of the portfolio. These funds are primarily hybrid funds that tend towards debt fund and return can be compared with such mutual funds. One, two and three years' average return of Debt-oriented Conservative Funds estimated by Value Research (2011) is 6.05 per cent, 7.39 per cent and 7.44 per cent respectively (Table 9.8). The return under central government NPS as against this was recorded between 8.05 per cent and 8.45 per cent for one year and 10.19 per cent and 11.36 per cent since inception (April 2008), though equity investment including mutual funds under such funds are maximum up to 15 per cent. Pension funds thus provided better return than mutual funds. Similarly performance of pension funds under state government scheme was also better than mutual funds. State government funds recorded yearly return between 9.88 per cent and 11.34 per cent while two year returns (since June 2009) varied between 9.22 per cent and 9.80 per cent (Table 9.9). It can also be noted that one year return (2010–11) was higher in case of state government funds as compared to the central government funds due increased yield in the year as most of the state government funds came in 2010–11. Equity market was also volatile

Table 9.8 Average Return Selected Mutual Fund Schemes (as on 31 March 2011)

Type of Mutual Funds	*Average Return* One Year	Two Years	Three Years
Multi Cap Equity Funds	7.85	18.17	7.74
Debt oriented Conservative Funds	6.05	7.39	7.44
Income Funds	4.90	4.73	6.65
Debt Funds–Gilt Medium & Long term	3.91	3.25	6.76
BSE Sensex	9.20	12.48	4.70
S &P CNX Nifty	9.32	11.79	4.52
NSE G-Sec Composite Index	0.64	1.04	4.61

Source: Value Research Mutual Fund Performance Report, 31 May 2011.

and coupon on corporate debt increased in 2010–11 compared to the previous year as well as end of the year in comparison with beginning of the financial year (Table 9.7). Therefore, the overall performance of pension funds was better than mutual funds.

Return under All Citizens' Scheme

❖ SCHEME E

Scheme E is an equity-oriented scheme but maximum permissible investment in equity is 50 per cent of the portfolio assets. The performance of the fund managers in equity scheme E, in 2010–11, was inconsistence as most of them performed much below the performance index of NIFTY and Sensex in 2010–11 though they performed well if we consider performance since inception. In Tier-I, one year return (2010–11) varied between 8.05 per cent and 11.89 per cent and return since May 2009 was estimated between 8.36 per cent and 17.85 per cent. However, excluding the lowest return 8.055, other six funds generated return between 13.67 per cent and 17.85 per cent. However, only two funds ICICI and Kotak Mahindra could beat yearly performance of both the indices while other fared poorly, with return of 11.83 per cent and 11.89 per cent respectively (Table 9.9). This compares well with returns of Multi Cap equity funds, 7.85 per cent for one year and 18.75 per cent for two years, keeping in view that Pension fund could invest up to 50 per cent in equity and Multi Cap funds invest 60–80 per cent in equity. In Tier-II, pension funds return in 2010–11 varied between 7.05 per cent and 11.66 per cent, while the return since December 2009 varied between 5.88 per cent and 9.955 percent. It is to be mentioned here that in Tier-II of Fund E, there is frequent withdrawals and a large portion of funds are kept in low yield liquid assets resulting into low return. This can be tackled with superior fund management strategy and timely asset reallocation and reinvestment.

Table 9.9 Returns in NPS under Various Schemes

A. ***Returns under Central and State Government Schemes*** **(31 March 2011)**

Scheme: CG			*Scheme: SG*		
PFM	*One Year (per cent)*	*Since Inception (per cent)**	*PFM*	*One-Year (per cent)*	*Since Inception (per cent)**
LIC	8.30	10.19	LIC	10.77	9.53
SBI	8.05	11.36	SBI	9.88	9.22
UTI	8.45	10.20	UTI	11.34	9.80
* Inception date is 1 April 2008			* Inception date is 25 June 2009		

CG: Central Government Employees Scheme, SG: State Government Employees Scheme

(Continued)

(Continued)

B. Returns under All Citizens' Scheme

B (i) Return under Scheme E

Scheme E: Tier-I			*Scheme E: Tier-II*		
PFM	*One Year (per cent)*	*Since Inception (per cent)#*	*PFM*	*One Year (per cent)*	*Since Inception (per cent)*
ICICI	11.83	17.85	ICICI	10.12	7.99
IDFC	8.89	16.72	IDFC	7.05	5.58
Kotak	11.89	13.67	Kotak	11.66	9.95
Reliance	9.67	16.01	Reliance	9.51	9.77
SBI	8.05	8.36	SBI	7.86	6.18
UTI	8.35	17.60	UTI	10.16	8.01
# Inception date is 1 May 2009			# Inception date is 14 December 2009		
Index: S&P CNX Nifty 11.14			Index: S&P CNX Nifty 11.14		
Index: BSE SENSEX 10.94			Index: BSE SENSEX 10.94		

B (ii) Return under Scheme: C

Scheme C – Tier-I			*Scheme C – Tier-II*		
PFM	*One Year (per cent)*	*Since Inception (per cent)#*	*PFM*	*One Year (per cent)*	*Since Inception (per cent)#*
ICICI	9.41	10.17	ICICI	10.74	9.38
IDFC	6.26	8.41	IDFC	6.02	5.17
Kotak	10.86	10.92	Kotak	7.20	6.17
Reliance	7.82	6.45	Reliance 7.17	6.32	
SBI	12.66	11.81	SBI	14.46	12.88
UTI	9.20	6.87	UTI	7.62	6.52
# Inception date is 1 May 2009			# Inception date is 14 December 2009		

B (iii) Returns under Scheme G

Scheme G–Tier-I			*Scheme G–Tier-II*		
PFM	*One Year (per cent)*	*Since Inception (per cent)#*	*PFM*	*One Year (per cent)*	*Since Inception (per cent)#*
ICICI	7.71	6.37	ICICI	6.43	5.79
IDFC	6.97	4.91	IDFC	6.00	5.34
Kotak	9.14	6.56	Kotak	6.40	5.47
Reliance	7.7	1 5.36	Reliance	5.68	5.43
SBI	12.25	11.64	SBI	11.82	13.74
UTI	12.52	7.36	UTI	16.44	13.11
# Inception date is 1 May 2009			# Inception date is 14 December 2009		

Source: PFRDA, http://pfrda.org.in/writereaddata/linkimages/POP per cent20Wise per cent20Performance_030920115253910510.pdf

Note: Returns greater than one-year are compounded annually

CS: central government scheme ; SG: state government scheme.

Return under Scheme C

Return under scheme C in 2010–11, varied from 6.26 per cent and 12.66 per cent, while the return since May 2009 varied from 6.45 per cent (IDFC) to 11.81 per cent (SBI). Out of six, three funds generated a return of more than 10 per cent. Return since inception under Tier-I of C, varied from 6.45 per cent (Reliance) to 11.81 per cent (SBI) in Tier-I. In Tier-II, one year return varied from 7.20 per cent (Kotak) to 14.46 per cent (SBI) and from 5.17 per cent (IDFC) to 12.88 per cent (SBI) since inception (Table 9.9). Scheme C which invests in corporate bonds could reap the benefits of improved coupon rates in 2010–11, which went up from 8.37 per cent in April 2010 to 9.23 per cent in March 2011. However, in Tier-II, investors can withdraw their money any time and fund managers keep a larger amount in more liquid and short- to medium-term assets. This may be one of the reasons of under performance in Tier-II. Again it is a reflection of asset management strategy and fund selection of fund managers.

Returns under Scheme G

Scheme G is a low risk G Sec fund investing gilt securities. Return of G Sec funds was impacted by G Sec yield and movement in money market rates. The yield of 10 year Central Government was 8.01 per cent in April 2010, but remained below 8 per cent between May 2010 and October 2010 and firmed up since November 2010 to end up at 85 in March 2011. Mutual Funds Gilt Schemes (medium- and long-term investment in gilt securities) generated average income of 3.91 per cent, 3.25 per cent and 6.76 per cent for one, two and three years respectively (Table 9.8). As against this pension funds generated better return in 2010–11, between 6.97 per cent and 12.52 per cent. UTI and SBI generated 12.52 per cent and 12.25 per cent respectively, while Kotak and ICICI generated 9.14 per cent and 7.71 per cent respectively. Even two-year returns of pension funds, which varied between 4.91 per cent and 11.64 per cent, were much higher than mutual funds. Relatively, Tier 2 return under G Sec funds was still better, 6 per cent–16.44 per cent in 2010–11 and between 5.34 per cent –13.74 per cent since December 2009. It can be recalled that more than 38 per cent investors selected G Sec funds under All Citizens Schemes and it is the public sector fund managers which generated relatively better return. Experience shows that beating market and providing superior return depend to a great extent on the size of the funds, market experience, understanding market movement, designing a medium- to long-term financial market and macroeconomic scenario, stock selection and portfolio rebalancing. Understanding and monitoring market movement and restructuring investment strategy (whenever required) will to a great extent determine the return on investment. This, however, calls for strong research base in a pension fund. However, experience indicates that research is virtually missing in all the funds, primarily due to cost consideration as the fund management fee is too low.

STRUCTURAL AND REGULATORY CONSTRAINTS IN NPS

The NPS, introduced on 1 January 2004 to attend to several national goals like extending pension coverage to billions of workers in the unorganised/informal sector, providing an avenue to save for retirement by this segment of society, to reduce the pressure on exchequer by replacing the government financed DB pension system by partially self financed DC for civil servant who will join services in future, to offer better return to pension saving through diversified and high return portfolio managed by PFMs. However, very little has been achieved, particularly in respect of the extension of coverage to the unorganised/informal sector workers. However, the scheme could make little progress in extending coverage and achieving its goals due to several structural, organisational and administrative problems.

Absence of Legislative Support

Pension reform is a critical socio-economic and political issue effecting life of millions of subscribers and impacting national economic policy. In absence of legislative support, confident subscribers weaken and regulator is not able to take many required initiatives and necessary developmental and punitive actions. Many administrative problems also arises due to absence of any legislative approval of the system and legal authority. To bring the NPS within a statutory regulatory jurisdiction, an ordinance was promulgated setting up a statutory Pension Fund Regulatory and Development Authority (PFRDA) on 29 December 2004. Subsequently, a bill was introduced in the Parliament in March 2005 to replace the ordinance and to provide legislative authority to PFRDA. However, till October 2011 the bill had not been passed. The bill provides for establishing a statutory authority to promote old age income security by establishing, developing and regulating pension funds and protecting the interest of subscribers to schemes of pension funds. Delay in passing the PFRDA Bill and proving legislative sanction to the NPS has undoubtedly hampered the progress. Not much serious efforts have been made by PFRDA in the areas of capacity building and pushing the new system so vigorously to extend coverage. Supervision, monitoring, surveillance need to be improved further and this is possible only if the authority is empowered with legislative approval.

Low Level of Awareness

The NPS has failed to create enough awareness among the investors and enthusiasm among the various stakeholders. The NPS, particularly the All Citizens Scheme elicited poor response due to several structural problems implicit in demand side as well as supply side. However, the most important factor seems to be the low level of awareness. We have noted earlier that there is a low level of retirement though the overall domestic and household savings rates are reasonably good and improving. However, savings for the old age is still quite low. A survey of household savings conducted by NCAER and Max New York Life revealed, 'nearly 69 per cent of households in India save for reasons old age financial security where as 63 percent households save to meet future expenses towards marriages, births and other social ceremonies. Financial risk is quite severe in India'; an overwhelming 56 per cent of households feel that they cannot survive for more than one year on their own current savings in case they lose their major source of household income (Shukla 2007). Therefore there is need to improve the level of awareness about systematic savings for old age income through channels like pension funds. But neither the government nor the regulator initiated any meaningful programme to educate people to save through NPS. The PFMs are not authorised to do that and the point of presence (POPs) have never initiated such programmes as there is neither any obligation nor any incentives. This requires a concerted action programme by the public and private agencies. Public private support is basically a confidence building, awareness developing financial education programme for retirement savings, the core component being NPS. This is a national-level literacy mission with the major objectives to create awareness about the potential adverse impact of ageing and population explosion, benefits of NPS, necessity for financial savings, long-term impact of early savings for retirement, understanding and analysing individual risk tolerance level and taking informed need-based and risk-based retirement savings decisions, etc.

Absence of Effective Distribution Channel

Experience indicates that financial products, particularly, in India are sold not bought. Agents, brokers and other distributors play the key role in product positioning and distribution, which are absent in NPS due to the cost factors. Advisors-who do not have any accountability for success or failure may provide much support. Therefore, an active role is to be played by the PFRDA and other stakeholder who have opted to be associated with NPS System. It seems that the current thoughts of increasing NPS sales through spread of financial literacy by advertising in news papers have not prompted the potential investors to invest in NPS. It is a fact that only advertising does not help effective product positioning.

Financial products like insurance, mutual fund, pensions are distribution driven. In a country like India with low per capita income and lower level of awareness about such products and their importance and necessity, distribution mechanism is immensely important. Distributors not only sale the products but also act as first line educator. Unfortunately, the regulator, in order to keep the cost as low as possible does not focus on this. Insurance and mutual funds have grown faster due to effective distribution network and distributors. The importance of agents in selling financial products can be seen from the fact the by the end of March 2010, there were 2,978,283 individual agents and corporate agents licensed by IRDA for selling life insurance products (IRDA 2010). Total individual agents of LIC, the largest insurer in India, were 1,402,807, which is one of the prime drivers of business. The importance incentives to derive financial product sales can be assessed from the example of mutual fund industry, which abolished entry loads in 2009 causing a drastic fall in the sale of equity mutual funds from ₹119,838 crore in 2007–08 to ₹61,114 crore in 2009-10 (PFRDA 2011).

POPs are the major contact and sales points for All Citizens Scheme at the ground level and they take NPS products to the customers. Most of the POPs are branches of commercial banks which have been designated by the respective banks and approved by the PFRDA. These branches undertake selling of other financial products like insurance and mutual funds also in addition to banking business. The PFRDA has introduced an incentive structure for POPs which includes ₹40 for every new account, and ₹20 per transaction and ₹150 as a supplementary support for every enrolment, to encourage them to promote NPS products. But this has not resulted into effective sales growth, as the monetary incentives are considered to be unattractive as compared to the huge promotional costs. Moreover, NPS sales are additional jobs for branch employees, which does not help much in career advancement and for banks and other sponsors of POPs, it is not core business. Further, there is no driving force to motivate POPs and not much training has been proved to them. All these factors have led to poor performance of POPs. Performance of POP seems to be dismal considering the high hopes put on them by PFRDA. Initially PFRDA appointed 22 POPs which rose to 29 by 30 April 2020. There was a marginal increase in the number of POPs by 3 September the number of POPs were 35. Similarly the number of POP-SP branches increased from 3,091 by 30 April 2010 to 12,226 by 3 September 2011 and the number forms collected by these branches increased from 5,532 to 55,611. It shows that on an average the number of forms collected per branch rose from 1.7 application to 4.5 applications. In a country like India, which has a large number of banks and financial institutions the number of POPs are very insignificant. The number of forms collected by them is also very insignificant; this indicates lack of involvement and motivation on the part of POPs (Annexure 9A.1).

Therefore, in order to derive NPS sales there is a need to look into these two aspects namely professional sales force and appropriate incentives without harming interest of investors. Two steps can be taken by PFRDA–creating a specialised sales force/distribution channels and secondly allowing the PFMs to market pension products. A model of mutual funds can be replicated for NPS–allowing pension funds to mobiles money and invest the same. (This author as a fund manager has advocated this for long time since 2007–2010.) It should be kept in view that in the early stage of any financial industry all the stake holders have to a play a developmental role, while driving the sales. This happened in India when mutual fund industry began its journey in the late 1980s (Sadhak 2002). Cost is no doubt an element of consideration in Pension industry, but expanding coverage is also essential. Further, net cost can be minimised by superior fund management and investment return which would finally impact the accumulation of wealth. The report of Committee to Review Implementation of Informal Sector Pension (CRIISP) (PFRDA 2011) has also provided some suggestions such as increase in the number of branches of Postal Department, allowing the PFMs to sell NPS but not directly but through POP within their corporate structure, work out a comprehensive marketing action plan, developing a branding programme, etc. (Annexure 9A.1).

Lack of Confidence

A system tends to be sound and able to attract potential investors when the system itself and other who manage it at the ground level induce confidence among the potential investors. In a country like India, where there is little awareness about old age savings, low per capita income and a large number of people living in villages, there is no effective awareness programme, no effective distribution channel and legislative approval of NPS. These factors together weaken the confidence of investor in NPS to a great extent. Moreover, in India people, particularly the low income and less educated ones, have tremendous confidence in government institutions. The poor response to NPS thus may not be only due to the structural weakness of system but perhaps due to the failure of generating enough confidence. This can be noted from the fact that out of about ₹125 crore mobilised under All Citizens Scheme ₹91 crore was mobilised by the two public sector funds while about ₹34 crore was mobilised by four private sector funds (Table 9.9). This shows the level of confidence about public sector funds and the regulator should think about increasing the number of public sector PFMs in NPS.

However, simply by increasing the number of public sector PFMs will not increase the investors' confidence. Intermediaries have some role to play to remove the misconception if any and take the NPS forward. The NPS is a national initiative and for the citizens of the country as a whole, who are engaged not only in the government sector but also in the private and informal sector.

Various stakeholders like PFMs and POPs accepted to be the part of this new initiative knowing the architecture, business model and other business considerations. Media has emerged as a strong medium of opinion making and is playing a crucial role in educating the public about the various aspects of any new initiative. Though the government and regulator have their own role but responsibilities of other stake holders are also essentially critical. Therefore, coordinated efforts and actions by public and private entities are required to implement NPS successfully. This action can be called as public private support (PPS) for NPS (Sadhak 2009).

Absence of Return Guarantee

Another factor weakening the confidence of potential investor is the absence of performance guarantee. Though guarantee of minimum return is an important characteristics of most of the countries that have undertaken pension reform by introducing individual account–based DC system, in India there is no such guarantee from PFMs, sponsors, regulator or government. We have seen in Chapter 2 of Section 1 that there are guarantee of investment return in most of the countries. Generally there are two types of guarantee, namely fixed rate guarantee and relative rate guarantee. A fixed rate guarantee is a pre-determined flat rate and fixed return on pension investment (for example, bank savings deposit rate in Hungary, 2.5 per cent nominal return in Malaysia, etc.). Countries like Argentina, Hungary, Malaysia, Mexico, Singapore Uruguay, etc., have introduced fixed rate guarantee. Relative rate return guarantee is linked to a bench mark return, which is often the average of the return of other funds, bank fixed deposit rates, government bond index, etc. Counties like Chile, Colombia, Peru, Poland, etc., have introduced relative rate of return guarantee for the pension funds.

There are various practices regarding the guarantee providers and arranging the resources for guarantee. Guarantee providers can be the fund managers, sponsors, central pension guarantee fund or by the government. In many Latin American countries fund managers are required to set up yield fluctuation reserve fund and the sponsors are required to set cash reserve fund. For example, in Chile the Yield Fluctuation Fund (YFF) is made up of pension funds where the actual yield surplus over the last year has exceeded the average actual yield of all the funds for that year by more than two percentage points or by more than 50 per cent whichever is higher. Cash Reserve (CR) is equivalent to at least 1 per cent of the value of pension fund and is paid by using the AFPs own resources, that is, out of shareholders fund. When a pension fund is unable to provide guaranteed minimum return even by using fund YFF and CR, the government steps in and makes up the deficits and proceeds to wind up the fund. In countries like Poland and Hungary, central pension guarantee funds are established through contribution of fund managers. For example, in Hungary the Central Guarantee Fund (GF) is a pre funded institution. Pension funds pay 0.3 per cent–0.5 per cent of members contribution into the GF. The government steps in when resources of GF is exhausted to fulfil the guarantee.

Minimum Return Guarantee (MRG) has its own advantages and disadvantages. MRG make the DC partially DB pension and transfer a part of investment risks to the PFMs. Second, guarantee is a sort of insurance which may make the PFMs take unmanageable higher risks. However, advantages seem to underscore the disadvantages while a MRG offered by PFMs.

First, pension savings is a critical old age income generated by investors through savings with pension funds, with expectations of a higher return than the risk free return on bank deposits and bonds, in anticipation that the pension fund managers are experts. Therefore, pension funds need to perform to provide the expected return so that investors in their old age receive regular income.

Second, when the responsibility of providing minimum return is put on the PFMs, a more cautious and scientific investment approach will be followed by them by minimising the risk of decline in return. This will strengthen the risk governance and regulatory oversight which is a pre-condition for efficient supervision of pension funds.

Third, when some responsibility for good performance is fixed for the sponsors, only the best and competent organisations will enter into pension business, which will promote a healthy fund management industry in the pension sector.

Fourth, minimum return guarantee on pension fund returns induces confidence among the investors in investing in pension funds which will provide a boost to domestic savings through pension funds. It has been mentioned by many potential pension investors that are unsure about long-term performance of pension funds in absence of any accountability in respect of return by the PFMs, regulator or government. Therefore, provision of minimum return in NPS will to some extent remove the anxiety of investors and subscription is expected to increase manifold.

A MRG became a necessity due to another structural condition of pension, that is, tax financed universal pension in a multi pillar system which has been strongly advocated by World Bank and implemented by many developing countries and exists in most of the developed countries as a redistributive mechanism. In India there is no universal pension and in such a situation MRG becomes a necessity. Pension reform is not to be seen from a short term perspective but a longer view is to be taken to provide social protection to the people of ageing India. A MRG will partially support this objective.

Pension funds are critical financial intermediary playing an unparallel role in the economy confronted by the problems of ageing, financial market instability and many dimensional pressure on scarce financial resources. Pension funds need to survive as commercial entity but at the same time need to protect the old age survival of its members. Therefore, any reform regarding pension and retirement policy must be based on protecting the best interest of all the stake holders and perceived challenges that may be thrown up by the unpredictable future.

Higher Enrolment Cost

NPS has been considered to be one of the low cost pension systems in the world, but not necessarily that low when compared with the other industry like insurance, mutual funds, etc. The CRIISP report has pointed out that a minimum contribution of ₹6,000, the cost works out to 8 per cent, is quite high by any standards, especially when compared with some of the other competing products in the market–such as banks deposits, insurance policies or mutual funds. The cost of NPS Lite though claimed as a low cost product is actually not so. Under NPS Lite an account holder needs to pay ₹35 as joining fees for a Permanent Retirement Account Number (PRAN) card and ₹70 every year. The CRIISP has also pointed out that NPS charges a flat ₹436 per year plus 0.0084 per cent per annum. Whereas other similar mutual funds and life insurance schemes charge on an ad valorem basis in the range of 2.3–2.8 per cent of the amount invested during a year (Table 9.10).

Table 9.10 NPS Costs Compared with Similar Products of Mutual Funds and Pension Funds

Column 1	*NPS*	*Mutual Funds*	*Insurance PF Scheme*
1	CRA Flat Charge (@ ₹366)	Entry Load : Nil	
2	Custodian Charge (@0.0075)	Expense Ratio (@1.25 per cent)	Policy Administration Charges @0.25 per cent
3		STT(@0.125 per cent	STT (0.125)
4	PFMs / FMC Charge (@0.0009 per cent)		FMC charges** (@1.50)
5	POPs collection Charge @₹120 + 40)	Distribution Expenses @ 1 per cent on amount collected*	Agents Commission @2 per cent on amount collected
6	₹526 + 0.0084	2.38 per cent	2.88 per cent

Source: Report of the Committee to Review Implementation of Informal Sector Pension (2011).
Note: The above data is based on the information available on the AMC's and Insurance Companies websites. Some of the pension schemes offered by Insurance companies may also have life insurance components and their pricing in addition to this. Many of these schemes offer additional benefits like guarantee feature and may not be comparable.* SEBI in August 2009 abolished entry loads on investment in mutual funds but distributors can charge customers directly for the services. ** FMC = Fund management charges.

The flat charges of the NPS are very steep, which tilts the scheme in favour of wealthier investors. The high cost in NPS is primarily due to high CRA cost, as other costs are quite comparable with mutual funds and life insurance products. Therefore, basic solution lies with reduction and rationalisation of CRA costs. One fails to understand why there is only one CRA while there are more than one intermediaries in case of PFMs, POPS. The monopoly of CRA by one institution should be ended by inducting at least one more CRA. Competition among the CRAs will put down ward pressure on cost and further improve service quality.

Fund Managers

The most important driving force of individual account–based private pension system is the fund managers who are managing the assets and others are service providers. In a large country like India with diverse geographical spread must have sufficient number of pension fund managers (PFMs). But for a huge number of employees in the central and state government only three fund managers have been authorised and for a large unorganised sector only six fund managers have been authorised. One fails to understand this. Moreover, the selection process adopted by PFRDA, though technically fair does not offer much support to the system. There are technical and financial bidding. It was found the many well-known financial institutions with strong market presence, which were technically qualified, were excluded in the final round due to low financial bids. This situation needs to be avoided by rationalising selection process to induct reputed large financial organisations. Therefore, PFRDA should take immediate steps to increase the number of PFMs.

Low Fund Management Fee

Low cost syndrome has also reflected in fund managers fees. Presently the PFRDA approved fund managers fees is 0.0009 per cent decided through a competitive bidding in 2009. It is a fact that this low fee was quoted by a PFM and applied to all PFMs irrespective of the nature of the scheme. But the problem lies in the nature of bidding decided by the PFRDA. The PFRDA decided to accept only lowest bidding that applied to all PFMs. The lowest bidders perhaps wanted to ensure entry into pension market irrespective of cost consideration. None of the PFMs can recover the fund management expenses with this low cost and may not be able to break even in the near future. This author as fund manager has several time advocated the need to give up administer pricing in a competitive market. It was suggested that PFRDA should keep in place a cap to avoid high fund management fees and also a floor to restrain uneconomical lower fees. We need to keep cost of NPS as low as possible including fees for fund management, but too low fees will impact the quality of fund management, as it will not be possible to hire competent and experienced fund managers, quality research will not be undertaken and no incentive will be provided for better performance.

Ownership of NPS

Unless the ownership is clearly identified no programme can be effective enough to achieve the desired goal. Therefore, we need to clearly spell out ownership, responsibility and accountability of the owners. Since NPS is a national programme, it needs to be owned by a cross section of entities in addition to the government and regulator. Intermediaries like the sponsors of PFMs, POPs, CRA, etc, who have opted to be a part of NPS, have an important role to play in the process since in course of time they will receive financial and non-financial benefits either directly or indirectly. Corporates also have an important role to play for making NPS a success, since it will provide retirement benefit support to the workers (Sadhak 2009).

Voluntary Savings

Tier 2 NPS is considered to be voluntary savings by the members of NPS, to augment pension savings and to accumulate some funds which may help them to mitigate non-pension expenditure. FIAP defines voluntary savings as

> *a mechanism whereby dependent and self-employed workers can save over and above the amount they contribute mandatorily to pension plans, in order to increase the amount of their pension or advance their retirement age. With this type of savings, workers can partially or fully compensate the financial impact on the amount of their pensions caused by pension gaps during their working lives (periods with no contributions), increases in life expectancy and/or decreases in long-term rates of return.*

Tier 2 of NPS is more flexible than Tier 1 as the investors are free to withdraw from this account. It's an important way of saving through fund management expertise of pension funds. However, it seems the response has been quite poor. Perhaps one of the reasons for this poor response is that there is no special incentive like tax benefits as we find in many countries. In most of the Latin American countries tax incentives and other benefits are given for voluntary savings, For example in Brazil tax incentives are given to workers up to 12 per cent of income; companies up to 20 per cent of salaries. In Chile there is no tax incentive but a bonus of 15 per cent of savings in a calendar year (no tax relief) or contribution discounted from taxable income (maximum US$27,175 in one year) is given. In Columbia tax incentives are given if funds are withdrawn after five years and are used for housing. In Mexico, tax incentives up to 10 per cent of income (no more than five minimum salaries) are given for voluntary savings. In Uruguay income tax is deducted from employers' deposits up to 20 per cent of contributions but in Peru and Bolivia no tax incentives are given for voluntary savings (in Peru there is no tax on pension). In most countries, the liquidity of voluntary pension savings also enables their use for financing non-pension benefits. However, withdrawals for purposes other than pensions are liable to tax penalties. A couple of countries allow contributions to be made, from the beginning, for short-term non-pension purposes, and they can therefore be withdrawn, but without receiving any tax benefits (FIAP 2010). However, in India there are no tax incentives for Tier 2 savings in NPS. The PFRDA/government should consider providing some tax incentives in the Tier 2 of NPS. These incentives can be linked to minimum period of savings and purpose of withdrawal. Speculative savings/withdrawal need to be discouraged and penalised.

NPS for Rural Sector

NPS Lite is a well-conceived programme which has tremendous potential to extend pension coverage to low income people and already created quite good response. But it seems this response is primarily from urban segments as the aggregators selected an urban bias. We need to take this programme deep into country side for those who have little or no regular income. Chinese Rural Pension can be an ideal example of such an initiative. Even agricultural workers tied to land and working for a landlord should be provided old age income support by those who have utilised the services of workers. Swavalamban benefit may be extended to them and the balance contribution should be made by the land lord or for whom they work for a minimum period. *A National Rural Pension Policy* should be designed by incorporating NPS Lite and Swavalamban Scheme to cover rural informal segments. The PFRDA should make special efforts to designate rural aggregators with extended monetary support to encourage them to focus on workers in rural areas.

Pension as Corporate Social Responsibility

The state has been gradually withdrawing itself from business and industrial activities and the space is left for private initiatives. Private corporate have extended their activities in almost all areas of economy and expected to increase further. Corporates have the responsibility to take care of the old age income security of their employees. NPS offers an opportunity to provide such old age support through employer–employee contribution. A mandatory provision would facilitate such a move by the corporate. While in many corporate houses such initiatives exist and mostly for the senior employees, covering the low income employee through mandatory occupational pension through NPS would be a welcome step.

Market Development Programmes

In a new system like NPS market development programme is an integral and important activity of a regulator. Regulatory focus should combine (*a*) setting up of the system and regulatory structure, (*b*) implementing the system and (*c*) undertaking the market development. This author had suggested such a programme which has also been echoed by CRIISP report. There is need for well conceived market development initiatives including business like actions and accountability of the stake holders. All the stakeholders like PFMs and POPs need to be actively involved in financial literacy campaign and to provide active support to increase NPS subscription. Accountability, responsibility and expected role of stakeholders in promoting the NPS and mobilisation of funds need to be spelt out directly.

Resource Support of Stake holders

Huge resources are available with the sponsors of PFMs and the organisations selected as POPs. These organisations should volunteer to provide initial support to the NPS. The Life insurance companies which have sponsored either PFMs or POPs together have more than 20 lakh agents.

Market Discovery

One important market segment for NPS would be unorganised but associated group of self-employed. Large number of people who are not employed in the organised sector but independently work for them would form huge potential market. It can be mentioned here that recently a top level executive of a life insurance company desired that their agency organisation with few million agents can be covered under NPS. There are many such associations which like to take the benefits of NPS. To bring this large potential subscribers under NPS some amount of marketing initiatives, at least in the form of organised interaction are required.

Structured Co-ordination

Success of market development programmes would however depend on a business target planning (BTR), active coordination and regular monitoring on the part of PFRDA. The BTR needs to work like long range planning apparatus which explore market potential and initiate policy response to tap the potential market. In order to implement the BTR, a high-level coordination committee needs to be formed including Chairman/MD of all the stake holders, to activate their participation. Subsequently, regular monitoring at the operational level would be required. Such a market-oriented approach would not only increase alertness among the stakeholders but would also enhance the sense of urgency. A structured programme with targeted attempt including increase in PFMs, resource support of stake holder and through market discovery would enable the NPS to mobilise market development programmes would be initiated by the regulator and a new department needs to be created to undertake and manage the development programmes. This department of the regulatory body will act as the nodal point and co-ordinate all such activities.

Public Private Support Programme (PPSP)

The crux of the problem is lack of awareness, absence of stake holders' accountability and to some extent structural weakness which are pulling back the well thought out NPS system. NPS is a national programme and needs national level initiatives and actions including awareness creation, while removing the regulatory bottlenecks and building required capacity at various level of regulatory and administrative set up. The regulator or government intervention is not sufficient to bring effective awareness for NPS, particularly when participation of unorganised sector is voluntary. Further awareness needs to be created among the immediate potential investors and also among the future investors, corporate and other social organisations directly or indirectly involved in economic activities. Therefore, national level awareness campaign is a must for NPS, which can be created through a specially designed programme with private and public participation. This programme can be called as PPSP for NPS.

PPS would cover all young and old, educated and illiterate, organised and unorganised sector. It should cover schools, colleges, higher education institutions, factory offices, organised and unorganised labour force, etc. Hence, the material, the mode of delivery should be uniquely designed to suit the purpose of specific section to be covered. *PPS transmission mechanism* needs to be crafted carefully. NPS is a socio-economic programme (SEP), therefore, the trainers need to be highly skilled, they should motivate and be purpose oriented. A special band of trainers drawing from all the entities involved in execution of the programme should be trained first, who in turn take the NPS education to the people. Media and journalists are also to be trained, since they play a critical role in educating their readers. Effective implementation of PPS calls for coordinating the programme without any leakage. Also, we need to set up a National Co-ordination Committee (NCC) drawing experts from stake holder of public and private sector. A national-level programme like PPSP requires a huge budget and owners of PPSP need to translate ownership into responsibility through financial contribution to PPSP fund. Further, since it is a national priority programme, contribution from other profitable entities may also be accepted. The government may provide suitable tax benefits for such contribution. PPSP would have immense beneficial impact on NPS in terms of increasing awareness, enrolment and contribution. In most of the countries such awareness programmes were launched along with the pension reforms. Pension awareness campaign had significant influence on expanding pension awareness, increasing the number of contributors and contribution.

ANNEXURES

Annexure 9A.1: Extract from Report of the Committee to Review Implementation of Informal Sector Pension [CRIISP]

❖ EXECUTIVE SUMMARY

1. India's economic growth and demographic transition is resulting in a falling birth rate, a slowing down of the death rate and a subsequent rise in the proportion of the aged population. A large part of the informal sector remains without any funded social security scheme.
2. In a significant move in December 2003, the Interim Pension Fund Regulatory and Development Authority was created as the watchdog and promoter for the pension sector, and, all government employees joining service on or after January 1,

2004, were compulsorily brought under the coverage of the 'New Pension System' (NPS)–a defined contribution scheme replacing the defined benefit scheme available to the Government employees until then. Most of the states have also migrated to the DC system under NPS, except three states. NPS was introduced for all citizens from May 2009.

3. The NPS was created with a unique and defining feature of individual retirement account with portability.
4. Despite its unique features and the potential to address the issue of old age income security in the informal sector, NPS has remained unpopular, possibly due to the faulty assumption that pension products do not need to be sold. From this basic flaw flow all the other infirmities in the product design and micro-structure.
5. The biggest problem with NPS is the absence of any clear idea about who owns the customer. While the existing unbundled architecture has its own advantages, it has ended up fragmenting responsibility for not only attending to customer grievances but for also selling the product to potential contributors.
6. The POPs have so far not actively marketed the product, despite some incentives announced by the PFRDA; nor have the PFMs, primarily because of a tacit arrangement that discourages them from active canvassing of accounts, possibly to avoid any mis-selling.
7. The reluctance by the POPs—especially bank-POPs—in pushing NPS products might also be due to an inherent conflict with other products sold through the branch, with incentives higher compared with NPS. The main reason behind the lukewarm response appears to be the low-to-negligible distribution incentive incorporated in the system architecture.
8. Costs are a deterrent too. The cost structure followed by PFRDA is based on the absolute amounts every subscriber is required to pay to each stakeholder in the NPS architecture. Although the amount seems small enough, but these absolute costs look pretty high in percentage terms.

❖ SUMMARY OF RECOMMENDATIONS

1. The committee recommends an ad valorem structure for POPs which has the potential of merging the advantages of volumes (from small investors) with value (high ticket investments from rich investors). The committee feels that the ideal rate should be 0.5 per cent of the amount subscribed by the NPS subscriber, subject to an upper limit of ₹50,000 and a lower limit of ₹20.
2. The Committee suggests that PFRDA engage with the postal department proactively to increase the number of branches selling NPS. Another option is to appoint the numerous mobile telecommunications service providers which have taken mobile telephony to the remote corners of this country.

3. The committee feels that there should be no upper limit or qualitative restriction on any category of distributor. Popularising NPS is a national priority and, as long as the basic criterion of 'fit and proper' is met, PFRDA can look at appointing all categories of distribution agents to distribute NPS.
4. PFMs should be allowed to sell NPS but not directly. If within their corporate structure they have a POP, they should synchronise their actions. For all PFMs which do not have a POP, the committee recommends that they should be allowed to float POP subsidiaries which can then be used to source NPS accounts. These subsidiaries would be subject to PFRDA's extant rules and regulations applicable for POPs and would receive the same incentives as earned by other POPs.
5. PFRDA may consider changing the current rule requiring a minimum annual subscription of ₹6,000 for NPS Main to bring it down to ₹.1000 per year so that any account-holder with this contribution can access the POP network in the country, and also avail of the benefits of Swavalamban.
6. PFRDA should take a fresh look into a break-up of the annual maintenance charge of ₹280 or even the per transaction charge of ₹6 levied by the current CRA. PFRDA should also revisit the suggestion of inducting in a few more CRAs, as was originally planned. [paragraph 5.30]
7. PFRDA should commission fresh research into calculating the costs of NPS delivery, especially in the light of the emergence of new cost-effective transaction channels.
8. Promotion of NPS should be a part of the national financial inclusion agenda. It would allow PFRDA to access the national pool of investor education funds and funded outreach programmes, since the target audience for PFRDA and the other programmes are common.
9. PFRDA should work out a comprehensive marketing action plan, including a branding programme. In addition, PFRDA should conduct an exercise to design a market development unit within the regulatory structure. This unit will be responsible for devising short and long term marketing plans for achieving PFRDA's developmental role. This unit may also develop a suitable branding and communication programme that would lead to desired level of customer acquisition and retention
10. PFRDA should continue with the Tier-II for the moment but put in place adequate regulatory safeguards for this product in consultation with the Reserve Bank of India (with regard to the savings bank characteristic of the product) and the Securities and Exchanges Board of India (from the viewpoint that the funds management activity takes on the features of a liquid mutual fund).
11. The government should extend the Swavalamban incentive of ₹1,000 every year for a longer period, if not for perpetuity.
12. PFRDA should consider introducing a dynamic element to the fee structure for the PFMs, a sort of sliding scale, which ensures that an increase in the assets under management automatically results in a lowering of the fee

13. PFRDA needs to re-examine the extant criteria for selection of PFMs. PFRDA can adopt the rules framed by Securities and Exchanges Board of India rules– with suitable changes. PFRDA can determine the number of PFMs it can optimally supervise.
14. PFRDA should be financially autonomous to help it discharge its duties as an independent regulator and to nurture a pension sector that is free from controversy or regulatory capture. [paragraph 5.67+ 5.69]
15. There might be a case for issuing pre-paid PRAN cards. The KYC has to be the responsibility of the aggregator/POP. The distribution network of telecom companies selling pre-paid cards and Bill payment companies must be included as channels for mobilising subscriber contributions to PRANs.
16. PFRDA should actively encourage Bank POPs to make available on their websites the pay online option in order to bring NPS within the easy reach of those with internet access.
17. It is recommended that the capital protection feature for the NPS product be offered to subscribers. Inflation indexed bonds of different maturities could allow NPS to hedge inflation risk and in turn offer investment products to retail clients that are protected against inflation.
18. PFRDA needs to evolve a regulatory framework for detecting and penalising instances of mis-selling. The committee feels that PFRDA should probably institute a separate committee to draft new rules and regulations to keep mis-selling at a minimum.
19. PFRDA should probably draft a code of conduct for all the participants in the NPS chain. This is necessary to avoid any ambiguities about their role.
20. PFRDA should also step up its inter-action with external researchers, especially by making clean data available to them. PFRDA, apart from actively publishing all research on its web-site, should also commission research and development from time to time.
21. PFRDA should find a way to work jointly with the insurance sector regulator, Insurance Regulatory and Development Authority, for developing a proper market for annuities. (Report of the Committee to Review Implementation of Informal Sector Pension [CRIISP], Chairman: G. N. Bajpai, http://www.pfrda.org.in/writereaddata/ linkimages/CRIISP per cent20Report9681894859.pdf.)

Annexure 9A.2: India's Pension Reform: Some Important Landmarks

India embarked on pension reforms in 1998. India's pension reform spans many agencies and has made remarkable progress in laying sound foundations of a modern, well designed pension system.

The Ministry of Social Justice and Empowerment, Government of India, had set up a Committee on Old Age Social & Income Security (OASIS) in 1998 under the chairmanship Dr S. A. Dave.

In August 2008, MoSJE sets up an eight-member inter-ministerial expert committee under Project OASIS.

1 February 1999, First Project OASIS Report (dealing with improvements to existing pension and PF provisions) presented to the Union Finance Minister of India).

21 October 1999, Government constitutes Working Group for 'Assessment of Pensionery Liability of the Government of India' (under the Chairmanship of A. M. Sehgal).

11 January 2000, OASIS Committee (Chairman Dave) submitted OASIS Report to the Ministry of Social Justice and Empowerment, Government of India. *In May 2000,* Asian Development Bank (ADB) commissions a technical assistance project on reform of Employees' Provident Fund Organisation (EPFO).

February 2001, Road-map for DC pension scheme for civil servants and the general public announced during the Union Budget by then finance minister.

In March 2001, A working group on pension reforms for the unorganised sector was set up under N. Rangachary, the then Chairman, IRDA.

5 April 2001, World Bank submitted its report 'India–The Challenges of Old Age Income Security' to Government of India.

25 June 2001, A. M. Sehgal Committee report on Pensionery Liabilities of the Government of India, was submitted to the Finance Minister, Government of India.

In October 2001, IRDA Committee (Chairman N. Rangachari) submitted its report on Unorganised Sector Pension Reforms.

In February 2003, The then finance minister, Government of India announced a new DC pension scheme for civil servants and other workers during the Union Budget 2003–04.

February 2003, Reserve Bank of India (RBI) sets up a Group to Study the Pension Liabilities of the State Governments (Chairman B. K. Bhattacharya).

In August 2003, The Union Cabinet approves the proposal to implement the 2003–04 Budget proposal for introducing a new DC pension scheme for new central government employees (except armed forces) and unorganised sector workers. The Union Cabinet also approves the establishment of the interim Pension Fund Regulatory and Development Authority (PFRDA).

10 October 2003, Interim Pension Fund Regulatory and Development Authority was established through a notification of the Department of Economic Affairs, Ministry of Finance, Government of India.

29 December 2003, The Department of Economic Affairs, Ministry of Finance, Government of India issued an ordinance on the issue of interim PFRDA.

24 October 2003, Bhattacharya Committee submitted the Report of the Group to Study the Pension Liabilities of the State Governments to Reserve Bank of India. *22 December 2003,* The Department of Economic Affairs, Government of India, issued notification on new pension and provident fund rules effective on a mandatory basis for central government employees recruited on or after 1 January 2004; DEA also notifies the features of this New Pension System (NPS).

1 January 2004, NPS introduced for central (civil) government employee Union Budget 2004–05 announcement specifies an EET treatment for pensions under the NPS.

In June 2004, Announcement made of government's intent to put in place suitable legislation to provide a regulatory framework for NPS.

In January 2005, The Union Cabinet decides to introduce the PFRDA Bill, 2005 in the BudgetSession2005–06.

In March 2005, The government tables the PFRDA Bill, 2005 during the Budget session of the Parliament.

March 2005, The Parliament refers the PFRDA Bill, 2005 to the Standing Committee on Finance.

In April 2005, The government appoints D. Swarup as chairman of PFRDA for a period of five years.

22 January 2007, PFRDA, invited Expression of Interest (EoI) from public sector entities with experience of developing and managing technology based central administration and recordkeeping systems, for functioning as CRA responsible for opening and maintenance of personal retirement accounts of the subscribers under the NPS and providing a number of related services.

11 May 2007, The Pension Fund Regulatory and Development Authority (PFRDA) issued a Primary Information Memorandum and Expression of Interest (EOI) package for appointment of Pension Fund Managers for the New Pension System (NPS).

26 November 2007, The Pension Fund Regulatory and Development Authority (PFRDA) and National Securities Depository Limited (NSDL) entered into a formal agreement on 26th November 2007 relating to the setting up of a Central Recordkeeping Agency (CRA) for the New Pension System (NPS).

21 November 2007, LIC Pension Fund Ltd. was incorporated by the ROC Mumbai, as the First Pension Fund Company under NPS in India by *Registrar of Companies Maharashtra.*

27 November 2007, PFRDA announced the appointment of Life Insurance Corporation (LIC), State Bank of India (SBI), UTI Asset Management Company (UTI-AMC).

29 March 2008, the Chairman of NPS Trust and the Chief Executives of three newly incorporated and PFRDA approved Pension Funds Signed separate Investment Management Agreement. Dr H. Sadhak, CEO LIC Pension Fund Ltd signed the Agreement for LIC Pension Fund.

31 March 2008, LIC Pension Fund issued the *Commencement of Business Certificate* by PFRDA.

31 March 2008 (midnight), Trustee Bank, Bank of India, First time transferred the Pension Funds of the Central Government Employees.

2 April 2008, Three Pension Funds invested NPS Funds in the Indian Capital Market.

22 May 2008, Stock Holding Corporation Ltd was appointed as the Custodian for the NPS Trust.

21 November 2008, LIC Pension Fund completed one year since incorporation and released its Accounts and First ever Annual Report, by any PFRDA approved Pension Fund Company in India.

26 December 2008, PFRDA invited EOI for appointment of Pension Fund Managers for managing pension fund assets for All Citizens Scheme.

12 January 2009, PFRDA invited EOI for appointment of Point of Presence (POP) for Managing pension funds for All Citizens Scheme.

1 May 2009, NPS was extended to all citizens of India through *All Citizens Scheme.*

14 December 2009, Tier II of All Citizens Scheme was introduced.

22 July 2010, PFRDA introduced NPS Lite Scheme.

10 August 2010, PFRDA constituted Committee to Review implementation of Informal Sector Pension (CRIISP).

1 July 2011, Committee to Review implementation of Informal Sector Pension (CRIISP) submitted its Report to PFRDA.

1 August 2011, PFRDA invited Expression of Interest (EOI) for selection of Annuity Service Providers.

REFERENCES

Federation of International Association of Pension Funds (FIAP) (2010), *Voluntary Pension Savings in Individually Funded Systems of FIAP Member Countries.* Santiago: FIAP, December 2010.

Insurance Regulatory and Development Authority (IRDA) (2010), *Annual Report 2009–10.* Hyderabad: IRDA.

Pension Fund Regulatory and Development Authority (PFRDA) (2011), *Report of the Committee to Review Implementation of Informal Sector Pension (CRIISP).* New Delhi: PFRDA, 1 July 2011.

Reserve Bank of India (2011), *Annual Report 2010-11*, section Domestic Rates in Financial Market. Available at: http://www.rbi.org.in/scripts/PublicationsView.aspx?id=13332.

Sadhak, H. (2002), *Mutual Funds in India- Marketing Strategies and Investment Practices' Response.* New Delhi: SAGE, 2002 (4th Reprint 2007).

——— (2009), 'Public Private Support Key to NPS Success', *Financial Express*, 24 August 2009, New Delhi (edition).

Shukla, Rajesh (2007), 'How India Earns, Spends and Save–Results from the Max New York Life NCAER India Financial Protection Survey', Max New York Life Insurance and National Council of Applied Economic Research, New Delhi, 2007

Value Research (2011), *Mutual Fund Insight*, volume 1x Number 1 (15 September–14 October). New Delhi: Dhirendra Kumar.

SECTION THREE

Pension Reforms in India

Some Critical Issues and Unfinished Agendas

10 Pension Payouts, Mandatory Annuitisation and State of Annuity Market in India

DEFINED CONTRIBUTION PENSION AND PAYOUTS

India has introduced defined contribution pension and all the attention has been focused on fund management, collection, etc., which is considered to be the accumulation phase of the NPS. But the success of NPS will depend on evolution management of a well-regulated payout system. In fact payout phase is the virtual backbone of any mandatory pension system. A defined contribution pension (DC) system is broadly divided into two phases—*accumulation phase* covering the collection of contribution and funds management and a *decumulation phase/pension payout* which arranges payment of pension to the pensioners. Compared to accumulation phase, payout seems to be more complex and complicated, as it requires well-designed instruments and mechanism to deliver pension payments in accordance with pension policy which should also remove structural impediments to liquidity, safety and free flow of funds for uninterrupted delivery of pension payments. Payout phase of any DC pension system also faces the challenges of investment risks like accumulation phase, but additionally it also faces the longevity risk which is not present in accumulation phase. In this section we propose to discuss about payouts that have been slated to be introduced in NPS. However, we would also like to discuss about the conceptual framework of payouts and practices of few countries which have introduced pension reforms and mandatory defined contribution system.

Designing an Appropriate Payout System

Reforming pension system by switchover from DB to DC has attracted more attention to accumulation phase rather than deccumulation/payout phase, though it is the core to retirement survival. Fund management has become more glamorous than pension payouts. In fact payout needs more critical attention of policymakers, since at that stage pension investors are out of jobs and depend on the money saved during service/working life. This is the phase when a pension investor has to protect the risk arising out of over stressing longevity, expenses for medical care, maybe some money for repayment of debt or building a house for living, etc., which calls for prudent and efficient allocation of retirement wealth already saved. One of the most important aspects of Defined Contribution system is to design an appropriate payout system keeping in view the state of Financial Market, system of taxation, changing lifestyle, longevity, profile, etc. Further, consideration for payout designs needs to be considered keeping in view the variety of requirements in the post-retirement period, when regular earnings cease to exist except pension through past income generated during working life. Therefore, a rationale and realistic payout system should take into consideration protection against longevity, costs of payouts, liquidity, bequest motives, etc. There may be several expectations of pension savings, but the important expectations are:

- *Protection against longevity risk*: There is an uncertainty in the longevity of a person, though in general longevity has been increasing steadily. With the increase in longevity, a pensioner is living a longer life, but it is uncertain how long, and it is this uncertainty that makes an individual savings decision risky, and longevity risks tend to be most critical risk factor in the pension payout stage. Any policy, thus, designed for pension payout must consider this risk factor and try to minimise longevity risk as far as possible.
- *Liquidity*: The next most important consideration for pension payout design is the liquidity to support the needs for cash. Cash requirements have two components—one can be assessed in advance and other which is unforeseen. Assessed cash requirements at the post-retirement period arise out of certain obligations like house buildings, marriage, etc., in absence of alternative savings. Unforeseen cash requirements arise from unvisualised exigencies. There the system must provide some liquidity out of accumulated savings in the post-retirement period.
- *Bequest:* Third most important consideration is the bequest motive; this may arise out of several factors—love and affection, to pass on wealth to someone including next generation. This is possible if the system is flexible and allows to posses liquidity in the payout stage.

Methods of Payout Payments

There are various forms of payments in the payout stage of any pension system. In accumulation stage money is saved and assets are accumulated which are used to create a stream of income for old age consumption. Payout in post-retirement or on withdrawal in the post-accumulated phase can be achieved through a one-time or a stream of regular income or a combination of both, in a DC system. The system design, however, will depend on the level of development of the country, level of alternative savings and disposable income, system of public social security and public assistance programmes, development of capital market, etc. The main forms of payouts that have been introduced as a part of DC pension system in various countries can be classified into three categories as *lump sum payments, programme withdrawal,* and *life annuity*. All the three types can serve the payout programme in a DC pension system and these have certain merits and demerits. For payout under the DC System either any one of these options or a combination of options can be introduced, and the same has been followed in many countries. Each of these options has a certain characteristic feature and therefore a combination of two is often considered to be a good option. Let us examine the important feature of the above options.

❖ LUMP SUM PAYMENTS

Under the lump sum payment system pension investors receive all the accumulated wealth by a single payment. This wealth can be spent by her/him in any manner she/he desires—spending a part of money to purchase a life annuity, investing a part of money for health care, investing some portion in stock market, spending for house construction or preserving some cash for emergency need.

Advantages of Lump Sum Payments

This is a very simple system as far as the administration of the scheme is concerned and has a very *insignificant administration cost. This also provides flexibility and liquidity to the pensioners.* Since Lump sum allows the investors to withdraw entire amount she/he can spend the money according to the spending need, like buying a house, medical expenses, marriage, education, etc., Therefore, lump sum system provides full and flexible freedom of spending.

Lump Sum Payments Help Self Annuitisation and Avoid over Annuitisation and Liquidity

Lump sum payment provides full liquidity which is not available in other forms of payments. It helps an investor to annuitise a part or full payment according to her/his needs and risk tolerance level and can choose the type and quantity of annuity from among the different kinds of annuity products. She/he can invest a part of funds in annuity, some money debt or equity according to the needs and risk tolerance level and also can avoid over annuitisation, depending on the other form of income security like state-sponsored pension benefits in the form of regular annuity payment. Lump sum payments also take care of *bequest* motive of a pensioner which may be an important objective of savings. A part of the lump sum amount can be set aside for heirs or loved ones or for community/social welfare.

Disadvantages of Lump Sum Withdrawal

In spite of all these benefits, full lump sum payment is not considered as an ideal method for pensioners as it can be dangerous and can defeat the very purpose of pension saving. If a pensioner is not prudent and educated enough about old age income, money can be spent for the purpose other than old age income. Again lack of knowledge and skill for asset allocation may see that entire money is lost and there is nothing to protect longevity risk. In view of this, lump sum payments are not allowed in mandatory pension schemes in many countries like USA, Japan and Soviet Union. However, partial withdrawal of lump sum is allowed in Argentina, Peru and Chile and in some other countries.

Programme Withdrawal

Under the programme withdrawal system payments may be spread over a period of time and the pension investor receives a series of payments. Programme withdrawals may also have a provision that the pension investor receive some lump sum payments in certain emergency cause.

Programme withdrawal has the advantage of liquidity and flexibility, but to a lower extent than that under the lump sum payment. Programme withdrawal also provides to fulfil the bequest motive of the investors. To some extent the programme withdrawal system is better than lump sum as money is received in a programmed manner and possibility of losing entire accumulated funds due to wrong allocation and mismanagement of funds are less than that in the lump sum payment system. However, it also fails to provide full longevity risk of a pension investor. Valdes-Prieto (1998) has drawn attention to some drawbacks of programme withdrawal since no portion of wealth is annuitised, single bequest and absence of any portfolio which reduces investment risk to zero, etc.

Deferred Withdrawal

Under deferred withdrawal, subscribers can defer a part or full amount of accumulated pension assets upto a certain specified period. This facility allowed the subscribers invested in pension account to earn higher return but has a disadvantage of market fluctuation. Deferred annuity may work well when a part of accumulated pension assets converted into annuity and payment of remaining portion of accumulated assets are deferred.

❖ LIFE ANNUITY

Annuities are special type of contract sold by the life insurance companies or any specialised annuity company to the individuals who purchase them as financial instrument to receive a series of specified payments in future. In DC private pension system, long-term accumulated savings are savings transferred to an annuity company through an annuity contract and accordingly the savers who purchase such a contract receive a series of payments; sometimes these payments are lifelong. Among the various systems of retirement payments life annuities are most favoured and accepted by most of the countries either as a single option or clubbed with payout options like lump sum or programme withdrawals. A life annuity is like DB pension which provides lifetime income to the annuitant. Under life annuity an individual receives pension till he is alive. There are different types of life annuities such as:

- *Lifetime annuity without return of purchase price,* the annuitant receives pension as long as she/he lives. But ceases on occurrence of an eventuality and the insurance contract comes to an end.
- *Life Annuity with a return of the purchase price,* when an annuitant receive pension till he is alive but on death, the purchase price of the annuity including the basic sum assured plus the bonuses/additions, if any, is paid out to his nominees/beneficiaries.
- *Lifetime annuity guaranteed for a certain number of years provides* a pension for a certain number of years (as prescribed by the plan) irrespective of whether he is alive for the said period or not. Annuities have certain distinctive features, which provide 'protection against two broad classes of risks namely *Biometric Risk* such as longevity and mortality risk and Macroeconomic and Financial Market Risk such as inflation, interest rate, and equity market and credit market risk' (Sigma No3/2007).

Benefits of Life Annuities

Life annuities provide certain benefits including:

- *Longevity Risk:* Under Life Annuity, a pension investor receives a series of payments as per determined contract as long as she/he lives. Life Annuity thus provides full longevity risks. Since a life annuity guarantee lifelong pension, the pensioner is free from the problem of retirement asset allocation.

- *Inflation Risk:* Risks arising out of increased inflation causing erosion of purchasing power of an annuitant can be protected.
- *Credit Risk:* Life Annuity also protects the annuitant from unanticipated risk arising out of investment in bonds, equities or other instruments.
- *Post-retirement Consumption Planning: Life Annuity helps to plan Consumption* as the pensioner who bought a life annuity knows the extent of cash flow in the post-retirement period and accordingly plan her/his consumption.

There are certain disadvantages of life annuity, though it is very popular and is a widely used financial instrument in mandatory pension system as a payout method. Buying a life annuity at retirement or at a pre-determined flow of income stream may protect the pensioners from longevity and investment risks; it also deprives her/him 'future control over investments and losing the potential to earn superior investment returns. It also runs counter to the bequest motive' (Antolin 2008). Another important drawback of life annuity is that it does not help the annuitant to fulfil her/his bequest motive due to future flow of contracted amount. Annuitant cannot create any estate for loved one or social cause as possible in case of lump sum payment system. Though life annuities protect risk against longevity and provide guaranteed regular flow of income, they are illiquid, inflexible and fail to fulfil bequest motive of a pension investor.

However, in spite of some drawbacks of annuity as an instrument of pension payout, it has been recommended by experts and is widely used by countries globally for managing payouts in defined contribution pension system, because the life annuity can take care of the most important requirement of pension investment, that is, covering longevity risk, while lagging in respect of liquidity and bequest motive, the other two systems, namely, lump sum payments and programme withdrawal provide liquidity and allow bequest but fail to take care of longevity risk. Therefore, countries having well-developed financial market, prevailing DB pension benefits, etc., go for more flexible payout system like lump sum payments, programme withdrawal, while countries without any other pension benefits, low savings and lower level of financial literacy generally focus more on life annuity or annuitisation. A combination of at least two methods which impart protection, liquidity and flexibility is preferred over any single method. This, however, calls for striking a balance between protection and flexibility. According to Antolin (2008),

> *Countries where much of individuals' retirement income comes from assets accumulated in the DC pension may need to Annuitise a large amount of those assets. In the case of countries where participation in DC pension is mandatory, policy makers may consider mandating a certain level of annuitisation or at least, mandate annuitisation at old age.*

Therefore, due to necessity of maintaining a balance between the two most important pension objectives, most of the countries, including India, adopted a DC system, and opted for mandatory annuitisation of a part of pension payouts. We may examine in brief the payout system in some countries which have introduced pension reforms.

Mandatory Annuitisation

Though annuities are considered to be most favoured instrument in the pension payout phase, experts have different opinion about introducing mandatory annuitisation in a DC pension system. The major arguments against mandatory annuitisation are that it takes away the freedom of individual choice to invest accumulated funds according her/his choice and often may lead to over annuitisation. The most significant drawback is the timing of annuity purchase. If the investor has to purchase an annuity at the time of retirement or at any particular time, it may adversely impact the return if the market is not favourable at that time. However, these arguments seem to be weak when judged against the advantages of Mandatory Annuitisation. Mandatory annuitisation has the advantages of covering longevity risk and protecting inflation and investment risks, through pre-planned arrangement of regular income flow.

Mandatory annuitisation forces the employees to invest full or a part of accumulated savings in annuity to ensure regular income during retirement period which in turn reduces the risk arising from unwise spending of accumulated funds mandatory annuitisation helps the development of annuity market, induce competition and improve market efficiency which ultimately benefits the annuity holders/pensioners. An important requirement of mandatory annuitisation is existence of a well-regulated developed annuity market having flexibility in choice and availability of annuities which can serve the wide variety of demand with different levels of risks tolerance that annuitant would like to satisfy. Though the deferred and immediate annuities of various types are mostly preferred as payout instruments, there are many innovative annuity products in developed markets, which not only provide regular income but also aim at managing inflation and interest risks (Indexed linked Annuity), higher return (Variable Annuity), etc. Some of these annuities are discussed in Annexure 10A.1

PAYOUT OPTIONS IN SELECTED COUNTRIES

We have noted earlier that there are basically three types of payouts including life annuity and life annuity has several variations. There are guidelines about option and nature of products which a pensioner can choose. These guidelines/regulations are to protect the interest of investors keeping in view the various types of risks associated with pension products. Further, while some countries allow the investors themselves to buy annuities with the accumulated funds, in other countries, fund managers arrange to purchase annuity products for the investors at the end of accumulation period.

Argentina

In Argentina, under the fully funded pension system, pension money is accumulated in private individual accounts, 'workers may choose, on retirement, between receiving an annuity-based pension, draw–down periodic payments or, in certain special cases, a split pension' (Rofman 2001). Argentina law restricts the choice of annuity products only to a joint and survivor annuity. Further annuities are based on standard mortality table and nominal interest rate of 4 per cent. Disability benefits are paid as draw-down or as fixed annuity depending on the available fund size. According to Argentina law, annuity choice is limited to a joint and survivor annuity. Retirement annuity in Argentina is provided by registered retirement insurance companies. In 2001, roughly 21 insurance companies were doing retirement business out of 217 insurance companies (Orszag and Cardinale 2002).

Brazil

In Brazil, annuities are paid by life insurance companies and participants are given four options including a standard annuity, a term annuity, a guaranteed period annuity and an annuity with survivor benefits. Annuity products in Brazil are basically tax-efficient deferred annuity contracts, escalating with guarantee of a revaluation at least equal to the inflation rate (Orszag and Cardinale 2002). These annuities combined with accumulation policies annuities with revaluation at least are equal to inflation.

Chile

In Chile, an individual member at the time of retirement is allowed to split the accumulated amount in two parts—one part being used to buy a Deferred Annuity Policy and the other part used for programme withdrawal. The annuity, however, must be inflation indexed fixed annuity. Retirement annuities are provided by licensed life insurance companies in Chile.

Mexico

Mexico broadly follows the Chilean practice in respect of retirement payment and allows the pensioners either to opt for a life annuity or for an income drawdown product. In Mexico, consumer price index linked life annuity can be offered as retirement annuity. The payment of life annuity adjusted in February every year. Payouts under income drawdown adjusted mortality and financial assumptions. Authorised life insurance companies provide the retirement annuities.

Uruguay

In Uruguay authorised life insurance companies are allowed to sell retirement annuities and only single premium immediate annuities are authorised by law (Orszag and Cardinale 2002). Annuities are joint life annuity with survivor benefits. Pensioners are allowed to buy annuity only from the four life insurance companies.

Hungary

According to the Pension Law 1997, workers in payout phase are allowed to opt for either annuities or lump sum withdrawals during the first 15 years after the reform. However, after 2013 life annuities were mandatory. Workers were allowed to choose from four types of annuities, namely, single life annuity, joint life annuity, fixed term joint annuity, covering the spouse or other beneficiary for a fixed period, combined with a single life annuity for the primary beneficiary and a single life annuity combined with a fixed term annuity covering the spouse or other beneficiary for a fixed period after the death of the main beneficiary (Impavido and Rocha 2006). These annuities are fixed real annuities, and are indexed to the price and wage inflation.

Sweden

In Sweden, public pillar pensions are received by the workers through Life Annuities determined by accumulated account balance and cohort life expectancy, while in the Occupational plans, there is a choice between *life and term annuities.* Participants may select either this state-provided guaranteed annuity, which is priced at a fixed low discount rate but pays out bonuses if returns exceed this (Palmer 2000). However, in Sweden, no *lump sum withdrawals are allowed under the public or occupational plans.* Under the funded scheme life and term annuities are allowed in the form of either (a) with-profits annuities with minimum guaranteed benefits and annual bonuses or (b) unit linked annuities. The presence of a public entity, the Premium Pension Authority (Premium Pensions Myndigheten, or PPM), and the operation of private occupational plans under collective labour agreements ensure that the interests of workers and retirees are well protected (Rocha et al. 2011).

ANNUITY MARKET CONSTRAINTS

Though annuity is considered to be the best form of payment in the payout phase under the DC system, implementation of mandatory annuitisation programme confronted with several hurdles as there are a fair number of risks for annuitant and annuity providers. The inherent risks in annuity prohibit the growth of annuity market, create indifference among annuity providers to supply enough annuity products and investors to buy large annuity which could expand annuity market. *However, in a mandatory annuitisation programme, these constraints are required to be removed through regulatory intervention in the interest pension investors.* It is a fact that in most of the countries, except a few like UK, USA, Australia, etc., the annuity market is under developed. Estelle James (2001) has noted that

> *Annuities markets are still poorly developed in virtually all the countries. The underdevelopment of the industry manifests itself in its small size relative to other kind of insurance, the absence of mortality tables which are pre-requisite to sound pricing and funding policies and the relative paucity of long term financial instruments with which to match assets and liabilities, thereby creating substantial reinvestment risk.*

There are several constraints for the underdevelopment of annuity market which arises due to supply factors, demand factors and government regulatory inertia.

Supply Constraints

This arises due to unwillingness of life insurance companies to market this products aggressively as it is quite difficult to price products appropriately. This is because of difficulties in mortality forecasting and fast-changing lifestyle and life expectancy. Insurers are further constrained by short-supply long-term financial instruments for risk management; since there is uncertainty in the longevity of annuitants, annuity, and asset liability management is a key issue in annuity business. In annuity risk is transferred to annuity providers but absence of sufficient financial instruments like long dated bonds, inflation indexed bonds make insurers disinclined to push annuity products.

❖ ADVERSE SELECTION

In annuity business, adverse selection is one of the most critical risk factors called mortality risk. Mortality risk may arise out of the various factors like fast changing longevity, continued improvement in mortality, outdated mortality table, etc. It is assumed that mostly the people who volunteer to purchase annuity are people who believe that they would live longer. Since an individual is the best judge of her/his health condition and fully aware of the medical requirements which an insurance company/annuity company may not know. This makes mortality assessment difficult. As a result, annuity provider may charge higher rates for such group resulting into lower annuity value, which may discourage the prospective buyers. Outdated annuity table also may prove a constraint for pricing of the products appropriately.

❖ FINANCIAL RISKS

Annuity providers encounter various risks and three important financial risks associated with annuities are *Inflation Risk, Investment Risk and Reinvestment Risk.* These risks also create asset–liability mismatch. However, inflation risk can be avoided by purchasing an Inflation Index Annuity. *Interest rate risk* arises due to unexpected changes in interest rates offered by government securities. Since annuity rates are influenced by the yield of Government Security, changes in the interest rate are an important risk factor. Interest rate risks, however, can be partially offset by investing in long-term government bonds.

Investment and *Reinvestment Risk* arises out of changes and volatility in the capital market, particularly in the bond. Since retirement annuity covers long-term unanticipated mortality risk, annuity providers need to invest in long-term financial instruments to hedge such risks. However, there is a shortage of such instruments even in the developed markets. They are virtually rare in developing markets like India. Therefore, assets are often invested in short to medium term instrument which may not provide required yield for guaranteed return and to maintain asset–liability matching.

❖ LOW MARGIN

Compared to life business, the margin in annuity business is low, which dampens the spirit of insurers. Stewart (2007) has observed, '[G]iven that annuities are relatively low margin financial products, if incorrect mortality assumptions are used they can prove unprofitable for providers'.

Insurers are further constrained by *short supply long-term financial instruments* for risk management. Since there is uncertainty in the longevity of annuitants, annuity, asset liability management is a key issue in annuity business. In annuity, risk is transferred to annuity providers but absence of sufficient financial instruments like long dated bonds, inflation indexed bonds make insurers disinclined to push annuity products.

Demand Side Constraints

Major demand-related constraints are lack of understanding of annuity products, lack of concern about retirement saving, availability of competing products in the market and alternative source of retirement income like public pension, bequest motives or state-supported social security, etc. There is often indifference about retirement annuity, which arises out of several factors like underestimating longevity, alternative savings like public pension, social security, joint family income, etc. Several studies have indicated that men and women usually underestimate their longevity, which deter them to go for retirement annuity. For example, a study conducted by the Society of Actuaries (SOA 2001) observed that men tend to underestimate longevity at 65 years as against current longevity of 81–83, whereas women estimated their longevity of 65 years as against 85–86. This causes indifference among people to buy retirement annuity. *Regulatory constraints* are often cited as one of the causes of underdevelopment of annuity market. Inflexible investment regulation, inertia to provide special regulation for retirement products, adverse tax treatment encouragement to product innovation, etc., related to regulatory constraints.

PAYOUTS IN NPS AND PROPOSED ANNUITY PROGRAMME

The Government of India introduced New Pension System (NPS) in January 2004 which is mandatory for employees joining services w.e.f. January 2004. NPS has been extended to all citizens as a voluntary pension w.e.f. 1 May 2009. However, two different types of payout mechanisms have been introduced by PFRDA. In fact, NPS has included all three forms of payouts with mandatory annuitisation. At the end of accumulation period, there is mandatory annuitisation of a part of wealth, and remaining wealth can be withdrawn as lump sum in **Central Government employees'** fund. In case of accumulation under all citizens, in addition to annuitisation and lump sum withdrawal, there is also provision for deferred withdrawal.

Payout in NPS for Central Government Employees

At the time of retirement/age of 60, when accumulation period ends, an employee has the option to invest at least 40 per cent accumulated wealth in purchasing an annuity plan from a life insurance company approved by IRDA and to take maximum 60 per cent as lump sum.

Payout in NPS for All Citizens

Voluntary NPS allows an investor to withdraw before age 60 at any point of time, but she/he has to invest at least 80 per cent of accumulated wealth to purchase an annuity from a life insurance company approved by IRDA and 20 per cent as lump sum withdrawal. However, under voluntary NPS, when an investor exits at age 60 from the system, she/he has to invest at least 40 per cent of wealth in annuity and the remaining amount can be withdrawn as lump or can be deferred upto the age of 70. This provision of deferred withdrawal is an additional facility in NPS. Effective implementation of mandatory annuitisation will, however, depend on a vibrant and dynamic life insurance market to supply appropriate annuity products. Annuitisatin will also need support of a debt capital market to facilitate long-term investment of pension assets like long-term inflation linked bonds. Also, there would be need for a separate regulation for annuity business, which would in course of time expand manifold.

Proposed Annuity Products in NPS

One of the important features of NPS is the mandatory anuitisation at the time of exit from the scheme. Annuity will be provided by IRDA and PFRDA approved life insurance companies. In order to enlist such life insurance companies, PFRDA has invited expression of interest (EOI) from IRDA licensed life insurers for acting as designated annuity service providers and for providing annuity products to the subscribers of National Pension Scheme (NPS). The subscribers will buy annuity directly from the list of such annuity service providers (ASPs) companies. The PFRDA has also set certain eligibility criteria for ASPs which include that life insurance companies should be licensed by IRDA and have experience of selling annuity products in the Indian market for at least three years. They should have minimum net worth of 250 crore. In the EOI, some indication about the annuity products to be offered by ASP is given.

There are seven options which include a variety of products like *Immediate Annuity, Deferred Annuity, Inflation Indexed Annuity and any other annuity.* This is a very sound policy as it will allow the ASPs to come out with non-conventional products like variable annuity, investment linked annuity, etc. There have always been supply side constraints as far as annuity products are concerned. Indian market lacks innovative products and PFRDA proposal will induce insurance companies to manufacture innovative annuity products and the savers will have wider options (Annexure 10A.2).

INDIAN LIFE INSURANCE INDUSTRY AND ANNUITY MARKET

Life insurance industry is an important and integral component of macro economy and has emerged as a dominant institutional player in the financial market, impacting the health of economy through its multi-dimensional role in savings and capital market. While the primary role of a life insurance company is to provide insurance coverage for managing personal financial risks, it plays a very crucial role in promoting savings by selling a wide range of products and also actively contributes in promoting and sustaining the capital market of a country. In the emerging economy, characterised by the reduced role of state and declining state-supported social security, the importance and the role of the life insurance industry has increased significantly not only as a risk manager but also as retirement security and annuity provider (Sadhak 2009).

There are serious and far-reaching financial implications of ageing on life insurance industry. Life insurance plays an important role in the economy by providing avenues for long-term savings and capital formation. It also helps individuals to manage financial and longevity risks and through annuity it provides old age income, through the pension plans and annuity plans. A pension plan covers both accumulation and decumulation of retirement savings, while an annuity plan plays the critical role in deccumulation phase. In a defined contribution pension system, accumulation phase is managed by the specialised fund managers but an annuity company takes the responsibility to provide pension/regular income through annuity contracts. Private pension arrangement in DC system transfers the longevity risk, inflation risk, interest risk, etc., to the pensioners unlike DB system where these risks are borne by the pension providers. However, the longevity risks can be transferred back to insurance companies and inflation and interest rate risks to annuity companies.

Trend in Growth of Life Insurance Business

India has a reasonably developed life insurance market—a well-developed regulatory mechanism, a good basket of insurance product, well-managed network of distribution. In the year 2010, 23 life insurance companies (in the public and private sector) were operational. Further, the public sector Life Insurance Corporation of India (established in 1956 by the Government of India) is one of the largest life insurance companies in the world. The LIC is the dominant market leader in India, providing life insurance service in India and abroad since 1956. By the end of March 2010, these 23 companies operated through network of 12,018 offices. Indian insurance sales were primarily led by Agents. By the end of March 2010, there were 2,978,283 licensed individual agents (1,402,807 belonging to LIC) and 2,930 corporate agents (IRDA 2010). A large number of the offices and agents are located in rural and semi-urban areas. Since nationalisation, Indian life insurance has registered a very significant growth and gradually increased its share in household financial savings which was 23.8 per cent in 2010–11. The number of enforced policies and SA of life insurance industry as a whole stood at 3,189.27 lakh policies (Table 10.1) and ₹3,338,540.67 crore SA by 31 March 2010 (Table 10.2). The market leader LIC, which started with ₹1,474 crore SA under 56.86 lakh in force policies in 1958, reached to ₹2,341,937 crore SA under 2,785 lakh in force policies in 2010. Growth in life fund and assets under management are considered to be an important indicator of growth of life insurance industry. LIC, after nationalisation of 256 life insurance companies started with a life fund of ₹410.47 crore (in India), which in course of time increased significantly and by the end of 31 March 2011, total life fund stood at ₹247,993 crore (RBI 2011), while total assets of life insurance companies under management stood at ₹2,078,691 crore of which LIC had 87.3 per cent, that is, ₹1,815,388.19 crore by 31 March 2010. In the year 2009–10, Indian life

Table 10.1 Life Insurance Business (within India)—in-force Policies (number in '000)

In-force Policies ('000)	*31.03.06*	*31.03.07*	*31.03.08*	*31.03.09*	*31.03.10*
Total in-force Policies	193,601.29	226,200	257,911	291,618	318,926.6
Life	183,108.83	194,164	198,168	217,687	235,064.88
General Annuity and Pension	3,186.08	3,193	3,135	3161	3,183.66
Health	40.43	165	494	824	815.91
Linked Business	7,265.95	28,678	56,114	69,946	79,862.15
B. Policies in per cent					
Life	94.58	85.83	76.84	74.65	73.7
General Annuity and Pension	1.65	1.41	1.22	1.08	1
Health	0.02	0.07	0.19	0.28	0.26
Unit linked	3.75	12.68	21.76	23.99	25.04
Total	100	100	100	100	100

Source: Insurance Regulatory and Development Authority (IRDA), Annual Report 2009–10.

Table 10.2 Individual Business in Force (within India) (sum assured in ₹ crore)

Business In-force Sum Assured (₹ Crore)	*31.03.06*	*31.03.07*	*31.03.08*	*31.03.09*	*31.03.10*
Total Sum Assured under in force Policies	1,554,044.68	2,034,640	2,396,646	2,913,703	3,338,540.67
Life	1,374,364.41	151,3876	1,620,876	1,962,562	2,273,516
General Annuity and Pension	68,424.96	91,557	51,867	52,081	52,952.36
Health	887.88	72,770	36,618	52,800	44,607.09
Linked Business	110,367.43	35,6437	687,284	846,261	967,464.45
B. Per cent of total Sum Assured					
Life	88.44	74.4	64.63	67.35	68.09
General Annuity and Pension	4.4	4.5	2.16	1.79	1.59
Health	0.06	3.58	1.53	1.81	1.34
Unit Linked	7.1	17.52	28.68	29.04	28.98
Total	100	100.01	100.00	100	100

Source: Insurance Regulatory and Development Authority (IRDA), Annual Report 2009–10.

insurance industry recorded an overall growth of 19.69 per cent in premium income of ₹2,65,450 crore, the fastest growth rate being registered by ULIP (27.44 per cent), as against growth rate of 14.33 per cent of traditional products. This shows the emerging trend in life insurance market in India since 2000–01, growing popularity of unit linked policies replacing the predominant position of endowment policies. This trend initially induced by the private insurance companies by launching of several unit linked policies which changed the product market structure of life insurance industry in India. India, the fourth largest economy of the world in terms of GDP at PPP ranking in 2009 will overtake the US in 2050 with projected GDP at PPP (constant 2009) of US$ 43180 billion next to China (Hawksworth et al. 2011). This is an indication that India has the potential of becoming a world giant in the insurance sector.

Market Structure: Life Insurance

An analysis of recent trend in life insurance business in India will indicate the emerging trend. Post-liberalised market has witnessed the increase in number of life insurance companies (LIC and 22 Private insurance Companies), diversified life insurance products (Life Products, Pension Products, Annuity Products, Health Insurance Products, Unit Linked Products, Unit Linked Pension Products, Unit Linked Health insurance Products, etc.). It is evident from the data in Tables 10.1 and 10.2 that the relative importance of life products has been gradually declining in the recent times while the unit linked and health products are prominently becoming favourable in the market place. The number of in-force life policies in total in-force policies declined from 94.58 per cent in 2005–06 to 73.70 per cent in 2009–10, while the share of unit linked policies increased from 3.75 per cent to 25.04 per cent during the same period (Table 10.1).

Similarly, health insurance is also increasing gradually which went up from 0.02 per cent to 0.26 per cent during the same period. But the pension and general annuity policies declined significantly from 1.65 per cent in 2005–06 to 1.00 per cent in 2009–10 (Table 10. 2).

This is a cause of concern in view of crisis of ageing and need for old age income protection. The same trend has also been noticed in terms of SA in respect of in-force policies. While SA under life policies declined from 88.44 per cent in 2005–06 to 68.09 per cent in 2009–10, the same for unit linked policies increased from 7.10 per cent to 28.98 per cent during the same period. Similarly the share of SA of Health policies increased from 0.06 per cent to 1.34 per cent. But the share of pension and general annuity declined drastically from 4.40 per cent in 2005–06 to 1.34 per cent in 2009–10. This can be examined in terms changing pattern of sales of LIC of India, the largest insurer of the country. One of the reasons is the increased popularity of unit linked policies and some insurance companies also launched unit linked pension plans. For example, LIC sold 22.42 lakh unit linked policies in 2005–06, of which 19.02 lakh were linked pension policies. In 2009–10, LIC sold 82.18 unit linked policies, of which 51.32 lakh were unit linked pension policies. Total SA under unit linked policies increased from ₹4,045.91 crore in 2005–06 to ₹36,951.06 crore in 2009–10 including SA under linked pension plans of ₹279.41 crore and 1196.28 crore, respectively (LIC Annual Report 2005–06 and 2009–10).

However, the market structure and emerging life insurance market may be further examined in terms of the assets under different class of insurance policies. Total assets under management for life fund, pension and general annuity and unit linked plans during 2005–06 to 2009–10, increased from ₹397,189 crore to ₹732,613 crore, ₹37,264

Table 10.3 Assets under Management of Life Insurance Companies in India

Column 1	*Column 2* 2005–06	*Column 3* 2006–07	*Column 4* 2007–08	*Column 5* 2008–09	*Column 6* 2009–10
Life Funds (A)					
LIC of India	38,94,448	4,53,440	5,22,985	6,06,487	6,99,475
Private Sector	7,741	12,115	18,645	23,163	33,137
Total (A)	3,97,189	4,65,555	5,41,630	6,29,650	7,32,613
A as per cent of D	43.1	42.06	38.72	37.93	35.24
Pension & General Annuity (B)					
LIC of India	36,158	35,062	87,744	1,07,135	1,30,885
Private Sector	1,107	2,001	3,518	6,817,	10,038
Total (B)	37,264	37,064	91,262	1,13,952	1,40,923
B as per cent D	4.04	3.35	6.52	6.86	6.78
Unit Linked Insurance (C)					
LIC of India	4,63,771	5,59,201	6,78,403	7,99,593	9,85,028
Private Sector	23,380	44,979	87,567	1,16,772	2,20,127
Total (C)	4,87,151	6,04,180	7,65,969	9,16,365	12,05,155
C as per cent D	52.86	54.59	54.76	55.2	57.98
Grand Total (A+B+C) = (D)	9,21,604	11,06,799	13,98,86	16,59,967	20,78,691
Assets under Management of LIC of India	8,89,377	10,47,703	1289132	15,13,215	1815387
As *per cent of D*	96.5	94.7	92.2	91.1	87.3
Assets under Management of Private Insurers	32,227	59,096	1,09,730	146752	2,63,304
As per cent D	3.5	5.3	*7.8*	*8.9*	*12.7*

Source: Insurance Regulatory and Development Authority (IRDA), Annual Report 2009–10.
Note: Figures in Italics indicate percentage of total.

crore to ₹140,923 crore and from ₹4,87,151 to ₹12,05,155. In terms of percentage share of different class of life insurance, there has been a significant decline in the share of life funds to total assets from 43.10 per cent in 2005 ₹06 to 35.24 per cent in 2009 ₹10 (Table 10.3).

However, percentage share of assets to total assets under management in respect of Pension and general annuity as well as Unit Linked Policies has increased. While the share of pension and general annuity has increased from 4.04 per cent in 2005–06, the share of Unit linked assets from has increased from 52.86 per cent to 57.98 per cent during the same period. Thus, unit linked plans occupied more than half of life insurance space in India, which is not a very healthy sign since unit linked plans are basically investment products serving short to medium term investment objectives.

MARKET STRUCTURE: PENSION AND GENERAL ANNUITY

Though life insurance industry has come a long way since nationalisation of life insurance industry in 1956 and further opening up of industry to private players in 2000–01,

Indian annuity market not only remained narrow but declined in terms of relative importance. The first annual report of LIC for the period September 1956 to December 1957, showed total annual payment of ₹9.95 lakh under 575 annuities. Since then Indian life insurance industry travelled a long way, witnessed a significant growth in life insurance business, moved from monopoly to competitive market environment, but the annuity market remained virtually non starter and dormant, when compared with growth of life insurance industry.

Data in Table 10.4 provides some idea about the in-force annuity policies and Sum Assured. Total number of in-force policies during 2005–06 to 2009–10 declined from 31.86 lakh to 31.84 lakh while sum assured declined sharply from ₹68,424 crore to ₹52,952.36 crore. In the total market share, the share of in-force pension and general annuity policies, market share declined from 1.65 per cent to 1.0 per cent, while share in total sum assured declined at a sharper rate from 4.40 per cent to 1.59 per cent during the same period. However, the assets under management increased from ₹37,264 crore to ₹1,40,923 crore. (Table 10.4)

Annuity Plans Launched by LIC of India

Encouraged by very favourable tax benefits, LIC launched some annuity plans during 1987–92 and there was tremendous market response. During this period, LIC launched participating deferred annuity plans Jeevan Dhara in October 1987, participating

Table 10.4 In-force Pension and General Annuity Policies—Market Concentration

	31.03.06	*31.03.07*	*31.03.08*	*31.03.09*	*31.03.10*
Actual in-force Policies (no. in '000)					
i. Private Companies	263.32 (8.26)	284 (8.9 0)	306 (9.76)	372 (11.73)	403.82 (12.69)
ii. LIC of India	2922.87 (91.74)	2909 (91.10)	2829 (90.24)	2789(88.23)	2779.84 (87.31)
iii. Total (i+ii)	3186.08 (100.0)	3193 (100.0)	3135 (100.0)	3161 (100.0)	3183.66 (100.0)
B. SA under in force Policies (₹ crore)					
i. Private Companies	4513.42 (6.60)	4530 (4.95)	4598 (8.86)	5117 (9.83)	6025.80 (11.38)
ii. LIC of India	63911.54 (93.40)	87027 (95.05)	47269 (91.14)	46964 (90.17)	46926.56 (88.62)
iii. Total (i+ii)	68424.96 (100.0)	91557 (100.0)	51867 (100.0)	52081 (100.0)	52952.36 (100.0)

Source: IRDA Annual Report, Various Years.
Notes: (a) Total figures has been adjusted on the basis SA of each segments; (b) Health Policies and SA under health Policies also include Unit Linked Health Policies; (c) Figures in bracket indicate percentage share to total.

immediate plan Jeevan Akshay in February 1988, participating Jeevan Suraksha in August 1996, non-participating deferred annuity plan New Jeevan Dhara and non-participating immediate plan New Jeevan Akshay in June 2000. Even after withdrawal of tax benefits U/S 88, and introduction of Section 80CCA, which allowed exemptions up to ₹10,000, was attractive to some extent. During 2002–05, LIC launched immediate annuity plan New Jeevan Akshay in February 2002, Deferred Annuity plan New Jeevan Dhara and Jeevan Nidhi in November 2004, New Jeevan Suraksha. However, withdrawal of 80CCC further reduced exclusive tax benefits to insurance premium, and reduced market response, which dampened the spirit and introduction of annuity plans comparatively declined. The declining trend in sales of pension and general annuity will become more visible if we look into the sales of LIC. In the year 2009–10, LIC sold 18,661 pension policies as against sales of 259,515 pension policies in 2001–02. Similarly, sale of general annuity policies also declined from 515,948 in 2001–02 to 23,466 in 2009–10 (Table 10.5). Since, LIC is the industry leader, this had led to the overall decline in growth of pension and annuity market in India.

Market Concentration

Another issue of concern is the unwillingness among the insurance companies to enter annuity market aggressively. Therefore, LIC remains the major player in the annuity market with nearly 90 per cent of market share. The private companies have recently launched some pension plans and their market share in number of policies increased from 8.26 per cent in 2005–06 to 12.69 per cent in 2009–10, while the same in SA increased from 6.6 per cent to 11.4 per cent during the same period. Though market share of LIC declined, still it is the major player in the annuity and pension market. The share of LIC in pension and general annuity market in terms of in-force policies and SA was 87.31 per cent and 88.62 per cent, respectively (Table 10.4).

Table 10.5 Sales of Life Annuity by LIC

	Deferred Annuity (A)		*Immediate Annuity (B)*		*Combined (A+B)*	
Year	*No. of Annuity*	*Total Annual Payments (₹ in Crore)*	*No. of Annuity*	*Total Annual Payments (₹ in Crore)*	*No of Annuity*	*Total Annual Payments (₹ in Crore)*
1980–90	212124	26900.35	25616	659.35	237740	27559.7
	(89.22)	(97.61)	(10.78)	(2.39)	(100)	(100)
1991–01	305462	44027.00	134346	7649.00	439808	51676.0
	(69.45)	(85.20)	(30.55)	(14.800	(100)	(100)
Total	517586	70927.35	8308.35	136862	677548	79235.7
	(79.09)	(89.5)	(20.91)	(10.49)		

Source : Annual Report and LIC Fact Book 2010.

Narrow Product Range

Further, most of the annuity products are Immediate or Deferred Annuity—the new generation products like Variable Annuity, Inflation Indexed Annuity, Equity Linked Annuities are not there in India. Latest information about relative size of Immediate Annuity and Deferred Annuity market is not available. However, some information about sale of Deferred and Immediate annuity plans by LIC are available through its annual report up to the year 2000–01. Accordingly, during 1980–1990 to 1991–2001, 79 per cent of life policies sold LIC were deferred annuity and 21 per cent life policies were immediate annuity with SA of 90 per cent and 10 per cent respectively (Table 10.5). However, a change has been observed in the demand pattern in terms of sales as the per cent share of deferred annuity declined from 89.22 in 1980–90 to 69.45 in 1991–01. During recent times another development is the growing demands for joint life policy as some new policies (like joint life policies) are being issued by life insurance companies in India.

Most of the pension plans launched recently are the unit linked products allowing the investors to buy an annuity policy at the end of accumulation period. The unit linked pension policies are quite popular in India. Unit linked pension plans are basically deferred annuity type plans. Unit linked plans consist of two stages—accumulation and deccumulation. In the accumulation phase the investors accumulate assets towards retirement income under these plans and at maturity can withdraw 33 per cent retirement plans of accumulated amount as lump sum and the rest is to be invested in any annuity plan. Primary reason for higher growth in sales of annuity policies and poor growth of annuity business in recent times was unparalleled growth in unit linked business, which was strongly supported by upswing in Indian stock market encouraging the investors to assume higher risk for higher return. Insurance companies also pushed up sales of unit linked products to take advantage of stock market boom, lower capital requirement, and to expand market base among risk-oriented investors segments. All these factors provided impetus to unit linked segments and in the process traditional life assurance and annuity products were ignored. Another reason is the withdrawal of some tax benefits earlier given for investing in annuity and pension products. Products like Jeevan Dhara, Jeevan Akshay plans, etc., launched by LIC were highly successful basically due to favourable tax benefits and lost attraction when they were withdrawn. However, the present tax treatment is not very conducive for annuity investment.

STEPS TO BE TAKEN TO DEVELOP ANNUITY MARKET IN INDIA

Poor growth of annuity business in India indicates that life insurance companies could not or did not fully exploit the potential of pension annuity market. We have seen earlier the general supply and demand side constraints to annuity market development in India. As a result the market for annuity products is very thin, product range is very narrow, very few insurance companies supply immediate annuity, there is no inflation indexed annuity, no variable annuities in the market. Therefore, mandatory annuitisation in India needs to focus on developing a vibrant annuity market by removing the constraints as mentioned above, to achieve the objectives of NPS. The underdevelopment of annuity market is a global phenomenon and in most of the countries, except few like UK, USA, Australia, etc., Estelle James (2001) has noted that 'Annuities markets are still poorly developed in virtually all the countries'. The underdevelopment of the industry manifests itself in its small size relative to other kind of insurance, the absence of mortality tables which are prerequisite to sound pricing and funding policies and the relative paucity of long-term financial instruments with which to match assets and liabilities, thereby creating substantial reinvestment risk. Indian annuity market is on the verge of explosion and the NPS will force market players to shed complacency and be active in promoting annuity business due to huge demand for such products. As we indicated earlier, the demand will arise from the increased number of elderly population requiring old age income savings through long-term annuity products and the compulsory annuitisation programme of NPS. To promote a developed annuity market we need to focus on supply and demand side of constraints as discussed above, through regulatory and non-regulatory measures. We discuss below some required measures in this direction.

Updating Mortality Table

Fresh Mortality Investigation/Table: Longevity risks are one of the major risk factors associated with annuity market and the inability to assess these risks gives rise to adverse selection by annuity manufacturers. Annuity pricing requires close understanding of emerging changes in longevity across the various ethnic groups, among the people living in urban and rural areas, between the men and women, etc. Absence of required technical knowledge to investigate and forecasting mortality increases indirect financial risks deter the life insurance companies to enter into annuity market. Absence of updated mortality table makes it difficult to judge the longevity of a select group and inappropriate pricing may be disadvantageous for the annuity buyers or annuity producers. This risks can be minimised by the regulatory updating the mortality annuity table for annuity. Indian life insurance companies are still following the Mortality Rates of Annuities in LIC of India LIC A (96–98) Ultimate Table. It has been observed by James and Sane (2003) that

> *in absence of India specific data LIC has been using different British tables, In 1985 the LIC adopted a (90) ultimate tables based on the mortality experience of male and female annuitant in the UK over the period of 1967–70, with different adjustment from time to time.*

Considering the fast-changing life expectancy and lifestyle, this seems to be outdated and needs to replaced by a table with recent investigations. The mortality table for annuity should also incorporate changes in longevity due to improvement in health, longevity of different group of people, etc. Unless the mortality table is constantly improved, no realistic estimate can be made about longevity and price of the annuity according o the risks involved. Therefore, there is an urgent need for developing a specific mortality table for Indian annuity market based on recent mortality investigations.

Developing Long-term Financial Instruments

One of the reasons for the underdevelopment of the annuity market is the absence of a vibrant and developed debt market and supply of required long-term debt instruments to hedge future capital market risks. The Indian debt market is yet to develop to support the requirement of long-term instruments for an emerging pension industry like ours. Underdevelopment of debt market is the source of asset liability mismatch and prudent investment management. Annuity contracts are long term in nature and payments are to be made over an uncertain long period as asset liability matching becomes a critical factor in an annuity company. Therefore, there is a constant need for investment instruments matching return and payment obligations. There is also risk of inflation and change in interest rates over a long period of time. This calls for availability of sufficient number of quality instruments for investment, and hedging interest rate and inflation risks. These instruments are basically long term in nature and primarily the debt instruments. Therefore, absence of well-regulated and developed debt market deters life insurance companies to enter into annuity market. Importance of long-term bond/debt instruments are immense and short supply of such instruments may have immense negative impact on pension funds return and thus annuity return. The strong correlation between bond supply and bond demand of pension fund were examined by Xiao et al. (2009) and he noted that

> *one percentage point increase of pension flows lowers corporate yield by at least 28 basis points and treasury yields by 20 basis points...and the bond shortage would increase pension liabilities by at least 4 percent and normal cost by at least 8 percent in one year.*

It is therefore absolutely necessary that adequate bond supply is maintained to ensure smooth investment of pension and annuity funds so that cost can be maintained at minimum to ensure better return on investment and to provide adequate annuity. Though longevity risks, in a fixed income annuity, remain uncovered, the financial risks can be mostly covered by investing in long-term fixed income securities including inflation indexed bonds which will allow the annuity to manage ALM and in absence of financial instruments for investing funds to earn the guaranteed return, there will be long-term liability mismatch. Therefore, there should be asset liability matching long-term debt instruments like government securities, which are normally absent in the Indian market. In developed financial markets, innovative financial instruments like longevity bonds, Inflation indexed bonds have been introduced to hedge mortality and long-term financial risks. To hedge longevity risks, Longevity Index Bonds or Survivor bonds have been suggested. First Mortality Bond was issued by Swiss Re in 2002, and the first longevity index bond was structured by BNP Paribas and issued by European Investment Bank in 2003.

❖ MORTALITY BOND

In December 2002, Swiss Re issued a three-year Mortality Bond. The principal payment of this mortality bond was tied up to an index tracking mortality rate in five countries namely UK, USA, France, Switzerland, and Italy. The principal under the mortality bond would be repayable in full if the mortality index did not exceed 1.3 times the base level during any of the three years of the bond's life. However, it would be reduced by 5 per cent for every 1 per cent increase in the mortality index above this threshold, and would not be repaid if the index surpassed 150 per cent of the base level. The issue size was $400 million, and the quarterly coupons set at three months LIBOR plus 135 basis points.

❖ LONGEVITY BOND

In November 2004, the European Investment Bank (EIB) announced plans to issue the first longevity bond targeted to UK pension schemes and life insurers with exposure to longevity risk for the male population of England and Wales aged 65 in 2002. The initial issue of this 25 years bond was set at £540. Although the bond was launched by the EIB, issuance was arranged and managed by BNP Paribas. According to the structural arrangement BNP would effectively bear the investment risk and the longevity risk would be covered by the partner. However, the issue was withdrawn in late 2005, since the pension industry price was too high. The longevity bonds, though have immense potential for risk management, it could not succeed to encourage the investors mainly pension funds due to several factors. Thomsen and Andersen (2007) mentioned:

> *In general, the market is short of investors in longevity risk, and capital needs to be attracted by offering alluring risk adjusted returns. In addition, some externalities may hinder the development of markets. A factor such as the outstanding volume is often essential for a market to develop, but once the volume has passed a critical level, growth may potentially be very high.*

Antolin and Blommestein (2007) suggested developing Longevity Index for Longevity Risk may promote Longevity Index Bonds. Another capital market instrument to hedge financial risks is the Inflation Index Bonds. To manage financial risks many countries issue inflation indexed bonds. In the developed debt markets, such as, UK, USA, New Zealand, Canada, Sweden, and South Africa, such Inflation Indexed Bonds are issued by the Government These bonds are issued at a regular interval to enable the investors to hedge inflation risk. There are several variants of Inflation Indexed Bonds, the most popular being the Capital Indexed Bonds.

Risk Management Regulation

Though lot is being talked and written about the importance of risk management, experience indicates that very less is done and very little management space is provided for this in India. Often the race for market share, growth and performance, etc., forces the managers to ignore the risk associated with such objectives. Risk management should not be an issue of compliance but should be the way of life in funds management and throughout the organisational operation. Regulation should not only focus on financial risk management but also the enterprise risk management. This call for a Standardised Risk Management Format (SRMF) is to be institutionalised by all the annuity providers. It is often observed that there are no full disclosures about various costs that an annuity provider would charge on distribution, administration, etc.

Widen Product Market

The Indian annuity market is quite narrow in respect of product range, as most plans launched are participating and non-participating deferred annuities. Immediate annuities are few and mostly launched by LIC. In developed markets, a new generation of annuity products is available for retirement investment, namely, variable annuity, equity-indexed annuity, inflation-indexed annuity, impaired annuity, enhanced annuity, in addition to fixed and guaranteed annuity.

Increase Tax Incentives

Tax incentives play an important role in annuity market development. We have mentioned earlier that the annuity products like Jeevan Dhara, Jeevan Suraksha were very successful in Indian market primarily due to tax incentives and annuity sales declined when the incentives were withdrawn. During the 1987–92 period, annuity investment attracted tax incentives under Section 88 of the Income Tax Act, 1969 and 88, the entire premium amount paid for annuity plans was fully exempted for income tax.

During 1987–92, LIC launched Jeevan Dhara, Jeevan Akshay and Jeevan Suraksha which received a huge market response. Tax benefits under Section 88 were withdrawn from 1992 onwards and there was a decline in sales of annuity policies by LIC in many countries. There are several ways to provide special incentives for annuity investing. Three important ways to provide tax incentives for annuity investment are through age-based tax allowance and preferential tax treatment for retirees with modest income, and pension income exemption from social security contribution (Sigma 2007). The government should consider this aspect and introduce a liberal tax regime for the annuity market. Since 1992, tax incentives for investment have gradually become unattractive.

Reduce Emphasis on Unit linked Insurance Plan (ULIP) Business

Whatever may be the reasons, Indian life insurance companies focused more on unit linked pension rather than annuity products. It is high time our attention shifted to need-based selling to maximise long-term benefits of customers. Annuity needs to be popularised by spreading financial literacy and the role of annuity and pension products.

Annuity Market Regulation

❖ PORTFOLIO REGULATION

Portfolio regulation in annuity becomes necessary because market risk is transferred to annuitant and the fund managers may take excessive risk to show higher return to retain or improve market share, though it may not be favourable. Moreover, annuity is a long-term product and undergoes several market cycles—interest rate and stock market cycles, which call for care and prudence in portfolio investment. Therefore, in order to stop such activism and to reduce portfolio risk, portfolio regulation for annuity business is essential. Portfolio regulation also indirectly acts as a guarantee, since annuity providers need to purchase specified quantity of specified securities prudently decided by the regulator to prevent long-term asset liability mismatch. However, only quantitative regulation may not be very effective in a volatile globalised market and it should be supported by Prudent Person (Rule) Regulation which will improve the accountability and responsibility of fund managers and fund management.

Pricing and Transparency Regulation

Annuity pricing has a significant implication on retirement payment through annuity. Pricing is a complex matter and annuity providers consider several long-term aspects related to the cost of annuity service and various kinds of risk associated with pricing.

Therefore, realistic assessment of mortality with the help of updated investigation will help the manufacturers to price products appropriately. Investors are often doubtful about the price in absence of public information on product pricing. Disclosing the pricing information will remove misunderstanding and encourage the investors to buy such products.

Cost of annuity is an important area of concern for the investors, since very often actual costs are not explicitly spelt out in offer document by many life insurers and annuity providers. There are often hidden costs which an investor may not know. Often distribution and service costs vary from one company to another, even in the same type of products. Since total costs have an impact on the long-term return on investment and subsequent flow of retirement income, regulation must force the annuity provider to disclose various initial and subsequent costs. In this respect, one can think about Cost Bench Marking (CBM) to protect investors' interest.

In absence of any specific regulatory guidelines on pricing, distortions may occur and annuitant may not get fair value for the price they pay. The major factors influencing the annuity prices are mortality, future interest rate, administrative cost, etc. Mortality tables are often outdated, and there is also age discrimination; forecasting future interest rate may often be biased due to wrong assumptions of changes in future macro economic variables and incompetence of forecaster; administrative cost including marketing and distribution cost may have some hidden costs, etc., while the updated standard mortality table needs to be introduced and periodically modified, the government should also come out with a standard interest rate to be used for calculating annuity pricing. This practice is followed in many Latin American countries like Argentina, Chile, Peru Colombia, etc.

Information Regulation

Information asymmetry is considered to be one of the important factors for financial market failure. Unless sufficient and necessary information related to financial, operational, management and corporate governance, etc., are provided by the annuity provider, the investor may be misled and may take wrong decision and enter into an annuity contract and which may also lead to serious adverse financial consequence regarding retirement income. It is therefore necessary that such financial and non-financial information, that help the investors to take informed prudent purchase decision, may be mandatory on the part of the annuity provider.

DESIGNING ANNUITY PROGRAMME FOR NPS

As discussed above, the present annuity market in India is very under developed which is a cause of concern, particularly in view of ageing, need for old age saving instruments and mandatory annuitisation of NPS accumulated funds. Indian pension market is still very small compared with other countries having similar GDP. Pension assets as a percentage of GDP were only 5.7 per cent in 2007 However, this is going to change drastically when NPS strengthens and penetration improves in next few years. Available estimates indicate a significant growth in very near future since NPS will expand the coverage. A survey of ADB and Ministry of Finance in 2004 shows that 310 million workers in the unorganised sector are uncovered and 20 millions are able and willing to join NPS immediately. In addition to that all the new employees in central and state governments are to join NPS. This will give a boost to annuity demand and market will expand exponentially. There are some estimates of future growth in pension assets in the post-reformed period. According to a study conducted by FICCI–KPMG, pension assets in India, after the reform, would increase to ₹4,064 billion in 2025. Another estimate of *Helen K. Poirson* of IMF shows that pension assets would grow from ₹1,500 billion in 2010 to ₹3000 billion in 2020 and further to 4,000 billion in 2025. These estimates, however, includes, growth of non-NPS funds,.

The increase in number of pension subscribers under NPS and spending of minimum 40 per cent pension wealth to purchase annuity policy from life insurance companies would support multifold increase in demand for annuity products in Indian life insurance market. But as we have noted above that the life insurance market is not fully ready to provide necessary annuity products to the prospective buyers of annuity. Indian market is also not innovative enough to supply preference-oriented annuity products that would be demanded in future. Further, the financial market, the debt market is in poor shape and unable to provide enough financial instruments for risk and asset and liability management. We have suggested some of the necessary steps to develop annuity market in India. In addition to that annuity programme for NPS would require certain structural measures including selection of the annuity products, licensing the annuity providers, designing an annuity-friendly tax regime, introducing capital market solution to risk transfer, etc. The initiatives to develop annuity market should also be supported by a well-functioning efficient regulatory regime. Some such initiatives are out lined below.

Payout Policy

It is a fact that not much has been done in the area of insurance market product innovation and research on buying behaviour. These would be essential, because of changing product market relationship in the emerging annuity market. Moreover, healthy annuity market would need strong support of capital market which needs to provide long-term financial instruments like index linked and other types of bonds/fixed income securities. The emerging annuity market would also call for a more focused regulatory mechanism for annuity market.

The primary objective of annuity programme in any DC pension system with partial mandatory annuitisation is to ensure reasonable retirement income through efficient asset allocation which will take care of longevity, inflation and reinvestment or timing risks. Hence, there is a need to reduce demand and supply side constraints in annuity market as discussed earlier. Therefore, a broad-based annuity policy must consider few important aspects like annuity providers, type of annuity products to be offered as retirement annuity, costs of such products, timing of post-accumulation annuity investment, risk management in annuity programme, regulatory responsibility to protect interest of annuity policy holders.

Payout in New Pension System (NPS) has already been outlined and India has adopted a flexible partial mandatory annuitisation programme. Accordingly a pension investor in NPS would be required to invest at least 40 per cent of accumulated wealth in purchasing an annuity policy. This policy of partial annuitisation takes care of several needs of a pension investor—annuity would provide regular flow of retirement income, withdrawal of lump sum payment (60 per cent or less) will provide the liquidity to fulfil other financial need and also to satisfy bequest motive. However, in the new system, an employee needs to wait till retirement for lump sum withdrawal and cannot utilise that part of pension savings for which he would be entitled at the time of retirement. In India, average income of an employee is low and may not have other source of income to take care of other financial needs like house construction, etc. It may be considered whether like PPF, investors in NPS would be allowed to withdraw a portion of savings without tempering the basic objectives of retirement income.

Selection of Annuity Providers

One of the important annuity policy aspects is to decide the annuity providers as per the provision in NPS in India, an investor is required to use at least 40 per cent of accumulated amount to purchase an annuity policy from any life insurance company approved by IRDA. It means that annuity can be purchased by any life insurance company.

Traditionally annuity providers are the life insurance companies due to their understanding of mortality risk and their experience in providing life insurance. However, experience indicates that life insurance companies are often reluctant to undertake annuity business due to inherent business risks arising out of changes in mortality, adverse selection and non-availability of sufficient financial instruments for hedging long-term risk. Many life insurance companies may not have necessary experience and required solvency capital and risk management experience to protect retirement capital of the annuitant. Therefore, the regulators usually adopt a selectivity criterion to authorise life insurance companies to sell retirement annuity. Therefore, certain regulatory differences are noted in respect of retirement annuity providers, and also there are profit and non-profit organisation to sell annuity products, in some countries, though their presence is miniscule in annuity market.

- Life insurance companies can directly sell retirement annuity products in Italy, Colombia, etc.
- Life insurance companies need to obtain an authorisation license from the regulator to sell retirement annuity in UK, Chile, Mexico, Uruguay, etc.
- Life insurance companies need to set up separate affiliate to sell retirement annuity. In Argentina, retirement annuity sold by registered retirement insurance companies set up by life insurance companies. In 2001, there were 21 such companies.
- In some countries retirement annuities are also provided by authorised organisation in addition to life insurance companies. For example, in Brazil, authorised profit and non-profit organisation can sell retirement annuities.

In India no regulation has so far been introduced but PFRDA is in the process of selecting the sponsors who will set up separate companies to provide annuity products to the investors in NPS.

The PFRDA, however, decided to authorise separate annuity company sponsored by IRDA licensed life insurance companies to provide annuity to the members of NPS at the payout stage. This is a welcome decision since annuity market in India is very underdeveloped and lot of concentration is required to promote annuity culture, full-time attention is required to promote products and market. Separate annuity companies will be in a position (under strict regulatory norms) to financial literacy about annuity, initiate market development and business promotion.

Licensing Annuity Providers

However, the experience in different countries shows that very few life insurance companies are usually active in annuity market. Orszag and Cardinale (2002) mentioned that in Chile only 20 life insurance companies were authorised to sell retirement annuities and in Mexico, 14 life insurance companies are authorised to sell annuity products. He has further mentioned that in 2001, in Argentina only 21 companies were doing purely retirement business out of 217 companies. The similar trend in lack of interest in selling annuity products in developed market is also noted by David Blake (1999) who has mentioned: 'in UK of around 240 authorised life companies, only about 10 are at any time serious providers of life annuity'. Managing mortality risks in life insurance and retirement annuity are different. While insurance covers the mortality risks for a defined period covering the policy terms, in retirement annuity mortality is unknown and the annuitant may live beyond the expected period of the annuity providers. Therefore, annuity provider needs different knowledge, expertise and better solvency margin and risk capital for the business. Since annuity business is relatively risky and profit projections are very often hazy, there is a possibility of unethical practices in pricing and distribution, which calls for strict regulatory controls. Licensing would enable the regulator to exercise selective control over the annuity providers. Moreover, annuity market in India is still undeveloped and needs to be developed further to enable it to serve the growing demand of the NPS payouts. A regulator would be required to initiate development measures.

International experience shows that in most of the countries annuity providers are licensed and limited in number and controlled by tight regulations. These regulations are relaxed with market maturity. For example, the registered annuity issuers may each be allocated a basket of contracts, with price and conditions set by the regulator. Subsequently migration between issuers at regulated transfer fees may be permitted followed by some price regulations (Doyle and Piggott 2002).

In the light of the above argument, it is to be examined whether pension fund regulator should also authorise the annuity providers through licensing mechanism. It also needs to be examined whether certain technical and financial criteria need to be fixed for such authorisation.

Annuity Service Providers in NPS

Pension Fund Regulatory and Development Authority (PFRDA) has empanelled six IRDA approved life insurance companies for providing annuity services to the subscribers of National Pension System (NPS).The six companies are :

1. Life Insurance Corporation of India
2. SBI Life Insurance Co. Ltd.
3. ICICI Prudential Life Insurance Co. Ltd.
4. Bajaj Allianz Life Insurance Co. Ltd.
5. Star Union Dai-ichi Life Insurance Co. Ltd.
6. Reliance Life Insurance Co. Ltd.

The subscriber in the NPS system can choose from any of the six above mentioned annuity service providers and can opt for any annuity scheme from amongst the schemes being offered by these ASPs.

ASP for Default Option

The NPS has an provision of Default Option and for this a separate ASP has been selected by the PFRDA. Life Insurance Corporation of India has been selected as the Default Annuity Service Provider which will offer A Default Annuity Scheme to the subscribers of Default Option. The Default Annuity Scheme is Annuity for life with a provision of 100% of the annuity payable to spouse during his/her life on death of annuitant' and Under this option, but the payment of monthly annuity would cease once the annuitant and the spouse die without return of purchase price.

In case of inadequate corpus to buy the default annuity from the default ASP, the subscriber has to mandatorily choose an ASP who would offer an annuity at the available corpus in the account of the subscriber.

Identifying Annuity Products

Mandatory annuitisation under the NPS indicates that at least 40 per cent of accumulated money to be invested in annuity and no mention has been made about the type of annuity to be purchased by the pension investors. Therefore there is flexibility in annuity selection. However, certain guidance is required to ensure that the pension investors do not go for wrong selection and put their retirement income at stake. The importance of such guidance becomes essential because of low-level financial literacy in India.

The most crucial objectives of an annuity are to transfer longevity risk to annuity providers, ensure regular and guaranteed income. Many of the annuity products do not have these desired benefits. Moreover, need and risk tolerance of pension investors in the post-accumulation phase differ with their savings and financial position. Therefore, the basket of annuity products which would not only provide the required pension benefits to the different categories annuitant according to their needs and risk tolerance level but also have inbuilt provision to tackle underlying risks of a particular product.

One important consideration to design the annuity products for defined contribution system is the explicit and implicit product risk. This is important because in a DB system risk is borne by the employers, whereas in a DC System the same is born by the pensioners. There are different types, some of them are borne by the annuitants, some by annuity providers, that is, life insurance companies. For example, mortality and investment risks in ordinary, enhanced and impaired life annuities are borne by the annuity providers while the same in unit and investment linked are borne by the annuitants. The design objectives as indicated above may not be achieved with a single product and therefore there should be a variety of products to cover the various needs of the people. Though of late product innovations are taking place, in reality the product range varies around conventional endowment and unit linked products in India. In the countries with developed annuity market like UK, USA, Australia, a large number of annuity products are available to the consumers. Therefore, annuity/pension regulation innovations in annuity products have underlying linkage to the capital market and investment strategies. Since needs of pensioners differ according to their pre-pension wealth and the level of risk tolerance, the product range should be reasonably wide. Though the basic objectives of pension and annuity investing is to receive a regular flow of income, it has also certain ancillary objectives like concern for other family members, timing of payment and receipt of pension, income objectives, risk tolerance, bequest motives, etc. Life annuity seems to be most preferred, for having two basic groups, namely, *Immediate Life Annuity and Deferred Life Annuity*, in the real world there are variety of products having different features which may impact the amount of pension. Immediate annuity has found favour with large number of countries including UK, USA, Canada and South Africa. 'More recently joined by Chile and other individual account reformers, are dominated by annuities that are purchased at retirement, converting a lump sum into a life time income stream' (Rusconi 2008).

However, many countries like Germany Denmark, etc., find favour with Deferred Annuity which are purchased during the working years. They attract a relatively low guaranteed return throughout the accumulation and payout phase with bonuses added as investment returns emerge. Further, some countries like Netherland allow both the Immediate and Deferred Annuity. Immediate Annuity, though popular, runs the investment risk which may arise at the time of purchase. Interest rate market may be down with low interest rate which will be reflected in annuity return and pensioners may be at loss. This problem may be solved by purchasing Deferred Annuity during working period at least few years before retirement. The PFRDA has taken very appropriate steps by proposing to allow investors to opt from different annuity product combination. Accordingly an investor can choose Immediate Annuity, Deferred Annuity and Inflation Indexed Linked Annuity. She/he would also be able to opt for variable annuity. This is a positive step to widen annuity market range and depth. The PFRDA should also ensure in consultation with IRDA that sufficient products are available in the market. In fact it should be a precondition to give license to any annuity sponsor.

Minimising Timing Risk

Understanding and minimising timing risks in DC system is an important consideration which relates to annuitisation and switching option. Timing risks, which arise due to the decision to buy annuity and to switch over from one portfolio to another have important bearing on annuity outcome in the form of return. Timing risks may arise in the accumulation phase (for fund managers) as well as at annuitisation. In the accumulation stage it may arise due to switchover from one portfolio to another by an investor at wrong time which may alter the risk exposure considerably, for example, switching over to a debt portfolio when interest rate may be moving upward causing decline of portfolio yield or to an equity portfolio at a very high level of equity index causing lower or negative return at an inappropriate time. These may happen due to unbridled freedom of active choice by the investor during accumulation phase. One of the methods, suggested by Valdes-Prieto (1998), to eliminate timing risks in DC pension is to force the employees to choose a single benchmark portfolio when they enter the pension system. Another way to solve this problem to a great extent is to introduce in the system a process of interaction between investors and fund managers. Timing risks in payout phase arises if annuitisation is mandated and if product is Immediate Annuity to be purchased only at the time of retirement or only at the time of exit. Unfavourable depressed market may adversely affect the interest of annuitant.

In NPS timing risks also arise due to strictly stipulated annuitisation timing. NPS mandated annuitisation of at least 40 per cent accumulated amount at the time of exit/ retirement by an investor. However, market at that point of time may not be favourable and the price of annuity may be high resulting into lower regular income during the rest of the life of the annuitant. This may be called unfavourable entry time. The problems of timing can be tackled by introducing a flexible period in the system to invest in annuity. For example, instead of mandatory purchase of annuity at the time of retirement, an employee may be allowed to buy annuity within a given period according to her/his choice. If an employee retires at the age of 60, she/he may be allowed to purchase annuity from age 55–60, with staggered vesting age. Thus an employee can take advantages of market movement and purchase, required annuity at a price beneficial to her/him.

Enhancing Tax Benefits for Retirement Investing

Taxation has an important promoting retirement savings and many experts suggest leniency in pension savings taxation, particularly in the countries where pension market is relatively underdeveloped. Therefore, a pro pension tax policy in terms of nil or reduced tax on savings and investment return on savings are advocated. However, in most of the counties it is EET, that is, tax exemption on contribution, return on investment and tax on withdrawal. For example, EET is attracted by retirement savings in USA, UK, Canada, Italy, Netherlands, Sweden, etc., while in Japan it is ETT. NPS in India attracts EET. However, even in EET lower tax rate would make pension and annuity more attractive. It has been noted that tax benefits on retirement savings play an important role in annuity market. Jeevan Dhara, Jeevan Akshay, etc., of LIC was highly successful basically due to favourable tax benefits and lost attraction when it was withdrawn. However, present tax treatment is not very conducive for annuity investment. At present *contribution* paid as Premium for an insurance plan up to ₹100,000 per annum is eligible for deduction under Section 80C, while premium contribution towards pension plans are eligible for deduction under Section 80CCC—the limit being set at ₹10,000. However, the deduction under Section 80CCC falls under the overall limit of ₹100,000. For example, if an individual pays a premium of ₹15,000 for a pension plan, then the tax benefit of ₹10,000 only. Also, his overall tax benefit will stand reduced to ₹90,000 (that is ₹100,000 less ₹10,000). *The maturity amount* in case of conventional insurance plans is treated as tax free in the hands of the individual. However, in case of pension plans up to one third of the maturity amount, which can be withdrawn, is treated as tax free in the hands of the investors. Further, in case of conventional insurance plans, the individual receives the entire corpus on maturity but in case of pension plans, the individual has the option of withdrawing up to one third of the maturity amount in cash. The pension, receiving from the remaining two-thirds amount, is taxed according to the marginal rate of tax. Therefore, in order to make annuity investment more attractive to the investors for retirement savings, more attractive tax benefits need to be introduced.

Annuity Purchase Option

One important aspect needs to be examined about the entity when it comes to selecting the annuity products for a member who exits from NPS. In most of the countries there is open market option to buy annuity from any licensed annuity provider. However, in some market like Swiss market open market option is not allowed. In such a market annuity is generally provided by the pension fund. Though there are arguments like suppressing active choice, encouraging monopoly, etc., by such arrangement, there is enough merit also, particularly in countries with low level of financial literacy which prompted to introduce default option (auto choice in NPS). In India, due to lack of financial literacy and understanding about future financial flow, a wrong decision may be taken by a member and that may lead to serious consequences. It may therefore be prudent to decide whether fund manager in NPS would play a role in annuity selection of a member or at least an Annuity Advisory (AA) should be issued by the trustee indicating Risk–Return and Risk tolerance (RRR) of any annuity purchase decision.

The most important challenge before the NPS is not the accumulation of funds, but to evolve a smooth functional mechanism for payouts. Indian life insurance market is quite small and annuity market narrow; Indian capital market particularly the debt market is poorly developed. There are few financial instruments for hedging risks and very little awareness about the necessity of risk management, low-level financial literacy about retirement investing and particularly through annuity investing. Mandatory annuitisation will force the NPS members to invest in annuity. The challenge is really manifold and much deeper than we normally visualise. This will call for close coordination and active involvement of insurance companies, regulator, government, and other stake holders like media, educational institutions, corporate houses, etc. In order to reduce the existing institutional gaps, certain immediate steps are required to be taken immediately to make investors aware about the importance of annuity products for long-term retirement savings, transparency in product pricing so that investors do not think that they are cheated by annuity manufacturers, to remove supply constraints through regular updating of mortality table so that adverse selection is avoided by the annuity manufacturers and a proper regulatory regime is introduced to protect the interest of investors as well as annuity suppliers, etc.

ANNEXURES

Annexure 10A.1: Types of Annuities

There has been a significant development in annuity market in terms of product design and a large variety of annuity products are available to suit the needs of investors depending on their risk tolerance and other objectives. Various annuity products, which are available in the market, can be classified as per the payment arrangement, coverage of lives, payout duration, etc.

Annuities according to payment arrangement: Annuity products can be categorized as per the nature of purchase payment like *Single Premium Annuity*: when the cost or purchase price of annuity paid lump sum in one single payment, it is called *Single Premium Annuity.*

Regular Premium Annuity: This is also known as instalment annuity. When Premium or cost of purchase of annuity plan is paid by regular instalments it is called *Regular Premium Annuity or Instalment Annuity*: Payments, however, under this type of plans may be fixed or flexible as decided in the contact.

Annuities according to the coverage of Lives: Annuity products may be classified as per the coverage of lives under the plans. Three important categories are:

Single Life Annuity: Single life annuity covers the risk of life assured and payment of annuity or pension continues till the annuitant survives. Payments ceases on the death of the annuitant but the balance amounts, if any, are not refunded under this type of plans

Joint life annuity: Under this type of annuity plans payment of annuity does not stop with the death of first annuitant and continues till the joint annuitant survives. However, in case of joint life annuity, payment for the surviving annuitant continues at a reduced rate as per the contract.

Group Annuity: Group annuity plan covers a group of employees such as employees of a company or any recognized group on the basis of activities.

Annuities according to timings of payment: According to the timings of payments Pension Plans are classified as Immediate Annuity and Deferred Annuity:

Immediate Annuity: In case of immediate annuity plans, the annuity/pension commences immediately as per the terms of the plan but mostly within one year of having paid the premium.

Deferred Annuity: Under the Deferred Annuity Plans the commencement of annuity/pension is deferred up to a certain time as per the plans and as decided by the policyholder, which is called the deferment period. For example, if an individual buys a pension plan with tenure of 25 years (also known as the 'deferment period'), his annuity will begin 25 years hence. Premium under this policy can be paid as a single premium or as regular premium. In India, most of the pension plans are deferred annuity plans.

Phased Annuity: A series of annuities are purchased under the phased annuity programme, with staggered vesting. Phased annuity can take care of timing problems in mandatory annuity. Phased annuities if carefully purchased can provide benefit of income maximization as one can take advantage market decline when annuity prices are low.

Annuities according to Payout Duration: According to payout duration annuities may be categorized as:

Temporary Annuity: Under this type of plans annuitants receive pension/annuity payments for a fixed period or until his/her death, whichever is earlier as per the contract.

Fixed Term or Certain Annuity: In this case Annuity payments are made for a fixed term or certain period, for example, five or ten years, irrespective of the longevity of the annuitant. This is also called Annuity with Minimum Guarantee.

Annuities according to Payout Terms: Annuities can be classified as per the terms of payout sets in the contract. These are:

Level Annuity: Very common annuity products also called Standard Annuity. Under this plan the annuitant receive a fixed amount of nominal payment during the period of annuity contact. Level Annuity pay higher income during the initial period comparing to the escalating annuity.

Escalating Annuity: Under this type of pans, annuity/pension is not fixed, but amount of annuity changes annually at a fixed rate for certain period, say after five or ten years. However initial payments under such plans are generally lower than level annuity.

Other Annuity Products: Annuities as mentioned above are quite common but there are certain other types of annuities found in the developed markets. These annuities, in addition to providing future income also perform certain specific purpose. Some such annuities products are discussed below:

Variable Annuity: Variable Annuities (also called Investment Linked Annuities) are most attractive retirement annuity, particularly in developed market like USA. They provide twin benefits of insurance and investment. A variable annuity contract provides regular payments by the annuity provider to the annuitant for the life time and even at a guaranteed rate as per the contact. A variable annuity can be purchased by a single payment or by a series of payments. There are two types of variable annuities, namely, *Immediate Variable Annuity* under which an annuitant starts receiving annuity immediately and *Deferred Variable Annuity* under which payments are deferred for a stipulated period. Under the deferment period, assets get accumulated and invested and therefore annuity payments may be higher than immediate annuity option. Investment options under variable annuity are quite flexible and funds are invested in different financial instruments like equity, bonds, etc., return from investment fluctuates depending on the underlying securities. The risk is higher in variable annuity because of wider investment choice. This risk is borne by the investors and not by insurers. Variable annuity may also offers death benefits, tax deferred earnings growth.

A Variable annuity plan has got two phases, namely, accumulation phase and payout phase. While at the accumulation phase an investor allocates investment option through purchase price, at the payout phase she/he receive a stream of income.

Equity Indexed Annuity: Equity indexed annuities are basically investment products with life insurance benefits. The payout in equity index annuity linked to price variation of underlying stocks. Equity index annuity guarantee a minimum payment if the contract holds till maturity and also pay a part of the capital appreciation of the underlying stock index. The equity index annuity was first launched in the US in 1995 and since then grown significantly.

Price Index Linked Annuity: Under this type of plan Annuity/Pension amount are linked to the Retail/Consumer Price index of the country. Annuity providers invest the premium in indexed linked bonds and the coupon payments are used to make payments for annuity. There can be *Limited Price Index Linked Annuity* which partially compensates changes in price, but annuity payment varies only up to a certain percentage *Point*.

Unit Linked Annuities: Unit Linked Annuities are another type of investment linked annuities; retirement income being directly linked to the value of underlying investment fund. There are various types of unit linked fund mostly into three types of risk characteristic, namely, High Risk Funds, Medium Risk Funds and Low Risk Funds. Risk Characteristics, however, determined by the underlying securities in the fund which impact the pattern of income growth. There are high, medium and low risk linked funds. High Risk Funds primarily invest in equity and equity-related stocks with potential to provide higher income. Medium Risk Funds are mostly the balanced funds having invested in low-risk Bond/Debt stocks and high-risk equity stocks, while Low Risk Funds primarily invest in Low risk Bonds/Debt stocks. Generally, Unit linked annuities do not offer any guaranteed income. In India, Life Insurance Companies offer various types of annuity products as Pension Annuity in two phases, namely, Accumulation and Payout, while investors make payment during a particular period (accumulation period). At the end of accumulation period, they can commute one third of accumulated amount as tax-free withdrawal and balance to be used to purchase an annuity policy from any life insurance company.

Annuity with Capital Protection: Annuities with capital protection allows the annuitant to receive regular annuity till she/he is alive. However, after the death of annuitant, the balance capital amount is paid to the annuitant's legal nominee or heir. The balance amount can be refunded either as lump sum cash enhanced annuity as per contract.

Impaired Life Annuities: Impaired Annuity products are being offered in many developed markets. These instruments can take the form of an enhanced annuity. Impaired life annuity policy provides higher annuity to an annuitant having health (like cancer, heart attack, etc.) or lifestyle (like smoking, overweight, etc.) problems which reduce the lifespan and therefore qualify the annuitant to receive higher pension/annuity.

Annexure 10A.2: Annuity Service Providers under NPS

In the month of August 2011, PFRDA has floated an Expression of Interest (EOI). Invitation for expression of interest from IRDA-licensed life insurers for acting as designated Annuity Service Providers and for providing annuity products to the National Pension Scheme (NPS) subscribers. The following annuity options are indicated in the PFRDA advertisement:

❖ OPTION I

The Monthly Pension/Annuity: should be paid to the subscriber for life and, upon death of subscriber, the monthly annuity shall be paid to the family members.

A. *Deferred Annuity*: Same as above with the difference being that *the annuity will be purchased well before the age of 60 years* and the payment of monthly pension/annuity needs to begin upon attainment of 60 years for non-government employees and at the retirement age as stipulated, for government employee *or* at an age prior to this.

❖ OPTION II

A. *The Monthly Pension/Annuity* should be paid to the subscriber for life and upon death of subscriber the monthly annuity (100 per cent) shall be paid to the spouse of the subscriber for life and upon the death of such spouse the purchase price of the annuity to be returned to the legal heirs of the subscriber.
B. *The Monthly Pension/Annuity* should be paid to the subscriber for life and upon death of subscriber the monthly annuity (60 per cent) shall be paid to the spouse of the subscriber for life and upon the death of such spouse the purchase price of the annuity be returned to the legal heirs of the subscriber.
C. *Deferred Annuity*: Same as A and B above with the difference being that the annuity will be purchased well before the age of 60 years and the payment of monthly pension/annuity needs to begin upon attainment of 60 years for non-government employees and at the retirement age as stipulated, for government employee *or* at an age prior to this.

❖ OPTION III

A. *Monthly Annuity* as per Option I and with Annuity increasing at a simple rate of 5, 6 or 7 per cent or any other option on similar lines.
B. *Deferred Annuity*: Same as above with the difference being that the annuity will be purchased well before the age of 60 years and the payment of monthly pension/

annuity needs to begin upon attainment of 60 years for on-government employees and at the retirement age as stipulated, for government employee *or* at an age prior to this.

❖ OPTION IV

A. *Monthly Annuity as per Option II* and with Annuity increasing at a simple rate of 5, 6 or 7 per cent or any other option on similar lines.
B. *Deferred Annuity*: Same as above with the difference being that the annuity will be purchased well before the age of 60 years and the payment of monthly pension/ annuity needs to begin upon attainment of 60 years for non-government employees and at the retirement age as stipulated, for government employee *or* at an age prior to this.

❖ OPTION V

A. *Annuity Plans with Impairment Annuity as an Option*
B. *Deferred Annuity*: Same as above with the difference being that the annuity will be purchased well before the age of 60 years and the payment of monthly pension/ annuity needs to begin upon attainment of 60 years for on-government employees and at the retirement age as stipulated, for government employee *or* at an age prior to this.

❖ OPTION VI

A. Inflation indexed annuity plans
B. *Deferred Annuity*: Same as above with the difference being that the annuity will be purchased well before the age of 60 years and the payment of monthly pension/ annuity needs to begin upon attainment of 60 years for non-government employees and at the retirement age as stipulated, for government employee *or* at an age prior to this.

❖ OPTION VII

Any other annuity type designed or proposed by the life insurer for this purpose (these options are tentative and PFRDA is at liberty to choose any or all the options or any other option that it deems fit, without assigning any reason).

REFERENCES

Antolin, P. and H. Blommestein (2007), 'Governments and the Market for Longevity-Indexed Bonds'. OECD Working Paper Series on Insurance and Private Pensions No. 4.

Antolin, P., C. Pugh and F. Stewart (2008), 'Forms of Benefit Payment at Retirement'. *OECD Working Papers on Insurance and Private Pensions*, No. 26, OECD publishing, © OECD. doi:10.1787/238013082545

Blake, David (1999), 'Annuity Markets: Problems and Solutions', *The Geneva Papers on Risk and Insurance*, vol 24, No. 3, July 1999.

Doyle, Suzanne and John Piggott (2002), 'Mandatory Annuity Design in Developing Economies'. Social Protection Discussion Paper Series No. 0208, May 2002.

Hawksworth, John and Anmol Tiwari (2011), 'The World in 2050'. Price Waterhouse Coopers LLP, London.

Heller, Peter S. (1998), Rethinking Public Pension Reform Initiatives. IMF Working Paper, International Monetary Fund.

Impavido, Gregorio and Roberto Rocha (2006), 'Competition and Performance in the Hungarian Second Pillar'. Policy Research Working Paper Series 3876, The World Bank.

IRDA (2010), 'Annual Report 2009-10'. Insurance Regulatory and Development Authority.

James, Estelle and Renuka Sane (2003), 'The Annuity Market in India: Do Consumers Get Their Money's Worth? What are the key Public Policy Issues?' *Economic and Political Weekly*, 22 February 2003.

James, Estelle and Xue Song (2001), 'Annuities Markets around the World: Money's Worth and Risk Intermediation'. Technical Report, CERP Working Paper 16/01.

Jens, Thomsen (Governor) and Jens Verner Andersen (2007), 'Longevity Bonds—A Financial Market Instrument to Manage Longevity Risk', *Monetary Review*, 4th Quarter. Available at: http://www.oecd.org/dataoecd/56/9/41668679.pdf

Orszag, Mike and Mirko Cardinale (2002), 'Paying Out Private Pension in Latin America'. Watson Wyatte Technical Report, December 2002.

Palmer, E. (2000), 'The Swedish Pension Reform Model: Framework and Issues'. World Bank Social Protection Discussion Paper 0012, June 44.

Poirson, Helen K. (2007), 'Financial Market Implications of India's Pension Reform'. IMF Working Paper, WP/07/85, Asia and Pacific Department, International Monetary Fund. Available at: http://fic.wharton.upenn.edu/fic/india/15poirson.pdf

RBI (2011), 'Annual Report 2010-11' Reserve Bank of India, Mumbai.

Rocha, Roberto, Dimitri Vittas and Heinz P. Rudolph (2011) 'Annuities and Other Retirement Products—Designing the Payout Phase'. The International Bank for Reconstruction and Development/The World Bank.

Rofman, Rafael P. (2001). 'Annuitization in Pension Schemes—The Case of Argentina'. Seminar for Actuaries and Statisticians, 21–22 November at Montevideo, International Social Security Association.

Rusconi, R. (2008), 'National Annuity Markets: Features and Implications'. OECD Working Papers on Insurance and Private Pensions, No. 24, OECD publishing, OECD.doi:10.1787/240211858078

Sadhak, H. (2009), *Life insurance in India-Opportunities, Challenges and Strategic Perspective.* SAGE Response: New Delhi.

SEBI–NCAER (2001), 'Survey of Indian Investors (2000–01)'. SEBI, Mumbai 2001.

Shukla, Rajesh (2008), 'How India Earns, Spends and Saves: Results from the Max New York Life', NCAER India Financial Protection Survey.

Sigma (No. 3/2007), 'Annuities: A private solution to longevity risk', *Economic Research & Consulting*, Swiss Re Insurance Company Ltd., Zurich, Switzerland.

——— (2011), 'World insurance in 2011' Swiss Re, Sigma No 2/2011.

SOA (2001), 'Retirement Risk Survey: Key Findings'. Available at: http://www.soa.org/sections/retirement/framework.html

Stewart, Fiona (2007), 'Policy Issues for Developing Annuity'. OECD Working Papers on Insurance and Private Pensions No 2. OECD Publishing.

Valdes-Prieto, Salvador (1998), 'Risk in Pensions and Annuities: Efficient Design'. Social Protection Unit, Human Development Network, The World Bank. Available at: http://www.worldbank.org/sp

Vittas, Dimitri, Heinz Rudolph, John Pollner (2010), 'Designing the Pay Out Phase of Funded Pension Pillars in Central and Eastern European Countries'. Policy Research Working Paper 5276, The World Bank, Europe and Central Asia Region, Private and Financial Sector Development Department and Central Europe and the Baltic Country Department, April 2010.

Xiao, Y Julia and Yingbin Xiao (2009), 'Adequacy of Bond Supply and Cost of Pension Benefits: A Financial Economics Perspective, SOA Research Projects in Pension. Available at: http://papers.ssrn.com/sol3/papers.cfm?abstract_id=1447526

11 Pension Products, Default Option and Public Policy

INTRODUCTION

The primary motive of saving through pension plans is to receive regular flow of income in the post-retirement period or in the old age. Present saving for future consumption comes at a cost of squeezing current income by different *risk tolerance levels.* Therefore, the *secondary objectives* of pension fund investing are dictated by safety, security and growth. Investors with higher income and higher risk tolerance levels may prefer pension plans containing higher risks, while investors with low level of risk tolerance would prefer even lower growth but better safety and security of investment. Therefore, there should be a basket of pension products to satisfy the varied needs of the investors. Another significant issue related to pension plans is the portfolio choice, that is, how to select an appropriate pension portfolio depending on the individual need and limit of risk tolerance. In an individual account based pension system, choice is left to the investors, which is called active choice. An investor can select a plan most suitable for her/him. However, in reality active choice is very difficult and thus often the plan selection is left to the PFMs which are called a default option. Active choice is a risk-based asset allocation, while default option is an age-based asset allocation. Default option is structurally a pre-determined portfolio which is based on the age of an investor, but the portfolio goes on changing with the increase in the age of the investors. Default option is thus an alternative investment approach to the active choice of portfolio selection in a defined contribution pension plan. Due to a variety of reasons, when someone is unable to take an active decision, she/he may leave it to the professional fund manager under a default option having an outline of pre-determined pattern of asset allocation and often have legislative support to the default option. In a default option, asset allocation is based on age instead of risk, as in the case of active choice. In a default option portfolio, portfolio risks tend to be reduced gradually as the investment terms get nearer. However, it must be remembered that in both the cases, investment risks are transferred to the investors. In an active choice, investors directly select the portfolio having different risk contents, while in a default option, investors have fairly good idea about the portfolio risk contents, but future risks remain uncertain.

TYPES OF PENSION PLANS

Pension plans/products are primarily identified by the investment and asset allocation pattern imposed by the quantitative restriction and regulatory mechanism in case of both DB and DC pension systems. From the point of view of investment decision, funds are often identified as active choice funds, where investment decisions are actively taken by the investors but in case of default option most often investment decisions and selection of funds are left to PFMs who manage a pre-determined investment portfolio. Funds are also classified as risk-based investing funds and age-based investing funds. In case of former, investment decisions are driven by the risk tolerance level of the investors through active choice and in case of the latter, investment decisions are driven by the age profile related to the implicit risk perception and risk tolerance level of the investors.

Growth of pension business and pension market has also encouraged innovation in pension products. A variety of funds are available for retirement investing. However, most wide variation in the pension market has been observed in respect of pension plans and products in developed countries like the US, UK, Sweden, etc. For example, in the US where DB and DC system exists simultaneously, a large number of plans like DB plans, DC plans, hybrid and cash balance plans, qualified retirement plans, simple IRAs, SEP IRAs, 'HR 10' or Keogh plans, non-qualified plans, etc., are in existence. There are also a number of investment plans under DC schemes, which are mostly the combination of risks and returns of different degrees. There are equity-oriented schemes, debt-oriented schemes, balanced schemes, and government security-oriented schemes. These plans are operated by pension funds and mutual funds. There are a variety of pension plans in the pension market but we may categorise these plans into two categories, that is, active choice pension funds and default option pension funds.

Active Choice/Risk-based Investment Funds

These are primarily risk-based funds akin to mutual funds products. There are a variety of funds but few most important fund types are:

❖ EQUITY FUNDS

These are high-risk/high-return funds, and portfolio may consist even up to 100 per cent of equity and equity-related instruments. Investors having higher risk tolerance ability and interested in high growth prefer these funds.

❖ DEBT FUNDS

Debt Funds can be purely government debt security (G Sec) funds, corporate debt funds or hybrid funds having both G Sec and corporate debt instruments in the portfolio. Debt funds are less risky and may generate lower return than equity funds. Investors with lower risk tolerance and more interested in safety of capital prefer these types of funds.

❖ BALANCED FUNDS

Balanced Funds are somewhere in between equity and debt funds in terms of risks and returns. Portfolio of such funds may consist of 50 per cent equity and 50 per cent debt instruments or some mixture of the both, which may generate return higher than the debt funds but lower than the equity funds. Similarly, risk contents of such funds are higher than the debt funds but lower than the equity funds.

Active choice funds primarily follow the risk-based investment strategy and the fund managers focus on risk-adjusted return through portfolio diversification, like mutual funds. Mutual funds investment and asset allocation is basically driven by the concept of mean variance analysis, which lay emphasis upon risk minimisation through portfolio diversification over a single period and the same assets are maintained in the portfolio irrespective of changes in risk tolerance level of an investors based on age factor. Risk-based investing does not consider age-based risk and therefore, fails to take care of risk that is associated with retirement investing. This deficiency of active risk-based investment gave room for age-based investment, which is considered to be a better concept and a better solution for retirement investment.

Default Option/Age-based Investment Funds

In general, the basic principle of investment is the age-based investment rather than risk-based investment as in the case of active choice, though some risk-based investment funds are broadly categorised as *default option funds.* Under this category there are a variety of funds, some funds having risk-based portfolios and some having age-based, but both types of funds follow diversification of portfolio for risk minimisation and achieving growth. The important fund types in this category are Life Style Funds, Life Cycle Funds, Target Dated Funds, etc., catering to investors with different risk perception and level of risk tolerance. However, such wide varieties of fund are usually present in the US market but not in the emerging market countries like in Latin America, Eastern Europe, etc.

❖ LIFE STYLE FUNDS

Life Style Funds are often termed as default funds, which follow diversified investment portfolio but rebalancing is carried out periodically. However, risk exposure of such funds remains more or less the same. According to Viceira (2007), 'the main characteristics of Life Style Funds is that they change the stock exposure of the fund as a function of investors risk tolerance whereas Life Cycle fund reduce the stock exposure of the fund as their target maturity date approach.' These are basically mutual funds and are found mostly in the US market.

❖ LIFE CYCLE FUNDS

In many respects, Life Cycle Funds reflect the Life Style Funds and aim at maximising portfolio return through diversification. But these funds are distinctly different from Life Style Funds in terms of risk perception. Life Cycle Funds are age-based asset allocation funds and portfolio gets readjusted not with the changes in the market but with the changing age profile of investors. Portfolios are pre-determined, indicative of assumed risks. According to Kintzel (2007), 'The General Life Cycle proposition calls for investment portfolios that hold a decreasing proportion of assets in equities (associates with higher risk) and a greater proportion in fixed return investments (associated with lower risk) as an individual ages.' Since Life Cycle Funds are age-based, a higher proportion of assets are invested in equity at the initial stage and gradually tend towards low-risk assets like bonds and cash to maintain a fair level of risk exposure over the long period of investment.

❖ TARGET DATED FUND

Target Dated Funds are also called Target Dated Retirement Funds launched by Mutual Funds. There are two main types of Target Dated Funds, Risk Life Cycle Funds and Target Dated Life Cycle Funds. Risk Life Cycle Funds are usually risk-based funds and can be in the form of Aggressive Funds, Moderate Funds and Conservative Funds. An investor can select one of them on the basis of risk profile and risk tolerance. These are not age-based retirement funds. Target Dated Life Cycle Retirement Funds are simple investment instruments, for retirement savings. There can be a series of funds specifying different retirement dates with pre-determined portfolio composition. An investor can select a fund depending on his/her date of retirement. Like general Life Cycle Funds, Portfolio is based on age-related risk perception, that is, risk tolerance diminishes with advancement of age and towards the date of retirement. Target Dated Funds contain two portfolios: one is growth (shares) and the other safe (bonds) assets. However, the

Retirement Date Directed Funds do not normally follow any uniform age pattern. At the end of 2006, there were 168 Target Dated Funds with assets of $109 billion which had grown to 226 funds having assets worth of $164 billion by 31 October 2007, which represent 35 per cent increase in number of funds and 50 per cent increase in assets (Surz 2012).

IMPORTANCE OF DEFAULT OPTION INDIVIDUAL ACCOUNT BASED FUNDS

The DC pension system characterised by self-financing and risk sharing by the employees (or members), emphasises upon active participation of individual by exercising choice—choice of PFM, choice of investment plan, choice of asset allocation, etc. Ideally, an investor should take informed investment decision through active participation, since the risk tolerance and return requirements and time horizon of investment differs from investor to investor. However, very often, this does not happen and the members may be unable to select a fund or fund manager, due to lack of understanding, paucity of time, etc., and these are left to someone. Cronqvist and Thaler (2004) in their study of Retirement Funds in Sweden have observed that when the Social Security was privatised in Sweden (in 2000), 43.3 per cent of new participants chose the default plan for retirement savings, despite the fact that 456 plans were available for selection. This percentage further increased to 91.6 per cent after three years, in spite of several attempts by the government to motivate employees to choose specific plans. In recent times, American employees are going in a big way to select default option for retirement savings. In their study, Choi et al. (2002) observed that in the US, between 42 and 71% participants accept the default contribution rate and between 48 and 81% of plan assets are invested in default fund. The same trend is also noted in UK. A study conducted by the consulting firm Hewitt Bacon and Woodrow observed that 80 per cent of the members of group personal pension schemes in UK accepted the default option provided by the plans (Bridgeland 2002). Pension Decision Research, a pension research company in the US, after studying 31 large plans across eight different sectors found that 80 per cent of employees favoured default funds rather than alternatives put forward by their employers. In the US, where Life Cycle and Life Style Funds are used as Default, Funds have grown significantly during recent times. ICI Research Fundamentals (July 2007) has reported that the assets in these funds have grown by 50 per cent in 2006 to $303 after rising 57 per cent in 2005. Most of the mutual funds in the US providing retirement plans experienced the growing phenomenon of preference for default funds. For example, Fidelity has more than doubled its life cycle assets since the end of September 2005 and managed $91 billion in May 2008.

Asset allocation is a technical job requiring wide spectrum of knowledge in economic and financial parameters, understanding of duration and timing for rebalancing of assets risk assessment in respect of financial instruments and total portfolio, etc.

In fact, in a highly developed literate country like the US, the employees find it difficult to take decision to select a fund for their savings plan. Survey of DC Savings Plan in the US conducted by John Hancock Services (2002) reported that 38 per cent of respondents have little or no financial knowledge, 40 per cent respondents reported that they believe money market funds contain stocks and two thirds of respondents did not know that it was possible to lose money in government bonds. However, it is improper to think that a large number of investors as indicated above do not understand economic and financial parameters to take asset allocation and investment decision. Probably there may be something else inducing investors to prefer default plans.

Similar trend was also observed in Japan in a survey on financial literacy conducted by the Pension Fund Association of Japan in 2007 among the DC plan sponsors and participants. The survey found that principal guaranteed products account over 50 per cent assets while investment trusts' share accounts for 4.5 per cent of total assets. It was further noted that 53.2 per cent respondents do not understand how DC plans work. This shows why it is so difficult for any employee to select an appropriate investment plan for their retirement savings and default effects in 401(K) plan and self-control problems. The complexity of asset allocation also leads the employee to delay enrolment—this has been noted by Iyengar, Hebarman and Jiang (2004). They also observed a negative relationship between number of funds offered in 401(k) plan and 401(K) participation rate. More the funds, less the participation rate and less the funds, more the participation. Viceira (2007) has observed that 'a large number of DC plan participants, particularly among those with lower levels of education, wealth and income show a considerable degree of inertia, in their contribution and investment decision'. Behavioural Economics has forwarded some explanation through non-standard theory of self-control problems. Della Vigna (2007), in the pioneering research paper 'Psychology and Economics', mentioned, 'Evidence from the field observed that individual preferences are assumed to be time consistent and independent of the framing of the decision—but laboratory experiment shows that the decisions are time—inconsistent.' All these observations show that the standard perception of rational informed decision-making by the investors is not necessarily true in retirement investment decision. Researches and behavioural economists have attempted to trace the reasons for reluctance/avoiding to take active decision by the investors. The most important factors seemed to be lack of financial/macroeconomic knowledge, time constraints, information overload, decision inertia, etc. Some of the important factors are:

Lack of Financial Knowledge: Relatively low level of financial knowledge is an impediment to select pension products with long-term return implications.

Lack of Macroeconomics Knowledge: Financial Market movement is significantly influenced by long-term macroeconomic trend and business cycles. These are technical and complicated phenomena and often difficult to predict even by a financial analyst. An ordinary employ may be confused while analysing them.

Time Constraints: It is often time-consuming to analyse the various macrofinancial parameters to understand the financial market and long-term delivery of returns of various financial instruments.

Decision Inertia: It is often seen that members often do not actively exercise their option to select a fund simply due to inertia to take a decision, though they may be having time to take active decision and knowledge to select a fund.

Wide Range of Financial Products: It is also observed that investors/members get confused with availability of a number of funds and lots of funds-related information, due to information overloads.

In view of the factors mentioned above and due to other reasons, the regulators, particularly in emerging markets, moved very cautiously in designing pension products. During the first two decades of pension reforms in Chile, participants were not allowed to exercise active choice of fund selection, and in 2002, the fund managers were allowed to offer only five investment options. Mexico introduced a still more conservative approach. There are only two investment options for the participants in the new pension system. In order to overcome these constraints of DC pension, attention has been diverted towards default option, which provides some answers to the choice-related problems.

LIFE CYCLE INVESTMENT IN DEFAULT OPTION

In spite of the proliferation in number of plans, the most popular pension plan in the US and many other countries like the UK, Sweden, etc., default option has emerged as the most popular pension plan. Default option is a variant of Life Cycle Funds used for enhancing retirement savings and risk-adjusted returns in a DC pension system. The concept of Life Cycle Funds is basically built upon the theory of Life Cycle consumption and Life Cycle Portfolio choice, which help in designing financial plans for retirement savings. Concept of life cycle savings is centred on, among others, the age of the investors which is a determinant of risk tolerance limit. The model assumes that age of the investors has a significant implication on the risk exposure; as such risk exposure tends to reduce with an ageing investor. Life Cycle Portfolio model also broadly provides guidance to investors about present and future savings and investing; therefore, it is a great help to our investors, to plan retirement savings and investment. Bodie et al. (2007) emphasised upon Life Cycle Portfolio approach for such retirement savings plan. They distilled three principles from the Life Cycle approach which are essentially cornerstone of Life Cycle Consumption and investment. According to the first principle, the focus is not on the financial plan itself, but on the consumption profile. Second principle implies financial assets as vehicles for moving consumption from one location in the Life Cycle to another, while according to the third principle, money is more valuable to an investor in a low-consumption situation than in a high-consumption situation. Future consumption, however, does not depend on the current savings only but on total wealth. Total wealth is the sum total of savings and human wealth, which is the present discounted value of the future expected earnings. Therefore, in any default pension plan built upon Life Cycle savings and consumption, the consideration of total wealth needs to be reflected.

Default Option and Age-based Investment

It has been indicated earlier that investing strategy and asset allocation assumption is a default option based on the age of an investor, as it has a direct bearing on the financial risk tolerance level of an investor. Therefore, its focus on the age of investors and the horizon of investment, and the model is called age-based investing as against risk-based investing by mutual funds and asset management companies. The age-based time horizon investment model is also influenced by human capital concept, which signifies that it enhances the risk tolerance level of investors over the risk level which can be supported by current financial savings. Life Cycle Funds thus create a portfolio with higher allocation in equities at the initial years but gradually shifts towards bonds and cash as the years pass and the investors move towards the date of retirement. As the risk-based asset allocation, which is usually undertaken in a mean variance framework, may not take care of retirement savings objectives, some experts have suggested an alternative investing model based on time horizon of investment and on the assumption that the long-term equity investing is safe and provide better return. A study on default investment options in DC plans in Australia by Basu and Drew (2006) reports that strategies with higher allocation to stocks can be expected to result in higher wealth outcomes for participants; downside risk of falling short of target wealth outcomes reduces with increased allocation to stocks. The study of Basu and Drew revealed, '[V]ery high allocations to stocks may actually prove to be less risky on most occasion if risk is viewed in the context of falling short of the participant's wealth accumulation target, in terms of probability and magnitude of shortfall.'

However, Viceira (2007) has noted that the annualised volatility of real or inflation-adjusted US stock returns appears to decline with holding horizons, from about 16 per cent per annum at a one-year horizon, to about 8 per cent per annum at a horizon of 25 years. Further, though equity investing for retirement income is widely advocated, some studies indicate that risk apprehension of equity investing keeps many household away from large exposure. Daniele Fano (2005) has observed that the direct and indirect stock ownership was very low across the industrialised nations. Accordingly,

> *only 15 per cent of French households owned stock directly and 23 per cent indirectly through mutual funds and other instruments in the late nineties. The corresponding figures are 19 per cent and 48 per cent for the USA, 27 per cent and 34 per cent for the UK, 7 per cent and 15 per cent for Italy.*

This is an indication of risk perception of household about equity which should act as an eye-opening fact for those who vehemently argue for equity-centric retirement products for NPS.

Allocating Assets in an Age-based Default Option

There are several innovative Life Cycle Default Option Plans in the US and other countries based on a variety of assumptions, but mostly focusing on the age-based allocation in equities. Kintzel (2007) has cited four life cycle approaches. Most popularly known as Thumb of Rule approaches '100 Minus Age'. This Rule dictates that equity portion would be an amount equivalent to 100–Age. If age of an investor is 30 years, the equity in the portfolio would be 70 per cent (100–30). This has been extended further to '110 Minus Age', '120 Minus Age' by many financial planners. Similarly, there is another thumb rule, 'Your Age in Bond' which dictates the per cent of bond in portfolio would be equivalent to the age of investor, that is, if the age of an investor is 30, the bond in the portfolio would be 30 per cent. In fact, this is similar to age minus equity rule. Hickman et al. (2001) analyse 'Your Age in Bond' by using Monte Carlo simulation. There are several other studies by eminent authors on how to determine allocation of assets for retirement funding. The Shillar Plan (2005) is a life cycle model that is aggressive at young age and tending to be conservative at later age.

Asset Allocation in Target Date Retirement Funds

One of the important variants of Default Life Cycle Fund is Target Retirement Dated Funds; these are very popular in the US and were launched by mutual funds. For example, Fidelity Retirement 2015 Fund and Fidelity Retirement 2035 Fund, Vanguard Retirement 2015 Fund and Vanguard Retirement 2035 Fund, T Row Price Retirement 2015 Fund and T Row Price Retirement 2035 fund, Fidelity Freedom 2015 Fund and Fidelity Freedom 2035 Fund, etc., are Life Cycle Funds that were launched in November 2003. While the Fidelity 2015 was launched for the employees who would retire between 2013 and 2017, Fidelity 2035 was launched for those who would retire between 2033 and 2037. Vanguard Target dated 2015 and 2035 funds are Life Cycle Balanced Funds, both were launched in October for those who would retire between 2013–2017 and 2033 and 2037, respectively. T Row Price 2015 Retirement Fund and T Row Price Retirement Fund 2035 were launched in February 2004 for the people who would retire in 2015 and 2035, respectively. Both the Funds seek the highest total return over time, consistent with an emphasis on objective of the fund, which is capital growth and income to achieve by investing in a diversified portfolio of T. Rowe Price Stock and Bond Funds.

Though in general, portfolio of Target Dated Funds consists of stocks, bonds cash, etc., Jennings and Reichenstein (2007) observed in their study of four US Life Cycle Funds that portfolio consists of US stocks, international assets, US high yield bonds, US high grade bonds, and cash plus short-term bonds. They have also noted that that these funds follow fixed weight strategy, though in some funds target asset allocation slowly changes with time, the actual allocation is not allowed to deviate materially from the target allocation at any point of time (Vanguard), and some funds allow its target asset allocation to be based on perceived market prospects (T Row Price). Further, the composition of the portfolios changes over time from higher weight from equity to bond. The funds asset allocation strategy tends to be more conservative over time. Since the Life Cycle Funds have inverse relationship between the age and risk profile of an investor, risk weight in Target Dated Funds changes as the retirement date approaches. There will be higher percentage of risky assets in Target Dated Funds with distant retirement date than in a fund nearer to the date of retirement.

PUBLIC POLICY FOR DEFAULT OPTION AND ASSET ALLOCATION

Often there is a debate among the policymakers and investment experts whether there should be any public policy about the nature and structure of default option in DC pension plans or it should be left to fund management companies and market participants. Majority opinion, however, favours the regulatory guidelines in the form of public policy keeping in view the critical importance of pension savings in the life of retiree and the fact that entire asset allocation choice is left to the funds. The public policy aims at protecting interest of investors selecting default option by providing guidelines on product design and asset allocation pattern. The public policy also focuses on quantitative restrictions on asset allocation and required changes in the portfolio over a period of time depending on changing age profile which influences the risk tolerance level of subscribers/members. The public policy is therefore an attempt to put in place an age-based investment model in place of risk-based model. Other objective of such regulation is to moderate risk-return profile, so that safety security and return of the fund is protected. We may examine the nature of such policies in some countries.

Chile

In Chile, the legislative measures for default funds are linked to the age of the members. There are five funds, differentiated by the limit of equity investment. Maximum and minimum equity investment in Fund A is 80 per cent and 40 per cent, while for Fund B, it is 60 per cent and 25 per cent, for Fund C it is 40 per cent and 15 per cent and for Fund D it is 20 per cent and 5 per cent. Fund B is mainly a fixed income securities fund.

The rule divides the members into three age groups and allows default investment in B, D and C type of Funds.

Fund B: Assigned to men and women below 35 years of age.
Fund C: Assigned to men between 36–35 years and women between 30–50 years of age.
Fund D: Assigned to men older than 56 years and women older than 51 years of age.

Default option asset structure in Chile shows that a significant percentage of assets (34.2 per cent to 15 per cent) can be invested in foreign securities, while investment in equity varies from 17.3 per cent to 8.9 per cent. However, overwhelming percentage of assets invested in public and private bonds and investment tend to move to become highly conservative from Fund B to Fund D.

Mexico

In Mexico, AFORES are the private companies which manage individual accounts and investment management companies called SFEROEs. There are two types of default funds called SIEFORE Basica. All workers who are below 56 years of age are assigned SIEFORE Basica-2, while workers who are 56 years or more can be assigned SIEFORE Basica-1.

Peru

Although in Peru there is no default fund, the workers who do not specify choice can be assigned one of the three different funds on the basis of age groups. Members who are younger than 60 years are assigned to mixed fund (higher equities) and those who are above 60 years will be assigned to conservative fund (higher fixed income).

Sweden

Sweden introduced the contribution-based DC system of financial accounts, or the FDC system administered by Premium Pension Authority (PPM). Insured may choose a maximum of five different funds, approved by FDC. There were 744 funds. However, when an individual does not choose a fund, her/his contribution is deposited in a default fund, called *Seventh AP Fund*, which is an independent government agency. 'This fund, which has broad discretion in the allocation of investments, has invested about 90 percent in equities and 10 percent in bonds' (Sattergren 2005). Further evidence showed that in Sweden the per cent of active choosers was steadily falling since

2000, when the first time such request to choose a fund was sent to the individuals. The per cent of active choosers sharply fell from 66 in 2000 to 8 in 2003.

Australia

In Australia, regulatory requirements call for trustees to identify a default strategy whenever an investment choice is offered to standard employee-sponsored members and most of the superannuation funds have default option—which is basically a balanced fund following a balanced diversified portfolio—spreading investment across the regions and across the instruments. There is no age-based portfolio differentiation but a wide range of instruments have been included in the portfolio with relatively higher weightage to stocks (Australian and international shares).

It can be noted from the asset allocation data that *Chilean and Mexican default fund* allocation give higher weight to the age factor. Accordingly, lower the age group, higher the asset allocated to instrument like equity in default portfolio of Chile, which, however, gradually reduces with the increase in age of the employees. For higher age group more weight is given to low-risk debt instruments. Chilean default plans also allowed international investment for better diversification. Mexican default portfolio on the other hand basically weighed in favour of public securities and does not allow investment in foreign securities.

US

The Pension Protection Act in the US requires that the Department of Labour (DOL) provide fiduciary protection for default investment in DC plan. In the light of this provision, DOC issued the regulation for Qualified Default Investment Alternatives (QDIA). According to this regulation, Default Funds would include diversified portfolios including balanced funds; Life Cycle or Target Dated Funds and managed accounts. Accordingly, the Sponsors must fulfil the requirement to be a QDIA, assets must be invested in QDIA, participants and beneficiaries would be given an opportunity to give directions, participants and beneficiaries to be given an explanatory notice and also materials such as investment prospectus, the plan should offer a broad range of investment alternatives and fees should not exceed a certain limit. Default options are also legalised in many other countries including Italy, Russia, Slovakia, etc.

Default Option in NPS

In NPS, there are two choices, namely, active choice and auto choice. Auto choice is nothing but the default option which also incorporates life cycle investing strategy. *Auto*

Choice has been designed for those investors who are not in a position to exercise active choice. Auto choice fund has a predetermined portfolio which balances risk tolerance based on the age of the investors. In auto choice life cycle default option, investment in higher risk class assets like equity gradually declines along with increasing age of the investors. For example, initial pattern of allocation (up to the age of 35 years) includes 50 per cent in asset class E (equity), 30 per cent in asset class C (corporate debt) and 20 per cent in asset class G (government securities). The proportion of asset classes E and C in the portfolio gradually declines to 10 per cent at the age of 55 years, while the proportion of asset class G tends to increase to 80 per cent at the age of 55 years. Auto choice is thus an age-based risk adverse investment portfolio, quite natural and significant for NPS.

PRODUCT PORTFOLIO OF NPS—ARGUMENTS FOR EXPANSION

A broad conceptual framework about various types of pension products and importance of default option in individual account based DC system has been briefly discussed above. Some critical areas of importance including the basis of asset allocation, investment strategy and importance of public policy and practices in some countries have also been focused on. It has been observed that default option has emerged as the single most important pension product for the largest number of investors due to several personal and institutional factors. However, one missing link of such policy is the income and risk tolerance ability of investors, which have been assumed as uniform for all such investors. Therefore, a single default option may not be able to serve the interest of investment objectives of all investors coming from heterogeneous social groups. Carroll et al. (2005), in their study *Optimal Default and Active Decision*, state, 'Defaults may be socially optimal when agents have a shared optimum and the default leads them to it. But even a well chosen default may be undesirable if agents have heterogeneous needs.' It is therefore felt that a single default model may not be sufficient for heterogeneous group of Indian investors. Moreover, risk-based active choice products like mutual funds may not necessarily serve the objectives of retirement saving. Even in risk-based funds an element of age-based assumption of allocation would be welcomed by the investors who prefer risk-based investment through active choice. Keeping these two major views in sight, we may discuss the current product portfolio of NPS including default option and the further scope for expansion.

Current NPS Product Portfolio

We have discussed about investment plans/products under NPS in Chapter 7 and noted that there are two types of products (schemes), namely, Active Choice Funds and Auto Choice Funds.

❖ ACTIVE CHOICE FUNDS

In case of government employees, there are two schemes—Scheme I, basically a balanced fund tilted towards debt investing and Scheme II, a pure debt fund (not yet operational). For All Citizens Scheme there are four options, namely, scheme (called as three asset classes) and one auto choice fund. According to the PFRDA, the pension fund managers will manage three separate schemes, each investing in a different asset class, which are listed below:

Asset class E (equity market instruments): The investment by an NPS participant in this asset class would be subject to a cap of 50 per cent. This asset class will be invested in index funds that replicate the portfolio of either BSE Sensitive index or NSE Nifty 50 index.
Asset class G (Government Securities): This asset class will be invested in central government bonds and state government bonds.
Asset class C (credit risk bearing fixed income instruments): This asset class contains bonds issued by any entity other than the central and the state government. This asset class will be invested in liquid funds of mutual funds, credit-rated debt securities which include rated bonds/securities of public financial institutions and public sector companies, rated municipal bodies/infrastructure bonds and bonds of all firms (including PSU/PSE).

Proposal for New Funds

The current product basket of NPS seems to be quite narrow, considering the heterogeneity of investors and market competition with the similar products of mutual funds and life insurance companies, as well as wide divergence of income and risk tolerance level of investors. It is therefore necessary that the regulator urgently considers to expand the product basket by including some risk products and another default option (auto choice). To start with, at least the following types of new funds can be introduced for NPS subscribers.

Life Style Fund

Active choice category must have a new risk-based Life Style Fund having features as discussed above. Asset allocation under this Life Style diversified fund can be flexible keeping the overall limit of equity investment (maximum up to 50 per cent) of portfolio, but fund managers may be allowed to rebalance the portfolio keeping the changing age profile in view. It would be a dynamic fund unlike existing active choice funds which do not consider age profile of investors while deciding investment strategy and asset allocation. Life Style Funds are basically diversified mutual funds and Indian investors are quite aware of mutual fund market. Therefore, such funds in the NPS will have easy access to the market.

Target Dated Retirement Funds

Target Dated Retirement Funds have special appeal to an important section of investors who have higher risk tolerance ability, focused on retirement income, and would retire in a particular year in future. Retirement date for all the government and public sector employees and for many private sector employees are pre-determined, and the Target Dated Funds would enable the unorganised and organised private sector employees to save for retirement.

Insurance Linked Savings and Retirement Income Fund

India is a country with low per capita income and a large segment of population has lower propensity to save specially for old age income. Even those low-income people do not have enough disposable income to save for longevity risk, old age income and short income requirement. Often they choose one among the many requirements. However, if a product can take care of all these needs, then it would be more acceptable to them; NPS should therefore consider *a Savings Insurance Pension (SIP)* product. There is provision of mandatory annuitisation in NPS but no provision for life insurance. Moreover, many low-income people may not be able to manage two portfolio—Pension (tier I) and Savings (tier II). Having these three provision would be an inducement for low-income subscribers, particularly that of NPS Lite. Most of the Latin American countries have introduced pension products with inbuilt provision of life insurance.

Low Risk Age in Bonds (Second Auto Choice Fund)

Currently available auto choice funds can invest up to 50 per cent portfolio assets in equity and rest in corporate debt instruments seem to contain a high degree of risk and may be suitable for groups having higher income and higher risk tolerance level, but may not be suitable for other groups. In view of wide divergence in income and wealth distribution, and low level of financial literacy, a *low risk debt centric auto choice fund (LRDCACF)* will serve the investors better, whose risk tolerance is low. Many unorganised sector employees depend on casual and seasonal employment, having low income and their tolerance is naturally lower than those in the organised sector, who have a regular high-pay job, and they would find this LRDCACF more suitable for them than the existing one (Sadhak 2009).

❖ RATIONALE FOR SECOND AUTO CHOICE FUND

India is a vast country with wide gap of income, earnings and saving disparity. A very large percentage of wealth, income and saving capacity are cornered by a small percentage while the vast majority has limited income and poor saving capacity. Accordingly, the risk-bearing capacity of this large section of population is very limited and a second auto choice fund instead of single one is absolutely essential. No doubt India has developed good saving habit and Indian household sector saving is the driver of domestic saving which was more than 33 per cent of GDP. During recent times, India has achieved significant improvement in GDP growth of over 8 per cent. Also, India now boasts of growing number of billionaires. However, we should not forget that more than 35 per cent of the Indian population is below the poverty line and there exists a wide inequality in household and personal wealth and income distribution. Disproportionate distribution household wealth has been indicated in a discussion paper on the World Distribution Household. Accordingly, the share of the lowest 30 per cent in household wealth was recorded as only 2.5 per cent in 2002–03, while the share of top 10 per cent was 52.9 per cent of household wealth, top 5 per cent had 38.3 per cent share of wealth and the top 1 per cent had 15.3 per cent of household wealth in India Wealth (Davis et al. 2008). In the year 2002, 46.1 per cent of total income was earned by the richest 20 per cent of the population, while the poorest 20 per cent of population earned only 8.1 per cent of total income. Gini Coefficient, an indicator used to measure inequality, was also found to be 38, (Gini coefficient [0=perfect equality; 100=perfect inequality] http://earthtrends.wri.org). A Survey conducted by SEBI-NCAER (2000–01), revealed some facts about *income distribution* pattern of households which was highly skewed as more than 59 per cent households fall in the low monthly income group of up to ₹5,000 per month. Concentration of wealth and uneven distribution of wealth reduces the size of investment market. There are a large number of risk concerned small investors without much access to financial knowledge and information and a small segment of High Net Worth Individual with higher risk tolerance, having access to financial information and knowledge.

Secondly, the large majority of low income and less literate or illiterate people will be the majority who do not have much knowledge to select a retirement fund and also fund managers are expected to opt for auto choice funds based on the assumption of same level of risk tolerance for all investors opting for such a fund, which is not a reality. Poor or low income people have less risk tolerance limit and safety and moderate growth are the prime objectives of investment. This reinforces the argument for the second auto choice fund for NPS to cater to the need of low income investors. Assuming that this class of investors have less risk tolerance ability, but at the same time, need to augment accumulated asset through age-based diversified growth of portfolio.

Feature of the Second Auto Choice Fund (Default Options) NPS

This is default option structured around age-based investment concept, portfolio being heavily biased in favour of government securities, though it contains corporate debt and equity instruments. We developed this fund keeping in view of risk return relationship that is impacted by the age factor and risk tolerance level of low-income investors. This fund can be called as a fund of *Age in Bond* Default Option due to its emphasis on Bond/Debt investing.

Asset Allocation in the Second Auto Choice Fund (Age in Bonds)

Asset Allocation under this option has been formulated on the assumption of two major considerations, namely, investment horizon and level of risk tolerance. This Option is less aggressive and tends to become more conservative in terms of asset allocation over a period of time. Asset Allocation pattern has been arrived by assuming that an investor will retire at the age of 60, she/he has lower level of Risk tolerance, is more concerned about safety and security of capital and at the same time desires to have better risk adjusted return compared to pure G Sec active choice funds (Table 11.1).

❖ LIQUIDITY CONSIDERATION

Age in Bond Fund is a low-growth high-safety fund meant for low-income investors. Due to several financial factors there may be urgent need for cash. Since debt market is not that liquid and equity market often exhibits volatility in India, 10 per cent funds are allocated for short-term investment in bank deposits, mutual funds, cash, etc.

Table 11.1 Asset Allocation under Age in Bond Fund

Age Group	*Government Bonds (A)*	*Corporate Debt (Max) (B)*	*Domestic Equity (C)*	*Cash/Other (D)*
25–35	65	(25)	25	10
35–45	75	(15)	15	10
45–55	85	(05)	05	10
55–60	90	(00)	00	10

Source: Author's assumption.

❖ EQUITY ALLOCATION

Since risk is the major concern, we began with allocation of high-risk equity first by taking Higher Age (HA) in each group and the age of Retirement (R) to determine the maximum investment in equity (R-HR). Therefore, maximum investment in equity will be 25 per cent of portfolio (60–35) for the age group of 25–35 years and so on.

❖ G SEC ALLOCATION

Allocation to the Government Securities (G Sec) will be determined after allocation to equity and allocation to liquid funds (which is constant at 10 per cent). Therefore, after investment of 25 per cent in (C) and 10 per cent (D) equivalent to 35 per cent (C+D), we have an amount of 65 per cent (100–35 per cent = B) assets to invest in government bonds for the age group of 25–35. Similarly, investment of 75 per cent may be made in government bonds for the age group of 35–45 and so on.

❖ ALLOCATION TO CORPORATE BONDS

However, for the sake of better growth some amount of funds out of the allocation for government bonds may be invested in corporate bonds by the fund managers. Since corporate bonds are riskier than government bonds, allocation to corporate bonds are proportionate to equity allocation at all stages (B = C). But this allocation to corporate bonds/debt would be out of the overall limit of bond investment; for example, out of 65 per cent allocation earmarked for government bond, 25 per cent may be allocated to corporate bonds for the age group of 25–35 years. Similarly, 5 per cent may be allocated to corporate bonds for the age group of 45–55 years.

This Age in Bond Default Life Cycle Model is designed for investors with lower level of risk tolerance. In this fund initial equity component would be higher (25 per cent), and thereafter it tends to be nil at the age of 55 and above. However, allocation to government bonds would gradually increase to 90 per cent in the age group of 55–60, but equity investment stops at the age of 55 per cent five years prior to retirement, because of uncertainty in equity market (remember 2007–08 market crash) may wipe out equity gain totally (The Opposite may also happen when market may move up during last five years of retirement, but that is uncertain and no risk to be taken for such risk averse investors.)

This is a better approach to determine a default portfolio, though it may not be totally scientific. But superior than the existing auto choice as there is no benchmark correlation between age and asset allocation. It is felt that this portfolio would better serve the need for unorganised sector, particularly those who are with low income and lower level of risk tolerance and opted for auto choice or failed to decide any active choice portfolio.

Further, a regulatory mechanism needs to be designed for allocation of auto choice funds according to the income and risk tolerance level of the investors. Fund managers must be accountable to invest according to certain laid down principles for auto choice investment and asset allocation governed by public policy and fund management regulation.

Investment Strategy

When compared with the auto choice fund as at present in the NPS, the second default option called Age in Bonds is a less aggressive investment strategy with required diversification biased in favour of bonds (debt). Rebalancing of portfolio on time scale based on age is an important feature of investment strategy, which would take care of changing risk profile of the investors. In such a predetermined model, normally the fund managers follow the strategic allocation strategy, but since the rebalancing is pre-determined, there is enough scope during the intermediate period to apply tactical asset allocation strategy by following the scientific market timing. Since Indian market very frequently exhibits volatility, we have earmarked certain amount for investing in other instruments like mutual funds, fixed deposit, cash, etc. We have also considered Investing in domestic corporate debt. However, the percentage of foreign equity will be out of overall domestic equity investment limit, and investment in domestic corporate debt will be out of the limit of the domestic government bonds.

PUBLIC POLICY AND FUND MANAGER'S ACCOUNTABILITY

In an individual account based DC pension fund, almost entire investment decision is left to the fund manager's prudence as such performance and fund return depend on the prudence, expertise and experience of the fund managers. Experience indicates that quantitative investment management regulation (as in place for NPS) cannot effectively stop non-performance, fraud and lack of integrity in general. Moreover, active involvement of the fund managers would be required once two default options are in place. Fund managers need to identify the appropriate auto choice fund (default option) on the basis of risk level of the investors determined through certain *Risk Tolerance Index* based on income, occupation and other factors. Regulators must determine such an index and the default option regulation should clearly lay down the principles of auto choice investment and allocation of auto choice funds to the investors who have neither opted for any such fund, nor exercised active choice option. Therefore, there should be strict regulatory norms supported by countries Legislation. The accountability should not only rest with the fund managers but also with the sponsor of the fund. The government also has a responsibility in seeing that the system performs well and investors' interests are protected. A comprehensive public policy and regulatory mechanism approved by the country's legislative system will induce confidence of investors and protect the interest of beneficiaries.

Pension Products and Regulatory Conflicts

One area of concern in the market of pension products is the conflict among regulators as such products are launched by life insurance companies, mutual funds, in addition to dedicated pension fund. In India life insurance companies are regulated by the Insurance Regulatory and Development Authority (IRDA), mutual funds are regulated by Securities and Exchange Board of India (SEBI), pension funds are regulated by Pension Fund Regulatory and Development Authority (PFRDA). Although product characteristics are different for pension funds launched by these companies, they are directed towards achieving similar objectives of creating retirement income for the investors. Since various costs related to fund management, administration, etc., are different, they will impact the accumulated return and final return. One concern will be introducing uniformity in costs across the funds regulated by different regulators. It happened in the past in respect of distribution costs of ULIP, which became a matter of contention between IRDA and SEBI. Therefore, a general framework pension funds feature, various costs, etc., can be decided by the regulators with necessary operational flexibility. Apart from costs, portfolio structure, asset allocation pattern, portfolio valuation, etc., should have some similar practice across the funds launched by pension funds, mutual fund and life insurance companies.

REFERENCES

Bashears John, James J Choi, David Laibson and Brigitte C. Madrian (2007), 'The Importance of Default Options for Retirement Saving Outcome: Evidence from the United States'. Available at: http://papers.ssrn.com/so/3/papers.cfm?abstruct

Basu, Anup and Michael Drew (2006), 'Appropriateness of Default Investment Options in Defined Contribution Plans: The Australian Evidence'. Available at: http://mpra.ub.uni-muenchen.de/3314

Bodie Zvi, Jonathan Treusgard and Paul William (2007), 'The Theory of Life Cycle Saving and Investing', in Public Policy Discussion Paper, (No 07–3), Federal Reserve Bank, Boston.

Bridgeland, Skyara (2002), 'Choices, Choices'. Pension Management Institute Trustee Group News, December.

Carroll, Gabriel D, James J. Choi, David Laibson, Brigitte Madrian and Andrew Metric (2005), 'Optimal Defaults and Active Decisions'. Available at: http://www.nber.org/w11074.

Choi James, David Laibson, Brigitte Madrian and Andrew Metric (2002), 'Default contribution Pensions: Plan rules,participant decisions, and the path of least resistance', in J. Poterba (ed.), *Tax Policy and the Economy*, 16. Cambridge MA: MIT Press.

Choi James, David Laibson, Brigitte Madrian and Andrew Metric (2004), 'For Better or for Worse: Default Effects and 401(K) Saving Behavior', in David Wise (ed.) *Perspectives in Economics of Aging.* Chicago: University of Chicago Press.

Cronqvist, Henrik and Richard H Thaler (2004), 'Design Choices in Privatised Social Security System: Learning from Swedish Experience'. *American Economic Review, Papers and Proceedings,* 94(2).

Della Vigna, Stefano (2007), 'Psychology and Economics: Evidence from the Field'. NBER Working Paper Series, Working Paper 13420. Available at: http://www.nber.org/papers/w13420

Fano, Deniele (2005), 'Assessing Risk in Household Portfolios: Progress and Open Issues at the Macro and Micro/Survey Level'. Luxembourg Wealth Study, S.A.DI.BA. Perugia. Available at: http://www.lisproject.org/iws/introduction/files/fanorevised.pdf

Hickman, Kent, Hugh Hunter, John Byrd, John Beck, and Will Terpening (2001), 'Life-cycle Investing, Holding Periods, and Risk'. *Journal of Portfolio Management* 27(2): 101–111.

Iyengar, Sheena S, Gur Hebarman and Wei Jiang (2004), 'How Much Choice Is Too Much? Contribution to 401 (K) Retirement Plans', PRC WP 2003-10. Pension Research Council Working Paper Pension Research Council, The Wharton School, University of Pennsylvania, Philadelphia.

Jennings, William W and William Reichenstein (2007), 'Choosing the Right Mix: Lesion from Life Cycle Funds'. *AAII Journal* (January 2007). Available at: http://www.aaii.com/journal/article/choosing-the-right-mix-lessons-from-life-cycle-funds

John Hancock Financial Services (2002), *Eight Defined Contribution Plan Survey: Insight into Participants Investment Knowledge & Behaviour.* Boston: John Hopkins Financial Services.

Kintzel, Dale (2007), 'Portfolio Theory, Life Cycle Investing and Retirement Income'. Social Security Policy Brief (No 2007-02).

Kurod, Yusuke (2008), 'Importance of Investor Education in DC Pension Schemes', in Lakyara Nomura Research Institute Ltd. Available at: http://www.nri.co.jp/english/opinion/la

Pension Fund Association (2007), *Survey of Financial Literacy.* Tokyo: Pension Fund Association.

Sadhak, H (2009), 'Does Not India Need a Default Option in the New Pension System?' *Economic & Political Weekly* (46), 14 November.

Shiller, Robert J. (2005), 'The Life Cycle Personal Accounts Proposal for Social Security: An Evaluation'. NBER Working Paper No. 11300, National Bureau of Economic Research, Cambridge, MA.

Surz, Ron (2012), 'Finding Sharpshooters of Target Date Life Cycle Funds'. Available at: http://www.advisorperspectives.com/newsletters07/newsltr29-1.html.

Viceira, Luis M (2007), 'Life Cycle Funds'. Available: http://ssrn.com/abstract=988362\

12 Investment, Risk Management, Corporate Governance and State of Capital Market

INTRODUCTION

Investment Management is considered to be the core of pension fund management as the performance in terms of risk-adjusted return will determine the end accumulation of asset size of the individual account. The end result of fund management performance would however be determined by a number of factors like investment regulation and restriction, fund managers' competence and integrity, system of risk management, asset valuation and governance. Efficiency in investment and risk management is further influenced by non-institutional factors like government policy and state of capital market in country. These factors will have combined effect on final outcome of fund management and asset accumulation. Few of the many related issues discussed here have strong bearing on efficiency of investment and risk management and they are closely correlated to each other, which ultimately augments the beneficiary interest.

INVESTMENT MANAGEMENT

Investment management is carried out under the regulatory guidelines and most of the countries, including India, have introduced quantitative regulation to restrict portfolio investment and create way for diversification investment policy and strategy plays an important role in efficient fund management, which primarily depends on the formulation of investment policy and strategy by the funds. Thus, the fund managers' expertise, experience and technical knowledge are important for efficient investment management. Fund managers play the most critical role in designing strategy for investment, managing investment of funds, liability and risks. Most of the countries have introduced fit and proper test for fund managers' selection.

Investment Restriction

The primary purpose of imposing investment limit and restrictions is to curtail excessive risk-taking attitude and undue competition that may harm investors' interest which may arise out of disproportionate investment in a risky securities (equity), concentration of investment in few securities, limited or wide diversification, investing in unknown or foreign markets, etc. Adverse investment impacts such activities and calls for strict investment regulation and limiting investment in security class, issuers and particular market, which are being followed by most of the newly reformed countries. Pension funds invest with a longer time frame in horizon and longer the time horizon, more the uncertainty and risks of capital and return. No doubt equity can provide higher return than bonds, but it is also accompanied by higher degree of risks. However, higher return would also depend on the state and stability of the capital market. Capital markets in emerging countries are relatively more volatile, governance and surveillance system is poor as compared to the developed countries. However, bond market is also not that developed in emerging countries but they suffer less as bond return is relatively stable, though there is constraint of liquidity and depth in the market. Therefore, there is an emphasis on bond investing. Restrictions are also imposed on pension fund investment to avoid *overinvestment or concentration* in securities issued by a single or few issuers company or in a single or few sectors as it defeats the objectives of diversification. Therefore, restrictions are put to a maximum investment, say 5 to 10 per cent, of total assets in a single issuer or in a single sector. By this sector and issuer restriction over concentration (risky strategy) is avoided and fund managers are pushed towards optimal diversification. In case of debt investment, sometimes restrictions are imposed on investment duration to avoid overconcentration and overexposure risks. Investing heavily either in the short-term or long-term *bond is risky.* Concentration in the short-term bond is associated with interest rate risk while too much investment in the long-term bond has left the fund managers out of portfolio rebalancing or strategy reorientation. Further, excessive investment either in G Sec or Corporate Bond may be very risky. Interest rate in the G Sec fluctuates with liquidity and fiscal policy of the government (market borrowing) among others, while corporate bond rates are influenced by the demand for investment, money supply and market liquidity.

There is also an intense debate on overseas or *foreign investment* by the pension funds. It is argued that investment in foreign market would protect the funds from the risk arising out of market volatility and foreign investment would provide stability in investment return. Further, the emerging markets are often too small in size and number of goods rated securities are few. Pension assets are huge in terms of GDP and there is limited scope of diversification and cost of investment is also high if listed securities are few. The capital markets of developed countries offer better opportunities as they can absorb huge investment, volatility is less compared to emerging/developing markets, well governed, etc. However, any decision to allow pension funds to invest abroad need to be taken with careful consideration of domestic market environment, available expertise with domestic funds and long-term outlook of domestic and international economy and also experience of other countries, which have allowed domestic pension funds to invest abroad.

Pension fund managers in a newly reformed system may not have required skill, expertise and operating expertise abroad. Outsourcing such expertise may be a costly exercise and investors may end up with higher cost and lower return. Domestic markets in many emerging countries are not totally integrated with global market and less effected by global turmoil, whereas developed markets are more integrated globally and more susceptible to global volatility.

Often there is also an argument that overseas investment by pension funds allows flight of domestic savings offshore which may adversely affect the domestic market and growth 'since there is a positive linkage between domestic savings, and particularly pension assets, and economic growth and financial' (Davis and Hu 2005). In addition to the above argument, there is often the political resistance to overseas investment of domestic savings if the savings rate in country of savings is low, there is any constraint of liquidity and capital market is reasonably developed. In India often there is a clamour for investing in foreign market, but recent experience of Latin American pension fund would be an eye opener for us. Foreign investment as a percentage of total assets by June 2009 was highest in Chile (32 per cent), followed by Peru (15 per cent), Colombia (10 per cent), Mexico (7 per cent), Uruguay (3 per cent). No foreign investment by pension funds of Bolivia. (OECD/IOPS 2009).

Prudent Person Rule

The primary focus of quantitative regulation is controlling the diversification of portfolio investment through certain pre-determined quantitative restriction as such investment risks associated with certain securities are minimised. Quantitative regulation thus tries to ensure reasonable diversification across the asset class and across the various geographical markets. Quantitative regulation also provides uniform choice to the investors and attempts to induce uniform investment practices as far as the fund managers are concerned and the fund managers are restrained from investment activism. But there are some critical views like quantitative restrictions that limit the choice of the investors, reduces the incentives for fund managers, adversely impact the competition and the efficiency of fund managers, which is detrimental to investors interest. Further, quantitative regulation does not make fund managers and other decision-makers accountable for poor decision.

Prudent Person Rules, on the other hand, 'focus on the behaviour of the person concerned, more specifically the behaviour of the asset manager, the institutional investor and the process of decision making' (Davis 2001). According to (Daykin 2002),

> *This may imply laying down general requirements of prudence, setting out investment principles, imposing a requirement to take investment advice from a qualified and or registered professional, and requiring the trustees or board of directors to take personal fiduciary responsibility for the investment of assets.*

Prudent Person Rule thus provides greater flexibility and freedom to the investors and fund managers and increases the level of competition. At the same time, it also imposes responsibility of the fund managers, board of directors and trustees as the regulation relies more on the wisdom and expertise of the fund managers, and board members to diversify portfolio and on the internal control mechanism to manage the portfolio-related risks. Davis (2001) also observed that 'portfolios with prudent person rules have fewer bonds, more equities and foreign assets than those with quantitative restrictions'. It is argued that mere quantitative regulation fails to protect the interest from numerous risks that are associated with fund management practices and the behaviour of the fund managers which often leads to frauds and incompetency in absence of strict accountability rule. However, the appropriateness and suitability would depend on the prevailing market condition, overall financial regulation, legal system, culture of regulation and governance in general and particularly in the funds of management industry.

It has been observed that most of the countries reforming its pension system and introducing mandatory defined contribution system opted for quantitative investment regulation. We have noted in chapter two of section one that quantitative limits to investment in various instruments have been introduced in Chile, Colombia, Peru, Mexico, Brazil and others. It has also been noted in respect of Hungary and Poland. This is perhaps due to the fact that during the transitional period, a more strict control is required for fund management, risk minimisation, and to prevent funds management activism and in prudent practices and other factors are indicated above.

Investment Policy and Strategy

Investment management in a funded private pension system is undertaken by complying with the investment regulation and various related guidelines issued by the regulator and the government, which to some extent restrict the choice of portfolio selection. But designing the investment policy and asset allocation strategy is generally left to the board of the fund management company. While this policy has to be drawn keeping in view the investment guidelines issued by the regulator, it also has to incorporate provision for risk management, avoid concentration, lay down accountability of fund managers, and the strategy for risk-adjusted return maximisation. Investment policy should clearly and unambiguously lay down the investment strategy as it impacts the portfolio selection, rebalancing and reinvestment in a systematic manner. Investment management policy should also aim at introducing discipline in fund management and to curtail tendency of investment management activism.

Asset allocation strategy aims at building an optimum portfolio, to achieve the long-term investment objective of pension fund investment. Since the DC pension system funds are invested for long periods which usually experience a number of *risk cycles*, pension fund portfolio allocation, therefore, is a critical issue. Risks in pension fund investing can be to a great extent minimised through a diversified portfolio of various instrument like debt, equity and alternative instruments like real estate, mutual funds, securitised instruments, etc. However, the allocation strategy cannot be static but also not be too flexible which may distort the portfolio and become vulnerable to short-term changes in the market. These objectives, can be achieved by combining the *Strategic Asset Allocation (SAA)* and *Tactical (or Dynamic) Asset Allocation Strategy (TAA)*, which is also called *Dynamic Asset Allocation (DAA)*.

Strategic asset allocation has a long-term investment perspective and aims at maximising the return through diversification of portfolio assets which help in risk minimisation and also provide an opportunity to derive benefits of better return from diverse asset class which are associated with risks of varying degree, that is, there are different sub portfolios with different types of return and risks. Over a period of time fluctuation in investment gets smoothened out and excess return or excess losses are minimised. Tactical Asset Allocation is a dynamic strategy which actively readjusts the portfolio built on the basis of SAA, according to the expected short-term changes in the market arising out of financial and economic factors which may influence return of some instruments not all. These factors are monetary policy, money supply or liquidity in the system, expected demand for money in the economy, inflation, interest rate, expected overall and sectoral growth rate, industrial output, export, import, etc. Tactical Asset Allocation quickly adjusts portfolio which reduces the adverse impact of changes on the overall portfolio return. A concept called market timing is applied and portfolio is readjusted for a short period keeping the overall long-term portfolio intact in terms of composition.

Though some talked about building an optimum portfolio by using SAA, in reality no such long-term optimum portfolio can be constructed as the market is so dynamic and volatile, frequent rebalancing of portfolio becomes a necessity for better long-term risk-adjusted return. Investment policy must provide a direction of investment strategy to be followed by the fund managers, and the investment committee/board must ensure implementation of such a strategy.

CAPITAL MARKET AND PENSION FUNDS' INVESTMENT MANAGEMENT

One of the important preconditions for pension reform is the existence of well-developed capital market—both equity and debt, supported by developed infrastructure, prudential market regulation. Since investment is the core business of pension funds, efficiency in investment and risk management will depend on the market structure, depth, delivery and settlement system. India since structural reform in 1990s has come a long way and promoted a well-developed capital market, particularly the equity market which can be compared with developed market, though much remains to be done to develop corporate debt market. India has put in place an independent regulator for capital market, Securities and Exchange Board of India (SEBI), which has put in place global standard regulation.

Growth and Domestic Savings

India is one of fastest growing country registering 8.6 per cent average growth rate in Gross Domestic Product (GDP) at factor cost during 2005–06 to 2010–11 (10 per cent growth rate in service sector and 11 per cent in financial service, insurance, real estate and business services). The gross domestic saving as percentage of GDP in 2009–10 was 33.7 per cent as against the average growth rate of 33.9 per cent during 2004–05 to 2009–10. During the year 2009–10, household saving was 23.5 per cent of GDS and 11.8 per cent was invested in financial assets, of which 47.3 per cent was bank deposit, 23.8 per cent in life insurance, 9.1 per cent in pension and provident funds.

Investment by Foreign Institutional Investors (FIIs)

Liberalisation of norms for entry of FIIs saw a large numbers of foreign players operating in Indian capital market and by the end of March 2011, there were 1,722 FIIs operating with 5,686 sub accounts (SEBI 2011). They have a significant presence in Indian market as they are holding 10.32 per cent of shares of all listed stocks. There has been a steady increase in cumulative investment by FIIs since 1992–93, which was only $4 million. By the end of March 2011, cumulative investment by FIIs increased to $121,561 million. With such a presence, FIIs have tremendous power to influence market movement.

State of Stock Market

As indicated above, Indian stock market is one of the most vibrant markets among the emerging countries in terms of market capitalisation, trading frequency, and turnover, etc. Market capitalisation of Bombay Stock Exchange (BSE) in terms of GDP of the oldest stock of India has gone up from 43.4 per cent in 2003–04 to 86.8 per cent in 2011, while that of National Stock Exchange of India (NSE) increased from 40.5 per cent to 85.1 per cent during the same period (SEBI 2011). Though market capitalisation of

India as percentage of GDP at 55.7 per cent was above the middle income countries at 49.5 per cent but much lower than high income countries 62.9 per cent in 2008. In terms of turnover ratio, India at 116.3 per cent was marginally above the middle income countries (213.8 per cent) but much behind the high income countries (9187.1 per cent) in 2009 (World Bank 2010). Trading frequency, an indicator of market liquidity, was also quite good and improving steadily in BSE and NSE. During 2010–11, the number of stocks traded in BSE and NSE was 3,752 and 1,541, respectively. The percentage of stocks traded more than 100 days declined to 88.6 per cent but increased to 93.7 per cent in 2010–11, over the previous year (SEBI 2011).

However, one of the concerns for institutional investors like pension fund is the market concentration in terms of promoters holding. Shareholding pattern in India is heavily skewed in favour of promoters. According to NSE Fact Book (2011), by the end of March 2011, 1,574 companies were listed with NSE (Market Capitilisation of ₹6,702,616 crore) and 51.7 per cent shares were held by Indian promoters and 5.65 per cent by foreign promoters. Institutional investors held 18.78 per cent shares (domestic investors 5.56, FIIs 10.32, mutual funds 2.59, venture cap funds 0.15 and others 0.16), while non-institutional public holding was 21.51 per cent (corporate 5.97 + individual 11.72 + other 3.82). Against the issue depository receipt, 2.29 per cent shares were held by the custodian. With this large holding promoters have tremendous power to influence the market, which may not be in the interest of institutional investors like pension funds and others.

State of Bond Market

Developed bond market is a necessity for long-term investment and risk management by pension funds, life insurance companies and absence of vibrant and liquid bond market create constraints for long-term investment and to mange risks for long-term investment. Bond market in India comprises government securities or G Sec. (central and state government securities) and corporate bonds (bonds of financial institutes, public sector and private corporate) though government bond market is quite well functioning, the corporate debt market is lagging in India. Government bond market in India has grown steadily, and at 38 per cent of GDP, it compares well with other markets like Thailand, Singapore, Malaysia and China, but corporate debt market at 3 per cent of GDP is less developed than most in emerging East Asia (ADB 2008).

Recent trend in the bond market shows that during 2009–10, an amount of $178,799 million was raised in the primary market through bond issue and 77.3 per cent was though government bond and 22.3 per cent through corporate bond. Corporate bonds are very illiquid as can be seen in terms of secondary market turnover, which was $1900311 million. Secondary market turnover of corporate bond was merely 1.7 per cent of total turnover, the rest 98.3 per cent of that came from government securities (NSE 2010). However, the turnover ratio of government securities in NSE wholesale debt market was only 58.15 per cent and that of PSU/Institutional Bonds was still lower at 15.4 per cent indicating overall lower trading.

Corporate Bond Market in India

The corporate bond market in India is only 10–15 per cent of the bond market of India. It has languished both in terms of market participation and structure, though in recent times some upward movement was noticed in corporate bond market. Bond issues in India witnessed an improvement in India since 2005, $2,118 which went up to $2,150 in 2009. But when compared with other emerging markets, India stands poorly in 2009 in terms of value of corporate bond issued by Mexico ($15,541), UAE ($13,004), Brazil ($10,167) Indonesia ($5,454) as against bond issued by India ($2,150) (NSE 2010).

The yield on corporate bond is much better compared with government securities. In the month of September 2010, yield on 0–1 years, 5–6 years, 9–10 years and above 10 years corporate bond was 7.73 per cent, 7.97 per cent, 8.64 per cent and 8.73 per cent, respectively, as against yield on the G Sec with same duration was 6.16 per cent, 7.40 per cent, 7.92 per cent, 8.23 per cent, respectively (RBI 2011). Institutions often avoid corporate bonds as there are very few papers with good rating (AAA or AA), there are doubts about corporate governance, poor liquidity, etc. Other constraints to development of corporate bond market are: predominance of bank loans, limited participation of FIIs, pension and insurance companies, households and crowding out by government bonds.

Government Bond Market

As compared to the corporate debt market, the government debt market is better developed in India. The government securities market in India has undergone significant change since 1990s, with the introduction of financial sector reforms which facilitated introduction of market based price discovery, new instruments, widening of investors base, establishment of primary dealers, electronic settlement and trading, etc. But the current market for government securities lacks depth in trading and is narrow in terms of product offering. These are not only the major inhibiting factors for investment management performance but also come in the way of risk management in pension funds.

Concentration of Holding of Government Securities

The commercial banks and Life Insurance Corporation (LIC) are holding the bulk of government securities in India. While all the commercial banks together held 46.93 per cent of all central and state government securities, LIC held 22.76 per cent, and EPFO

4.42 per cent of such securities in 2007. Therefore ownership is primarily concentrated, which adversely reduces the trading volume, since LIC, Employees Provident Fund, etc., and other long-term investors prefer to retain such securities on maturity basis.

Demand–Supply Gap in Government Securities

The growing demand for government securities and increased demand–supply gap can be further assessed in terms of bids received and bids accepted by the Reserve Bank of India in auction of central and state government securities. Let us now consider the notified amount minus bids received as an indication of the extent of excess demand and bids received minus bids accepted as received as an indication of extent of supply shortage in government securities. The demand–supply gap can be noted in terms of gap between bids for government securities and bids accepted by RBI. This gap increased from ₹138,776.97 crore in 2004–05 to ₹395,707.63 crore in 2008–09. Demand–supply gap is on an average of 20.5 times for central government securities and is more than three times in respect of state government securities. Short supply of long-term securities not only poses investment risk and yield problem but also generates reinvestment risk. In an uncertain interest rate market, short duration investment does not allow long-term asset liability matching and mismatch carries unbundled risk in a fund.

Decline in Supply of Long-term Central Government Securities

The problem of short supply of long-term government securities in India, the average tenor of central government dated securities has been declining for the past few years. Maturity distribution of long-term central government dated securities over 10 years has declined from 74 per cent in 2005–06 to 39 per cent in 2008–09, while medium term securities of 5–10 years became more than double—26 per cent to 55 per cent during the same period; there is a severe shortage in supply of long-term securities over 30 years, which is only 23.37 per cent of all central government dated securities, while 51.35 per cent securities had maturity below 15 years. This makes long-term hedging and risk management difficult for pension funds, provident funds and life insurance companies. Risk management is a critical function for these institutions and that function can be successfully carried out with the help of long-term debt instruments.

Depressed Secondary G Sec Market

A vibrant debt market to support long-term investors must have an active secondary market, allowing the long-term institutional investors to buy and sell securities.

This would however depend on the transparent liquid and active secondary market. However, low trading in the secondary market for central and state government securities is due to the concentration of holding, supply shortage, etc.

Absence of Inflation Indexed Bonds

Mortality and financial risks associated with pension and annuity business are major concerns for pension fund managers. Though longevity risks, due to future uncertainty, mostly remain uncovered, the financial risks can be hedged by investing in long-term fixed income securities including inflation indexed bonds. Financial innovation in developed market led to the introduction of such instruments like longevity bonds, inflation indexed bonds to hedge mortality and long-term financial risks.

To hedge longevity risks, longevity index bonds or survivor bonds have been suggested. First time such longevity index bond was structured by BNP Paribas and issued by European Investment Bank in 2003 on realised mortality rate of 65 years, in England and Wales but was not very successful (Antolin and Blommenstein 2007) suggested developing longevity index for longevity risk, which may promote longevity index bonds. While successful longevity indexed bonds can help longevity risk management, ultra long term inflation indexed bonds can protect capital and yield against inflation. Inflation index bonds are therefore tremendous support to the pension funds and other long-term investors who are large-scale investors in fixed income debt securities. Inflation index bonds are quite popular and a large number of bonds have been issued primarily by the sovereign government and the major buyers are the pension funds and life insurance companies. These bonds are mostly linked to consumer price index, for example, Treasury Inflation Protected Securities (TIPS) in the US, Index-linked Gilts in the UK, Real Return Bonds in Canada, CPI-linked Bonds in Japan, etc. Some of these bonds are for very long duration and are called ultra long term bonds, for example, the UK Debt Management Office (DMO) issued the world's longest inflation-linked bonds. The ultra long 50-year inflation-protected government bonds were issued in September 2009, which was a huge success and well received by pension funds and insurance companies. Japan has been issuing long-term bonds regularly but the 40 years ultra long term bonds issued first time in financial year in November 2007 was oversubscribed by more than five times. These bonds aimed at domestic insurance companies and pension funds.

India has also made an unsuccessful experiment with Capital Index Bonds. Only such Capital Index Bond was issued in India in 1997 which, however, failed to attract investors' interest. The 6 per cent Capital Indexed Bond 2002 was issued for the first time on 29 December 1997. The reasons for lacklustre response to the bonds are cited as the bond only offered inflation hedging for the principal, while the coupons of the bond were left unprotected against inflation and complexities involved in pricing of the instrument. The huge demand for long-term government bonds can be assessed from the emerging size of Indian pension market in terms number of potential investors to NPS and the expected flow of funds. Indian Pension Market is still very small compared with other countries. However, available estimates indicate a significant growth in very near future since NPS will expand the coverage. Investment and allocation pattern as discussed above under different options clearly indicates that NPS is basically debt instruments oriented system. Therefore, the NPS will generate huge demand for debt instruments, particularly for government securities at the accumulation phase of NPS. Further mandatory annuitisation would also create huge demand for annuity products in Indian Life Insurance market. Therefore, the success of NPS and performance of fund managers in accumulation period and that of annuity providers would primarily depend on the well-managed diversified government securities market having a wide range of long-term products like CPI Linked Inflation Indexed Bonds. The discussions above clearly indicate a close relationship among pension fund investment, valuation, risk management, capital market and governance system, but governance plays the most critical role by integrating them and providing necessary impetus to accountability, fairness in the prudential management. The role of the government is to provide necessary long-term investment instruments and capital market regulators to ensure smooth functioning of the market and retain fair value of investment.

INVESTMENT REGULATION AND PORTFOLIO RESTRICTION IN NPS

The PFRDA has issued guidelines on investment management, including portfolio composition, formation of investment management committee, risk management committee, etc.

Investment Restriction

The PFRDA has introduced quantitative investment regulation for pension fund management. However, these restrictions are not uniform for the government NPS and All Citizens Scheme. While investment in equity and equity mutual funds allowed up to 15 per cent in government NPS, and in All Citizens Scheme investment in equity is allowed up to 50 per cent (Chapter 7). There are also certain limits/restrictions on investment in G Sec and corporate debt, bank deposit, investment in short-term instruments, etc. Indian pension funds (under NPS) are not allowed to invest in foreign markets. According to the circular issued by the Ministry of Finance, Department of Economic Affairs, Government of India, dated 14 August 2008, the pension fund managers are allowed to invest government NPS funds up to 55 per cent of funds in government securities, up to 40 per cent of funds can be invested in debt securities with maturity of not less than three years tenure issued by corporate bodies including banks and public financial institutions (provided that at least 75 per cent of the investment in this category is made in instruments having an investment grade rating from at least one credit rating agency). In this (40 per cent) category PFMs are also allowed to invest in term deposit of one year and above (provided that the scheduled commercial banks must meet conditions of continuous profitability for immediately preceding three years; maintaining a minimum capital to risk weighted assets ratio of 9 per cent; having net non-performing assets of not more than 2 per cent of the net advances, minimum net worth of not less than ₹200 crore) and also in the *rupee bonds* having an outstanding maturity of at least three years issued by institutions of the International Bank for Reconstruction and Development, International Finance Corporation and the Asian Development Bank. The PFMs are also allowed to invest up to 5 per cent of funds in money market instruments including units of money market mutual funds, up to 15 per cent of funds can be invested in shares of companies on which derivatives are available in Bombay Stock Exchange or National Stock Exchange or equity linked schemes of mutual funds regulated by the Securities and Exchange Board of India (see annexure Chapter 7).

The above notification has further restricted the turnover ratio (the value of securities traded in the year/average value of the portfolio at the beginning of the year and the end of the year) should not exceed 2. It is expected that throughout the year the investments are in conformity with the above pattern; however, at no time investments in any category should exceed by more than 10 per cent of the limit prescribed and the investment pattern may be achieved by the end of the financial year. The circular further stated that the investment of the funds of a trust is the fiduciary responsibility of the trustees and needs to be exercised with appropriate due diligence. Therefore, the trustees are solely responsible for the investment decisions taken in accordance with the pattern of investment specified above (Department of Economic Affairs 2008). It may be mentioned here that that so far no restrictions have been imposed on investment in a sector or issuer of a company but pension funds themselves impose certain restriction on exposure (up to 5 per cent) in a group and avoid overexposure in any sector. This is one of the areas that require attention of the regulator to avoid risk due to overexposure.

The PFRDA has issued a separate investment guidelines indicating permissible asset classes and certain restrictions. We discuss here some of the important points. The PF will manage three separate schemes, each investing in a different asset class, namely, *Asset class E (equity market instruments), Asset class G (government securities) and Asset class C (credit risk bearing fixed income instruments).*

❖ ASSET CLASS E

The investment in asset class is subject to a cap of 50 per cent, and the funds can be invested in index funds that replicate the portfolio of either BSE sensitive index or NSE Nifty 50 index. The assets are not to be encumbered and investment in any equity stock is limited to the higher of its weight in the chosen index or a maximum of 10 per cent of the issued capital of a company, as held by the PF in aggregate. The investment in the issued stock of a related party (such as the PF's sponsor or group companies) is limited to its weight in the chosen index. No investment is allowed in IPO, unlisted equity shares or equity related instruments, or in any unlisted security of an associate or group company is allowed. PFMs are not allowed to advance any loans for any purpose but the PF can invest the funds of the scheme in short-term deposits of scheduled commercial banks or in call deposits up to 10 per cent of the scheme corpus for up to two days, pending deployment of funds of a scheme in securities in terms of investment objectives of the scheme.

❖ ASSET CLASS G (GOVERNMENT SECURITIES)

The authorised investments include Government of India bonds and state government bonds subject to the restrictions that the assets are not to be encumbered and no loans for any purpose can be advanced by the PF.

❖ ASSET CLASS C (CREDIT RISK BEARING FIXED INCOME INSTRUMENTS)

Authorised Investments include *Liquid Funds* of AMCs regulated by SEBI, with average total assets under management (AUM) for the most recent six-month period of, at least, ₹5,000 crore, *fixed deposits of scheduled commercial banks* (subject to the restriction that net worth of at least ₹500 crore and a track record of profitability in the last three years, capital adequacy ratio of not less than 9 per cent in the last three years. Net NPA of under 5 per cent as a percentage of net advances in the last year), *debt securities* with maturity of not less than three years tenure issued by corporate bodies including scheduled commercial banks and public financial institutions [as defined in Section 4(A) of the Companies Act] (provided that at least 75 per cent of the investment in this category is made in instruments) having an investment grade rating from at least one credit rating agency. Credit Rated Public Financial Institutions/PSU Bonds and Credit Rated Municipal Bonds/Infrastructure. The PFMs can invest the funds of the scheme in short-term deposits of scheduled commercial banks or in call deposits up to 10 per cent of the scheme corpus for up to two days.

There are some other restrictions which include restricting the PFMs to purchase or sell securities only through an associate broker, which is an average of 5 per cent or more of the aggregate purchases and sale of securities made by the scheme, not to use the NPS Funds to buy securities/bonds held by the PFM or its subsidiary in their own investment portfolio or any other portfolio held by them, buy and sell securities on the basis of deliveries, and in no case put itself in a position whereby it has to make short sales or carry forward transactions or engage in badla finance (carry forward).

Derivative transactions through recognised stock exchanges are allowed if it is in the interest of the subscribers, only for the purpose of hedging and portfolio balancing, in accordance with the guidelines issued by SEBI/RBI. Transfer of investments from one scheme to another scheme in the same PF, under certain conditions.

There is also an *Auto Choice (default option)* in the All Citizens' Scheme of NPS. When an investor fails to exercise her/his option, NPS Trust allocates the Auto Choice fund. It's a Life Cycle fund and asset allocation changes according to the changes in age. Lower the age, higher the investment in equity (max 50 per cent) and higher the age, lower the investment in equity.

For example, investment asset classes E, C and G up to the age of 35 years will be 50 per cent, 30 per cent and 20 per cent, respectively. The pattern of allocation will constantly change and portfolio will be more and more debt oriented. At the age of 40, the portfolio will contain and change to 40 per cent E, 25 per cent C and 35 per cent G. At the age of 50, the portfolio will contain 20 per cent assets of E, 15 per cent assets of C and 65 per cent assets of G and at the age 55 years, the portfolio will have only 10 per cent assets of E, 10 per cent assets of C and 80 per cent assets of G.

Investment Management Committee

As per the Investment Management Agreement signed between NPS Trust and PFMs, all the PFMs are to form an *Investment Management Committee* and a *Risk Management Committee.* Investment committee consists of at least three members including the CEO, CIO and an independent director of the board. The committee draws an *investment policy* approved by the board of the pension fund. The investment policy is guided by the issue relating to liquidity, prudential norms, exposure limit, stop loss limits in securities trading, investment and market risks, management of asset liability mismatch, investment audits, etc. The investment policy is to be reviewed periodically by the board and to be submitted to the NPS trustees. The operational guidelines are prepared by the management with the approval of the concerned board of directors which need to be approved by the regulatory authority.

Guaranteed Return in Pension Funds

Guarantee of return or performance of the fund managers is an important regulatory issue. As we have noted in chapter two, section one, that performance guarantee has become virtually a well-accepted norm for the fund management in almost all countries in Latin America (for example, Argentina, Chile, Peru, Uruguay, Colombia) and East European countries (Hungary, Poland) which have introduced pension reforms. However, in India no regulatory provision has been made for such a guarantee.

In India, EPS has implicit guarantee as the yearly rate of interest (return) is decided by the government. IRDA has also made it mandatory for the insurance companies to provide at least 4.5 per cent guaranteed return on ULIP (withdrawn later on). ULIPs are basically pension products which manage accumulation of funds for annuity purchase. However, in India no such provision has been introduced by the regulator. There is no guarantee for minimum return, and as such there is no legal accountability of the sponsors of the pension fund to ensure minimum return on the funds. Indian government has also no responsibility in respect of returns. Return and performance is only market driven. There is no penal provision for poor performance of the fund managers. However, centralised allocation of government NPS takes into account the relative performance of the three fund managers, and yearly allocation depends on the relative rate of return achieved in the previous year. However, there is no penalty for poor performance by the fund managers. There is resistance to performance guarantee in many quarters. The issue of providing minimum return guarantee has emerged as one of the most critical factor in the way of passing the PFRDA Bill in the Indian Parliament.

Need for More Transparency

In a privatised pension system, entire investment risk is transferred to the investors, and fund managers virtually have no accountability as far as performance is concerned. Selection of fund and fund managers is the responsibility of the investors but the way funds are to be managed is the discretion of fund managers. It is therefore necessary that the ability, experience, past track record be made public to help an investor take an informed decision. Moreover, investment strategy plays an important role in fund management. Experience shows that long-term funds are often invested with short-term perspective to register better results and to attract more subscription, which ultimately may not be in the interest of the investors. Therefore, every pension fund must publicly declare the investment policy and strategy that they are following and at the end of the year publish how effective these policies are.

VALUATION OF PENSION FUNDS ASSETS

A great deal of discussions are going on in India and abroad about the appropriate valuation models for pension funds. In India, so far no specific valuation regulation for pension funds under NPS has been issued but currently the pension fund assets are valued following the guidelines issued by Securities and Exchange Board of India (SEBI) for valuation of assets of mutual funds, which is primarily the Mark to Market (MTM) model. However, following the mutual fund valuation model (MTM) to assess the assets of pension fund in Indian context may not be appropriate from beneficiary point of view. A specific valuation model needs to be designed keeping in view the long-term pension savings, operational and market constraints, valuation of pension assets, etc. The investment objectives of mutual funds and pension funds are different. Mutual funds mobilise resources from investors for investing in capital markets on a short to medium term basis. Investors want to maximise risk-adjusted return from capital market using the mutual fund vehicle, primary objective being the maximisation of investment return. Most of the mutual funds are open-ended schemes and an investor can enter and exit from the fund any time depending on the market volatility and fluctuation in asset prices. Further entry into a scheme and exit from a scheme is determined though the unit value called *Net Asset Value (NAV)* per unit. It is therefore very critical for mutual fund that they evaluate their asset value on an ongoing basis by using a method which reflects current appreciation or depreciation of funds.

Valuation Models

There are several valuation models but few most important models are Mark to Market (MTM) model, Fair Value (FV), Book Value/Held to Maturity (HTM) model, etc. The MTM model is widely a valuation model which suggests that all the assets in a portfolio should be valued at current market prices, irrespective of whether assets market exists or not at that point of valuation. However, for illiquid assets, mostly, debt instruments which are not traded, MTM suggests some methods to bench mark the yield/return of similar assets with similar tenure which have been traded. *Fair value concept for asset valuation* is applied when market price/value of an asset is not available due to absence of regular market for such assets. Fair value is an estimate of what a buyer and a seller is ready to accept for an illiquid financial instrument. The HTM model valuation is based on the historical cost of assets. The HTM has been criticised on the ground that it does not capture the true value of an underlying asset, as the value remains static. Yet this method of asset valuation is considered to be an important method to measure value of an asset when a large number of securities in the portfolio are not traded in the market and determining their true market value is impossible.

However, the appropriateness of a valuation model would depend on the nature of investing organisation, objective of investment and the very purpose of valuation of assets. Apart from the distinctive investment objectives, there are market constraints like the size of equity market, depth of debt market, liquidity in the market, etc. Therefore, same valuation method may not be very appropriate in all the countries and at all the times. In a very liquid market having competitive trading environment, buying and selling an asset can take place in the market place through prevailing market price. But in an illiquid market, though assets may exist, there may not be an open trade but through negotiated deals, which often depends on the bargaining powers of the parties and necessity and priority of the buyers and sellers to have such assets in their portfolio.

Therefore, while deciding a method of asset valuation, the state of market for such assets needs to be kept in mind.

Valuation of Assets under NPS

In NPS debt instruments constitute a large per cent of portfolio. But in India, debt market is yet to be developed to support price discovery through regular trading in debt instruments. Though some activities are observed in government securities market, trading in corporate debt and state development loans is virtually absent. Therefore, illiquid debt market forces the fund managers to resort to off-market negotiated deals. In an illiquid market of long-term debt instruments like corporate bonds, state loans, etc., pricing and thus yield, in MTM valuation, depend on MTM model, which marks down the prices and makes the instrument more illiquid and drives away the buyers. However, real value of the long-term debt instruments like government guaranteed bonds, state loans does not decline and the buyers will receive contacted return on maturity of the holding period. Therefore, in absence of developed debt market, application of MTM valuation for illiquid debt securities would lead to subjectivity in valuation but under the book value or HTM, this problem of under-valuation does not arise. As per the current practice, pension fund assets under NPS are valued by following the MTM model. Simple MTM valuation to determine assets prices and allocating units can be often discretionary. The principle of equity demands that no one should pay more or less than the real value of assets at the time of entry. MTM valuation, however, generates inequity in unit allocation and none of the methods indicated above can be considered as the most ideal method in any market as the markets are mostly inefficient or semi-efficient and are never the reflection of true value of a security.

A Suggested Valuation Model for NPS

We need to have one realistic model for valuation of assets. It is therefore suggested that a Composite Model of Valuation (CMV) may be adopted for valuation of assets of NPS. The CMV would incorporate security class wise valuation method depending on the nature of security, trading frequency, etc. Equities are to be valued at the market price, while G Sec is to be valued at market price wherever traded, but non-traded securities are to be valued at book value method (due to sovereign guarantee), state guaranteed bonds, state developed loans to be valued on book value basis (due to the payment guarantee by the government) and corporate bonds will be valued at market price and non-traded bonds are to be valued by using MTM or book value/purchase price (depending on the changes in rating, if any). For operational reasons, fund portfolio under CMV needs to be divided into three sub portfolios, namely, Portfolio A, Portfolio B and Portfolio C.

❖ PORTFOLIO A (TRADING AND TO BE TRADED PORTFOLIO)

Portfolio A would consist of all the equity securities and that portion of debt securities are earmarked for future trading by the fund. Portfolio A would be valued on MTM basis.

❖ PORTFOLIO B

Portfolio B would consist of G Sec, state government bonds, state development loans and would be valued on book value/HTM basis.

❖ PORTFOLIO C

Portfolio C would consist of corporate bonds including private corporate and PSU Bonds. They should be valued at market price and in absence of active trading should be valued on the basis of MTM model. This model would take care of valuation and would remove the distortions generated by unrealistic MTM model and under-valuation of government securities. This will also eliminate the impact on asset price volatility on NAV and allocation of units to the investors. Further, in order to introduce consistency and fairness in asset valuation in NPS, PFRDA has appointed an independent agency to undertake asset valuation on quarterly basis on the basis of actual data on investment performance by the PFMs.

IMPORTANCE OF CORPORATE GOVERNANCE IN PENSION FUND MANAGEMENT

Governance challenges in pension funds are multi-faceted and multidimensional and the extent of challenges may differ from country to country depending on the pension fund regulatory regime, market environment, sponsors of the funds, real expectation of the sponsors, ethical practices in business, quality of management and governing board, etc. However, certain generalisation is possible in view of the basic objective of pension funds, that is, to provide maximum risk-adjusted return to its members. The nature of challenges confronted by pension funds in DC system differs from that of DC system. We, however, would focus on pension funds in DC System like NPS. The distinctive character between the two is the investment risks. While investment risks in the DB system is borne by the pension providers, investment risks in the DC system is transferred to the investors. This makes governance of the funds essentially more complex and critical. The *major objective* of the governance system would be to ensure that pension system through its intermediaries is capable of providing either guaranteed or maximum risk-adjusted return to its members. Good governance has a strong linkage between pension fund administration, investment management, risk management and provide a leadership direction to achieve these objectives and finally ensure protection of beneficiary interest.

Factors Effecting Good Governance

Good governance practices in a pension fund depend on a number of factors like prudential regulation with clear direction, company governing board with clear vision, a competent operational management team with knowledge, expertise, commitment to excellence and superior performance. Important sources of good governance are *regulatory regime, investment policy and strategy, risk management policy and strategy,* well-documented *internal control system, composition of board, and competence of corporate management.*

Regulatory Regime

Regulatory regime has an important role in promoting good governance practices in pension funds. The foundation of good governance system in an individual account based defined contribution system is laid down by the regulatory system covering issues of licensing, sponsors, characteristics of board, background and competency of the corporate managers, investment and risk regulation and supervisory mechanism, etc. Regulation can provide an overall governance culture in the industry by curtailing the tendency of market concentration and promoting healthy competition in the market place. Regulation also provides guidance in selection and efficiency of fund management companies including functional management and the company board, investment strategy, day-to-day management of investment, valuation practices, overall operational costs, technical experience of functional managers, overall risk management culture and its implementation, etc. Regulation, however, needs to be development oriented and regulators are also to be facilitators with enough flexibility to change as per market condition and guiding to install good governance system.

Internal Control System

Internal control system not only improves the efficiency of management and good administration but also promotes good governance system. Internal control system therefore establishes a link between the two and imparts efficiency in pension fund administration which in turn influences fund management performance, the ultimate objective of pension funds. Internal control improves the management efficiency while regulation acts as a safety measure to protect the investors' interest. However, these are basic instruments of good governance, but need to be sincerely implemented by the operating management team under guidance and monitoring of the governing board. Good governance, however, primarily depends on the sense of responsibility, accountability, self-governance of the management team. Some of the important areas of control system, which promotes good governance, are: efficiency in internal administration, compliance management, cost management, investment management, timely information disclosure, etc. Able and efficient internal administration of a pension will enable the fund to reduce the time lag between collection and investment, minimise the collection and distribution costs, minimise the operation and investment costs, etc., which will be ultimately reflected in the enhancement of accumulated assets. Cost management in fund administration assumed great importance because higher costs may reduce the quantum of terminal assets.

Investment Management

The major area of governance concern in a pension fund is the investment management function, the core to pension fund operation. Primarily the fund management activities are governed by the investment regulation/guidelines issued by the regulator, which are quantitative in nature in India. However, prudence is required even while managing funds with reference investment guidelines. Investment strategy is very critical for investment management since investment is made in an uncertain market environment, which undergoes several market cycles, changes in interest rate regime, and inflationary threat. In such a situation, an appropriate investment strategy is very essential. Investment activities like stock selection, duration matching, portfolio reallocation, secondary market trading, etc., need careful consideration based on experience and knowledge. Fund management activism may ruin the portfolio and put the investor into great difficulties in the form of reduced return. Therefore, governance in investment management is very critical for return and safety of funds. It basically determined well-designed investment strategy. Investment strategy is very critical for investment management since investment is made in an uncertain market environment, which undergoes several market cycles, changes in interest rate regime and inflationary threat. In such a situation, an appropriate investment strategy is very essential. Investment activities like stock selection, duration matching, portfolio reallocation, secondary market trading, etc., need careful consideration based on experience and knowledge. Fund management activism may ruin the portfolio and put the investor into great difficulties in the form of reduced return.

Therefore, *governance in investment management* is very critical for return and safety of funds. A study of Ambachtsheer et al. (2008) identified four most important specific challenges of pension fund governance and challenges which include agency/context issues, oversight effective issues, investment belief/risk management issues and strategic planning/management effectiveness issues. Understanding these issues and taking necessary actions by the board is crucial for effective governance system. Quality of governance has direct bearing on the efficiency and performance of pension funds which are crucial for protection and enhancement of retirement income. An interesting study by Ambachtsheer (2007) observed, 'High quality funds outperformed low quality funds by about 2 per cent per annum. Therefore Institutionalisation of high quality governance is very essential for performance management in pension funds.'

Board of Directors and Active Management

The external regulation and internal control set the governance format and operating management required to manage the funds to promote good governance practices. However, these idealistic expectations often remain unfulfilled due to several pressure and constraints. *Vision, mission and intention* of good governance remain merely statement of intent. Here the role of corporate governing board assumes great significance. A competent board without any outside/external pressure can emerge as a guiding force behind the operating management and good governance can become a reality. Many studies have indicated that good governance and high performance of a pension fund is influenced to a great extent by the governing board. But there are certain preconditions for an active and performance-oriented governing board. The sponsors are responsible to see that the board members have requisite knowledge, expertise and willingness to spare time as per their role and act only in the interest of fund and the beneficiaries. Board members must be capable to withstand any undue pressure from the sponsors or stakeholders and be able to take independent decision to protect the interest of the beneficiaries.

The Committee on Fund Governance Best Practice Principles (Chair: Peter Clapman), in its report (31 May 2007), provided certain best practice principles for fund governance. Five sets of principles basically focus on *transparency, leadership, attributes and core competencies, conflicts of interest and disclosure, and delegation.* According to Clapman committee report, a fund should clearly define its governance rule which should be publicly available, and would disclose its leadership structure. The governing body should consist of appropriately qualified and experienced individuals, to fulfil fiduciary duties to fund beneficiaries, the governing body should be vested with powers to select and dismiss and '[s]tandards of performance should be clearly set, measured with the results communicated, each trustee should have thorough understanding of funds obligations to its beneficiaries'. The Committee further states, 'The Board should at all time include individuals with investment and financial market experience and expertise relevant to the fund's ability to exercise its fiduciary obligations to its beneficiaries' and the fund should evaluate trustee skills annually. Since pension funds management involves several conflicting situation, the committee suggested public disclosure of its policy on *conflict of interest.* The committee has also focused on *delegation* and suggested to permit governing body to rely on the expertise and advice of appropriately selected and uncomplicated consultants and staffs. The important focus of the committee is on fiduciary responsibilities, competency of trustees and board members, integrity and transparency, etc.; the most vital issues in good governance are reflected here. Ideal qualities and principles of good governance may be also at conflict if the sponsors, board and active managers are more motivated by the profit motive and agency problem remains unsolved. Good governance is not merely a technical and compliance issue but an issue of commitment and governance culture.

An efficient governance system, however, evolved under the suitable *national law* providing autonomy and support to the pension fund regulators and supervisor. A system of efficient governance would depend in addition to legal support on the pension fund regulatory regime, market environment, sponsor of the funds, real expectation of the sponsors, ethical practices in business, quality of management and governing board, etc. It will finally be determined by the determination of regulator and sponsors as there is a conflict between the two— while the regulator desires to maximise the investors' benefits, sponsors may be interested in seeking to enhance their own interest by reducing costs, influencing board and management decision which may not be totally in the interest of investors. Managing this conflict is the function of supervisor and their efficiency counts a lot in promoting good governance in pension fund management.

Corporate Governance in NPS

Many of the governance issues discussed above have been reflected in PFRDA guidelines/instructions. To avoid market concentration and to encourage competition, seven pension funds (till December2011) sponsored by public and private sector entities have been issued licences, various administrative and fund management costs have been determined by the regulator, pension products have been identified, due diligence has been done by PFRDA before selecting intermediaries through open competitive bidding. There is a centralised NPS trust and custodian, trustee bank. This helps to keep costs at minimum, introduce a uniform supervision and monitoring system for better governance. Fund managers are closely monitored, they submit a day-to-day report on investment of funds to the NPS Trust, and the trust reviews the performance on a quarterly and yearly basis. Valuation of assets is carried out by an independent agency appointed by the regulator.

Pension funds under NPS have been formed as companies and they are sponsored by financial institutions that fulfil the fit and proper test. There is a fire wall between the sponsors and pension fund companies. Pension funds are board managed and, as per the provision, at least 50 per cent of the board members are independent directors. Appointment of the chief executive, chief investment officer, risk officer and the board directors are to be informed to the NPS Trust. There is a mandatory *Investment Management Committee* constituted with at least two independent directors, chief executive officer, and chief investment officer and a *Risk Management Committee* constituted with at least one independent director, chief executive officer and designated risk officer. The performance and investment activities are also regularly monitored and reviewed on quarterly basis by the NPS Trust. It is the responsibility of the governing board and operating management team to implement it. However, these are basic instruments of good governance, but need to be sincerely implemented by the operating management team under guidance and monitoring of the governing board. Good governance, however, primarily depends on the sense of responsibility, accountability and self-governance of the management team.

Corporate Governance

Good governance in pension funds is not only beneficial for the funds but also has immensely influencing role in promoting quality corporate governance in the corporate sector. Pension funds play a very significant role in promoting capital market by creating demand for various financial instruments in order to diversify investment risk of portfolio. There are strong evidences that pension reforms through introduction of DC scheme exerted significant influence on capital market development in Latin American countries like Chile, which was the first country to introduce such reforms in 1981. Pension funds mobilise a very large portion of household savings, invest in capital market, particularly in securities of a large number of corporates, and are able to exert pressure on them to adopt good corporate governance which would ultimately be beneficial for all the investors including pension funds. But to exert a meaningful influence on the corporate governance of capital market entities, pension funds themselves need to have quality governance practices.

RISK MANAGEMENT IN PENSION FUNDS

The world around us, of late, has been changing so fast that neither the information system nor the management practices are able to capture the potential trend in the direction of change; there exists uncertainty and inability to initiate proactive action. The major changes that have been noticed include changes in demographic structure impacting the demographic composition leading to increase in longevity, convergence and volatility in financial markets, emergence of complex new products, fast-changing computer technology and information system. All these have brought unanticipated changes in financial services. These changes have immense impact on financial institutions like pension funds, because new changes are faster and thus have reduced the time and space for managerial response, which has also made the future more unpredictable. Risk management in pension funds particularly in the privately managed defined contribution funds emerged as the most critical concern, since the entire risks are transferred to the investors. Unless the risks associated with administration, funds management and pension payouts through annuities are managed properly, the investors may suffer huge loss which may even defeat the very purpose of pension investing. This was observed in 2007–08, when global financial crisis washed away a large portion of assets of individual accounts, which has reinforced the importance and necessity of risk management in pension funds. There are several sources of risks associated with pension fund management right from licensing to a company to sponsor fund to pension payout through annuity payment. Therefore, risks in pension funds arise from regulation, supervision, management, investment policy and strategy, and sources external to company like economic and fiscal policy. Risk management policy thus needs to cover wider operational and non-operational areas related to pension fund functioning. Risk management in pension funds is primarily an issue of governance and *risk governance* would be a better term to incorporate the entire gamut of risk management.

Risk Governance

Sound governance system is an important mechanism which plays a crucial role in promoting transparency and soundness in management of a corporate and thus creates a culture of disclosure, vigilance, accountability and sensitivity about risk management among managers and other employees. Since corporate governance also promotes strategic vision of the organisation, it also strengthens the organisation's risk management strategy.

Risk governance is an important function of the board. Though it is a component of overall corporate governance, it is also a distinct function in a pension as its primary objective is to ensure maximise risk-adjusted return for the investors. As such it is a major area of operation of a pension fund and the major concern for board members. Efficient risk management under the directives and guidance of the board call for total awareness of the board members about the importance of various aspects of risk management like importance of risk management in pension funds, risk identification, risk mitigation models and serious desire to ensure that risk management strategies are implemented not as a compliance but as a serious business. There should be a well-documented procedure and reporting system to be followed by the management and any departure should be viewed seriously by the board. Risk policy as approved by the board is to be reviewed periodically. Risk officer who reports directly to the board should submit his report periodically and directly to the board.

Types of Risks in Funded Pension Schemes

There are a number of risks affecting a fund management operation directly and indirectly, since operational objectives are basically a futuristic function. The future extending a long horizon is uncertain and mostly unpredictable, only a part of that uncertainty may be predicted and precautionary initiatives can be taken. Pension fund managers operate within the given regulatory framework and changing market environment in an uncertain future. However, scientific prediction and projection of probable changes would to some extent mitigate the risk associated fund management, capital protection and future provision of annuity to the members. We may outline here some of such risks associated with funded pension fund management.

In a funded pension scheme, fund managers are expected to attain twin objectives, namely, protecting capital and ensuring reasonable risk-adjusted return for the members of the scheme. Return enhancement becomes crucial because the investor defers present consumption for future with an expectation of increased and regular payment for future consumption. Risk is an important component of return and needs careful understanding, especially its nature and its dimension. Risk elimination is never possible but a portion investment risk may be handled through diversification of portfolio asset allocation while some portion of risk is non-diversifiable. Therefore, there are two components of investment risk—diversifiable and non-diversifiable. Risk element in investment may be reduced through portfolio diversification by investing in various financial instruments like equity, debt, money market instruments within the given regulatory framework. Some regulators also allow alternative investment like real estate, commodities, etc. Further, a liberal investment regulation regime may also be investment of pension assets in foreign equity and debt.

The non-diversifiable portion of risks composed of capital risk, re-investment risk, credit risk, inflation risk, fiscal risk, etc. Capital risk arises when value of portfolio declines owing to erosion of portfolio value due to decline in the price of equity, decline of market value of debt instruments of default, etc., due to systemic or market factor which may be hedged but cannot be fully diversified. Re-investment risks arise due to changing interest rate regime. Maturity proceeds received from early investment will earn a very low interest causing erosion of portfolio value, while liquidity risks arise from sudden changes in a situation which causes unexpected large claims arising out of unnatural changes, which may cause mismatch between available liquidity and demand for liquidity. Fiscal risks arise due to changes in the fiscal policy of the government. Most significant is the taxation rule, which may adversely affect the accumulation and final payout. Frequent changes in the rules of taxation may turn pension fund investment into an unattractive proposition. Inflation risk is accompanied by changes in macroeconomic factors and monetary policy cannot be avoided over a long period of time. However, the adverse impact of changes in inflation factor can be hedged by investing in long-term inflation protected bond.

❖ MORTALITY RISK

Mortality risk is not a concern for fund managers in accumulation stage in a funded DC pension system but becomes an important risk factor in payout stage of DC system and in DB plans. Mortality risk arises out of longer life expectancy than estimated. In an annuity contract between a pensioner and the annuity provider (normally a life insurance company), the annuity provider may underestimate the longevity and end, providing more annuity benefits than the purchase price. This may happen due to obsolete mortality table, absence of mortality research and regular updating of mortality data.

❖ OPERATIONAL RISK

Operational risks are associated with management, human resources, system, strategy, marketing incentives, etc. Marketing incentives to the sales people may often promote future risks since sales people tend to maximise their own commission instead of focusing on the interest of customers or company.

Management Risks

Management risks are associated with incompetency of management which is unable to provide management efficiency, predict potential changes and provide necessary direction to handle adverse development detrimental to the financial health of the fund and interest of the investors.

Regulatory risk

Regulatory Risk arises out of the regulators' inability to assess the market reality and those affecting operation of pension funds. Market and investors' expectation are dynamic and regulation should reflect these changes to provide investors interest centric prudential guidelines/regulation, but regulation sometimes becomes a rigid bureaucratic instrument driven by political interest. Regulatory risks also arise out of frequent changes in the guidelines, impacting overall operational policy and investment strategy of the fund.

Political risk

Pension reform is significantly influenced by the political intervention. In order to achieve political mileage, the political parties may interfere in the framing of regulation and operation of pension funds which may not be in the interest of investors and contain operational and other risks. Licensing, investment guidelines and operation, etc., may be influenced for certain political purpose.

SUGGESTED ACTION PLAN FOR RISK MANAGEMENT

Risk management Policy is not a Statement of Intent (SI) but a Statement of Plan of Action (SAP), providing an outline of objectives and structure of risk management framework, methods of identification of various risks associated with operation of a fund, probable sources of risks, risk measurement and risk oversight. Risk management is not an exclusive function of the risk officer but an overall responsibility of all, including board members, CEO, management team, risk officer and all the employees. Risk policy must involve them all into this action plan.

Objectives

The broader objective of the Action Plan for Risk Management (APRM) is to put in place an workable framework under which roles and responsibilities would be defined and sufficient provision for necessary support is to be identified. The action plan should identify the fiduciary responsibility, role of independent risk officer and risk office, role and responsibility of CEO and other members of the management including CIO, COO and CFO. It should also identify the role of investment policy and investment strategy in risk management and risk reporting. The action plan should include methodologies for risk identification and risk mitigation and risk limit/risk budgeting, and the contents and periodicity of risk reporting to the board. Risk measurement may include valuation method, risk-adjusted return, stress testing, tracking error, etc.

Risk Measurement Technique

The action plan should also include one or more suitable techniques for portfolio risk measurement as an indicator of investment performance and risk management. Risk evaluation is however more complicated than evaluation of investment performance as the former is an exercise on past actions while the latter indicates the outcome which could have been better if risk management was done with more precision.

There are several methods to risk measurement of a portfolio but most widely used methods for fund management are *value at risk*, *tracking error* and *volatility measure.*

Value at Risk (VaR)

Value at Risk (VaR) is a measure of expected loss on a particular investment over a long period of time under certain confidence level, for example, confidence level of 95 per cent or 99 per cent, and this method is used to measure market risks. VaR is a general concept and has a wider application, but is most commonly used to measure the *market risk* of the asset portfolios. It can measure the maximum loss within the given confidence level over a given period of time. VaR can be incorporated into asset allocation strategy by using shortfall constraints which is generally used as market risk measure. 'VaR is used as an ex post measure to evaluate current exposure to market risk and other decisions to whether exposure ought to be reduced' (Huisman 1999). There are other risk measurement models and the Board and Management need to accept one or more such models for risk measurement and need to include in the action model. Risk reporting to the board and to the regulation (as prescribed in the regulation is also important). A standard format incorporating all relevant aspects needs to be incorporated in such format.

Tracking Error

It is an analysis to measure how closely a portfolio follows a benchmark/index. It measures the *standard deviation* of the difference between the return of the portfolio and the return of the index. Tracking error (also called *active risk*) is a measure of the deviation from the benchmark. When portfolio active return is divided by portfolio tracking error, we get the *information ratio*, which is a risk-adjusted performance metric. Tracking Error can be backward looking or forward looking. The most usual sort of backward risk measure adopted in the fund management industry is the retrospective or the backward looking *tracking error*, which shows the risk that have been run within the portfolio, but they are less helpful to identify the future risks that are likely to be experienced by the portfolio, while forward looking risk is estimated by calculating the forward looking tracking error which shows the risk that portfolio would experience if the same remain unaltered (Kemp et al. 2000). Other risk measures are: *Volatility Measure* (indicates the variability or dispersion of price of a financial instrument at a time and also shows the probability of achieving certain price at future date, is commonly used for measuring risk and r option pricing); *Beta Analysis,* (used for investment risk based on the volatility of returns based on certain baseline); *Sharpe Ratio and the Information Ratio* (used to indicate risk-adjusted returns), etc. Action Plan needs to identify one or more such measures to be adopted for risk management.

❖ RISK OVERSIGHT

Another important component of action plan is the *risk oversight compliance* policy, risk monitoring, independent review and necessary modification in review, monitoring and implementation.

❖ RISK MANAGEMENT STRATEGY

Risk in pension funds has wider dimension in terms of sources and ramification and there are a variety of techniques and strategies to control risks, which cannot be totally eliminated. Some of the strategies are discussed here.

❖ LEGISLATION

Legislation provides a broad legal framework under which a pension fund functions. It often prescribes the limits of functional freedom to limit the risk exposure of a company.

❖ REPORTING AND COMPLIANCE

Legislation provides powers to the regulatory authority, which frames rules and regulations for the industry and the company. Regulators also supervise implementation of various rules/regulations by the companies. Regulation provides the overall framework; risk management strategy includes the standard risk management measures through investment regulation for portfolio diversification, quantifying investment limit in various financial instruments, regulating costs and expenses, building up management and board-level capacity through fit and proper test. Regulation also includes standard compliance and reporting by the pension funds and thus monitors the risk management practices in pension funds.

❖ RISK-BASED SUPERVISION

Risk-based supervision has emerged as a powerful tool for risk management. Risk-based supervision is the process that identifies various risks critical to the financial viability of a fund in the long run. This involves issues relating to management including company board, operational and technical issues, investment management processes and strategies, changes in the capital market, economic and fiscal policies impacting the performance of the fund. Globally, pension fund regulators are introducing risk-based regulation and supervision.

❖ INVESTMENT POLICY AND STRATEGY

Pension Funds are required to adopt an investment policy as per the regulation. Investment policy aims at attaining the obligations like providing the safety, security and growth of the fund. Actual investment function carries through the asset allocation strategy. As noted above, in a defined contribution pension system, long-term objectives are met through strategic asset allocation which tends to provide maximum return with some estimated risk through an optimum portfolio over a long period of time. Tactical asset allocation strategy is used to minimise the impact of short-term volatility and market risks. Effectiveness of investment strategy to control and manage risks to a large extent depends on the fund managers expertise and ability to forecast future trend in domestic and international economy, financial market, changes in political environment, regulatory regime, etc., and the probable impact of such changes. These will immensely influence strategic asset allocation. A short-term market perspective and market movement will determine market timing and risks due to market volatility. These can be controlled through Tactical Asset Allocation.

❖ ASSET–LIABILITY MANAGEMENT

Asset–Liability Management (ALM) is a dynamic concept and an important tool of risk management and also an integral part of strategic investment management. 'ALM involves developing mathematical scenarios of the future evolution of pension fund assets and liabilities, given certain assumptions about the statistical properties of economic, financial and biometric variables that affect the evolution of assets and liabilities' (Blome et al. 2007). Having contracted fund management practice in a DC pension system, investment risks remain with the members and are not transferred to the fund managers. However, since the fund managers are responsible for managing retirement savings prudently to provide maximum possible risk-adjusted return to the investors, long-term risk management is not only a concern but also an important responsibility of investment management. However, risk management still remains a critical issue for investment management in DC system. Sometimes, even in DC system, there is a minimum bench mark return to be achieved by the fund managers (though it is not yet a condition for the fund management in India, but may be in the future. This brings us to the core of liability management, keeping in view the current and future funds inflow in view. Asset–Liability thus emerges as an issue of importance even in a funded DC system. The ALM study thus provides an insight of liability of an asset portfolio and the degree of risk associated with the portfolio against the notional bench mark return set out by the funds.

Institutionalisation of Risk Management

Institutionalisation of risk management depends on creation of an organisation-wide risk management culture supported by a policy of risk governance, well-defined risk management objectives, policies and practices, responsibilities and monitoring and suitable risk standard. Institutionalisation of risk management practices calls for separating risk monitoring (RM) from operational function (OF). Therefore, monitoring should be entrusted to the entity not involved in operational matters. Though implementation will be reviewed by a primary fiduciary such as the board or top management, yet there is a necessity for independent monitoring through designated persons. Many organisations appoint a chief risk officer (CRO) for this purpose and the person appointed as the CRO is reasonably a senior-level executive reporting to the chief executive/board. The CRO should have a proven record and expertise to handle such a job independently and without any inhibition. The CRO would monitor the implementation of risk management, keeping the risk budget and risk policy as a benchmark. He would also keep a watch on the deviation of actual risk from the risk tolerance limit and implementation of risk standard, and risk strategy. CRO functions independently and submits periodic report to the board either on a quarterly or a half-yearly basis, through the chief executive of the organisation. However, the success of the CRO system largely depends on real independence. If top management is not very sincere and committed to the cause of risk management, there will never be real independence.

❖ RISK MANAGEMENT CULTURE

Risk management is a philosophy which needs to be accepted by an individual employee of an organisation. But this philosophy cannot be imposed and will not work if thrust upon them only through control mechanism. For acceptance of the risk management philosophy, it is required to promote a culture of risk management. Individuals throughout the organisation must own this philosophy in such a way that they become the owners of risk management. To facilitate the ownership of risk management, there should be awareness about importance, criticality of the concept and ultimate benefits to the employees and the organisation that could be achieved out of implementation of risk management. However, the awareness campaign requires the commitment of the board and top management of the organisation. Sincerity, seriousness and commitment of the top management need to be seen by the other employees down the line. One of the important instruments to promote corporate risk management culture is well-meaning Long-Term Policy (LTP) with corporate vision, mission, goal and various stakeholders' interest. However, policies need to be effectively supported by well-designed procedures. Procedures are often seen as a control mechanism. No doubt controls are required and are essential components of risk policy. However, internal control needs to be seen as an instrument of empowering people and providing them with guidelines to control activities to mitigate various risks.

❖ INCENTIVES FOR RISK MANAGEMENT

Incentives are important to create a culture of risk governance and risk management. Risk governance can be established either through 'risk control' or through 'risk reward'. In either of these models, there is a necessity of improving risk knowledge, risk information and competitive risk practices. Genuine risk reporting and risk information will strengthen risk governance. Risk management has its costs as well. Professional training, technology, short-term loss due to rigid implementation of risk policy, etc., may cost in the short-term, though the benefits out of risk management practices may accrue in the long-term. However, management must be willing to bear this cost in the long-term interest. Further, the review of risk management practices and risk measurements are required to be conducted at frequent intervals by the fiduciary. This review should include the policy compliance, due diligence, monitoring investment guidelines, investment strategies, risk limits and evaluation of investment models. If required, revision or redesigning of models, strategies, risk limits may be done within the overall guidelines and parameters of the regulators. However, the goal of risk governance and risk management can be achieved if the top management and board are actively interested in it. Therefore, risk management should not be thought of only as a regulatory requirement, but an integral part of corporate strategy and a way of corporate life in the interest of all the stakeholders.

Risk Management in NPS

Under NPS, the broad risk management guidelines have been issued by the PFRDA, which all the fund managers comply with. Risk management is implemented through a committee approach. Accordingly, all the PFMs should constitute a *Risk Management Committee* consisting of chief executive officer, chief investment officer, the risk/compliance officers and an independent director of the board. The risk management policy is approved by the board of directors, which should include risk management functions, disaster recovery and business contingency plans, insurance cover against risks, ensuring risk-adjusted return to the subscribers consistent with the protection, safety and liquidity of such funds. The risk management policy approved by the board will be implemented by the management committee and the board would be kept informed periodically. The board should review the policy on a half-yearly basis and suggest modifications/changes to bring it with the requirement of law and regulations and also inform the NPS Trust. The risk management committee may engage services of outside risk management professionals.

As per the guidelines provided by the Regulator PFRDA, all the fund managers have drawn detail risk management policy approved by their board of directors. The operational policy is much wider and has enlisted the objectives and detailed implementation mechanism, risk monitoring and review system. However, the current practice of risk management that is based on the broad guidelines of PFRDA is too narrow in scope and centred around investment operation and financial risks. Therefore, many sources of risk remain unattended; for example, management risks, technology risks, policy risks have not surfaced in the present policy. These risks can be suitably addressed by incorporating Prudent Person Rule in the risk management policy. Moreover, the regulator should design a risk standard for the pension fund industry in a specially designed risk regulation.

ROLE OF CAPITAL MARKET IN INVESTMENT AND RISK MANAGEMENT

Issues of fund management, valuation of assets, and state of capital market of the country and risk management are interrelated as one component has bearing on the other. Therefore, efficiency in pension fund investment management requires competent fund managers, market-related workable valuation methodology and well-regulated and well-functioning capital market with sufficient number of debt and equity securities. There is an important role of rating agencies as the pension funds are required to invest mostly in rated instruments and high-quality rating would make the investment safe and secure the interest of investors in NPS. Risk management is also most critical to pension fund investment management which is influenced by the regulation, fund managers competency, risk management products and the system of risk governance (SRG) and commitment of the governing board. Experience shows that these factors are still below the desired level in NPS. There is need a for competency building at all levels including regulation, supervision, fund management and fund governance.

REFERENCES

ADB (2008), 'Asia Bond Monitor 2008'. Manila: Asian Development Bank.

Ambachtsheer, Keith (2007), 'The Three Grades of Pension Fund Governance Quality: Bad, Better and Best'. Available at: http://kpa-advisory.com/pdf_documents/Three per cent20 Grades per cent20of per cent20Pension per cent20Fund per cent20Governance per cent20Quality_July per cent202007.pdf

Ambachtsheer, Keith, Ronald Capelle and Hubert Lum (2008), 'The Pension Governance Deficit Still with US'. *Rotman International Journal of Pension Management*, 1(1), Fall 2008.

Antolin, Pablo and Hans Blommenstein (2007), 'Governments and the Market for Longevity —Indexed Bonds'. OECD Working Papers on Insurance and Private Pensions, No. 4, OECD Publishing. doi:10.1787/260561411283.

Blome, S., K. Fachinger, D. Franzen, G. Scheuenstuhl and J. Yermo (2007), 'Pension Fund Regulation and Risk Management: Results from an ALM Optimization Exercise'. OECD Working Paper on Insurance and Private Pension, No. 8.

Clapman, Peter (2007), 'Committee on Fund Governance—Best Practice Principles (Peter Clapman, Chair). The Stanford Institutional Investors' Forum, 31 May 2007.

Davis, E Philip and Yu-Wei Hu (2005), 'Saving, Funding and Economic Growth'. Economics and Finance Discussion Papers from Economics and Finance Section, School of Social Sciences, Brunel University. Available at: http://www.brunel.ac.uk/329/efwps/05-02.pdf

Davis, E. Philip (2001), 'Portfolio Regulation of Life Insurance Companies and Pension Funds'. Discussion Paper PI-0101, The Pension Institute, London, January,http://www.pensions-institute.org/

Daykin, Christopher D. (2002), 'Risk Management Regulation of Defined Contribution Schemes'. Presented at Actuarial Aspects of Pension Reform, Seminar for Social Security Actuaries and Statisticians, International Social Security Association, Moscow, 3–5 July.

Department of Economic Affairs (2008), Circular On 'The Pattern of Investment to be followed by Non-Government Provident Funds, Superannuation Funds and Gratuity Funds', issued by Government of India, Ministry of Finance, Department of Economic Affairs Circular: F.No.5(88)/2006-PR, dated 14 August.

Huisman, Ronald, Kees G. Koedijk, Rachel, A. J. Ponwal (1999), 'Asset Allocation in a Value-at-Risk Framework'. Available at: http://www.smartquant.com/references/VaR/var6.pdf

Kemp, Malcom (Chairman), Martin Cumberworth, Daniel Gardner, Julie Griffiths and Christopher Sandford (2000), 'Portfolio Risk Measurement and Reporting: An Overview for Pension Funds', January 2000.

NSE (2010), 'Indian Securities Market—A Review'. Mumbai: National Stock Exchange of India.

NSE (2011), *Fact Book 2011*. Mumbai: National Stock Exchange of India.

SEBI (2011), 'Annual Report 2010–11'. Mumbai: Securities and Exchange Board of India.

OECD/IOPS (2009), 'Pension reform and developments in Latin America, Conference Proceedings of the OECD/IOPS Global Forum on Private Pensions', Rio de Janerio, Brazil, October 2009. http://www.oecd.org/site/iops/documents/46142448.pdf

RBI (2011), *Handbook of statistics on the Indian Economy 2010–11*. Mumbai: Reserve Bank of India.

World Bank (2010), 'World Development Indicators'. Washington D.C.: World Bank.

13 Pension Fund Regulation and Supervision

Issues and Challenges

INTRODUCTION

Designing an effective regulation and supervisory mechanism for privately managed individual account based defined contribution (DC) pension funds is not only an important and necessary component of pension system but is also a very critical and complex job. It is so important because an individual entrusts the lifelong savings for old age income to a private entity (fund manager) with the expectation that her/his funds will be prudently managed and will grow and provide regular flow of income for old age protection. There are other entities also associated with the fund management system. Therefore, well-coordinated activities of these institutions and efficient management of funds would enable the investors to achieve that goal. Pension fund regulation is further complex as there are a number of stakeholders—government, sponsors, beneficiaries, etc., who are involved with pension system. In a DC system pension funds are managed by the fund managers but payouts come from life insurance or annuity service providers, so the life insurance industry also plays an important role. Further, pension assets are invested in capital market/financial instruments, governed by a separate regulatory organisation/regulator. These regulators also impact the fund management operation of the pension funds. The government also plays an important role by providing a broad outline and legislative framework of the pension system. Pension fund regulation is thus a critical combination of pension system, capital market and life insurance. Involvement of all these entities in pension accumulation and pension delivery often generates conflict of interests. The pension regulator needs to manage these conflicts, supervise the intermediaries so that they perform efficiently. Therefore, a well-designed regulatory mechanism and efficient delivery mechanism not only facilitates smooth functioning of pension system but also induces confidence among the pension savers.

Regulation and supervisions are two distinct functions but very often a single agency performs both the functions, though often regulation is designed by the government and regulatory authority undertakes supervision functions with the help of specialised departments. Therefore, regulatory efficiency also depends on the authority and accountability of the regulator. In an individual account based DC system, choice is left to the individual to decide the fund managers, select the portfolio, option to switch over, etc. The entire risk of investment and other choices are borne by the investors and always remain susceptible to risk of market failure arising out of information asymmetry, externalities and market concentration, etc. It is necessary that pension fund investors are protected against such market failures through appropriate regulation to reduce the risk of investment through portfolio regulation, capital/solvency regulation, monopoly/market concentration. There are other areas like costs of pension fund administration (marketing and servicing) and pension payouts, etc., which could not be left to the private service providers and need to be controlled through regulation. Therefore, the role of regulator in a pension system is very important and the scope is quite wide.

REGULATIONS AND SUPERVISION

Though regulation and supervision are two distinct concepts, and regulatory functions differ from supervisory functions, in reality these functions are overlapping and the regulator acts as the supervisor and regulatory norms are submerged in supervisory practices.

Regulation

Financial institutions are very important in the entire socio-economic–political set-up of a country and occupy centre stage developing and delivering financial products and services so that the aspiration of growth objectives of the country and expectations of individual member of the respective financial institutions (pension funds, life insurance, banking, asset management companies, etc.) are achieved. Pension funds are somewhat different from other financial institutions as there is an implicit contractual agreement between the contributors and fund managers for payment of contribution by the contributors and delivery of accumulated wealth which is expected to be more than contribution. Though in a DC system there is no guarantee of exact return but expectation is that it would be higher than what a contributor would get by self-investment. Regulation of activities of fund managers and other intermediaries are therefore essential to ensure the objectives of safety, security and reasonable return by preventing the exposure to market failure. Market failure may occur due to a variety of reasons like information asymmetry, externalities, monopoly, power, etc. There is a need to prevent such occurrences in order to protect the investors. Davis (2000) puts it beautifully, as he says, 'The main economic reasons for pension fund regulation are asymmetric information, monopoly power and certain non-market failure based reasons such as ensuring tax subsidies are directed to retirement income provision'. Therefore, pension funds are to be protected from market failure and regulation plays the most critical role in protecting institutions and interest of investors.

Regulation, however, accompanied the process and speed of liberalisation. Therefore, the process of liberalisation emerges as a determinant of regulation. Liberalisation is a structural and a cultural change, which is accompanied by shock, resistance and doubts and these factors are to be kept in mind while focusing on the areas and speed of regulation. 'The recognition that changes cannot occur overnight and that time is needed to build up regulatory capacity suggests that a process of gradual liberalisation may be preferable to the rapid liberalisation ...' (Stiglitz 2001). Managing the regulatory change in a liberalised environment depends on the building up of the regulatory capacity by filling up the capacity gap. The objective of regulation in a newly established pension regime needs to be clearly spelt out or publicly announced as it will create confidence in the minds of people.

Regulatory Approach

The successful implementation of any regulation depends on the underlying regulatory approach in relation to objective, market of environment and legal system. Therefore, there has always been a dilemma about the most appropriate form of regulation. Vittas (1998) has identified four approaches, namely, Centralised Management by a public agency (Eastern Europe and Central Asia as well as National Provident Fund in Singapore and Malaysia), Regulatory Vacuum or Rudimentary Legislation (as in Russia), *Draconian* regulation covering most aspects of operation (Chile and other Latin American countries) and Quantitative *Prudent Regulation.* The Prudential Regulation aims at protecting the pension fund beneficiaries and the pension funds. Fiduciary responsibilities of trustees are expected to ensure fair play and efficiency of the fund managers and protection of beneficiaries' interest. Investment management regulation restricting the investment limit in various instruments and prohibiting investment in certain areas is expected to ensure misuse of funds, reducing the risks through investment diversification. While investment activities are strictly controlled (through quantitative restriction, pension fund valuation, benefit calculation, etc.), it also focuses on information dissemination on regular basis, with the objective to ensure efficiency in fund management, to avoid excessive risk-taking by the funds. However, prudential regulation has certain weaknesses and there is a growing tendency among the countries to switch over to *risk-based regulation* as quantitative prudential regulation is not enough to protect the investors' interest as often risk arises from incompetency, managerial actions and inactions, etc. In the evolving world of regulation, a large number of countries adopted a regulatory philosophy that aligns with country's legislative mandate of pension reforms though the methods may be different. The most preferred kind of regulation in the newly reformed pension system is some sort of strict regulation covering the whole gamut of pension fund operation, in line with what Vittas called *Draconian Regulation* and others like Demarco and Rofman (1998) called *Proactive Model.*

> *The main choice in designing the supervisory system is between Pro·ıctive and Reactive Models. While the first approach involves detailed regulation of most activities of pension fund managers, the second approach relies on self regulation, with much less detailed instructions from supervisors. The proactive model is mostly adopted in newly created pension in less developed countries (Demarco and Rofman 1998).*

The regulatory approach in most of the countries introducing individual contribution based DC system revolves around individual choice to select funds, fund managers, etc., which contains a variety of risks—product pricing, investment management, service delivery, payouts, etc. Therefore, the government and regulatory authorities in the newly reformed countries introduced somewhat stricter regulation restricting the entry to the pension fund industry, fixing the minimum capital requirement, limiting the product offerings, limiting the choice of investment portfolio, minimum performance guarantee by the fund managers, etc. This is often termed as draconian and many authors, Srinivas et al. (2000), felt:

> *Draconian regulation of pension funds has prevented the achievement of many of these objectives, as it forces the workers to choose one manager and one fund preventing the workers to diversify investment across the funds, and preventing the portfolio adjustment according to the individual age. 'Strict asset-allocation rules and relative performance criteria mean that pension funds often invest and perform almost identically, removing any substantive choice for workers over the allocation of their pension fund's assets and the portfolio's risk and returns.'*

Since in the new individual based account system the entire pension risk is transferred to the investors while in the DB system pension providers bear the pension risks, there is total uncertainty of return, accumulated assets and amount of final pension that one can buy with accumulated amount in the privatised DC pension system, and such a strict regulatory regime is absolutely necessary. However, at the same time it should be kept in mind that regulation has a cost which is ultimately borne by the investors and overregulation may be reactionary at times. Further, a newly reformed pension system (for example, NPS in India), should not blindly follow the regulation adopted by some other countries. Every country has peculiar social and economic consideration, constraints and aspiration which should be reflected in regulation.

Principles of Regulation

Regulatory Objectives, regulatory approach and regulatory principles are closely interlinked and strongly influence each other which, however, flow from the format of reform. An efficient regulatory system should however be based on sound principles which covers the requirements of institution building, efficient management of pension system including investment management, risk management, benefit design and benefit delivery system, governance and supervision.

> *An adequate regulatory framework for private pensions should be enforced in a comprehensive, dynamic and flexible way (taking into account the complexity of the schemes) in order to ensure the protection of pensions plan members and beneficiaries, the soundness of pensions plans and funds and the stability of the economy as a whole. (OECD 2009a)*

OECD has recommended certain core principles of pension fund regulation, which include: Conditions for effective regulation and supervision (Core Principle 1); Establishment of pension plans, pension funds, and pension fund managing companies (Core Principle 2), Pension plan liabilities, funding rules, winding up, and insurance (Core Principle 3); Asset Management (Core Principle 4), Rights of members and beneficiaries and adequacy of benefits (Core Principle 5); Governance (Core Principle 6) and Supervision (Core Principle 7) (OECD 2009b).

OECD principles cover the whole gamut of regulatory canvas and any regulatory mechanism based on these principles will be able to protect the interest of investors as well as the interest of sponsors and other intermediaries. Various criteria prescribed for asset management also cover the area of prudential regulation and move forward towards risk-based supervision. However, the regulation for pension fund system will be determined by the nature of the mandate. The mandate is given to the regulator through legislative approval of the country. It provides a broad outline of the reformed system, nature of the industry, regulators' power and authority, composition of regulatory authority, benefits and contribution of system, role of various intermediaries, scope of investment, payouts and annuity, system of governance and supervision of the system, etc. The regulators function under the legally approved framework and implement the regulatory control over the pension system. In India such a legislative approval so far (October 2011) is not provided to the interim PFRDA, and it is functioning under administrative instructions of Government of India (the PFRDA bill which was introduced in 2005 in the Parliament yet to be passed.)

Role of Pension Fund Trust

Pension Fund Trust plays an important role in a mandatory defined contribution pension system in protecting beneficiary interest supporting supervision and implementing regulatory controls. Pension fund trusts are expected to ensure that the intermediaries function as per regulatory norms, fund management is carried as per investment guidelines, funds are managed prudently to ensure that effective risk mitigation framework are in place. It also monitors the policy implementation and initiates necessary intervention in the interest of the investors. Trust is a legal entity and holds the pension fund assets on behalf of the pension fund investors. In fund management industry and occupational pension fund usually there are fund-specific trusts (such as mutual funds in India). However, in case of the NPS there is a single centralised trust, namely, NPS, established by the PFRDA on 27 February 2008, with three members to begin with. Subsequently, three more members were included in the board and one of the trustees was appointed as the CEO of the NPS Trust. The NPS Trust always acts in the interest of the beneficiaries. It ensures that the funds are managed by the PF(s) in accordance with the NPS Trust deed and the PFRDA guidelines/directions. The NPS Trust controls all the property of the pension funds and holds these in the trust for the beneficiaries. The trust is also responsible to take necessary steps to ensure that the transactions of the PFs are in accordance with the provisions of the NPS Trust deed. The trust monitors and periodically reviews the functions of the intermediaries and takes necessary actions to rectify the deviations if any. In Indian NPS, the NPS Trust is the most critical interface and plays an important role in protecting beneficiaries' interest.

MAJOR AREAS OF PENSION FUND REGULATION AND SUPERVISION

Regulation for privately managed pension funds in a transitional liberalised pension system like India must be different from that of a well-established pension system, since transitional problems are quite different from that of established system. The role of regulator and supervisor cannot be restricted only to regulation and control. They are also expected to play the role of developer and facilitator in market development, institution building, regulating the entities in the pension market and controlling their activities to promote healthy market practices, to minimise various types of risks, cost control and enhancing investors' benefits. The regulation, therefore, must aim at establishing a regulatory process that provides robust system of supervision, control and monitors the implementation of the regulation and any deviation which may generate future risks and adversely impact the investors' benefits.

Institution Building

Since the responsibility of regulator, particularly in a newly promoted pension system, is not only to design regulatory and supervisory mechanism to control the pension industry but also to promote and strengthen newly established market system. The regulation must induce confidence among all the stakeholders, particularly among the members of the pension system. There are constraints to development—lack of awareness, low level of literacy and habit of pension savings, absence of expertise for fund management and operation, competent persons as trustees and board members, etc.

Therefore, institution building and market development would occupy an important place in the regulation. These activities will mostly be carried out by the supervisor, but regulatory back up would make it an essential function of supervisors. The regulation, therefore, aims at capacity building and institutionalising the culture of pension fund savings and pension fund management, and to contribute to institution building to strengthen the pension system.

The regulation for pension fund must be country and environment centric. Sometimes it is seen that many regulatory conditions borrowed from others do not suit the local environment, and in the long run create chaos. For example, the valuation of debt portfolio in India, which has a debt market without depth and less liquidity, cannot be the same as a developed country with well-developed debt market. For the regulation to be effective, it should be market centric in a local condition. Further, regulation must be realistic so that those who are regulated should not try to find an escape route to violate it. Regulation should be institutionalised and a way of operational life of a company (pension fund and other intermediaries). In real life we often observe that some regulation—though designed with good intention—is either difficult to implement (even by the supervisor) or unreasonable in a given situation and market environment. Regulation should not be so rigid that it fails to capture changing market environment and stakeholders' expectation. But at the same time, it should not be so flexible that the investors lose confidence. Regulation must be drawn with a clear vision and future perspective. The core to success of any regulatory regime is the clearly defined regulatory/supervisory objectives, operational transparency and the confidence of stakeholders of the pension system.

Regulation for Market Entry

A market-centric regulation to translate national aspiration through regulation can be designed with the market structure in view. Pension industry is composed of several components like DB pension, DC pension, insurance company pension plans, etc. Individually funded pensions can be voluntary or mandatory. Further, a country may have single pension system like mandatory individual funded pension or a parallel system with mandatory individual-funded system along with employer-sponsored DB system. The market structure can be either homogeneous or heterogeneous. Regulation in a homogeneous market will differ from a heterogeneous market. However, pension regulation in a newly established market needs to have a considered view about the entry of various market intermediaries, namely, pension fund managers, record keeping agency, distributors, banking agency, custodians, annuity service providers, etc. While a competitive environment needs to be promoted, there should be an optimum number of these entities to avoid excessive competition which may create confusion in the marketplace and produce adverse results. Another critical issue is the nature of promoting companies. Generally existing financial institutions are barred from direct entry but they are allowed to sponsor such intermediaries. It is also necessary to see that the sponsored have core competency, reputation, sound capital base and business practices, which would support the new entities to grow and perform in the interest of investors. In India there has been an entry barrier. For the government NPS, only the government or public sector entities were allowed to sponsor fund managers, while for the private sector fund managers, a fit and proper test was imposed. Further, there is often restriction on ownership of an intermediary company like pension fund managers, record keeping agency, etc. India has taken a gradual step in allowing intermediaries in the NPS. There is a reasonable competition in funds management as there are seven fund managers (three for government NPS, seven for All Citizens' Scheme and NPS Lite). However, other functions carried are out by single centralised agency in respective areas, as there is one centralised NPS Trust, one central record keeping agency, one centralised NPS trustee bank and one centralised custodian for the entire NPS system. There are also certain restrictions on ownership control of the pension fund. For example, direct foreign investment in a pension fund company under NPS is restricted up to 26 per cent equity capital.

Licensing Regulation

Licensing is an important instrument to ensure that desired institutions enter into pension business. Licensing is also an instrument to limit future risks like agency and systematic risk associated with an entity operating in the pension market. Through licensing unwanted institutions (which can even be a liability of the system) can be prohibited to enter into the market. This is more important for a new system because many without core competence and track record may be induced into it with a mere profit motive. Such non-serious players should be barred through a well-designed licensing system. Licensing conditions can be utilised to assess the past record, core competence, management and operational capability of the company before issuing licences. Licensing also can be used as an instrument of disclosure for the licensed company.

In India we have seen in the past, when banking and mutual industries were opened up to private sector, a large number of new banks and mutual funds were set up and many of them closed shortly, often putting the investors in difficulties. Therefore, a close scrutiny would be necessary in issuing licences. The PFRDA followed a procedure of minimum capital requirement, minimum funds managed, other fit and proper tests and a two-way public bidding system to offer licenses—technical bidding and commercial bidding. However, there was an overemphasis on financial bidding and as a result many less experienced bidder quoted unsustainable lower fees just to get a license. Many of these institutions did not have country-wide presence and experience of managing long-term investment. Many in India feel that they could not induce enough confidence among the pension investors as response to their collection is very poor. Though keeping the cost low is undeniably an important regulatory issue, but marginally higher cost by more efficient fund managers may ultimately generate better return and the fund which induces confidence needs to be in the marketplace to increase the reach.

Regulation for Pension Products

Pension products (plans), distribution and fees charged by the distributors are important areas of regulation and supervision. In a mandatory DC system workers are forced to participate in the pension system and individually choose the funds and fund managers. Selecting an appropriate fund is sometimes a difficult choice. Regulation, therefore, plays an important role in helping the investors. Pension plans/funds are approved by the regulator considering various aspects of future risks and probable return on accumulated assets. Generally pension funds are limited in number. In the early stage of reform, most of the Fund managers in Latin America offered two funds and subsequently after few years the number of funds offered increased. *Chile* introduced multi-fund system in August 2002, prior to that, the Pension Fund Administrators (AFP) were authorised to offer two types of funds: Fund Type 1 (that includes a percentage of fixed and variable income) and which all members of the pension system could join, and Fund Type 2 (which only had fixed income) and which only retired members and members who were 10 years or less from reaching retirement age could join. But as of August 2002, each fund manager offered its members five portfolios (or funds). The funds are denominated A, B, C, D and E. Fund A has the highest proportion invested in variable income (80 per cent), whereas Fund E is authorised to invest a maximum of 5 per cent in this type of assets. Members who do not choose a fund type on joining the system are assigned to one of them according to their age. *Mexico* introduced multi-fund system on 28 March 2008 and each pension fund manager is authorised to offer five investment alternatives (SB1, SB2, SB3, SB4 and SB5). The funds differ mainly in their limits on variable income instruments. SB1 can only invest in fixed income instruments, whereas SB5 can invest up to 30 per cent in variable income. The regulations pre-establish a fund that varies according to the age of those members who do not exercise their right to choose the investment fund. *Peru* put in place the multi-fund system in January 2005. Each fund manager was allowed to offer three types of funds: a capital preservation fund (Type 1), a balanced or mixed fund (Type 2) and a growth fund (Type 3). Fund Type 1 can invest up to 10 per cent in shares, Fund Type 2 up to 45 per cent and Fund Type 3 up to 80 per cent. Members who do not choose a fund type on joining the system are assigned to one of them according to their age. *Hungary* introduced the multi-fund system in January 2007. This system was initially voluntary, but as of January 2009, it became mandatory. Each fund manager is authorised to offer three types of funds: a conservative fund (up to 10 per cent in variable income), a balanced fund (up to 40 per cent in variable income) and a growth fund (up to 100 per cent in variable income). Members who do not choose a fund type on joining the pension system are assigned to one of them according to their age (FIAP 2010).

Indian regulator, however, introduced a product basket with larger number of funds (schemes) right from the beginning. As we have discussed in Chapter 7, there are two schemes for government employees, namely, a low-risk scheme restricting equity investment up to 15 per cent and a very low risk G Sec fund (not yet operational). However, there are four funds for All Citizens' Scheme, one fund allowing equity investment up to 50 per cent and others are Corporate Debt fund, G Sec fund and Auto Choice fund (Default Option). The NPS Lite which has been introduced for low-income disadvantaged segment has, however, adopted the schemes offered to the government employees. One of the objectives of the regulator is to limit the risk associated with equity investment. Further, Indian pension funds are not yet allowed to invest in foreign markets.

Collection of Contribution

Regulatory and supervisory focus on collection of contribution is directed with a view to minimise costs, improve service quality and improve the reach of the pension system. Agencies collecting the contributions can also play an important developmental role. However, the newly reformed countries have adopted two different models of collection, namely, centralised collection system and decentralised collection system. For example, in Latin America, countries like Argentina, Mexico, Uruguay, and in Eastern Europe, Poland adopted the centralised collection system to collect pension contributions, whereas Bolivia, Chile, Colombia and Peru have adopted the decentralised collection system. In the decentralised system pension contributions are collected jointly with the collection of contributions to other social security programs or the collection of some taxes. But in the decentralised system, pension contributions are collections exclusively for the pension fund system (in Chile pension fund contributions are collected jointly with the contributions for unemployment insurance). Collection cost is an issue in the new system and many feel decentralised collection system is costlier. However, AFP has noted,

> *[C]ontrary to what one would expect, the costs reported by the decentralized collection models are in general lower than the centralized models. This could be explained by the fact that part of the potential advantages of the centralized systems lie in the lower costs for the employers and in the lower costs of crediting individual accounts assumed by the Fund Managers, which processes are not included in cost measurement as they do not fit into the definition of 'collection' adopted for this study. (AFP 2006)*

India has adopted a mixture of centralised and decentralised system of collection. Contributions under the government NPS are collected through a centralised channel while other contributions to All Citizens' Scheme and NPS Lite are collected through a decentralised channel. For the government NPS, contribution of employees is collected by the respective pay and account office and sent to the collecting bank (NPS Trust bank) while the collected funds are distributed by CRA among the three designated fund managers. For the All Citizens' Scheme, there are 35 POPs which collect the contribution and send it to the trustee bank, which transfers the fund to the six designated fund managers.

However, in the NPS Lite scheme, collection of contribution is the responsibility of the aggregators, which collect the contribution from the members and deposit the amount to the trustee bank which in turn transfers the same to the fund managers as per choice of the aggregators. The POPs and the aggregators are also expected to popularise the NPS products by creating awareness among the potential investors in NPS. India has not appointed any distributors or agents to sell pension products but introduced some incentives for aggregators to motivate them to increase sales and to create awareness.

Banking System

Though NPS has adopted a decentralised model of contribution collection, it has entrusted the collection of contribution under the NPS scheme to a single public sector bank, Bank of India. This bank acts as the trustee bank and all the banking transactions are carried out through it.

Custodian

Custodian's role in a pension system is very important as they hold all the pension fund assets in their custody. Though fund managers manage the assets under their funds but they cannot hold these assets in their name. All assets are the property of the trust on behalf of the individual investors. There is a centralised custodian system under NPS and Stock Holding Corporation of India (SHICL), a company promoted by the public sector financial institutions has been appointed as the custodian for the NPS.

Investment Regulation

Mandatory DC pension system is centred on the investment management pension fund managers and its associated activities like risk management, asset valuation practices risk management and governance of funds management. Therefore, investment management regulation occupies the centre stage of any regulation for occupational pension fund management, particularly in the post-reform new pension system of any country. Investment regulation is also most talked about piece of regulation as there are different views about the approach of an appropriate regulatory format. We have already indicated about two important schools of thoughts as *quantitative prudential regulation* and *prudent person rule*, both of which have certain merits and demerits and the issue is which should be more suitable in a given situation.

Pension reform and introduction of DC system by replacing the old DB system is not only a cultural shock and perception reversal, but it also appears with significant amount of doubt. This is further impacted by transfer of risk from the pension providers to the investors, as well as the entry of numerous fund managers and other entities in the pension market without or with less credential and track record. The regulation needs to take care of investor confidence as well as control the activities of fund managers to protect investors' interest. Three important regulatory aims would be to create an environment of *competition* in the fund management industry, *control* the activities of pension fund managers in tune with the regulatory objectives and *confidence* building among the investors by protecting and ensuring beneficiary interest. Though investment regulation primarily focuses on the management of portfolio of various investment products ensuring that there is diversification of portfolio assets according to regulation to avoid undue risks, the regulation also focuses on valuation of assets, investment practices and governance, monitoring risk management and risk mitigation mechanisms, performance evaluation, system of compliance and periodic disclosure of activities of fund managers. Investment regulation in a mandatory DC system must attempt to introduce a regulatory regime that can enhance the value for the investors, effectively control risks, keep the costs minimum, market-related realistic system of valuation, performance accountability, good governance and accountability of fund managers, sponsors and responsibility of the government to promote an investors-centric pension system. Pension fund investment is a long-term proposition and thus associated with high degree of uncertainty and risks. The capital market is not efficient; at best in some cases like India, it is semi-efficient, liquidity is also a constraint in the debt market and high-quality papers are few in supply. Given these investment constraints and absence of strong corporate governance and risk management practices, *neither the quantitative regulation nor prudent person rule alone will be sufficient guiding factors for sound investment management but quantitative regulation supported by prudent person rule will be the most effective.* The PFRDA has introduced quantitative regulation for restricting NPS investment, but *it would be prudential if the quantitative regulation is supported by prudent person rule to introduce accountability, efficiency and more transparency.*

Investment Restriction

Asset class restrictions are basically related to limiting equity investment as it is considered to be riskier than bond/debt investing. Another objective of imposing restrictions on pension fund investment is restrain over concentration in securities issued by a single or few issuers company or in a single or few sectors as it defeats the objectives of diversification. Further excessive investment of either G Sec or corporate bond may be very risky. Interest rate in the G Sec fluctuates with liquidity and fiscal policy of the government (market borrowing) among others while corporate bond rates are influenced by the demand for investment, money supply and market liquidity. As such regulation aims at restraining fund managers to take risky exposure either in G Sec or Corporate Bond or either in the short-term or long-term bond (mostly in the short-term bonds). Foreign investment by Indian pension funds are not allowed but a powerful section in India is putting constant pressure to allow pension funds to invest in capital market abroad. Any such decision, however, needs to be taken keeping in view the sufferings of pension funds abroad during 2007–08 due to market decline. Moreover, the experience of pension reforms in Latin America and the asset allocation of pension funds in many countries need to be kept in mind. It has been mentioned in chapter 12 that investments by some countries, including Bolivia, are very minimal. There is no foreign investment by pension funds of Bolivia (IOPS 2009). Indian market is also well developed compared to the capital markets in many emerging countries and foreign fund managers put their money in Indian market; therefore, it does not make sense at this stage to invest in foreign markets by Indian Pension Funds.

The risk policy as provided by the regulator, PFRDA, all the fund managers have drawn detail risk management policy approved by their board of directors. The operational policy is much wider and has enlisted the objectives and detail implementation mechanism, risk monitoring and review system. However, the current practice of risk management that is based on the broad guidelines of PFRDA is too narrow in scope and is centred on investment operation and financial risks. Therefore many sources of risk remain unattended, for example, management risks, technology risks, policy risks have not surfaced in the present policy. *These risks can be suitably addressed by incorporating prudent person rule in the risk management policy. Moreover, the regulator should design a risk standard for the pension fund industry in a specially designed risk regulation.*

Investment Regulation and Infrastructure Investment by Pension Funds

Pension fund regulation is conservative by nature and emphasises upon allocating a major portion of assets to debt and debt-oriented low-risk securities to avoid high risks, volatility, and to ensure liquidity. However, due to recent changes in the interest rate regime, volatility in the stock market, pension fund managers find it difficult to maintain the target of investment yield and prudentially invest the growing corpus, due to short supply of long-term quality debt instruments and there is a growing demand for alternative investment avenues. In this context investing in infrastructure, private equity, etc., has been advocated by many and pension funds abroad are gradually resorting to alternative investment.

Though it is an accepted fact that infrastructure is one of the prime movers of economic growth, yet this sector was overlooked for a long time by the developing countries including India. However, in recent times there has been an awareness and urgency to promote infrastructure through increased investment, but states are unable to fulfil the huge growing demand and public–private partnership has emerged as the focal point of development. The spectrum of infrastructure is varied. It includes social (health care, education, etc.) and economic infrastructure (communications, transportation, housing, utilities), the demand of which would grow continuously with the growth of population and the rate of growth of economy (alternatively economy needs support of infrastructure to grow faster). According to India Infrastructure Finance Ltd (IIFCL), investment in infrastructure in the 11th Five Year Plan (2007–2012) would be $514 billion, which would further go up in 12th Five Year Plan. Emerging infrastructure, therefore, offers tremendous opportunity for emerging pension fund industry in India. There are several arguments for pension fund investment in infrastructure:

Portfolio Diversification

Pension funds invest for a very long term ranging 30–35 years which is associated with huge uncertainty and risk. Limiting the risk through portfolio diversification is one of the well-tested strategies. Allowing pension funds to invest in infrastructure along with equity and debt instruments would further support the strategy of diversification for risk minimisation.

Long-term Investment

Infrastructure sector requires long-term investment and the pension funds prefer to invest for a longer horizon. Therefore, there is a natural match between both. Ultra Long Term Bond (40–50 years) government or corporate bond market has not yet developed in India. Infrastructure sector can fill this gap and provide an opportunity for institutional investors like pension funds.

Long-term Investment Planning by Pension Funds

Infrastructure investment is also considered to be attractive due to relatively higher return and for longer duration as 'Infrastructure industry characterized by high entry barriers, economies of scale, low operating costs, longer duration, inelastic demand, etc., would allow the funds long term planning' (Inderst 2009).

Facilitate Social Sector Expenditure

Fiscal Benefits, the participation of pension funds in financing infrastructure projects helps the fiscal consolidation of the public budget, facilitating resources for other social expenditure items or by reducing the fiscal pressures of the respective country, improves the allocation of resources (Alonso et al. 2010).

Reduces Political Risk

It is also argued that infrastructure investment by pension funds would reduce political and regulatory risk. Greater discipline would be expected on the part of the governments with regard to the contracts and the rules of the game if resources are involved that will finance the pensions of local workers. It will also find favour with investors as their savings will be invested for social and local development oriented activities (Vives 2000).

Pension funds (including funds under NPS) are however not totally debarred from infrastructure investing and the fund managers under NPS are investing selectively in the infrastructure companies but through the secondary market through third party dealing and only in the unlisted with higher investment grade rating. But it vey insignificant (less than 1 per cent) and also does not get return advantage that would have been available by investing directly. However, a country like Chile invested over 9 per cent of pension assets in the infrastructure sector in 2008 (BBVA 2008).

World Bank (2006) has suggested three mechanisms through changes in investment guidelines to encourage Indian pension funds to invest in infrastructure sector. This include pension fund investment in the projects where multilateral and central government extend guarantee of minimum rate of return, pension funds depositing funds with banks for long period for infrastructure financing and in the longer run pension funds are to be allowed to invest in the project appraised by All India FIIs. However, except for the first suggestion of government guarantee, others may not be very useful for pension funds at this juncture as the constraints and concerns are deeper and much wider. There are many concerns that restrain the pension funds to take a sizeable and early exposure to infrastructure sector, particularly those that are promoted by the private sector or through the PPP Mode. There are several constraints like poor quality of management, corporate governance and credential of the promoter and poor quality of the balance sheet; longer construction period causing probable cost overrun, interest rate and exchange risk; absence of standardisation of product pricing, often doubtful entry of promoters without past experience, doubtful past track record and fear of default by the promoters; absence of a strong regulatory regime and legally established escape route for pension funds, poor rating of the papers, no guarantee from government, etc. Due to all these reasons pension funds in India have a tendency to avoid investing in infrastructure sector. Once these concerns are taken care of through strong regulatory regime, the pension funds would be encouraged to invest in infrastructure. However, selected liberalisation of investment regulation with strong safeguard through government guarantee would encourage fund managers to increase infrastructure investment but the pension fund regulation should also strengthen risk management regime by introducing prudent person rule.

PERFORMANCE REGULATION AND GUARANTEED RETURN

Guarantee of return or performance of the fund managers is an important regulatory issue. As we have noted in Chapter 2 in Section 1 that guaranteed return has virtually become a well-accepted norm for the fund management regulation in almost all countries in Latin America, East Europe and other countries which have introduced pension reforms. The instruments of guarantee are, however, different in different countries but they are a reality, which makes the fund managers accountable to generate a minimum return. For example, countries like Chile, Argentina, Peru, Uruguay and Colombia require pension funds to achieve rates of return above a prescribed minimum, typically related to the industry average. Argentina and Chile define their profitability band in relative terms: the minimum of 2 percentage points and 50 per cent (Chile) or 70 per cent (Argentina) above or below the average annual return of the industry. In Uruguay, the guarantee is expressed in both absolute and relative terms (OECD/IOPS 2009). In order to implement this guarantee, all the fund managers establish *a reserve fund, sometimes called liquidity fluctuation fund* with their own capital. If the reserve is insufficient to top up the fund's return to the minimum, *the government guarantees the minimum*. However, in Peru the minimum return is not guaranteed by the government. In countries like Poland and Hungary, central pension guarantee funds are established through contribution of fund managers. For example, in Hungary the central guarantee fund (GF0) is pre-funded institution. Pension funds pay 0.3 per cent–0.5 per cent of members' contribution into the GFO. The government steps in when resources of GFO get exhausted to fulfil the guarantee. In India, EPS has implicit guarantee as the yearly rate of interest (return) is decided by the government. Recently IRDA had also made it mandatory for the insurance companies to provide a guaranteed return for the ULIP products (though withdrawn later on). Minimum Return Guarantee (MRG) has its own advantages and disadvantages. The MRG can make the DC partially DB pension and transfers a part of investment risks to the fund managers. Secondly, guarantee is a sort of insurance which may prompt the fund managers to take unmanageable higher risks. However, advantages seem to underscore disadvantage when an MRG is offered by a fund manager.

Firstly, pension savings is a critical old age income generated by investors through savings with pension funds with expectation of a higher return than the risk-free return on bank deposits and bonds, in anticipation that the pension fund managers are experts. Therefore, pension funds need to perform to provide the expected return so that investors in their old age receive regular income.

Secondly, when the responsibility of providing minimum return is put on the fund managers, a more cautious and scientific investment approach will be followed by them minimising the risk of decline in return. This will strengthen the risk governance and regulatory oversight which is a precondition for efficient supervision of pension funds.

Thirdly, when some responsibility for good performance is fixed for the sponsors, only the best and competent organisations will enter into pension business, which will promote a healthy fund management industry in the pension sector.

Fourthly, MRG on pension fund returns induces confidence among the investors in investing in pension funds which will provide a boost to domestic savings through pension funds. It has been mentioned by many potential pension investors that are unsure about long-term performance of pension funds in absence of any accountability in respect of return by the fund managers, regulator or government.

Therefore, provision of minimum return in NPS will to some extent remove the anxiety of investors and subscription is expected to increase manifold. The MRG became a necessity due to another structural reason of pension reform, that is, tax financed universal pension in a multi-pillar system which has been strongly advocated by the World Bank and implemented by many developing countries and exists in most of the developed countries as a redistributive mechanism. In India there is no universal pension and in such a situation MRG becomes a necessity. Pension reforms are not to be seen from a short-term perspective but a longer view should be taken to provide social protection to the people of ageing India. The MRG will partially support this objective.

Pension funds are critical financial intermediaries playing an unparalleled role in the economy confronted by the problems of ageing, financial market instability and many dimensional pressure on scarce financial resources. Pension funds need to survive as commercial entity, but at the same time, need to protect the old age survival of its members. Therefore, any reform regarding pension and retirement policy must be based on protecting the best interest of all the stakeholders and perceived challenges that may be thrown up by the unpredictable future development. However, in India no such provision has been introduced by the regulator. There is no guarantee for minimum return, and as such there is no legal accountability of the sponsors of the pension fund to ensure minimum return on the funds. Indian government also has no responsibility in respect of returns. Return and performance is only market driven. There is no penal provision for poor performance of the fund managers. However, centralised allocation of government NPS takes into account the relative performance of the three fund managers and yearly allocation depends on the relative rate of return achieved in the previous year. However, there is no penalty for poor performance. There is resistance to performance guarantee in many quarters. But perhaps this is one of the reasons for poor response to the NPS.

REGULATION FOR ASSET VALUATION

Pension funds operate with an objective of long-term asset accumulation to provide retirement income to the members by investing their funds in capital markets. The valuation method must be linked to the primary objective of fund. Since there are a number of pension funds with varying risk characteristics, one single method may not be ideal to evaluate funds with different risk characteristics. Even with broader assessment methodology flexibility is required to achieve the desired goal through objective assessment. Since a portfolio consists of a number of financial securities for different duration with different yield pattern, which may be purchased by a mutual fund, pension fund or a life insurance company, no realistic objective assessment may be possible by using a uniform single method of valuation. Therefore, the purpose of valuation needs to be decided before applying any valuation methodology.

Apart from the distinctive investment objectives, there are market constraints like the size of the equity market, depth of debt market, liquidity in the market, etc. Therefore, same valuation method may not be very appropriate in all the countries and at all the times. In a very liquid market having competitive trading environment, buying and selling an asset can take place in the market through prevailing market price. But in an illiquid market, though assets may exist, there may not be an open trade but through negotiated deals, which often depends on the bargaining powers of the parties and necessity and priority of the buyers and sellers to have such assets in their portfolio. Therefore, while deciding a method of asset valuation, the state of market for such assets needs to be kept in mind. In NPS debt instruments constitute a large per cent of portfolio. But in India, debt market is yet to be developed to support price discovery through regular trading in debt instruments. Though some activities are observed in government securities market, trading in corporate debt and state development loans is virtually absent. Therefore, in absence of developed debt market, application of Mark to Model (MTM) for illiquid debt securities would lead to subjectivity in valuation but under the book value or Held to Maturity (HTM), this problem of under-valuation does not arise.

As per the current practice, pension fund assets under NPS are valued by following the MTM Model. Simple MTM valuation to determine assets prices and allocating units may often be discretionary. The principle of equity demand is that no one should pay more or less than the real value of assets at the time of entry. The MTM valuation, however, generates inequity in unit allocation. Allocation of higher number of units under MTM would mean that value of accumulated assets exceeded her/his real investment at the entry point. This creates an imbalance between what is due to her and what has been offered to her. When an excess unit is offered to the investor, fund has to bear the excess value at the end of the contracted term having long-term strain on the fund. Similarly allocation of lower number of units would be detrimental to beneficiary interest. None of the methods indicated above can be considered as the most ideal method in any market. Because markets are mostly inefficient or semi-efficient and never reflect the true value of a security, we need to have one realistic model for valuation of assets. It is therefore suggested that a *Composite Model of Valuation* (CMV) may be adopted for valuation of assets of NPS. CMV would incorporate security class wise valuation method depending on the nature of security, trading frequency, etc. An outline of such a model has been given in Chapter 12.

ANNUITY REGULATION

The NPS is a DC pension system having two phases, namely, accumulation and payout phase. The regulatory aspects discussed above so far focus on accumulation phase. But payout is also an important area of regulation. We have discussed in chapter 10 about various aspects of payouts and noted that annuity is the first choice for payouts, and India has adopted mandatory annuitisation model for pension payouts. According to NPS architecture, the PFRDA will authorise selected life insurance companies licensed by IRDA. In view of immense significance, annuity regulation must specifically focus on the issues given below.

Selection of Annuity Providers

Traditionally annuity providers are the life insurance companies, but experience indicates that life insurance companies are often reluctant to undertake annuity business due to inherent business risks arising out of changes in mortality, adverse selection and non-availability of sufficient financial instruments for hedging long-term risk. However, the experience in different countries show that very few life insurance companies are usually active in annuity market. David Blake (1999) has mentioned, 'in UK of around 240 authorised life companies, only about 10 are at any time serious providers of life annuity'. Therefore, the regulators usually adopt selectivity criteria to authorise life insurance companies to sell retirement annuity. We have noted in Chapter 10, the practices of authorisation of annuity providers in some countries in Latin America. Indian regulators need to keep in view the fact that annuity market is very underdeveloped and except Life Insurance Corporation of India, none have much experience and track record of annuity business. Therefore, a cautious approach is required and strict regulatory conditions need to be imposed while issuing licenses. Another important component of annuity regulation is the annuity products. Regulation should provide wider choice of products to the members of NPS at the annuity phase.

The most crucial objectives of an annuity are to transfer longevity risk to annuity providers, ensure regular and guaranteed income. Though life annuity seems to be simple, having two basic groups, namely, Immediate Life Annuity and Deferred Life Annuity, in the real world there are a variety of products having different features which may impact the amount of pension. Regulations, therefore, in many countries put restrictive conditions on annuity as payout method. These restrictions are often in the form of type of annuity, minimum income through annuity investment, etc.

Mandatory annuitisation under the NPS indicates that at least 40 per cent of accumulated money is to be invested in annuity and no mention has been made about the type of annuity to be purchased by the pension investors. Therefore, there is flexibility in annuity selection. However, certain guidance is required to ensure that the pension investors do not go for wrong selection and put their retirement income at stake. The importance of such guidance becomes essential because of low-level financial literacy in India. A general guideline on suitable annuities to take care of longevity, investment and inflation risks in the post-retirement period would be necessary and beneficial for the members. The fund manager can also play an important role in identifying the suitable annuity products for a member of the NPS. Therefore, annuity regulation must identify the role of PFMs as a facilitator in the annuity regulation.

It was discussed in Chapter 10 that there is a timing risk if annuity purchase is stipulated only at the time of retirement/exit. For example, instead of mandatory purchase of annuity at the time of retirement, an employee may be allowed to buy annuity within a given period according to her/his choice. If an employee retires at the age of 60, she/he may be allowed to purchase annuity from age 55–60, with staggered vesting age. Thus, an employee can take advantages of market movement and purchase required annuity at a price beneficial to her/him.

Annuity regulation needs to be carefully crafted to incorporate price regulation, risk management, governance system, capital adequacy of annuity company, etc. NPS supervisor also has to play an important role to protect beneficiaries' interest through close monitoring of annuity service providers and initiating timely actions to any deviations on the part of ASPs. However, there may be a mechanism of regulatory conflict resolution as there may be possible conflict between the two regulators, namely, PFRDA and IRDA.

REGULATION AND PENSION FUND GOVERNANCE

Designing the pension fund governance regulation is a multidimensional, complex and challenging task as a number of issues are to be brought in its purview and many conflicting interests of the stakeholders need to be addressed. Since there is a wide range of functional areas having direct and indirect links with other regulators and entities operating in the financial market and economy, governance regulation for pension fund needs to be sensitive about those issues, as the governance quality immensely impacts the administrative efficiency and performance of a pension fund translating into the retirement income. A study conducted by Ambachtsheer, Campelle and Scheibelhut, in 1997, found a positive correlation between proxy metrics for pension fund governance quality and for pension fund performance. High-quality funds outperformed low-quality funds by about 1 per cent per annum (Ambachtsheer 2007). They repeated this statistical analysis with the new 81 CEO scores based on the 2004 survey and the four-year NVA metrics for these 81 funds, as reported by CEM (CEM Benchmarking is an organisation that measures the cost-effectiveness of pension fund organisations around the globe). Taking the CEO score range to be effectively from 3 to 6, a coefficient of 0.8 implies the top CEO score funds outperformed the bottom ones by an average of 2.4 per cent per annum (that is 3 × 0.8) over the 2000–2003 period (Ambachtsheer et al. 2008). It is therefore essential that the issue of governance should occupy an important place in regulation of pension funds and the regulatory format must contain a mechanism to address various governance issues, implementations of regulatory mechanism and accountability of supervisors, active management and the board of directors. Therefore, a holistic approach must be taken while designing the mechanism for pension fund governance.

OECD (2009b) has issued a framework of good governance for pension fund governance which covers the governance structure and the governance mechanism. According to OECD principles, the governance structure is based on identification and separation of operational and oversight responsibilities, vesting the governing body with power to administer the pension funds, to protect the interest of pension plan members and beneficiaries, *accountability of the* governing body to pension plan members, beneficiaries, supervisory body and the other competent authorities. There should be a condition of minimum *sustainability for* membership in the governing body, and the governing body may delegate functions to internal staff, or to subcommittees or to external service providers. For conducting periodic audit, an independent auditor should be appointed, and an actuary should be appointed in case of defined benefit plans. There should be an independent custodian for custody of pension fund assets or this can be carried out by the pension entity or financial institutions which manage pension assets. OECD guidelines also indicated a format of *governance mechanism* based on *risk-based internal controls,* which should control all the organisational and administrative procedures, *reporting system*—timely dissemination of accurate and relevant information and *disclosure* of relevance to all parties. These issues have been discussed in details in the OECD guidelines.

Many of the governance issues discussed above have been reflected in PFRDA guidelines/instructions. To avoid market concentration and to encourage competition, seven pension funds (till December 2011) sponsored by public and private sector entities have been issued licenses, various administrative and fund management costs have been determined by the regulator, pension products have been identified, due diligence done by PFRDA before selecting intermediaries through open competitive bidding. There is a centralised NPS Trust and custodian, trustee bank. This helps to keep costs at minimum, introduce a uniform supervision and monitoring system for better governance. Fund managers are closely monitored, they submit a day-to-day report on investment of funds to the NPS Trust, and the trust reviews the performance on a quarterly and yearly basis. Valuation of assets is carried out by an independent agency appointed by the regulator.

Pension funds under NPS have been formed as companies and sponsored by financial institution which fulfilled the fit and proper test. There is a firewall between the sponsors and the pension fund companies. Pension funds are board managed and as per the provision, at least 50 per cent of the board members are independent directors. Appointment of the chief executive, chief investment officers, chief risk officers and the board directors have to be approved by the NPS Trust. There is a mandatory investment committee constituted with at least two independent directors, chief executive officer and chief investment officer and a risk management committee constituted with at least one independent director, chief executive officer and designated risk officer. The performance and investment activities are also regularly monitored and reviewed on quarterly basis by the NPS Trust. It is the responsibility of the governing board and operating management team to implement. However, these are basic instruments of good governance, but they need to be sincerely implemented by the operating management team under guidance and monitoring of the governing board. Good governance, however, primarily depends on the sense of responsibility, accountability, self-governance of the management team.

SUPERVISION OF PENSION FUNDS

A well-designed regulatory system for the pension fund with clearly defined objectives and sound principles is the prerequisite for establishing a robust supervisory system. Since regulator plays the twin role of development and support, the growth of orderly development focusing on the elements of growth in regulation, supervision is centred on these twin objectives and implements the regulatory control and facilitates the growth of pension industry. Therefore, if a regulator generates regulatory inputs, supervision takes it to the output level to achieve the desired results. A robust system of supervision is thus important for efficient implementation of regulatory conditions to promote a sustainable pension system. Effective supervision thus is not only important for effective implementation of regulation but is also a prerequisite to protect beneficiary interest. Robust supervisory regime is necessary for the development and successful operation of any financial system, institutional development and strengthening the operating environment, creating confidence among members of the system, particularly at the early stage of development. Some experts argue that strong supervisory intervention may tend to be a disincentive for innovation and performance and thus supervisory role may be minimum. However, global financial crisis in 2008 had shown us the importance of proactive continuous supervision, even a mature system needs to be rigorously supervised and developments need to be closely monitored. The role of supervision, however, may be sometimes less flexible as they are expected to implement what the regulatory and legislative authorities have laid down. Therefore, regulatory flexibility within the given legislative framework is absolutely essential for effective supervision.

Institutional Structure

Pension supervision has a distinctive role in the whole pension system, as it is the supervision which enforces the regulation and creates condition for smooth implementation of regulation protecting the interest of beneficiaries. Effective supervision however depends on the structure of supervisory organisation and is a clearly defined and legally supported authority with scope for supervision. However, the institution of supervision may structurally vary. Supervisory functions may be carried out by an existing supervisor like central bank or insurance supervisor or by an exclusive institution like pension supervisor. Regulator and supervisor may perform two different functions separately or a single institution can perform both the regulatory and supervisory function. There are certain advantages and disadvantages in both the system.

> *Using a single institution has the advantage of defining control routines regardless of the personal preferences of regulators. The second allows supervisors to approach their job without preconceptions. A combination of both alternatives is possible. This corresponds more closely to the experience of countries that have introduced private pension funds. In most countries a 'super intendancy of pension funds' was created, while the regulatory framework was defined partly by this agency, and partly by other authorities, such as finance and labour ministries, the social-security administration, and regulators of other financial services. (Demarco and Rofman 1998)*

However, it may be remembered here that most of the newly reformed countries in Latin America having less number of population, entrusting regulatory and supervisory function to a single agency may bring economies of scale, close monitoring and active supervision, but in a large country with huge population it may be difficult for a single institution to perform both the functions effectively. A country like India needs to have two institutions functionally different but closely integrated legally.

Another issue of supervision is the autonomy of supervisory institutions. Autonomy of supervisory institutions is required for independent implementation of regulation in order to protect the beneficiary interest without any outside pressure. Autonomy is to be provided through legal mechanisms and it should be made dependent on its own source of income to manage its functions. Dependence on the fiscal support from the government may make it vulnerable to pressure. However, there are certain preconditions to provide full autonomy to a supervisory institution in a newly reformed pension system. It would depend on the quality and scope of regulation, experience, knowledge and understanding of the board and supervisory staff of the institutions, strength and attitude of the supervisor to withstand any pressure coming out of the group of vested interest. Often these are not found in a new system and therefore some sort of legislative intervention becomes unavoidable. Demarco and Rofman (1988) pointed out that supervisory agencies in Chile, Bolivia, Colombia and Uruguay are not autonomous, while supervisory agencies in Argentina, Mexico and Peru are autonomous. Further, the funding source of autonomous supervisors like Argentina, Peru is supervision fees, while for Mexico it is partial. Though in Bolivia supervisor is not autonomous, its source of funding is supervision fees. Countries like Chile, Uruguay depend on the national budget for its funding.

Role of Supervisor in Pension Administration

It has been indicated above that effective supervision is a critical component of pension fund administration, and the role of supervisor in terms of scope, coverage, efficiency and independence are needed to be clearly identified and legally supported. There are certain universal principles which provide a general framework for supervision. The Organisation for Economic Co-operation and Development (IOPS) has come out with 10 principles of supervision which are quite comprehensive and can support to promote an efficient system of supervision for pension system. Supervisory authority should be independent and the operational objectives should be clearly defined and legally supported. Supervisory authority should have necessary resources and sufficient and efficient manpower. The IOPS also emphasised upon proportionality and consistency in investigation and risk mitigation, and consultation with bodies which they supervise. Other important issues of supervision are the confidentiality, transparency and governance. The IOPS advocates risk-based supervision, which is critical for managing risks of pension funds. These principles set the ground for the role of pension fund supervisor. These are the principles to set up an efficient supervisory system, but in reality there may be much variation. Supervisory authority are often not granted full autonomy; resources may not be adequate from own source and the supervisor may need to depend on the government support which may invite political intervention. In a new system sufficient number of technically qualified and experienced people (staff) may not be available and regulator may be a political appointee, which may not necessarily be the best choice. Therefore, the task of putting in place an efficient supervisory authority is often confronted with many institutional and non-institutional factors hindering the development of a healthy supervision system for pension fund.

In NPS, still there is no role clarity for regulator and supervisor of pension funds. In fact, the NPS Trust performs a large number of supervisory functions like appointment of intermediary, monitoring the operation and functions of intermediaries, evaluating the performance of fund managers (through a consultant appointed for this purpose), valuation of funds (through SHCIL), conduct on-sight and off-sight inspection, attend investors complaints as per the various guidelines/instructions issued by the PFRDA. Fund managers are required to submit daily report on investment made by them. NPS Trust also conducts quarterly review of PFMs. In a sense, the trust undertakes implementation of PFRDA regulation, supervises and monitors the activities of pension fund managers and other intermediaries of NPS, but it is not yet legally the pension fund supervisor for NPS. However, once the PFRDA Bill is passed by the Indian Parliament, there is likely to be a clarity and role distinction of the regulator and supervisor.

Supervision Approach

There are several variants of supervisory models depending on the nature of the management of economy, social security system, financial and regulatory environment, etc. However, two major distinctive systems of supervision of financial institutions including pension funds are compliance-based model and risk-based model of supervision.

Compliance-based Supervision

This is focused on the limited number of risks based on the pension fund regulation primarily related to investment management. These risks are basically market risks, credit risks, liquidity risks, interest rate risks, default risks, etc. These are operation-linked risks and the management tries to mitigate these risks within the regulatory guidelines. The compliance-based model thus attempts to ensure that a company operates within the regulatory framework and fulfils the regulatory conditions so that the regulatory and the legislative objectives of operation are met without exposing them to undue risks. This is done through periodic review, offshore and onshore inspection and auditing the system and operation. These objectives are achieved through analysis and evaluation of financial result and balance sheet of the company and identify any deviation of established rules and procedures and take necessary actions to prevent such occurring which may adversely affect the interest of the stakeholders. Compliance-based model, however, overlooks many other hidden risks that are outside the purview of regulation and originate due to external factors and internal actions or no actions.

Risk-based Supervision

Risk-based Supervision (RBS), while retaining the compliance-based review process, focuses further to identify the various financial, operational, management process risks associated with the operation and management of a company. Risks are also associated with changing external environment, strategic decision of management, process of operation, the system of governance, etc., which are most often ignored by the compliance-based approach of supervision but become major focus of RBS. The RBS is a more flexible approach as it has the scope of investigating and risk mitigation initiative with a futuristic perspective in areas of organisational strategy, process and operation and management actions. The RBS focuses on the enterprise implicit and explicit risks and resulting impact. 'The process is said to be *Structure* because it systematically considers all of the key aspects of the company's business and within each looks at the risks to that areas of operation' (Thompson 2001). The RBS is a comprehensive risk management approach. It enables a company to put in place a risk management policy and practice in line with regulatory guidelines, constantly monitor the implementation and revise them in accordance with any expected development—internally and externally—so that adverse impact of potential risks is either diminished or avoided. On the other hand, it (RBS) becomes a more sophisticated and more effective supervisory tool for any supervisory authority as '[u]nder the RBS, there is a continuous updating risk assessments through on site reviews, offsite reviews, market intelligence that creates an early warning or rating system for the supervisory authority to anticipate and deal with emerging issue' (Randle 2009). Since the operation of financial institutions in the globalised market has become more complex and there are several manifestations of risks from known and unknown external sources, RBS has emerged as the most potent instrument to manage them.

Pension funds, particularly those that are run on DC basis, are distinct financial institutions due to several reasons including the objective of pension investment for retirement income, a very long-term perspective of investment, transfer of risks to the investors, etc., which are confronted by agency problems, market risks, strategy risks, regulatory risks, legal risks, governance risks, etc. These risks can be efficiently managed by RBS, and therefore there is an increasing emphasis on risk-based supervision of pension funds. The IOPS also advocates risk-based approach in its 'Principles of Private Pension Supervision' as it allows 'scarce supervisory resources to be targeted at the pension funds which seem to be at most risk and allows supervisory authorities to take a more pro-active approach, attempting to avoid potential problems before they occur (as opposed to a reactive compliance based regime)' (IOPS 2007). Many pension supervisors in developed and emerging countries including Australia, the UK, Germany, Netherlands, Denmark, Mexico, South Africa, Croatia, etc., introduced the RBS Model. India has followed the first approach, that is, proactive model of supervision for the NPS as all the activities of all the intermediaries and stakeholders was brought under regulatory supervision, namely, selection of intermediaries, investment management, portfolio restrictions, risk management, fees/costs structure of various activities, payouts and annuity products, etc.

FINANCIAL CRISIS, REGULATION AND SUPERVISION OF PENSION FUNDS

Global financial crisis originating from subprime problems virtually brought the financial sector to near collapse, but it was rescued by the huge package of costly stimulus. The menacing impact of financial market crisis was most felt in the pension industry globally, but more in the mature economy. Financial crisis brought forth many challenges for the regulators and supervisor of pension funds. Globally, a debate has cropped up about viability and sustainability of the present form of reforms and regulation. The financial crisis has significantly eroded the assets of pension funds, particularly in the OECD Countries, as reported in Pension Market Focus (December 2008). The study noted that the total pension assets of OECD declined by 3.3 trillion or nearly 20 per cent from December 2007. Including other pension assets, like assets in personal pension plans, this loss was about $5 trillion. The crisis in the financial market also impacted the return on pension fund investment, which marked a decline of more than 30 per cent. Further this decline was significant in countries having higher investment in equities. For example, a country like Ireland having 66 per cent exposure in equities witness more than 30 per cent decline in return. However, the decline in assets and return would have been much higher but for the shift in asset allocation pattern which was taking place in mature economies. A study by Watson Wayatt (2009), Global Pension Study, indicated that that there has been a significant shift in asset allocation since 2005. During the period 2005–2008, equity investment declined from 59.7 per cent to 41.4 per cent and bond investment increased from 24.5 per cent to 40.2 per cent. The increased weight in favour of bond portfolio in pension funds restrained the decline in overall return.

However, NPS in India could remain isolated from the crisis due to the cautious and prudent investment guidelines of PFRDA which reduces the risk content of fund management operation. Therefore, the fund managers, namely, LIC Pension Fund, SBI Pension Fund and UTI Retirement Solutions, which stated investment management operation from 2 April 2008, could beat the street crisis to deliver reasonably higher return on NPS funds. These three funds could withstand the market pressure and could generate return of 12–14 per cent by 30 March 2009 (PFRDA 2009). This has been possible due to the prudent allocation pattern prescribed by the regulator PFRDA: 85 per cent investment in debt market instruments, up to 10 per cent in corporate bonds/equity mutual funds and up to 5 per cent in equity for the pension assets of the government employees. This composition, however, has changed now, allowing up to 15 per cent in equity and equity mutual funds.

As a result of the fallout, many are even questioning the individual account based privately managed pension reform which transfers entire risks to the investors. Some of the countries are rethinking about such reforms and even Argentina and Hungary reversed the reform by nationalising pension system. Questions have been raised about the excessive emphasis on equity investment which is very risky and the appropriate trade-off between risk and return for retirement savings (different from short to medium term investing through mutual funds). Valuation methodology of pension assets has also been questioned as the MTM model was unable to capture long-term value and the fall in assets value during the crisis was owing to the MTM valuation. People who exited during the crisis suffered more than those who continued with the funds. There is a need to look into the present valuation method of pension funds. There has been an ongoing debate on the fund managers, sponsors and the government accountability in the individual account based DC system. Many countries have introduced minimum pension guarantee, but still a debate on the feasibility, rationality and cost of such guarantee is going on. Financial crisis has prompted many countries to rethink about strengthening social safety net. For example, the Finish government announced that it would introduce a guaranteed minimum pension in 2011 and considering reform to redistribute government contribution to lower income workers account (Antolin and Stewart 2009). Further, the financial market crisis has reinforced the need for such guarantee and accountability of the fund managers, sponsors and the government.

The financial market crisis also raised serious question about the efficiency of regulation and particularly the supervision of pension funds. Supervisors are not only responsible to implement regulation but also need to keep a close watch on the functioning of funds and monitor the emerging potential market challenges and it seems they failed in this respect. Therefore the crisis has alerted many regulators and supervisors to the need for monitoring and to devise an early warning system. Antolin and Stewart (2009) mentioned that as an immediate response to the crisis, pension regulatory and supervisory authorities have increased the monitoring and supervisory activities of pension funds around the world. This includes stress testing, scenario testing, reporting liquidity, stepping up of on-site and off-site inspection, etc.

There is also a question of fund managers' investment strategy and market forecasting practices and expertise of pension fund managers. Crisis was developing for quite some time and there was enough scope to take proactive action by restructuring investment strategy, rebalancing portfolio, which failed. Therefore, time has come to underline the accountability of fund managers and sponsors. But it is also a fact that the rigidity of investment regulation and portfolio limit often come in the way to adopt such an investment strategy. Therefore, it is suggested that there should be enough flexibility in the regulation to cope with such adverse developments in the financial market impacting pension industry. Financial crisis has also reinforced the regulatory control and limit of investment, a robust risk management regime, stringent punishment for regulatory violation and fund management activism, and supervisory accountability, etc.

REFERENCES

Alonso, Javier, Jasmina Bjeletic, Carlos Herrera, Soledad Hormazabal, Ivonne Ordóñez, Carolina Romero, David Tuesta and Alfonso Ugarte (2010), 'Projections of the Impact of Pension Funds on Investment in Infrastructure and Growth in Latin America'. Working Paper No. 1002, Economic

Research Department. Available at: http://www.bbvaresearch.com/KETD/fbin/mult/WP_1002_tcm348-213944.pdf?ts=15102012

Ambachtsheer, Keith (2007), 'The Three Grades of Pension Fund Governance Quality: Bad, Better and Best'. Available at: http://kpa-advisory.com/pdf_documents/Three per cent20 Grades per cent20of per cent20Pension per cent20Fund per cent20Governance per cent20Quality_Jul

Ambachtsheer, Keith, Ronald Capelle and Hubert Lum (2008), 'The Pension Governance Deficit : Still with Us', *Rotman International Journal of Pension Management,* 1(1), Fall 2008.

Antolin, P. and F. Stewart (2009), 'Private Pensions and Policy Responses to the Financial and Economic Crisis'. OECD Working Papers on Insurance and Private Pensions, No. 36. OECD Publishing © OECD. doi:10.1787/224386871887

BBVA (2008), 'Infrastructure Investment and Pension Funds in Latin America'. A Presentation to OECD/IOPS Meeting by BBVA Economic Research Department, Mumbasa, Kenya, 31 October.

Blake, David (1999), 'Annuity Markets: Problems and Solutions'. *The Geneva Papers on Risk and Insurance,* 24(3), July 1999.

Davis, E. Philip (2000), 'Regulation of Private Pensions—A Case Study of the UK'. Discussion Paper PI-0009, The Pension Institute, Birkbeck College, University of London, Available at: http://www.pensions-institute.org/

——— (2001), 'Portfolio Regulation of Life Insurance Companies and Pension Funds'. Discussion Paper PI-0101, the Pension Institute, London, January 2001. Available at: http://www.pensions-institute.org/

Demarco, Gustavo and Rafael Rofman with contributions from Edward Whitehouse (1998), 'Supervising Mandatory Pension Funds: Issues and Challenges'. Social Protection Discussion Paper Series No. 9817, December 1998, Social Protection Unit, Human Development Network, The World Bank. Available at: http://www.worldbank.org/sp

Inderst, George (2009), 'Pension Fund Investment in Infrastructure'. OECD Working Papers on Insurance and Private Pensions, No. 32, OECD Publishing©, OECD, 2009. Doi:10.1787/227416754242.

International Federation of Pension Fund Administrators (FIAP) (2010), *Description and Analysis of the Multifund Systems in the Latin America and Eastern European Pension System,* FIAP, Santiago, January 2010.

IOPS (2007), 'Experiences and Challenges with the Introduction of Risk-based Supervision for Pension Funds'. International Organisation for Pension Supervisors, Working Paper No. 4, 1 August 2007.

OECD (2009a), 'OECD Guidelines for Pension Fund Governance'. OECD, 5 June 2009.

——— (2009b), 'OECD Recommendation on Core Principles of Occupational Pension Regulation' (approved by the OECD Council on 5 June 2009). Available at: http://www.oecd.org/dataoecd/14/46/33619987.pdf

OECD & IOPS (2009), 'Pension Reform and Developments in Latin America'. Conference Proceedings of the OECD/IOPS Global Forum on Private Pension, Rio de Janerio, Brazil, October 2009. Available at: http://www.oecd.org/dataoecd/24/17/46142448.pdf

Pension Fund Administrators (AFP) (2006), *Collection Costs in Pension Fund Systems,* AFP, Santiago, March 2006.

Pension Fund Regulatory and Development Authority (PFRDA) (2009), 'Detailed Investment Guidelines for All Citizens under the New Pension System'. Available at: http://www.pfrda.org.in/writereaddata/linkimages/investment per cent20guidelines per cent2030_04_092418358081.pdf

Randle, Tony (2009), 'Risk Based Supervision'. Primer Series on Insurance Issue, The World Bank, 14 December 2009.

Srinivas, P. S., Edward Whitehouse, Juan Yermo (2000), 'Regulating Private Pension Funds' Structure, Performance and Investments: Cross-country Evidence'. Social Protection Discussion Paper Series, Social Protection Unit Human Development Network, The World Bank, July 2000.

Stiglitz, Joseph E. (2001), 'Principles of Financial Regulation: A Dynamic Portfolio Approach'. *The World Bank Research Observer,* 16(1), Spring 2001, The International Bank for Reconstruction and Development/The World Bank.

The World Bank (2006), 'India-Financing Infrastructure: Addressing Constraints and Challenges'. Finance and Private Sector Development Unit, South Asia Region, The World Bank, June 2006.

Thompson, John (2001), 'Risk Based Supervision of the Insurance Companies, An Introduction'. Paper prepared for The World Bank, 19 March 2001. Available at: http://www1.worldbank.org/finance/assets/images/Risk-Based_Supervision_-_Feb_21.pdf

Vittas, Dimitri (1998), 'Regulatory Controversaries of Private Pension Funds'. Developing Research Group, The World Bank. Available at: http://www-wds.worldbank.org/external/default/WDSContentServer/IW3P/IB/1998/03/01/000009265_3980429111149/additional/113513322_20041117163033.pdf.

Vives, Antonio (2000), 'Pension Funds in Infrastructure Project Finance-Regulations and Instrument Design'. Infrastructure and Financial Market Division, Inter-American Development Bank, Washington DC, March 2000.

Wayatt, Watson (2009), 'Global Assets Pension Study', Watson Wayatt Worldwide, January 2009.

14 Financial Literacy

Promoting Awareness and Protecting Interest of Investors

INTRODUCTION

The importance of financial literacy is to promote financial products to assist the investors to take informed decision and to protect the interest of investors recognised worldwide irrespective of the level of literacy, economic and market development. Financial market of late has tended to become very complex and makes the investors confused and perplexed. Expansion and global integration of financial market, innovation of a variety of new financial instruments and entry of numerous financial institutions of varied characteristics profile increased the investors' confusion and anxiety. An aggressive market penetration and market expansion approach by a large number of financial service providers often led them to adopt unethical market practices, putting the consumers' interest at stake. Financial regulation and laws relating to financial services often seem to be static and unable to confront irregularities emanating from fast changing market environment. All these developments necessitated the need to empower the financial services consumers with financial market knowledge through financial education and financial literacy programme.

Critical importance of financial literacy has been well recognised globally (though quite late) and several initiatives have been launched, particularly in the developed countries including New Zealand, United Kingdom, the US, Australia, etc., to educate financial services consumers to take informed decision for financial well-being and to protect their financial interest. Many developing and emerging market countries including India also realised the necessity and importance of financial literacy and undertook some initiatives. However, a close scrutiny of such initiatives in India reveal that most of such organization-specific initiatives are directed with an intention of pushing their products and expanding their own consumer market, instead of empowering the consumers with general understanding, market information, critical evaluation of various financial products, relative strength and weaknesses of services, and to take need-based informed decisions. In a sense, often these programmes tend to be a marketing exercise rather than empowering the individual with financial knowledge. However, there is no harm to promote a sector-specific financial literacy programme with a holistic view and with sole objective of empowering the consumers to take informed decision for their financial well-being.

In a complex financial market and given a limited amount of investible funds, an individual needs to take a cautious need-based informed decision having the important investment perspective in view. While personal knowledge and expertise about investment is crucial, the regulatory and market environment also has significant impact on the financial well-being of an investor. Financial market is very dynamic and changes continuously and sometimes adversely in the interest of investors. Moreover, free market today is not completely free to provide any equilibrium between embedded cost and embedded value, as often there are outside intervention distorting the free market mechanism. This brings to the fore the necessity of a robust supervisory and regulatory mechanism to protect investors' financial well-being. Therefore financial regulation is a critical factor for financial well-being of an investor and financial literacy needs to be an integral part of any regulation.

WHAT IS FINANCIAL LITERACY?

There are several terms like financial literacy, financial capability, financial education, etc., which are used to denote the same meaning in general but all these, in real sense, are directed towards different meaning. In general terms, financial literacy is used to indicate the knowledge and understanding of financial matters, products, process and implications of any financial decisions in the matter of personal finance. The Retirement Commission, New Zealand (2008) defines Financial Literacy 'as the ability to make informed judgments and take effective decisions regarding the use and management of money throughout the life course'. This is a simple but a powerful definition of financial literacy. The OECD defined financial literacy as 'the combination of consumers'/investors' understanding of financial products and concepts and their ability and confidence to appreciate financial risks and opportunities, to make informed choices, to know where to go for help, and to take other effective actions to improve their financial well-being' (World Bank 2010). (An alternative term is financial capability, mostly used in UK, to convey the same.) Financial capability on the other hand is defined by Kempson (2008) as:

> *A financially capable person is one who has the knowledge, skills and confidence to be aware of financial opportunities, to know where to go for help, to make informed choices, and to take effective action to improve his or her financial well-being while an enabling environment for financial capability building would promote the acquisition of those skills.*

Both the concepts, in general, convey the same meaning of empowerment of an individual to take financial well-being enhancement decision. Though both the terms used to mean the same purpose, perhaps the term Financial Capability is more focused to decision-making ability of an individual regarding personal finance and thus would be more appropriate for designing a format for Financial Education. Orton (2007) says that

> *the terms* financial capability *and* financial literacy *are often used interchangeably, and sometimes the terms* economic literacy *and* economic capability *are used, even though the latter pair has a different meaning. Recent usage favours financial capability and financial literacy, and also distinguishes between the two.*

However, no financial literacy is complete without general understanding of economic environment, impact of changing economic variables/factor. While talking about financial well-being, we should not forget that it is actually economic well-being which is achieved through consumption. In case of pension income through retirement savings, the objective is mainly to maintain post-retirement/old age consumption. Financial education is a way to enhance the financial and economic literacy of an individual to take a more capable decision. Therefore, any initiative to improve financial literacy/capability must be attempted within a broader framework of economic literacy.

INTERNATIONAL EXPERIENCE OF FINANCIAL LITERACY PROGRAMME

In the post-reform period many countries have undertaken financial literacy programmes for educating public about privatised pension system. International Organisation of Pension Supervisors (IOPS) (2008) cited many case studies. For example, Poland launched two stages of such campaign—the first stage of such campaign was launched in 1997 when the parliament was passing the new pension legislation and targeted the 'opinion leaders' and the second stage launched in 1999 and targeted 'individual effected by the new system'. Sweden started a campaign by sending a pension statement in 1999 to 5.3 million individuals. The core objective of campaign was to build trust and knowledge about new pension system and to encourage people to read and understand the pension statement. Countries like Hungary, Mexico, etc., also undertook campaign about pension reform and the new pension system. Two more effective financial literacy programme launched by Ireland and New Zealand quoted below provide some interesting insight and inputs for such programmes in India.

Ireland

In *Ireland*, the pension board, established by the Pensions Act, 1990, conducts the National Pensions Awareness Campaign (NPAC) on behalf of the government as recommended in the 'Securing Retirement Income' report of the national pensions policy initiative published in 1998. The objectives of the NPAC 2003–2006 are 'to heighten pensions awareness with the view to increasing pension coverage in Ireland, ensure those with pension provision address the adequacy of that provision and promoting pensions development and building an educational foundation about retirement planning for the future is an associated objective' (Hutch 2006). Following Hutch (2006), some of the key features of NPAC are indicated below.

❖ KEY TARGET GROUP

NAPC has two target groups namely the *Primary targets,* which include population aged 25–39 years old, women, graduates and first job seekers, farming/rural community, while the *secondary target* group includes migrants, young people/graduates.

❖ AWARENESS STRATEGY

It includes intensified advertising promotion to focus on the key targets (25-year-olds to 39-year-olds) through media, TV, cinema, radio, Internet and lifestyle magazines, newspapers, etc., to encourage people to be *aware and informed* about the adequacy of their existing pension and directing consumers to be personally *responsible and take action* for their future retirement planning as well as promoting employers responsibility, to draw consumers to the pensions board website, particularly the pensions calculators, etc.

❖ SUPPORT AGENCIES PROMOTING NPAC

A large number of agencies are assisting in delivering the NPAC message to their members. These agencies include Trade Unions, Business and Employers Confederation, Small Firms Association, Chambers of Commerce, Small and Medium Enterprises, Institute of Personnel and Development, Citizen Information Centres, Farmers Association, Women's Association, National Library Network, Rural Leader Groups, Hotels Federation, Restaurants, etc., in Ireland.

❖ FINANCIAL PLANNING EDUCATION INITIATIVES

The pension board has taken initiative to build educational foundation about retirement planning for the future through establishment of the pension board, financial regulator, government departments, state agencies, to establish a formal 'Financial Planning Education'. Financial planning education targets schools and colleges. The Irish schools' curriculum includes this module and pension checklists are sent to career guidance offices in all the third-level colleges and universities, asking about pension to those who seek their first job, producing pension information in different languages including French, Spanish, Polish, Russian, Chinese and Arabic and conducting media interviews on the subject matter, producing articles and information for newspapers, magazines, newsletters, etc.

New Zealand

Financial literacy programme in *New Zealand* carried out by the Retirement Commission, New Zealand, under its *National Strategy for Financial Literacy* announced on 1 December 2006, 'as Retirement Commission Financial Knowledge Survey found that many New Zealanders have low financial knowledge' (Crossan 2008). The National Strategy for Financial Literacy focuses on reaching people by extending the delivery of financial education/information and sharing the outcomes with others.

❖ REACHING PEOPLE

The first objective is to reach people through financial education/information programme which is timely, culturally fit, accessible and flexible.

❖ EXTENDING DELIVERY

The second component of the programme is to extend the delivery system by offering professional development and resource support to teachers, identifying location and channels for effective delivery of financial education with the community partnership, developing partnership with employers, workers union, pacific communities, etc.

❖ SHARING WHAT WORKS

Towards this objective the 'Retirement Commission will take the lead in bringing together interested parties to develop an evidence base, sharing of best practice and experiences through which others may learn, and launching a database of financial education/information providers.

Evaluation of outcome and effectiveness of financial literacy/information is important component of such a programme. The national strategy, therefore, made a provision for *monitoring and reporting* of financial literacy programme. Accordingly the financial knowledge of the adult New Zealand population was measured every four years through a survey, to capture the long-term effects of financial literacy on personal financial well-being, etc.

STATE OF LITERACY, SAVING AND INVESTMENT PERSPECTIVES OF INDIAN HOUSEHOLDS

Investment decision of a household depends on several factors including the income of the family, current and future income, current and future expenses, understanding about various opportunities to invest, access to financial instruments and financial infrastructure, level of education in general and financial education in particular. Some of these factors are discussed below.

Population Profile—Rural–Urban Divide

Literacy profile of population has significant importance to design any financial literacy campaign for pension programme, as population constitutes the core for pension system. India is the second most populous country of the world with 1.21 billion people in 2011, 62.37 million, that is, 51.5 per cent being male and 58.64 million, that is, 48.5 per cent being female population (Population Census 2011). Further, Most of the Indians still live in rural areas (68.84 per cent) and urban population constitutes only about one third (31.16 per cent) of total population. Locational factors have a significant bearing on investment decision. Rural population in general mostly depends on agro-based seasonal income, rate of literacy is also lower than urban population, financial market infrastructure is also poorer than urban areas, and financial institutions pay lower attention to rural market as it is associated with higher marketing costs.

Trend in Literacy in India

General literacy in India is much below the developed world, though the overall literacy rate has improved in recent years but this improvement is geographically and genderwise uneven in India meaning that no single programme would fulfil the requirement and special efforts need to be made for lower literacy segments. Overall 82.1 per cent of Indian male population is literate but rural male literacy rate recorded at 78.6 per cent was much lower than urban male literacy rate at 89.7 per cent. Overall female literacy was recorded at 65.5 per cent, while literacy among female in rural and urban areas was recorded at 58.8 per cent and 79.9 per cent respectively (Population Census 2011). This low rate of general literacy, particularly in the rural areas and among the female population, has a strong bearing on the level of financial literacy. It was observed in study of Lusardi and Mitchell (2006) that financial literacy is highly correlated with schooling and financial condition is acute among those with less than high school degree. It was also noted that those with college degree display better understanding about risk diversification. Therefore, any financial literacy programme must keep in view the special needs and requirements of this huge number.

Employment Characteristics

Informal sector workers dominate the employment market in India. According to National Sample Survey 61st round (2004–05), 86.34 per cent workers were employed in the informal sector as against only 13.66 per cent employment in the formal or organised sector consisting of public and private sector.

Skewed Income Distribution

India is a country of many contrasts and there exists a wide disparity in distribution of wealth and income. A country with the fourth largest number of billionaires in the world is also one of the poorest countries with more than 35 per cent below the poverty line. Concentration of wealth and uneven distribution of wealth reduces the size of investment market. There are a large number of small investors who are mostly concerned about investment risks, very less access to financial knowledge and information. At the same time, there exists very small segment of High Net Worth Individual (HNI) who has higher risk tolerance ability, better access to financial information and knowledge. It is the former group which needs more access to information, and needs to be equipped with financial literacy and market knowledge. The need for the latter is different from the former.

Households, Investors, Non-investors and Savers

SEBI-NCAER Survey (2011) indicated that out of 227.48 million households only 24.48 millions are investors and 203.36 million are non-investors. Locational bifurcation indicates that 73.38 millions are unban households and 154.46 millions are rural households, but rural areas have only 9.25 million investors as against 15.24 million investors in rural areas (Figure 14.1).

Savers and Investors

Savings and investments are correlated and it is expected that higher the savings higher would be the investment in financial assets. But it is not happening, though India is

Figure 14.1 Investors and Non-investors Household

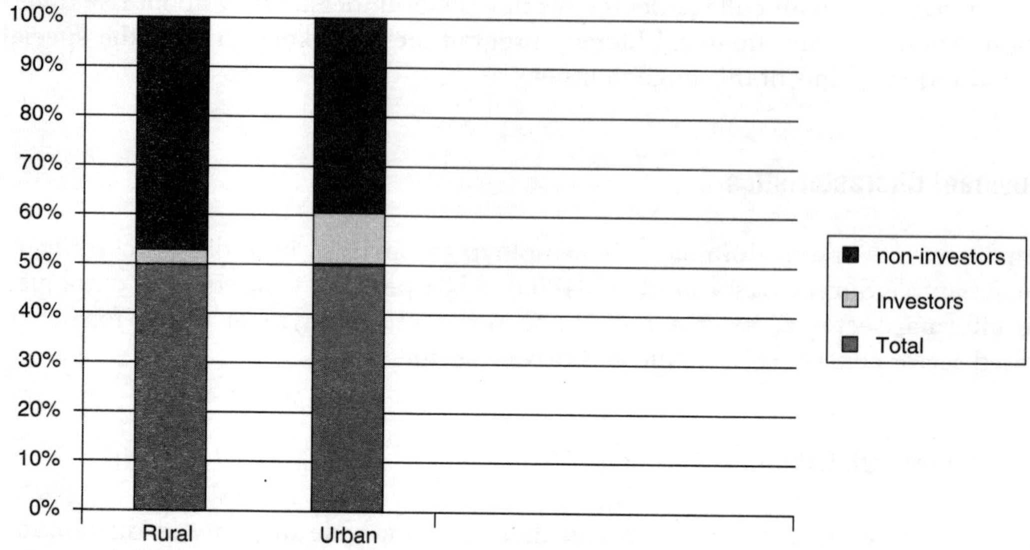

Source: National Council of Applied Economic Research (2011).

maintaining a steady growth rate in savings, investor population has grown by only 6 per cent in the last 10 years (SEBI-NCAER 2011). SEBI-NCEAR study estimated that there were 34 million savers (46 per cent) and others 25 million (33 per cent). This 'Others' households may be putting their money in gold, real estate, etc., but keeping them away from formal financial sector saving is the lack of knowledge, absence of accessible financial instruments and infrastructure, or any proper guidance. Financial education can play an important role in bringing them in the financial market and inducing them into investing (Figure 14.2).

Household Savings

Trend in household savings in financial instruments indicate a direction of savings preference and investment perception. Reserve Bank of India's Annual Report (2010–11) report provides an idea of the household preference for financial savings in India. During the year 2010–11 (ending September 2011) household sector invested an amount of ₹1,043,977 crore (as against ₹991,582 crore in the previous year) in various financial instruments, bank deposits, mutual funds, life insurance, pension and provident funds, etc. Major preference for the household sector was the deposit with commercial banks, life insurance policies and pension and provident funds and the percentage share of these instruments was 42 per cent, 23.8 per cent and 9.1 per cent, respectively. However, most significant emerging trend in distribution of household

Figure 14.2 Savers and Investors

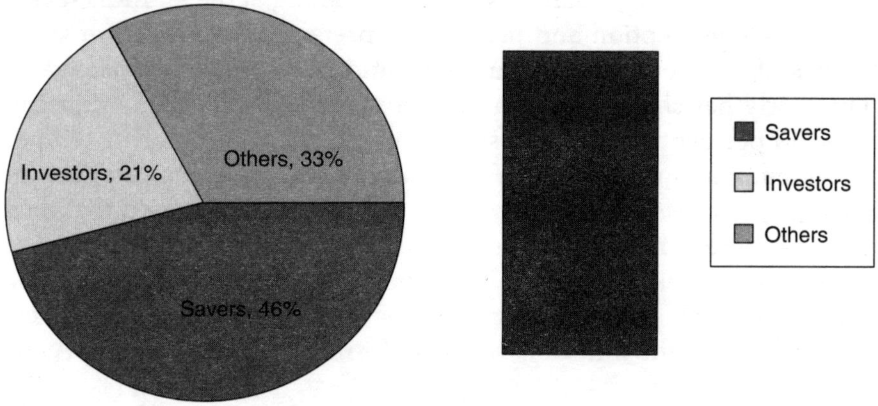

Source: National Council of Applied Economic Research (2011).

savings in India is gradual decline of the share of deposit with commercial banks and provident and pension funds, while that of life insurance policies has been steadily increasing.

It has been reported by RBI that the percentage share of commercial banks in household savings in financial assets declined from 52.8 per cent in 2008–09 to 42 per cent in 2010–11, while that of provident and pension funds declined from 10 per cent to 9.1 per cent. However, the percentage share of life insurance in household savings went up from 21 per cent to 23.8 per cent during the same period. However interestingly, NCAER (2011) household survey shows that investment with commercial banks is still the most preferred as 38.84 per cent household preferred commercial banks followed by life insurance 33.67 per cent (Chapter 4, Table 4.4).

Indian Investors Are Risk Averse

SEBI–NCAER Survey of Indian Investors (2000–01) revealed certain interesting facts about Indian investors investing in capital market instruments like equity, bonds mutual funds. According to this study, estimated 13.1 million or 7.4 per cent of all-India household directly invested in equity share or bonds or on both and estimated 11.8 million investor household invested in units of mutual funds. But more significant finding of the study is the risk perception of investing household. There was very low level of risk consciousness. 'The behaviour of investor households has generally shown negative correlation between the degree of risk and choice of instruments of investment…it is because Indian investors are risk averse and they go for investment offering moderate return and lower or NIL credit risk' (NCAER 2011). Similar trend in risk aversion was also noted in NCAER (2011) survey which commented, 'majority (53 per cent) of surveyed investing households fall in the least risk taker category. The degree of risk was highest among investors with more than 15 years of schooling at the all India level.'

A further evidence of risk perception and investment preference observed in study by MCX-SX (2010) has also revealed a similar trend and investment perspective of Indian Investors. This study has shown that top five most preferred investment instruments were insurance (86 per cent), fixed deposits (49 per cent), gold or silver (43 per cent), real estate (25 per cent) and mutual funds (23 per cent). Another important revelation is that the investors prefer *guaranteed return* as 66 per cent had indicated that they do not invest in stocks as there is no guaranteed return, 65 per cent indicated that too much price fluctuation in the stock market, while 62 per cent indicated that investing in capital market is very risky. This should be an eye opener for pension policymakers in India who vehemently oppose the introduction of performance guarantee in NPS by the fund managers.

Education and Investment Decision

The study has also noted that the level of education is an important determinant of investment decisions as of all graduate households heads, 17 per cent were investors. When the heads of households had primary and higher secondary education, the proportion of investors was just 2 per cent and 5 per cent, respectively, and among non-educated households, less than 1 per cent were investors. This indicates that financial education can significantly influence the investment decision of a household and the needs of financial education of households with different background would be different.

Importance of Pension Plans in Household Savings

A recent study by NCAER (2011) revealed certain interesting facts about household preference for pension savings. The study of NCAER based on sample of 38,412 households from 44 cities and 40 villages. The percentage of investors household was 20 per cent in urban areas and 6 per cent in rural areas and the estimated number of urban investors household is 15.23 million of all the urban households, while the estimated number of savers household was 34 million (46 per cent) (other household 25 million [33 per cent]).

The survey shows that the most preferred investment choice is the commercial bank (38.84 per cent), followed by life insurance (33.67 per cent), post office savings (20.33 per cent), and preference for pension was merely 4.28 per cent. It was also observed that *pension plans* are more preferred by households (5.8 per cent) *with higher level of education (with schooling above 15 years) and females referred pension plans marginally higher (7.4 per cent) than males (4.1 per cent). Occupational break-up shows that preference for pension plans was higher (5.20 per cent) among agricultural and allied workers followed by blue collared employees (4.88 per cent) and white collard employees (4.31 per cent). Further preference for pension was higher (4.67 per cent) among upper income group, followed by middle upper (4.14 per cent), middle income (4.11 per cent), and lower income group (3.74 per cent)* (Table 14.1).

Distribution of Estimated Savers in Pension and Others

Out of 34 million savers' households only 6.02 million, that is, 17.7 per cent saved in pension plans. However, more savers (3.26 million) (54.13 per cent of pension savers) were in the category of 11–15 years of schooling, lower than those were people with schooling above 15 years. But highest number of pension savers 1.68 million (27.94 per cent) were in the highest income group, monthly income more than ₹25,000.

Table 14.1 Choice of Saving Instruments (in per cent)

Household Profile	*Post Office Savings*	*Pension*	*Life Insurance*	*Commercial Banks*	*Regional Banks*	*Total*
Year of Schooling						
Up to 5 years	14.92	**1.66**	33.72	45.36	4.38	100
6 to 10	15.61	**2.98**	37.95	40.99	2.48	100
11 to 15	20.93	**4.15**	33.26	38.66	3.01	100
Above 15	22,87	**5.81**	31.75	36.91	2.65	100
Occupation						
Agriculture & Allied	10.54	**5.20**	39.26	42.04	2.96	100
White Collar	21.08	**4.31**	33.66	38.13	2.82	100
Blue Collar	19.25	**4.88**	39.53	33.17	3.17	100
Business, Transfer and Others	18.73	**3.31**	27.96	47.01	2.99	100
Income						
Lower	11.90	**3.74**	41.81	39.08	3.47	100
Middle Lower	17.34	**4.00**	37.94	37.27	3.45	100
Middle	22.18	**4.11**	33.52	37.81	2.38	100
Middle Upper	21.98	**4.14**	32.76	38.65	2.48	100
Upper	21.29	**4.67**	30.83	40.19	3.02	100
Sex						
Male	20.54	**4.09**	33.63	38.99	2.75	100
Female	16.78	**7.42**	34.20	36.42	5.18	100
TOTAL	20.33	**4.28**	33.67	38.84	2.88	100

Source: National Council of Applied Economic Research (2011).

Note: Lower Income: All participants having monthly income less than or equal to ₹10,000.

Lower Middle Income: All participants having monthly income between ₹10,001–15,000.

Middle Income: All participants having monthly income between ₹15,001–20,000.

Middle Upper Income: All participants having monthly income between ₹20,001–25,000.

Upper Income: All participants having monthly income between ₹20,001–25,000.

Interestingly, male savers in pension outnumbered the female savers though in choice the female savers outnumbered the male savers. There were 5.28 million male savers as against 0.73 million female savers in pensions (Table 14.2).

Table 14.2 Profile of Savers' Households by Saving Option (estimated)

Household Profile	*Post Office Savings*	*LIC*	*Pension Scheme*	*Commercial Banks*	*Regional Banks*
1. *Savers by Education (Million)*					
Year of Schooling					
Up to 5 years	0.66	2.54	**0.13**	3.76	0.23
6 to 10	4.09	12.24	**1.20**	14.24	1.07
11 to 15	12.89	28.95	**3.26**	34.74	3.08
Above 15	4.28	8.72	**1.43**	9.30	0.83
TOTAL	**21.92**	**52.45**	6.02	**62.04**	**5.21**
2. *Savers by Education (in per cent)*					
Year of Schooling					
Up to 5 years	3.02	4.82	**2.20**	6.06	4.37
6 to 10	18.66	23.33	**19.97**	22.95	20.51
11 to 15	58.79	55.20	**54.13**	56.00	59.25
Above 15	19.53	16.62	**23.70**	14.98	15.87
TOTAL	**100**	**100**	100	**100**	**100**
3. *Savers by Income (Million)*					
Monthly Income (in ₹)					
Up to 10,000	2.73	8.67	**0.69**	11.59	0.95
10,001–15,000	5.49	13.54	**1.36**	16.12	1.52
15,001–20,000	6.04	13.30	**1.26**	15.07	0.95
20,001–25,000	3.38	7.72	**1.03**	9.00	0.62
More than 25,000	4.29	9.21	**1.68**	10.25	1.17
TOTAL	21.92	52.45	**6.02**	62.04	5.21
4. *Savers by Income (in per cent)*					
Monthly Income (in ₹)					
Up to 10,000	12.44	16.54	**11.47**	18.68	18.33
10001–15000	25.04	25.82	**22.64**	25.98	29.26
15001–20000	27.55	25.35	**20.90**	24.30	18.17
20001–25000	15.41	14.72	**17.05**	14.51	11.85
More than 25000	19.56	17.57	**27.94**	16.53	22.39
TOTAL	100	100	**100**	100	100
5. *Savers by Gender (Million)*					
Male	19.92	48.32	**5.28**	57.69	4.75
Female	2.00	4.12	**0.73**	4.36	0.46
TOTAL	21.92	52.45	**6.02**	62.04	5.21
6. *Savers by Gender (in per cent)*					
Male	90.87	92.14	**87.81**	92.98	91.23
Female	9.13	7.86	**12.19**	7.02	8.77
TOTAL	100	100	**100**	100	100

Source: National Council of Applied Economic Research (2011).

Information and Investment

Access to information has important bearing on investment decision of the household. Information increases awareness about products, process and benefits and lack of timely and sufficient information blocks the investment decision. MCX-SX study revealed that lack of information is one of the major barriers to invest (in stock market), and across the country, 56 per cent of those surveyed conveyed lack of information about investing as a major barrier to participating in the market. Lack of information has been identified as a major reason for non-participation in the market. It was identified as 47 per cent in tier-1 cities, 59 per cent in tier-2 cities, and by 63 per cent in tier-3 cities. This study also indicated the required information content as 59 per cent of those surveyed demanded increased awareness about the products and 53 per cent demanded increased awareness about the process (MCX-CX 2010). Expansion of market coverage and increasing market participation was to a great extent determined by the timely and adequate information about product, process and benefits.

Financial Literacy and Awareness about Retirement Savings

There are several challenges to successfully develop and implement the NPS. However, the most significant seems to educate the subscribers to take active informed decision. According to Swaroop (2008), Chairman PFRDA,

> *The main challenges, to my mind, are to empower the subscribers to take appropriate investment decisions based on their risk and return profile, provide safety and high returns, extending coverage to as many people as possible and to improve financial literacy levels. All stakeholders in pension reforms will have to make extra efforts to educate potential participants about benefits and advantages of saving for retirement. Here the role of financial planners is crucial and of great significance.*

However, in India, not many structured study on financial literacy and the process of financial decision-making by the individual investors are available to assess the level of financial literacy and its impact on active investment decision.

Investment Objectives and Perception of Retirement Savings

There are some evidence on why Indian investors save and what are their perception about savings for old age income. A Survey conducted by the NCAER-Max-New York Life (Shukla 2008) throws further light on savings behaviour of Indian household—their income level, investment preference and investment objectives, etc., which may be useful for us in designing a default option. The survey noted that in 2004–05, there were 205.9 million households in India and the average household in India has an annual income of ₹65,041 and expenditure of ₹48,902. Due to lack of social security system over 80 per cent of Indians save and less than one fourth in financial instruments and two third of all savings are kept in liquid assets. Overwhelmingly, 83 per cent of household save for emergency including marriages and social events, children education and gifting, and nearly 69 per cent of households in India save for old age financial security. The findings of NCAER—Max New York Study revealed quite alarming signal in view of the fact that only 69 per cent of households save for old age financial security and that means 31 per cent of household do not have any provision for old age financial savings. Some further insight into saving behaviour, particularly about the consciousness about retirement savings of Indian households revealed in a study *India Income and Savings Survey* (IISS 2007) conducted by Dataworks. The respondents were asked to nominate whether building retirement savings was a primary savings objective. The result obtained through the survey indicate that 'fewer than one in fourteen uncovered workers presently are consciously saving for retirement and the amounts being saved in most cases are patently inadequate as they represent, in the average case, between only one and one and one half times their average annual earnings'.

The studies cited above shows that Indian households are basically averse to risk and prefer to save through financial instruments which contain lower risks. They prefer to put a large part of savings in liquid assets and 31 per cent households even do not save for old age financial security. All these put immense responsibility on the NPS to educate the households about the necessity for old age savings through financial literacy programme and to offer suitable financial products to channelise savings into old age pension. In such an environment of low level of financial literacy, low level of awareness of retirement savings, it can be assumed that we yet have to promote an active decision-making environment, particularly in the unorganised sector for retirement investing.

FINANCIAL LITERACY CAMPAIGN IN INDIA

So far no centralised/national-level financial literacy campaign has been promoted in India. However, some industry-specific financial awareness and literacy campaigns have been promoted by industry regulators like RBI, IRDA, SEBI. These programs are mostly directed to respective industry regulated by them.

Reserve Bank of India

The Reserve Bank of India has undertaken banking-specific project "Project Financial Literacy" with the objective to disseminate information about the central bank and general banking concept to various target groups including school and college going children, women, rural and urban poor, defence personnel and senior citizens.

The Insurance Regulatory and Development Authority of India (IRDA)

IRDA has undertaken mass awareness advertising campaign on insurance through 'Bima Bemisaal' to create awareness among people about insurance and importance of insurance in our lives, to educate policyholders about their rights and obligations, protections made available by IRDA through regulations, existence of various grievance redressal channels, etc.

Securities and Exchange Board of India (SEBI)

SEBI has introduced financial literacy programme for various segments of society to about financial market and investment. This programme is coordinated through:

❖ SCHOOL PROGRAMME

This programme is conducted jointly with National Institute of Securities Market for 8th and 9th standard school children which covered more than 4300 school children from 32 schools in 2008–09.

❖ ASSOCIATION WITH NON-GOVERNMENT ASSOCIATIONS (NGOS)

SEBI is conducting financial literacy programme partnering with NGOs which have experience in promoting financial literacy at school level.

❖ FINANCIAL LITERACY PROGRAMME THROUGH RESOURCE PERSON

SEBI tied up with resource person to increase understanding about various financial concepts among the School and College Students, Middle income Group, Executives, Housewives, Retirement Planning, Self-help Groups, etc.

❖ VISIT TO SEBI

Through this programme SEBI invites students from School, College and Professional Institutions to increase understanding about financial market regulation.

❖ JOINT PROGRAMME WITH OTHERS

SEBI also conducts Investor Education Workshops with the help of Investor Associations, Joint Programs with exchanges/Depositories/Trade Bodies. SEBI also conducts Investor Education Workshops by Exchanges/Depositories/Trade Bodies. In addition to the above, SEBI also conducts Regional Seminars. SEBI has also prepared financial education reading materials in English and various regional languages for school children, college children, homemakers, executives, middle income group, investment planning for retired people. SEBI has also launched a dedicated website for investor's awareness: http://investor.sebi.gov.in/Reference per cent20Material/Guajarati/executivesguj.pdf.

In addition to the above, many financial organisations conduct investor's awareness programmes, independent of the programmes conducted by the regulators.

Minimum Common Standards for Financial Advisers and Financial Educators

The Government of India formed a committee on Investor Awareness and Protection, chaired by Swaroop (2008), Chairman PFRDA. The committee released its recommendation in November 2009. The recommendations of the committee included some radical changes in the commission given to agents and brokers, and some proposal for financial education and financial literacy. The recommendation has very far-reaching implications for Agents/Distributors of insurance, mutual fund distributors, and financial advisors. The recommendations include scrapping the commissions on insurance products, a common regulator for all financial advisers, a common minimum standard for all sellers of mutual funds, insurance products and pension products, setting up *Financial Well-being Board of India* (FINWEB) that will regulate all financial advisers and spread financial literacy in India. The committee also recommended adopting an SRO-driven regulatory system for financial advisers.

The FINWEB should consist of two operational arms, namely, a *Self Regulatory Organisation* (SRO) focus on bringing all financial advisers under one common standard and a *Financial Literacy Cell* focusing on financially literacy. The FINWEB should function under a board of directors to be drawn from the existing regulators, ministry of finance, financial sector, industry associations, independent entities and academics. There should be independent funding for the FINWEB either through a capital grant or the annual budget. The committee favoured the principle-based regulation.

So far no formal decision has taken on the implementation of full report though upfront commission to mutual fund agents have been stopped. While some suggestions like setting up FINWEB are welcomed, there was vehement opposition to withdrawal of incentives to distributors and agents. Moreover, the proposed FINWEB seems to be another bureaucratic organisation, which many doubt would be able to provide necessary leadership to carry on financial literacy in India.

A PROPOSAL FOR NATIONAL FINANCIAL LITERACY PROGRAMME FOR RETIREMENT SAVINGS (NFLPR)

The recommendations of FINWEB are very generic and any specific direction lacks market perception, any specific solution to enhance financial capability of individual, particularly in respect of retirement saving. We need to have retirement saving directed programme for India. Financial literacy programme adopted in many developed countries with higher literacy rate and fairly good level of financial literacy may not be suitable for India with low level of general literacy and lower level of understanding about economic, financial matters and personal finance.

A majority of households have very low income and marginal propensity to save, though retirement/old age income is equally necessary for them. International experience as discussed above shows that for achieving effectiveness of any financial literacy/information programme to develop financial capability of people, it needs to be designed very carefully in a simple language that is understood by a large section of target oriented population, and the programme needs to be continuously evaluated and its progress monitored.

One of the important determinants of financial literacy in a country is the overall rate of literacy, which is quite low in India. Distribution of wealth and income is skewed and there is much less awareness about retirement savings. Moreover, NPS is a new system not even known to a large section of Indian population. When any existing system changes and products are introduced, there is a knowledge gap, uncertainty, anxiety, absence of trust and confusion. This is applicable to pension reforms and new pension products as well. We have discussed about the various issues associated with pension reforms and introduction of DC system financed by individual investors and absorbing risks of all kinds. There is a cultural change and psychological pressure when a country switches over from a known system to an unknown system, like through pension reform and there is a huge gap between the perceived understanding of investors and actual impact of the changed system. This gap needs to be narrowed through information dissemination and by improving general understanding about the system, products, market mechanism, regulation, and governance, accountability of various stakeholders and benefits of beneficiaries. Financial education and financial literacy is therefore considered to be the cornerstone for success of any reforms, particularly the pension reform. The effort towards improving financial literacy for NPS needs to be targeted within a general framework of financial education, to serve the best interest of investors as it would improve the understanding, skill assessment for informed decision, and to provide a comparative perspective across the financial market and products to improve financial well-being of the self. Keeping this broad perspective in view, an attempt has been made to provide a working format for financial literacy programme targeted for NPS. However, an effective programme for financial literacy must be designed keeping in view the socio-economic profile of potential market and investors. This is needed to identify the various aspects of the programme like course contents, delivery system, coordinates, etc. Several studies have been conducted in India about investors' socio-economic background, investment preference, risk perspectives, understanding of financial products and markets, etc., which would provide a broader view about the proposed focus of such a programme. The financial literacy and capacity building for personal financial well-being needs to be carried out through well-designed programme, and can be *called National Financial Literacy Programme for Retirement Savings* (NFLPR), an outline of which is given below.

NATIONAL FINANCIAL LITERACY PROGRAMME FOR RETIREMENT SAVINGS (NFLPR)

Objective

The objective of NFLPR would be three fold. *Firstly*, the programme would aim at building financial capability and empowering those without financial knowledge to take decision for personal financial well-being through financial and economic education. *Secondly*, the NFLPR needs to be designed in a way that it educates the people about various features of NPS, various aspects of risks associated with the scheme, the way to minimise risks, various regulatory provisions to protect investors' interest, etc. *Thirdly*, the NFLPR would aim at reaching out to the maximum people particularly in the rural and semi-urban areas, low-income and less educated people.

Programme Contents

The contents of the programme should be designed keeping the above objectives in view to serve two primary objectives of promoting financial literacy and building capability for retirement investing.

❖ IMPROVING GENERAL AWARENESS ABOUT SAVINGS FOR OLD AGE INCOME

Due to lack of general literacy and absence of appropriate mechanism to disseminate economic and financial information, most of the people are not aware of the emerging threats to their old age existence due to increased longevity and ageing and importance of savings to overcome the financial difficulties that would emerge with longer survival. Financial literacy programme, therefore, needs to focus on the changing population dynamics, and related financial requirements and needs to promote a culture of retirement/old age savings, etc.

❖ IMPROVING FINANCIAL AND ECONOMIC KNOWLEDGE

Firstly, the objective of such programme should be to empower the potential consumers of pension services with knowledge and understanding of various economic and financial issues impacting individual's financial and economic well-being and to strengthen the individual to take informed decision which would enhance their financial well-being. It should also aim to improve the general understanding in financial issues like financial products/instruments, various financial institutions and their way of functioning, governance, financial markets and operational mechanism, relative importance, benefits, costs, and risks associated with any investment decision. Role of regulators in various markets, investors' protection, etc., along with general understanding about financial products, system, costs, benefits and risks, etc., are needed to enable a consumer to decide the priority and relative importance of any financial decision.

Developing Financial Capability for Retirement Savings Through NPS

It has been indicated that pension reform and switchover from DB to DC system brings with it lots of transitional difficulties and dislocation of cultural beliefs and people fail to understand the long-term implicit benefits of the new system. Therefore, an economic-cum-financial literacy campaign is necessary to create awareness about the need for change and the expected national and individual benefits of the new system. Economic and financial campaigns also aim at educating people about likely challenges emanating from the changing population age profile, increased longevity, importance of pension savings, etc.

❖ FEATURES, ARCHITECTURE AND ADMINISTRATION OF NPS

Experience of this author as the CEO of one of best performing large pension funds in India shows that most of the people are not aware of the NPS features, administration, architecture, benefits and risks, etc. Unless people understand these, they may not be interested in investing. Currently no agency (government, regulator, fund managers, etc.) has taken any serious and effective steps in this regard. Lack of awareness is one of the important reasons for poor acceptance of NPS. Therefore, to increase pension coverage through NPS, an effective awareness campaign needs to be brought in.

❖ FUNDS MANAGEMENT, INVESTMENT VALUATION, RISKS AND PERFORMANCE

Funds management is the most important area of concern in a privately managed pension system. It is fund managers who are responsible for investment performance. Investors should therefore know about fund managers' background, skill, experience, performance and track record, capability of investment management, funds management strategy, etc.

❖ VALUATION

This is a critical issue in pension fund asset management which determines entry and exit prices and accumulation of assets. The method of financial asset valuation is a controversial issue. Therefore, regulator approved valuation methods and its strength and weaknesses are required to be made public and brought to the notice of investors.

In a privately managed pension system entire investment risks are transferred to the investors. There are several types of risks associated with investment which may have significant impact on the risk tolerance level of individual investors. Therefore, investors need to be educated about these risks and their probable impact on accumulated assets in order to be able to take an informed decision by considering the risk factors. There is a tendency in the privatised fund management system to focus on the brighter side and suppress the adverse features like risks. Financial literacy programme must provide the correct picture on various risks and needs to be impartial in the interest of investors.

❖ GOVERNANCE AND ACCOUNTABILITY

Financial literacy must include the information about regulation and governance system, in NPS. Various regulatory and supervisory positions should be known to public. The system, norms and regulatory provisions regarding accountability of the government, PFRDA, NPS trust, board of fund managers, fund management company, CRA, etc., should be disclosed and informed to the investors.

❖ INVESTORS PROTECTION

One of the most important objectives of financial literacy programme is to protect the beneficiary interest by making them aware about the various provisions in regulation aimed at protecting their interests. Responsibilities and accountability of various service providers, management and board of various entities should be known to the investors.

Unless the investors are aware about the inbuilt provision, no action can be taken by them to redress their grievances.

Funding

The NFLPR is a national programme and for the benefits of workers/employees and other citizens of the country. Financially literate workers/employees, asset of any organization, who will make a difference in productivity, and financially literate population, who save for their own retirement income prudently, will reduce burden on government. Therefore, the cost of NFLPR programme needs to be borne by the government and the corporates, as they are also going to be the beneficiaries.

Target Group

Five star culture of financial literacy and financial inclusion, as often noticed, will not really serve the purpose. The programme needs to be taken to the people who need it. The programme should target farmers, workers, particularly the informal sector employees, students in school and college, teachers, media and opinion makers. Moreover, those who are involved in policymaking and running pension systems need to be targeted particularly in the areas of risk, regulation and protection of investors' interest.

Public–Private Partnership (PPP)

A National Literacy Programme of huge magnitude cannot effectively be carried out by the government only or the PFRDA. A wider participation by a large number of financial and social organisations is required. A *financial literacy forum* may be formed comprising the fund management industry, sponsors of pension funds, other association of industries, association of workers, teachers, NGOs, students, media, etc., and the government. They will undertake the responsibility in the respective areas to provide economic and financial education.

Format of NFLPR

Programme design is an important factor and such programme formats need to be simple. They should be easily comprehensible to a layman. All the media, including print and electronic, need to be used, but designs should be target oriented. Literacy background of targeted persons needs to be taken into consideration while designing specific programmes.

Monitoring and Review

The programme must be continuously reviewed and evaluated through close monitoring system and mid-course correction measures need to be taken. Review should be conducted to assess the impact of programme, perhaps survey can be conducted for this purpose. On the basis of the survey findings, necessary modification in programme contents, campaign format, delivery system, etc., can be modified for better results. A well-designed monitoring and review mechanism needs to be put in place.

Accountability

Since a large number of entities and institutions are involved in this non-commercial and non-incentive driven programme, there is a possibility of lack of interest to actualise the declared objectives. In order to overcome the inertia on the part of those who are selected to take forward the programme, some amount of accountability needs to be imposed through regulation. Care should be taken to ensure that these institutions are not turned into a parking place of bureaucrats in their post-retirement period. People with proven track record and necessary background and experience should to be placed with the institution.

These are few of the required features and many more factors can be added to improve it further. However, the final outcome will depend on the quality of inputs, but will be finally determined by the commitment and ownership of the programme.

REFERENCES

Committee on Investment Awareness Programme (2009), 'Minimum Common Standards for Financial Advisers and Financial Education' (Chairman: D Swaroop). Consultation paper, available at: http://pfrda.org.in/writereaddata/eventimages/Consultation per cent20Paper3411776713.pdf

Hutch, Mary (2006), 'National Pensions Awareness Campaign (NPAC)'. Presentation in OECD Conference on Financial Education New Delhi, India 21-22 September (2006). Available at: http://www.oecd.org/finance/financialeducation/37396801.pdf

IIMS (2008), 'India Investment Survey (2007)', cited in *The Sleeping Giant-Private Pension Market in India 2008*, an IIMS Data works Research Report, New Delhi.

Kempson, Elaine. (2008.), 'Financial Education Fund: Monitoring and Evaluation Policy and Procedures'. Financial Education Inception Report (mimeo), November, cited in Robert Holzmann (2010), 'Bringing Financial Literacy and Education to Low and Middle Income Countries: Need to Review, Adjust, and Extend Current Wisdom', . World Bank, IZA and CES SP Discussion Paper, July 2010.

Lusardi, Annamaria and Mitchell Olivia (2006), 'Financial Literacy and Planning: Implications for Retirement Wellbeing'. Available at: http://www.dartmouth.edu/~alusardi/Papers/FinancialLiteracy.pdf

MCX-SX (2010), 'Indian Equity Investors Survey 2010'. MCX-SX, Mumbai. Available at: www.mcx.sx.com

NCAER (2011), 'How Households Save and Invest: Evidence from NCAER Household Survey'. Sponsored by SEBI of India, National Council of Applied Economic Research, New Delhi, July 2011.

OECD/IOPS. (2008), 'Private Pensions and Government Information Campaigns: Lessons from OECD Countries'. Presented at OECD/IOPS Global Forum on Private Pensions. Available at: http://www.oecd.org/document/9/0,3746,en_2649_34853_41005769_1_1_1_1,00.html

Orton, Larry. (2007), 'Financial Literacy: Lessons from International Experience'. Canadian Policy Research Networks Inc. (CPRN), September 2007. Available at: http://www.cprn.org/documents/48647_EN.pdf

Registrar General and Census Commissioner. (2011), 'Census of India, 2011'. Rural Urban Distribution of Population (Provisional Population Totals), Registrar General and Census Commissioner, India. Available at: http://censusindia.gov.in/2011-prov-results/paper2/data_files/india/Rural_Urban_2011.pdf

Reserve Bank of India (2011), 'Annual Report 2010–11'. Mumbai: RBI.

Retirement Commission, New Zealand (2008), 'National Strategy for Financial Literacy–A Summary' (Foreword by Diana Crossan). Retirement Commission, New Zealand, June 2008.

Securities Exchange Board of India (SEBI) (2001), 'SEBI-NCAER Survey of Indian Investors–2000–01'. Securities Exchange Board of India.

Shukla, Rajesh (ed.) (2008), 'How India Earns, Spends and Saves', Results from The Max New York Life–NCAER India Financial Protection Survey. The Max New York Life Insurance, New Delhi.

Swaroop, D. (2008), 'India's Pension Reform Initiative', *Indian Journal of Public Audit and Accountability*, Vol. 1 (April–June 2007).

15 Summary and Some Suggestions

PENSION REFORM IS A MUST BUT SHOULD BE WITH A HUMAN FACE

The most critical socio-economic problem of this century is the emerging challenges of changing population dynamics and growing threat of ageing and how to prevent it by providing sustainable old age income securities to millions by maintaining fiscal health of the system. Pension reform thus emerged as the most critical social and economic policy of concern for the policymakers, researchers and academic world. Some even find it as the most emerging business proposition. There is no denying the necessity of pension reforms, but differences arise over the structure, contents, and conceptualisation of the entire exercise.

Unfunded DB pension system, having many advantages in general, suffers from many inbuilt weakness: benefits are disproportionate to contribution, distribution of benefits are uneven, low rates of return, and there is also pressure on state exchequer due to state funding. Pension reforms directing to replace PAYG system by privately managed individual accounts based DC system has been widely advocated and introduced by many countries. It has been argued that individual account based DC system is better than DB system to face the emerging pension challenges as it generates better return on investment, establishes closer link between contribution and benefits, induces the individual to reduce present consumption and force him/her to save more for old age, remove labour market distortions, improve the national savings rates via increased private savings and economic growth. Several studies have been conducted and analyses have been made by the experts to assess the impact of pension reforms. It has emerged that initial success of Chilean type of reforms could not be an ideal model for every country and therefore alternative models were advocated and implemented by many countries. However, the reform experience in these countries provided us valuable lesson, which can be institutionalised while undertaking pension reforms in countries like India.

Growth is painful and transition is costly. There are explicit and implicit pain and costs in any change over which need to be thought while undertaking any reform. There are systemic risks and social costs which need to be assessed in the light of risk tolerance ability of the country and its people and the agenda of change should be set for the benefits of the pension investors and greater good for the country. Pension reforms thus aim at promoting financial stability of the system as well as maximum pension benefits for those who save for old age income.

SOME SIGNIFICANT FEATURES OF PENSION REFORMS

Pension reform through introduction of individual account based funded pension in Latin America and Central and Eastern Europe (CEE) countries has many important characteristics. The new system is basically a *multi-pillar system* with the core contribution coming from the individual members, but the state also assumes an important role by providing universal social security. While the first pillar basically remained as *universal social security* or social insurance or basic minimum pension programme financed by states, the second pillar is usually a fully funded DC pillar managed by private pension fund managers. The third pillar is primarily voluntary savings plans for additional retirement benefits. The first and second pillars are mandatory in most of the countries studied in this book. In order to reduce the intensity of various risks associated with privatised DC scheme and to provide some comfort to the investors/members, most of the reformed countries have introduced some safety measures either through minimum pension guarantee or through minimum/benchmark return for the second pillar DC plans which are managed by independent fund managers. By introducing the *social assistance/minimum pension guarantee* the state has tried to mitigate these problems and implicitly carried out its social obligation. These steps have reduced the hardship of retirees and fulfilled the social obligation of states.

One of the most significant aspects of pension reforms and introduction of mandatory DC system is the *rapid increase in the size of pension assets* in the countries which have introduced pension reforms. Latin America and CEE countries which have introduced pension reforms witnessed significant growth in pension assets.

One of the most crucial issues associated with fully funded second pillar managed by private fund managers in a multi-pillar pension system is the *uncertainty in investment* return and investment risks which are borne by the members. Investment restrictions, diversification and prudent person, etc., through investment regulations are attempt to protect the *account holder's interest.* Moreover, most of the countries which have introduced DC system managed by private fund managers have introduced some *benchmark or guaranteed return* to be provided by the private fund managers, when fund managers fail the sponsors and the government step in to protect the interest of account holders.

Pension Reforms have gone beyond the old age income security and most of the countries are concerned about old age health of elderly population *and health insurance and health care benefits are part of the new system.* For example, Colombian Health Care system is a part of social security and pension reforms. The Law 100 put in place a single insurance system based on cross-subsidies. China has also taken a bold step to provide affordable health care facilities to its citizens along with the introduction of various measures to reform old age pension system and to expand coverage. China has also taken a bold step to improve health care system and to bring entire population under health care network.

Recent reforms also focused on rural pension. Generally, it is the organised urban employees who become major beneficiaries of any reforms due to their massive organised strength, but recent reforms in *Brazil and China* focused on rural pension. The Brazilian constitution granted the right of retirement for rural workers independently of their contribution and rural workers receive social security benefits equivalent to minimum wages subject to the proof of 10 years' rural activities. Their contributions are based on a fraction of commercialised products from workers' excess production, rural workers' retirement systems are important steps which create incentives for workers staying in the rural sector and support the local economy. China has been making serious efforts to promote a pension insurance scheme for rural people since 1986. In January 1991, the state council decided to develop old age social insurance in rural areas having two components under the 'Basic Plan for Old Age Social Insurance in the Countryside. While Basic Pension component financed by local and central government and a Personal Account component based on contributions from enrolled individuals.'

While there are many positive features of the multi-pillar pension system, there are certain concerns also. One of the concerns is the coverage. One strong argument in favour of the privately managed pension system is that it would extend pension and provide pension benefits to people who are beyond the *social security coverage.* New pension system has been able to achieve this objective to some extent, particularly in countries where joining a new system was mandatory. While in some countries membership increased, in some countries it declined after reform (Chapter 9). But most serious concern is the very *low level of active contributors* which has been estimated at below 40 per cent of the members.

It has also been argued that pension reforms would increase domestic *savings, investment and support economic growth.* However, in all these areas there are different observations by the experts. While some experts observed through cross country study that 'the development of funded pension does indeed contribute to higher aggregate savings,' Independent Evaluation Group (IEG) of world bank, however, commented that the *impact of multi-pillar reform on savings is inconclusive.* Similarly there are different views about the impact of pension reforms on the growth country's GDP. There is no significant evidence from Latin America that post reforms, GDP growth rate was better in LAC countries. Further, yet there is no conclusive evidence that pension reform has reduced the fiscal burden of state and will provide long-term fiscal sustainability, since most of the countries except Chile do not have long track record, it may take little longer time to realise the real impact on fiscal sustainability. One of the desired objectives of pension reforms and privatisation of pension system is to generate higher rate of return, through competitive fund management system. However, in reality such an objective has not realised in Latin America, since the pension market is being controlled by few fund managers who *promoted market concentration and weakened the competition.* Some studies even commented that overall the pension fund management market is inefficient as pension fund managers could have produced the same level of output with around 35 per cent fewer assets.

An intense debate has emerged after the global financial crisis in 2007–08 about ongoing pension reforms on two counts: (*a*) long-term viability of fully mandatory defined contribution system totally replacing the defined benefit system, and (*b*) designing pension fund portfolio heavily biased in favour of equity. It has been noted that during 2008 turmoil countries with fully defined contribution system and investing a significantly large amount of assets in equity have suffered most in terms of decline of pension fund assets. The OECD estimated total assets of all pension funds by October 2008, had declined by USD 3.3 trillion (nearly 20 per cent) compared to December 2007. This decline was severe in countries having higher exposure in equities, for example, Irish pension funds with 66 per cent investment in equities. Similar decline was also noted in emerging countries. Estimated loss of aggregate value of pension assets was 33 per cent in Chile, 23 per cent in Argentina, 15 per cent in Uruguay, 11 per cent in Mexico, etc. This development has thrown challenges before the policymakers about structure reform. It has also reinforced the view that portfolio design needs to be decided very carefully, in the context of uncertainty and risks. Risk governance and accountability of fund managers and board are under focus and the structure of robust regulation and careful supervision is being reinvented.

WHAT AILS NPS AND PENSION REFORM IN INDIA

India has taken a very well-conceived decision to reform its pension system and to introduce a contributory pension for the new employees joining government services keeping the old DB pension system for the existing employees as well as current provisions for EPS and EPS managed by EPFO undisturbed. However, the system launched in January 2004 and operationalised in April 2008 has not been well accepted by the potential investors and made only marginal progress by covering about 50,000 employees till the end of 2011, contributors mostly from the government services for whom it is mandatory to join. The new system suffers from many structural problems and implementation is not only slow but has failed to induce confidence, due to absence of capability and conceptual clarity at the level of implementation (discussed throughout this book particularly in chapter 9). Most significant structural weaknesses are given below.

Low Level of Awareness

The NPS has failed to create enough awareness among the investors and enthusiasm among the various stakeholders. The NPS, particularly the All Citizens Scheme, elicited poor response due to several structural problems implicit in demand side as well as supply side constraints. However, most important factor seems to be the low level of awareness. But neither the government nor the regulator initiated any meaningful programme to educate people to save through NPS. Pension fund managers are not authorised to do that and the POPs have ever initiated such programmes as there is neither any obligation nor any incentives.

Absence of Effective Distribution Channel

Financial products, particularly in India, are sold not bought. Agents, brokers and other distributors play the key role in product positioning and distribution, which are absent in NPS due to the cost factors. Therefore, an active role is to be played by the PFRDA and other stakeholders who have opted to be associated with the NPS System. It seems that the current thoughts of increasing NPS sales through spread of financial literacy by advertising in newspapers has not enthused the potential investors to invest in NPS. It is a fact that only advertising does not help effective product positioning. Financial products like insurance, mutual funds, pension funds are distribution driven. In a country like India with low per capita income and lower level of awareness about such products and their importance, a necessity distribution mechanism is immensely important. Distributors not only sell the products but also act as first-line educators. Unfortunately, the regulator, in order to keep the cost as low as possible, did not focus on this and even probably they thought some advertisement about scheme would attract the investors. But it turned to be misleading. Insurance and mutual funds industry has grown faster due to effective distribution network and distributors.

Lack of Investors Confidence

A system tends to be sound and attracts potential investors when the system itself and the others who manage it at the ground level are able to induce confidence among the potential investors. In a country like India, factors such as little awareness about old age savings, low per capita income, large rural population, no effective distribution channel and no legislative approval of NPS, weaken the confidence of investor in NPS to a great extent. Moreover, in India the low income and less educated people have tremendous confidence in government institutions. While on one hand, more public sector entities need to be given licence to manage funds, on the other hand, intermediaries should play an active and effective role to remove such misconception and take the NPS forward.

Absence of Guaranteed Return

One of important factors that would play an important role to take forward NPS, and induce investors' confidence is the performance guarantee or guaranteed return by the fund managers. Though guarantee of minimum return is an important feature of individual account based private pension in most of the countries which have undertaken pension reforms, there is no such performance guarantee either by the fund managers, sponsors, regulators or by the government. We have seen in chapter 2 of section 1 that there are guarantee of investment return in most of the countries. Minimum return guarantee has many advantages, as the guarantee makes the DC partially DB pension and transfers a part of investment risks to the fund managers. Secondly, guarantee is a sort of insurance which may push the fund managers to take unmanageable higher risks. Guarantee of return linked to bench mark is absolutely necessary to induce investors' confidence. Further, minimum return guarantee will make the fund managers more accountable and responsible, introduce a more strategic risk management approach, better governance, healthy competition among the fund managers, will remove the anxiety of investors about future return.

Fund Managers Selection

The most important driving force of individual account based private pension system are the fund managers who are managing the assets and the service providers. In a large country like India with a diverse geographical spread, the NPS must have sufficient number of fund managers, but for huge number of employees in the central and state governments only three fund managers have been authorised and for a large unorganised sector only six fund managers have been authorised. Moreover, the selection process adopted by PFRDA, though technically fair, is not of much support to the system. There are technical and financial bidding. It was found that many well-known financial institutions with strong market presence, which were technically qualified, were excluded in the final round due to financial bid.

Low Fund Management Fee

Another weak link between the fund managers and investment management is the low fees. Presently, the PFRDA-approved fund managers fees is 0.0009 per cent decided through a competitive bidding in 2009, which continued subsequently (fund management fee has been revised upward to 0.0102 per cent for central government and state government NPS; it has been revised to 0.25 per cent for All Citizens Scheme w.e.f. 1 November 2012). It is a fact that this low fee was quoted by one fund but is applicable to all fund managers irrespective of the nature of the scheme. But problems lie in the process of bidding adopted by the PFRDA. The PFRDA decided to accept only the lowest bid and applied it to all fund managers. The lowest bidder perhaps wanted to ensure entry into pension market irrespective of cost considerations. None of the fund managers can recover the fund management expenses with this low cost and may not be able to break even in near future. It is dangerous to keep fund management fees low, as it will impact the quality of fund management, as it will not be possible to hire competent and experienced fund managers, quality research will not be undertaken and no incentive will be provided for better performance.

Institutional Capacity

Many feel that the capacity to provide a dynamic push and strengthen the NPS through innovative market-oriented initiatives is not sufficient enough as the institutional capacity remained below the desired level. The NPS cannot be promoted only through administrative initiatives but also needs to be taken forward by market-oriented development programmes through professional involvement. Understanding the market expectation and market dynamics are very essential at the early stage of any reform process to avoid the gap between policy direction and its acceptability. There is a need for continuous market exploration, analysis of changing expectations of investors, making the regulation a dynamic process to institutionalise the potential changes through robust system of supervision.

Ownership of NPS

Ownership seems to be fragmented in NPS, and as a result, it is a child of nobody and no one seems to be accountable for its implementation. Regulator without any legislative authority takes only administrative initiative, role of fund managers is limited to investment management, while CRA is concerned with account maintenance, and POPS limit their role in collecting applications. As a result, institutions-driven business initiatives and accountability-based performance is missing in NPS. The regulator and other entities have been entrusted with the responsibility of NPS and should be jointly accountable to make success. There should be a broader framework and integrated mechanism of coordination and accountability of each constituent. Unless the ownership is clearly identified, no programme can be effective enough to achieve the desired goal.

SOME FURTHER STEPS TO STRENGTHEN PENSION REFORM AND TAKE FORWARD NPS

Legislative Support

Pension reform is a critical socio-economic and political issue affecting lives of millions of subscribers and impacting national economic policy. In absence of legislative support, confidence of subscribers weakens and regulator is not able to take required initiatives and necessary developmental and punitive actions. The PFRDA is still functioning under the ordinance which was promulgated on 29 December 2004. The bill to replace this was introduced in the Parliament in March 2005. However till October 2011 the bill had not been passed. Delay in passing the PFRDA bill and providing legislative sanction to the NPS has undoubtedly hampered the progress. Not much serious efforts were made by PFRDA in the areas of capacity building and pushing the new system so vigorously to extend coverage. Supervision, monitoring and surveillance need to be improved further which is possible only if the authority is empowered with legislative approval.

Financial Literacy Programme

We have seen in Chapter 14 through various studies that there is low level of financial literacy and awareness about retirement saving. The NPS is a new programme and most of the people are not aware of the basic features. It is therefore a challenge to reach out to the millions with low level of education and even lower level of financial literacy. Therefore, a comprehensive national-level financial literacy programme, *National Financial Literacy Programme for Retirement Savings* (NFLPR), needs to be launched. A comprehensive framework has been given in Chapter 14. The objective of NFLPR would be building financial capability and empowering those without financial knowledge to take decision for personal financial well-being through financial and economic education, educate people about various features of NPS, risks associated with the scheme, the way to minimise risks, various regulatory provisions to protect investors' interest and reach to maximum people, particularly those in the rural and semi-urban areas, low-income and less educated people. The NFLPR is a national programme and for the benefits of workers/employees and other citizens of the country. Financially literate workers/employees are assets of any organisation which will make difference in productivity, and financially literate population who save for their own retirement income prudently will reduce burden on government. Therefore the cost of NFLPR programme needs to be borne by the government and the corporate, as they are also going to be the beneficiary. A National Literacy Programme of huge magnitude cannot effectively be carried out only by the government or the PFRDA and a wider participation by a large number of financial and social organisations is required. A financial literacy forum may be formed comprising the fund management industry, sponsors of pension funds, other association of industries, association of workers, teachers, NGOs, students, media, etc., and the government. They will undertake the responsibility in the respective areas to provide economic and financial education.

Market Development

In a new system like NPS, market development is an integral and important activity of a regulator. Regulatory focus should combine (*a*) setting up the system and regulatory structure, (*b*) implementing the system and (*c*) undertaking the market development. This author had suggested such a programme which has also been echoed by CRIISP Report. There is a need for well-conceived market development initiatives including business-like actions and accountability of the stakeholders. All the stakeholders like fund managers, POPs need to be actively involved in financial literacy campaign and to provide active support to increase NPS subscription. Accountability, responsibility and expected role of stakeholders in promoting the NPS and mobilisation of funds need to be spelt out directly.

❖ MARKET DISCOVERY

One important market segment for NPS would be unorganised but an associated group of self-employed people. Large number of people who are not employed in the organised sector but independently work for them would form huge potential market. It can be mentioned here that recently a top-level executive of a life insurance company desired that their agency organisation with few million agents should be covered under NPS. There are many such associations which like to take the benefits of NPS. To bring large potential subscribers under NPS, some amount of marketing initiatives, at least in the form of organised interaction, is required.

❖ STRUCTURED COORDINATION

Success of market development programme would however depend on a business target planning (BTR), active coordination and regular monitoring on the part of PFRDA. BTR needs to work like long-range planning apparatus which explores market potential and initiates policy response to tap the potential market. In order to implement the BTR, a high level of coordination committee needs to be formed including chairman/MD of all the stakeholders, to activate their participation. Subsequently, regular monitoring at the operational level would be required. Such a market-oriented approach would not only increase alertness among the stakeholders but would also enhance the sense of urgency. A structured programme with targeted attempt including increase in fund managers, resource support of stakeholders through market discovery would enable the NPS to mobilise participation. Market development programme should be initiated by the regulator and a new department should be created to undertake and manage market development. This department of the regulatory body will act as the nodal point and coordinate of all such activities.

Rural Pension

NPS Lite is a well-conceived programme which has tremendous potential to extend pension coverage to low-income people and has already created quite a good response. But it seems this response is primarily from urban segments as the aggregators selected have an urban bias. We need to take this programme deep into the country side for those who have little or no regular income. Chinese rural pension can be an ideal example of such initiative. Even agricultural workers tied to land and working for a landlord should be provided old age income support by those who have utilised the services of workers. The Swavalamban benefit may be extended to them and the balance contribution should be made by the landlord or for whom they work for a minimum period. A national rural pension policy should be designed by incorporating NPS Lite and Swavalamban scheme to cover rural informal segments. The PFRDA should make special efforts to designate rural aggregators with extended monetary support to encourage them to focus on workers in rural areas.

Voluntary Savings

Tier 2 NPS is voluntary savings by the members of NPS, to augment pension savings and to accumulate some funds which may help them to mitigate non-pension expenditure. Tier 2 of NPS is more flexible than Tier 1 as the investors are free to withdraw from this account. It's an important way of saving through fund management expertise of pension funds. However, it seems the response towards it is quite poor. Perhaps one of the reasons for this poor response is that there is no special incentive like tax benefits as we find in many countries. In most of the Latin American countries, tax incentives and other benefits are given for voluntary savings. Therefore, to make voluntary savings an attractive proposition, the PFRDA/government should consider providing some tax incentives to save in the Tier 2 of NPS; the incentives, however, can be linked to minimum contribution and period of savings and purpose of withdrawal. Speculative savings/withdrawal, however, should to be discouraged and penalised.

Return Guarantee

In order to create confidence among the potential investors and induce pension savings through NPS, minimum return guarantee (MRG) should be introduced, as it will remove to some extent the uncertainty of fund managers performance and future return. We have discussed earlier that return guarantee, in addition to improving investors guarantee, will increase competition and accountability of the fund managers, which will better protect the interest of account holders. The benchmark can be decided through average return of pension fund industry or by the G Sec yield or fixed deposit rate. Mechanism of guarantee can be decided like other countries by designing a Yield Fluctuation Fund (YFF), or a Dedicated Pension Guarantee Fund (DPGF) by the sponsor. Above all, there should be National Pension Development and Guarantee Fund (NPDGF), as discussed below.

Set Up a National Pension Development and Guarantee Fund (NPDDGF)

The NPDGF is a central level fund to be promoted by the Government of India with paid-up capital contributed by the central government, state government and public sector entities.

❖ OBJECTIVES

The NPDGF will have twin objectives to promote NPS through awareness programme including financial literacy and to act as the last resort for pension guarantee to be provided by the fund managers and sponsors.

❖ SOURCES OF FUNDS

In addition to the paid-up capital, the NPDGF will receive a portion of disinvestment proceeds, a social security cess from corporate profits, and a portion of revenue generated by the State Lottery, and investment income of its own fund.

❖ MANAGEMENT

A national-level advisory committee/trust comprising nominee from government, PFRDA, fund management industry and institutional experts from the financial sector.

Investment Regulation

Investment regulations need to be revisited and the regulation has to be NPS focused instead of general guidelines for pension funds, and pension as NPS has a different objective and structure. It should aim at providing flexibility within restriction and should be based on a quantitative investment limit along with prudent person rule.

Rationalisation of Fund Managers Selection

The PFRDA should encourage serious and long-term players with proven track record to enter into fund management business. It's not only profit but also a social responsibility that should derive the sponsors. The PFRDA should also prevent market concentration by allowing optimum number of fund managers. This calls for rationalisation of selection process to induct a reputed large financial organisation. Further, lowest cost syndrome needs to be given up and based on technical criteria and track record; the fund managers can be appointed and allowed to operate within the prescribed upper limit of fund management fees. Even if commercial bidding is followed, the lowest fee criteria should be given up, instead the PFRDA can decide a cap to avoid high fund management fees and also a floor to restrain uneconomical lower fees by a bidder.

Second CRA

We have noted that a portion of NPS cost arises out of the CRA cost. There is competition among fund managers and the same can be extended to CRA, by appointing another CRA. The monopoly of current CRA by one institution needs to be removed by inducting at least one more CRA. Competition among the CRAs will put downward pressure on cost and further improve service quality.

Pension Product: Second Auto Choice Fund

Auto Choice Fund has been introduced for the subscribers of NPS by assuming the same risk tolerance level throughout the life cycle of investors. Auto Choice (Default Option) are essential in a basket of pension products basically for two reasons, namely, the inability of an investor to select a need-based option as well as to match her/his risk tolerance with the implicit risks of a pension product. However, by introducing a single Auto Choice fund regulators have ignored varying degree of risks associated with investors of different risk tolerance ability, particularly the NPS Lite Investors. It is therefore suggested that a second auto choice fund combining low risk but moderate growth is needed. An outline of such a debt-centric Auto Choice Fund is provided in the text.

NPS Lite: A Composite Micro Provision

Annuity Lite is primarily a micro pension product designed to provide an avenue for old age pension/income, particularly for the low-income and vulnerable sections of society. The investors in the NPS Lite have low income and their financial literacy is even lower. It may be difficult for them to select a need-based annuity product independently at the time of exit. It is therefore suggested that NPS Lite should combine accumulation and pay pension stage, defining the pension on exit from the scheme (at the age of 60). This will not only be an incentive to join NPS Lite but would also act as a deterrent to early exit.

Further, the low-income people are financially as well as health-wise vulnerable. But they may not have enough means to go for health insurance separately. A health insurance element along with pension would be a welcome step. A portion of contribution can be set aside towards Group Health Insurance scheme, with a provision for limited withdrawal in case of serious disease/emergency situation.

Realistic Valuation Method

Currently followed Mark To Market valuation model is not only suitable for valuation of NPS assets but also generates internal inequity. A partially liquid narrow government bond market, a virtually illiquid and depressed corporate debt market do not support any rational logic for Mark To Market valuation and *suggested* Composite Model of Valuation (CMV) for NPS. The CMV would incorporate security class wise valuation method depending on the nature of security, trading frequency, etc. Equities are to be valued at the market price, while G Sec are to be valued at market price wherever traded, but non-traded bonds are to be valued at book value basis. Similarly, state-guaranteed bonds, state-developed loans need to be valued on book value basis and corporate bonds will be valued at market price and non-traded bonds to be valued by using Mark to Model or book value. For the operational reasons, fund portfolio under CMV needs to be divided into three sub-portfolios, namely, portfolio A, portfolio B and portfolio C. *Portfolio A* (trading and to be traded portfolio) would consist of all equity securities and that portion of debt securities earmarked for future trading by the fund. *Portfolio A* would be valued at Mark to Model basis. *Portfolio B* would consist of G Sec, state government bonds, state development loans and would be valued at book value/HTM basis, and the *Portfolio C* would consist of corporate bonds including private corporate and PSU Bonds. They should be valued at market price and in the absence of active trading should be valued at Mark to Model. This model of valuation would remove the distortions generated by unrealistic overall Mark to Model and also eliminate the impact of asset price volatility on net asset value and allocation of units to the investors.

Risk Governance

As per the Risk Policy provided by the regulator PFRDA, all the fund managers have drawn a detailed risk management policy approved by their board of directors. The operational policy is much wider and enlisted in the objectives and detailed implementation mechanism, risk monitoring and review system. However, the current practice of risk management that is based on the broad guidelines of PFRDA is too narrow in scope and is centred on investment operation and financial risks. Therefore, many sources of risk remain unattended, for example, management risk, technology risks, policy risks have not surfaced in the present policy. Currently prescribed risk management measures are totally inadequate and will not be able to protect account holders' long-term interest. Regulator should therefore consider introducing risk-based governance, introduction of prudent person rule in addition to quantitative restriction for investment, a comprehensive risk regulation including risk audit and risk standard for the pension fund industry, to be put on place. There should be guidelines for the fit and proper test for the risk manager/officer. A broader outline for the functions and responsibility for the risk management committee and its accountability and reporting should be issued. Risk management is a culture and needs to be institutionalised through active and effective participation of regulators, pension fund board and management.

Retirement Age

Retirement age is an important instrument of pension reforms and has important socio-economic implications. Though changing the retirement age upward is essentially an ingredient for parametric Pension Reform, it is being gradually incorporated in a Systemic Pension Reform because of long-term positive impact. Since longevity has increased significantly, increasing the age of retirement has become a necessity rather than mere deferment of pension burden as often seen by many. When a person is living 80 years and above, early retirement, say at 60, suddenly stops her/his contribution to organizational growth, and the country loses the experienced and skilled manpower. The lower pension entitlement can be reversed by increasing the working age by extending the age of retirement and to allow the older persons work longer. Secondly, higher retirement age is also a boost to domestic savings since at a higher age propensity to save is higher than propensity to consume. It also provides relief to exchequer, though temporarily; allows the government to channelise funds for development work to boost up growth. Higher retirement and pensionable age thus found favour in not only developed countries but also emerging market countries like Chile, Argentina, Brazil, Poland, Greece which are not that burdened with aged population and shortage of labour supply. In India mostly the retirement age of the working employees is 60 years. India is going to be the most populous country of the world in 2030. Population aged 60+ will go up from 8 per cent to 21 per cent, while population above 80+ will go up from 8 per cent to 15 per cent during 2008–2050. India has introduced NPS, which is DC pension and in NPS it is the individual who has to save for his own retirement. But early retirement in the age of increased longevity will not only reduce post-retirement pension entitlement, it will also be a drain on human capital and strain on national economy and impact growth of savings. Moreover, increase in retirement age will provide a cushion to the government to rebalance the strained fiscal. Further, increase in retirement age would help to boost up much needed household and domestic savings as the propensity to consume declines and propensity to save increases at a higher age. Retirement age of some section of employees is already 62 years and in some other sections it is 65 years. It is therefore suggested that Indian government should consider increasing the retirement age of its employees beyond 60 years.

Means Tested Pension Tax

Tax policy of a funded pension has to encourage retirement savings by keeping revenue loss and cost of tax concession at minimum, distributional justice and also ensure incentives for deferred consumption, etc. While unrealistic higher tax rate on pension contribution or pension payment will discourage pension savings, excessive tax benefits for retirement savings on the other hand is not socially tenable and also generates adverse revenue consequences. Generous tax exemption will disproportionately benefit rich individuals and there will be erosion in government revenue which would constrain public spending by the government. Therefore, pension savings should not be totally tax exempt or there should not be uniform generous tax exemption. In order to encourage savings through tax incentives and to maintain equity Means Tested Pension Tax can be introduced, by imposing lower rate of taxes on lower income investors and higher rate of taxes for higher income investors in pension funds.

Pension Products and Regulatory Conflicts

One area of concern in the market of pension products is the conflict among regulators as such products are launched by life insurance companies, mutual funds, in addition to dedicated pension fund. In India life insurance companies are regulated by the Insurance Regulatory and Development Authority (IRDA), mutual funds are regulated by Securities and Exchange Board of India (SEBI), pension funds are regulated by PFRDA. Though product characteristics are different of pension funds launched by these companies but are directed to achieve similar objectives of creating retirement income for the investors. Since various costs related to fund management, administration, etc., are different, they will impact the accumulated return and final return will vary due to cost effect. One concern will be introducing uniformity in costs across the funds regulated by different regulators. It happened in the past in respect of distribution costs of ULIP, which became a matter of contention between IRDA and SEBI. Therefore, a general framework pension funds feature, various costs, etc., can be decided by the regulators with necessary operational flexibility. Apart from costs, portfolio structure, asset allocation pattern, portfolio valuation, etc., should have some similar practice across the funds launched by pension funds, mutual fund and life insurance companies.

Ownership of NPS

Unless the ownership is clearly identified, no programme can be effective enough to achieve the goal. Therefore, we need to clearly spell out ownership, responsibility and accountability of to the owners. Since NPS is a national programme, it needs to be owned by a cross-section of entities in addition to the government and regulator. Intermediaries like the sponsors of the fund managers, point of presence, central record keeping agency, etc., who have opted to be a part of NPS, have the important role to play in the process since in course of time they will receive financial and non-financial benefits directly or indirectly. Corporates also have an important role to play for making NPS a success, since it will provide retirement benefit support to the workers.

Long-term Inflation Protected Bonds

NPS is basically debt investment oriented since a large amount of total funds need to be invested in debt instruments, particularly in government securities. The demand for debt instruments particularly for the government securities will arise at two stages, that is, at the accumulation stage and at the decumulation or payout stage. Investment and allocation pattern in NPS under different options clearly indicate that NPS is basically a debt-oriented system. The mandatory annuitisation would create huge demand for annuity products in Indian life insurance market. Demand for long-term government securities would also arise for necessary hedging instrument to manage inflation and interest rate risk and to generate inflation-adjusted income. Therefore, the success of NPS and performance of fund managers in accumulation period and that of annuity providers would primarily depend on the well-managed diversified government securities market having a wide range of long-term product. But the current market for government securities lacks depth in trading and is narrow in terms of product offering. These are not only the major inhibiting factors for investment management performance but also come in the way of risk management in pension funds. Pension funds are long-term investors and one of the most severe risk factors for investment management is the uncertain inflation. However, the negative effects of inflation can be negated by investing in inflation protected bonds. These bonds are mostly in the nature of government or corporate bonds but provide the inflation-protected return and thus an important and necessary hedging instrument for the long-term investors like pension funds, life insurance companies, etc. Inflation index bonds are therefore tremendous support to the pension funds and other long-term investors who are large-scale investors in fixed income debt securities and concerned about protecting long-term investment return.

Steps to be Taken to Develop Annuity Market in India

Success of NPS and mandatory annuitisation programme will depend on a vibrant well-regulated and well-functioning annuity market, which so far is poorly developed in India. The demand for annuity product will arise from the increase in number of elderly population requiring old age income savings through long-term annuity products sold by life insurance companies and mandatory annuitisation programme of NPS. To promote a developed annuity market, we need steps to remove supply and demand side constraints, which include *updating mortality table developing long-term financial instruments, long-term debt instrument, promote an active and liquid debt market.* Therefore, there should be asset liability matching long-term debt instruments like Government Securities, which are normally absent in Indian market. In developed financial markets, innovative financial instruments like longevity bonds, inflation-indexed bonds have been introduced to hedge mortality and long-term financial risks. There are also longevity index bonds and survivor bonds to hedge long-term risks. Product market should be expanded by introducing new generation annuity products like variable annuity, equity-indexed annuity, inflation-indexed annuity, impaired annuity, enhanced annuity, in addition to fixed and guaranteed annuity, etc. There is also a necessity for introducing a separate regulation for annuity incorporating *portfolio regulation, pricing & transparency regulation, information dissemination.*

Public Private Support Programme (PPSP)

The crux of the problem is lack of awareness, absence of stakeholders' accountability and, to some extent, structural weakness which are pulling back the well-thought-out NPS system. NPS is a national programme and needs national-level initiatives and actions including awareness creation, while removing the regulatory bottlenecks and building required capacity at various levels of regulatory and administrative set-up. The regulator or government intervention is not sufficient to bring effective awareness for NPS, particularly when participation of unorganised sector is voluntary. Further awareness needs to be created among the immediate potential investors but also among the future investors, corporate and other social organisations directly or indirectly involved in economic activities. Therefore, national-level awareness campaign is a must for NPS, which can be created through a specially designed programme with private and public participation. This programme can be called as *Public Private Support Programme* (PPSP) for NPS.

Pension as Corporate Social Responsibility

The state has been gradually withdrawing itself from business and industrial activities and the space is left for private initiatives. Private corporate has extended its activities in almost all areas of economy and it is expected to increase further. Corporate has the responsibility to take care of the old age income security of their employees. NPS offers an opportunity to provide such old age support through employer–employee contribution. A mandatory provision would facilitate such a move by the corporate. While in many corporates such initiatives exist and mostly for the senior employees, covering the low-income employee through mandatory occupational pension through NPS would be a welcome step.

Pension Fund Terminology

Accumulated Assets: Assets that accumulated in a pension fund out of the contributions of a member, during a certain period, say till the date of retirement or before her/his exit from the fund.

Active Member: A member of a pension fund or pension plan who regularly contribute as per the condition laid down in the plan

Actuarial Valuation: A method of valuation of pension funds, carried out by an actuary to assess the future solvency, value of the fund, liability and funding requirements. Actuarial valuation is more significant for Defined Benefit schemes than Defined Contribution Schemes.

Actuarial Surplus: Actuarial valuation of a pension fund is conducted to find out the health of the fund. When actuarial value of assets is higher than liability, then Actuarial Surplus arise but if assets value is less than liability, actuarial liability arises.

Aggregator: Aggregators are the interface between the subscriber and NPS Lite intermediaries. They are approved by PFRDA and perform a number of functions in NPS Lite scheme including the registration of subscribers, verification of Know Your Customer (KYC), receive contributions and instructions from the subscribers and transmit the same to the intermediaries

Annuity Service Providers (ASPs): ASPs licensed by PFRDA would be responsible for delivering a regular monthly pension to the subscriber for the rest of his/her life.

Applicable NAV: 'Applicable NAV' is the Net Asset Value at the close of a Working Day.

Annuitant: The person who purchases an annuity policy and normally receives annuity benefits as per the terms and condition of policy is called an Annuitant.

Annuity: A form of financial contract mostly sold by life insurance companies that guarantees a fixed or variable payment of income benefit (monthly, quarterly, half-yearly, or yearly) for the life of a person(s) for a specified period of time. An annuity may be bought through instalments or as a single lump sum payment. Benefits may start immediately or at a pre-defined time in the future date or at a specific age.

Arbitrage: A trading strategy of buying securities and selling them simultaneously at a profit.

Asset Allocation: Asset allocation refers to diversification of portfolios among different asset classes in order to minimize risks and maximize risk adjusted return.

Basis Point: Basis Point is one hundredth of one percent, used in measuring interest rates, yield on investment, cost management fees for funds management, etc.

Bear Market: Refers to prolonged retreat in stock market when prices of stocks go down month to month.

Book Value: Value of assets included in the balance sheet of a company. The book value is the net value of an organization arrived at by subtracting its liabilities from its assets.

Bonds: Bonds are fixed income securities also known as debt instruments created to raise capital. Under most of the bonds, issuers pay fixed amount of interest to the investors.

Capital Asset Pricing Model (CAPM): CAPM is a theory which shows the relationship between risks and returns of an investment portfolio.

Cash Balance Plan: These are the defined benefit pension plans but appear as defined contribution plans, designed by the employers for their employees. These plans are based on some notional balances, in a hypothetical account. In cash balance an employer credit a percentage of employee salary to her/his account.

Compounding: Compounding is a powerful tool to measure the exponential growth in value of an investment which includes interest earnings—current and previous payment of interest.

Consumer Price Index (CPI): CPI measures the changes in consumer prices and thus indicates the trend in inflation. CPI is based on the prices of a basket of goods and services and changes all measures with reference to base prices.

Coupon Equivalent Yield (CEY): CEY is the effective interest rate earned on bond investment.

Coupon Rate: The stated interest rate on a bond.

Current Yield: It refers to the prevailing interest rate which the investors are entitled to get from investment in bonds and other fixed income securities.

Coverage Ratio: The coverage ratio is arrived at dividing the number of workers who contribute to contributory pension or retirement scheme, by the total number labour force.

CRA: Central Recordkeeping Agency. CRA perform some core activities in NPS such as Recordkeeping, Administration and customer service functions for all subscribers of the NPS.CRA also Issue Permanent Retirement Account Number (PRAN) to each subscriber, maintain a database of all PRANs issued and recording transactions relating to each subscriber's PRAN.CRA also act as an operational interface between PFRDA and other NPS intermediaries such as Pension Funds, Annuity Service Providers, Trustee Bank etc

Custodian: Custodian is the designated agency responsible for holding assets of the NPS Trust. Stockholding Corporation of India Limited (SHCIL) Is the Custodian under NPS.

Defined Benefit (DB) Scheme: DB schemes/Plans are unfunded pension schemes with predetermined pension benefits. The benefits are determined by a special formulae and pensions are usually paid at a certain percentage of terminal (at the time of retirement) salary of an employee.

Defined Contribution (DC) Schemes: DC Schemes are also called *Money Purchase Schemes* and are fully funded pension scheme. The benefits under DC schemes are not pre determined and depend on the value of contribution and interest earned over it but the contributions are pre determined. In a DC scheme entire investment and mortality risks are transferred to the members (investors).

Dependency Ratio: Dependency Ratio is the ratio of dependent persons (generally under age 15 and over age 60) to the working age population (normally age group 15–64 years). Dependency Ratio can be divided into Child Dependency Ratio (Ratio of population under age 15 to working age population (age 15–60 years) and Old Age Dependency (Ratio of older people age 60 years and above to working age population 15–60 years).

Discounting: The process of finding the present value of a series of future cash flow.

Dividend Yield: This refers to the dividend under a stock as a percentage of the stock prices.

Diversification: Refers to the investment strategy under which investment is made into various financial instruments including stocks, bonds, real estate, money market, etc.

Effective Rate of Interest: The percentage rate of return on annual basis.

Effective Yield: Refers to the annual rate of return including periodic interest rate from a bond investment.

Expected Mortality: Refers to the expected incidence of death in a group during a given period at any specified age.

Fiduciary: Refers to the relationship of confidence and trust between a person and an organization which exercises controls over assets of pension plans/life insurance assets.

Fair value: Fair Value is the market price at which a buyer is willing to buy an asset and a seller would sell that asset, both of them having reasonable knowledge about relevant information.

FEMA: Foreign Exchange Management Act

Fertility Rate: Fertility Rate refers to the number of live births per 1,000 women during the reproductive age normally consider as 15–49 in a given year

Financial Intermediation: Indicates transactions of financial institutions in financial market to acquire financial assets incurring liabilities in its own amount

Formal sector: The formal sector in an economy consist of the enterprises which comply with the government requirements for taxation, contributions for employee benefits like Provident Funds, Gratuity, pension etc.

EET system: Exempt–Exempt–Tax (EET) is a form of taxation imposed on pension plans, Under the EET, contributions, investment income, capital gains of the pension fund are tax exempt but benefits are taxed at the time of exit from the scheme.

ETE system: Under ETE (Exempt–Tax–Exempt) contribution to pension funds and benefits are tax exempt but investment income and capital gains of the pension fund are taxed

Fundamental Analysis: Refers to the analysis of value of shares, future profits, dividend, etc., based on accounting statements, economic and market information.

Funds Flow Statement: A statement showing flow of funds of a business firm over a period of time.

Futures: Futures are financial contracts between a buyer and a seller with an obligation to buy and sell assets at an agreed price at a future date set out in the contract.

Fully Funded: Refers to a pension scheme/fund which has enough assets to pay all current and future liabilities.

Generally Accepted Accounting Principles (GAAP): This is a common set of accounting procedures and standards.

Global Depository Receipts (GDR): These are receipts for shares in foreign companies traded in capital markets GDR. GDRs allow companies in USA, Europe and Asia to offer shares in many global markets.

Group Superannuation: Refers to the superannuation scheme offered to a group of employees.

Growth Fund: Funds that invest in growth stocks. Growth stocks are growing companies with potential of future earnings. Mutual funds, ULIP generally launch growth funds.

Hedging: A mechanism to protect the value of a portfolio against changes in market prices in future.

High Yield Bond: Refers to junk bond characterized by lower rating and higher possibility of default.

HTML: Hyper Text Mark up Language.

Human Life Value: Refers to a method used to assess life insurance needs of a person by considering his/her income, expenses future earnings and depreciation, etc., in monitory terms

Hybrid Pension Plan: The Pension Plans which combined features of Defined Benefit and Defined Contribution plans.

IMA: Investment Management Agreement, entered into between NPS Trust and the Pension Funds

Indexation: Indexation is an adjustment method followed in pension funds to change the level of pension benefits following the changes in cost of living due to changes in price, earnings etc. The can be price indexation, wage indexation or a mixture of the both.

IRDA: Insurance Regulatory and Development Authority(IRDA), regulate Insurance industry in India

Inkomstpension: Inkomstpension is the sub system of Swedish National Public Pension system under which a portion of earnings-related old age-pension linked to 16 percent of the pension base.

Immediate Annuity: Refers to the annuity plan under which the annuitant starts receiving annuity payment in the first month after the purchase of the annuity plan.

Immediate Vesting: Under a retirement plan of this kind, the employee benefits begin as soon as she/he purchases the plan.

Life Annuity: It is a kind of insurance products sold by Life insurance companies. When a life annuity purchased, annuitants receive a predetermined periodic payment till they survive. Life annuities are important means of payment in the payout stage for defined contribution pension system. In NPS, a member need to buy a life annuity by using at least 40% of her/his accumulated amount at the time of exit at the age of 60 years and by using at least 80% accumulated amount if exit takes place before the age of 60 years.

Life Expectancy: Life expectancy is the number of years someone lives if the current mortality continues. Generally life expectancy is determined with reference to birth

LIC: Life Insurance Corporation of India (LIC) is a state owned largest life insurance company in India founded in 1956 with the merger of 243 insurance companies and provident societies.. The Government of India own 100% stakes of the company.

Mandatory Annuitization: It is a process of payout in a defined contribution pension system under which a certain portion of accumulate assets (value)is used to buy a life annuity in the payout stage. Mandatory annuitization exists in NPS in India and is also followed by many countries particularly those which have introduced pension reform

Mandatory Contribution: Mandatory contributions are compulsory contribution for all the workers/ employees or for a specified section/s in the country.

Means-tested Pension benefits: Means Tested Pension Benefits are determined with reference the income and/assets of the targeted individual group.

Money Purchase Plan: A pension plan purchase with the contribution of both employer and employees at a pre determined percentage of contribution. Final accumulated amount arrived on the basis of the contribution and investment return will be utilised to purchase an annuity.

Multi-Pillar System: Generally a Multi Pillar Pension system consist of three pillar—a first pillar is the PAYG Public pillar, the second pillar is the mandatory funded pillar and the third pillar is the voluntary contribution by the members.

Net Asset Value (NAV): NAV is calculated by adding the value of investments in a fund and dividing the same by number of outstanding units.

Net Present Value (NPV): NPV refers to the present value of benefits minus present cost of purchase of an investment asset.

Net Rate of Return: The rate of return of a pension fund portfolio over a specified time period, after discounting fund management fees, custodian fees, record keeping fees. Distribution costs (if any) etc from the gross rate of return.

Notional Defined Contribution (NDC): NDC system resembles a defined contribution pension plan consisting of individual accounts for the members. All contributions and investment returns are accumulate in a notional account which finally converted into an annuity at retirement. However, return in the individual account is a notional which is set by the government but not by the market rate of return as in case of Defined Contribution Plan. In an NDC system entire risk is not transferred to the members as in case of DC system.

NPS Trust: PFRDA has established the NPS Trust under Indian Trust Act, 1862 and appointed NPS Board of Trustees in whom the administration of the "National Pension System" vests under Indian Law. The Trust is responsible for taking care of the funds under the NPS. The Trust holds an account with the Bank of India and this bank is designated as the NPS Trustee Bank

Occupational Pension Scheme: Pension Plans set up by an employer to provide retirement benefits to employees. The nature of the Occupational Pension Scheme may not be uniformed in all organisations and may differ from employer to employer.

Portability: Portability allows a member to transfer her/his NPS account at the time of changing her jobs.

Parametric Reform: Parametric Pension Reform do not follow the structural change but changes the key parameters of existing pension system depending on the need of reform requirement by maintaining the existing structure. Important parametric changes are usually related to contribution rates, retirement ages, or benefit levels etc. Parametric reform is primarily followed by developed countries

Pay-As-You-Go (PAYG): PAYG schemes are basically unfunded pension schemes. Pension payment employees in a PAYG system to the outgoing employees are made by the current contributions of existing employees. Government and public sector pensions are primarily PAYG. This system based on the intergenerational transfer- as to days workers support the pension of outgoing workers.

Pension Fund: Fund set up by the employer, employees or any other organisation with a view to pool resources for retirement or old age income through regular pension are generally termed as pension fund. The contribution of members and employers in a pension fund are invested in financial assets by the fund managers.

Personal Disposable Income: Personal income is derived by deducting savings of private corporate and corporate taxes from private income. Personal disposable income is derived by deducting direct taxes paid by the household and miscellaneous receipts of the government from personal income.

PFRDA: Pension Fund Regulatory and Development Authority (PFRDA), is the prudential Regulator for the National Pension System (NPS). PFRDA was established by the Government of India, Ministry of Finance; vide Notification F.No.5/7/2003-ECB & PR dated 10th October, 2003 to promote old age income security by establishing, developing and regulating pension funds, to protect the interests of subscribers to schemes of pension funds and for matters connected therewith or incidental thereto. PFRDA has been authorized by the Central Government through Notification in November 2008 to appoint/establish various intermediaries in the system such as Central Record Keeping Agency (CRA), Pension Funds (PFs), Points of Presence, Trustee Bank, NPS Trust, Custodian, etc. for operationalising the NPS roll out to unorganized sector subscribers.

Provident Fund (PF): Provident funds are special type of retirement saving plans for employees and contribution of a certain portion of salary is mandatory. There may be a matching contribution by the employer. Generally the payout in provident fund takes place at the time of retirement but partial withdrawal under special circumstances is also allowed. The payout amount is equivalent to contribution plus interest earned over a period of time.

PFMs: Pension Fund Managers (PFMs) are appointed by the PFRDA to manage pension funds under the National Pension System (NPS). PFMs, manage the retirement savings of subscribers under the NPS schemes. The PFMs are required to invest strictly in accordance with guidelines issued by the Government/PFRDA.

POP: Point of Presence are authorised by PFRDA to collect application forms from the subscribers to NPS scheme for onward transmission to CRA.

POP-SP: Point of Presence-Service Provider (Authorized branches of POP for NPS)

Portability: Ability to transfer individual pension account from one fund manager to another fund manager

PRAN: Permanent Retirement Account Number provided to every member (subscriber) of NPS.

Premium Pension: Premium Pension is a part of Swedish Earnings-related old-age pension, which has been designed as a funded system. Under premium pension system 2.5% pension credit invested in securities chosen by members.

RBI: Reserve Bank of India, established under the Reserve Bank of India Act, 1934.

Prudent Person Rule: Also called Prudent Man principle/rule, which focus on the qualitative aspects of investment decisions. In many countries, either it is imposed instead of Quantitative Regulation or along with quantitative regulation to regulate investment activities of pension funds. Under the prudent Person Rule fiduciaries, trustees etc are expected to take investment decision carefully as knowledgeable professional. Prudent Person rule induce accountability, reduces the investment risk, and help proper diversification of portfolio.

Replacement Rate: Replacement rate is an important indicator to judge the effectiveness of a pension system. It is the percentage of pay of a worker/employee before retirement which is paid as pension in the post retirement period

Securitization of Risks: Refers to a mechanism under which an insurance risk is diversified by using capital market. For this an insurance company raised money through capital market to cover risks.

Solvency Margin: Refers to the amount by which the assets of an insurer exceed the liability which is available to cover its required solvency margin. It also refers to the capital base and is defined as surplus assets over liabilities. An insurance company must maintain minimum solvency margin.

SEBI: Securities and Exchange Board of India (SEBI), which is the regulator for Indian Capital Market.

Subscriber: An individual who becomes a member of the National Pension System. Subscriber is also referred to as unit holder with respect to the units he/she owns.

Self Help Group (SHG): SHG is a small group of poor, who have voluntarily come forward to form a group to improve the social and economic status of the members.

Systemic Pension Reform: Systemic Pension reforms usually replace the existing system (Generally DB PAYG) normally by introducing a multi-pillar pension system. Systemic reform based on structural changes in respect of contribution, benefits, administration etc.

TEE System: Another form of taxation in Pension fund. TEE indicates Tax–Exempt–Exempt. Under this system, tax is imposed on pension contribution but investment income, capital gains of the pension fund and benefits are tax exempt.

Trust Deed: In NPS the Trust Deed entered into between the NPS Trust and PFRDA, as may be amended from time to time.

Trustee: A person or company appointed to carry out the function of a trust that is responsible to manage assets of a pension fund. In NPS there is a centralised single Trust appointed by PFRDA as per Indian Trust Act.

Trust Fund: In NPS there is a single Trust which owns the corpus of the Trust and all property belonging to it.

Trustees Bank: Trustee Bank manages the banking of the Pension Funds in accordance with applicable provisions of the NPS schemes as per the guidelines/notifications, issued by PFRDA, Ministry of Finance, and Government of India.

Uncovered workers: Workers those are not included in a formal pension plans/system in a country

Unfunded pension plans: Unfunded pension Plans are normally employer managed retirement plans. Pension is provided to the plan participants out of the current income of the employer.

Unit linked Pension Plans (ULIPPs): These are market linked pension plans offered y Life insurance companies, which provide opportunities for long term investment benefits as well as retirement pension. ULIPPs also offer life and health insurance covers to the investors. ULLIPs have two phases like NPS. Phase one is accumulation phase- funds are accumulated through regular contribution by an investor which are invested in capital market instruments. Phase two is the pension payout. At the time of exit/Retirement, one third of the corpus is paid to the investors as lump sum and remaining two third is invested in an annuity plan for regular payment as pension to the investors as per the contract.

Wage indexation: Wage indexation method in pension funds used to capture the changes in wages and adjust pension benefits accordingly.

Variable Annuity: Annuity benefits payment which varies from year to year depending on the value of portfolio of securities.

Index

About the Author

H. Sadhak is Advisor (Market and Industry) at Price Waterhouse Coopers (PwC) Pvt. Ltd, Mumbai. He has rich experience in financial services industry and has worked in leadership roles in pension fund, mutual fund, life insurance and banking industry. Prior to joining PwC, Dr Sadhak was the founder MD/CEO of LIC Pension Fund Ltd. Dr Sadhak is also an independent researcher and associated with many management institutions and universities as a guest faculty and examiner of PhD work.

Dr Sadhak has held many important posts such as Executive Director with LIC of India (2004–06) and Joint General Manager with LIC Mutual Fund (1989–99). He was also an officer with a public sector bank and a lecturer in economics at a degree college. In the recent past he was a member/expert of many high power working groups/ technical committees including Technical Committee on Accounting Policy for NPS, PFRDA; Technical Advisory Group, Real Estate Price Index, Government of India; Working Group on Household Savings, 11th Five Year Plan, Government of India; Working Group on Household Savings, 10th Five Year Plan, Government of India; Working Group, Fifth Economic Census, Government of India; Working Group on Insurance Sector Statistics, National Statistics Commission; Founder Convener, Research and Statistics Committee, AMFI.

An accomplished author, Dr Sadhak, has published more than 200 articles/research papers and five well appreciated books—*Life Insurance in India: Opportunities, Challenges & Strategic Perspective* (SAGE, 2009), *Mutual Funds in India: Marketing Strategies and Investment Practices* (SAGE, 1997), *Role of Entrepreneurs in Backward Areas* (1989), *Impact of Incentives on Industrial Development in Backward Regions* (1986).

He is widely travelled and has delivered lectures in many national and international seminars/conferences in India and abroad. He is a director on the board of many companies and is also associated with many trade and industry associations. He has received many awards for his contribution to research in finance and economic development.

Dr Sadhak obtained his PhD (Industrial Finance) from the University of Poona, MA (Economics) from University of Kalyani, West Bengal, and Diploma in Operation Research for Management from University of Mumbai.

He is also a distinguished poet and novelist having 12 collections of published works in Bengali, English and Hindi to his credit.